Chronology of the War at Sea

1939-1945

Volume One: 1939-1942

J. ROHWER AND
G. HUMMELCHEN

Chronology of the War at Sea

1939-1945

TRANSLATED FROM THE GERMAN BY
Derek Masters

Volume One: 1939-1942

Arco Publishing Company, Inc.

NEW YORK

Published by Arco Publishing Company, Inc.
219 Park Avenue South, New York, N.Y. 10003

Library of Congress Catalog Card Number 73-78526

ISBN 0-668-03308-8

Printed in Great Britain

Translator's Note

For this English translation of the *Chronik des Seekrieges 1939-45* the authors have substantially amplified and revised the original German text so that the present book in effect represents a new edition of the work.

In the case of most navies—but not the Royal Navy and the US Navy—the authors use the expressions *Kapitänleutnant, Korvettenkapitän* and *Fregattenkapitän* to describe certain officer ranks: in agreement with the authors I have translated these Lieutenant-Commander Commander and Commander* respectively (the asterisk denoting the senior of two Commander grades).

In dealing with Japanese units, I have used the normal British nomenclature i.e. battleship, cruiser and carrier *squadrons* and destroyer and submarine *flotillas:* but the reader should bear in mind that much of the literature on the subject today uses the American nomenclature i.e. battleship, cruiser and carrier *divisions* and destroyer and submarine *squadrons.*

Because of the difficulty in finding an English equivalent, I have left most German Air Force nomenclature in the original in the text but included the relevant formations in the Glossary.

Tonnage is normally GRT (Gross Register Tons).

D.R.M.

Preface

We have tried in this book to include both important and typical events of the war at sea 1939–45 in all the oceans of the world. It has not been our purpose to provide an historical account in abbreviated form or a simple enumeration of dates recalling certain operations and engagements, but something between the two—an aid to the quick understanding of the many happenings at sea. In doing so, we have tried, as far as possible, to place the events in their tactical or operational context. It was, therefore, necessary to lump together the events for certain periods instead of entering them on a purely day-to-day basis. But, to make it as easy as possible for the reader to find specific events, the first and last dates of the periods in question are reproduced in heavy type on the left followed by the maritime area. The order is chronological from the first date. In addition, the detailed indexes of persons and ship names, of operational code names and of convoys will provide further help in a specific quest.

We have quite deliberately given an international basis to the work. Many publications of the recent decades limit themselves to describing events essentially from one side and some authors continue to rely on what are inevitably often unreliable reports of the war period. It has been our aim to give as correct a picture as possible, on the basis of the best available sources, of what actually happened, on both sides and of who participated in the events.

A few figures will show in what detail the navies of all the countries engaged in the war have been treated. In addition to approximately 1,100 German warships and auxiliary warships and another 1,000 German U-boats, there are mentioned in the text more than 1,600 British and Commonwealth ships; almost 1,600 American; nearly 700 Soviet; about 700 Japanese; 700 Italian; more than 300 French; as well as 300 warships of the smaller sea powers—Brazil, Bulgaria, China, Colombia, Cuba, Denmark, Finland, Greece, Holland, Iran, Norway, Poland, Rumania, Spain, Sweden, Thailand, Turkey and Yugoslavia. Further, about 1,600 merchant ships of all seafaring states are mentioned—generally more than once and even up to thirty times.

If, in spite of the more than 9,600 ships and approximately 3,100 persons named, a reader fails to find his own ship or commander, he should bear in mind that in some places another individual or another ship might equally have been mentioned, but that, generally speaking, it would have been impossible to include more in the available space. Likewise, it was not possible to mention the responsible commanders and officers in the staffs ashore on both sides in each of the larger operations. We had to confine ourselves to the officers on the ships.

In addition to the official and semi-official works on the war at sea, the special investigations and memoirs of commanders and senior officers, we have also made use—particularly on the German side—of unpublished material. It is not possible here to mention all the sources used and all the relevant literature. We would refer to the *Bibliothek für Zeitgeschichte* in Stuttgart for specific bibliographical information. In what follows we can only mention the most important sources for our work: *Germany:* In the nature of the case German literature on the subject of the war at sea in the Second World War has only to a small extent been based on original documents. We have therefore tried to counter this deficiency by making greater use of central war diaries (for example, the war diary of the Navy Staff (*Seekriegsleitung*), the war diary of the Commander U-boats and various officers commanding U-boats, the war diaries of other commands, situation reports of the C-in-C *Luftwaffe* and Operational Staff I c, etc). Considerable space has been given to submarine warfare, and the defence against it, on both sides, which decisively influenced the course of the war at sea in the Atlantic, the Mediterranean and Pacific. We have included not only these operations which have so far received almost exclusive attention, ie those in which important results were achieved in attack or defence, but also the 'no result', the abortive and unsuccessful actions which have been largely neglected in the framework of over-all operations. This applies particularly to the actions of the last two war years whose range has been greatly underestimated. We have largely omitted the names of the ships sunk by submarines since they can be found in another publication.*

The air war at sea has, on the basis of the source material available, been more precisely described than has hitherto been the case. The same is true of the activities of the motor torpedo boats. We have also tried to pay more attention than hitherto to the daily war routine of the escort forces by dealing with typical events in all theatres of war without striving after a completeness which would have exceeded the limits of the book.

Great Britain and the Commonwealth: the basis of the account is provided by the many volumes of *History of the Second World War*—especially the four volumes by S. W. Roskill *The War at Sea* published by H.M. Stationery Office, London; the work of Joseph Schull, *The Far Distant Ships*, published by the Department of National Defense in Ottawa; the series *Australia in the War of 1939–45* from the Australian War Memorial in Canberra; the *Official History of New Zealand in the Second World War 1939–1945* of the War History Branch in Wellington; for South Africa the volume by L. C. F. Turner *War in the Southern Oceans 1939–1945;* and for India *The Royal Indian Navy 1939–1945*, by D. J. E. Collins. Apart from the relevant literature and a considerable correspondence, particular use was made of the *Weekly Naval Notes*, published by the Naval

*Jürgen Rohwer (1968) *Die U-Boot-Erfolge der Achsenmächte 1939-45*, Munich Lehmann.

Intelligence Division in London during the war, to clear up many points of detail.

USA: Here use could be made of the very detailed accounts by S. E. Morison, *History of United States Naval Operations in World War II* (Fifteen vols), for amphibious operations the official series *United States Army in World War II*, *Marine Corps Monographs*, *History of U.S. Marine Corps Operations in World War II;* and various publications of the Naval History Division—*Dictionary of American Naval Fighting Ships*—and of the U.S. Naval Institute, particularly, the *U.S. Naval Chronology World War II*, and the volumes of Th. Roscoe *Destroyers* and *Submarines;* as well as many individual publications.

USSR: the very comprehensive Soviet naval literature on the history of the Second World War has been systematically assessed, particularly the memoirs of the most important commanders and the accounts by the official naval historians. Thanks to the knowledge gained, it was possible to check, elaborate and clarify many details in the German documents of the war period, so that few gaps now remain.

Japan: In addition to the Anglo-American literature, it was possible to refer to a number of Japanese works both original and translated. Of particular importance were the *Japanese Monographs* composed by Japanese officers with the Allied Supreme Command in Tokyo, studies of operations of individual branches of the Japanese Navy and of specific battle areas.

Italy: The basis for the account of the activities of the Italian Fleet is the very detailed official work of the Ufficio Storico della Marina Militare *La Marina Italiana nella Seconda Guerra Mondiale* (18 vols).

France: For the period up to June 1940 much use was made of the unpublished volumes of the Service Historique about the operations 1939–40: for the subsequent period use was made chiefly of the work by Amiral Auphan and

Jacques Mordal, *La Marine Française pendant la Seconde Guerre Mondiale.*

Smaller navies: In addition to the relevant, and in some respects extraordinarily detailed, specialist literature, official publications were particularly used: eg for Brazil, C. A. Machado da Fonseca *A Marinha Brasileira e a Segunda Guerra Mundial (1939-1945)* and for Finland, the official *Suomen Sota 1941-1944* (vol IX), for Greece, K. A. Alexandre *To Nautikon Mas Kata ten Polemiken periodon 1941-1945,* for Holland, K. W. L. Bezemer *Zij vochten op de zeven zeen,* for Norway, E. A. Steen *Norges Sjökrig 1940-1945* (7 vols), for Poland, J. Pertek *Wielkie dni Malej Floty.*

Ships and Ship Losses: For the warships use was made of the well-known international annual fleet handbooks and of the many reference books which have appeared since the war on individual fleets and their classes of ship. For the merchant ships, use was made of Lloyd's Annual Register and Gröner's *Die Handelsflotten der Welt,* as well as of much documentation in international technical periodicals.

Apart from the various official national lists of losses of warships and merchant ships, which have appeared in the years since the Second World War, List B.R. 1337 *British and Foreign Merchant Vessels lost or damaged by Enemy Action during Second World War* and its supplements, prepared by the Naval Staff (Trade Division) of the Admiralty in London, was an indispensable source.

Appointments: for the German Navy use was made of Lohmann-Hildebrandt's *Die Deutsche Kriegsmarine 1939-1945* and in the case of foreign navies details were taken from the relevant literature.

Despite these ample sources and the extensive literature it would not have been possible for us to give so much detail and to keep it within the permissible framework without the kind help of numerous correspondents, officers of the German, Axis and Allied Navies and merchant marines and of many ship-lovers all over the world. Our thanks are due to all who helped in the past years, even if, for reasons of space, they cannot all be named. In particular, we should like to thank the historical departments of the various navies with their directors and staffs for their generous help over the years: Rear-Adm R. M. Bellairs, Commander M. G. Saunders (†), Lt-Cdr P. K. Kemp, H. C. Beaumont, J. D. Lawson, and recently Rear-Adm P. N. Buckley and Capt D. Macintyre of the Historical Section of the Admiralty and the Naval Historical Branch of the Ministry of Defence in London; Rear-Adm Ernest M. Eller and Capt F. Kent Loomis of the Naval History Division in Washington; Dr G. N. Tucker and E. C. Russell of the Naval Historical Section and Col C. P. Stacey and S. F. Wise of the Division of History in the Defense Department, Ottawa; Prof L. C. F. Turner, J. A. I. Agar-Hamilton and J. E. Betzler (†) of the Union War Histories Section in Pretoria; Contre-Amiral Rostand, Médecin en chef Hervé Cras, Contre-Amiral Brossard and Contre-Amiral Fliche of the Service Historique de la Marine in Paris; Orlogskaptein E. A. Steen of the Forsvarets Krigshistoriske Avdeling in Oslo; Ammiraglio di squadra G. Fioravanzo, Ammiraglio di squadra A. Cocchia (†), Contraammiraglio V. E. Tognelli and Contraammiraglio A. Donato of the Ufficio Storico della Marina Militare in Rome; and Rear-Adm Sakamoto of the Office of War History in the Japanese Self-Defence Forces in Tokyo.

Equally helpful were the authors of the British history of the war at sea, Capt S. W. Roskill, and of the American History of the War at Sea, Rear-Adm Professor S. E. Morison and his colleagues, Dr R. Pineau and Dr J. Bauer. In many difficult questions of the war at sea in East European waters we were helped by our friends Jürg Meister, Siegfried Breyer, Claude Huan, Rolf Erikson, and Pierre Warneck. Of the numerous ship-lover correspondents, we should mention in particular, Erich Gröner (†), L. L. von Münching, Paul Scarceriaux, David Irving and, from the participants in the Battle of the Atlantic, Fregattenkapitän G. Hessler (†) and Capt J. M. Waters (USCG). We express our warm thanks to them all and to many anonymous helpers, not least the members of our own families without whose co-operation the comprehensive indexes could not have been prepared in time.

The English edition is a revised and in parts considerably amended version of the German edition. Best thanks are due to Mr Derek Masters, translator, to Mr A. J. Watts, who was concerned with the illustrations, and not least to the publishers for their splendid assistance in preparing this edition.

Despite all efforts the present work will not answer every question and will contain some mistakes and errors because it has been impossible to fill gaps in the source material and to clear up contradictions; or because information has been incorrectly interpreted and printing errors have been overlooked. We shall, therefore, be grateful for any information which may give a truer or a more complete picture. We hope that the book will prove to be a useful reference work for all those who use it.

JÜRGEN ROHWER
GERHARD HÜMMELCHEN

Abbreviations and Glossary

AA	Anti-Aircraft
AF	(*Artillerie-Fährprahm*) gun ferry barge
AK	Supply Transport (Auxiliary Kargo)
AKA	Attack Supply Transport (Auxiliary Kargo Attack)
AP	Troop Transport (Auxiliary Personnel)
APA	Attack Troop Transport (Auxiliary Personnel Attack)
APD	Fast Transport (Auxiliary Personnel Destroyer)
A/S	Anti-submarine
ASV-Radar	Anti-Surface-Vessel-Radar
Batdiv	Battleship Division
BB	Battleship
BF	Base Force
BKA	Russian armoured cutter
BLT	Battalion Landing Team
Bn	Battalion
BO	Large Russian submarine chaser, patrol boat
Bord Fl Gr	(*Bordfliegergruppe*) Ship-borne wing, originally earmarked for uncompleted aircraft carrier
Capt 1st Class	Russian Captain
Capt 2nd Class	Russian Commander* (German *Fregattenkapitän*)
Capt 3rd Class	Russian Commander (German *Korvettenkapitän*)
*Cdr**	Fregattenkapitän (or corresponding rank) in the German, French, Italian, etc, navies
Cdr	Korvettenkapitän
DD	Destroyer
DE	Destroyer Escort
Desdiv	Destroyer Division (US)
Desron	Destroyer Squadron (US)
Div	Division
EG	Escort Group
EMC	Moored Mine (Last letter denotes Mark of mine)
ES	Escort Squadron
F	F1-10 (*Flottenbegleiter*) Fleet Escort Vessel F100-1200 (*Fährprahm*) Landing Craft Tank
FAA	Fleet Air Arm
Fl Div	(*Fliegerdivision*) German Air Division. The *Fliegerdivision* was later renamed *Fliegerkorps* and could operate within, or independently of, a *Luftflotte* (Air Fleet)
Fl K	(*Fligerkorps*) German Air Corps
Front	Russian Army Group
GB	Gunboat

xiii

Geschwader	German Air Group
Gruppe	German Air Wing
	(The *Geschwader* was the largest air formation with a nominal fixed strength. It usually comprised 90 aircraft in 3-4 *Gruppen*, with each *Gruppe* consisting of 3-4 *Staffeln* or squadrons)
HF/DF	High Frequency Direction Finding
Inf	Infantry
JG	(*Jagdgeschwader*) Fighter Group
K Fl Gr	(*Küstenfliegergruppe*) Coastal Air Wing
KFK	(*Kriegsfischkutter*) Naval fishing cutter
KG	(*Kampfgeschwader*) Bomber Group
LAT	(*Leichter Artillerieträger*) Light aux gunboat
LCF	Landing Craft Flak
LCI	Landing Craft Infantry
LCI (G)	Landing Craft Infantry Gunboat
LCI (M)	Landing Craft Infantry Mortar
LCM	Landing Craft Mechanised
LCS	Landing Craft Support
LCT	Landing Craft Tank
LG	(*Lehrgeschwader*) Air Trainer Group
LMB	Ground Mine (Laid by aircraft)
LSD	Landing Ship Dock
LSI	Landing Ship Infantry
LSM	Landing Ship Medium
LST	Landing Ship Tank
LSV	Landing Ship Vehicle
Luftwaffe	German Air Force
M	(*Minensucher*) Minesweeper
MAD	Magnetic Airborne Detector
MAS	Italian Motor Torpedo Boat, originally submarine-chaser
MFP	(*Marine Fährprahm*) Naval ferry barge
MGB	Motor Gun Boat
MMS	Motor Minesweeper
MO	Russian submarine-chaser (small)
MS	Italian motor torpedo boat
MS	Minesweeper
MTB	Motor Torpedo Boat
OKH	(*Oberkommando des Heeres*) Army High Command
OKM	(*Oberkommando der Marine*) Naval High Command
OKW	(*Oberkommando der Wehrmacht*) Armed Forces Command
PC	Patrol Craft
PCE	Patrol Craft Escort
PT boat	Patrol Torpedo Boat
R	(*Räumboot*) Motor Minesweeper
RA	(*Räumboot Ausland*) Captured MMS in German Navy

RAAF	Royal Australian Air Force
RAN	Royal Australian Navy
RCAF	Royal Canadian Air Force
RCN	Royal Canadian Navy
RCT	Regimental Combat Team
Regt	Regiment
RIN	Royal Indian Navy
RN	Royal Navy
RNZN	Royal New Zealand Navy
RT	Trawler
S	(*Schnellboot*) Motor Torpedo Boat, E-boat
SAT	(*Schwerer Artillerieträger*) Heavy auxiliary gunboat
SC	Submarine-chaser
SG	(*Schnelles Geleitboot*) Fast escort vessel
SKA	Russian patrol boat
SKL	(*Seekriegsleitung*) German Navy Staff
SKR	Russian patrol ship
SM	Submarine
Sqdn	Squadron
Stavka	Russian headquarters
St G	(*Stukageschwader*) Dive Bomber Group
Supermarina	Italian Navy Staff
T	(*Torpedoboot*) Torpedo Boat
TA	(*Torpedoboot Ausland*) Captured foreign T-boat in German Navy
TB	Torpedo Boat
TF	Task Force
TG	Task Group
TKA	Russian motor torpedo boat
TMA	Ground Mine
Trägergruppe	Air carrier Wing, originally earmarked for uncompleted aircraft carrier
TU	Task Unit
U	(*U-Boot*) U-boat
UDT	Underwater Demolition Team
UJ	(*Unterseebootjäger*) Submarine-chaser
UM	Submarine Mine
USAAF	US Army Air Force
USCG	US Coast Guard
USN–VP	US Navy Reconnaissance Squadron
USN–VPB	US Navy Patrol Bomber Squadron
V	(*Vorpostenboot*) Auxiliary patrol vessel, trawler, drifter, etc
Wehrmacht	German Armed Forces
W/T	Wireless telegraphy
YMS	Yard Mine Sweeper
Z	(*Zerstörer*) Destroyer
ZG	(*Zersrtörergeschwader*) Heavy Fighter Group
†	CO killed

1939

19 Aug   North Atlantic
Owing to the critical international situation, the German Navy Staff (Seekriegsleitung) sends 14 U-boats into the North Atlantic to take up waiting positions there. *U45, U46, U47, U48* and *U52* set out from Kiel; and *U28, U29, U33, U34, U37, U38, U39, U40* and *U41* from Wilhelmshaven.
21 Aug   South Atlantic
Pocket-battleship l*Admiral Graf Spee* (Capt Langsdorff) sails from Wilhelmshaven towards evening to head for an appointed position in the South Atlantic. The fleet tanker *Altmark* (Capt Dau), whose function is to refuel the pocket-battleship, is sent on 5 Aug to Port Arthur/USA to take on diesel oil there and then to join *Admiral Graf Spee*.
22-23 Aug   North Atlantic
U30 and *U27* leave Wilhelmshaven for the North Atlantic.
24 Aug   North Atlantic
Pocket-battleship *Deutschland* (Capt Wennecker) sails from Wilhelmshaven to the North Atlantic to take up a waiting position S of Greenland. The fleet tanker *Westerwald* (Cdr Grau), whose function is to refuel the pocket-battleship, puts to sea two days earlier.
25 Aug   General Situation
In the morning first warning telegram from Norddeich Radio to German merchant shipping overseas.
27 Aug   General Situation
All German merchant ships overseas are asked by W/T to do everything to reach their home ports 'within the next four days' or to make for ports of friendly or neutral states.
31 Aug-7 Sept   North Sea
British Home Fleet (Adm Sir C. Forbes), comprising the battleships *Nelson, Ramillies, Rodney, Royal Oak,* and *Royal Sovereign,* the battlecruisers *Hood* and *Repulse,* the carrier *Ark Royal,* 12 cruisers and 16 destroyers of the 6th DD Flotilla (8 'Tribals') and the 8th DD Flotilla ('F' Class), searches in the waters between Scotland, Iceland and Norway for returning German merchant ships, in particular, for the fast Atlantic liner *Bremen.*
1 Sept   Baltic
0445 hrs: start of German attack on Poland. German naval forces consist of: Naval Group Command East (Adm Albrecht, Chief of Staff Rear-Adm Schmundt) with overall responsibility. Under its command: Commander Reconnaissance Forces, Vice-Adm Densch, with the light cruisers *Nürnberg, Leipzig* and *Köln*; Officer Commanding Torpedo Boats, Rear-Adm Lütjens, with the destroyers *Leberecht Maass, Georg Thiele, Richard Beitzen, Friedrich Ihn, Erich Steinbrinck, Friedrich Eckoldt, Bruno Heinemann, Wolfgang Zenker, Bernd von Arnim* and the 1st MTB Flotilla with *S10, S11, S12, S13, S18, S19* and tender *Tsingtau*; Officer Commanding Minesweepers, Capt Ruge, on torpedo boat *T196* with the escort boats *F7, F8, F9, F10,* the 1st MS Flotilla with the minesweepers *M1, M3, M4, M5, M7, M8, M111, M132,* the Experimental Barrage Command with the old minesweepers *Nautilus, Otto Braun, Pelikan, Arkona, Sundewall,* and the 3rd MMS Flotilla with the tender *Von der Gröben* and *R33, R34, R35, R36, R38, R39, R40*; Officer Commanding U-boats East, Cdr* Schomburg, with *U5, U6, U7, U14, U18, U22, U31, U32, U35* and *U57*; Officer Commanding Naval Air Forces East, Maj-Gen Coeler, with ten marine air squadrons; in addition, harbour protection flotillas and the old battleship *Schleswig-Holstein* (Capt Kleikamp) in Danzig-Neufahrwasser.
Polish Navy: C-in-C Rear-Adm Unrug. Destroyers *Wicher,* (*Blyskawica, Burza* and *Grom* set out for Britain on 30 Aug), minelayer *Gryf,* submarines *Sep, Orzel, Wilk, Rys, Zbik,* two old torpedo boats, two gunboats, six small minesweepers, as well as auxiliary and training vessels. *Schleswig-Holstein* shells Westerplatte, whose defenders beat off attack by a naval assault company. Ju 87s of IV Stuka/LG 1 (Capt Kögl) sink at about

1

1400 hrs the Polish torpedo boat *Mazur* in the naval harbour of Oksywie (Oxhöft).

2 Sept Baltic
Commander Reconnaissance Forces and *U31*, *U32*, and *U35* are transferred to the North Sea. IV/L.G. 1 sinks the Polish Auxiliary ships *Gdynie* (538 tons) and *Gdansk* (538 tons) in the Gulf of Danzig. Polish submarine *Wilk* damaged by depth charges.

3 Sept General Situation
Great Britain and France declare war on Germany.

3 Sept Baltic
Early in the morning the Officer Commanding Torpedo Boats makes a sortie towards Hela with the destroyers. Engagement with *Gryf*, *Wicher*, and 15cm battery. The latter obtains hits on *Leberecht Maass* (four dead).

3 Sept North Sea
Staff of the General on 'special employment' with Air Fleet 2 becomes 10th Fl Div (Lt-Gen Geisler). Task: Air war against British shipping.

3 Sept North Atlantic
U30 (Lt Lemp) mistakes British passenger liner *Athenia* (13581 tons) for auxiliary cruiser south of Rockall Bank and torpedoes her. About 1300 survivors from the sinking ship are rescued by the British destroyers *Electra* and *Escort*, the Norwegian motor ship *Knute Nelson*, the American ship *City of Flint* and the Swedish yacht *Southern Cross* which come to the scene. 112 lose their lives.

As a result of this first sinking—without warning—the British Admiralty believes that Germany has started unrestricted U-boat warfare.

In fact, following the report of the sinking of the *Athenia*, the Germans issue additional instructions curbing mercantile warfare.

3 Sept North Atlantic
The first U-boat wave, sent into the Atlantic as a precautionary measure, from 19 Aug onwards, begins its operations: 2nd U-boat Flotilla W of the British Isles and the Channel with *U27*, *U28*, *U29*, *U30*, *U33* and *U34*. Later also *U26*, *U31*, *U35* and *U53* (mining operations off Portland) and *U32* (mining operations in the Bristol Channel). Successes achieved up to 3 Oct (including those by mines): *U26* (Lt-Cdr Ewerth) sinks three ships of 17414 tons with mines and damages corvette *Kittiwake* with a mine; *U27* (Lt-Cdr Franz) sinks two ships of 624 tons; *U28* (Lt-Cdr Kuhnke) one ship of 4955 tons; *U29* (Lt-Cdr Schuhart) three ships of 19405 tons (see also 3-17 Sept); *U30* (Lt Lemp) two ships of 9625 tons (excluding *Athenia*); *U31* (Lt-Cdr Habekost) sinks two ships of 8706 tons (see also 16 Sept); *U32* (Lt-Cdr Büchel) sinks two ships of 5738 tons and damages two ships of 17525 tons with mines; *U33* (Lt-Cdr von Dresky) three ships of 5914 tons; *U34* (Lt-Cdr Rollmann) two ships of 11357 tons and one ship of 2534 tons taken as a prize; *U35* (Lt-Cdr Lott) sinks four ships of 7850 tons and damages one ship of 6014 tons; and *U53* (Lt-Cdr Heinicke) sinks two ships of 14018 tons. *U27* is lost on 22 Sept. Of the 7th U-boat Flotilla W of the Bay of Biscay, comprising *U45*, *U46*, *U47*, *U48* and *U52*, and the 6th U-boat Flotilla W of the Iberian peninsula, comprising *U37*, *U38*, *U39*, *U40* and *U41*, *U38* (Lt-Cdr Liebe) two ships of 16698 tons; *U41* (Lt Mugler) brings in two prizes of 2172 tons. *U47* (Lt-Cdr Prien) sinks three ships of 8270 tons; and *U48* (Lt-Cdr Schultze) three ships of 14777 tons. The boats are recalled on 7 Sept.

3 Sept North Sea
54 Blenheims and Wellingtons of RAF Bomber Command are deployed without result against German warships sighted in the North Sea.

3 Sept Baltic
4/Trägergruppe 186 sinks the Polish destroyer *Wicher*, 3/K. Fl. Gr 706 the minelayer *Gryf* and 3/K. Fl. Gr 506 some smaller ships and the gunboat *General Haller* in Hela.

3 Sept North Sea
German cruisers, destroyers, torpedo boats and minelayers begin to lay the 'Westwall' mine barrages in the North Sea. Up to 20 Sept, generally in more than one operation, there take part: Commander Reconnaissance Forces (Vice-Adm Densch) with the cruisers *Nürnberg*, *Leipzig*, *Köln*, *Königsberg* and *Emden*; Officer Commanding Torpedo Boats (Rear-Adm Lütjens) with

the 1st DD Flotilla (Capt Meisel) with *Georg Thiele, Richard Beitzen, Friedrich Ihn, Erich Steinbrinck* and *Friedrich Eckoldt*; the 2nd DD Flotilla (Capt Bonte) with *Theodor Riedel, Hermann Schoemann, Bruno Heinemann,* and *Leberecht Maass*; the 4th DD Flotilla (Cdr* Bey) with *Bernd von Arnim, Hans Lody,* and *Erich Giese*; the 5th DD Div (Cdr* H. Hartmann) with *Diether von Roeder, Hans Lüdemann, Hermann Künne* and *Karl Galster*; the 5th TB Flotilla (Cdr Heyke) with *Greif, Möwe, Albatros, Kondor* and *Falke*; and the 6th TB Flotilla (Cdr Waue) with *Leopard, Seeadler, Iltis, Wolf* and *Luchs,* and the minelayers *Cobra, Kaiser* and *Roland.*

3 Sept   South Atlantic
The British cruiser *Ajax* stops the German freighters *Olinda* (4576 tons) and *Carl Fritzen* (6594 tons) between Rio Grande do Sul and the estuary of the River Plate. They avoid capture by scuttling themselves.

3-6 Sept   North Sea
U13 (Lt-Cdr Daublebsky v. Eichhain); *U15* (Lt-Cdr Buchholz); *U16* (Lt-Cdr Weingaertner); and *U17* (Lt-Cdr v. Reiche) lay magnetic mines on the British East Coast off Orford Ness, Flamborough, Hartlepool and the Downs. On *U13*'s mine barrage two ships of 11301 tons sink and another of 10902 tons is damaged. On *U15*'s mine barrage two ships of 4274 tons sink.

3-10 Sept   North Sea
U12, U56, U58 and *U59* are stationed on Great Fisher Bank and *U9* and *U19* off the Scottish East Coast against British naval units. No result. *U20* operates off S Norway.

3-17 Sept   North Atlantic
Aircraft carriers of Home Fleet are employed against U-boats; *Ark Royal* off the North-Western Approaches, *Courageous* and *Hermes* off the South-Western Approaches. On 14 Sept *U39* (Lt-Cdr Glattes), after an unsuccessful attack on *Ark Royal* due to torpedo defects, is sunk by her screening destroyers *Fame, Faulknor, Firedrake, Forester* and *Foxhound.* On the same day aircraft from the carrier damage *U30,* but two Skuas are lost. On 17 Sept *U29* (Lt-Cdr Schuhart) sinks the

carrier *Courageous* (Capt Makeig-Jones†) west of Ireland. 514 lives are lost. The carriers are then withdrawn from the U-boat search.

3-17 Sept   North Sea
On 3 Sept the British Government announces the blockade of Germany. First operation to control contraband: Submarines are stationed off Hornsriff, the estuaries of the Elbe and Jade and near Terschelling as well as between the Shetlands and Norway. But only German U-boats are sighted and they are attacked without success. On 10 Sept the submarine *Triton* sinks another British submarine *Oxley* off Obrestad and on 14 Sept *Sturgeon* only just misses her sister boat *Swordfish.* The submarines are withdrawn from the Shetland narrows on 20 Sept.
From 3 Sept to 6 Sept the Humber Force operates with the cruisers *Glasgow* and *Southampton* and eight destroyers off the Norwegian coast; at the same time, the Home Fleet cruises W of the Hebrides and searches for the *Bremen* (51731 tons), the flagship of the German Merchant Navy, on her way back from New York. But she has already arrived at the North Base near Murmansk. On the basis of a false report that heavy German units have put out to sea parts of the Home Fleet cruise E of the Orkneys until 6 Sept.
From 6 Sept to 10 Sept the Home Fleet (Adm Forbes) with the battleships *Nelson* and *Rodney,* the battlecruiser *Repulse,* the cruisers *Aurora* and *Sheffield* and 10 destroyers operates against German blockade-runners off the Norwegian coast. From 7 Sept to 12 Sept the battlecruisers *Hood* and *Renown,* the cruisers *Belfast* and *Edinburgh* and four destroyers cruise in the waters between Iceland and the Faeroes. The carrier *Ark Royal* provides air cover and reconnaissance.
From 6 Sept the Northern patrol is formed from the cruisers of the 7th and 12th Cruiser sqdns: *Caledon, Calypso, Diomede, Dragon*; and *Effingham, Emerald, Cardiff* and *Dunedin.* Two cruisers receive orders to operate permanently between the Shetlands and the Faeroes and three between the Faeroes and Iceland. Up to 28 Sept 108 merchant ships are stopped, 28 of

which are ordered to Kirkwall for inspection.

4 Sept North Sea
First attacks by RAF Bomber Command on German warships in the Heligoland Bight: Five Blenheims of No. 110 Sqdn (Fl-Lt Doran) get three hits (unexploded) on the pocket-battleship *Admiral Scheer* in the Schillig Roads and lose one machine to AA defence. Four of five Blenheims of No. 107 Sqdn are destroyed by AA fire. One aircraft, which is shot down, crashes on the side of the light cruiser *Emden* and causes casualties.
14 Wellingtons of Nos. 9 and 149 Sqdns make an unsuccessful attack on the battleships *Gneisenau* and *Scharnhorst* in Brunsbüttel and lose two aircraft to Me 109's of II/JG 77.
Five Blenheims of No. 139 Sqdn fail to find their targets and have to return.

4 Sept Baltic
Schleswig-Holstein, *T196* and *v.d. Gröben* shell Westerplatte. The Officer Commanding Torpedo Boats proceeds to the North Sea with the destroyers.

4 Sept General Situation
Advance parties of the British Expeditionary Force are transported in destroyers from Portsmouth to Cherbourg.

4-6 Sept Baltic
Polish submarines *Rys*, *Wilk* and *Zbik* lay a total of 50 mines N of the estuary of the Vistula, E of Hela and NE of Heisternest. The first two mine barrages are cleared, but *M85* is sunk on the last on 1 Oct. Submarines *Rys*, *Sep* and *Wilk* are damaged by depth charges from the 1st MS Flotilla.

6 Sept North Sea
First convoys on the British East Coast between the Firth of Forth and the Thames estuary.

7 Sept Baltic
Surrender of Westerplatte after renewed shelling by *Schleswig-Holstein* and attack by naval assault company with Army engineers.
Withdrawal of German U-boats from the Baltic.
New operational area of Polish submarines between Bornholm and the Gulf of Danzig: no successes.
Up to 13 Sept *Schleswig-Holstein* shells Polish positions and batteries near Hochredlau and on Hela daily.

7 Sept Atlantic
First British Atlantic convoys set out— from the English Channel (OA), from Liverpool (OB) and to Gibraltar (OG).

8 Sept North Sea
The Dutch Navy loses the minesweeper *Willem van Ewijck* (460 tons) near Terschelling when she runs on her own mine barrage.

9 Sept General Situation
First troop transport convoy of the British Expeditionary Force sails from Southampton to Cherbourg.

9-10 Sept North Sea
British destroyers *Esk* and *Express* lay during the night the first offensive mine barrage on the suspected German exit channels in the German mine-warning area.

11 Sept Baltic
Polish submarines receive orders to get through to Britain—*Wilk* actually arrives on 20 Sept—or to allow themselves to be interned in Sweden when they have used up their reserves. *Sep* at Landsort on 17 Sept, *Rys* at Stavnäs on 18 Sept and *Zbik* at Stavnäs on 25 Sept. *Orzel* puts into Reval (Tallinn) on 14 Sept.

11-16 Sept North Sea
British minelayers *Adventure* and *Plover* and auxiliary minelayers lay 3000 mines in the Straits of Dover. Escort provided by cruiser *Cairo* and the 19th DD Flotilla.

11-29 Sept North Sea
Unsuccessful operations by six German U-boats against British naval units off the Scottish East Coast. First torpedo failures (premature fuses and depth-keeping defects) in attacks on British destroyers and submarines.

12 Sept Baltic
German experimental vessel *Otto Braun* hit by Polish battery on Hela.

12 Sept Western Atlantic
US Navy organises neutrality patrols: 'Zero' with the destroyers *Davis*, *Jouett*, *Benham* and *Ellet* between Halifax and Placentia Bay.
'1' with destroyers *Hamilton* and *Leary* near the Georges Shoals.
'2' with the destroyers *Goff*, *Hopkins*, and the Patron 54 with the tender *Owl* working from Newport.
'3' with the destroyers *Decatur*, *Barry*, *Reuben James* and *Manley* and Patrons

52 and 53 working from Chesapeake Bay.
'6' with destroyers *Babbitt* and *Claxton* in the Straits of Florida.
'7/8' with cruisers *San Francisco* and *Tuscaloosa*, destroyers *Truxton*, *Sampson*, *Broome*, *Borie* and Patrons 33 and 51 with the tenders *Gannet*, *Lapwing* and *Thrush* in the area of the Caribbean.
'9' with cruisers *Quincy* and *Vincennes* off Cape Hatteras.
Reserve in Hampton Roads: battleships *New York*, *Texas*, *Arkansas*, *Wyoming* and carrier *Ranger*.

13 Sept   Atlantic
The French fast minelayer *La Tour d'Auvergne* (ex-*Pluton*) sinks in the harbour of Casablanca after an internal explosion.

14 Sept   Baltic
Gdynia taken by the Kaupisch Korps. Polish minesweepers *Jaskolko*, *Rybitwa* and *Czajka* lay a barrage of 60 mines S of Hela.

14 Sept   Atlantic
Departure of first SL convoys from Freetown.

14 Sept-12 Oct   Atlantic
Operations by French submarines *Agosta*, *Ouessant*, *Persée*, and *Poncelet* against German blockade-runners in the area of the Azores. *Poncelet* (Cdr de Saussine) captures the steamer *Chemnitz* (5522 tons) on 28 Sept.

15-23 Sept   Atlantic
First Transatlantic convoys.
On 15 Sept convoy KJF1. sets out from Kingston (Jamaica).
On 16 Sept Convoy HX1. (18 ships) sets out from Halifax with destroyers *St Laurent* and *Saguenay* as anti-U-boat screen. On 17 Sept Convoy HXF.1 follows with the destroyer *Fraser*. Ocean escort for these convoys provided by cruisers *Berwick* and *York*. On 23 Sept Convoy HX.2 follows with destroyer *Skeena*.

15 Sept-4 Oct   North Sea
Off the Norwegian Southern Coast in mercantile warfare, in accordance with prize regulations, *U3* (Lt-Cdr Schepke) sinks two ships of 2348 tons; *U4* (Lt-Cdr v. Klot-Heydenfeldt) three ships of 5133 tons; *U6* (Lt-Cdr Weingaertner) one ship of 3378 tons; *U7* (Lt Heidel) three ships of 5892 tons; and

U36 (Lt-Cdr Fröhlich) two ships of 2813 tons.

16 Sept   North Atlantic
First U-boat attack on a convoy: *U31* sinks the steamer *Aviemore* (4060 tons) in convoy OB.4.

18 Sept   Baltic Sea
The Polish submarine *Orzel* (Lt-Cdr Grudzinski) breaks out of Reval. She reaches England on 14 Oct after an adventurous voyage without maps.

19 Sept   Baltic
The Officer Commanding Minesweepers (Capt Ruge) with *M3*, *M4*, *Nautilus*, *Nettelbeck*, *Fuchs*, *Otto Braun*, *Pelikan*, *Arkona*, *Sundewall* and *Drache*, and supported by *Schleswig-Holstein*, shell Polish positions near Oxhöft, Ostrowogrund, and Hexengrund.

19-20 Sept   North Atlantic
After two trawlers are sunk by *U27* off the Hebrides the C-in-C Home Fleet deploys 10 destroyers of the 6th and 8th DD Flotillas to search for U-boats. They are supported by air reconnaissance. On 20 Sept *U27* is found and sunk by *Faulknor*, *Fearless*, *Forester*, and *Fortune*. The last-named is able to salvage secret documents with a boarding party shortly before the U-boat goes down.

20 Sept-15 Jan   North Sea
Submarines of the Home Fleet (Rear-Adm Watson) operate against German naval movements in the North Sea and off Norway. Large boats of the 2nd Flotilla (*Thames*, *Oberon*, *Triton*, *Triumph*, *Thistle* and later, *Triad*, *Trident* and *Truant*) off Norway; medium boats of the 2nd Flotilla (*Swordfish*, *Sturgeon*, *Seahorse*, *Starfish*, *Seawolf*, *Sunfish*, *Spearfish* and *Sterlet*), of the 3rd Flotilla (*Salmon*, *Sealion*, *Shark* and *Snapper*) and of the 6th Flotilla (*Undine*, *Unity*, *Ursula*, *L23*, *L26*, *L27*, and *H49*) off the Skagerrak, Jutland, Hornsriff, in the Heligoland Bight, off Terschelling, and W of the German 'Westwall' minefield. Owing to rare sightings, initial successes are few. (Compare 20 Nov and 4 Dec-14 Dec). From October the Polish submarines *Orzel* and *Wilk*, having broken out of the Baltic, also take part.

22-23 Sept   North Sea
Raid by British 2nd Cruiser Sqdn with

Southampton, Glasgow, Sheffield, and *Aurora* and eight destroyers of the 7th DD Flotilla is broken off because of collision of two destroyers. The Home Fleet comes out to cover the operation.

22 Sept-3 Nov   Atlantic
The French submarines *Achille, Casabianca, Pasteur* and *Sfax* are stationed in turn near Cape Ortegal to keep watch on German merchant ships in North Spanish ports.

22 Sept-27 Dec   Atlantic
The French submarines *Agosta, Bévéziers, Ouessant, Sidi-Ferruch* are moved to Martinique to watch for blockade-runners using the passages between the Antilles.

24 Sept   General Situation
The restrictions in the orders relating to mercantile warfare against France are lifted. Permission is given to open fire on merchant ships using W/T.

25-26 Sept   North Sea
British Home Fleet with 2nd Cruiser Sqdn (*Southampton, Aurora, Sheffield* and *Glasgow*) and six destroyers of the 7th DD Flotilla, comes out to recover the submarine *Spearfish* badly damaged in the central North Sea. Cover provided by the C-in-C (Adm Forbes) with the battleships *Nelson* and *Rodney*, the battlecruisers *Hood* and *Renown*, the carrier *Ark Royal*, the cruisers *Norfolk, Newcastle* and *Edinburgh* and destroyers of the 4th and 8th DD Flotillas. The force is located by German air reconnaissance. Four Ju 88's of I/KG 30 attack. One (2nd-Lt Storp) has a bomb rebound off *Hood*, another (L/Cpl Francke) gets a near-miss on *Ark Royal* which leads German propaganda to report the sinking of the carrier. 9 He 111's of 1/KG 26 miss the 2nd Cruiser Sqdn.

25-27 Sept   Baltic
Polish artillery positions on Hela are shelled by the old battleships *Schlesien* (Capt Utke) and *Schleswig-Holstein* (Capt Kleikamp).

25 Sept-23 Oct   North Sea
Deep anti-U-boat mine barrages laid in Straits of Dover (3636 mines between Folkestone and Cape Gris Nez). In October *U12, U16* and *U40* are lost. Passage of U-boats through the Channel is stopped.

26 Sept   North Atlantic
First convoy sets out from Gibraltar to Britain (HG.1). Permission for operations given to pocket-battleships *Admiral Graf Spee* (South Atlantic) and *Deutschland* (North Atlantic).

26 Sept   Baltic
According to Soviet claims the Soviet tanker *Metallist* (968 tons) is sunk in Narva Bay ostensibly by a Polish submarine. However, the submarine *Orzel*, having broken out of Tallinn is on the way to Britain; the boats *Rys, Sep* and *Zbik* are interned in Sweden; and *Wilk* is already in the North Sea. According to Finnish information, based on statements made by Soviet prisoners, the *Metallist* was, in fact, sunk by the torpedo boat *Tutch*, on the orders of the Leningrad Party Secretary, Zhdanov, following an unsuccessful attack by the submarine *Shch-303*, in order to provide an excuse to move against Estonia.

26-28 Sept   North Sea
German Destroyers and torpedo boats conduct mercantile warfare in the Skagerrak. 45 merchant ships are stopped and inspected.

29 Sept   North Sea
In a reconnaissance sortie by No. 144 Sqdn of RAF Bomber Command over the Heligoland Bight five out of 11 Hampdens are shot down by German fighters. Unsuccessful attack on two German destroyers near Heligoland.

30 Sept   South Atlantic
Admiral Graf Spee achieves her first success in sinking the British steamer *Clement* (5051 tons) off Pernambuco.

30 Sept   North Atlantic
Deutschland begins operations on Bermuda-Azores route. 5 Oct: steamer *Stonegate* (5044 tons) sunk.

30 Sept-6 Oct   North Sea
German destroyers, torpedo boats and minelayers, employed in mercantile warfare, in the Skagerrak and Kattegat, halt another 72 merchant ships and inspect them.

1 Oct   General Situation
British merchant ships receive orders to ram U-boats when they sight them.

1 Oct   Baltic
The German minesweepers *M4, M111, M132* and *Nettelbeck* shell the Hela

peninsula in co-operation with army batteries and a naval railway battery in preparation for the infantry attack. The garrison of Hela (Rear-Adm Unrug) capitulates. Last resistance on the coast broken.

2 Oct General Situation
Pan-American Security Zone proclaimed.

2-4 Oct General Situation
Permission given for the use of German arms against camouflaged ships in defined areas round Britain and in the Bay of Biscay.

4 Oct General Situation
Permission given to use all weapons against armed Allied merchant ships.

4 Oct Western Atlantic
The largest convoy yet, KJ.3 (45 Ships), leaves Kingston, escorted by the British cruiser *Berwick* and the Australian *Perth* which, halfway to Britain, is then relieved by the British cruiser *Effingham*.

5 Oct Atlantic
Eight British and French hunting groups are formed to search for the German pocket-battleship *Admiral Graf Spee* operating in the South Atlantic:
Force F (North America/West Indies): British cruisers *Berwick* and *York*.
Force G (East Coast of South America): British cruisers *Cumberland*, *Exeter* later *Achilles* and *Ajax*.
Force H (Cape of Good Hope): British cruisers *Shropshire* and *Sussex*.
Force I (Ceylon): carrier *Eagle*, British cruisers *Dorsetshire* and *Cornwall*.
Force K (Pernambuco): British carrier *Ark Royal* and battlecruiser *Renown*.
Force L (Brest): French battleship *Dunkerque*, carrier *Béarn*, cruisers *Georges Leygues*, *Gloire* and *Montcalm*.
Force M (Dakar): French cruisers *Dupleix* and *Foch*.
Force N (West Indies): French battleship *Strasbourg*, British carrier *Hermes* and British cruiser *Neptune*. From 5 Oct to 12 Oct *Admiral Graf Spee* sinks four ships of 22368 tons on the Cape Town-Freetown route and proceeds to supply ship *Altmark* for replenishment.

7 Oct English Channel
So far 161000 troops, 24000 vehicles and 140000 tons of supplies belonging to the British Expeditionary Force have been landed in France without loss.

7-9 Oct North Sea
The Commander of the German Fleet (Adm Boehm) makes a sortie towards the Southern coast of Norway with the battleship *Gneisenau*, the light cruiser *Köln* and nine destroyers (*Max Schultz, Paul Jacobi, Bernd von Arnim, Friedrich Ihn, Erich Steinbrinck, Friedrich Eckoldt, Diether von Roeder, Karl Galster* and *Wilhelm Heidkamp*) to draw the Home Fleet across a concentration of U-boats (four boats) and within range of the Luftwaffe and, in this way, to take the strain off the pocket-battleships. The German formation is sighted on 8 Oct by a Hudson of No. 224 Sqdn, RAF. Humber Force, comprising light cruisers *Edinburgh, Glasgow, Southampton* and battlecruiser squadron consisting of *Hood, Repulse*, cruisers *Aurora* and *Sheffield* and four destroyers sets out, as well as the Home Fleet with the battleships *Nelson* and *Rodney*, the carrier *Furious*, the cruiser *Newcastle* and eight destroyers. 12 Wellington bombers miss their targets. 127 He 111's of KG 26 and of LG 1, as well as 21 Ju 88's of I/KG 30 are deployed; but they achieve no success. The operation ends without result for both sides.

9 Oct North Atlantic
British cruiser *Belfast* of the Northern Patrol captures the German passenger steamer *Cap Norte* (13615 tons). From 29 Sept to 12 Oct another 63 merchant ships are halted, 20 of which are ordered to Kirkwall for inspection.

9-16 Oct North Atlantic
Pocket-battleship *Deutschland* operates on the HX route. US freighter *City of Flint* (4963 tons) is captured with contraband. The Norwegian freighter *Lorentz W. Hansen* (1918 tons) is sunk.

10-19 Oct North Atlantic
First attempt to conduct a U-boat group operation with a tactical commander on board (Cdr W. Hartmann) on *U37*. Only six boats of the intended nine set out. Of these *U40* (Lt-Cdr v. Schmidt) is sunk in the Channel after hitting a mine: and *U42* (Lt-Cdr Dau) and *U45* (Lt-Cdr Gelhaar) are sunk respectively by the escorts of convoys OB.17 and KJF.3 after these have been attacked. On 17 Oct an operation is conducted with the remaining three boats—*U37* (Cdr Hartmann), *U46* (Lt-

Cdr Sohler) and *U48* (Lt-Cdr Schultze) —against the still unprotected convoy HG.3. Each boat sinks one ship: torpedo failures prevent greater successes. Total sinkings by the boats of this group: *U37* eight ships of 35306 tons; *U45* two ships of 19313 tons; *U46* one ship of 7028 tons; and *U48* five ships of 37153 tons. In addition, *U42* torpedoes one ship of 4803 tons.

12-26 Oct   North Atlantic
The Northern Patrol stops 112 neutral ships and orders 23 of them to Kirkwall. Light cruisers *Delhi* and *Sheffield* and auxiliary cruisers *Scotstoun* and *Transylvania* of the Northern Patrol stop the German merchant ships, *Bianca* (1375 tons), *Biskaya* (6386 tons), *Gloria* (5896 tons), *Gonzenheim* (4574 tons), *Poseidon* (5864 tons) and *Rheingold* (5055 tons). The latter three ships avoid capture by scuttling themselves.

14 Oct   North Sea
U47 (Lt-Cdr Prien) penetrates into the Bay of Scapa Flow and in two approaches, despite several torpedo failures, sinks the British battleship *Royal Oak* (Capt Benn†). 833 dead including the Commander of the 2nd Battle Sqdn, Rear-Adm Blagrove.

16 Oct   North Sea
Ju 88's of I/KG 30 (Capt Pohle) attack shipping targets in the Firth of Forth. Light cruisers *Edinburgh* and *Southampton* and destroyer *Mohawk* are slightly damaged by unexploded bombs. Two aircraft are shot down including that of the Gruppe Cdr.

16 Oct   Atlantic
During the searches by the Anglo-French hunting groups in the Atlantic the German freighter *Halle* (5889 tons) is encountered by the French cruiser *Duguay-Trouin* on 16 Oct W of Dakar and scuttles herself.

16 Oct-5 Nov   North Sea
U-boats lay magnetic mine barrages off the British East Coast: *U16* (Lt-Cdr Wellner†) in the Straits of Dover—but runs on a mine and sinks; *U19* (Lt-Cdr Meckel) off Inner Dowsing; *U21* (Lt-Cdr Frauenheim) in the Firth of Forth; *U23* (Lt-Cdr Kretschmer) off Cromarty; *U24* (Lt-Cdr Jeppener-Haltenhoff) off Hartlepool. On the West Coast *U31* (Lt-Cdr Habekost) lays a barrage in Loch Ewe and *U33* (Lt-Cdr v. Dresky)

off North Foreland. The following losses occur on these barrages: on *U16*'s one auxiliary minesweeper (67 tons) sunk; on *U19*'s three ships of 12344 tons sunk; on *U21*'s one ship of 2266 tons and the netlayer *Bayonet* sunk and the cruiser *Belfast* damaged (see 21 Nov); on *U24*'s one ship of 961 tons sunk; and on *U31*'s two auxiliary minesweepers of 160 tons sunk and battleship *Nelson* damaged (see 4 Dec); on *U33*'s two ships of 11929 tons sunk and one ship of 13647 tons damaged.

17 Oct   North Sea
Four Ju 88's of I/KG 30 (Capt Doench) attack ships in Scapa Flow losing one aircraft. Training ship *Iron Duke* has to be beached after near-misses.

17 Oct   General Situation
The German Navy Staff permits the use of all weapons against all enemy merchant ships, passenger ships excepted.

17-18 Oct   North Sea
Offensive mining operation off the Humber Estuary by the Officer Commanding Torpedo Boats (Rear-Adm Lütjens) with the destroyers *Wilhelm Heidkamp*, *Hermann Künne*, *Friedrich Eckoldt*, *Diether von Roeder*, *Karl Galster* and *Hans Lüdemann*. Total results: seven ships of 25825 tons sunk.

21 Oct   North Sea
9 He 115s of 1/K.Fl.Gr. 406 are intercepted by fighters when approaching a British convoy off the Humber estuary and four are lost.

21-30 Oct   Atlantic
The French Force de raide (Vice-Adm Gensoul), consisting of the battleship *Dunkerque*, the cruisers *Georges Leygues*, *Gloire* and *Montcalm* and the large destroyers *Mogador*, *Volta*, *L'Indomptable*, *Le Triomphant*, *Le Malin*, *Le Fantasque*, *Le Terrible* and *L'Audacieux*, operates on the route Antilles-English Channel to cover the large convoy KJ.4 against an attack by the pocket-battleship *Deutschland* at sea in the North Atlantic. In this operation the German blockade-runner, *Santa Fé* (4627 tons) is captured on 25 Oct by *Le Fantasque* and *Le Terrible* with support from the cruiser *Dupleix*.

23 Oct   Western Atlantic
The German tanker *Emmy Friedrich* (4372 tons) coming from Tampico

(Mexico) is reported in the Yucatan Channel by the British cruiser *Orion* and the Canadian destroyer *Saguenay* and scuttles herself on being stopped by the British cruiser *Caradoc*.

23-31 Oct   Norway
British ore convoy from Narvik is escorted by the British cruiser *Aurora* and four destroyers. The Home Fleet (Adm Forbes), consisting of the battleships *Nelson* and *Rodney*, the battlecruiser *Hood* and six destroyers, operates as a covering force.

24 Oct-13 Nov   North Sea
Four German U-boats operate against units of the British Fleet W of the Orkneys. On 30 Oct *U56* (Lt-Cdr Zahn) attacks the battleship *Nelson* but, owing to torpedo failure, without result. In subsequent operations against merchant ships *U13* (Lt-Cdr Daublebsky v. Eichhain) sinks one ship of 4666 tons and *U59* (Lt Jürst) three ships of 1470 tons.

25 Oct-15 Nov   North Atlantic
Planned sortie by three German U-boats into the Mediterranean fails. *U25* (Cdr Schütze) is damaged after attack on French convoy 20.K—one ship of 5874 tons sunk; *U53* (Lt-Cdr Heinicke) has to break off sortie; only *U26* (Lt-Cdr Ewerth) reaches the Mediterranean after abandoning plan to sow mines off Gibraltar, but she has no success. *U34* (Lt-Cdr Rollmann), which operates on her own further to the N, sinks four ships of 16546 tons, including two on 27 Oct and 29 Oct from the convoy HX.5A.

28 Oct-6 Nov   Central Atlantic
Whilst British Force K (Rear-Adm Wells), comprising carrier *Ark Royal*, battlecruiser *Renown* and destroyers *Hardy*, *Hostile*, *Hasty*, and *Hereward*, operates against German pocket-battleships from Freetown, a carrier aircraft sights the German blockade-runner *Uhenfels* (7603 tons) on 5 Nov. The ship is captured by the destroyer *Hereward*.

29 Oct   General Situation
German warships and U-boats are given permission to attack without warning passenger ships travelling in convoy.

31 Oct   North Sea and Baltic
So far, of the several hundred ships which have been searched for contraband by German surface naval units, U-boats and aircraft in the North Sea and Baltic, a total of 127, representing 245455 tons, have been brought into German harbours.

4 Nov   General Situation
The American Neutrality Law comes into force which forbids American ships and citizens to enter clearly-defined war zones.

5-15 Nov   North Atlantic
The pocket-battleship *Deutschland* is recalled and returns through the Denmark Strait and the Shetland passage. On 17 Nov the ship anchors in Gotenhafen (Gdynia).

6 Nov-2 Dec   Indian Ocean/
South Atlantic
German pocket-battleship *Admiral Graf Spee* (Capt Langsdorff) operates S of Madagascar. On 15 Nov she sinks tanker *Africa Shell* (706 tons) and on 16 Nov halts a Dutch steamer. On receipt of this news the British C-in-C East Indies, Vice-Adm Leatham, forms several groups to search for the German ships: battleships *Malaya* and *Ramillies* and carrier *Glorious* in the area of Socotra; carrier *Eagle*, cruisers *Cornwall* and *Dorsetshire* and Australian destroyers *Vendetta* and *Waterhen* in the area of Ceylon; cruisers *Kent* and *Suffren* (French) and Australian destroyers *Vampire* and *Voyager* in the area of Sumatra; Australian cruiser *Hobart* S of the Arabian Sea; cruiser *Gloucester* and French sloop *Rigault de Genouilly* in area N of Madagascar to the Seychelles; and Australian destroyer *Stuart* and one submarine in the area of the Maldives and Chagos Archipelago. Whilst the *Admiral Graf Spee* returns to the South Atlantic from 17 Nov to 26 Nov to replenish from the supply ship *Altmark* the C-in-C South Atlantic, Vice-Adm d'Oyly Lyon, forms search groups in the South Atlantic, too: Force H, comprising the cruisers *Shropshire* and *Sussex*, is reinforced by Force K which is summoned from Freetown and which includes the battlecruiser *Renown*, the carrier *Ark Royal* and the cruiser *Neptune*. On 21 Nov the German blockade runner *Adolf Woermann* (8577 tons), which has been reported by a British steamer, is found by the

Neptune near Ascension and scuttles herself. On 2 Dec the blockade-runner *Watussi* (9552 tons) which has been reported by a South African aircraft and intercepted by the cruiser *Sussex*, is sunk by her own crew off South Africa when the *Renown* opens fire. The cruisers of Force G (Commodore Harwood) *Ajax*, *Achilles*, *Exeter* and *Cumberland* operate in the area off the Falkland Islands and off South America. The submarine *Clyde* and the destroyers *Hardy*, *Hostile*, *Hasty* and *Hereward* patrol on the Freetown-Natal coastal route and the carrier *Hermes* from Dakar with the French cruisers *Dupleix* and *Foch*.

7 Nov   North Sea
First sortie by a torpedo-carrying aircraft of Air Commander West against British destroyers E of Lowestoft. It misses its targets.

12-13 Nov   North Sea
Offensive mining operation off the Thames Estuary by the Officer Commanding Destroyers, Capt Bonte, with the destroyers *Karl Galster*, *Wilhelm Heidkamp*, *Hermann Künne* and *Hans Lüdemann*. Successes achieved: destroyer *Blanche* and 13 merchant ships totalling 48728 tons sunk. The four destroyers are met by the Commander Reconnaissance Forces (Vice-Adm Densch) with the light cruisers *Königsberg* and *Nürnberg* and the 6th TB Flotilla comprising *Leopard*, *Seeadler*, *Iltis* and *Wolf*.

12-17 Nov   Norway
Home Fleet acts as covering force for a second ore convoy from Narvik (see 23 Oct).

14 Nov   Central Atlantic
The French auxiliary cruiser *Koutoubia* captures the German blockade-runner *Trifels* (6198 tons) in the area of the Azores.

15-20 Nov   North Atlantic
Second attempt to conduct U-boat group operations against a convoy. On 15 Nov *U53* (Lt-Cdr Heinicke) sights the French convoy KS.27 W of Gibraltar. Although *U53* is repeatedly driven off by a seaplane, the escorting destroyers *Frondeur* and *Sirocco*, the sloop *Chevreuil* and the large destroyer *Chevalier-Paul*, which is summoned to the scene, she is able to keep in con-

tact until 20 Nov. But the arrival of *U41* (Lt-Cdr Mugler), *U43* (Lt-Cdr Ambrosius) and *U49* (Lt-Cdr v. Gossler) brings no success because the boats are partly held up by independents and the approaching convoy OG.7 and because repeated torpedo failures with all the boats frustrate the attacks. In their operations against stragglers and independents *U41* and *U43* each sink four ships of 12941 tons and 16030 tons respectively.

15-24 Nov   North Sea
In operations on the British East Coast *U15* (Lt-Cdr Frahm) lays magnetic mines off Lowestoft; *U19* (Lt-Cdr Müller-Arnecke) off Orford Ness; and *U20* (Lt-Cdr Moehle) near Newarp lightship. *U15* is responsible for one ship of 258 tons sinking on a mine barrage; *U19* for one ship of 6371 tons; and *U20* for two ships of 7929 tons. In simultaneous torpedo operations on the East Coast *U18* (Lt Mengersen) sinks one ship of 345 tons and *U22* (Lt-Cdr Jenisch) one ship of 500 tons. Near the Noordhinder lightship *U57* (Lt-Cdr Korth) sinks two ships of 2949 tons.

15 Nov-5 Dec   North Atlantic
U28 (Lt-Cdr Kuhnke), on the way to a mining operation, in the Bristol Channel, sinks two ships of 10277 tons by torpedo. One ship of 9577 tons sinks on the mine barrage. *U29* (Lt-Cdr Schuhart) has to break off her mining operation because of the strong defence.

17-18 Nov   North Sea
Offensive mining operation by the destroyers *Hermann Künne* (Cdr of 5th DD Div, Cdr* H. Hartmann), *Bernd von Arnim* and *Wilhelm Heidkamp* off the central Thames Estuary. Overall result: destroyer *Gypsy*, one trawler and seven ships totalling 27565 tons sunk. The force is met near Terschelling Bank by the Commander Reconnaissance Forces with cruisers *Leipzig* and *Nürnberg* and *Leopard*, *Seeadler*, and *Iltis* of the 6th TB Flotilla.

18-19 Nov   North Sea
Offensive mining operation by the destroyers *Erich Steinbrinck* (Cdr 4th DD Flotilla, Cdr* Bey), *Friedrich Eckoldt* and *Hans Lody*, off the Humber Estuary. Overall result: seven ships totalling 38710 tons sunk including the Polish passenger ship *Pilsudski* (14294

tons) on 26 Nov. The destroyers are met by the cruiser *Leipzig* and the 6th TB Flotilla comprising *Leopard, Seeadler, Iltis* and *Wolf.*

20 Nov   North Sea
First British submarine success: *Sturgeon* (Lt Gregory) sinks the patrol vessel *V209* (428 tons) in the Heligoland Bight.

20 Nov   North Sea
First use of air mines by seaplanes of the Commander Naval Air Forces (Air Commander West) off the British East Coast. 41 air mines are dropped in three sorties in November. By 23 Nov Lt-Cdr Ouvery succeeds in defusing one of these mines off Shoeburyness, where it is discovered on the mud flats.

21 Nov   North Sea
British cruiser *Belfast* runs on a mine laid by *U21* (Lt-Cdr Frauenheim) in the Firth of Forth.

21-22 Nov   North Sea
Commander Reconnaissance Forces (Vice-Adm Densch) operates against merchant shipping in the Skagerrak with the pocket-battleship *Lützow* (ex-*Deutschland*), the cruisers *Köln* and *Leipzig* and the 6th TB Flotilla with *Leopard, Seeadler* and *Iltis.*

21-27 Nov   North Atlantic
Sortie by the German Fleet Commander (Vice-Adm Marschall) with the battleships *Gneisenau* (Capt Förste) and *Scharnhorst* (Capt Hoffmann) into the North Atlantic against the Northern Patrol. Its purpose: to relieve pressure on the pocket-battleship *Admiral Graf Spee* in the South Atlantic. On the way out they are accompanied until 22 Nov by the Commander Reconnaissance Forces with the light cruisers *Köln* and *Leipzig* and the destroyers *Bernd von Arnim, Erich Giese* and *Karl Galster* which are then dispatched for operations against shipping in the Skagerrak together with the torpedo boats *Leopard, Seeadler, Iltis* and *Wolf* (until 25 Nov). The battleships make a sortie into the Faeroes-Iceland passage. There on the evening of 23 Nov the auxiliary cruiser *Rawalpindi* (Capt Kennedy†) is surprised and sunk by *Scharnhorst* in a brief gun duel. Whilst rescuing survivors the German force sights the British cruiser *Newcastle* in the vicinity, but is able to avoid her in a rain squall and

withdraw to a waiting position in the Arctic. In response to *Rawalpindi*'s distress signal and the *Newcastle*'s report, all available ships are deployed in a search: first the old cruiser, *Delhi*, which, together with the *Newcastle*, is stationed in the vicinity, then the cruiser *Sheffield* coming from Loch Ewe with three destroyers from Scapa. To cover the Iceland-Faeroes passage, apart from the old cruisers *Calypso* and *Ceres*, which are stationed there, the heavy cruisers *Norfolk* and *Suffolk* are brought up from the Denmark Strait, where the watch is taken over by the battleship *Warspite* detached from an HX convoy. The watch over the Faeroes-Shetland passage, apart from the old cruisers *Caledon, Cardiff* and *Colombo* which are stationed there, is undertaken by the cruisers *Diomede* and *Dunedin* coming from the S. The cruisers *Aurora, Edinburgh* and *Southampton* set out with three destroyers from the Firth of Forth to cover the Fair Isle passage and a fourth destroyer guards the Pentland Firth. The convoy ON.3, which has just put to sea, returns and its three destroyers join the cruiser *Glasgow* which is cruising off Norway with two destroyers in the expectation that the German passenger ship *Bremen* will pass there from Murmansk. The C-in-C Home Fleet, Admiral Forbes, sets out from the Clyde with the battleships *Nelson* and *Rodney*, the heavy cruiser *Devonshire* and seven destroyers of the 8th DD Flotilla (*Faulknor*). On 24 Nov and 25 Nov the cruisers form a close reconnaissance line W of Bergen, whilst the *Aurora* with the destroyers from the cruiser squadrons stand on the alert off Utsire and the Home Fleet cruises N of the Shetlands until 29 Nov. The submarines *L23, Sturgeon, Thistle* and *Triad* are stationed off the Skagerrak and all the submarines in the Firth of Forth and Tyne are sent to the area off Lister. Because there is also a danger of the German ships breaking out into the Atlantic, the battlecruiser *Repulse* sets out from Halifax with the carrier *Furious*. On 25 Nov the French Force de raide (Vice-Adm Gensoul), comprising the battleship *Dunkerque*, the light cruisers *Georges Leygues* and *Montcalm* and the large destroyers *Mogador*, and

Volta, puts to sea from Brest and joins the battlecruiser *Hood* (Vice-Adm Whitworth) coming from Plymouth with the destroyers *Exmouth, Echo* and *Eclipse* for a sortie into the area S of Iceland. Many ships suffer considerable damage from a heavy storm beginning on 26 Nov. Taking advantage of the bad weather, the German ships are able to reach the North Sea unnoticed on 26-27 Nov. The French battleship *Strasbourg* which leaves Dakar on 21 Nov and is escorted from Casablanca by the large destroyers *Guépard, Valmy* and *Verdun*, is met on 25 Nov by the large destroyers *Le Malin, Le Triomphant* and *L'Indomptable* W of Spain and accompanied to Brest.

21-30 Nov   North Atlantic
The U-boats *U31* (Lt-Cdr Habekost), *U33* (Lt-Cdr v. Dresky), *U35* (Lt-Cdr Lott), *U47* (Lt-Cdr Prien) and *U48* (Lt-Cdr Schultze) are stationed in the area of the Orkneys to support the Fleet operations. *U33* sinks five trawlers and a prize of 5088 tons; *U47* is unsuccessful in attacking the cruiser *Norfolk* on 28 Nov because of a torpedo failure. On 29 Nov *U35* is annihilated by the destroyers *Kingston, Kashmir* and *Icarus*.

21 Nov-4 Dec   Baltic
The German patrol vessels *V701* (21 Nov), *V301* (25 Nov), *V704* (30 Nov) and the submarine-chaser *UJ117* (4 Dec) are lost on the German and Danish defensive mine barrages laid in the Belt and Sound.

24-25 Nov   North Sea
Commander Reconnaissance Forces (Densch) with pocket-battleship *Lützow* (ex-*Deutschland*), the cruisers *Köln* and *Leipzig* and the 6th TB Flotilla with *Leopard, Seeadler, Iltis* and *Wolf*, are employed in mercantile warfare in the Skagerrak.

27 Nov-7 Dec   North Sea
On the British East Coast *U58* (Lt-Cdr Kuppisch) lays magnetic mines off Lowestoft; *U59* (Lt Jürst) off the Cockle lightship; and *U61* (Lt-Cdr Oesten) off Newcastle. Two ships of 705 tons sink on *U59*'s barrage and one ship of 4434 tons is damaged on *U61*'s barrage. In torpedo operations on the East Coast *U21* (Lt-Cdr Frauenheim) sinks one ship of 1277 tons; *U31* (Lt-Cdr Habe-

kost) sinks six ships of 12338 tons; and *U56* (Lt-Cdr Zahn) sinks one ship of 2119 tons and torpedoes one ship of 3829 tons.

28 Nov   North Sea
12 British Blenheim bombers attack the Borkum seaplane base.

30 Nov-1 Dec   Baltic
Start of Soviet attack on Finland. After an air attack by the air forces of the Baltic fleet (Brigade Cdr Ermachenko) a part of the force of light naval units (Capt 1st Class Ptokhov), consisting of cruiser *Kirov* and two destroyers, shells the Finnish island of Russarö which returns the fire.

30 Nov-2 Dec   Arctic
Soviet Northern fleet (Flagman 2nd Class Drozd) attacks Finnish harbours in Petsamo Fjord. Supported by the destroyer *Karl Libknecht*, the patrol ship *Groza*, two NKWD patrol ships and three minesweeping trawlers, elements of the 104th Rifle Div of the 14th Army are landed in the barely defended Liinahamari and at Petsamo. Cover of sea approaches provided by destroyers *Grozny* and *Kuibyshev*, and N of the Varanger peninsula by submarines *Shch-402* and *Shch-404*.

30 Nov-6 Dec   Baltic
Supported by units of the Soviet Baltic Fleet (Flagman 2nd Class Tributs), Soviet assault forces (Capt 1st Class Ramishvili) land on the islands of Seiskari and Lavansaari (30 Nov- 3 Dec), Someri and Narvi (1 Dec), Suur- and Pien-Tytärsaari (4-5 Dec) and Suursaari (5-6 Dec), lying in the inner Gulf of Finland.

2-13 Dec   South Atlantic
German pocket-battleship *Admiral Graf Spee* (Capt Langsdorff) sinks the British freighters *Doric Star* (10086 tons) and *Tairoa* (7983 tons) between St Helena and South Africa and on 7 Dec the *Streonshalh* (3895 tons) S of Trinidad. On the first report on 2 Dec the C-in-C South Atlantic (Vice-Adm d'Oyly Lyon) orders Force H with the cruisers *Shropshire* and *Sussex* to proceed to the Cape Town-St Helena route. Force K, comprising the battlecruiser *Renown*, the carrier *Ark Royal* and the cruiser *Neptune*, searches along the route to Freetown from the Central South Atlantic; Force G assembles with the

cruisers *Achilles, Ajax* and *Exeter* off the River Plate; and the *Cumberland* covers the Falkland Islands. During these movements, the *Shropshire* locates the blockade-runner *Adolf Leonhardt* (2990 tons) on 9 Dec and the *Ajax* and *Cumberland* the *Ussukuma* (7834 tons) on 5 Dec. Both ships scuttle themselves.

2-15 Dec   North Atlantic
In operations W of the English Channel *U47* (Lt-Cdr Prien) sinks three ships of 23168 tons and *U48* (Lt-Cdr Schultze) four ships of 25618 tons.

3-13 Dec   Norway
In an operation off the Norwegian North Coast *U38* (Lt-Cdr Liebe) sinks three ships of 13269 tons.

3 Dec   North Sea
Unsuccessful attack on German warships near Heligoland by 24 Wellington bombers of Nos. 38, 115 and 149 Sqdns RAF.

3-20 Dec   Baltic
Submarines of the Soviet 1st and 2nd SM Brigades (Capt 1st Class Kuznetsov and Capt 1st Class Kosmin) operate in the Gulf of Bothnia (including *S-1, Shch-317, Shch-319*) and in the Gulf of Finland (including *Shch-322* and *Shch-323*). *S-1* (Lt-Cdr Tripolski) sinks the German steamer *Bolheim* (3324 tons) off Rauma on 10 Dec; *Shch-323* (Lt Ivantsov) the Estonian steamer *Kassari* (379 tons) off Utö on 10 Dec. On 7 Dec the Soviet Union declares the Finnish coast from Tornio to Helsinki a blockade zone. On 17 Dec the Aaland Islands are also included.

4 Dec   North Atlantic
British battleship *Nelson* runs on a mine dropped near Loch Ewe by *U31* (Lt-Cdr Habekost).

4-6 Dec   Norway
Mining operation by the cruiser *Nürnberg* (Capt Klüber) off Kristiansand.

4-9 Dec   Baltic
Unsuccessful operations by Finnish submarines: *Vetehinen* against Soviet ice-breaker *Ermak* off Libau, *Iku-Turso* against Soviet ships off Stockholm and *Saukko* against Soviet forces shelling off Koivisto.

4-14 Dec   North Sea
In operations by British submarines in the Heligoland Bight *Salmon* (Lt-Cdr Bickford) sinks the outward-bound German *U36* (Lt-Cdr Fröhlich†). On

12 Dec Bickford tries to halt the passenger liner *Bremen* returning from the Kola Inlet, but has to submerge when a Do 18 flying boat appears. On 13 Dec he fires a salvo at great range against a German naval force (three light cruisers) which have met five destroyers returning from a mining operation off Newcastle). The *Leipzig* receives a serious hit amidships and the *Nürnberg* a hit in the bow. On 14 Dec the submarine *Ursula* (Lt-Cdr Phillips) attacks the force with the damaged *Nürnberg*. The torpedoes are intercepted by the fleet escort vessel *F9* which sinks.

5 Dec   Pacific
The British cruiser *Despatch* captures the German freighter *Düsseldorf* (4930 tons) in Chilean waters off Punta Caldera.

6-7 Dec   North Sea
Naval seaplanes of Air Commander West (3/K.Fl.Gr. 106, 3/506 and 3/906) drop 27 mines in the Humber and Thames estuaries and in the Downs.

6-7 Dec   North Sea
Offensive mining operation by destroyers *Erich Giese* and *Hans Lody* off Cromer. Results: two ships (5286 tons) sunk, one other damaged. As she withdraws, *Erich Giese* torpedoes the British destroyer *Jersey*.

6-27 Dec   North Atlantic
To protect the North Atlantic convoys HXF.11, HX.11 and HX.12 against attacks by German pocket-battleships or battlecruisers, the British and French submarines *Narwhal, Seal, Sfax, Casabianca, Pasteur* and *Achille* proceed in the convoys.

7-22 Dec   North Sea
On the British East Coast *U13* (Lt-Cdr Scheringer) lays magnetic mines off Dundee; *U22* (Lt-Cdr Jenisch) off Blyth; *U60* (Lt-Cdr Schewe) off Cross Sands; *U61* (Lt-Cdr Oesten) off the Firth of Forth on *U13*'s barrage one ship of 1421 tons sinks; on *U22*'s four ships of 4978 tons; on *U61*'s one ship of 1086 tons; and on *U60*'s one ship of 4373 tons. In torpedo operations on the East Coast and in the southern part of the North Sea *U20* (Lt-Cdr Moehle) sinks one ship of 1339 tons; *U21* (Lt-Cdr Frauenheim) two ships of 2827 tons; *U23* (Lt-Cdr Kretschmer) sinks one ship

of 2400 tons; *U57* (Lt-Cdr Korth) one ship of 1173 tons; and *U59* (Lt Jürst) three ships of 4148 tons.

9-10 Dec Baltic
The Finnish coastal batteries near Saarenpää on Koivisto carry out a gun duel with a Soviet shelling force consisting of the flotilla leader *Minsk*, the destroyers *Karl Marx* and *Volodarski*, and the gunboats *Sestroretsk*, *Kronstadt* and *Krasnaya Gorka*.

9 Dec-5 Jan Atlantic
The German tanker *Nordmeer* sails from Curaçao and reaches Vigo in spite of being pursued by the French submarine *Ouessant*.

10-23 Dec North Atlantic
First Canadian troop convoy TC.1 with 7400 men of the 1st Canadian Div sets out from Halifax with the transports *Aquitania*, *Empress of Australia*, *Empress of Britain*, *Duchess of Bedford*, and *Monarch of Bermuda*. Protection against U-boats in Canadian home waters provided by destroyers *Ottawa*, *Restigouche*, *Fraser* and *St Laurent*. Ocean escort: battlecruiser *Repulse*, battleship *Resolution* and carrier *Furious*. At approximately 20°W it is met by A/S escort comprising twelve destroyers of the 6th and 8th DD Flotillas led by *Faulknor*.

12 Dec North Sea
Attack by eight Whitley bombers of the RAF against the German seaplane bases at Borkum and Sylt, from where the minelaying aircraft operating against the British East Coast take off.

12 Dec Western Approaches
British destroyer *Duchess* sinks after collision with battleship *Barham*.

12-13 Dec North Sea
Offensive mining operation in Newcastle area by the Officer Commanding Destroyers (Commodore Bonte) with destroyers *Hermann Künne*, *Friedrich Ihn*, *Erich Steinbrinck*, *Richard Beitzen*, and *Bruno Heinemann*. Result: 11 merchant ships of 18979 tons sunk. After carrying out the operation the destroyers are met by the cruisers *Nürnberg*, *Leipzig* and *Köln*. Attacks by British submarines see 4-14 Dec).

13-17 Dec South Atlantic
Battle off the estuary of the River Plate: pocket-battleship *Admiral Graf Spee*, against the cruiser force of the Com-

mander South American Squadron, Commodore Harwood, with *Exeter* (Capt Bell), *Ajax* (Capt Woodhouse) and *Achilles* (Capt Parry). Heavy cruiser *Exeter* is put out of action (61 dead and 23 wounded); light cruiser *Ajax* (seven dead and five wounded) severely damaged; and *Achilles* (four dead) slightly damaged. *Admiral Graf Spee* (36 dead and 60 wounded) has to put in to Montevideo because of the damage sustained.
The C-in-C South Atlantic (Vice-Adm D'Oyly Lyon), summons to the area of the Plate Estuary the cruiser *Cumberland* from the Falkland Islands (she arrives 16 Dec) and the cruisers *Dorsetshire* and *Shropshire* from the Cape of Good Hope (they arrive 19 Dec). Force K, comprising the battlecruiser *Renown*, the carrier *Ark Royal* and the cruiser *Neptune*, is ordered to Rio de Janeiro to refuel, where on 17 Dec it joins the destroyers *Hardy*, *Hostile*, *Hasty*, and *Hereward* which have come from Freetown via Pernambuco (15 Dec), and then proceeds at full speed to the River Plate.

14 Dec Baltic
The Soviet destroyers *Gnevny* and *Grozyashchi* shell the Finnish island of Utö, whose battery returns the fire.

14 Dec North Sea
12 Wellington bombers of No. 99 Sqdn are deployed against a German warship force reported by a submarine in the Heligoland Bight. They are intercepted by Me 109's and they lose six of their number.

14-16 Dec North Sea
The German torpedo boats *Jaguar* and *Seeadler* capture six ships in mercantile warfare in the Skagerrak.

14-19 Dec Western Atlantic
On 14 Dec the German freighter *Arauca* (4354 tons) and the passenger ship *Columbus* (32581 tons) leave Vera Cruz (Mexico) in an attempt to get home. The Australian cruiser *Perth*, which is employed in watching the Yucatan Channel and is constantly shadowed by the US cruiser *Vincennes* with the destroyers *Evans* and *Twiggs*, does not come up. In the Gulf of Mexico, the Straits of Florida and as far as Cape Hatteras the *Columbus* is continually escorted by two of the US destroyers

Benham, Lang, Jouett, Bagley, Doran, Philip, Upshur and *Greer* which relieve each other and then by the cruiser *Tuscaloosa.* On 19 Dec the British destroyer *Hyperion* comes into sight, having been directed there by regular position reports passed by the US ships in plain language with the result that the *Columbus* has to scuttle herself. The *Arauca* is sighted on the same day off Miami by three US naval aircraft which lead the British cruiser *Orion* to the scene. While still in US waters the *Arauca* is able to avoid capture and puts in to Port Everglades.

14-20 Dec   Baltic
Unsuccessful operation by Finnish submarine *Vesikko* against Soviet forces off Koivisto. The Finnish submarine *Vesihiisi* lays a mine barrage off Baltischport on which the steamer *Edith Hasseldiek* (?) is said to have been lost.

17 Dec   South Atlantic
Because repairs are impossible in the time allowed by the Uruguayan Government the German pocket-battleship *Admiral Graf Spee*, which was damaged in the battle off the River Plate (see 13 Dec), is scuttled by the crew. The Commander, Capt Langsdorff, commits suicide on 20 Dec.

17-18 Dec   North Sea
British destroyers *Esk, Express, Intrepid* and *Ivanhoe* drop 240 mines off the Ems Estuary.

17-19 Dec   North Sea
Bombers of X Fl. K. sink 10 vessels, chiefly trawlers, with a total tonnage of 2949 tons off the East Coast of Britain.

18 Dec   North Sea
24 Wellington bombers of Nos. 9, 37 and 149 Sqdns are intercepted by German fighters when they carry out armed reconnaissance over Wilhelms-haven. They lose twelve machines. No. 37 Sqdn alone loses five out of six machines taking part. Another three damaged bombers are destroyed when they make forced landings.

18-19 Dec   Baltic
Ships of the squadron of the Baltic Fleet (Flagman 2nd Class Nesvitski) shell the Finnish coastal battery at Saarenpää on Koivisto: on 18 Dec battleship *Oktyabrskaya Revolutsia* (Capt 2nd Class Vdovichenko) with five destroyers and on 19 Dec battleship *Marat* (Capt 1st Class Belousov) with one flotilla leader, six destroyers five patrol ships and two gunboats.

19 Dec-22 Jan   North Atlantic
When proceeding to a mining operation *U30* (Lt-Cdr Lemp) sinks an A/S trawler of 325 tons with torpedo and torpedoes the battleship *Barham* (28 Dec). Four ships of 22472 tons sink on the mine barrage laid off Liverpool on 6 Jan and another ship of 5642 tons is damaged. One ship of 959 tons sinks on the mine barrage laid by *U32* (Lt Jenisch) off Ailsa Craig.
U46 (Lt-Cdr Sohler), operating on her own W of Ireland, sinks one ship of 924 tons.

25 Dec-19 Jan   Baltic
A second group of Soviet submarines forces its way through the Södra-Kvarken passage into the Gulf of Bothnia; it includes *Shch-311* (with the Commander of the 17th Div, Capt 2nd Class Orel, on board), *Shch-309, Shch-324* and *S-2*. The last is lost on 2 Jan in the passage on a mine barrage laid by the Finnish minelayer *Louhi*. *Shch-311* (Lt-Cdr Vershinin) sinks the Finnish steamer *Wilpas* (775 tons) on 28 Dec off Vasa and the Swedish steamer *Fenris* (484 tons) on 5 Jan near the Sydostbrottens lightship. *Shch-324* (Lt-Cdr Konyaev) attacks a Finnish convoy in the Aaland waters on 13 Jan; the Finnish yacht *Aura II* (563 tons), belonging to the escort, is lost through a leak caused by depth charges.

28 Dec-12 Jan   North Sea
U58 (Lt-Cdr Kuppisch) sinks two ships of 4426 tons off the East Coast of Britain. One ship of 1333 tons sinks on a mine barrage laid by *U56* (Lt-Cdr Zahn) on Cross Sand.

1940

3 Jan   North Atlantic
The American steamer *Mormacsun*, while on route to Bergen, is brought into Kirkwall by British blockade forces. Following the sharp reaction of the American press, Churchill gives instructions not to halt any more American merchant ships or to bring them into the forbidden fighting zone.

6-7 Jan   North Sea
Offensive mining operation in the Thames Estuary by the 1st DD Flotilla (Cdr* Berger), comprising *Friedrich Eckoldt*, *Erich Steinbrinck* and *Friedrich Ihn*. Results: destroyer *Grenville* and six merchant ships totalling 21617 tons sunk and one ship damaged.

6-9 Jan   North Sea
In submarine-hunting operations in the Heligoland Bight the British submarine *Undine* is forced on 6 Jan to surface by depth charges from the auxiliary minesweepers *M1201*, *M1204* and *M1207* and scuttles herself. On the next day, the 1st MS Flotilla sinks the submarine *Seahorse*. On 9 Jan the submarine *Starfish*, after a depth charge attack by the minesweeper *M7*, has to surface and scuttles herself. Following these losses, the submarine operations in the Inner Heligoland Bight are halted.

6-16 Jan   North Sea
Off the Scottish East Coast *U19* (Lt-Cdr Schepke) sinks one ship of 1343 tons; *U20* (Lt-Cdr Moehle) one ship of 1524 tons; and *U23* (Lt-Cdr Kretschmer) two ships of 11667 tons. Further successes by *U24* are frustrated by torpedo failures.

6 Jan-12 Feb   Indian Ocean
The first New Zealand and Australian contingents (13500 men) are brought to Suez in the convoy US.1. On 6 Jan the transports *Orion* (23371 tons), *Empress of Canada*, (21517 tons), *Strathaird* (22281 tons) and *Rangitata* (16737 tons) set out from Wellington escorted by the battleship *Ramillies* and the Australian cruiser *Canberra*. In Cook Strait they are joined by the transports *Dunera II* (11162 tons) and

Sobieski (Polish—11030 tons) coming from Lyttelton with the New Zealand cruiser *Leander*, and off Sydney on 10 Jan the transport *Orcades* (23456 tons), *Strathnaver* (22283 tons), *Otranto* (20026 tons) and *Orford* (20043 tons) join the convoy and the Australian cruisers *Australia* and *Sydney* (only as far as Jervis Bay) relieve the *Leander*. On 12 Jan the transport *Empress of Japan* (26032 tons), which comes from Melbourne, joins the convoy. On 20 Jan the Australian cruisers are relieved off Fremantle by the British cruiser *Kent* and the French *Suffren*. On 30 Jan these two cruisers are relieved by the Australian *Hobart* and the carrier *Eagle*. The French transport *Athos II* (15276 tons) joins the convoy as far as Djibouti. On 8 Feb the convoy passes Aden and reaches Suez on 12 Feb, the escort ships having turned away beforehand.

7 Jan-6 Feb   Western Atlantic
The German freighter *Consul Horn* (8384 tons) gets through the Anglo-French watch at Aruba unnoticed, escapes from the French submarine *Agosta* and deceives US naval reconnaissance aircraft and the British cruiser *Enterprise* as she is disguised as a Soviet freighter. She reaches Norwegian waters.

9-30 Jan   North Sea
Bombers of the X Fl.K. in attacks on shipping off the British East Coast sink twelve freighters of 23 944 tons and one trawler.

10-11 Jan   North Sea
Offensive mining operation in the Newcastle area by Officer Commanding Destroyers (Commodore Bonte) with *Wilhelm Heidkamp*, *Karl Galster*, *Anton Schmitt*, *Friedrich Eckoldt*, *Richard Beitzen* and *Friedrich Ihn*. Result: one trawler of 251 tons sunk.

At the same time the 4th DD Flotilla (Cdr* Bey), comprising *Bruno Heinemann*, *Wolfgang Zenker* and *Erich Koellner*, drops mines off Cromer causing the sinking of three ships of 11155 tons.

C   17

15 Jan-13 Feb North Atlantic
In individual operations in the North Atlantic *U25* (Cdr Schütze) sinks six ships of 27335 tons; *U44* (Lt-Cdr Matthes) eight ships of 29688 tons; and *U51* (Lt-Cdr Knorr) two ships of 3143 tons. *U55* (Lt-Cdr Heidel), which has already sunk one ship of 1304 tons on the way out, attacks the convoy OA.80G (OG.16) early on 30 Jan and in two approaches sinks two ships of 10111 tons. She is then damaged by depth charges from the sloop *Fowey* and, after surfacing, is attacked by the Sunderland flying boat *Y/228*, which brings up the destroyers *Whitshed* and *Valmy* (French). When they open fire *U55* scuttles herself. On 5 Feb *U41* (Lt-Cdr Mugler), after torpedoing a tanker of 8096 tons and sinking a steamer of 9874 tons from the convoy OA.84, is sunk by depth charges from the British destroyer *Antelope*. *U34* (Lt-Cdr Rollmann) lays a mine barrage off Falmouth on which one ship of 7807 tons sinks and she sinks with one torpedo one ship of 5625 tons. A mine barrage laid by *U31* (Lt-Cdr Habekost) off Loch Ewe has no success.

18 Jan Baltic
In a Soviet air attack on the Finnish port of Kotka the icebreaker *Tarmo* is severely damaged.

18-27 Jan North Sea
In torpedo operations on the British East Coast and in the southern part of the North Sea *U59* (Lt-Cdr Jürst) sinks one ship of 1296 tons; and *U61* (Lt-Cdr Oesten) one ship of 2434 tons; *U9* (Lt Lüth) sinks two ships of 2367 tons; *U22* (Lt-Cdr Jenisch) the destroyer *Exmouth* and one ship of 1469 tons; *U57* (Lt-Cdr Korth) one ship of 1328 tons and also one ship of 8240 tons on a mine barrage; *U18* (Lt Mengersen) one ship of 1000 tons; *U19* (Lt-Cdr Schepke) four ships of 8855 tons; *U23* (Lt-Cdr Kretschmer) one ship of 1085 tons; *U14* (Lt Wohlfarth) one ship of 1752 tons; *U20* (Lt-Cdr v. Klot-Heydenfeldt) four ships of 6848 tons. *U15* and *U60* return without success owing to torpedo failures.

27 Jan-10 Feb North Sea
In torpedo operations on the British East Coast and in the southern part of the North Sea *U13* (Lt Schulte) sinks two ships of 3659 tons; *U21* (Lt Stiebler) two ships of 4900 tons; *U58* (Lt-Cdr Kuppisch) one ship of 815 tons; and *U59* (Lt-Cdr Jürst) three ships of 2400 tons. *U56*, *U24* and *U17* have no success. *U15* (Lt-Cdr Frahm) collides on setting out with the torpedo boat *Iltis* and is lost.

Jan Feb Arctic
To protect the occupied territory of Petsamo against possible Anglo-French operations the Soviet minelayers *Pushkin* and *Murman* lay 200 mines in January between Vardö and the Fisherman's Peninsula. In February *Murman* lays another 170.

4-22 Feb North Atlantic
In their individual operations in the Atlantic *U26* (Lt-Cdr Scheringer) sinks three ships of 10580 tons; *U37* (Cdr Hartmann) eight ships of 24539 tons; *U48* (Lt-Cdr Schultze) four ships of 31526 tons (the mine barrage laid off Weymouth has no success); *U50* (Lt-Cdr Bauer) four ships of 16089 tons; and *U53* (Cdr Grosse) five ships of 13298 tons and torpedoes one ship of 8022 tons. On the return *U53* is sunk by the British destroyer *Gurkha* on 23 Feb.

9-10 Feb North Sea
Offensive mining operations by 1st DD Flotilla (Cdr* Berger), comprising *Friedrich Eckoldt*, *Richard Beitzen* and *Max Schultz* in the Shipwash area. Results: six ships of 28496 tons sunk, one other ship damaged. At the same time the 4th DD Flotilla (Cdr* Bey) consisting of *Bruno Heinemann*, *Wolfgang Zenker* and *Erich Koellner* carries out an operation in the area of Haisborough (Cromer Knoll). Three ships of 11855 tons sink on this mine barrage.

10 Feb-3 Mar North Atlantic
To operate against six German merchant ships which have broken out of Vigo, search forces under the C-in-C, Western Approaches, Adm Dunbar Nasmith, are formed consisting of ships of the Home Fleet (battlecruiser *Renown*, carrier *Ark Royal*, cruiser *Galatea* and destroyers), of the Western Approaches Command, the Northern Patrol and of the French Admiral-West. On 11 Feb the French sloop *Elan* captures the *Rostock* (2542 tons) and on 12 Feb the British destroyer *Hasty* seizes the *Morea* (4709 tons). The *Wahehe* (4709 tons) is

captured on 21 Feb by the cruiser *Manchester* and the destroyer *Kimberley* of the Northern Patrol. The *Orizaba* (4354 tons), after successfully breaking the blockade, is lost off Skjervöy (Northern Norway) where she goes aground. The *Wangoni* evades the British submarine *Triton* off Kristiansand on 28 Feb and reaches Kiel. The last ship, the *Arucas* (3359 tons), has to scuttle herself on 3 Mar when approached by the British cruiser *York* E of Iceland.

10-14 Feb   North Atlantic
Unsuccessful attempt by three U-boats (*U26, U37, U48*) to locate a British force consisting of the aircraft carrier *Ark Royal*, the battlecruiser *Renown* and the heavy cruiser *Exeter* W of the Channel. The force had been identified by radio intelligence.

11-13 Feb   Atlantic
The German freighter *Wakama* (3771 tons), coming from Rio de Janeiro, is stopped by the British cruiser *Dorsetshire* in the area of Cabo Frio and scuttles herself.

12 Feb 40   North Atlantic
U33 (Lt-Cdr Dresky†) is sunk by the British minesweeper *Gleaner* as she tries to lay mines in the estuary of the Clyde.

16 Feb   Norway
British destroyer *Cossack* (Capt Vian) attacks the German supply ship *Altmark* (Capt Dau) in Jössing-Fjord inside Norwegian territorial waters and frees 303 crew members on board belonging to ships which the pocket-battleship *Admiral Graf Spee* has sunk in the South Atlantic.

17-18 Feb   North Atlantic
Third attempt to conduct a U-boat group operation against convoys with a tactical commander on board (Cdr Hartmann on *U37*). Of the five intended boats *U54* (Lt-Cdr Kutschmann) probably ran on to the mine barrage laid by British destroyers on the German exit route and sank (see 22 Feb). When on 17 Feb the 'B' Service learns of the rendezvous point of the French convoys 10.RS and 65.KS W of Portugal, *U26* and *U50* are still too far away. *U53* (Cdr Grosse) summons *U37* which at first is held up by the convoys OG.18 and independents; but the U-boats are only

able to fire successfully at independents and stragglers encountered near the convoy. *U37* sinks three ships and *U53* one ship. Two attacks fail because of torpedo defects.

18-20 Feb   North Sea
Operation 'Nordmark'. Sortie against convoy traffic between England and Scandinavia by battleships *Gneisenau* (Capt Netzbandt) and *Scharnhorst* (Capt Hoffmann), the heavy cruiser *Admiral Hipper* (Capt Heye) and two destroyers (*Karl Galster* and *Wilhelm Heidkamp—Wolfgang Zenker* returns because of ice damage) under the command of Fleet Commander (Adm Marschall). The sortie reaches the passage between Shetland and Norway but has no success. The 2nd DD Flotilla, comprising *Paul Jacobi*, *Theodor Riedel*, *Hans Schoemann* and *Leberecht Maass*, and the torpedo boats *Luchs* and *Seeadler*, at first employed as a screen, are sent off on a mercantile warfare mission in the Skagerrak. Of the U-boats employed in the operation *U9* (Lt Lüth) sinks one ship of 1213 tons; *U14* (Lt Wohlfarth) four ships of 5320 tons; *U61* (Lt-Cdr Oesten) two ships of 5703 tons; *U63* (Lt Lorentz) one ship of 4211 tons; *U57* (Lt-Cdr Korth) one ship of 10191 tons and torpedoes one ship of 4966 tons. The latter is sunk by *U23* (Lt-Cdr Kretschmer) which also sinks the destroyer *Daring*. *U10* (Lt Preuss) sinks two ships of 6356 tons in the southern part of the North Sea.

22-23 Feb   North Sea
Operation 'Wikinger'. When the Officer Commanding Destroyers (Commodore Bonte) with the 1st DD Flotilla (*Erich Koellner, Friedrich Eckoldt, Leberecht Maass, Max Schultz, Richard Beitzen,* and *Theodor Riedel*) proceeds towards British trawlers reported by air reconnaissance in the area of the Dogger Bank, the force is attacked in error by He 111's of II/K.G.26 (the aircraft crews are not informed about their own ships in this part of the sea). Three bombs hit *Leberecht Maass*. In taking evasive action *Leberecht Maass* (Cdr Bassenge†) and *Max Schultz* (Cdr Trampedach†) run on to a mine barrage newly laid by two British destroyers in the German mine-free path and sink with the majority of their

crews. Only 60 men are rescued from *Leberecht Maass*.

25 Feb   North Sea
When *U63* (Lt Lorentz) tries to attack the Britain-Norway convoy HN.14, she is sighted by the British submarine *Narwhal* and sunk by the escorting destroyers *Escort, Imogen* and *Inglefield*.

29 Feb-9 Mar   North Sea
In operations off Cross Sand and in the southern part of the North Sea *U14* (Lt-Cdr Wohlfarth) sinks four ships of 5290 tons; *U17* (Lt-Cdr Behrens) two ships of 1615 tons; and *U20* (Lt-Cdr v. Klot-Heydenfeldt) two ships of 9551 tons.

1-2 Mar   Western Atlantic
The German freighters *Troja* (2390 tons) and *Heidelberg* (6530 tons) try to reach home from Aruba. The *Troja* is encountered on 1 Mar by the British cruiser *Despatch* near Aruba and the *Heidelberg* on 2 Mar by the British cruiser *Dunedin* off the Windward Passage. Both freighters scuttle themselves.

2 Mar   English Channel
First attack by German aircraft (K.G. 26) on shipping targets in the southern part of the Channel. Passenger ship *Domala* (8441 tons) is set on fire near the Isle of Wight.

2-11 Mar   North Atlantic/ English Channel
U28 (Lt-Cdr Kuhnke), *U29* (Lt-Cdr Schuhart) and *U32* (Lt Jenisch) lay mine barrages off Portsmouth, Newport and Liverpool on the British West and South Coasts. One ship of 710 tons sinks on *U29*'s barrage and one ship of 5068 tons on *U32*'s.
In torpedo attacks before and after this *U28* sinks two ships of 11215 tons; *U29* two ships of 9789 tons; *U32* one ship of 2818 tons. Further attacks end in torpedo failures.

2-13 Mar   North Atlantic
The British cruiser *Berwick* of the Northern Patrol stops the German blockade-runners *Wolfsburg* (6201 tons) and *Uruguay* (5846 tons) on 2 Mar and 6 Mar respectively. The ships scuttle themselves. On 13 Mar *La Coruna* (7359 tons) scuttles herself when approached by the armed merchant cruiser *Maloja*.

5 Mar-2 Apl   North Sea
On 5 Mar *U38* and *U52*, which are setting out for the Atlantic are recalled, and with *U30, U43, U44, U46, U47,*

U49 and *U51* are concentrated against British naval forces both sides of the Shetlands and Orkneys. In these operations *U38* (Lt-Cdr Liebe) sinks five ships of 14309 tons and *U47* (Lt-Cdr Prien) one ship of 1146 tons. *U44* (Lt-Cdr Mathes), in trying to attack British battlecruisers, is sunk on 20 Mar by their destroyer screen, *Fortune, Faulknor* and *Firedrake*.

5 Mar-8 Apl   Western Atlantic/ North Atlantic
On 5-6 Mar the German freighters *Hannover, Mimi Horn* and *Seattle* leave Curaçao. The *Hannover* is encountered in the Mona Passage in the night 7-8 Mar by the Canadian destroyer *Assiniboine*. She is prevented from scuttling herself inside Dominican waters by a boarding party from the British cruiser *Dunedin*. During the hunt for the *Hannover*, in which the French cruiser *Jeanne d'Arc* also takes part, the two other ships are able to break out of the Caribbean. But the *Mimi Horn* has to scuttle herself in the Denmark Strait on 28 Mar when approached by the British armed merchant cruiser *Transylvania*. The *Seattle* becomes involved in the beginnings of the Norwegian operation off Kristiansand on 8-9 Apl and is lost.

9 Mar   North Sea
Auxiliary minelayer *Schiff II* (Cdr Betzendahl) drops barrages E of the North Foreland. Results: five ships of 14152 tons sunk.

11 Mar   North Sea
A Bristol Blenheim of RAF Bomber Command sinks the German U-boat *U31* (Lt-Cdr Habekost†) in Schillig roads. The boat is later raised.

11 Mar-10 Apl   North Atlantic
The heavy French cruiser *Algérie* and the battleship *Bretagne* transport 1179 and 1200 bars of gold respectively from Toulon to Halifax, accompanied by the destroyers *Vauban, Aigle* and *Maillé Brézé*. On the return from 29 Mar to 10 Apl the *Aigle* and *Algérie* accompany the freighters *L. D. Dreyfus* and *Wisconsin* with cargoes of aircraft.

13 Mar   General Situation
Peace Treaty signed between the USSR and Finland.

14-29 Mar   North Sea
Unsuccessful operation to hunt down British and French submarines in the

North Sea by *U7*, *U9*, *U19*, *U20*, *U23*, *U24*, *U56*, *U57* and *U59* and off southern Norway by *U1*, *U2*, *U3* and *U4*. When the boats are then ordered to the British East Coast *U19* (Lt-Cdr Schepke) sinks four ships of 5517 tons and *U57* (Lt-Cdr Korth) two ships of 7009 tons. From 16 Mar there is a large-scale operation by British submarines of the Home Fleet in the North Sea and off Norway. At times there are up to 14 boats in the operational area and up to six coming into and leaving the area. Of these *Trident* (Lt-Cdr Seale) sinks the steamer *Edmund Hugo Stinnes 4* (2189 tons) and *Ursula* (Lt-Cdr Cavaye) the steamer *Heddernheim* (4947 tons) off the Danish coast.

16 Mar   North Sea
18 Ju 88's (K.G. 30) and 16 He 111's (K.G. 26) of XFl.K attack units of the British Fleet in Scapa Flow, AA positions and the airfields at Stromness, Barthhouse and Kirkwall. They believe they have hit three battleships and one cruiser. In fact, only the heavy cruiser *Norfolk* is damaged.

19 Mar   North Sea
30 Whitleys and 20 Hampdens of RAF Bomber Command attack the German seaplane base at Hörnum.

20 Mar   English Channel
In a second attack by German aircraft in the sea area off the Isle of Wight the British freighter *Barn Hill* (5439 tons) is sunk.

22 Mar-20 Apl   North Sea
The first boats of the French 10th SM Flotilla *Sibylle*, *Antiope* and *Amazone* arrive in Harwich with their depot ship *Jules Verne* to reinforce the submarines of the Home Fleet. On 14 Apl *Orphée*, *Doris* and *Circé* follow, on 20 Apl *Calypso* and *Thétis*. In addition the 2nd SM Div (*Casabianca*, *Sfax*, *Achille* and *Pasteur*) arrives on 17 Apl and the minelaying submarine *Rubis* on 1 May. On 31 Mar *Sibylle* is the first boat to set out on an operation in the North Sea.

23 Mar   Indian Ocean
Formation of the British Malaya Force to keep watch on German merchant ships in Dutch East Indies harbours. The destroyers *Stronghold* and *Tenedos* off Sabang (*Lindenfels*, *Moni Rickmers*, *Sophie Rickmers*, *Wasgenwald*, *Werdenfels*); cruiser *Durban* off Padang (*Bitter-*

feld, *Franken*, *Rheinland*, *Soneck*, *Wuppertal*); submarines *Perseus* and *Rainbow* off Sunda Strait; cruiser *Dauntless* off Batavia (*Nordmark*, *Rendsburg*, *Vogtland*); cruiser *Danae* off Surabaya (*Cassel*, *Essen*, *Naumburg*); and sloop *Falmouth* off Tjilatjap (*Stassfurt*).

31 Mar   North Sea
Schiff 16 Atlantis (Capt Rogge) is the first German auxiliary cruiser of the Second World War to receive orders to put to sea.

31 Mar-8 Apl   Norway
British cruiser *Birmingham* with the destroyers *Fearless* and *Hostile* looks for German fishery vessels along the Norwegian coast up to Vestfjord.

3 Apl   Norway
The first ships of the export echelon for use in the operation 'Weserübung'— seven freighters of 48693 tons—set out from Hamburg for Narvik, Trondheim, and Stavanger.

5-8 Apl   Norway
Operation 'Wilfred': British mining operation in Norwegian waters. Force WB simulates minelaying with two destroyers off Bud/Kristiansund-North. Force WS, consisting of minelayer *Teviot Bank* and destroyers *Inglefield*, *Ilex*, *Imogen* and *Isis*, is recalled on 8 Apl before the beginning of the minelaying. Force WV, consisting of minelaying destroyers *Esk*, *Icarus*, *Impulsive* and *Ivanhoe*, escorted by the 2nd DD Flotilla with the destroyers *Hardy*, *Havock*, *Hotspur* and *Hunter*, lays mine barrage near Bodö. Covering force (Vice-Adm Whitworth): battlecruiser *Renown* and destroyers *Hyperion*, *Hero*, *Greyhound* and *Glowworm*. The last remains behind in a heavy storm to recover a rating who has fallen overboard and loses contact. On 8 Apl the *Glowworm* (Lt-Cdr Roope†) is encountered by the German Trondheim group and is sunk by the cruiser *Admiral Hipper* after she has previously rammed the cruiser. The landing of troops in Norway (Operation 'R4'), which was intended as an answer to the German counter moves against Operation 'Wilfred', is called off when the strength of the German forces is recognized and the troops on board are disembarked (see 7 Apl).

6 Apl North Sea
Schiff 36 Orion (Cdr* Weyher) is the second German auxiliary cruiser to receive orders to put to sea.

7 Apl North Sea/Norway
The first German naval forces set out for the Operation 'Weserübung'. Operational command: Naval Group Command East (Admiral Carls) for the area E of the Skagerrak mine barrage; Naval Group Command West (Adm Saalwächter) for the area W of the Skagerrak mine barrage, under the orders of the Navy staff (Seekriegsleitung).
Cover for groups 1 and 2: Vice-Adm Lütjens with the battleships *Scharnhorst* (Capt Hoffmann) and *Gneisenau* (Capt Netzbandt).
Group 1 (Narvik): Commodore Bonte with the destroyers *Wilhelm Heidkamp, Georg Thiele, Wolfgang Zenker, Bernd von Arnim, Erich Giese, Erich Koellner, Diether von Roeder, Hans Lüdemann, Hermann Künne* and *Anton Schmitt*. Group 2 (Trondheim): Capt Heye with the heavy cruiser *Admiral Hipper* (Heye) and the destroyers *Paul Jacobi, Theodor Riedel, Bruno Heinemann* and *Friedrich Eckoldt*.
Group 3 (Bergen): Rear-Adm Schmundt with the light cruisers *Köln* (Capt Kratzenberg) and *Königsberg* (Capt Ruhfus), the gunnery training ship *Bremse* (Cdr* Förschner), the torpedo boats *Leopard* and *Wolf*, the motor torpedo boat tender *Carl Peters* and the motor torpedo boats *S19, S21, S22, S23* and *S24*, and the auxiliary ships *Schiff 9* and *Schiff 18*.
Group 4 (Kristiansand South and Arendal): Capt Rieve with the light cruiser *Karlsruhe* (Rieve), the torpedo boats *Greif, Luchs, Seeadler*, and the motor torpedo boat tender *Tsingtau* and the motor torpedo boats *S7, S8, S17, S30, S31, S32* and *S33*.
Group 5 (Oslo): Rear-Adm Kummetz with the heavy cruisers *Blücher* (Capt Woldag) and *Lützow* (Capt Thiele), the light cruiser *Emden* (Capt Lange), torpedo boats *Albatros, Kondor* and *Möwe*, the 1st MMS Flotilla (Lt-Cdr Forstmann) with *R17, R18, R19, R20, R21, R22, R23, R24* and the whalers *Rau 7* and *Rau 8*.
Group 6 (Egersund): Cdr Thoma (Cdr of the 2nd MS Flotilla) with the minesweepers *M1, M2, M9* and *M13*.

Group 7 (Nyborg and Korsör): Capt Kleikamp with the old battleship *Schleswig-Holstein* (Kleikamp), the experimental vessels *Claus von Bevern, Nautilus, Pelikan*, the transports *Campinas* (4541 tons) and *Cordoba* (4611 tons), two tugs and the Training Flotilla of Commander Naval Defence Forces, Baltic, (Cdr* Dannenberg) with six trawlers.
Group 8 (Copenhagen): Cdr Schroeder with the minelayer *Hansestadt Danzig* (Schroeder) and the ice-breaker *Stettin* escorted through the Belt by vessels of the 13th Patrol Boat Flotilla (Lt-Cdr Fischer).
Group 9 (Middelfart and Belt Bridge): Capt Leissner (Officer Commanding Patrol Boats East) with the steamer *Rugard* (1358 tons), the minesweepers *Arkona, M157, Otto Braun*, the motor minesweepers *R6* and *R7*, the patrol vessels *V102* and *V103*, the submarine-chaser *UJ172* and the naval tugs *Monsun* and *Passat*.
Group 10 (Esbjerg and Nordby on Fanö): Commodore Ruge (Officer Commanding Minesweepers West) with command vessel *Königin Luise* (F6), the minesweepers *M4, M20, M84, M102*, the 12th MS Flotilla (Cdr Marguth) with *M1201* to *M1208* (large trawlers) and the 2nd MMS Flotilla (Cdr v. Kamptz) with *R25, R26, R27, R28, R29, R30, R31* and *R32*.
Group 11 (Tyborön on Limfjord): Cdr Berger (Cdr of the 4th MS Flotilla) with *M61, M89, M110, M111, M134* and *M136* and the 3rd MMS Flotilla (Lt-Cdr Küster) with the tender *Von der Groeben* and the motor minesweepers *R33, R34, R35, R36, R37, R38, R39* and *R40*.
In addition, the old battleship *Schlesien* (Capt Horstmann) operates in Danish waters from Kiel.
U-boat groups (individual boats directly under the orders of Commander U-boats, Rear-Adm Dönitz):
1 (Vestfjord): *U25, U46, U51, U64* and *U65*.
2 (Trondheim): *U30* and *U34*.
3 (Bergen): *U9, U14, U56, U60* and *U62*.
4 (Stavanger): *U1* and *U4*.
5 (E of Shetlands): *U47, U48, U49, U50, U52* and later *U37*.

6 (Pentland Firth): *U13, U19, U57, U58* and *U59.*
8 (Tindesnes): *U2, U3, U5* and *U6.*
9 (Shetlands-Orkneys): *U7* and *U10.* The U-boat operations end as a total failure, despite favourable firing opportunities, because of defects in the depth-keeping mechanisms and in the magnetic fusing of the torpedoes. The only successes: *U4* sinks one submarine and *U13* sinks one transport and torpedoes one tanker. In addition, *U59* sinks one ship on outward trip and *U37* three ships in returning from a special operation. Four German U-boats are lost.

7-8 Apl   Norway
When the news is received that a German operation has started, the C-in-C Home Fleet, Adm Forbes, sets out on the evening of 7 Apl from Scapa Flow for the Shetlands-Norway Passage with the battleships *Rodney* and *Valiant,* the battlecruiser *Repulse,* the cruisers *Penelope* and *Sheffield* and the destroyers *Somali, Matabele, Mashona, Bedouin, Punjabi, Eskimo, Kimberley, Kelvin, Kashmir* and *Jupiter.* They are followed later by the French cruiser *Emile Bertin* (Rear-Adm Derrien) with destroyers *Maillé-Brézé* and *Tartu.* Vice-Adm Edward-Collins sets out from Rosyth on the afternoon of 7 Apl with the cruisers *Arethusa* and *Galatea* and the destroyers *Codrington, Griffin, Electra* and *Escapade.* There also come from the escort of convoy HN.24 the destroyer *Tartar* and the Polish destroyers *Blyskawica, Burza* and *Grom.* Convoy ON.25 is recalled and the escort under Vice-Adm Layton, comprising the cruisers *Manchester* and *Southampton* and the destroyers *Janus, Javelin, Grenade* and *Eclipse,* are ordered to join the Home Fleet. After disembarking the troops on board, Vice-Adm J. Cunningham puts to sea from Rosyth on 8 Apl with the cruisers *Devonshire, Berwick, York* and *Glasgow* and the destroyers *Afridi, Gurkha, Sikh, Mohawk, Zulu* and *Cossack.* On 8 Apl when he receives the *Glowworm's* distress signal Adm Forbes detaches the *Repulse, Penelope* and destroyers *Bedouin, Punjabi, Eskimo* and *Kimberley* to join Vice-Adm Whitworth's force, comprising the *Renown* and the destroyers *Esk, Ivanhoe, Icarus,* *Greyhound, Hardy, Havock, Hotspur, Hunter* and *Hostile.*

7-29 Apl   North Sea/Norway
The Flag Officer Submarines, Vice-Adm Horton, orders all operational submarines of the British 2nd, 3rd and 6th and the French 10th SM Flotillas to take up positions off the SW and S coasts of Norway, in the Skagerrak and Kattegat and in the North Sea, in order to be able to intercept possible German counter-measures against the Operation 'Wilfred'. On 9 Apl the following have taken up their positions: the British submarines *Clyde, Sealion, Seawolf, Shark, Severn, Snapper, Spearfish, Sunfish, Triad, Truant, Triton, Unity, Thistle, Ursula, Tarpon* and *Sterlet* and *Trident,* the Polish *Orzel* and the French *Amazone, Antiope* and *Sibylle.* In addition, the British mine-laying submarines *Narwhal, Porpoise* and later the boats *Swordfish, Tetrarch,* and the mine-laying submarine *Seal* are employed.
At 1200 hrs on 8 Apl *Orzel* sinks the transport *Rio de Janeiro* on the Norwegian coast; at 1330 hrs *Trident* sinks the tanker *Posidonia* and at 1906 hrs *Trident* misses the *Lützow* with ten torpedoes off Skagen. At 1324 hrs on 9 Apl the submarines are given permission to attack transports without warning and at 1956 hrs on 11 Apl to attack all ships without warning within 10 nautical miles of the Norwegian coast. Of the Allied submarines engaged, *Orzel* (Lt-Cdr Grudzinski) sinks one ship of 5261 tons; *Trident* (Lt-Cdr Seale) one ship of 8036 tons; *Truant* (Lt-Cdr Hutchinson) torpedoes the cruiser *Karlsruhe* (eventually sunk by the torpedo boat *Greif*); *Sunfish* (Lt-Cdr Slaughter) three ships of 12034 tons and damages one ship of 2448 tons; *Triton* (Lt-Cdr Pizey) sinks two ships and *V1507* totalling 9221 tons; *Sealion* (Lt-Cdr Bryant) one ship of 2593 tons; *Triad* (Cdr Oddie) one ship of 3102 tons; *Snapper* (Lt King) one ship, *M1701* and *M1702* totalling 1319 tons; *Porpoise* (Cdr Roberts) U-boat *U1*; *Seawolf* (Lt-Cdr Studholme) one ship of 5874 tons; and *Sterlet* (Lt Haward) the training ship *Brummer.* In addition, *Spearfish* (Lt-Cdr Forbes) torpedoes the cruiser *Lützow* on her return (11 Apl). *Thistle* is lost on 10 Apl as a result of a

torpedo from *U4*; *Tarpon* on 14 Apl following depth charges from the minesweeper *M6*; and *Sterlet* on 18 Apl following depth charges from the submarine-chasers *UJ125*, *UJ126* and *U128*.

One trawler (709 tons) is lost on the mine barrage laid on 4 Apl by *Narwhal* (Lt-Cdr Burch) off Heligoland and the submarine-chasers and minesweepers *M1101*, *M1302*, *M1703* and *U-Jäger B* (totalling 1625 tons) on the mine barrier laid on 13 Apl near Cape Skagen. The patrol vessel *V403* (432 tons) is damaged.

9 Apl Norway
The new heavy cruiser *Blücher* is lost with many lives as a result of Norwegian coastal artillery and torpedo hits in the Dröbak Narrows (Oslofjord). Off Vestfjord there is a brief engagement between the German battleships *Gneisenau* and *Scharnhorst* and the British battle-cruiser *Renown* (Capt Simeon). Both 28cm shells which hit *Renown* fail to explode and do little damage. *Gneisenau* receives three hits, one of them from a 15in shell.

While Adm Forbes cruises with the main body of the Home Fleet (battleships *Rodney* and *Valiant*, cruisers *Galatea*, *Devonshire*, *Berwick*, *York* and *Emile Bertin*, destroyers *Codrington*, *Griffin*, *Jupiter*, *Electra*, *Escapade*, *Tartu* and *Maillé-Brézé*) about 100 nautical miles SW of Bergen, he detaches Vice-Adm Layton to make an attack on Bergen with the cruisers *Manchester*, *Southampton*, *Sheffield* and *Glasgow* and the destroyers *Afridi*, *Gurkha*, *Sikh*, *Mohawk*, *Somali*, *Matabele* and *Mashona* and the approaching cruiser *Aurora*. But the force is compelled to turn away by an attack by 47 Ju 88's of K.G.30 and 41 He 111's of K.G.26 in which the destroyer *Gurkha* is sunk and the cruisers *Glasgow* and *Southampton* are damaged by near misses. With the main body of the fleet the *Rodney* and *Devonshire* are slightly damaged. 4 Ju 88's are shot down. III/K.G.4 sinks the Norwegian destroyer *Aeger* in an attack on Stavanger.

As Group 1 comes into Narvik *Wilhelm Heidkamp* sinks the Norwegian coastal defence ship *Eidsvold* (Cdr* Willoch†)— eight survivors, and *Bernd von Arnim*

the coastal defence ship *Norge* (Cdr* Askim)—97 survivors with torpedo hits following abortive negotiations.

10 Apl Norway
15 British Skua dive-bombers of Nos 800 and 803 Sqdns sink the light cruiser *Königsberg* in Bergen.

10 Apl Norway
Early in the morning and in poor visibility the British 2nd DD Flotilla (Capt Warburton-Lee†), consisting of *Hardy*, *Hunter*, *Hotspur*, *Havock* and *Hostile* enters Ofotfjord and, in a surprise attack, sinks, in addition to a number of merchant ships caught up in the hostilities there, the German destroyers *Wilhelm Heidkamp* (Officer Commanding Destroyers, Commodore Bonte† on board) and *Anton Schmitt*. *Diether von Roeder* and *Hans Lüdemann* are damaged. In an engagement with the other destroyers of the German Narvik force *Hardy* and *Hunter* sink, while *Havock* and *Hotspur* are damaged. As they withdraw, the German supply transport *Rauenfels* (8460 tons) falls victim to the remaining British destroyers. Two attacks by *U51* (Lt-Cdr Knorr) on the British destroyers entering Vestfjord on 10 Apl, and one attack each by *U51* and *U25* (Cdr Schütze) on the British destroyers as they leave, fail in part because of torpedo defects. The cruiser *Penelope*, which entered Vestfjord to support the destroyers, runs aground at night on 11 Apl and is towed away, badly damaged, by the destroyer *Eskimo*.

10-11 Apl Norway
Battleship *Warspite* and aircraft carrier *Furious* join the Home Fleet, which continues the unsuccessful search for German forces W of Norway. On 11 Apl the light cruisers and some of the destroyers have to be detached for refuelling. Admiral Forbes makes a sortie towards Trondheim with the battleships *Rodney*, *Valiant* and *Warspite*, the carrier *Furious* and the heavy cruisers *Berwick*, *Devonshire* and *York*. 16 torpedo aircraft from *Furious* attack without success the remaining three German destroyers, after the cruiser *Admiral Hipper* has set out undetected with the destroyer *Friedrich Eckoldt* and escapes to the S.

On 11 Apl the heavy cruisers *Berwick*,

Devonshire and *York* are ordered to search for German forces on the Norwegian coast between Trondheim and Vestfjord, and later further up to Kirkenes. Two attacks by *U48* (Lt-Cdr Schultze) on the force W of Trondheim fail because of torpedo defects. The cruisers *Glasgow* and *Sheffield* receive orders after refuelling to scour the Inner Leads. One attack by *U37* (Cdr Hartmann) fails on 13 Apl because of torpedo defects.

12 Apl Norway
British air reconnaissance locates the battleships *Gneisenau* and *Scharnhorst* and the cruiser *Admiral Hipper* on their return SW of Stavanger. By taking advantage of the bad weather and with the help of W/T intelligence they have avoided the forces of the Home Fleet. 92 bombers of RAF Coastal Command and Bomber Command take off to attack but none finds a target.

13 Apl Norway
In fighting a British naval force (Vice-Adm Whitworth), consisting of the battleship *Warspite* (Capt Crutchley) and the destroyers *Icarus, Hero, Foxhound, Kimberley, Forester, Bedouin, Punjabi, Eskimo* and *Cossack*, the remaining eight German destroyers of the Narvik group are lost or are scuttled by the crews when their fuel and ammunition supplies are used up. *Punjabi* receives a shell hit; *Eskimo* loses her bow from a torpedo from *Georg Thiele*; and *Cossack* is more seriously damaged by shellfire from *Diether von Roeder* and by hitting a wreck. The aircraft of *Warspite* sinks the German U-boat *U64*. Attacks by *U25* on the destroyers of the force as it enters and leaves Ofotfjord on 13 Apl and one attack each by *U25* and *U48* on the battleship *Warspite* in Vestfjord on 14 Apl fail because of torpedo defects.

13-14 Apl North Sea
First British mining operation with 15 Hampden bombers (No. 5 Group RAF Bomber Command, Nos. 44, 49, 50, 61 and 144 Sqdns) off the Danish coast.

13-15 Apl Norway
The troop convoy NP.1, which left the Clyde and Scapa Flow for Harstad on 11-12 Apl, is divided on 13 Apl. The transports *Chrobry* and *Empress of Australia* proceed to Namsos with the 146th Infantry Brigade, escorted by the cruisers *Manchester* (Vice-Adm Layton), *Birmingham* and *Cairo* and three destroyers. There on 14 Apl advance parties are landed from the cruisers *Glasgow* and *Sheffield* and the destroyers *Afridi, Somali, Nubian, Sikh, Matabele* and *Mashona*. There follow on 15 Apl the transports which at first go further N because of the threat from the air. (Operation 'Maurice'). An attack by *U34* (Lt-Cdr Rollmann) on 'Tribal' class destroyers on 15 Apl fails because of torpedo defects.
The remainder of the convoy NP.1, consisting of the troop transports *Batory, Monarch of Bermuda* and *Reina del Pacifico*, continues its journey to Harstad where on 14 Apl the cruisers *Southampton*—unsuccessfully attacked by *U38* (Lt-Cdr Liebe) on 14 Apl—and *Aurora* (Admiral of the Fleet Lord Cork and Orrery) arrive. The battleship *Valiant* and nine destroyers cover the convoy. As they proceed *U65* (Lt-Cdr v. Stockhausen) misses the *Batory* and *U38* the *Valiant*. Off Vaagsfjord the destroyers *Brazen* and *Fearless* locate the U boat *U49* and sink her with depth charges. From the debris coming to the surface secret documents are recovered including a map with U-boat positions. The landing of the 24th Guards Brigade goes smoothly. In the night 15-16 Apl *U47* (Lt-Cdr Prien) fires two salvoes of four torpedoes against the troop transports and cruisers lying at anchor; but they are failures. On 15 Apl the C-in-C Home Fleet returns to Scapa Flow with the *Rodney* and *Renown* and six destroyers, whilst the *Warspite* and *Furious* are ordered to the area W of the Lofotens.

15 Apl-17 May Indian Ocean
Second Australian troop convoy US.2. On 15 Apl the transports *Ettrick, Neuralia, Strathaird* and *Dunera* set out from Melbourne, escorted by the battleship *Ramillies* and the Australian cruiser *Adelaide*. On 19 Apl the Australian cruiser *Sydney* joins it and on 22 Apl the transport *Nevasa* in Fremantle. There the *Adelaide* remains behind. In the area of the Cocos Islands the French cruiser *Suffren* relieves the *Sydney* on 30 Apl. From 3 May to 5 May the convoy is in Colombo; then it

continues its journey with the *Ramillies*, the *Suffren* and the British cruiser *Kent*. It is met off Aden on 12 May by the destroyers *Decoy* and *Defender* and reinforced in the Red Sea by the cruiser *Liverpool* and the sloop *Shoreham*. The convoy reaches Suez on 17 May.

16 Apl   North Atlantic
Landing by British troops on the Faeroe Isles with the agreement of the Danish Governor.

16-18 Apl   Norway
Operation 'Sickle'. On 16 Apl the British sloops *Auckland*, *Bittern*, *Black Swan* and *Flamingo*, sail with 700 advance troops who are landed on 17 Apl in Andalsnes. On 18 Apl Vice-Adm Edward-Collins, with the cruisers *Galatea*, *Arethusa*, *Carlisle* and *Curaçao* and two destroyers lands the 148th Infantry Brigade under Maj-Gen Paget in Andalsnes.
With this the German position in Trondheim is threatened from N and S.

17 Apl   Norway
Because of the critical situation which has developed for the defenders in Narvik, Hitler wants to permit Maj-Gen Dietl to cross to Sweden. But at the insistence of Gen Jodl, the order is given in the evening to 'hold on as long as possible'.
The British heavy cruiser *Suffolk* shells the seaplane base at Stavanger. Installations are badly damaged and four seaplanes are destroyed. In attacks by Ju 88's of II/K G. 30 *Suffolk* receives heavy bomb hits and can only get back to Scapa Flow with difficulty and with flooded quarter deck. The cruiser arrives on the morning of 18 Apl.

17 Apl   North Sea
Aircraft of the 9th Fl.Div. drop 24 mines in the Downs and in the Edinburgh Channel. Results: two ships of 6417 tons sunk.

18-19 Apl   Norway
The French auxiliary cruisers *El Djezair*, *El Kantara* and *El Mansour* under Rear-Adm Cadart land the 5th Chasseurs Alpins Demi-brigade in Namsos. Convoy FP.1 is escorted by the destroyers *Bison*, *Epervier* and *Milan*. Supplies on the transport *Ville d'Oran* (Convoy FP.1 B) escorted by the destroyers *Chevalier-Paul*, *Maillé-Brézé* and *Tartu*. Cruiser escort: *Emile Bertin*

(Rear-Adm Derrien) and cover at sea provided by battlecruiser *Repulse*. As they approach there is an attack on the evening of 18 Apl by *U34* on the cruiser and on the morning of 19 Apl an attack by *U46* (Lt-Cdr Sohler) on one of the destroyers, but they fail because of defective torpedoes. During the unloading of the convoy, which is met by the AA cruiser *Cairo*, on the afternoon of 19 Apl, there is an attack by Ju 88's of II/K.G.30 when *Emile Bertin* is damaged by bomb hits. On withdrawal an unsuccessful attack is made on the cruiser by *U51* (Lt-Cdr Knorr).

19-20 Apl   Norway
Namsos is almost completely destroyed in a German air attack.

19-21 Apl   Norway
SW of the Lofotens *U38* (Lt-Cdr Liebe) attacks the cruiser *Effingham* by night and *U47* (Lt-Cdr Prien) the battleship *Warspite* in the afternoon; no success is achieved owing to torpedo failures. In the evening of 19 Apl an attack by *U65* (Lt-Cdr v. Stockhausen) on the cruiser *Enterprise* fails because of a premature fuse. The British destroyers *Faulknor*, *Escapade*, *Jupiter*, *Grenade*, *Fortune*, etc. patrol this area to screen the heavy ships against German U-boat attacks, but they register no successes. On 19 Apl the British destroyer *Escort* sets out from Scapa Flow with the Polish *Grom*, *Blyskawica* and *Burza* as reinforcements for Harstad, but the *Burza* has to return because of storm damage. On 20 Apl an attack by *U9* (Lt Lüth) on *Blyskawica* fails because of a premature fuse. On 21 Apl the Polish destroyers and *Bedouin*, *Escort* and *Faulknor* make a sortie into Rombaksfjord.

20 Apl   North Sea
British Hampden and Wellington bombers attack the airfield at Aalborg.

21 Apl   North Sea
The 9th Fl.Div. drops 26 mines in the sea off Ramsgate-North Foreland and in the King's Channel. Results: three ships of 5540 tons are sunk.

21-25 Apl   Norway
Allied supply transports for Andalsnes. On 21 Apl *U26* (Lt-Cdr Scheringer), which is on a supply mission, sinks the transport *Cedarbank* (5139 tons), while escorted by two destroyers.

On 22 Apl the cruiser *Arethusa* brings supplies and personnel for an RAF airfield. On 23 Apl the cruisers *Galatea* (Vice-Adm Edward-Collins), *Glasgow* *Sheffield* and six destroyers land the first part of the 15th Infantry Brigade, followed by the remainder on 24 Apl on the cruisers *Birmingham, Manchester* and *York* and three destroyers. Air escort from the carriers (Vice-Adm Wells) *Ark Royal* and *Glorious* which fly in Gladiator fighters. AA cover off Andalsnes and Molde provided by AA cruisers *Carlisle* and *Curaçao* and sloops *Black Swan, Flamingo, Bittern* and *Fleetwood*. On 24 Apl *Curaçao* is damaged in a German air attack. On 25 Apl the A/S trawlers *Bradman, Hammond* and *Larwood* are lost to air attacks (they are later raised and repaired as German patrol vessels *Friese, Salier* and *Franke*); the Norwegian torpedo boat *Trygg* is also lost. Two attacks by *U23* (Lt-Cdr Beduhn) on the departing cruiser *York* on 25 Apl fail because of defective torpedoes.

22 Apl   North Sea
Another 34 mines are dropped off Harwich and in the Downs. Results: two ships of 2607 tons sunk.

22-23 Apl   Norway
The French transport *Ville d'Alger*, led by the cruiser *Birmingham*, the AA cruiser *Calcutta* and the French destroyers *Bison* and *Foudroyant* and met by the British destroyer *Maori* and the sloop *Auckland*, can only land 750 of her 1100 troops in Namsos because of a snowstorm.

23-24 Apl   Skagerrak
Brief action between the 8th French DD Div (Capt Barthes), comprising the large destroyers *L'Indomptable, Le Malin* and *Le Triomphant* and *V702* and *V709* of 7th Patrol Boat Flotilla (Lt-Cdr G. Schulze) in the Skagerrak. An attack by German bombers on the destroyer force on 24 Apl is unsuccessful.

24 Apl   Norway
Admiral of the Fleet Lord Cork shells Narvik with the battleship *Warspite*, the cruisers *Effingham* (F), *Aurora* and *Enterprise* and the destroyer *Zulu*. But assault troops held in readiness on the training cruiser *Vindictive* cannot be used. The force is screened against U-boats in Vestfjord and Ofotfjord by

the destroyers *Faulknor, Encounter, Escort, Foxhound, Havock, Hero, Hostile Grom* and *Blyskawica*.

24-27 Apl   Norway
Troop convoy FP.2 with the French 27th Demi-Brigade of Chasseurs-Alpins (Brig-Gen Fleischer) on the transports *Djenné, Flandre,* and *Président Doumer* from Scapa Flow to Harstad. Escort provided by destroyers *Chevalier-Paul, Milan, Tartu* and the British *Codrington* and *Fame*.
Supply convoy FS.2 with the freighters *Brestois, Château Pavie* and *Firmin* arrives on 28 Apl.

26-27 Apl   Norway
Supply convoy FS.1 with the French freighters *Amienois, Cap Blanc* and *Saumur* escorted by the destroyers *Boulonnais, Brestois* and the British *Matabele,* arrives in Namsos. The supplies are unloaded and the troops are partly embarked.

27 Apl   General Situation
The 'Inter-American Neutrality Committee' in Rio de Janeiro lays before the American Governments proposals to prevent further incidents in the Pan-American Security Zone.

29 Apl   Norway
Evacuation of 'Sickle Force' from Andalsnes and Molde. On 29 Apl the cruiser *Glasgow* in Molde takes the Norwegian King and Crown Prince on board and brings them to Tromsö. In the night 30 Apl—1 May the cruisers *Galatea* (Vice-Adm Edward-Collins) and *Arethusa, Sheffield* and *Southampton,* the transports *Ulster Monarch* and *Ulster Prince* and the destroyers *Tartar, Sikh, Mashona, Walker, Westcott* and *Wanderer* take on board 2200 troops in Andalsnes and Molde.
In the night 1-2 May Vice-Adm Layton with the cruisers *Birmingham* and *Manchester* evacuates 1500 troops from Andalsnes; the AA cruiser *Calcutta* and the sloop *Auckland* take nearly 1000 troops of the rearguard on board. The destroyer *Somali* evacuates a battle group from Alesund and the destroyer *Diana* transports the Norwegian C-in-C, Maj-Gen Ruge, to Tromsö.

29 Apl-20 May   Norway
Deployment of the Allied submarines *Severn, Porpoise, Triton, Trident, Taku, Achille, Sfax* and *Casabianca* off the

Norwegian SW and W coasts. *Severn* (Lt-Cdr Taylor) sinks one ship of 1786 tons; *Taku* (Lt-Cdr v.d. Byl) torpedoes the torpedo boat *Möwe* (9 May); *Trident* (Lt-Cdr Seale) torpedoes one ship of 5295 tons; *Narwhal* (Lt-Cdr Burch) lays a mine barrage off Frederikstad (29 Apl) and attacks a convoy on 1 May from which one ship of 6097 tons is sunk and another of 8580 tons torpedoed. One ship of 174 tons sinks on a mine barrage laid on 11 May near Haugesund. The French submarine *Rubis* (Cdr Cabanier) lays a mine barrage near Egersund on 10 May on which one ship of 1706 tons sinks. The British submarine *Seal* lays a mine barrage off Vinga in the southern exit of the Kattegat on which four ships of 6895 tons sink but she herself is damaged by a mine detonation on 4 May and, unable to submerge, has to surrender to German patrol vessels after a seaplane of 1/Bord Fl. Gr. 196 (Sub-Lt Karl Schmidt) has taken her captain, Lt-Cdr Lonsdale, prisoner.

30 Apl North Sea
Torpedo boat *Leopard* is rammed in a mining operation in the Skagerrak by the minelayer *Preussen* and sunk.

30 Apl North Sea
Aircraft of the 9th Fl. Div drop 11 mines in the Tyne Estuary, 10 in the Humber Estuary and two in the approach to Dunkirk.

30 Apl–3 May Norway
Evacuation of 'Maurice' Force from Namsos.
In air attacks on 30 Apl Ju 87's of I/St.G.1 sink the AA sloop *Bittern* (mistaken for a cruiser). On 1 May thick mist sets in with the result that ships cannot enter. Only Capt Lord Mountbatten with *Kelly*, *Maori* and two other destroyers gets through the mist into the fjord, but he has to return because of air attacks. In the night 2-3 May Capt Vian with the destroyers *Afridi*, *Nubian*, and the cruiser *York*, followed by Rear-Adm Cadart, with the French auxiliary cruisers *El Djézair*, *El Kantara* and *El Mansour* and the destroyer *Bison* enter and take aboard 5400 troops, including 1850 French. The cruisers *Devonshire* (Vice-Adm J. H. D. Cunningham) and *Montcalm* (Rear-Adm Derrien) with the destroyers *Grenade*, *Griffin* and

Imperial cruise at sea as a covering force. The AA cruiser *Carlisle* (Rear-Adm Vivian) provides AA protection in the harbour.
On its return the force is attacked several times from the air on 3 May and loses the destroyers *Afridi* (Capt Vian) and *Bison* (Capt Bouan) through Stuka attacks from I/St.G.1 (Capt Hozzel).

1 May North Sea
German aircraft drop 42 airmines in the Tyne and Humber estuaries and in the harbour approaches of Middlesbrough and Dunkirk.

1-6 May Norway
Troop convoy FP.3 with the Foreign Legion Demi-Brigade (Col Magrin-Verneret) and the Polish Brigade (Gen Bohusz) on the transports *Ville d'Alger*, *Monarch of Bermuda*, *Colombie*, *Chenonceaux* and *Mexique*, escorted by five British and one French destroyers, arrives in Harstad and Tromsö from Scapa Flow on 5 May. Supply convoy FS.3 with the freighters *Albert Leborgne*, *Enseigne Maurice Préchac*, *St Clair* and *Vulcain* follows on 6 May.

1 May–16 June Indian Ocean/Atlantic
Third New Zealand and Australian troop convoy U.S.3. On 1 May the transports *Aquitania*, *Empress of Britain* and *Empress of Japan* set out from Wellington and the *Andes* from Lyttelton. They reach Sydney on 5 May, escorted by the Australian cruisers *Australia* and *Canberra* and the New Zealand cruiser *Leander*. There the transports *Mauretania* and *Queen Mary* join the convoy, as does the *Empress of Canada* off Melbourne on 6 May. After stopping in Fremantle from 10 May to 12 May the convoy, with the exception of *Leander*, is diverted to the Cape route while on the way to Colombo because it is feared that Italy will enter the war. After the *Canberra* has been relieved by the British cruiser *Shropshire* on 20 May, the convoy skirts the minefield laid by the German auxiliary cruiser *Schiff 16 Atlantis* off Cape Agulhas and discovered on 13 May and reaches Cape Town on 26 May. Leaving the *Empress of Japan* behind, the convoy proceeds to Freetown with the cruisers *Cumberland* and *Shropshire* from 31 May to 7 June. From there it goes N on 8 June. Until 10 June it is additionally

escorted by the carrier *Hermes* and from 12 June to 14 June by the cruiser *Devonshire*. On 14 June it is met W of Gibraltar by a force comprising the battlecruiser *Hood*, the carrier *Argus* and three Canadian (*Restigouche*, *St Laurent* and *Skeena*) and three British (*Brooke*, *Wanderer* and *Westcott*) destroyers. These are reinforced on 15 June by Sunderland flying boats and the destroyers *Warwick* and *Witch*. Following W/T messages decoded by the German 'B' Service, the Commander U-boats deploys from 12 June to 15 June the U-boats *U43*, *U101*, *U29*, *U48* and *U46* as the group Rösing against the convoy, but it is not sighted. It arrives in the Clyde on 16 June.

3 May   North Sea/English Channel
Another 39 airmines are dropped off Dunkirk, Calais, Boulogne and in the Downs.

3-4 May   North Sea
Unsuccessful sortie by the French destroyers *Chevalier-Paul*, *Milan* and *Tartu*, and the British destroyers *Sikh* and *Tartar* into the Skagerrak.

4 May   Norway
A He 111 of K.Gr.100 sinks the Polish destroyer *Grom* off Narvik.

6-28 May   North Sea
Unsuccessful Allied submarine operations off the Dutch coast and in the southern part of the North Sea to cover the Eastern entrance to the English Channel by the British submarines *Sturgeon*, *Triad*, *Snapper*, *Seawolf* and *Shark* and the French boats *Orphée*, *Calypso*, *Antiope*, *Circé*, *La Sibylle*, *Thétis* and *Doris*. Of the German U-boats *U7* and *U9* (Lt Lüth) operating in the same area the latter sinks the *Doris* and two ships of 3838 tons. On 10 Apl the British minelayer *Princess Victoria* with the destroyers *Esk*, *Express* and *Intrepid* lay a barrage of 236 mines in the area of Egmond which is extended with 60 more mines by *Intrepid* on 15 May. On the same day the destroyers *Esk*, *Express* and *Ivanhoe* lay a barrage of 164 mines off the Hook of Holland. On 26 July the German minesweepers *M61*, *M89* and *M136* sink on these barrages.

7 May   Pacific
President Roosevelt orders the U.S. Pacific Fleet, which is in the Hawaiian area for manoeuvres, to remain in Hawaii until further notice.

9-10 May   North Sea
During a sortie by the cruiser *Birmingham* and seven destroyers against German minelayers in the Skagerrak the 1st MTB Flotilla, comprising four boats attacks the force. *S31* (Lt Opdenhoff) hits the destroyer *Kelly* with one torpedo amidships. The badly-damaged ship is towed with difficulty to Newcastle by the destroyer *Bulldog*.

10 May   North Sea
Beginning of the German offensive in the W. Attack on Belgium, Holland and Luxembourg. In the previous night German aircraft drop 100 airmines off Belgian and Dutch ports.

10 May   South Atlantic
The German auxiliary cruiser *Schiff 16 Atlantis* (Capt Rogge) drops 92 mines off Cape Agulhas, South Africa. The barrage is prematurely discovered and causes no shipping losses.

10 May   North Atlantic
British troops land in Iceland.

10-11 May   North Sea
He 111 bombers of K.G.4 sink the Dutch passenger ships *Statendam* (28291 tons) and *Veendam* (15450 tons) and the destroyer *Van Galen* in the harbour of Rotterdam.

10-15 May   Norway
Advance by German battle group Feurstein from Mosjoen to Mo. To avoid British 'Scissor Force' near Mosjoen, 300 mountain troops are embarked on Norwegian steamer *Nord Norge* and landed near Hamnesberget before the steamer is sunk by the British cruiser *Carlisle* and the destroyer *Zulu*. 'Scissor Force' has to be evacuated from Sandnessjoen to Bodö by destroyers *Janus* and *Javelin*.
The bulk of the British Guards Brigade is ordered to Bodö to block the southern approach to Narvik. Cruisers *Cairo* and *Enterprise*, destroyer *Hesperus*, sloop *Fleetwood* and freighter *Margot* land reinforcements near Mo in spite of air attacks.
On 14-15 May the transport *Chrobry* (11442 tons) takes a battalion to Bodö escorted by the destroyer *Wolverine* and the sloop *Stork*. But in the process

she is hit by Ju 87 bombers of I/St.G.1 and has to be abandoned.

12 May   North Sea/ English Channel
Another 32 airmines are dropped by German aircraft in and outside Dutch and Belgian harbours. The operations are continued in the following nights. From 17 May the French Channel ports (Dunkirk, Calais, Dieppe, Boulogne and Le Havre) are the target of mining operations; from 25 May British harbours (Portsmouth, Dover, Southampton, Folkestone and Newhaven) are also again mined. In all, 575 more airmines are dropped.

12-13 May   Norway
Two battalions of the French Foreign Legion land in Bjerkvik (Herjangsfjord-Narvik). The 1500 troops are transported by the cruisers *Effingham* (Adm of the Fleet Lord Cork) and *Aurora* and are disembarked. The battleship *Resolution* puts out two MLC landing boats each with two light tanks. Fire support is provided by the cruiser *Enterprise* and five destroyers, including *Havelock* with a French mountain battery on board.

13 May   North Sea
British destroyer *Hereward* brings Queen Wilhelmina to Britain from Holland. In the evening the Dutch government follows on the British destroyer *Windsor*.

14 May   North Sea
German bombers sink the Belgian passenger steamer *Ville de Bruges* (13869 tons) in the Scheldt Estuary. Air attack on Rotterdam.

15 May   General Situation
Capitulation of the Dutch forces.

15 May   North Sea
German bombers sink the British destroyer *Valentine* and badly damage the *Winchester* in the Scheldt Estuary.

16-17 May   North Sea
French destroyers *Fougueux*, *Frondeur*, *Cyclone* and *Sirocco*, supported by two squadrons of the naval air force, intervene in the fighting round Zuid Beveland and Walcheren.

16 May-8 June   English Channel
In operations in the Channel *U9* (Lt Lüth) sinks one ship of 3256 tons; *U62* (Lt Michalowski) sinks the British destroyer *Grafton* off Dunkirk. Attacks on the destroyers *Blyskawica* and *Vimy*

by *U60* (Lt-Cdr Schewe) fail because of torpedo defects. *U13* (Lt-Cdr Schulte) is lost on a mine.

17 May   Norway
The British cruiser *Effingham*, in trying to bring reinforcements to Bodö, runs on a shoal and capsizes. Survivors are rescued by the cruisers *Cairo* and *Coventry* and the destroyers *Echo* and *Matabele*.

17 May   Western Atlantic
To prevent further incidents in the Pan-American Security Zone, caused by the seizure of German merchant ships, the Venezuelan Government orders the German freighters *Durazzo* (1153 tons) and *Sesostris* (3987 tons) lying in Maracaibo to be taken over by units of the Navy and their engines to be dismantled.

18 May   Norway
In an attack by Ju 88's of II/K.G.30 on shipping targets near Narvik, the battleship *Resolution* is hit by a 1000 kg bomb which penetrates three decks.

18-21 May   Norway
The British aircraft carriers *Furious* and *Glorious* operate off the Lofotens. On 18 May No 701 Sqdn FAA with Walrus amphibious aircraft is sent to Harstad for reconnaissance and defence against U-boats. On 21 May *Furious* flies 18 Gladiator fighters of No 263 Sqdn RAF to Bardufoss. The *Ark Royal*, which is operating off Vestfjord to provide air support, has to go to Scapa on 21 May for replenishment.

19 May-2 June   North Atlantic
U37 (Lt-Cdr Oehrn) is the first U-boat to operate again after a lengthy pause in the area NW of Cape Finisterre. She sinks nine ships of 41207 tons and damages one other of 9494 tons.

20 May-30 June   Norway
In Allied submarine operations off the Norwegian coast the French submarine *Rubis* (Cdr Cabanier) lays three mine barrages: near Haugesund (27 May), in Hjeltefjord (9 June) and off Gripholen (26 June) on which, in all, six ships and the submarine-chaser *UJD*, totalling 3772 tons, sink. *Narwhal* (Lt-Cdr Burch) lays a barrage near Utsire on 12 June (on which one ship of 908 tons sinks). On the way to the Norwegian coast the Polish submarine *Orzel* runs on to new German mine barrages on 8 June. On

16 June *Tetrarch* (Lt-Cdr Mills) sinks one ship of 5978 tons and *Truant* (Lt-Cdr Haggard) sinks one ship of 8230 tons off Northern Norway.

21 May   English Channel
German troops reach the Channel near Abbéville.

22 May-12 June   North Sea
U8, *U56* and *U58* (Lt-Cdr Kuppisch) operate from Bergen W of the Orkneys and in the North Minch. Torpedo defects prevent successes. Only *U58* sinks one ship of 8401 tons.

23-24 May   English Channel
The British destroyers *Whitshed*, *Vimiera*, *Wild Swan*, *Venomous*, *Venetia* and *Windsor* evacuate 4368 troops under heavy German artillery fire and air attacks. On her second trip alone *Vimiera* takes 1400 from Boulogne. Before this, the large French destroyers *Chacal* and *Jaguar* and the ordinary destroyers *Fougueux*, *Frondeur* (*L'Adroit* sunk 21 May), *Bourrasque*, *Orage*, *Foudroyant*, *Cyclone*, *Sirocco* and *Mistral* under the command of Captain Urvoy de Porzamparc intervene and temporarily halt the German advance. *Orage* is sunk by German bombers and *Jaguar* is sunk by the motor torpedo boats *S21* (Lt v. Mirbach) and *S23* (Lt Christiansen).

24 May   Norway
Decision by Allied Supreme Command to evacuate Norway. Narvik is first to be occupied in order to destroy its installations.

24-26 May   English Channel
British cruisers *Arethusa* and *Galatea* and the destroyers *Wessex*, *Vimiera*, *Wolfhound*, *Verity*, *Grafton*, *Greyhound* and *Burza* (Polish) give support to the defenders of Calais from the sea. *Wessex* is sunk by German bombers. The large French destroyer *Chacal* suffers the same fate off Boulogne on 24 May.

26 May   Norway
The carrier *Glorious* brings Hurricane fighters of No. 46 Sqdn RAF to Skaanland (Northern Norway).

26-28 May   Norway
The AA cruiser *Curlew*, which is intended to be the Flagship of Admiral of the Fleet Lord Cork, is sunk on 26 May by German Ju 88's of K.G.30 off

Skaanland. For this reason attack on Narvik in the night 27-28 May is made with AA cruisers *Cairo* (Lord Cork) and *Coventry* (Rear-Adm Vivian) and destroyers *Whirlwind*, *Fame*, *Havelock*, *Walker* and *Firedrake* and sloop *Stork*. They support the Foreign Legion's crossing of Rombaksfjord and the advance with light tanks along the ore railway to Narvik, which has to be evacuated by the Germans on 28 May. Cruiser *Southampton* gives fire support to the Polish Brigade W of Narvik. Flagship *Cairo* is damaged by bomb hit.

28 May   English Channel
King Leopold capitulates with the Belgian Army. Beginning of the Operation 'Dynamo' (Return of the British Expeditionary Force). Up to 4 June following warships participate: British AA cruiser *Calcutta*, destroyers *Anthony*, *Basilisk*, *Blyskawica* (Polish), *Codrington*, *Esk*, *Express*, *Gallant*, *Grafton*, *Grenade*, *Greyhound*, *Harvester*, *Havant*, *Icarus*, *Impulsive*, *Intrepid*, *Ivanhoe*, *Javelin*, *Jaguar*, *Keith*, *Mackay*, *Malcolm*, *Montrose*, *Sabre*, *Saladin*, *Scimitar*, *Shikari*, *Vanquisher*, *Venomous*, *Verity*, *Vimy*, *Vivacious*, *Wakeful*, *Whitehall*, *Whitshed*, *Wild Swan*, *Winchelsea*, *Windsor*, *Wolfhound*, *Wolsey*, *Worcester*, sloops *Bideford*, *Guillemot*, *Kingfisher*, gunboats *Locust*, *Mosquito*, minesweepers *Albury*, *Dundalk*, *Gossamer*, *Halcyon*, *Hebe*, *Leda*, *Lydd*, *Niger*, *Pangbourne*, *Ross*, *Salamander*, *Saltash*, *Skipjack*, *Speedwell*, *Sutton*, *Sharpshooter*, four patrol ships, 53 minesweeping and A/S trawlers, five Q ships, 24 drifters, six MTBs, four MSABs, 28 personnel transports, eight hospital transports, and numerous auxiliary and private craft. In addition, the French destroyers *Branlebas*, *Bourrasque*, *Cyclone*, *Foudroyant*, *Mistral*, *Sirocco*, the torpedo boats *Bouclier*, *La Flore*, *L'Incomprise*, and the sloops *Amiens*, *Amiral Mouchez*, *Arras* and *Belfort*, as well as auxiliary and merchant ships. On the first day 17804 troops are evacuated from the mainland. One small steamer (694 tons) is sunk by the German motor torpedo boat *S34*; the British destroyer *Windsor* is damaged by bombs and other auxiliary ships and transports are sunk and damaged.

28 May-22 June   North Atlantic/ Bay of Biscay

The U-boats *U43*, *U101*, *U29*, *U48* and *U46* operate as the first wave concentrating on the area NW of Cape Finisterre. From 12 June- 15 June the boats are concentrated without success to operate as the group 'Rösing' against the troop convoy US.3. On 22 June *U46* attacks the carrier *Ark Royal* which is proceeding with the battlecruiser *Hood* to Gibraltar, but she is unsuccessful owing to torpedo defects. *U43* refuels in Vigo on 18 June and *U29* in El Ferrol on 20 June from German tankers and they continue the operations until 15 June and 4 July respectively. In all the U-boats sink in their individual operations: *U43* (Lt-Cdr Ambrosius) four ships of 29456 tons; *U101* (Lt-Cdr Frauenheim) seven ships of 42022 tons; *U29* (Lt-Cdr Schuhart) four ships of 26638 tons; *U48* (Cdr Rösing) seven ships of 31533 tons and damages one ship of 5888 tons; *U46* (Lt Endrass) five ships of 35347 tons and damages one ship of 8782 tons. Among the ships sunk are the auxiliary cruiser *Carinthia* (20277 tons) by *U46* on 6 June and the refrigerator ships *Wellington Star* (13212 tons) and *Avelona Star* (13376 tons) by *U101* and *U43* on 16 June and 30 June respectively.

29 May   English Channel

Second day of the Operation 'Dynamo': 47310 troops evacuated. British destroyer *Wakeful* sunk by *S30* (Lt Zimmermann); *Grenade* by German bombers; and *Grafton* by *U62* (Lt Michalowski). *Gallant*, *Jaguar*, *Greyhound*, *Intrepid*, *Saladin*, *Wolfhound* and *Mistral* (French) and the sloop *Bideford* are severely damaged by bombs. Destroyers *Mackay* and *Montrose* are damaged in collision and by running aground. The German Air Force also sinks eight auxiliary ships of 6201 tons and seven merchant ships totalling 15830 tons.

30 May   English Channel

Third day of the Operation 'Dynamo': 53823 troops evacuated. French destroyer *Bourrasque* sunk by German artillery off Nieuport and the destroyers *Anthony*, *Sabre*, and *Worcester* damaged by air attacks. Three large transports and six fishery vessels are sunk.

31 May   English Channel

Fourth day of the Operation 'Dynamo': 68014 troops evacuated. French destroyer *Sirocco* sunk by the German motor torpedo boats *S23* (Lt Christiansen) and *S26* (Lt Fimmen); the destroyer *Cyclone* loses her bow through a torpedo from *S24* (Lt Detlefsen). Destroyers *Express*, *Harvester*, *Icarus*, *Impulsive*, *Malcolm*, *Scimitar* and minesweeper *Hebe* damaged by German bombers.

31 May   North Sea/Norway

British Home Fleet has the following ships available; 2nd BB Sqdn: *Resolution*, *Rodney* (FF) and *Valiant*. Being repaired: *Barham* and *Nelson*. Battlecruiser Sqdn: *Renown* (F), *Repulse*. Being repaired: *Hood*. Aircraft carriers: *Ark Royal* (F), *Furious* (Clyde), *Glorious*, destroyer *Westcott*. Allocated cruisers being repaired: *Cairo* and *Enterprise*. 1st Cruiser Sqdn: *Devonshire* (F), *Sussex*. Being repaired: *Berwick*, *Norfolk*, *Suffolk*. 2nd Cruiser Sqdn: *Galatea* (F), *Arethusa* (both in Sheerness). Being repaired: *Aurora*, *Penelope*. 18th Cruiser Sqdn: *Southampton* (F) and *Birmingham*, *Manchester* and *Sheffield* in the Humber, *York* in Rosyth and *Newcastle* in the Tyne. Being repaired: *Glasgow*. 3rd DD Flotilla: *Delight*, *Diana*. Being repaired: *Imogen*, *Inglefield*, *Isis*. 5th DD Flotilla: *Jackal*, *Kelvin* in Harwich and *Javelin* in Sheerness. Being repaired: *Kelly*, *Kipling*, *Kashmir*, *Jaguar*, *Jersey*, *Jervis*, *Jupiter*. 6th DD Flotilla: *Tartar* (F); *Ashanti*, *Bedouin*, *Mashona*. Being repaired: *Somali*, *Matabele*, *Punjabi*, *Eskimo*. 8th DD Flotilla: *Foxhound*, *Fortune*, *Fame*, *Firedrake*. Being repaired: *Faulknor*, *Fearless*, *Forester*, *Fury*. 9th DD Flotilla: *Havelock* (F), *Harvester*, *Havant* and *Highlander* in Sheerness. Being repaired: *Hesperus*.

1 June   English Channel

Fifth day of the Operation 'Dynamo': 64429 troops evacuated. In heavy German air attacks there sink the flotilla leader *Keith* (Flagship Rear-Adm Wake-Walker) the destroyers *Basilisk*, *Havant* and *Foudroyant* (French); the minesweeper *Skipjack*, the gunboat *Mosquito* and the transports *British Queen* (807 tons) and *Scotia* (3454 tons) with French troops on board. There are heavy losses of personnel. *S34* (Lt Obermaier) sinks in a sortie against Dunkirk the British trawlers *Argyllshire* and *Stella Dorado*. The destroyers *Ivanhoe, Venomous, Vimy, Vivacious, Whitehall,* the sloops *Bideford* and *Kingfisher* are damaged in air attacks.

1 June Mediterranean
In a German air attack on Marseilles the British passenger ship *Orford* (20043 tons) sinks.

2 June English Channel
Sixth day of the operation 'Dynamo': 26256 troops evacuated. Destroyers *Malcolm* and *Sabre* are again damaged in air attacks.

4 June English Channel
End of operation 'Dynamo' (27 May-4 June): in all, 338226 Allied troops, including 123000 French, are transported from Dunkirk on 848 ships of every kind and size. Eighty five per cent of the British Expeditionary Force is saved, but almost without equipment. Losses: 72 ships including nine destroyers and a large number of small and very small craft, most of them sunk in air attacks. At 0940 hours units of the 18th German Army take Dunkirk. 40000 French taken prisoner.

4-10 June Norway
Allied Evacuation of Narvik. In five successive nights up to 7-8 June, 4700, 4900, 5100, 5200 and 4600 men are embarked on troop transports assembled off Harstad under the command of Capt Stevens on *Havelock,* mainly with destroyers. The first convoy, consisting of *Monarch of Bermuda, Batory, Sobieski, Franconia, Lancastria* and *Georgic,* leaves Harstad on 4 June, accompanied only by the training cruiser *Vindictive* and reaches Scapa Flow on 8 June without loss. As a result of a false report from the Q-ship, *Prunella,* about two unidentified ships proceeding towards the Iceland-Faeroes passage, the C-in-C Home Fleet fears a break-out by the German battleships into the Atlantic. Because of this the battle-cruisers *Renown* and *Repulse,* the cruisers *Newcastle* and *Sussex* and five escorting destroyers are sent off. Only the battleship *Valiant* remains available to cover the evacuation convoys. On 7 June the second troop transport, consisting of the *Oronsay, Ormonde,*

Arandora Star, Royal Ulsterman, Ulster Prince, Ulster Monarch and *Duchess* of *York,* escorted by the cruisers *Southampton* (Lord Cork, Vice-Adm Layton), *Coventry* (Rear-Adm Vivian,) the destroyers *Havelock, Fame, Firedrake, Beagle* and *Delight* leaves Harstad as well as a slow convoy with the transports and tankers *Blackheath, Oligarch, Harmattan, Cromarty Firth, Theseus, Acrity, Cotswold* and *Conch,* escorted by the destroyers *Arrow* and *Veteran,* the sloop *Stork* and ten trawlers. The cruiser *Devonshire* sets out to sea from Tromsö with the Norwegian King. The carrier *Ark Royal* stands by in the area of the troop convoy. The carrier *Glorious,* after taking the last aircraft on board, leaves Bardufoss with her last two destroyers independently for the W. Likewise some independents from Vestfjord and the transports *Orama* and *Van Dyck* which were not ordered to Harstad.

4-10 June Norway
Operation 'Juno': sortie against British evacuation transports in the area W of Harstad by the Fleet Commander, Adm Marschall, with the battleships *Gneisenau* (Capt Netzbandt) and *Scharnhorst* (Capt Hoffmann), the heavy cruiser *Admiral Hipper* (Capt Heye) and the destroyers *Karl Galster, Hans Lody, Erich Steinbrinck* and *Hermann Schoemann.* On the way the empty troop transport *Orama* (19840 tons), the tanker *Oil Pioneer* (5666 tons) and the trawler *Juniper* (505 tons) are sunk on 8 June. After detaching themselves from *Admiral Hipper* and the destroyers, the battleships destroy the British aircraft carrier *Glorious* (Capt D'Oyly-Hughes†) and the destroyers *Acasta* (Cdr Glasford†) and *Ardent* (Lt-Cdr Barker†). But *Acasta* is able to obtain a torpedo hit on *Scharnhorst.* Only 43 survivors from the carrier and three from both destroyers are rescued. But the British evacuation convoys are not found and they reach Scapa Flow on 10 June. An operation started on 9 June by the Home Fleet with the battleship *Rodney* and the recalled battlecruiser *Renown* is unable to catch the German ships before they sail into Trondheim.

4-21 June Mediterranean
Beginning on 4 June and continuing until 9 June 54 Italian submarines, in all,

D

set out for positions in the Mediterranean. Except for 26 they return on 14-15 June and most of the remainder return by 21 June or are relieved: *Veniero, Neghelli, Gondar, Fieramosca,* and *Mocenigo* operate on the French Riviera: *H1, H4, H6,* and *H8* in the Gulf of Genoa; *Medusa* off Ajaccio; *Faa'di Bruno, Morosini, Provana, Dandolo* and *Marcello* (not in position owing to breakdown) between Oran and Cartagena; *Barbarigo* and *Nani* N of Algiers; *Axum, Turchese, Adua* and *Aradam* south of Sardinia; *Alagi* off Bizerta; *Beilul, Brin* and *Durbo* in the Sicilian Channel; *Bausan* off Malta; *Uarsciek, Balilla, Anfitrite* and *Sciesa* on the Greek/Albanian coast; *Salpa, Giuliani, Bagnolini* and *Tarantini* S of Gaudo (Crete); *Lafolé, Diamante, Topazio* and *Nereide* N of Sollum; *Galatea* (not in position owing to breakdown), *Fisalia, Argonauta, Naiade* and *Smeraldo* off Alexandria; *Jantina, Jalea, Delfino, Tricheco, Zaffiro* and *Velella* between Crete and Rhodes: *Ametista, Gemma* and *Squalo* in the Aegean; *Settimo* and *Uebi Scebeli* N and W of Crete. On 12 June *Bagnolini* (Cdr Tosoni-Pittoni) sinks the British cruiser *Calypso* and *Naiade* (Lt-Cdr Baroni) the Norwegian tanker *Orkanger* (8029 tons). *Dandolo* (Lt-Cdr Boris) attacks a French cruiser force on 13 June and just misses the *Jean de Vienne*. *Provana* (Cdr Botta) misses the French convoy IR.2F and is then forced to surface by the sloop *La Curieuse* and sunk by ramming. On 20 June *Diamante* is sunk by the British submarine *Parthian* (Lt-Cdr Rimington). Mine barrage (40 mines) laid off Alexandria on 12 June by *Micca* (Cdr* Meneghini) achieves no success.

**5 June-13 July Gibraltar/
Central Atlantic**
On 5-6 June the Italian submarines *Cappellini* and *Finzi* set out from Cagliari for the Atlantic. *Finzi* passes through the Straits of Gibraltar on 13 June and then operates without success in the area of the Canaries. She passes through the Straits of Gibraltar (6 July) again, returning to base on 13 July. *Cappellini* is attacked by the A/S trawler *Arctic Ranger* with depth charges on 14 June off the Straits of Gibraltar. Then she is pursued by the destroyer

Vidette and has to take refuge in Centa from 15-24 June, whence she returns.

**6 June-10 July Mediterranean/
Red Sea**
Major defensive mine barrages are laid on the Italian Mediterranean coasts. The mine layers *Crotone* and *Fasana,* and the auxiliary minelayers *Orlando* and *Sgarallino* lay in the Gulf of Genoa and in the Elba area 21 barrages against surface ships and 27 barrages against submarines involving 1960 mines. In the Naples area the minelayer *Buffoluto* and the steamer *Partenope* lay seven barrages involving 433 mines. Off Sardinia the minelayers *Durazzo* and *Pelagosa,* the auxiliary minelayer *Caralis,* the auxiliary ship *Deffenu* and the torpedo boats *Papa, Cascino, Chinotto* and *Montanari* lay 30 barrages consisting of 2196 mines, 12 of which are against submarines. In the area of Sicily the auxiliary ships *Adriatico* and *Brioni* and the torpedo boats *Aldebaran, Andromeda, Alcione, Aretusa, Ariel, Airone, Pallade, Calliope, Circe* and *Clio* lay 28 barrages consisting of 1375 mines, 11 of which are against submarines. In the Gulf of Taranto and in the southern part of the Adriatic, including Albania, the minelayer *Vieste,* the auxiliary ship *Barletta,* the cruiser *Taranto* and the destroyers *Mirabello* and *Riboty* lay 37 mine barrages consisting of 2335 mines, 28 of which are submarine defence barrages. In the Northern Adriatic the minelayers *Albona, Azio, Laurana, Rovigo* and the auxiliary minesweeper *S. Giusto* lay 21 barrages consisting of 769 mines, 18 of which are against submarines. In the Aegean-Dodecanese area the auxiliary ship *Lero,* the destroyers *Crispi* and *Sella* and the torpedo boats *Libra, Lince* and *Lira,* lay 28 barrages consisting of 800 mines, four of them against submarines. Off Libya the auxiliary ship *Barletta,* and off Tobruk the destroyers *Aquilone, Euro, Nembo* and *Turbine,* lay 14 barrages consisting of 540 mines.
In the Red Sea, the minelayer *Ostia* lays eight barrages of 470 mines off Massawa and the destroyer *Pantera* two barrages of 110 mines off Assab on 7 June.

8-12 June Mediterranean
Offensive mine barrages are laid out by Italian ships in the Sicilian Channel.

In the nights 8-9 June and 9-10 June the minelayers *Buccari* and *Scilla*, accompanied by the torpedo boat *Altair*, lay 640 mines each between Pantelleria and Sicily. In the night 9-10 June the cruisers *Da Barbiano* (Div Adm Marenco di Moriondo) and *Cadorna*, the destroyers *Corazziere* and *Lanciere* and the torpedo boats *Calipso* and *Polluce* lay the barrage LK consisting of 428 mines between Lampedusa and Kerkennah. After an interrupted operation, *Buccari* and *Scilla* with the torpedo boats *Airone* and *Ariel* lay another 800 mines in the night 11-12 June. To cover the operation the cruisers *Pola* (Div Adm Paladini), *Trento, Bolzano, Eugenio di Savoia* (Div Adm Sansonetti), *Attendolo, Duca d'Aosta* and *Montecuccoli* put to sea with destroyers on 10-11 June.

9 June-2 July   North Atlantic/ Bay of Biscay
The U-boats *U32, U47, U25, U38, U28, U51* and *U30* operate as second wave concentrating on the area W of the English Channel and in the Bay of Biscay. From 12 June to 15 June they are deployed as the group 'Prien' against the convoy HX.48 which is located by the W/T intelligence service ('B' Service); but they only encounter stragglers. *U30* is replenished in El Ferrol on 25 June and is the first U-boat to enter the new Lorient base on 5 July. In their individual operations *U32* (Lt-Cdr Jenisch) sinks five ships of 16098 tons; *U47* (Lt-Cdr Prien) eight ships of 51189 tons; *U25* (Lt-Cdr Beduhn) the auxiliary cruiser *Scotstoun* (17046 tons) on 13 June; *U38* (Lt-Cdr Liebe) six ships of 30353 tons; *U28* (Lt-Cdr Kuhnke) three ships of 10305 tons; *U51* (Lt-Cdr Knorr) three ships of 22146 tons and damages one ship of 3082 tons; *U30* (Lt-Cdr Lemp) six ships of 26329 tons. Among the ships sunk is the unnotified troop transport *Arandora Star* (15501 tons) which is taking German and Italian civilian internees to Canada (sunk by *U47* on 2 July).

10 June   Norway
Capitulation of Norwegian troops (Maj-Gen Ruge) in Northern Norway. This concludes operation 'Weserübung'. German naval losses: three cruisers, 10 destroyers, one torpedo boat, four submarines, one gunnery training ship, one motor minesweeper and a number of auxiliary ships. Allied losses: one aircraft carrier, two cruisers, nine destroyers, five submarines and many auxiliary ships.

10 June   Mediterranean
Italy enters the war. Strength of the fleet: six battleships (only the two oldest ready for operations), seven heavy cruisers, 12 light cruisers, 59 destroyers, 67 torpedo boats and 116 submarines. A third of the merchant marine, comprising in all 3.4m tons, is at the moment outside the Mediterranean and so cannot be put to war use. Allied forces: British and French Mediterranean fleets. Eastern Mediterranean: British: four battleships, one aircraft carrier, nine light cruisers, 21 destroyers (four more detached to the Red Sea), six submarines. French: one battleship, three heavy cruisers, one light cruiser, one destroyer, six submarines. Malta (British): one destroyer, six submarines. Western Mediterranean: French: two modern battleships, two old battleships, four heavy cruisers, six light cruisers, 37 destroyers, 6 torpedo boats, 36 submarines. Gibraltar: one battleship, one aircraft carrier, one light cruiser, nine destroyers.

10-11 June   English Channel
The taking off of the 51st British Div from St Valéry is only partly successful. 3321 British and French troops are evacuated: the rest are taken prisoner.

10-11 June   Norway
A sortie by the battleship *Gneisenau* with the heavy cruiser *Admiral Hipper* and four destroyers from Trondheim into the Arctic produces no results.

10-13 June   English Channel
11059 British troops are evacuated from Le Havre partly to Cherbourg and partly to Britain. In the process the transport *Bruges* (2949 tons) sinks after being hit by bombs.

10-25 June   Mediterranean
Allied submarine operations in the Mediterranean: in the Central Mediterranean the British submarines *Odin, Osiris, Oswald, Olympus, Orpheus* and *Grampus* operate from Malta off Italian harbours. Of these *Odin* is sunk by the Italian destroyer *Strale* in the Gulf of Taranto on 13 June; *Grampus* by the

Italian torpedo boats *Circe, Clio* and *Polluce* off Syracuse on 16 June; and *Orpheus* by the destroyer *Turbine* off Tobruk. The French submarines *Le Centaure, Pascal, Fresnel, Vengeur, Redoutable, Narval, Caïman, Morse, Souffleur, Monge, Pégase* and *Le Tonnant* operate from Tunisian ports, sometimes repeatedly. *Morse* is lost when she hits a mine off Sfax on 15 June. The British submarines *Parthian, Pandora, Proteus* and *Phoenix* operate in the Eastern Mediterranean from Alexandria and *Rorqual* lays a mine barrage off the African coast. The French submarines *Phoque, Espadon, Protée, Achéron* and *Actéon*, operate in the Dodecanese area from Beirut. The French submarines *Iris, Vénus, Pallas* and *Archimède* operate in the Tyrrhenian Sea from Toulon and the French submarines *Ariane, Eurydice, Diane* and *Danaé* off Gibraltar from Oran. The French submarine *Saphir* (Lt-Cdr Caminati) lays a mine barrage off Cagliari, sinking two ships of 1699 tons; *Nautilus* off Tripoli; *Turquoise* off Trapani and *Perlé* off Bastia.

10-26 June   Red Sea/Indian Ocean
First operations by Italian submarines from Massawa (Eritrea): on 10 June *Ferraris* proceeds to Djibouti, *Galilei* to Aden, *Galvani* to the Gulf of Oman, and *Macalle* to Port Sudan. On 14 June *Torricelli* relieves *Ferraris* which returns owing to a breakdown. On 15 June *Macallé* (Lt-Cdr Morone) runs on a shoal and is lost. *Galilei* (Cdr Nardi) sinks the Norwegian tanker *James Stove* (8215 tons) on 16 June. She stops the Yugoslav steamer *Drava* on 18 June but has to release her again and is encountered on 19 June by the A/S trawler *Moonstone* and forced in a gun duel to surrender after the commander becomes a casualty. On the basis of documents captured on board, the sloop *Falmouth* is able to sink *Galvani* (Cdr Spano) off the Persian Gulf on 24 June, the submarine having previously destroyed the Indian sloop *Pathan*. *Torricelli* (Cdr Pelosi) is encountered on 23 June off Perim and is sunk in a gun duel with the British destroyers *Kandahar, Khartoum, Kingston* and the sloop *Shoreham. Torricelli* obtains hits on *Shoreham* and *Khartoum*. The latter

is set on fire and sinks after an explosion in a magazine. Of the submarines *Archimede, Perla* and *Gugliel-motti*, which set out on 19-21 June, the latter runs on a shoal on 26 June but can be salvaged in spite of severe damage.

10 June-20 Sept   Indian Ocean
German auxiliary cruiser *Schiff 16 Atlantis* (Capt Rogge) sinks and seizes in the Indian Ocean seven Allied merchant ships of 49338 tons and the French passenger ship *Commissaire Ramel* (10061 tons).

11 June   Atlantic
Auxiliary cruiser *Thor* (Capt Kähler) sets out from Sörgulenfjord for her first operation in the Central and South Atlantic (left Kiel on 6 June).

11 June   Mediterranean
First Italian air attack on Malta. Other bombers attack Toulon.

11 June   Norway
N of Harstad (Norway) German aircraft sink the British auxiliary ship *Van Dyck* (13241 tons).

11-14 June   Mediterranean
First sortie by the British Mediterranean Fleet (Adm Cunningham) against Italian shipping heading for Libya S of Crete and towards Benghazi and Tobruk. Taking part: battleships *Warspite* (F) and *Malaya*, carrier *Eagle*, 7th Cruiser Sqdn (Vice-Adm Tovey) with *Orion, Neptune, Sydney, Liverpool* and *Glouc-ester*, nine destroyers and old cruisers *Caledon* and *Calypso*. Simultaneous sortie by French cruisers (Vice-Adm Godfroy) *Duquesne, Tourville, Suffren* and *Duguay Trouin* and three destroyers into the Aegean and against the Dodecanese. On 12 June *Calypso* is sunk by the Italian submarine *Bagnolini* (Cdr Tosoni-Pittoni). British cruisers *Glouc-ester* and *Liverpool* with four destroyers shell Tobruk and engage the floating battery *San Giorgio* (ex-armoured cruiser) and four small Italian auxiliary minesweepers, of which *Giovanni Berta* (Chief Petty Officer Paolucci) sinks, firing her only 7.6cm gun. When air reconnaissance reports this British force the 3rd Italian Cruiser Div sets out from Messina with *Pola, Trento* and *Bolzano* together with the 11th and 12th DD Flotillas. In addition, the 1st and 8th Cruiser Divs with *Zara, Fiume, Gorizia, Duca degli Abruzzi*, and *Garibaldi* and

the 9th and 16th DD Flotillas set out from Taranto. But no contact results.

11 June-20 Aug   Atlantic
First Southern operation by a German U-boat. *UA* (Lt-Cdr Cohausz) operates on the way out (11 June-19 June) against the Northern Patrol and, after a miss on 14 June, sinks the auxiliary cruiser *Andania* (13950 tons) on 16 June. On the way S one ship is sunk and another in the first half of the operations in the area of the Canary and Cape Verde Islands. By 10 Aug a fourth ship is sunk, the U-boat having been replenished off Freetown on 19 July from the auxiliary cruiser *Schiff 33*. On the return three more ships are sunk, making a total of seven ships with a tonnage of 40706 tons.

12-20 June   Norway
Climax in the operations of the third British submarine wave off Norway with the boats *Severn, Clyde, Sealion, Spearfish, Porpoise, Narwhal, Trident, Truant, Taku, Tetrarch* and the French *Rubis*. *Narwhal* (Lt-Cdr Burch) lays a mine barrage near Utsire, sinking one ship of 908 tons. *Rubis* (Cdr Cabanier) lays two mine barrages in the area of Bergen on which four ships of 1898 tons are sunk. *Tetrarch* (Lt-Cdr Mills) sinks the tanker *Samland* (5978 tons) near Lister on 16 June. *Clyde* (Lt-Cdr Ingram) torpedoes the battleship *Gneisenau* in the bows off Trondheim on 20 June. On the way out to Norway the Dutch submarine *O13* is lost, presumably on 20 June after being attacked in error by the Polish submarine *Wilk*.

12-14 June   Norway
Home Fleet (Adm Forbes) makes a raid on Trondheim with battleship *Rodney*, battlecruiser *Renown* and destroyers to cover the carrier *Ark Royal*. On 13 June 15 Skua dive bombers fly off to attack the German battleship *Scharnhorst*. They get a hit with a 225kg bomb but it does not explode. Eight aircraft are shot down by the defence. On the return the destroyers *Antelope* and *Electra* collide.

13 June   Pacific
Auxiliary cruiser *Orion* (Cdr* Weyher) lays 162 mines in Hauraki Bay (New Zealand) and another 60 between Cuvier Island and Great Barrier Island and in the Colville Channel. In Hauraki Bay

the British passenger ship *Niagara* (13415 tons) sinks on 18 June.

13 June-13 July   Central Atlantic
German auxiliary cruiser *Schiff 21 Widder* (Cdr v. Ruckteschell) sinks three Allied freighters of 18552 tons in the western part of the Central Atlantic and seizes the Norwegian motor tanker *Krossfonn* (9323 tons).

14 June   Mediterranean
Sortie by the French 3rd Sqdn (Vice-Adm Duplat) with four heavy cruisers and 11 large destroyers from Toulon against the Ligurian coast. The 1st Cruiser Div shells Vado with *Algérie* and *Foch* and the destroyers *Lion, Aigle, Tartu, Chevalier-Paul* and *Cassard*; the 2nd Cruiser Div (Rear-Adm Derrien) shells the harbour installations of Genoa with *Colbert* and *Dupleix* and the destroyers *Albatros* and *Vautour*, escorted by the destroyers *Guépard, Valmy* and *Verdun*. A courageous attack by the Italian torpedo boat *Calatafimi* and the 13th MTB Flotilla is not successful. Italian coastal artillery obtains a hit on *Albatros*. The deployment of the Italian submarines *Neghelli* and *Veniero*, which are still at sea, and the submarines *Iride* and *Scire*, coming from La Spezia, achieve nothing.

14 June   Mediterranean
The 1st Italian DD Flotilla (Cdr* Ruggieri), consisting of *Turbine, Nembo* and *Aquilone*, shells Sollum.

15-18 June   English Channel
British 52nd Div and 'Norman Force', comprising 30630 troops, are evacuated from Cherbourg without loss.

16-17 June   English Channel
Evacuation of 1st Canadian Div with 21474 troops from St Malo without loss. Off Brest 32584 men of the British Army and RAF, as well as Allied troops, are evacuated. The harbour is destroyed on 18-19 June. The French fleet sets out for Casablanca and Oran.

16-18 June   Bay of Biscay
St Nazaire and Nantes are evacuated. In all 57235 Allied troops are brought to Britain. Heavy losses—about 3000 men—are sustained when British transport *Lancastria* (16243 tons) is sunk by German bombers.

16 June-2 July   North Atlantic
U61 (Lt-Cdr Oesten) and *U62* (Lt Michalowski) operate from Bergen in

the area of the Hebrides. An attack by *U61* on an auxiliary cruiser fails; *U62* misses two ships and sinks a small trawler of 211 tons.

17 June   General Situation
France sues for an Armistice.

17-18 June   General Situation
Evacuation of the British Expeditionary Force from the Continent completed.

17 June-19 July   North Atlantic
U52, *U65*, *U122*, *U26*, *U34*, *U102*, *U99* and *U30* (which has set out again from Lorient) operate as third wave in the area between the North Channel and Cape Finisterre. Shortly after the first attacks off the North Channel *U122* (21 June) and *U102* (30 June) are lost from unknown causes (mines?). *U26*, when attacking a convoy on 1 July, is sunk by the corvette *Gladiolus*, supported by a Sunderland flying boat of No 10 Sqdn RAAF. This is the first success registered by a 'Flower' class corvette. In their operations *U52* (Lt-Cdr Salman) sinks four ships of 13542 tons; *U65* (Lt-Cdr v. Stockhausen) one ship of 1177 tons and damages *Champlain* (see below) and two other ships of 13958 tons; *U122* (Lt Cdr Looff) sinks one ship of 5911 tons; *U26* (Lt-Cdr Scheringer) one ship of 6701 tons and damages one other ship of 4871 tons; *U34* (Lt-Cdr Rollmann) sinks destroyer *Whirlwind* and seven ships of 21334 tons; *U102* (Lt-Cdr v. Klot-Heydenfeldt) two ships of 4505 tons; *U99* (Lt-Cdr Kretschmer) six ships of 20755 tons; *U30* (Lt-Cdr Lemp) one ship of 712 tons. The troop transport *Champlain* (28124 tons), which hit a mine on 18 June and rested on the bottom, is finished off on 21 June by a torpedo from *U65*.
U30, *U34*, *U52* and *U99* put into Lorient for replenishment.

17-28 June   Gibraltar
From 17 June to 23 June the battle-cruiser *Hood*, the carrier *Ark Royal* and the destroyers of the 8th DD Flotilla *Escapade*, *Faulknor*, *Fearless* and *Foxhound* move from Scapa Flow to Gibraltar. The force is attacked on 22 June by *U46* in gale force 11 winds; but *Ark Royal* is missed because of a torpedo failure. In the following days the battleships *Resolution* and *Valiant*, the cruiser *Enterprise* and the destroyers

Escort, *Foresight* and *Forester*, arrive. With the arrival of Vice-Adm Somerville on board the cruiser *Arethusa* on 28 June, Force H is formed. In addition, the 13th DD Flotilla, comprising *Active*, *Wrestler*, *Vidette* and *Douglas*, *Keppel*, *Vortigern*, *Wishart* and *Watchman* (the latter returns to Britain in July), is stationed in Gibraltar.

18 June   English Channel/ Bay of Biscay
The German 7th Armoured Div occupies Cherbourg. 30630 troops are evacuated beforehand under cover from battleship *Courbet* (Capt Croiset); in the dockyards five uncompleted submarines, including *Roland-Morillot*, are blown up. Before the occupation of Brest by the German 5th Armoured Div the submarines *Achille*, *Agosta*, *Ouessant* and *Pasteur*, the destroyer *Cyclone* and the sloop *Etourdi*, which are in harbour for repairs, are blown up.

18-27 June   Atlantic
On 18 June the not quite completed French battleship *Richelieu* (Capt Marzin) sets out from Brest for Dakar with the destroyers *Fougueux* and *Frondeur*. On 19 June the unfinished battleship *Jean Bart* (Capt Ronarch) is towed out of St Nazaire, and accompanied by the new destroyers *Le Hardi*, (with the Commander Naval Forces West, Rear-Adm Laborde on board) and *Mameluk*, reaches Casablanca on 22 June. There her movements are observed by the British destroyer *Watchman*. The *Richelieu* arrives off Dakar on 23 June. On the same day the cruiser *Dorsetshire* sets out from Freetown to keep watch and meets the carrier *Hermes* off Dakar. On 25 June the British C-in-C South Atlantic, Vice-Adm D'Oyly Lyon, comes from Freetown with the seaplane carrier *Albatross*. But before she arrives the *Richelieu* sets out at midday on 25 June for Casablanca, followed by the *Dorsetshire*. However, Adm Darlan orders the *Richelieu* back to Dakar where she arrives on 27 June with the auxiliary cruisers *El Djezair*, *El Kantara*, *El Mansour* and *Ville d'Oran* from Brest and the destroyers *Epervier* and *Milan*.

18 June-19 July   Mediterranean
Supply transports from Naples to Leros with the Italian submarine *Atropo*, and

o Tobruk with *Bragadino, Corridoni* and *Zoea*. The latter goes on to Leros.

19 June   English Channel
The German motor torpedo boats *S19* (Lt Töniges) and *S26* (Lt Fimmen) sink the British freighter *Roseburn* (3103 tons) off Dungeness.

19-25 June   Bay of Biscay
Evacuation of some 19000 troops, mainly Polish, from Bayonne and St Jean-de-Luz.

In all, in the operations 'Cycle' (French North Coast) and 'Ariel' (Biscay Coast) —in addition to 'Dynamo'—144171 British, 18246 French, 24352 Poles, 4938 Czechs and 163 Belgians are evacuated. Total 191870 troops.

19-27 June   Mediterranean
A second wave of Italian submarines is stationed in the Eastern Mediterranean: W of Crete *Bausan*; S of Crete *Manara* and *Menotti*; off Sollum *Sirena*; off Alexandria *Rubino*; off Famagusta *Liuzzi*; in the approaches to the Aegean *Delfino*, *Squalo*, *Brin* and *Tricheco*. *Sirena* is damaged with depth charges in an Anglo-French cruiser sortie on 21 June and puts in to Tobruk.

19 June-2 July   Mediterranean
A second wave of Italian submarines operates in the Western Mediterranean against French shipping between North Africa and the South of France. Taking part: in the Gulf of Genoa *H1*, *H4* and *H8* (twice); off the French Riviera *Fieramosca* (battery explosion) and *Gondar*; in the Gulf of Lyons *Iride*, *Aradam*, *Mocenigo* and *Malachite;* in the Narrows of the Balearics *Bandiera*, *Ascianghi*, *Santarosa* and *Nani*; off the Algerian Coast *Glauco*, *Tazzoli*, and *Toti*; off Bizerta *Medusa* and *Marcello*; and in the Sicilian Channel *Capponi*, *Da Procida* and *Pisani*. *Glauco* (Cdr* Corvetti) slightly damages one ship of 3657 tons with gunfire. *Capponi* (Lt-Cdr Romei) sinks an unidentified ship.

20-21 June   Mediterranean
Last joint Anglo-French operation in the Mediterranean. Vice-Adm Tovey with the French battleship *Lorraine*, the British cruisers *Neptune*, *Orion* and *Sydney* and the destroyers *Stuart*, *Decoy*, *Dainty* and *Hasty* sails out to shell Bardia. This is carried out in the night 20-21 June but causes only slight damage. At the same time five British destroyers advance along the coast as far as Tobruk without finding targets. As a result of inaccurate air reconnaissance reports about Italian forces, the French cruisers *Duguay-Trouin* and *Suffren* with three British destroyers set out from Alexandria.

20-23 June   Norway
To divert British air reconnaissance from the return of the damaged battleship *Scharnhorst*, the battleship *Gneisenau* and the heavy cruiser *Admiral Hipper* leave Trondheim on 20 June to make a sortie into the Iceland-Faeroes passage. 40 nautical miles NW of Halten the British submarine *Clyde* (Lt-Cdr Ingram) attacks the force and obtains a torpedo hit in the bows of *Gneisenau* with the result that the operation is abandoned. On 21 June the *Scharnhorst*, accompanied by the destroyers *Erich Steinbrinck*, *Hans Lody*, *Hermann Schoemann*, and *Karl Galster*, joined by the torpedo boats *Greif*, *Kondor*, *Falke* and *Jaguar*, begins the journey to Kiel. Attempted attacks by six Swordfish torpedo aircraft off Utsire are beaten off and two planes are shot down. The ship arrives in Kiel on 23 June.

20-26 June   Mediterranean
Eight Italian merchant ships break through undetected from Leros to Brindisi.

22 June   General Situation
Conclusion of the German-French Armistice in Compiègne. Provisions: occupation of France to the line W and N of Geneva-Dôle-Tours-Mont de Marsa-Spanish frontier. Thus the whole of the English Channel coast and the Atlantic coast are in German hands. Disarming of the French armed forces except for 100000 volunteers; no air force and no army. Disarming of large parts of the Fleet, but no handover. At this point there are in Plymouth and Portsmouth: two battleships, two large destroyers, eight ordinary destroyers and torpedo boats, seven submarines and 200 smaller vessels. Continuation of French Government in unoccupied France (transferred to Vichy at the beginning of July). Pierre Laval enters the French Government and becomes leading minister under Pétain.

22 June   Norway
German auxiliary cruiser *Schiff 33*

Pinguin (Capt Krüder (leaves Sörgulen-fjord to take part in mercantile warfare. Operational areas: Antarctic and Indian Ocean.

22-24 June Mediterranean
Sortie by the Italian 7th Cruiser Div (Div Adm Sansonetti) and the 13th DD Flotilla from Cagliari against French convoy traffic between Algiers and Toulon as far as Port Mahon. Operation broken off without result. Met by the 2nd Sqdn with 10 cruisers and 12 destroyers.

24 June English Channel
The German motor torpedo boat *S36* (Lt Babbel) sinks the British tanker *Albuera* (3477 tons) off Dungeness and the *S19* a small freighter of 276 tons.

25 June General Situation
Cease fire in France from 0135 hrs.

25-27 June Mediterranean
First Italian supply convoy from Naples to Tripoli: troop transports *Esperia* (11398 tons) and *Victoria* (13098 tons) with 1727 troops on board; escorted by the auxiliary cruiser *Ramb III* and the torpedo boats *Orsa* and *Procione*.

27 June General Situation
Britain announces the blockade of Europe from the North Cape to Spain.

27-30 June Mediterranean
Operations in Eastern Mediterranean: British destroyers *Dainty* (Cdr Thomas), *Ilex*, *Decoy* and *Voyager* carry out submarine-hunting operations against Italian submarines S of Crete. On the way the submarine *Liuzzi* is sunk on 27 June as she returns from Cyprus. On 29 June out of a patrol line SW of Crete the *Uebi Scebeli* is sunk and *Salpa* is damaged. In addition the *Argonauta* is very probably sunk as she returns from Tobruk. Sunderland flying boats of No 230 Sqdn RAF damage the *Anfitrite* as she goes to join the patrol line on 28 June and the *Sirena* returning from Tobruk on 29 June. They sink the *Rubino* when she returns from Alexandria on 29 June. Only *Ondina* S of Crete and *Gemma* and *Topazio* off Sollum reach their positions.

British convoys from the Dardanelles and Greek harbours to Port Said with the cruisers *Caledon*, *Capetown* and the destroyers *Garland*, *Nubian*, *Mohawk* and *Vampire* pass undetected the Italian submarines *Jalea*, *Zaffiro* and *Ametista* in the approaches to the Aegean.

Two British convoys (MA.3) proceed from Alexandria to Malta, covered by Vice-Adm Tovey with the 7th Cruiser Sqdn consisting of *Orion*, *Neptune*, *Sydney*, *Liverpool* and *Gloucester* with a covering force comprising the battle-ships *Ramillies* and *Royal Sovereign*, the carrier *Eagle* and eight destroyers. Italian destroyers *Espero*, *Ostro* and *Zeffiro* bring supplies from Taranto to Tobruk. British air reconnaissance leads the British 7th Cruiser Sqdn to the scene. *Espero* (Flotilla Commander Cdr Baroni) attacks the British force to cover the withdrawal of the two other des-troyers, and sinks after hits from the Australian cruiser *Sydney*. Expenditure of ammunition by the British cruisers raises acute logistic problems since there are only 800 rounds of 6in ammunition still available.

28 June Mediterranean
Italian AA defence, during a British air attack near Tobruk, inadvertently shoots down the aircraft of Marshal Balbo, the Italian Governor of Libya.

30 June-1 July English Channel
German occupation of the Channel Islands, Jersey, Guernsey and Alderney. 26656 persons are evacuated from the islands beforehand to Britain.

1-2 July Baltic
Bombers of the RAF, in an attack on German warships in Kiel, use a 1000kg bomb for the first time. Battleship *Scharnhorst* is missed; but the heavy cruiser *Prinz Eugen* is hit by two small bombs.

1-13 July Mediterranean
Italian submarines *Emo*, *Marconi*, *Dandolo* and *Barbarigo* operate E of Gibraltar. On 2 July *Marconi* misses the destroyer *Vortigern* from Force H; on 6 July *Emo* sights the Force with the *Ark Royal*; and on 11 July *Marconi* (Cdr Chialamberto) sinks the destroyer *Escort* from the returning Force H.

1 July-4 Aug Norway
In Allied submarine operations off Norway *Snapper* (Lt King) attacks convoys on 3 July and 7 July and sinks one ship of 1134 tons; *Swordfish* (Lt Cowell) sinks the torpedo boat *Luchs* (26 July); *Sealion* (Lt-Cdr Bryant) one ship of 3318 tons. Because of the heavy

losses (*Shark* is unable to submerge after being hit by bombs off Skudesnes on 5 July and sinks when taken in tow; *Salmon* (9 July), *Thames* (23 July), *Narwhal* (30 July) are all sunk by mines and *Spearfish* is sunk by *U34* on 2 Aug) the operations are broken off near the coast until the situation is clarified.

1-17 July   South Atlantic
German auxiliary cruiser *Schiff 10 Thor* (Capt Kähler) sinks five Allied merchant ships of 25911 tons in the South Atlantic and captures the Dutch motor ship *Kertosono* (9289 tons).

2 July   General Situation
Directive by OKW: Hitler has decided that 'in certain conditions' a landing in Britain might be considered.

2 July-6 Aug   Central Atlantic
Second unsuccessful Atlantic operation by the Italian submarines *Calvi* (Madeira) and *Veniero* (Canary Islands).

3 July   Mediterranean
Operation 'Catapult': attack by a British naval force (Vice-Adm Somerville) on a part of the French fleet in Mers-el-Kebir (near Oran). French forces: battleships *Dunkerque* (Capt Barrois), *Strasbourg* (Capt Collinet), *Provence* (with Commander of the 2nd BB Div, Rear-Adm Bouxin), *Bretagne* (Capt Le Pivain), destroyer flotilla (Rear-Adm Lacrois) consisting of the large destroyers *Mogador*, *Volta*, *Tigre*, *Lynx*, *Kersaint* and *Le Terrible*, as well as the aircraft depot ship *Commandant Teste* (Capt Lemaire). The French Commander, Adm Gensoul, rejects British ultimatum, whereupon Force H, comprising the battlecruiser *Hood*, the battleships *Resolution* and *Valiant*, the aircraft carrier *Ark Royal*, the light cruisers *Arethusa* and *Enterprise* and the destroyers *Faulknor, Foxhound, Fearless, Forester, Foresight, Escort, Keppel, Active, Wrestler, Vidette* and *Vortigern*, opens fire on the French ships lying at anchor, some of which are not ready for action. *Bretagne* sinks, after being heavily hit, with 977 of her crew; *Mogador* loses her stern as a result of a direct hit (42 dead); *Dunkerque* (210 dead) and *Provence* are badly damaged. *Strasbourg* and the five remaining large destroyers are able to sail out and escape at high speed in spite of attacks by British carrier aircraft. She reaches

Toulon with *Volta*, *Tigre* and *Le Terrible* on the evening of 4 July. Total losses of the French Navy: 1147 dead. On the same day the following units are seized by British forces in Britain: in Portsmouth the French battleship *Courbet*, the large destroyer *Léopard*, the torpedo boats *Branlebas, La Cordelière, La Flore, L'Incomprise, La Melpomène*, six sloops and the supply ship *Pollux*. In Plymouth: the battleship *Paris*, the destroyers *Mistral* and *Ouragan*, the torpedo boat *Bouclier*, three sloops, the large submarine *Surcouf* and submarines *Junon* and *Minerve*. In Falmouth; submarines *Ondine* and *Orion*, three sloops and the target ship *L'Impassible*. In Dundee the submarine *Rubis*. On *Mistral* and *Surcouf* the crews resist with resulting losses on both sides. In addition, three minelayers, sixteen submarine chasers, seven motor torpedo boats, 98 minesweepers and guard vessels, 42 tugs and harbour craft, and 20 trawlers are seized.

3 July   Arctic
Auxiliary cruiser *Schiff 45 Komet* (Capt Eyssen) leaves Gotenhafen. Her operational area is the Pacific and is to be reached with Russian help by way of the Siberian sea route (she sets out from Bergen on 9 July).

3-4 July   Mediterranean
The Italian minelayers *Buccari* and *Scilla*, escorted by the torpedo boats *Alcione, Altair, Andromeda* and *Aretusa*, lays another 640 mines between Pantelleria and Sicily. The Italian submarine *Zoea* (Cdr Bernabò) lays a mine barrage W of Alexandria.

3-5 July   Mediterranean
The British submarines *Pandora* and *Proteus* receive orders on 3 July off Algiers and Oran to attack all French warships. *Proteus* does not get within range of the aircraft depot ship *Commandant Teste* but *Pandora* sinks the colonial sloop *Rigault de Genouilly* which is part of a force proceeding from Oran to Algiers. On 5 July the order is rescinded.

3-12 July   Mediterranean
The Italian submarine *Tarantini* (Cdr Iaschi), operating off Palestine, sinks one ship of 3040 tons.

4 July   General Situation
The French Pétain Government breaks

off diplomatic relations with Great Britain.

4 July English Channel

Ju 87's of St.G.2 (Maj Dinort) sink from the British convoy OA.178 S of Portland the auxiliary AA ship *Foyle Bank* (5582 tons), the freighters *Britsum* (5255 tons), *Dallas City* (4952 tons), *Deucalion* (1796 tons), and *Kolga* (3526 tons), and they severely damage nine other ships of 40236 tons. In an attack by German motor torpedo boats *S19* (Lt Töniges) sinks the freighter *Elmcrest* (4343 tons) and *S20* and *S26* torpedo two ships of 12472 tons.

4-5 July Central Atlantic

As an answer to the British attack on Oran the submarines stationed in Dakar, *Le Glorieux* and *Le Héros*, and the auxiliary cruisers and destroyers there (see 18-27 June), receive orders to attack British ships. On 5 July the British steamers *Argyll, Gambia* and *Takoradian* and the Danish ships sailing under the British flag *Harald, Tacoma* and *Ulrich* are seized. *Le Glorieux* is attacked by a British aircraft.

5 July Mediterranean

Swordfish torpedo aircraft of the British aircraft carrier *Eagle* sink the destroyer *Zeffiro* and the freighter *Manzoni* (3955 tons) in the harbour of Tobruk. The destroyer *Euro* and two other freighters have to be beached. *Euro is* later salvaged.

6 July Mediterranean

Torpedo aircraft of the carrier *Ark Royal* attack the French battleship *Dunkerque* lying in Mers-el-Kebir and sink the auxiliary ship *Terre Neuve* (859 tons) lying alongside her with a cargo of depth charges. As a result of the cargo exploding the side of the battleship is ripped open. 150 dead among the crews.

6-10 July Mediterranean

Battle off Punta Stilo/Calabria. On the evening of 6 July an Italian convoy leaves Naples for Benghazi, consisting of the passenger ship *Esperia* (11398 tons), the freighters *Calitea* (4013 tons), *Marco Foscarini* (6342 tons), and *Vettor Pisani* (6339 tons). Escort provided by the 4th TB Div comprising *Orione, Orsa, Pegaso* and *Procione*. It is joined on 7 July by the freighter *Francesco Barbero* (6343 tons) from Catania with the torpedo boats *Abba* and *Pilo*. On

board there are 2200 troops, 300 armoured vehicles and lorries and 16000 tons of supplies. Close escort provided by the 2nd Div (Div Adm Casardi) comprising the cruisers *Bande Nere* and *Colleoni* and the 10th DD Div consisting of *Maestrale, Libeccio, Grecale* and *Scirocco*.

On 7 July a British cruiser force is reported to have arrived in Malta. Thereupon Supermarina orders the 2nd Sqdn (Sqdn Adm Paladini) to set out to cover the convoy; flagship, heavy cruiser *Pola* with the 12th DD Div (*Lanciere, Carabiniere, Corazziere* and *Ascari*) the 1st Div (Div Adm Matteucci) comprising the heavy cruisers *Zara, Fiume* and *Gorizia*, with the 14th DD Div (*Alfieri Carducci, Gioberti* and *Oriani*, the 3rd Div (Div Adm Cattaneo), comprising the heavy cruisers *Bolzano* and *Trento* with the 11th DD Div (*Artigliere, Camicia Nera, Aviere* and *Geniere*), the 7th Div (Div Adm Sansonetti) comprising the light cruisers *Eugenio di Savoia, Duca d'Aosta, Attendolo* and *Montecuccoli* with the 8th DD Div (*Granatiere, Fuciliere, Bersagliere* and *Alpino*). The Fleet Commander (Sqdn Adm Campioni) sets out with the first squadron to cover the operation: he has the 5th Div (Div Adm Brivonesi), comprising the battleships *Cavour* (flagship) and *Cesare* with the 7th DD Div (*Freccia, Saetta, Dardo* and *Strale*), the 8th Div (Div Adm Legnani), comprising the light cruisers *Folgore, Fulmine, Baleno* and *Lampo*, the 4th Div (Div Adm Marenco di Moriondo), comprising the light cruisers *Da Barbiano, Di Giussano, Cadorna,* and *Diaz* and the 14th DD Div (*Vivaldi, Da Noli* and *Pancaldo*), the 15th DD Div (*Pigafetta* and *Zeno*) and the 16th DD Div (*Da Recco, Pessagno* and *Usodimare*).

Italian submarine concentrations: E of Gibraltar *Emo, Marconi, Dandolo* and *Barbarigo;* NW of Sardinia *Argo, Iride, Scirè* and *Diaspro;* S of Sardinia *Ascianghi, Axum, Turchese, Glauco, Manara* and *Menotti*; Sicilian Channel *Santarosa*; Malta *Capponi* and *Durbo*; Ionian Sea (*Brin*); *Sciesa, Settimo* and *Settembrini*; between Derna and Gaudo, *Beilul, Tricheco, Lafolè* and *Smeraldo.* Shortly before midnight the Italian submarine *Beilul* sights the British Mediterranean Fleet (Adm Cunningham) which has come out to cover two convoys between Malta and Alexandria. It is composed of the following groups: Force A (Vice-Adm Tovey): cruisers *Orion, Neptune, Sydney* (RAN), *Gloucester, Liverpool* and destroyer *Stuart* (RAN).

Force B (Cunningham): battleship *Warspite*, destroyers *Nubian, Mohawk, Hero, Hereward* and *Decoy.*

Force C: (Vice-Adm Pridham-Wippell): battleships *Malaya* and *Royal Sovereign*, aircraft carrier *Eagle* (with Nos. 813 and 824 Sqdns FAA), destroyers *Hyperion, Hostile, Hasty, Ilex, Dainty, Defender, Juno, Janus, Vampire* (RAN) and *Voyager* (RAN) as well as the Malta group (Force D) with at first four, and later seven, destroyers.

On the morning of 8 July Force H (Vice-Adm Somerville) puts to sea from Gibraltar with the battlecruiser *Hood*, the battleships *Valiant* and *Resolution*, the aircraft carrier *Ark Royal*, the cruisers *Arethusa, Delhi* and *Enterprise* and the destroyers *Faulknor, Forester, Foresight, Foxhound, Fearless, Keppel, Douglas, Vortigern, Wishart* and *Watchman.* On the same day the Italian convoy reaches Benghazi without loss. The Italian Fleet assembles in the Ionian Sea to make a sortie against the British Mediterranean Fleet in the hope that the Air Force will weaken British fighting strength beforehand. The warding off of Force H is left to the submarines and the Air Force. But Supermarina orders the concentration of boats near to its own coast to prevent the bases being cut off—which is the British aim.

On 9 July British air reconnaissance establishes contact with the Italian fleet; but the Italian Air Force is unable to provide reconnaissance reports. Torpedo attacks by aircraft from the *Eagle* are out-manoeuvred. In the afternoon first the cruisers are seen, then also the heavy units. In a battle lasting 105 minutes the British battleship *Warspite* obtains a heavy hit on the Italian battleship *Giulio Cesare* and the heavy cruiser *Bolzano* is slightly damaged by the British cruisers. Adm Campioni then orders his destroyers (the 9th

Flotilla comprising *Alfieri, Oriani, Carducci* and *Gioberti*, the 7th Flotilla comprising *Freccia* and *Saetta*, the 11th Flotilla comprising *Artigliere, Camicia Nera, Aviere* and *Geniere*, the 12th Flotilla comprising *Lanciere, Carabiniere, Corazziere* and *Ascari* and the 14th Flotilla comprising *Pancaldo* and *Vivaldi*) to attack and lay smoke screens. Contact is then lost and the British Fleet turns away. The attacks by the Italian Air Force with 126 aircraft achieve only one hit on the British light cruiser *Gloucester*. In numerous attacks on Force H by Italian S79 bombers flying at great altitude many near-misses are registered near the *Hood*, the *Resolution* and *Ark Royal*, but they only cause splinter damage. The Italian submarine *Marconi* (Cdr Chialamberto) sinks the destroyer *Escort* in the force E of Gibraltar. On 10 July torpedo aircraft from the *Eagle* attack Italian ships in the roads of Augusta and sink the destroyer *Pancaldo* which, however, can be later salvaged.

7 July Mediterranean

Agreement between the Commander of the French Force X, Vice-Adm Godfroy, and the C-in-C of the British Mediterranean Fleet, Adm Cunningham, about the internment and demobilisation of the French Squadron in Alexandria. It consists of the battleship *Lorraine*, the heavy cruisers *Duquesne, Suffren* and *Tourville*, the light cruiser *Duguay Trouin*, the destroyers *Basque, Le Fortuné* and *Forbin* and the submarine *Protée.*

7-21 July Mediterranean

Of the British submarines employed in the Mediterranean two operate off the Gulf of Taranto, one N and one S of the Straits of Messina and one off Cagliari. On 7 July *Olympus* receives considerable damage in Malta during an Italian air attack. *Phoenix* is sunk by the Italian torpedo boat *Albatros* off Augusta on 16 July and *Rorqual* (Cdr Dewhurst) lays a mine barrage on 21 July off Tolmeita (Cyrenaica), on which a ship of 3865 tons sinks.

7-8 July Central Atlantic

On the morning of 5 July the British carrier *Hermes* (Capt Onslow) and the Australian cruiser *Australia*, coming from Freetown, have joined the cruiser

Dorsetshire which is observing the movements of the French naval forces off Dakar. On 7 July an order arrives from the Admiralty to give the French Commander an ultimatum similar to the one given at Mers-el-Kebir in order to eliminate the *Richelieu*. The French refuse entry to the sloop *Milford* which approaches with an emissary. Following this, a fast British launch from the *Hermes* under the command of Lt-Cdr Bristowe succeeds in the night 7-8 July in getting through the harbour booms unnoticed, dropping depth charges under the stern of the battleship *Richelieu* and escaping. Then six Swordfish aircraft from the *Hermes* attack and get one torpedo hit. The remaining ships, including the cruiser *Primauguet* and the sloop *Bougainville* and destroyers are undamaged. An attempt by French aircraft to attack the British ships fails, nor are the submarines deployed, *Le Glorieux*, and *Le Héros*, able to attack the ships.

8-9 July   Baltic
Five British aircraft of Bomber Command attack Kiel and secure a hit (unexploded) on the cruiser *Lützow* in the dockyard.

10 July   English Channel
Beginning of German air attacks on British convoys in the Channel. In all, 40 Allied merchant ships, totalling 75698 tons, are sunk by German aircraft in July 1940. In addition, the destroyers *Brazen*, *Codrington*, *Delight* and *Wren* are sunk.

10-23 July   North Atlantic
The Type II C U-boats *U61*, *U56*, *U58*, *U62* and *U57* operate from Bergen between the North Minch and North Channel. In attacks on independents and convoys *U61* (Lt-Cdr Oesten) sinks two ships of 11531 tons; *U58* (Lt Schonder) one ship of 1591 tons; *U62* (Lt Michalowski) one ship of 4581 tons; and *U57* (Lt Topp) two ships of 10612 tons. *U56* (Lt Harms) attacks the transport *Dunera*, which has German and Italian civilian internees on board but is unnotified. Torpedo defects frustrate this and some 10 other attacks made by the five U-boats. *U58* puts in to Lorient for replenishment.

14-16 July   North Sea
German aircraft lay mines in the Thames Estuary and off Harwich.

14-25 July   Mediterranean
The following Italian submarines are operating: E of Gibraltar *Morosini*, *Nani*, *Faa' di Bruno* and *Berillo*; in the Sicilian Channel *Bausan*; E of Malta *Brin* and *Pisani*; S of Crete *Bagnolini*, *Giuliani* and *Toti*; and in the approaches to the Aegean *Atropo* and *Delfino*.

16 July   General Situation
Führer Directive No 16 on preparations for a landing in Britain ('Seelöwe').

17-20 July   North Sea
German minelayers, escorted by the 2nd and 5th TB Flotillas, lay the mine barrage 'N.W.1' in the English Channel.

18 July   North Sea
The British submarine *H31* sinks the German submarine-chaser *UJ126* NW of Terschelling.

18 July   Mediterranean
All French merchant ships in the Suez Canal are seized by British warships.

19 July   General Situation/Political
President Roosevelt signs the 'Two Ocean Navy Expansion Act', which provides for the building of 1325000 tons of warships, 100000 tons of auxiliary ships and 15000 naval aircraft.

19 July   General Situation/Political
Hitler's Reichstag speech: last 'peace appeal' to Britain (rejected by Lord Halifax on 22 July).

19 July   Mediterranean
Battle of Cape Spada: the Italian light cruisers *Giovanni delle Bande Nere* and *Bartolomeo Colleoni* (under orders of Div Adm Casardi) are located by British air reconnaissance and are intercepted while proceeding from Tripoli to Leros by the Australian cruiser *Sydney* (Capt Collins) and the destroyers *Havock*, *Hyperion*, *Hasty*, *Ilex* and *Hero*. *Colleoni* receives unlucky hits in the battle with the result that she becomes incapable of manoeuvre. The cruiser sinks after torpedo hits from *Ilex* and *Havock*. *Bande Nere* (Capt Maugeri) continues the engagement until *Sydney* turns away after a hit and reaches Benghazi. The British destroyers rescue 525 crew members of the *Colleoni*, including the Commander, Capt Novaro.

19-20 July   North Sea
Bombers of the RAF unsuccessfully attack the battleship *Tirpitz* and the heavy cruiser *Admiral Scheer* in the naval dockyard at Wilhelmshaven.

20 July   Mediterranean
Torpedo aircraft of the British carrier *Eagle* (Capt Bridge) sink the Italian destroyers *Nembo* and *Ostro* and the freighter *Sereno* (2333 tons) in the Gulf Bomba near Tobruk.

21-30 July   Mediterranean
British convoy operation in the Aegean. On 21 July the cruisers *Capetown* and *Liverpool* and the destroyers *Diamond*, *Stuart*, *Dainty* and *Defender* set out with six merchant ships from Alexandria and Port Said comprising convoy AN.2 for Aegean harbours. On 23 July the cruiser *Orion* and the destroyers *Vampire* and *Vendetta* appear off Castellorizo as a diversion. The action is repeated on 26 July before the return of convoy AS.2 when the ocean boarding vessels *Chakla* and *Fiona* are used to simulate a landing. The Mediterranean Fleet, comprising the battleships *Malaya*, *Royal Sovereign* and *Warspite*, the carrier *Eagle* and the cruisers *Neptune* and *Sydney* and ten destroyers, cruises SW of Crete to cover the operations. During the return of the convoy there are several Italian air attacks on 27 July, 28 July and 29 July which, apart from an unexploded hit on the *Liverpool*, only obtain near misses. On 28 July *Neptune* and *Sydney* make a sortie into the Gulf of Athens and sink a small tanker, *Ermioni*, carrying petrol for the Dodecanese.

23-25 July   English Channel
The mine barrage (N.W.2) in the Channel is laid out by German minelayers, escorted by torpedo boats.

23-27 July   Bay of Biscay
Proposed carrier raid on Bordeaux by Force H, consisting of carrier *Ark Royal*, cruiser *Enterprise* and destroyers *Faulknor*, *Foresight*, *Escapade* and *Forester*, has to be abandoned because of mist. The Force arrives back in Gibraltar on 26 July, followed by the old carrier *Argus* and the destroyers *Encounter*, *Hotspur*, *Gallant* and *Greyhound*.

25 July   English Channel
The German motor torpedo boat *S27* (Lt Klug) sinks the unnotified French repatriation steamer *Meknes* (6127 tons) off the British South Coast. Of the 1100 French troops on board nearly 400 lose their lives.

25-26 July   English Channel
Ju 87's of II/St.G.1 (Capt Hozzel) and IV/L.G.1 (Capt v. Brauchitsch) attack the British convoy CW.8 in the Channel and of the 21 ships in the convoy sink five of 5117 tons. Two destroyers and five more freighters are damaged. On 26 July the 1st MTB Flotilla (Lt-Cdr Birnbacher), consisting of *S19*, *S20* and *S27*, attacks the same convoy and sinks three ships of 2480 tons.

25-27 July   Norway
The battleship *Gneisenau*, having received makeshift repairs after a torpedo hit from a submarine, is transferred from Trondheim to Kiel. She is escorted by the Commander Reconnaissance Forces, Rear-Adm Schmundt, on cruiser *Nürnberg* and four destroyers and by another six torpedo boats from Utsire onwards. On 26 July the torpedo boat *Luchs* is sunk by the British submarine *Swordfish*.

25 July-9 Aug   Arctic
The heavy cruiser *Admiral Hipper* (Capt Heye) undertakes mercantile warfare operations in the Arctic between Tromsö and Spitzbergen; but she only encounters neutral merchant ships. A small Finnish steamer with contraband is seized as a prize.

26-31 July   Red Sea
The Italian submarine *Guglielmotti* searches in vain for two Greek steamers which have sailed S from Suez. The torpedo boats *Battisti* and *Nullo* also return without result.

26 July-5 Aug   Mediterranean
The Italian submarines *Alagi*, *Aradam* and *Mocenigo* operate E of Gibraltar without success; *Durbo* E of Malta; *Narvalo*, *Speri* and *Mameli* (Cdr Maiorana), which sinks one ship of 1044 tons, between Alexandria and Crete. In addition, *Anfitrite*, *Zaffiro*, *Squalo*, *Ametista* and *Corridoni* operate in the Aegean and its approaches.

26 July-10 Aug   North Atlantic
U34, *U52*, *U58* and *U99* operate from Lorient off the North Channel and individually attack outward and homeward bound convoys there. On 26-27 July *U34* (Lt-Cdr Rollmann) sinks four ships of 29320 tons; *U99* (Lt-Cdr Kretschmer) sinks from 28 July to 31 July four ships of 32345 tons and torpedoes on 2 Aug three tankers of

25548 tons; *U52* (Lt-Cdr Salman) sinks on 4 Aug three ships of 17102 tons; and *U58* (Lt Schonder) on 4-5 Aug two ships of 9768 tons. On the way home on 1 Aug *U34* meets the British submarine *Spearfish* returning from an operation and sinks her near Cape Nose Head.

End of July-20 Aug   Bay of Biscay
British submarines begin to patrol the Biscay ports ('Bay Patrol') from the end of July.
The first to be employed are *Tribune*, *Tigris* and *Talisman*. The first success is scored by *Cachalot* (Cdr Luce) on 20 Aug when she sinks *U51*.

28 July   South Atlantic
In the South Atlantic an engagement takes place between the German auxiliary cruiser *Schiff 10 Thor* (Capt Kähler) and the British auxiliary cruiser *Alcantara* (22209 tons, Capt Ingham). The British ship is badly damaged and has to put in to Rio de Janiero; *Schiff 10*, after repairs to minor damage, is able to continue her mercantile warfare operations.

28 July-10 Aug   North Atlantic
The Type II C boats *U59*, *U57* and *U56* operate from Bergen off the North Channel. *U59* goes to Bergen for replenishment, the others to Lorient. The operations again suffer from torpedo failures. *U59* (Lt-Cdr Matz) sinks one ship of 2002 tons: *U57* (Lt Topp) one ship of 2161 tons; *U56* (Lt Harms) the auxiliary cruiser *Transylvania* (16923 tons) on 10 Aug.

28 July-10 Sept   Central Atlantic
Third Atlantic operation by the Italian submarines *Malaspina*, *Barbarigo* and *Dandolo* in the area of the Azores and off Madeira. Subsequently they are moved to the new base at Bordeaux. *Malaspina* (Cdr Leoni) sinks one ship of 8406 tons; *Dandolo* (Cdr Boris) one ship of 5187 tons and damages one ship of 3768 tons; *Barbarigo* (Cdr Ghilieri) secures some shell hits on a ship of 3255 tons.

30 July   General Situation
Extension of British Navicert system to all European ports.

31 July-4 Aug   Mediterranean
Operation 'Hurry': Force H sets out from Gibraltar with the battlecruiser *Hood*, the battleship *Valiant*, the carrier

Ark Royal, the cruisers *Arethusa*, *Delhi* and *Enterprise* and the destroyers *Faulknor*, *Forester*, *Foresight*, *Foxhound*, *Fearless*, *Escapade*, *Active* and *Wrestler*. On 2 Aug the carrier flies off her Swordfish aircraft to attack Cagliari (Sardinia) where mines are also laid. Simultaneously, the old carrier *Argus* (Capt Bovell) which is proceeding independently of Force H and is escorted by the destroyers *Encounter*, *Gallant*, *Greyhound* and *Hotspur*, flies off SW of Sardinia 12 Hurricane fighters she has on board for transfer to Malta. On the news that Force H has set out Supermarina concentrates six submarine lines consisting of *Scirè*, *Argo*, *Neghelli*, *Turchese*, *Medusa*, *Axum*, *Diaspro* and *Manara* N of Cape Bougaroni on 1 Aug. But they sight nothing up to 9 Aug. In an attempted attack on an Italian force the British submarine *Oswald* is rammed and sunk by the Italian destroyer *Vivaldi* off Cape Spartivento on 1 Aug.

1 Aug   General Situation
In Directive No 17 Hitler orders the intensification of the sea and air war against Britain.

3-6 Aug   General Situation
Estonia, Latvia and Lithuania become member states of the USSR.

4-10 Aug   North Atlantic
Force H is transferred from Gibraltar to Britain. On 9 Aug the Force is met W of Ireland by the destroyers *Punjabi*, *Tartar* and *Zulu* which escort the *Hood* and *Ark Royal* to Scapa Flow, while the *Valiant* and *Argus* and the 8th DD Flotilla proceed to Liverpool.

4-19 Aug   Red Sea/Gulf of Aden
Italian occupation of British Somaliland. On 5 Aug Italian troops occupy Zeila and Hargeisa and on 6 Aug Oodweina. On 11 Aug the attack on the main British position near Tug Argan begins. Between 14 Aug and 19 Aug Berbera is evacuated by British troops. 5690 troops, 1266 civilians and 184 sick are evacuated to Aden with the assistance of the Australian cruiser *Hobart*, British cruisers *Caledon*, *Carlisle* and *Ceres*, the destroyers *Kandahar* and *Kimberley*, the sloops *Shoreham*, *Parramatta* (RAN) and *Auckland*, the auxiliary cruisers *Chakdina*, *Chantala* and *Laomédon* and the transports *Akbar* and

Vita (hospital ship). The cruisers and destroyers carry out various shellings of the coast.

4 Aug-9 Sept   Central Atlantic
German auxiliary cruiser *Schiff 21* sinks six Allied merchant ships of 30769 tons in the Western part of the Central Atlantic, including the Finnish sailing ship *Killoran* (1817 tons) which is in British service.

5 Aug   General Situation
First preparatory studies drawn up for a campaign against the Soviet Union.

5-16 Aug   Mediterranean
Italian submarines deployed in operations in the Mediterranean: *Ascianghi*, *Gondar* and *Marcello* E of Gibraltar; *Settembrini*, *Dessiè*, *Naiade* and *Balilla* NW to S of Crete; *Jalea* NE of Crete; *Gemma*, *Tricheco* and *Delfino* in the Aegean; *Tembien* off Sollum (1-6 Aug). *Micca* (Cdr* Ginocchio) lays a mine barrage W of Alexandria on 12 Aug and attacks a destroyer two days later. *Sciesa* has to break off a voyage into the Eastern Mediterranean because of engine trouble.

5 Aug-10 Oct   Arctic
The Soviet submarine *Shch-423* (Capt 3rd Class Zaidulin) is the first submarine to be transferred by the Northern seaway from Murmansk to Vladivostok accompanied by ice-breakers and a tanker.

6-10 Aug   Mediterranean
Offensive mining operations by the Italians in the Sicilian Channel. On 6 Aug the cruisers *Da Barbiano* (Div Adm Marenco di Moriondo) and *Di Giussano* and the destroyers *Pigafetta* and *Zeno* lay 394 mines (Barrage 7 AN) SSE of Pantelleria. Escort of torpedo boats *Cassiopea*, *Cigno*, *Pleiadi* and *Aldebaran*. The British destroyer *Gallant* sinks on this barrage on 10 Jan, 1941. In the nights 8-9 Aug and 9-10 Aug respectively the minelayer *Scilla* lays 216 and 200 mines W of Pantelleria and the destroyers *Maestrale*, *Grecale*, *Libeccio* and *Scirocco* each lay 216 mines W of it (Barrages 5 AN and 6 AN). Torpedo boats *Antares* and *Sagittario* provide escort for the *Scilla*. The British destroyer *Hostile* is lost on 23 Aug on the mine barrage 5 AN laid by the destroyers.

7-8 Aug   English Channel
The minelayers *Roland* (Cdr* Kutzleben), *Cobra* (Cdr Brill) and *Brummer* (Cdr Koppe) under the orders of Officer Commanding Patrol Boats West (Capt Schiller) lay the offensive mine barrage 'S.W.1' in the south-western North Sea. Escort provided by the 5th TB Flotilla (Cdr Henne), comprising *T2*, *T7*, *Falke*, *Kondor* and *Jaguar*.

7 Aug-4 Sept   North Atlantic
The following U-boats operate off the North Channel in varying combinations: *U30* from Lorient: *U37*, *U38*, *U46*, *U48*, *U51*, *U59*, *U60*, *U65* and *U100* from home ports and from Bergen. On the way out *U25* is lost on a mine barrage laid by British destroyers in the North Sea and *U37* and *U65* have to return prematurely to Lorient because of damage. *U51* is sunk in the Bay of Biscay by the British submarine *Cachalot* (Cdr Luce). The U-boats attack chiefly independents or convoys on their own. The attempt to operate with *U38*, *U46* and *U48* from 13 Aug to 16 Aug against an HX convoy located by the 'B' Service does not succeed. *U30* (Lt-Cdr Lemp) sinks two ships of 12407 tons; *U37* (Lt-Cdr Oehrn) one ship of 9130 tons; *U38* (Lt-Cdr Liebe) two ships of 12493 tons; *U60* (Lt Schnee) one ship of 1787 tons; *U59* (Lt-Cdr Matz) one ship of 2339 tons; *U46* (Lt Endrass) five ships of 33425 tons, including the auxiliary cruiser *Dunvegan Castle* (28 Aug) and damages one ship of 6189 tons; *U48* (Cdr Rösing) five ships of 29169 tons; *U51* (Lt-Cdr Knorr) one ship of 5709 tons; *U100* (Lt-Cdr Schepke) six ships of 25812 tons and damages one ship of 5498 tons.

8 Aug   English Channel
Attack by the 1st MTB Flotilla (Lt-Cdr Birnbacher), consisting of *S20*, *S21*, *S25* and *S27*, on the British convoy CW.9 off Newhaven. *S21* and *S27* sink two small freighters of 1583 tons and two others are damaged. One freighter of 1004 tons sinks after a collision in avoiding a torpedo.

8-12 Aug   North Sea
Aircraft of the 9th Fl. Div sow mines in the Thames and Humber estuaries and in the harbour entrances of Penzance, Plymouth, Liverpool, Southampton, Falmouth and Belfast.

10 Aug Pacific

Japanese Navy extends the blockade of the Chinese coast to South China.

10-20 Aug Pacific

German auxiliary cruiser *Schiff 36 Orion* (Cdr* Weyher) sinks three Allied merchant ships of 16593 tons E of Australia.

13 Aug Air War/Britain

Beginning of the intensified air war against Britain with the aim of securing air supremacy as a condition of 'Seelöwe'.

13-14 Aug Red Sea

The Italian submarine *Ferraris* (Cdr Piomarta) tries unsuccessfully to attack the British battleship *Royal Sovereign* which is passing through the Red Sea.

14-15 Aug English Channel

The minelayers *Tannenberg* (Cdr* v. Schönermark), *Cobra* and *Roland* under the orders of the Chief of Staff of the Commander North Sea Defences, Capt Böhmer, lay the offensive barrage 'S.W.2.' in the south-western part of the North Sea. Escort provided by the 5th TB Flotilla (Cdr Henne) comprising *Falke*, *Kondor*, *Iltis*, *Jaguar*, *T5* and *T7*.

15 Aug Mediterranean

The Greek cruiser *Helli* sinks off Tinos after receiving a torpedo hit from an unknown submarine. Italy rejects responsibility for the incident on 16 Aug.

15-21 Aug Mediterranean

In the Mediterranean the British submarines *Pandora* and *Proteus* are used to transport supplies to Malta. On 16 Aug *Rorqual* (Lt-Cdr Dewhurst) lays another mine barrage off Tolmeita (Cyrenaica), on which one ship of 3298 tons sinks. An attack on a convoy on 21 Aug fails; *Rorqual* is heavily attacked by the torpedo boat *Papa* with depth charges. Off Durazzo (Albania) *Osiris* (Lt-Cdr Harvey) sinks one ship of 1968 tons on 16 Aug.

16-18 Aug Mediterranean

British battleships *Warspite* (Adm Cunningham), *Malaya* and *Ramillies*, heavy cruiser *Kent* and twelve destroyers of the 2nd, 10th and 14th DD Flotillas shell Bardia and Fort Capuzzo in Cyrenaica on the morning of 17 Aug. On the return to Alexandria an Italian air attack on the Fleet fails to register

a hit. Shore-based fighters from the carrier *Eagle* shoot down 12 aircraft.

17 Aug General Situation

The OKW announces the 'total blockade' of Britain in an operational area around the British Isles. In this area, which is almost identical with the American war zone, forbidden to American ships and citizens, all ships are to be sunk without warning.

17 Aug-7 Sept Mediterranean

The following Italian submarines operate in the Mediterranean: *Bianchi* off Gibraltar; *Des Geneys* SW of Crete; *Millelire* and *Velella* in the Kaso Strait; *Jantina* in the Aegean. *Dagabur* and *Da Procida* undertake patrols to the Palestine coasts and to Cyprus; *Atropo* and *Foca* act as transports between Taranto and Leros.

18 Aug-2 Sept Norway

The Dutch submarines *O22* and *O23* operate off Norway. Of the British submarines *Swordfish*, *Snapper*, *Seawolf*, *Sunfish*, *Triumph*, *Taku*, *Tetrarch* and *Sturgeon* (Lt Gregory) operating off Norway up to September, the *Sturgeon* sinks one ship of 3624 tons in a convoy on 2 Sept.

18 Aug-3 Sept North Atlantic

U28, *U32*, *U101* and *U124* coming from Germany and *U37*, *U56*, *U57*, *U59* and *U60* setting out from Lorient, operate against independents and convoys in the area between the Hebrides, the North Channel, Ireland and Rockall Bank. *U57* attacks OB.202 on 24 Aug (sinking two ships and damaging one). *U37*, sent as a weather reporting boat far to the W, attacks SC.1 on 24-25 Aug (sinking the sloop *Penzance* and one ship). *U48* attacks HX.65 on 25 Aug early in the day and *U124* attacks in the evening (the former sinking two ships and the latter sinking two and damaging one with two more sunk on 26 Aug by K.Fl.Gr. 506—see 26 Aug.); *U28* again attacks SC.1 on 27 Aug (sinking one ship); *U100* attacks on 29 Aug first HX.66 and then OA.204 (two ships sunk and one torpedoed in the first and two ships sunk in the second); *U32* attacks HX.66 on 30 Aug (sinking three ships); and *U59*, *U60*, *U59* again and *U38* successively attack OB.205 on 30-31 Aug (sinking one ship and damaging three). Including ships in

Above: Sept 1, 1939: The old battleship *Schleswig-Holstein* opens fire on Wester-platte, near Danzig, with her forward 11-inch guns. With these shots World War II at sea began. *[BFZ*

Below: Sept 17, 1939: Following the sinking of the liner *Athenia* the Admiralty instituted a system of aircraft carrier patrols to hunt U-boats. This did not prove as successful as hoped, the carrier *Courageous* being torpedoed by *U29*. After this tragedy the carriers were withdrawn from the anti-U-boat patrols. *[MOD*

Above: Dec 19, 1939: At the start of the war the Royal Navy commenced a close blockade of Germany. On Dec 14 the passenger ship *Columbus* left Vera Cruz (Mexico) for Germany. The liner was constantly shadowed by US warships of the Neutrality Patrol, who gave her position in plain language. This led the British destroyer *Hyperion* to the *Columbus* which was forced to scuttle. *[BFZ*

Below: Dec 17, 1939: On Dec 13 the British cruisers *Achillies*, *Ajax* and *Exeter* brought to action off the River Plate the pocket-battleship *Admiral Graf Spee*, which had been carrying out mercantile warfare in the South Atlantic and Indian Oceans. Unable to effect repairs in Montivideo the *Graf Spee* was scuttled by her crew. Before she was finally destroyed the Royal Navy was able to retrieve vital parts of the gunnery radar set which can be clearly seen on the director tower. *[IWM*

March 4, 1940: On Feb 16 the British destroyer *Cossack* attacked the German supply tanker *Altmark* in Jössing Fjord and freed 303 captured seamen from vessels sunk by the *Admiral Graf Spee*. The Norwegian minelayer *Olav Tryggvason* keeps watch on the *Altmark* with her stern aground. [BFZ

April 8, 1940: While covering a minelaying operation off Norway the British destroyer *Glowworm* became detached from the main force in a storm and encountered German landing forces heading for Trondheim. After ramming the cruiser *Admiral Hipper* the destroyer was sunk by gunfire from the German vessel. [Keystone Press

Above: April 9, 1940: Carrying troops for a landing at Oslo the heavy cruiser *Blücher* attempted to force her way up the Dröbak Narrows (Oslofjord). After being hit by shells and torpedoes from Norwegian defences the cruiser capsizes with heavy loss of life. *[Norsk Telegrambora*

Below: April 13, 1940: A British force, including the battleship *Warspite* and nine destroyers enters Ofot Fjord and destroys or forces the Germans to scuttle the eight destroyers still afloat after the first battle of Narvik. In Rombaks Fjord the *Georg Thiele* torpedoes the *Eskimo*, which has her bows torn off by the explosion. *[IWM*

Above: May 30, 1940: Between May 28 and June 4 the Royal Navy, assisted by thousands of small craft, successfully evacuated the bulk of the BEF from Dunkirk. *[IWM*

Below: May 30, 1940: A destroyer bringing men of the BEF into Dover harbour. *[IWM*

Below: July 14, 1940: On July 10 the Luftwaffe commence air attacks on British convoys in the English Channel. The illustration shows such an attack. *[IWM*

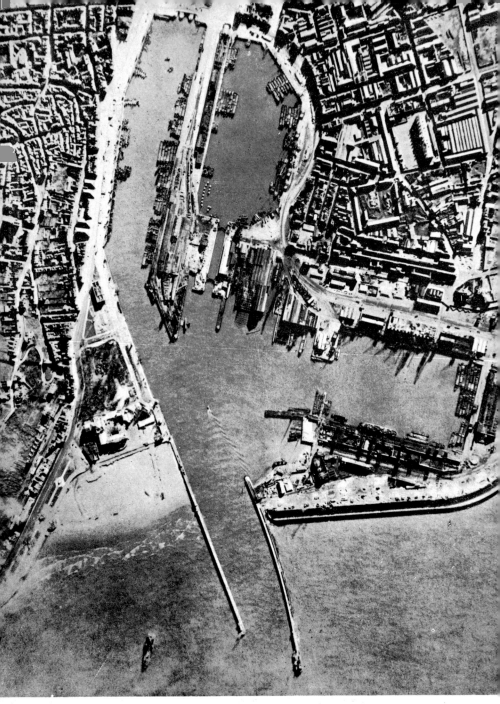

Sept 6, 1940: The people of Britain are given the first warning about a possible invasion by Germany. The operation was to be mounted from the Channel ports, in which the Kriegsmarine collected large numbers of barges for transporting the troops assigned to the invasion. The illustration shows barges assembled at Boulogne.

[A. Watts Collection

Above: July 3, 1940: Operation "Catapult". In Oran the French Commander rejects the British ultimatum, whereupon Force H opens fire on the French warships at anchor. In the foreground the heavy guns of the battleship *Provence* attempt to open fire on the British. Just behind the modern battleship *Strasbourg* is on fire (middle right), while the *Bretagne* (background) sinks with heavy loss of life. [BFZ

Below: Sept 24, 1940: Between Sept 23-25 1940 British naval forces assisted by vessels of the Free French Navy and Gaullist troops attacked the Vichy French port of Dakar. The two Vichy French cruisers in Dakar— *Georges Leygues* and *Montcalm*, and a destroyer, sail to attack the British. [BFZ

Below: June 9, 1941: Operations by British and Free French troops occupying Syria against strong Vichy French resistance.

British destroyers attack the Vichy French destroyers *Valmy* and *Guépard* off Sidon. [BFZ

Above: July 9, 1940: On June 10 Italy entered the war. A month later the British and Italian navies joined action at the battle of Punta Stilo/Calabria. The illustration shows Italian cruisers of the 1st Div firing on British forces.

[*Official Italian Navy*

Left: July 19, 1940: The Royal Navy scored its first major naval success in the Mediterranean when the Australian cruiser *Sydney* and five destroyers attacked two Italian cruisers off Cape Spada and sink the *Bartolomeo Colleoni*.

[*IWM*

Above: Nov 11-12, 1940: Fleet Air Arm Sqdns 813, 815, 819 and 824 embarked on the carrier *Illustrious*, carried out a raid on the Italian Fleet lying in Taranto. The battleship *Conte di Cavour* was torpedoed and sunk.

[*IWM*

convoy and independents, *U101* (Lt-Cdr Frauenheim) sinks three ships of 12311 tons; *U28* (Lt-Cdr Kuhnke) four ships of 9945 tons and damages one ship of 4768 tons (inclusive of SC.2); *U32* (Lt Jenisch) three ships of 13093 tons; *U124* (Lt-Cdr Schulz) two ships of 10563 tons and damages one ship of 3900 tons; *U57* (Lt Topp) three ships of 24088 tons and torpedoes one ship of 5407 tons; *U37* (Lt-Cdr Oehrn) six ships of 23384 tons and the sloop *Penzance*; *U60* (Lt Schnee) one ship of 1401 tons and torpedoes one ship of 15434 tons; *U59* (Lt-Cdr Matz) two ships of 7451 tons and torpedoes one ship of 8009 tons. On 1 Sept *U32* attacks the convoy which left the Clyde on 31 Aug with the transports for the Dakar operation (Operation 'Menace', see 23-25 Sept) and which is escorted by a naval force consisting of the cruisers *Devonshire* (Vice-Adm J. H. D. Cunningham) and *Fiji*, the battleship *Barham*, and the destroyers *Inglefield*, *Echo*, *Eclipse* and *Escapade*. *Fiji* receives a torpedo hit and has to be replaced by the Australian cruiser *Australia*. An attack by *U56* (Lt Harms) on this ship on 8 Sept is unsuccessful because of a torpedo failure. The *Barham* arrives in Gibraltar with the other ships on 3 Sept.

20 Aug   General Situation
First operational plan 'Felix' worked out to capture Gibraltar.
Italy declares the Mediterranean and the African coast an operational area.

20-29 Aug   North Atlantic
British force, comprising the battleship *Valiant*, the new carrier *Illustrious* and the AA cruisers *Calcutta* and *Coventry*, is transferred from British ports to Gibraltar. It is accompanied by the cruiser *Sheffield* and the 8th DD Flotilla (*Faulknor*, *Foresight*, *Forester*, *Fury*, *Firedrake*, *Fortune* and *Greyhound*) destined for Force H. The new flagship of Force H, the battlecruiser *Renown*, and the carrier *Ark Royal* have already arrived in Gibraltar.

21-31 Aug   Red Sea
The Italian submarines *Guglielmotti* (21-25 Aug), *Ferraris*, (25-31 Aug), the torpedo boats *Nullo* and *Sauro* (24-25 Aug), *Battisti* and *Manin* (30-31 Aug) and the destroyers *Pantera* and *Tigre* (28-29 Aug) search in vain for Greek

ships reported by agents and air reconnaissance in the Red Sea.

22-24 Aug   Mediterranean
Three Swordfish aircraft of No 824 Sqdn of the carrier *Eagle* sink the Italian submarine *Iride* and the depot ship *Monte Gargano* (1976 tons) in the Gulf of Bomba near Tobruk while the *Iride* is being prepared for the first operation by small battle units (*Maiali* human torpedoes) against Alexandria. Early on 23 Aug the destroyers *Stuart*, *Diamond*, *Juno* and *Ilex* set out from Alexandria to make a raid in the Gulf of Bomba in the night 23-24 Aug while the gunboat *Ladybird*, supported by the destroyer *Waterhen*, penetrates into the harbour of Bardia.

22-25 Aug   North Sea/English Channel
The 9th Fl. Div drops airmines off Dundee, Newcastle, Middlesbrough, Hartlepool, Dover, Portland, Poole, in Scapa, the Thames Estuary, the Downs and the sea around the Isle of Wight.

23 Aug   North Sea
He 115 torpedo aircraft of K.Fl.Gr. 506 from Stavanger attack the British convoy OA.203 in Moray Firth and sink the freighters *Llanishen* (5053 tons) and *Makalla* (6677 tons). The motor ship *Beacon Grange* (10119 tons) is badly damaged.

23-28 Aug   Norway
British cruiser *Norfolk* and Australian cruiser *Australia* make an unsuccessful sortie from Scapa Flow to the area of Bear Island to intercept German fishery vessels. An attack by the ships' aircraft on Tromsö has to be abandoned because of the weather.

25 Aug-3 Sept   Central Atlantic
The Vichy French submarine *Sidi-Ferruch*, which has been in the harbour of Duala (Cameroons) since 10 Aug, sets out on 25 Aug. On 27 Aug Capt de Hautecloque, later General Leclerc, takes over power on behalf of the Free French movement. On 28 Aug General de Larminat follows in Brazzaville (Congo). The submarine *Sidi-Ferruch* (Lt-Cdr de Kehror) which is sent to Libreville on 30 Aug, is able, at first, to stabilise the situation there, in favour of the Vichy Government. On 3 Sept Cdr* Morin sets out to her support from Dakar with the sloop *Bougainville*, the

E

submarine *Poncelet* and the transport *Cap des Palmes* with 100 Senegalese riflemen and 800 tons of supplies and arrives in Libreville on 10 Sept. On 3 Sept the sloop *D'Entrecasteaux* and the submarine *Ajax* are sent from Casablanca, on 4 Sept the tanker *Tarn* with the cruiser *Primauguet* and the sloop *Gazelle* and on the following days the sloops *D'Iberville*, *Surprise* and *Commandant Rivière*. Before the British cruiser *Delhi* arrives on 6 Sept off Pointe Noire (Congo), three French steamers set out from there. The *Jean Laborde* reaches Dakar on 8 Sept; the *Touareg* is captured by the British cruiser *Dragon* on 16 Sept and the *Cap Padaran* has to put in to Conakry on 23 Sept.

26 Aug   North Sea
Four He 115's of K.Fl.Gr. 506 from Stavanger attack the British convoy HX.65A off Kinnaird Head and sink the freighter *Remuera* (11445 tons) with a torpedo hit. Eight Ju 88's of the same Gruppe also damage the freighter *Cape York* (5027 tons) so badly with bomb hits that she has to be abandoned on 27 Aug.

26-29 Aug   North Sea
German aircraft drop airmines in the estuaries of the Thames and Humber, in the Downs and off Harwich.

26 Aug-16 Sept   Indian Ocean
German auxiliary cruiser *Schiff 33 Pinguin* (Capt Krüder) sinks and captures five Allied merchant ships of 27508 tons in the Indian Ocean.

27 Aug   General Situation
On the basic issue dividing OKH and OKM in connection with 'Seelöwe', Hitler decides in favour of the 'smaller solution' i.e. a landing on a front of approximately 140 KM on the British South-East Coast (Folkestone to Eastbourne).

27 Aug   North Atlantic
RAF Coastal Command establishes an advance air base on Iceland. The first squadrons stationed there are equipped with old Fairey Battle aircraft.

27 Aug-6 Oct   North Atlantic
A second wave of Italian submarines is moved in two groups from the Mediterranean to Bordeaux. The first group consisting of *Baracca, Emo, Faa' di Bruno, Giuliani, Tarantini,* and *Torelli*

operates in the area between Portugal, the Azores and Madeira; the second consisting of *Bagnolini* and *Marconi* off NW Spain. *Emo* (Cdr Liannazza) sinks one ship of 5199 tons; *Baracca* (Cdr Bertarelli) one ship of 3687 tons; *Marconi* (Cdr Chialamberto) one trawler of 330 tons; *Bagnolini* (Cdr Tosoni-Pittoni) one ship of 3302 tons. *Faa' di Bruno* makes three unsuccessful attacks.

29 Aug-6 Sept   Mediterranean
Operation 'Hats'/MB: a British force, Force F, consisting of the battleship *Valiant*, the carrier *Illustrious* and the AA cruisers *Calcutta* and *Coventry*, proceeds through the Mediterranean to Alexandria. In the Western Mediterranean, Force H (Vice-Adm Somerville), comprising the battlecruiser *Renown*, the carrier *Ark Royal*, the cruiser *Sheffield* and 12 destroyers, provides cover for the force. On 31 Aug nine Swordfish aircraft of the *Ark Royal* attack Port Elmas in Sardinia before Force H turns away. Force F is met S of Sicily by the Mediterranean Fleet (Adm Cunningham) consisting of the battleships *Malaya* and *Warspite*, the carrier *Eagle*, the 3rd Cruiser Sqdn (*Gloucester, Kent* and *Liverpool*) and the 7th Cruiser Sqdn (*Orion* and *Sydney*) and 13 destroyers of the 2nd, 10th and 14th DD Flotillas. They simultaneously cover a supply convoy for Malta comprising the transports *Cornwall, Plumleaf* and *Volo* and the destroyers *Jervis, Juno, Dainty* and *Diamond*. On 31 Aug the Polish destroyer *Garland* and the steamer *Cornwall* are damaged in attacks by the Italian Air Force. The Italian Fleet, consisting of five battleships, including the new 35000 ton ships *Littorio* and *Vittorio Veneto*, 13 cruisers and 39 destroyers, which sets out from Taranto and Messina, cannot find the British forces owing to inadequate air reconnaissance and turns back prematurely. Neither the Italian submarines *Corallo* and *Sirena*, stationed S of Crete, nor the *Berillo, Capponi* and *Durbo*, operating off Malta, sight the British ships, which arrive in Malta on 2 Sept (the convoy, *Valiant, Calcutta* and *Coventry*). Attacks by Italian Ju 87's dive-bombers on *Eagle* and the destroyers *Imperial* and *Janus* are unsuccess-

ful. On the return Cunningham divides his squadron into Force E (*Malaya*, *Eagle*, *Coventry* and six destroyers) and Force I (*Warspite*, *Valiant*, *Illustrious*, *Calcutta* and seven destroyers). The first proceeds S of Crete and the second N of Crete to the Dodecanese. The cruisers *Gloucester*, *Kent* and *Liverpool* with the destroyers *Mohawk* and *Nubian* are detached to the Gulf of Nauplia to meet a convoy there of five steamers. The cruisers *Orion* and *Sydney* and the destroyers *Decoy* and *Ilex* shell Scarpanto in the night 3-4 Sept. When the Italian *MAS 536* and *MAS 537* try to attack, the latter is sunk by *Ilex* in the Kaso Strait. Swordfish aircraft of the *Eagle* and *Illustrious* attack the Italian airfields of Kalatho and Maritza on Rhodes; four aircraft are shot down by Italian CR.42 fighters. An attack by the British submarine *Parthian* on an Italian cruiser force is not successful.

30 Aug   General Situation
Vichy France is forced to allow Japan to undertake the military occupation of harbour, airfields and railways in Northern Indo-China.

30 Aug   General Situation
OKM reports that the Navy's preparation for 'Seelöwe' cannot be completed by 15 Sept. Earliest possible date 20 Sept.

30 Aug-9 Sept   North Atlantic
First successful group operation with U-boats against Convoy SC.2 (53 ships). On 30 Aug the 'B' Service decodes the route instructions and the escort meeting point for 6 Sept. On 2 Sept *U124*, *U65*, *U47* and *U101* are accordingly deployed, but *U124* has to proceed far to the W to provide weather reports for 'Seelöwe'. Shortly after SC.2 is met by the Escort Group (sloops *Lowestoft* (Cdr Knapp) and *Scarborough*, destroyers *Skeena* (RCN) and *Westcott*, corvette *Periwinkle*, A/S trawlers *Apollo* and *Berkshire*), *U65* (Lt-Cdr v. Stockhausen) sights the convoy but is driven off by *Skeena* and *Periwinkle*. Towards midnight on 6-7 Sept *U65* again approaches and leads *U47* (Lt-Cdr Prien) to the scene which sinks three ships in succession. Flying-boats drive the U-boats off on 7 Sept and only in the late evening of 8 Sept do the U-boats *U65* and *U47* again approach. The latter sinks a fourth steamer. Towards morning on

9 Sept *U28* (Lt-Cdr Kuhnke) and *U99* (Lt-Cdr Kretschmer) approach and attack simultaneously. *U28* sinks a fifth ship. When light, *U99* is driven away from the North Channel. The surface night attacks by the U-boats cannot be prevented by the escorts which rely only on visual sightings and ASDIC detection. Total result: five ships of 20943 tons sunk.

31 Aug   English Channel
Result so far of Battle of Britain: 4779 German aircraft employed; 4447 tons of H.E. bombs dropped, and 191 tons of incendiary bombs. German losses: 252 fighters and 215 bombers. British losses: 359 aircraft.

31 Aug   North Sea
At sea NW of Texel the 20th British DD Flotilla runs into a German minefield and loses the destroyers *Esk* and *Ivanhoe*. The *Express* is severely damaged.

31 Aug-2 Sept   English Channel
The Officer Commanding Minelayers (Capt Bentlage) with the minelayers *Tannenberg*, *Roland* and *Cobra* lays the offensive mine barrage 'S.W.3' in the south-western North Sea. Escort provided by the 5th DD Flotilla (Cdr* F. Berger) with the destroyers *Erich Steinbrinck*, *Karl Galster* and *Paul Jacobi*, the 2nd TB Flotilla (Cdr Riede) with *T8*, *T5*, *T6* and *T7*, and the 5th TB Flotilla (Cdr Henne) with *Falke*, *I¹tis*, *Jaguar* and *Greif*.

31 Aug-13 Sept   North and Central Atlantic
Preparations for the British and Free French operation 'Menace'. On 31 Aug the convoy consisting of two troop transports, four freighters and one tanker (with 4200 British and 2700 Free French troops on board), three French sloops and one trawler, sets out from the Clyde. Cover and escort provided by Vice-Adm J. H. D. Cunningham with battleship *Barham*, cruisers *Devonshire* (F) and *Fiji* and destroyers *Inglefield*, *Eclipse*, *Echo* and *Escapade*. On 1 Sept the force is attacked W of the Hebrides by *U32* (Lt Jenisch). *Fiji* is hit by torpedo and has to return. On 6 Sept the Australian cruiser *Australia* sets out as a replacement; an attack on her by *U56* (Lt Harms) on 8 Sept fails because of torpedo defects. In the

meantime, Force H has set out on 6 Sept from Gibraltar with the battleship *Resolution*, the carrier *Ark Royal* and the destroyers *Faulknor*, *Foresight*, *Forester*, *Fortune*, *Fury* and *Greyhound* in order to meet on 13 Sept the convoy and the cruisers *Cornwall* and *Cumberland* and the sloops *Bridgewater* and *Milford* summoned from the South Atlantic and then to proceed together to Freetown (see 9-22 Sept for continuation).

1 Sept Bay of Biscay
Formation of the Italian submarine command BETASOM (Rear-Adm Parona) in Bordeaux. For operational purposes it is placed under the orders of the German Commander U-boats (Vice-Adm Dönitz).

1-24 Sept Bay of Biscay
The British Bay Patrol submarines in the Bay of Biscay are from time to time reinforced by submarines on the way to the Mediterranean. Off Brest *Tigris* (Lt-Cdr Bone) sinks a French trawler of 168 tons on 1 Sept and *Truant* (Lt-Cdr Haggard) encounters in the Bay of Biscay on 2 Sept the prize ship *Tropic Sea* (5781 tons) captured by the German auxiliary cruiser *Orion*: the ship is sunk by the prize crew. On 22 Sept *Tuna* (Lt-Cdr Cavanagh-Mainwaring) sinks the prize *Tirranna* (7230 tons) captured by the auxiliary cruiser *Atlantis* and, two days later, the catapult ship *Ostmark* (1281 tons).

2 Sept General Situation
Destroyer/Naval Base Deal between Britain and the USA signed: the USA makes over 50 old destroyers to Britain in return for the use of bases in the Bahamas, Jamaica, Santa Lucia, Trinidad, Bermuda, British Guiana and in Argentia in Newfoundland.

2 Sept North Sea
The German 9th Fl.Div drops mines in the Thames Estuary, in Scapa, in Moray Firth and off Aberdeen, Middlesbrough and Newcastle.

3 Sept General Situation
Hitler accepts 21 Sept as the possible date for the beginning of the landing in Britain ('Seelöwe').

4 Sept English Channel
In an attack by the 1st MTB Flotilla (Lt-Cdr Birnbacher) on a British convoy NE of Great Yarmouth *S21* (Lt Klug)

sinks the freighters *Corbrook* (1729 tons) and *New Lambton* (2709 tons); *S18* (Lt Christiansen) the freighters *Joseph Swan* (1571 tons) and *Nieuwland* (1075 tons) and *S22* (Lt Grund) the freighter *Fulham V* (1562 tons). *S54* torpedoes another steamer of 1350 tons.

5-6 Sept Mediterranean
The Italian torpedo boats *Altair*, *Alcione*, *Ariel* and *Aretusa* under Cdr* Del Cima lay the offensive mine barrages M.1 and M.2, consisting of 112 mines, NE and SE of Malta.

5-6 Sept English Channel
German minelayers, escorted by the 2nd TB Flotilla (Cdr Riede) comprising *T5*, *T6*, *T7* and *T8*, carry out the mining operation 'Walter' in the Straits of Dover.

5-7 Sept Red Sea
In the night 5-6 Sept the Italian torpedo boats *Battisti*, *Manin* and *Sauro*, and in the night 6-7 Sept the destroyers *Leone* and *Tigre* and the torpedo boats *Battisti* and *Sauro*, are deployed against a convoy from Aden to Suez located by air reconnaissance. But they do not find the target. The submarines *Ferraris* and *Guglielmotti*, stationed to the N, do not sight the convoy; but *Guglielmotti* (Cdr Tucci) sinks the Greek tanker *Atlas* (4008 tons) sailing as an independent.

6 Sept General Situation
First invasion warning in Britain.
America hands over the first eight of the old destroyers to the Royal Navy.

6-7 Sept English Channel
Offensive mining operation 'S.W.0' by the 5th TB Flotilla (Cdr Henne) comprising *Greif*, *Kondor*, *Falke*, *Iltis* and *Jaguar* and the 1st TB Flotilla (Cdr v. Rennenkampff) with *T1*, *T2* and *T3*.

6-8 Sept Norway
Unsuccessful sortie by the British aircraft carrier *Furious* against shipping targets off the Central Norwegian coasts.

6-9 Sept Mediterranean
The Italian Fleet sets out with five battleships, six cruisers and 19 destroyers to intercept Force H from Gibraltar S of Sardinia. The Force returns when it is learned that Force H has passed Gibraltar on a westerly course.

7 Sept North Sea
In an attack by the German motor torpedo boats *S33* and *S36* on the British convoy FS.273, *S33* (Lt Popp) sinks the Dutch freighter *Stad Almaer* (5750 tons) E of Lowestoft.

7 Sept Gibraltar
The Vichy Government orders a first 'trial convoy', consisting of the tug *Pescagel*, accompanied by the sloop *Elan*, to proceed from Casablanca to Oran through the Straits of Gibraltar. Up to November 1942 540 Vichy French convoys comprising 1750 ships pass through the Straits of Gibraltar in both directions.

7-8 Sept English Channel
British aircraft attack German assault craft in the Channel ports.

8-9 Sept English Channel
Offensive mining operation 'Hannelore' in the Straits of Dover by the 2nd TB Flotilla (Cdr Riede) comprising *T5*, *T6*, *T7* and *T8*.

8-23 Sept North Sea
In the North Sea the Allied submarine *Rubis* (French) operates on the Dogger Bank, the Dutch *O22* off SW Norway and *O23* off the Skagerrak.

9 Sept General Situation
The U.S. Navy gives building orders for 210 warships, including seven battleships and 12 aircraft carriers.

9-22 Sept North Atlantic
After the SC.2 operation *U47* acts as the weather boat. *U28*, *U65* and *U99* remain W of the Hebrides and off the North Channel where the newly-despatched *U48*, *U61*, *U59*, *U58*, *U100* and *U138* are stationed. They operate individually against independents and convoys. *U28* (Lt-Cdr Kuhnke) attacks OA.210 on 11 Sept; *U48* SC.3 on 15 Sept; and *U138* OB.216 on 20-21 Sept successfully. On 20 Sept the weather boat *U47* (Lt-Cdr Prien) sights the convoy HX.72 (41 ships) shortly after the ocean escort auxiliary cruiser *Jervis Bay* has turned away. With only one torpedo left *U47* maintains contact for *U29*, *U65*, *U48*, *U46* and *U43* which have been ordered to the scene in spite of the convoy's efforts to escape. Before the convoy is met by the escort group *U99* (Lt-Cdr Kretschmer) comes up in the evening and torpedoes three ships in succession, one of which sinks and two

of which are finished off on 21 Sept with torpedoes and gunfire with the help of *U47*. On the morning of 21 Sept *U48* (Lt-Cdr Bleichrodt) sinks one ship. From the Escort Group which arrives soon after—sloop *Lowestoft* (Cdr Knapp), corvettes *La Malouine*, *Calendula* and *Heartsease*—the only destroyer *Shikari* is sent to help the torpedoed ships. On the evening of 21 Sept *U100* (Lt-Cdr Schepke) reaches the convoy and, in the course of several approaches lasting four hours, sinks seven ships without being detected by the four escorts present. In the morning the destroyers *Scimitar* and *Skate* meet the ships of the scattered convoy and, together with *Lowestoft*, drive off *U32* (Lt Jenisch) which attacks a steamer of the convoy with gunfire. Total result in operating against HX.72: 12 ships of 77863 tons. In all, the first-named U-boats sink, inclusive of individual attacks: *U47* (Lt-Cdr Prien) five ships of 27544 tons and one ship of 5156 tons with *U99*; *U99* (Lt-Cdr Kretschmer) six ships of 20063 tons; *U48* (Lt-Cdr Bleichrodt) seven ships of 35138 tons and the sloop *Dundee* from SC.3 and damages, in addition, one ship of 5136 tons; *U65* (Lt-Cdr v. Stockhausen) two ships of 10192 tons; *U138* (Lt Lüth) four ships of 34644 tons; and *U100* (Lt-Cdr Schepke) seven ships of 50340 tons.

9-22 Sept Central Atlantic
Expedition by a French naval force (Rear-Adm Bourragué), consisting of the light cruisers *Georges Leygues*, *Gloire* and *Montcalm* and the large destroyers *L'Audacieux*, *Le Fantasque* and *Le Malin*, to re-establish the authority of the Vichy Government in the colony of Gabon which has gone over to De Gaulle. The squadron leaves Toulon on 9 Sept; it is first reported early on 11 Sept 50 nautical miles E of Gibraltar by the British destroyer *Hotspur* and it passes through the Straits of Gibraltar in the morning at high speed. On the way to Dakar it puts in to Casablanca to refuel on 12-13 Sept. The remaining British units of Force H in Gibraltar (see 31 Aug-13 Sept) receive orders too late to stop the French ships. On 14 Sept Vice-Adm Cunningham, who is approaching Freetown with the British forces for the

Operation 'Menace', receives orders to prevent the French ships getting to Dakar. A reconnaissance patrol undertaken 75 nautical miles NW of Dakar in the night 14-15 Sept by the 1st Cruiser Sqdn, comprising *Devonshire*, *Cumberland* and *Australia*, as well as the *Ark Royal*, is unable to find the ships whose entry into Dakar is reported by reconnaissance aircraft on 15 Sept. On 18 Sept the three French cruisers leave Dakar, after the older light cruiser *Primauguet* has been sent in advance to Libreville with the tanker *Tarn* to provide fuel supplies. But the latter are intercepted by the British cruisers *Cornwall* and *Delhi* and escorted to Casablanca. The cruiser force is at once shadowed by the heavy cruisers *Australia* and *Cumberland* patrolling in the area S of Dakar. When the *Gloire* has to remain behind because of engine trouble, the British escort this ship, too, to Casablanca. The operation against Gabon is then abandoned and the two remaining French cruisers return to Dakar.

10-20 Sept   Mediterranean
The Italian Expeditionary Corps for a campaign against Greece is brought from Brindisi to Albania without loss: 40310 troops, 7728 horses, 701 vehicles and 33535 tons of supplies.

13 Sept   North Sea
The Royal Navy transfers the battle-cruiser *Hood*, the battleships *Nelson* and *Rodney*, two cruisers and eight destroyers from Scapa Flow to Rosyth in order to be able to intervene in any German attempt to invade in the Channel.

14 Sept   North Sea
The 9th Fl.Div drops airmines in the Estuary of the Thames. The mining is continued on 15 Sept, 17 Sept, 18 Sept, 23 Sept and 30 Sept.

14-15 Sept   English Channel
Attacks by the RAF on shipping targets in the harbours of the French and Belgian coasts between Boulogne and Antwerp cause appreciable damage to the transport fleet assembled for 'Seelöwe'.

15-16 Sept   English Channel
Offensive mining operation 'Bernhard' by the 2nd TB Flotilla, comprising *T5*, *T6*, *T7* and *T8* in the Straits of Dover.

15-19 Sept   Mediterranean
British attack on Benghazi. On 15 Sept the battleship *Valiant*, the carrier *Illustrious* (Rear-Adm Lyster), the cruiser *Kent* and seven destroyers set out from Alexandria. On 16 Sept they join the 3rd Cruiser Sqdn, comprising the AA cruisers *Calcutta* and *Coventry*, W of Crete and proceed to the take-off position for the aircraft of the *Illustrious* which mine the harbour of Benghazi and attack ships with torpedoes in the night 16-17 Sept. The destroyer *Aquilone* is lost on a mine; and the destroyer *Borea* (later salvaged) and the freighters *Gloria Stella* (5490 tons) and *Maria Eugenia* (4702 tons) are lost as a result of torpedoes. On the return the cruiser *Kent* and two destroyers are detached to shell Bardia. The cruiser receives a heavy torpedo hit in the stern in an attack by Italian torpedo aircraft and is, with great difficulty, towed on 15 Sept by the destroyers to Alexandria. An attack by the Italian submarine *Corallo* (Cdr Albanese) on the *Illustrious* and *Valiant* fails. Of the submarines *Ondina*, *Uarsciek*, and *Settimo* stationed off Tobruk, the last misses two destroyers.

16 Sept   General Situation
No progress is made in the exploratory talks about Spain's participation in the war and in the conquest of Gibraltar when the Spanish Foreign Minister Serrano Suñer visits Berlin.

16-25 Sept   South Pacific
The Free French Governor of the New Hebrides, Sautot, is brought by the Australian cruiser *Adelaide* (16-19 Sept) from Vila to Nouméa (New Caledonia) to take over the area for De Gaulle. The plan is at first frustrated by the Vichy French sloop *Dumont d'Urville* (Cdr de Quièvrecourt) to whose support the sloop *Amiral Charner* sets out from Saigon on 20 Sept. But on 25 Sept *Dumont d'Urville* has to withdraw and returns to Saigon with *Amiral Charner*. Nouméa goes over to De Gaulle.

17 Sept   General Situation
Hitler postpones the operation 'Seelöwe'. But the preparations for a landing in Britain are to be continued and maintained.

17 Sept   Indian Ocean
The auxiliary cruiser *Schiff 16* (Capt Rogge) sinks in the Indian Ocean the

French passenger ship *Commissaire Ramel* (10061 tons) sailing in British service.

17-18 Sept   Air War/Britain
In an air attack on Glasgow the British heavy cruiser *Sussex* is severely damaged.

17-25 Sept   Mediterranean
The Italian submarines *Beilul*, *Delfino*, *Narvalo* and *Squalo* operate in the area N and NW of Crete.

18 Sept   North Africa
The Italian North African offensive (10th Army), which began on 13 Sept, comes to a halt as a result of supply difficulties after crossing the Egyptian/Libyan frontier and capturing Sidi Barrani (16 Sept).

19-21 Sept   Red Sea
The Italian destroyers *Leone*, *Pantera* and the torpedo boats *Battisti* and *Manin*, as well as the submarines *Archimede* and *Guglielmotti*, search in vain for a convoy of 23 ships reported by air reconnaissance. The steamer *Bhima* (5280 tons) is damaged by near-miss bombs and has to be beached. The escort for the British convoy includes the Australian sloops *Parramatta* and *Yarra*.

21 Sept   English Channel
So far 51 barges, nine steamers and one tug have been destroyed by British air attacks on Channel ports. In all, 155 transports (approximately 700000 tons), 1277 barges and lighters, 471 tugs and 1161 motor boats have been assembled for 'Seelöwe' between Le Havre and Antwerp.

22 Sept   General Situation
Following an agreement with the Vichy government Japanese troops occupy bases in Northern Indo-China.

22-28 Sept   Mediterranean
In British submarine operations in the Mediterranean *Osiris* (Lt-Cdr Harvey) attacks an Italian convoy off Durazzo (Albania) and sinks the escorting torpedo boat *Palestro*. The submarines *Regent*, *Triton* and *Truant*, newly transferred to the Mediterranean, report successes: *Truant* (Lt-Cdr Haggard) sinks one ship of 8459 tons off Ischia and *Triton* (Lt-Cdr Watkins) sinks one ship of 1434 tons off Genoa and shells installations in Vado and Savona. Off Benghazi *Pandora* (Lt-Cdr Linton) sinks one ship

of 813 tons and is heavily attacked by depth charges from the escorting torpedo boat *Cosenz*.

22 Sept-16 Oct   North Atlantic
The U-boats *U29*, *U43*, *U31*, *U32*, *U46*, *U37*, *U38*, *U137*, *U103* and *U123* arrive successively in the North Atlantic between the North Channel and Rockall Bank. The boats operate in varying concentrations against independents and convoys. An attempt to catch a convoy on 9 Oct with a reconnaissance line consisting of *U123*, *U103*, *U37*, *U38* and *U48* W of Rockall fails. There are only individual attacks in which the boats score the following successes (*U38* and *U123* include their successes against HX.79 and SC.7): *U29* (Lt-Cdr Schuhart) sinks one ship of 6223 tons; *U31* (Lt-Cdr Prellberg) two ships of 4400 tons; *U32* (Lt Jenisch) 8 ships of 42645 tons and damages one ship of 7886 tons; *U37* (Lt-Cdr Oehrn) five ships of 23237 tons; *U38* (Lt-Cdr Liebe) four ships of 30345 tons and damages one ship of 3670 tons; *U43* (Lt-Cdr Ambrosius) one ship of 5802 tons; *U46* (Lt Endrass) one ship of 3058 tons; *U103* (Cdr Schütze) five ships of 20279 tons and one ship of 3697 tons with *U123*; *U123* (Lt-Cdr Moehle) sinks four ships of 14589 tons and one ship of 3697 tons with *U103*, one ship of 5458 tons with *U101* and *U100* and one ship of 3106 tons with *U99*; *U137* (Lt Wohlfarth) sinks three ships of 12103 tons and damages one ship of 4917 tons. The missions undertaken by *U60* (Lt Schnee) off the Pentland Firth and by *U61* (Lt-Cdr Stiebler) off the North Minch have no success.

23-25 Sept   Central Atlantic
Operation 'Menace': British naval forces attack Dakar to prepare a landing by Free French troops. The British force under Vice-Adm J. H. D. Cunningham consists of the battleships *Barham* and *Resolution*, the carrier *Ark Royal*, the heavy cruisers *Devonshire*, *Cumberland* and *Australia* (RAN), the light cruiser *Delhi* and the destroyers *Faulknor*, *Foresight*, *Forester*, *Fortune*, *Fury*, *Greyhound* (from Force H) and *Inglefield*, *Eclipse*, *Echo* and *Escapade* as well as the sloops *Bridgewater* and *Milford*. In addition, there are the Free French sloops *Savorgnan de Brazza*, *Comman-*

dant Duboc and *Commandant Dominé.*
3670 Free French troops are embarked
on the troop transports *Pennland*
(16381 tons) and *Westernland* (16479
tons) and four freighters; and 4270
British troops on four more troop
transports and one freighter, which are
only to be landed in an emergency. One
tanker and one Free French armed tug
accompany the force. In Dakar the
following pro-Vichy units are stationed:
the unfinished battleship *Richelieu*, the
cruisers *Georges Leygues* and *Montcalm*,
the large destroyers *Le Fantasque*,
L'Audacieux and *Le Malin*, the destroyer *Le Hardi*, the sloops *D'Entrecasteaux*, *D'Iberville*, *Calais*, *Commandant Rivière*, *Le Surprise* and *Gazelle*,
five auxiliary cruisers and the submarines *Bévéziers*, *Persée* and *Ajax*.
Attempts by De Gaulle, through an
emissary and wireless messages, to
persuade the French naval forces (Rear-
Adm Landriau) to come over are
rejected by Governor Boisson, whereupon the French coastal batteries, open
fire on the assault fleet. In the process,
the cruiser *Cumberland* and the
destroyers *Foresight* and *Inglefield*
are hit.
The French submarine *Persée* is lost in a
surface attack on a cruiser and the large
destroyer *L'Audacieux* receives heavy
hits from the cruiser *Australia* and is
beached on fire (80 dead). An attempt
at landing by de Gaulle's troops in
Rufisque Bay is beaten off.
24 Sept: In trying to attack, the French
submarine *Ajax* is sunk by the destroyer
Fortune. After that *Barham, Resolution,
Devonshire* and *Australia* shell coastal
batteries and French ships lying in
harbour. The French defence obtains
four hits on *Resolution*; attacks by
carrier aircraft from *Ark Royal* achieve
no results and they lose six of their
number.
25 Sept: Renewed shelling of the harbour
by the British battleships. *Richelieu*
gets a 38cm (15in) hit on *Barham* and
the submarine *Bévéziers* (Lt-Cdr Lance-
lot) torpedoes the *Resolution*, whereupon
Churchill orders the operation to be
abandoned. The French armed forces
suffer 100 dead and 182 wounded; the
civilian population 84 dead and 197
injured.

23 Sept-6 Oct   Norway
Of the Dutch submarines *O21* and *O24*
operating off Norway *O21* just misses
the German *U61* near Bergen.

**23 Sept-5 Nov   Central and North
Atlantic**
A third wave of Italian submarines is
transferred to the Atlantic. The first
group, consisting of *Da Vinci, Otaria,
Glauco, Veniero, Nani* and *Cappellini*,
operates in the area of the Azores and
Madeira; the second, consisting of
Argo, Calvi and *Tazzoli* off the Spanish/
Portuguese coast. *Nani* (Cdr Polizzi)
sinks the A/S trawler *Kingston Sapphire*
in the Straits of Gibraltar and one ship
together totalling 1939 tons; *Cappellini*
(Cdr Todaro) one ship of 5186 tons; and
Tazzoli (Cdr Raccanelli) one ship of
5135 tons.

24-25 Sept   Gibraltar/Mediterranean
As a reprisal for the British attack on
Dakar 60 Vichy French aircraft from
Morocco bomb Gibraltar on 24 Sept
and drop 45 tons of bombs. On 25 Sept
81 aircraft make a second attack with
60 tons of bombs. Damage is slight.
Two aircraft are lost. The French destroyers *Epée, Fleuret, Fougueux* and
Frondeur from Casablanca carry out a
demonstration off Gibraltar in the night
24-25 Sept when the *Epée* opens fire
on the British destroyer keeping watch
before she continues the journey to
Oran.

24-27 Sept   North Sea
In operations in the area off Terschelling
the British submarine *H49* (Lt Coltart)
attacks two German convoys and sinks
one ship of 2186 tons.

24-30 Sept   North Atlantic
Heavy cruiser *Admiral Hipper* (Capt
Meisel) leaves Kiel to carry out mercantile warfare in the Atlantic. On 27 Sept
serious engine trouble develops W of
Stavanger which compels the ship to
return. The cruiser reaches Kiel on
30 Sept.

26 Sept   Pacific
The Canadian auxiliary cruiser *Prince
Robert* captures the German motor ship
Weser (9179 tons) off Manzanillo (Peru).

27 Sept   General Situation
Conclusion of the Three-Power Pact
between Germany, Italy and Japan in
Berlin. Purpose: to prevent the USA
intervening in the war by threaten-

ing a two-front war in the Atlantic and the Pacific. The relations of the three powers with the USSR are to remain unaffected.

27 Sept Gibraltar
First Vichy French convoy to pass through the Straits of Gibraltar from Casablanca since operation 'Menace'. It consists of three merchant ships accompanied by the sloop *La Gracieuse*.

28-29 Sept English Channel
Offensive mining operation in Falmouth Bay by the Officer Commanding Destroyers (Capt Bey) with the destroyers *Hans Lody, Karl Galster, Paul Jacobi, Erich Steinbrinck* and *Friedrich Ihn*. Covering group: *Friedrich Eckoldt* and *Theodor Riedel*. Results: five ships of 2026 tons sunk.

28 Sept-3 Oct Mediterranean
The British cruisers *Gloucester* and *Liverpool* leave Alexandria for Malta with 1200 troop reinforcements. Escort provided by the Mediterranean Fleet (Adm Cunningham) with the battleships *Valiant* and *Warspite*, the carrier *Illustrious*, the cruisers *Orion, Sydney* and *York* and 11 destroyers of the 2nd and 14th DD Flotillas (Operation MB.5). Italian air reconnaissance locates the Force whereupon the Italian Fleet sets out with the battleships *Littorio, Vittorio Veneto* (9th Div), *Cavour, Cesare* and *Duilio* (5th Div), the heavy cruisers *Pola, Zara, Gorizia* and *Fiume* (1st Div), *Bolzano, Trento* and *Trieste* (3rd Div), the light cruisers *Duca degli Abruzzi* and *Garibaldi* (8th Div), *Eugenio di Savoia* and *Duca d'Aosta* (7th Div) and 23 destroyers from Taranto and Messina. In the afternoon of 29 Sept many Italian air attacks (28 Savoia S79's) have no success.

When reconnaissance aircraft from the *Illustrious* report the Italian Fleet only 9 Swordfish aircraft are available. But they cannot be employed because of Italian air superiority. In consequence, the Italian Fleet returns on 30 Sept unmolested. The *Gloucester* and *Liverpool* are detached on 30 Sept, disembark their troops in Malta and rejoin the British Fleet on 1 Oct which then sets out for base. On 2 Oct *Orion* and *Sydney* shell Stampalia when they make a sortie into the Aegean. The Italian submarines *Ambra* and *Serpente* stationed S of Crete, and *Mameli, Tembien, Colonna* and *Berillo*, which are standing off the coast of Cyrenaica, do not approach the British forces; the last is sunk on 2 Oct by the British destroyers *Hasty* and *Havock*. The submarine *Gondar* which has set out to make a *Maiali* human torpedo attack on Alexandria is sunk on 30 Sept W of its target by the Australian destroyer *Stuart* and a Sunderland flying boat of No 230 Sqdn RAF.

29 Sept Mediterranean
The Italian submarine *Scirè* (Cdr Borghese), on her way to make a human torpedo attack on Gibraltar, is ordered back because Force H has set out for the Atlantic (Dakar operation).

29 Sept Central Atlantic
German auxiliary cruiser *Schiff 10* sinks the Norwegian whale-oil factory ship *Kosmos* (17801 tons) in the Central Atlantic.

29 Sept-4 Oct Central Atlantic
Force H with the battlecruiser *Renown* and destroyers is deployed against the French battleship *Richelieu* which, it is feared, is to be transferred from Dakar to a harbour in the Bay of Biscay. On 1 Oct the ships operate in the area of the Azores against a possible German assault on the Canaries. On 4 Oct Force H returns to Gibraltar.

30 Sept-1 Oct English Channel
Offensive mining operation 'Werner' by the 5th TB Flotilla (Cdr Henne) comprising *Greif, Kondor, Falke* and *Seeadler* off Dover.

1 Oct General Situation
Conclusion of a German-Finnish agreement on German arms deliveries to Finland. In return Finland gives Germany entire right to buy up all ore concessions (nickel mines near Petsamo).

1-8 Oct Mediterranean
The Italian submarines, *Ametista, Gemma* and *Tricheco* operate in the SE approaches to the Aegean. On 6 Oct *Tricheco* sinks the *Gemma* in error. *Zaffiro* operates in the Aegean.

1-30 Oct North Sea/English Channel
In many sorties off British ports and river estuaries the 9th Fl.Div drops in all 715 air mines, 317 of them in the Thames Estuary, 81 in the Humber Estuary, 46 in the Tees Estuary, 40 off Liverpool and 39 in the Firth of Forth.

The remaining mines are dropped partly off Hartlepool, Cardiff, Sunderland, Plymouth and Swansea.

2-9 Oct Central Atlantic
To protect the French Cameroons 1564 troops of a British brigade are sent on 2 Oct from Freetown to Duala on board the transport *Westernland*, escorted by the cruiser *Devonshire*, the destroyers *Escapade*, *Faulknor*, *Foresight* and *Fury* and the Free French sloops *Savorgnan de Brazza*, *Commandant Dominé* and *Commandant Duboc*. The troops are landed there from 7 Oct. to 9 Oct.

4-9 Oct Mediterranean
In the Gulf of Genoa the British submarine *Triton* (Lt-Cdr Watkins) sinks one ship of 1860 tons and off Durazzo *Regent* (Lt-Cdr Browne) two ships of 6088 tons.

5-16 Oct North Atlantic
In operations against independents and convoys in and just off the North Channel the Type II U-boats have the following successes: *U58* (Lt Schonder) sinks one ship of 4956 tons; *U59* (Lt-Cdr Matz) two ships of 12706 tons; *U137* (Lt Wohlfarth) torpedoes the auxiliary cruiser *Cheshire* (10552 tons). *U138* (Lt Lüth) one ship of 5327 tons and torpedoes two ships of 11555 tons.

7-10 Oct Mediterranean
The Italian 14th DD Flotilla (Capt Galati), comprising *Vivaldi*, *Da Noli* and *Tarigo* (*Malocello* out of action because of engine trouble), lays in the night 7-8 Oct the mine barrage 4 AN with 176 mines E of Cape Bon and in the night 9-10 Oct the mine barrage M3 with 174 mines S of Malta. The British destroyer *Hyperion* sinks on the first mine barrage on 22 Dec and the British destroyer *Imperial* sinks on the second on 11 Oct.

7-19 Oct Norway
The Dutch submarines *O22* and *O23* and the French *Rubis* operate off Norway. Of the British submarines *Snapper*, *Seawolf*, *Sunfish*, *Triumph*, *Tetrarch* and *Cachalot* continue to be employed off Norway.

8 Oct Bay of Biscay
In the Bay of Biscay the British submarine *Trident* misses the German *U31* with a torpedo and has a gun duel with the German boat.

8-9 Oct English Channel
The 5th TB Flotilla (Cdr Henne), comprising *Greif*, *Seeadler*, *Kondor*, *Falke*, *Wolf* and *Jaguar*, makes a sortie into the area near the Isle of Wight.

8-14 Oct Mediterranean
Operation 'MB.6': British supply convoy of four steamers, escorted by the AA cruisers *Calcutta* and *Coventry* and four destroyers, from Alexandria to Malta. Cover from the Mediterranean Fleet (Adm Cunningham) with the battleships *Warspite*, *Valiant*, *Malaya* and *Ramillies*, the carriers *Eagle* and *Illustrious*, the cruisers *York*, *Gloucester* and *Liverpool* (3rd Cruiser Sqdn), *Ajax*, *Orion* and *Sydney* (7th Cruiser Sqdn) and 16 destroyers. The convoy reaches Malta undetected in stormy weather on 11 Oct, but the destroyer *Imperial* is damaged on a mine. When an Italian civilian aircraft reports sighting the returning force, Supermarina tries to lay an ambush in the Ionian Sea. The 1st TB Flotilla (Cdr Banfi), comprising *Airone*, *Alcione* and *Ariel*, makes a surprise but unsuccessful attack on the cruiser *Ajax* (Capt McCarthy) in the night 11-12 Oct. *Airone* and *Ariel* sink in the defensive fire; *Alcione* rescues the crew of the sinking *Airone* and escapes. The 11th DD Flotilla (Capt Margottini), comprising *Artigliere*, *Aviere*, *Camicia Nera* and *Geniere*, which arrives on the scene of the fighting, is likewise caught in the defensive fire of *Ajax* as it approaches. *Artigliere* receives heavy, and *Aviere* light, hits. *Camicia Nera* takes *Artigliere* in tow; she is located on the morning of 13 Oct by a Sunderland flying-boat which leads Swordfish from the *Illustrious* to her but they do not hit her. When the British cruiser *York* (Capt Portal) approaches, *Camicia Nera* cuts loose and *Artigliere* is sunk after the crew have disembarked. The 3rd Cruiser Div, consisting of *Trieste*, *Trento* and *Bolzano*, and three destroyers of the 14th Flotilla, set out to help from Messina, but arrive too late. 225 survivors are recovered by the hospital ship *Aquileja*. On the return Swordfish bombers from the British carriers *Eagle* and *Illustrious* attack Leros (13-14 Oct) and on the evening of 14 Oct the cruiser *Liverpool* is hit in the bows by a torpedo from an Italian aircraft.

9 Oct North Atlantic

The Italian submarine *Malaspina* (Cdr Leoni) is the first to proceed to the North Atlantic from Bordeaux. In the course of October, *Dandolo*, *Otaria*, *Barbarigo*, *Finzi*, *Baracca*, *Bagnolini*, *Marconi* and *Faa' di Bruno* follow. At the end of October and the beginning of November there are more Italian submarines than German U-boats in the operational area.

9 Oct Central Atlantic

General de Gaulle lands in Duala (Cameroons) from the minesweeper *Commandant Duboc* and hoists the Free French flag for the first time on French territory.

9-20 Oct North Atlantic

Whilst *U47* and *U124* take up weather positions far to the W, *U48*, *U101*, *U93*, *U100*, *U46*, *U99* and *U28* operate with *U123* and *U38* (which have already been longer at sea) in varying concentrations in the area round the Rockall Bank and off the North Channel. On 11-12 Oct *U48* sinks three ships from the convoy HX.75. On 15 Oct *U93* sinks one ship from OB.227 and on 16 Oct she establishes contact with OB.228 from which *U138* has torpedoed two ships the day before. She shadows the convoy, which makes a wide detour to the N, until 20 Oct and sinks two ships on 17 Oct, but the other boats are too far off. On 17 Oct *U48* sights the convoy SC.7 with 30 ships (four stragglers) shortly after it has been met by the sloops *Scarborough* and *Fowey* and the corvette *Bluebell*; she sinks two ships but is then driven off by flying boats. *Scarborough* remains behind. On receipt of *U48*'s report, the Commander U-boats forms a patrol line with *U101*, *U46*, *U123*, *U99* and *U100*. In the night 17-18 Oct *U38* attacks the convoy twice and torpedoes one ship; but she is driven off by the corvette *Heartsease* which has arrived with the sloop *Leith*. In the evening the convoy runs into the patrol line. The escorts with the convoy *Leith* (Cdr Allen), *Fowey* and *Bluebell* are powerless with their Asdics against *U101*, *U46*, *U99* (which fires whilst moving in the convoy), *U123* and *U100* as they attack in the night in quick succession and sometimes more than once. 16 ships

are sunk, one other ship is torpedoed and the convoy is completely scattered. *U101* sinks three ships and torpedoes two; *U46* sinks two ships; *U99* sinks six ships and torpedoes one; *U100* sinks one straggler and again torpedoes two ships disabled by *U101*; *U123* sinks two ships as well as two previously disabled by *U101* and *U100* and by *U99*. *U99*, *U101* and *U123* have to return, having fired all their torpedoes. *U100*, *U46*, *U28*, which failed to get to the scene, and *U38* and *U48* which are further to the N, encounter on 19 Oct the convoy HX.79 located far to the W by *U47*. The convoy's Ocean Escort, the auxiliary cruisers *Alaunia* and *Montclare*, has already turned away and its Escort Group has only come up on the morning of 19 Oct, after releasing the westward-bound OB.229. In spite of its unusual strength (the destroyers *Whitehall* (Lt-Cdr Russell), *Sturdy*, the minesweeper *Jason*, the corvettes *Hibiscus*, *Heliotrope*, *Coreopsis*, *Arabis*, the A/S trawlers *Lady Elsa*, *Blackfly* and *Angle* and submarine *O21*), *U47* maintains contact and guides the other boats to HX.79 with its 49 ships. In the night 19-20 Oct the U-boats attack in succession and sometimes more than once. *U38* sinks two ships; *U46* sinks two ships and one ship hit by *U47*; *U47*, moving partly in the convoy, sinks three ships and torpedoes three others; *U48* sinks one ship previously disabled by *U47*; and *U100* sinks three ships. Only *U28* does not reach the scene before daylight. The boats taking part have fired all their torpedoes and have to return. In the west, in the meantime, *U124* attacks OB.229 and sinks two ships, but fails to get the Italian submarine *Malaspina* to the convoy. In all, in these operations the following sinkings are made by the U-boats (inclusive of some scattered ships and stragglers): *U48* (Lt-Cdr Bleichrodt) six ships of 37083 tons and one ship of 6023 tons with *U47*; *U101* (Lt-Cdr Frauenheim) three ships of 10645 tons and one ship of 5458 tons with *U100* and *U123* and torpedoes one ship of 4155 tons with *U100*; *U93* (Lt-Cdr Korth) three ships of 13214 tons; *U124* (Lt-Cdr Schulz) five ships of 20061 tons; *U46* (Lt Endrass) four ships of 20426 tons and one ship of 4947 tons with *U47*; *U99* (Lt-Cdr Kretschmer) six ships of 28066 tons and one ship of 3106 tons with *U123*; *U100* (Lt-Cdr Schepke) four ships of 24715 tons and one ship of 5458 tons with *U101* and *U123* and torpedoes one ship of 4155 tons with *U101*; *U47* (Lt-Cdr Prien) three ships of 17067 tons, one ship of 6023 tons with *U48*, one ship of 4947 tons with *U46* and torpedoes one tanker of 8995 tons. From the convoy SC.7, in all, 21 ships, including four stragglers, of 79592 tons are sunk and two more are torpedoed; from HX.79 12 ships of 75069 tons are sunk and one tanker torpedoed.

11 Oct Air War
In a heavy air attack on Liverpool four ships of 34744 tons are badly damaged in the harbour.

11-12 Oct English Channel
Second sortie by the 5th TB Flotilla (Cdr Henne), comprising *Falke, Greif, Kondor, Seeadler* and *Wolf*, into the sea area off the Isle of Wight. In engagements with light forces the Free French submarine-chasers *Ch6* and *Ch7* are sunk.

11-16 Oct Central Atlantic
The Vichy French submarine *Vengeur* goes from Toulon to Oran (11-13 Oct) and from there proceeds with the submarines *Monge, Pégase* and *L'Espoir* to Casablanca (16-18 Oct) and on to Dakar (23-26 Oct).

12-20 Oct Mediterranean
Two Italian submarines operate E of Gibraltar and fall victim to the British submarine hunt: *Durbo* is sunk on 18 Oct by the destroyers *Firedrake* and *Wrestler* with support from two London flying-boats of No 202 Sqdn RAF; *Lafolé* is sunk on 20 Oct by the destroyers *Gallant, Griffin* and *Hotspur*.

13-14 Oct Norway
British destroyer force (Capt Vian), comprising *Cossack, Ashanti, Maori* and *Sikh*, attacks a group of ships in German service near Egersund and sinks two of them in a confused engagement by night.

13-14 Oct Mediterranean
In mining operations by the Italian submarines *Foca* (Cdr Giliberto) on 13 Oct off Haifa and by *Zoea* (Cdr

Bernabò) on 14 Oct off Jaffa, the first is lost through an unknown cause.

15 Oct General Situation
The plan to attack Greece is decided on in the Italian War Council in Rome.

15 Oct General Situation
Finland gives a treaty undertaking to the Soviet Union not to fortify the Aaland Islands.

15-18 Oct North Sea/English Channel
In operations by British submarines in the Channel *L27* attacks a convoy on 15 Oct. On 18 Oct *H49* is sunk near Terschelling by the German submarine-chasers *UJ116* and *UJ118* under Lt-Cdr Kaden.

15-21 Oct Mediterranean
An Italian submarine group, consisting of *Bandiera, Santarosa, Speri, Ascianghi, Topazio* and *Anfitrite*, is stationed between Crete and Alexandria but has no success. The submarine *Toti* (Cdr Bandini), which is returning because of a breakdown and cannot submerge, encounters on 15 Oct off Calabria the British submarine *Rainbow* which is sunk in a gun duel. On approximately 20 Oct the submarine *Triad* is lost on a mine barrage in the Gulf of Taranto.

16 Oct Air War/Britain
The 9th Fl.Div (Lt-Gen Coeler), which since the spring has flown air mining sorties against British ports, is transformed into IX Fl.K. without there being any reinforcement of the flying formations.

16-17 Oct Air War/Germany
British bombers attack Bremen, Cuxhaven, Hamburg and Kiel by night.

17-18 Oct North Sea
In a sortie by German motor torpedo boats against the British SE coast *S18* (Lt Christiansen) sinks the British freighter *Hauxley* (1595 tons), and *S24* and *S27* torpedo two freighters totalling 6726 tons.

17-18 Oct English Channel
Sortie by the Officer Commanding Destroyers (Bey) with the destroyers *Hans Lody, Karl Galster, Friedrich Ihn* and *Erich Steinbrinck* towards the western exit of the Bristol Channel. There is an engagement with British cruisers and destroyers. *Steinbrinck* reports a so-far unconfirmed torpedo hit on a cruiser. The 5th TB Flotilla

operates as a support group with *Greif, Seeadler, Kondor, Falke, Wolf* and *Jaguar.*

18 Oct-1 Nov   Norway
The Dutch submarine *O24* operates off Holmangrund/Norway.

20-21 Oct   Red Sea
Unsuccessful attempt by the Italian destroyers *Pantera, Leone, Sauro* and *Nullo* to attack the British convoy BN.7 in the Red Sea (32 ships escorted by the cruiser *Leander* (RNZN), the destroyer *Kimberley*, the sloops *Auckland, Indus* and *Yarra* and the minesweepers *Derby* and *Huntley*). The attackers are driven off by the escort. *Nullo* (Cdr Borsini, has to be beached near Massawa after the engagement. The destroyer *Kimberley* is hit by coastal guns and has to be towed to Port Sudan. *Nullo* is destroyed on 21 Oct by three Blenheim bombers of No 45 Sqdn. The Italian submarines *Ferraris* and *Guglielmotti*, stationed further to the N, do not come up.

20 Oct-5 Nov   North Atlantic
After the great convoy operations only *U28* and *U124* remain for the present in the operational area. Some days later *U29*, *U31* and *U32*, which have recently set out, arrive. On 26 Oct *U28* (Lt-Cdr Kuhnke) torpedoes the freighter *Matina* (5389 tons), the wreck of which is sunk on 29 Oct by *U31* (Lt-Cdr Prellberg). On 26 Oct a FW200 (Lt Jope) of 2/K.G.40 obtains a bomb hit on the British passenger ship *Empress of Britain* (42348 tons) about 110Km NW of Donegal Bay (Ireland). The ship catches fire but is taken in tow by escort vessels. The U-boats *U28*, *U31* and *U32* (Lt Jenisch) are ordered to pursue: the latter reaches the ship on 28 Oct and sinks her with two torpedoes whilst she is escorted by two destroyers. In the attack on a convoy on 30 Oct, *U32* is sunk by the British destroyers *Harvester* and *Highlander*. *U31* is likewise sunk in an attack on a convoy on 2 Nov by the destroyer *Antelope* with aircraft support. *U99* (Lt-Cdr Kretschmer), which arrives shortly afterwards in the operational area, encounteres the two British auxiliary cruisers *Laurentic* (18724 tons) and *Patroclus* (11314 tons) W of Ireland, after sinking a steamer on 3 Nov. The *Laurentic* is first hit by a torpedo and then hit again half an hour

later in an attempt to finish her off. She is brought to a standstill and is sunk in the morning with a torpedo, the *Patroclus* having been hit and reduced to a wreck with three torpedoes. The *Patroclus* only sinks after two more hits. *U99* returns having sunk, in all, four ships of 42407 tons.
The first group of Italian submarines to be stationed in the North Atlantic W of the German U-boats, *Malaspina, Dandolo, Otaria* and *Barbarigo*, sights several ships and convoys but achieves no successes.

21 Oct   Mediterranean
Formation of the Italian Command 'Maritrafalba' (Capt Polacchini) in Brindisi to carry out, and escort, troop and supply transports to Albania. Under command are the destroyers *Mirabello, Riboty*, the torpedo boats *Calatafimi, Castelfidardo, Curtatone, Monsambano, Confienza, Solferino, Prestinari, Cantore, Fabrizi, Medici* and *Stocco*, the escort ships *Ramb III, Capit. Cecchi, Lago Tana, Lago Zuai* and the 13th MAS Flotilla with four boats. In addition, the 12th TB Flotilla, consisting of *Antares, Altair, Andromeda* and *Aretusa*, is allotted as a fighting force.

23 Oct   General Situation
Hitler meets General Franco in Hendaye on the Franco-Spanish frontier. The talks on Spain's entry into the war and the conquest of Gibraltar lead to no result.

23 Oct   Atlantic
Heavy cruiser *Admiral Scheer* (Capt Krancke) leaves Gotenhafen for mercantile warfare operations in the Atlantic. On 27 Oct the cruiser receives orders in Brunsbüttel to set out and reaches Stavanger on 28 Oct. From 31 Oct to 1 Nov the ship passes through the Denmark Strait undetected.

24 Oct-30 Nov   Atlantic
The German freighter *Helgoland* breaks out of the Colombian port of Puerto Colombia, eludes pursuit by the U.S. destroyers *Bainbridge, Overton* and *Sturtevant*, passes the Antilles chain near St. Thomas on 3 Nov and reaches St. Nazaire.

25-28 Oct   Mediterranean
British sortie into the Aegean to cover a convoy operation between Alexandria and Greece. The operation is covered

by the 2nd Sqdn of the Mediterranean Fleet, comprising the battleships *Malaya* and *Ramillies* and the carrier *Eagle*, as far as the Kaso Strait. Carrier aircraft attack the airfield at Maltezana. The cruisers *Orion* and *Sydney* with the destroyers *Jervis* and *Juno* make a sortie as far as the Dardanelles for contraband control.

25 Oct-2 Dec   Central and North Atlantic
The fourth group of Italian submarines is transferred to Bordeaux. *Marcello* and *Morosini* operate at first without success between Vigo and the Azores. *Bianchi* and *Brin* have to put in to Tangiers on 4 Nov after *Bianchi* has been bombed by a London flying-boat of No 202 Sqdn RAF and attacked by the destroyer *Greyhound* with depth charges and damaged.

27-30 Oct   Gibraltar
After three attempts have been abandoned because of the defence, the Italian submarine *Scirè* (Cdr Borghese) launches three *Maiali* human torpedoes off Gibraltar; but they do not reach their targets.

28 Oct   Mediterranean
Italian troops cross the Greek/Albanian frontier and invade Greece.

28 Oct-6 Nov   Mediterranean
The Italian submarines *Zaffiro*, *Narvalo* and *Corridoni* (after a transport mission from Taranto to Rhodes and Leros) operate in the south-eastern approaches to the Aegean. *Delfino* and *Jantina* cruise in the Aegean. *Atropo* (Cdr Manca) has to break off a mining operation off Zante on 29 Oct while actually laying mines; *Bragadino* (Cdr Vannutelli) lays 24 mines off Navarino on 30 Oct.

29-30 Oct   English Channel
Offensive mining operation 'Alfred' by the torpedo boats *Iltis* and *Jaguar* off Dover.

29 Oct-2 Nov   Mediterranean
Sortie by the British Mediterranean Fleet (Adm Cunningham) with four battleships, two carriers, four cruisers and destroyers into the Ionian Sea to cover convoys to Greece. No opposition. The Italian submarines *Menotti*, *Settembrini*, *Dessiè* and *Tricheco*, operating S of Crete from 28 Oct to 5 Nov, do not establish contact.

31 Oct   Mediterranean
British Army and Air Force units land on Crete.

31 Oct-1 Nov   Mediterranean
Sortie by Force H, comprising the battlecruiser *Renown*, the battleship *Barham* and the destroyers *Forester*, *Fortune*, *Firedrake*, *Gallant*, *Greyhound* and *Griffin* along the Moroccan West Coast against suspected movements by Vichy French warships.

1-20 Nov   Norway
Of the Allied submarines operating off Norway the French *Rubis* (Cdr Cabanier) lands agents in Korsfjord. The British *Sturgeon* (Lt Gregory) attacks two German convoys on 3 Nov and 6 Nov off Obrestad and sinks two ships of 2631 tons. She is relieved by the Dutch submarine *O23*. *O22* is sunk on 8 Nov off SW Norway by depth charges from the German submarine-chasers *UJ177* and *UJ1104*.

2-12 Nov   Bay of Biscay
In the Bay of Biscay the British submarine *Taku* (Lt-Cdr Van der Byl) sinks the tanker *Gedania* (8923 tons). The submarine *Swordfish*, which relieves the *Usk* off Brest, is probably lost (on a mine?) about 10 Nov. *Tigris* (Lt-Cdr Bone) sinks one trawler of 301 tons.

3 Nov   North Sea
A FW200 of I/K.G.40 severely damages the British passenger ship *Windsor Castle* (19141 tons) with a bomb hit W of Ireland.

4 Nov   Mediterranean
The British submarine *Tetrarch* (Lt-Cdr Mills) torpedoes one ship of 2532 tons in a convoy off Benghazi.

4-14 Nov   Mediterranean
British naval operations in the Mediterranean with carrier attacks on Taranto. On 4 Nov the convoys AN.6 and MW.3 set out from Port Said and Alexandria for the Aegean and Malta, accompanied by the AA cruisers *Calcutta* and *Coventry* and the destroyers *Dainty*, *Vampire*, *Waterhen* and *Voyager*. After bringing AN.6 into Suda Bay these ships, with the exception of the last, proceed westwards with MW.3. The cruisers *Ajax* and *Sydney* set out from Alexandria on 5 Nov, land supplies in Suda Bay on 6 Nov and then join the Mediterranean Fleet at sea on the same day.

Operation MB.8: Convoy MW.3 with five supply ships proceeds to Malta. It is covered by the Mediterranean Fleet (Adm Cunningham,) comprising the battleships *Warspite*, *Valiant*, *Malaya* and *Ramillies*, the carrier (Rear-Adm Lyster) *Illustrious*, the cruisers *Gloucester* and *York* (3rd Cruiser Sqdn), the *Orion* (and later *Ajax* and *Sydney*) (7th Cruiser Sqdn, Vice-Adm Pridham-Wippell) and 13 destroyers: *Nubian* (14th Flotilla,) *Mohawk*, *Jervis*, *Janus*, *Juno*, *Hyperion* (2nd Flotilla), *Hasty*, *Hero*, *Hereward*, *Havock*, *Ilex* and, detached from the 2nd Flotilla, *Decoy* and *Defender*.

Operation 'Coat': On 7 Nov Force H (Vice-Adm Somerville) goes to sea from Gibraltar with the carrier *Ark Royal*, the cruiser *Sheffield* and the destroyers *Faulknor* (8th Flotilla), *Duncan*, *Firedrake*, *Forester*, *Fortune* and *Fury*, in order to cover Force F (reinforcements for the Mediterranean Fleet comprising the battleship *Barham*, the cruisers *Berwick* and *Glasgow* and the destroyers *Encounter* (back), *Gallant*, *Greyhound* and *Griffin*), as far as S of Sardinia. On 9 Nov the Swordfish aircraft of Nos 810, 818 and 820 Sqdns make an attack on Cagliari. Italian bombers attack the force which is located on 9 Nov but only near misses are obtained near *Ark Royal*, *Barham* and *Duncan*. An Italian submarine group, comprising *Alagi*, *Axum*, *Aradam*, *Medusa* and *Diaspro*, is stationed SW of Sardinia on 9 Nov but is unable to find both forces. The 14th DD Sqdn (*Vivaldi*, *Da Noli*, *Pancaldo* and *Malocello*) which is sent to the Sicilian Channel passes by Force F (now detached from Force H) in the night 9-10 Nov. Force F joins the Mediterranean Fleet coming from the E on the morning of 10 Nov when S of Malta and then enters Malta to land 2150 troop reinforcements. Of the Italian submarines *Mameli*, *Corallo*, *Bandiera*, *Topazio* and *Capponi* (Cdr Romei), stationed E of Malta, only the last is able to fire—unsuccessfully—at the *Ramillies* as she comes into Malta with the *Coventry* and the destroyers and convoy MW.3. On 10 Nov the convoy ME.3 with four empty ships (unsuccessfully attacked on 11 Nov by the Italian

submarine *Topazio*) (Cdr Berengan) and the escort of MW.3 and the *Ramillies* set out eastwards, followed by the destroyer *Vendetta* (repaired in Malta) and the monitor *Terror*, which arrives in Suda Bay on 13 Nov. The destroyers *Faulknor*, *Fortune* and *Fury* which have led Force F as minesweepers to Malta return to Force H, S of Sardinia. The latter proceeds back to Gibraltar after the *Ark Royal* has flown off another three Fulmars to Malta. After meeting the units coming from the W on 10 Nov, the forces of the Mediterranean Fleet at first proceed eastwards. The Italian aircraft seeking to keep contact suffer losses from the Fulmar fighters from the *Illustrious*. On 11 Nov the *Illustrious* (Capt Boyd) with the cruisers *Gloucester*, *Berwick*, *Glasgow*, *York* and four destroyers turns to attack Taranto; the cruisers *Orion*, *Sydney* and *Ajax* and the destroyers *Mohawk* and *Nubian* turn to the N to make a raid on the Strait of Otranto.

Operation 'Judgment'; a Force composed of 12 and nine Swordfish aircraft from the carrier Sqdns Nos 813, 815, 819 and 824 from the *Illustrious* attacks the Italian Fleet lying in the harbour of Taranto during the night 11-12 Nov. In two waves under Lt-Cdr Williamson and Lt-Cdr Hale, the Swordfish aircraft obtain three hits on the modern battleship *Littorio* and one each on the older *Caio Duilio* and *Conte di Cavour*, *Cavour* sinks on the bottom; she is later salvaged but not put into service. The heavy cruiser *Trento* and the destroyer *Libeccio* are slightly damaged by bomb hits (unexploded). Two of the attacking aircraft are shot down by AA fire.

In the night the cruisers under Vice-Adm Pridham-Wippell find a convoy of four ships in the Strait of Otranto proceeding from Valona to Brindisi and escorted by the auxiliary cruiser *Ramb III* and the old torpedo boat *Fabrizi*. These escape while the steamers *Antonio Locatelli* (5691 tons), *Capo Vado* (4391 tons), *Catalani* (2429 tons) and *Premuda* (4427 tons) are sunk. Apart from a bomb hit on the destroyer *Decoy* on 13 Nov, the forces of the British Mediterranean Fleet return to Alexandria without further losses.

5-8 Nov   Mediterranean

The temporarily repaired French battleship *Provence* is transferred from Oran to Toulon, accompanied by the destroyers *Epée, Fleuret, Le Hardi, Lansquenet* and *Mameluck*. The force is met by the battleship *Strasbourg*, the cruisers *Algérie, Dupleix, Foch, La Galissonnière* and *Marseillaise* and five destroyers.

5-17 Nov   North Atlantic

The German heavy cruiser *Admiral Scheer* (Capt Krancke), after sinking an independent of 5389 tons, attacks on 5 Nov E of Newfoundland the convoy HX.84 (37 ships) proceeding from Halifax to Britain. The escorting auxiliary cruiser *Jervis Bay* (Capt Fegen†, 14164 tons) at once gives orders for the convoy to scatter under a smokescreen, while she tries to tie down the German ship in order to gain time. After she goes down, *Scheer* is able to sink five steamers of 33331 tons before dark and to damage three ships, including the tanker *San Demetrio*, totalling 27853 tons. On receipt of *Jervis Bay's* distress signal, the Home Fleet deploys the battleships *Nelson* and *Rodney* with destroyer escorts to block the Iceland-Faeroes passage and the battlecruisers *Hood* and *Repulse*, the *Renown* (recalled from Force H) and the cruisers *Dido, Naiad* and *Phoebe* of the 15th Cruiser Sqdn to block the approaches to the Bay of Biscay. Two HX convoys are recalled. Normal convoy traffic is not resumed until 17 Nov with HX.89. *Admiral Scheer,* however, proceeds to the South Atlantic.

6-7 Nov   North Sea

Sortie by the 1st and 2nd TB Flotillas (Cdr v. Rennenkampff and Cdr Riede), comprising *T1, T4, T6, T7, T8, T9* and *T10,* against the Scottish East Coast. *T6* (Lt-Cdr Wolfram) is lost when she hits a mine, whereupon the operation is broken off.

7 and 8 Nov   Pacific

The British freighter *Cambridge* (10846 tons) and an American freighter (5883 tons) sink on the mine barrage laid from 29 Oct to 2 Nov in the Bass Strait (Australia) by the German auxiliary minelayer *Passat* (Lt-Cdr Warning).

7-9 Nov   Central Atlantic

Free French attack on Libreville. The transports *Fort Lamy, Nevada* and *Casamaoce,* land troops of the Foreign Legion under Col Leclerc on 7 Nov in the Bay of Mondah, N of Libreville (Gabon). Escort provided by the Free French sloops *Commandant Dominé* and *Savorgnan de Brazza* (Cdr* d'Argenlieu) British forces, including the cruisers *Delhi* and *Devonshire,* confine themselves to blockading the coast of Gabon. The Vichy French submarine *Poncelet* (Cdr de Saussine), which tries to attack the British sloop *Milford,* is forced to surface by depth charges from the latter and has to scuttle herself. On 9 Nov, after several attacks by Free French aircraft on the French sloop *Bougainville* (Cdr* Morin) lying in Libreville, there is an engagement between this ship and the *Savorgnan de Brazza* in which the *Bougainville* is set on fire and sinks. By 14 Nov the whole of French Equatorial Africa has fallen into de Gaulle's hands.

8-30 Nov   North Atlantic

U137, U138, U93, U100, U103, U123 and *U104* operate in the area W of the North Channel; and further to the W as weather boats *U29* and *U47,* as well as the Italian boats *Baracca, Finzi* and *Marconi. Faa' di Bruno* must have sunk from an unknown cause when setting out at the beginning of November 1940. On 8 Nov *Marconi* (Cdr Chialamberto), in attempting to maintain contact with HX.84, which has been attacked by a FW 200 of K.G.40, is herself attacked by the British destroyer *Havelock* with depth charges, but is able on the following day to finish off the Swedish freighter *Vingaland* (2734 tons), set on fire by a FW 200 of I/K.G.40. On 16-17 Nov *U137* sinks three ships of an outward-bound convoy; following her report, *U47* and *U100* approach the convoy on 18-19 Nov but have no success. One of the two boats is located by a Sunderland flying-boat of the RAF with ASV-I radar equipment. This is the first radar locating of a U-boat by an aircraft. *U93, U103, Finzi* and *Marconi* are too far off. On 20 Nov *U103* sights OB.244 and sinks two of its ships but is driven off in a depth charge pursuit by the British corvette *Rhododendron.* On 23 Nov *U123* establishes contact with the dispersing convoy and sinks five ships. From the homeward-bound

Above: Nov 28, 1940: In November 1940 the Royal and Italian navies clashed again at the battle of Cape Spartivento. The picture shows British cruisers opening fire on the Italian forces which scored hits on the British cruiser *Berwick*, furthest from the camera. [IWM

Right: Nov 9, 1940: On 7 Nov Force H put to sea from Gibraltar to provide cover for reinforcements being sent to the Mediterranean Fleet. The Italians sighted the force on 9 Nov, and with the Luftwaffe attacked the British force in the Sicilian Narrows, but scored only near misses on the carrier *Ark Royal*. [IWM

Above: May 19, 1941: From Gibraltar Force H, with the battle cruiser *Renown* and carriers *Furious* and *Ark Royal*, launched Hurricane fighters south of Sardinia for Malta. [IWM

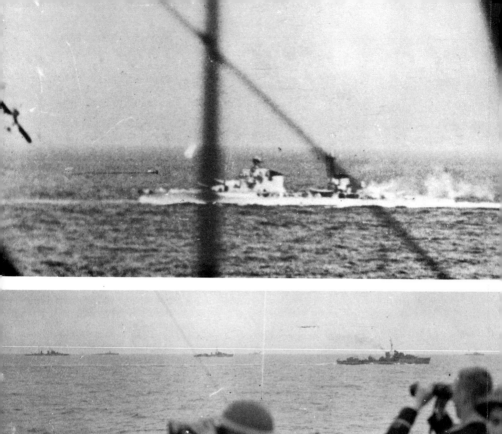

Top: March 28, 1941: In the battle of Cape Matapan Swordfish aircraft made an unsuccessful attack on the Italian cruiser *Bolzano*   [IWM

Above: May 22, 1941: In May the British were forced to withdraw from Crete when the Germans landed heavily armed parachute troops on the island. Force C of the Royal Navy, with four cruisers and three destroyers, attacked a German/Italian troop convoy north of Crete. The cruiser *Naiad* is to the left, and in the middle and right the destroyers *Nubian* and *Kingston*.   [IWM

Top right: May 22, 1941: Force C comes under heavy air attacks, which continue after the force has joined the powerful covering group. In the continuing air attacks mounted by the Luftwaffe, the cruiser *Gloucester* is sunk.   [IWM

Opposite: May 23, 1941: On May 22-23 the destroyers *Kashmir, Kelly* and *Kipling* shell the airfield at Maleme (Crete). On their return the following day *Kashmir* and *Kelly* are sunk, the *Kipling* rescuing the survivors under heavy bombing attacks.   [IWM

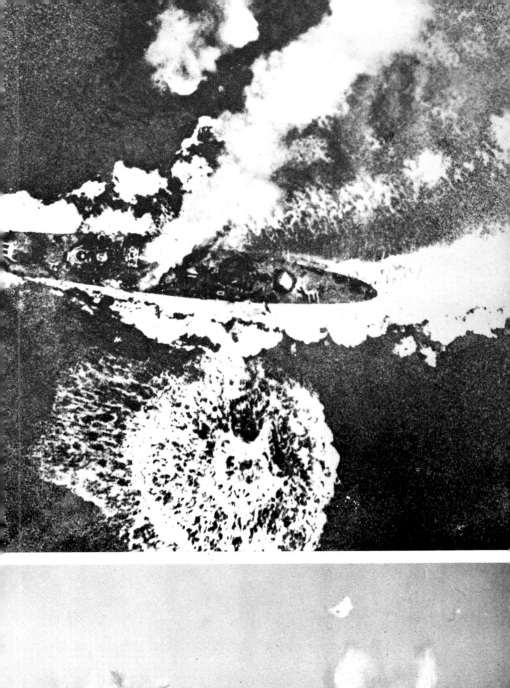

Above: March 31, 1940: Auxiliary cruiser *Atlantis* puts to sea on a cruise that will last 622 days, and in which she will sink 22 ships of 145,697 tons.　　　　*[BFZ*

Below: May 24, 1941: On 18 May the *Bismarck* and *Prinz Eugen* leave Gotenhafen on a cruise to carry out mercantile warfare in the Atlantic. Breaking through the Denmark Straits, the force is attacked by the *Hood* and *Prince of Wales*. In a five minute action the *Bismarck* opens fire and sinks the *Hood*.　　　　*[BFZ*

Below: May 27, 1941: Following the sinking of the *Hood*, every available British warship is concentrated in the hunt for the *Bismarck*. She is finally trapped by the battleships *King George V* and *Rodney*, and sent to the bottom by torpedoes from the cruiser *Dorsetshire*.　　　*[Keystone Press*

Above: Feb, 1941: The Luftwaffe joins the U-boats and surface warships in attacks on Atlantic convoys. FW 200s of I/K.G. 40 under von Merignac at Bordeaux provide search and attack forces to co-operate with the Kriegsmarine. *[Bundesarchiv*

Below: Until continuous air support from carriers or Coastal Command can be provided, merchantmen fitted with a catapult over the focsle sail with Atlantic convoys. The *Ariguani* is typical of such vessels which carried a single Hurricane fighter. *[IWM*

Below: Sept, 1941: To augment the escorts for Atlantic convoys US Escort Groups based on Iceland were provided for convoys. Such a group was permanently based on Hvalfjord to watch the Denmark Straits for German vessels attempting to break out into the Atlantic. One of the vessels was the *Mississippi.* *[IWM*

Above: Aug 8, 1941: In Loksa Bay the Russian destroyer *Karl Marx* is sunk by Ju 88s of K. Fl. Gr. 806.　　　　*[BFZ*

Below: Sept 23, 1941: The German Baltic Fleet is transferred to the Aaland Sea to prevent a possible breakout from Leningrad into the Baltic by the Soviet Fleet. The *Tirpitz,* accompanied by the *Admiral Scheer,* follows a torpedo boat, and is accompanied by the cruisers *Koln* and *Nurnberg* and three destroyers.　　　　*[IWM*

Below: Sept 21-24, 1941: The Luftwaffe mounts huge Stuka attacks against the Baltic Fleet in Kronstadt and Leningrad. The battleship *Marat* with demolished bow, settles on the bottom off the mole at Kronstadt.　　　　*[BFZ*

Above: Aug 16, 1941: German troops enter the Russian port of Nikolaev. On the stocks they find the battleship *Sovetskaya Ukraina,* a heavy cruiser, destroyers and submarines all wrecked by the retreating Russians.

[Bundesarchiv

Below: Sept 21, 1941: The destroyer *Frunze* leads Russian forces which are to land near Grigorevka to attack the Rumanians near Odessa in the rear. While going to the assistance of a gunboat damaged in an air attack, the *Frunze* is herself sunk by Stukas.

[BFZ

Above: Nov 13-14, 1941: On returning from an operation to fly off aircraft for the defence of Malta, the carrier *Ark Royal* is torpedoed by *U81*. With a salvage party on board the stricken carrier, the destroyer *Legion* stands by ready to take a tow line. Shortly after, however, the carrier sank.
[*IWM*

Below: Nov 25, 1941: Force K from Malta, supported by units of the Mediterranean Fleet, sails to attack German/Italian convoys bound for North Africa. Off Bardia *U331* penetrates the destroyer screen of the battleship force and torpedoes the *Barham* which capsizes and explodes. [*IWM*

SC.11, *U100* sinks seven ships in the night 22-23 Nov; *U93* does not approach nor are *U29*, *U43* and *Finzi* able to get to OB.244. In all, *U137* (Lt Wohlfarth) sinks four ships of 13341 tons; *U100* (Lt-Cdr Schepke) sinks seven ships of 24601 tons; *U103* (Cdr Schütze) seven ships of 38465 tons; *U123* (Lt-Cdr Moehle) six ships of 27895 tons; *U104* (Lt-Cdr Jürst) one ship of 8240 tons and torpedoes one ship of 10516 tons; *Baracca* (Cdr Bertarelli) one ship of 4866 tons; and *Marconi* (Cdr Chialamberto) one ship of 2734 tons, disabled by bombing from I/K.G.40. *U104* must have sunk from unknown causes on 27 Nov.

9 Nov   North Sea/North Atlantic
German aircraft drop mines in the estuaries of the Thames and Humber and off Liverpool. An FW 200 of I/K.G. 40 damages the British passenger ship *Empress of Japan* (26032 tons) in the North Atlantic.

10 Nov-2 Jan   Central Atlantic
U65 (Cdr v. Stockhausen), which set out on 15 Oct, operates off Freetown, after being replenished from the supply ship *Nordmark*, from 15 Nov to 19 Nov and sinks four ships. After being replenished on 29 Nov the U-boat sinks four other ships and torpedoes one tanker by 2 Jan. Total results: eight ships of 47785 tons sunk and one ship of 8532 tons torpedoed.

12 Nov   North Sea
He 115s of 3/K.Fl.Gr. 906 torpedo three freighters of 6604 tons in a British convoy off Middlesbrough.

14-16 Nov   Mediterranean
The British cruisers *Berwick*, *Glasgow*, *Sydney* and *York* transport 3400 troops from Alexandria to Piraeus.

14-22 Nov   Mediterranean
After the British raid of 11-12 Nov the Italian submarines *Jalea* and *Millelire* operate in the Strait of Otranto to cover their own convoys. Cruisers and destroyers are sent to Brindisi as a precautionary move.

15 Nov   Western Atlantic
Flying boats of US Navy Patron 54, based on the tender *George E. Badger*, begin reconnaissance flights from Bermuda.

15-20 Nov   Mediterranean
Operation 'White': British Force H (Vice-Adm Somerville) with battle-cruiser *Renown*, aircraft carrier *Ark Royal*, cruisers *Despatch* and *Sheffield* and the destroyers *Faulknor*, *Fortune*, *Fury*, *Wishart*, *Forester*, *Firedrake*, *Duncan* and *Foxhound*, accompanies the carrier *Argus* to the area SW of Sardinia where 12 Hurricane fighters and two Skua bombers are flown off to Malta. But because of the strong contrary winds only four Hurricanes and one Skua reach Malta. A raid by *Ark Royal* on the airfield at Alghero (Sardinia) planned for 17 Nov has to be abandoned because of the weather. The Italian submarines *Alagi*, *Aradam* and *Diaspro* are deployed but they are unable to find Force H.

On 17 Nov the cruiser *Newcastle* sets out for Malta with 200 RAF personnel and important spare parts and arrives on 19 Nov. From 15 Nov to 20 Nov the cruisers *Gloucester*, *York*, *Orion*, *Ajax* and *Sydney* bring 4000 troops from Alexandria to Piraeus and return without incident.

16-17 Nov   Air War/Germany
127 British bombers attack Hamburg.

16-18 Nov   Western Atlantic
The German freighters *Phrygia*, *Idarwald* and *Rhein* try to break through from Tampico (Mexico) to Western France. At once escorted by US destroyers, the *Phrygia* scuttles herself—in the belief that she has been found by the enemy; the other two return after unsuccessful attempts to throw off the pursuers.

16-29 Nov   Norway
Dutch submarine *O24* operates off Egersund.

18-28 Nov   Indian Ocean
German auxiliary cruiser *Schiff 33* sinks four Allied freighters of 35083 tons, including the British refrigerator ship *Maimoa* (10123 tons), in the Indian Ocean.

20-30 Nov   Mediterranean
In the Eastern Mediterranean the Italian submarine *Onice* operates NW of Alexandria (only until 24 Nov); *Narvalo* in the Kaso Strait; and *Delfino* in the Northern Aegean; *Atropo* carries out a supply operation from Taranto to Leros.

22-28 Nov   Red Sea
The Italian submarines *Archimede* and *Ferraris* search in vain for a reported British convoy.

F

23-24 Nov   Air War/Britain

Heavy German air attack on Southampton. Among other ships, the passenger steamer *Llandovery Castle* (10640 tons) is badly damaged.

23-28 Nov   North Sea/English Channel

German aircraft drop mines in the estuaries of the Thames and Humber, off Newcastle, Pembroke, Plymouth, Falmouth and Bristol.

23 Nov-1 Dec   Mediterranean

The Italian submarines *Nereide* and *Sirena* operate in the Strait of Otranto.

23 Nov-13 Dec   North Atlantic

The U-boats *U43*, *U47*, *U103* (weather boats) *U52*, *U94*, *U95*, *U99*, *U101* and *U140* operate in the North Atlantic, W of the North Channel and, further to the W, the Italian boats *Argo*, *Giuliani* and *Tarantini*. On 1 Dec *Argo* (Lt-Cdr Crepas) torpedoes the Canadian destroyer *Saguenay* belonging to the escort of the convoy HG.47. On the afternoon of 1 Dec *U101*, which is stationed the furthest W, sights the convoy HX.90, whose Ocean Escort, the auxiliary cruiser *Laconia*, soon after leaves the convoy. Before arrival of the Escort Group *U101*, *U52* and *U47* approach and continually attack the convoy in the night 1-2 Dec. In four approaches *U101* sinks four ships; *U47* sinks one ship and torpedoes the tanker *Conch*; and *U52* in two approaches sinks one ship and torpedoes two. On the evening of 1 Dec *U99* hits with one torpedo, a little to the N, the auxiliary cruiser *Forfar* proceeding westwards, and finishes her off with four torpedoes. The escorting destroyer HMCS *St Laurent* has been detached to HX.90. An attack by *Argo* fails. After the arrival of the Escort Group, comprising the sloop *Folkestone*, the corvette *Gentian* and the destroyer *Viscount*, *Tarantini* is attacked with depth charges. Contact is lost in the morning and air reconnaissance, made with three machines, produces no result. While *U95* and *U99* finish off and sink the disabled *Conch* from the rear, *U99* sinks another independent and *U43* attacks an outward-bound convoy making a detour to the N, and sinks two ships. *U94* finds HX.90 again in the afternoon of 2 Dec and in two approaches sinks two ships.

The convoy is scattered. On receipt of a 'B' Service report, *U43*, *U52*, *U94*, *U99* and *U103* are ordered on 3 Dec to look for convoy SC.13; but they do not find it. *Argo* sinks one of its ships.

In the convoy operation and in individual attacks *U43* (Lt Lüth) sinks three ships of 21262 tons and torpedoes one ship of 10350 tons; *U47* (Lt-Cdr Prien) sinks one ship of 7555 tons and one ship of 8376 tons with *U95* and *U99*; *U52* (Lt-Cdr Salman) sinks one ship of 5448 tons and torpedoes two ships of 8820 tons; *U94* (Lt-Cdr Kuppisch) sinks three ships of 13617 tons; *U95* (Lt-Cdr Schreiber) sinks one ship of 1860 tons, one ship of 8376 tons with *U47* and *U99* and torpedoes one ship of 1296 tons; *U99* (Lt-Cdr Kretschmer) sinks three ships of 25915 tons and one ship of 8376 tons with *U47* and *U95*; *U101* (Lt-Cdr Mengersen) sinks five ships of 28505 tons; *U140* (Lt Hinsch) sinks three ships of 13207 tons. *Argo* (Lt-Cdr Crepas) sinks one ship of 5066 tons and torpedoes the destroyer *Saguenay*.

On the return *Tarantini*, after being met by the German minesweeper escort, is lost on 15 Dec in the Bay of Biscay, as a result of an attack by the British submarine *Thunderbolt* (Lt Crouch).

In all, nine ships of 52817 tons belonging to HX.90 are sunk.

24-25 Nov   English Channel

Sortie by the Officer Commanding Destroyers (Capt Bey) with the destroyers *Karl Galster*, *Hans Lody* and *Richard Beitzen* into the area off Plymouth. Two ships of 2156 tons are sunk in the sortie.

24-29 Nov   Mediterranean

Operation 'Collar': battle off Cape Teulada (Sardinia). On 24 Nov Force D, consisting of the battleship *Ramillies* and the cruisers *Berwick* and *Newcastle*, leaves Alexandria for Gibraltar and the cruiser *Coventry*, the destroyers *Defender*, *Gallant*, *Greyhound*, *Griffin* and *Hereward* go to meet a convoy coming from Gibraltar S of Sardinia. They are accompanied until S of Malta by covering group (Force C) consisting of battleships *Barham*, *Malaya*, and carrier *Eagle* (which carries out a raid on Tripoli on 26 Nov). On 25 Nov the Mediterranean Fleet (Force A) (Admiral

Cunningham) leaves Alexandria with battleships *Valiant*, *Warspite*, the carrier *Illustrious*, the 7th Cruiser Sqdn with *Ajax*, *Orion* and *Sydney* and destroyers to cover a convoy to Suda Bay (Crete). In the process *Illustrious* makes a raid on Rhodes on 26 Nov. In addition, a supply convoy to Malta puts to sea with the 3rd Cruiser Sqdn (Force E) consisting of *Glasgow*, *Gloucester* and *York*. On 25 Nov the convoy, which is to go E, (Force F), with the cruisers *Manchester* (Vice-Adm Holland) and *Southampton* (each with 700 men on board) the destroyer *Hotspur*, the corvettes *Peony*, *Salvia*, *Gloxinia*, *Hyacinth* and the transports *Clan Forbes*, *Clan Fraser* and *New Zealand Star*, is met off Gibraltar by the covering group (Force B) consisting of the battlecruiser *Renown* (Vice-Adm Somerville), the carrier *Ark Royal*, the cruisers *Despatch* and *Sheffield* and the destroyers *Faulknor*, *Firedrake*, *Forester*, *Fury*, *Encounter*, *Duncan*, *Wishart*, *Kelvin* and *Jaguar*.
On the report that Force B has left Gibraltar and on the sighting of Force D, S of Malta, by an Italian civilian aircraft on 25 Nov, the Italian submarines *Alagi*, *Aradam*, *Axum* and *Diaspro* are stationed S of Sardinia, and *Dessiè* and *Tembien* off Malta. On 26 Nov the Italian Fleet Commander, Sqdn Adm Campioni, with the battleships *Giulio Cesare* and *Vittorio Veneto*, the 13th DD Flotilla (comprising *Granatiere*, *Fuciliere*, *Bersagliere* and *Alpino*), the 7th DD Flotilla (comprising *Freccia*, *Saetta* and *Dardo*) and the Commander of the 2nd Sqdn, Sqdn Adm Iachino, with the 1st Cruiser Div, consisting of *Pola* (F), *Fiume*, (Div Adm Matteucci), *Gorizia* and the 9th DD Flotilla (comprising *Alfieri*, *Carducci*, *Gioberti* and *Oriani*) set out from Naples; and the 3rd Cruiser Div (Div Adm Sansonetti), consisting of *Trieste*, *Trento*, *Bolzano* and the 12th DD Flotilla (comprising *Lanciere*, *Ascari* and *Carabinieri* (from Messina to intercept the forces coming from the W. Of the boats of the 10th TB Flotilla *Alcione*, *Vega*, *Sagittario* and *Sirio* sent into the Sicilian Channel from Trapani, the last fires unnoticed torpedoes at Force D in the night 26-27 Nov.

After reconnaissance aircraft from the *Ark Royal* have sighted elements of the Italian Fleet on the morning of 27 Nov, Admiral Somerville joins up two hours later with Force D approaching from the E. He orders the convoy with the three transports, the four corvettes and the destroyers *Duncan* and *Wishart*, as well as the cruiser *Coventry* coming from Force D and its destroyers, to proceed to the SE whilst he himself sails to meet the Italian Fleet with the *Ramillies* and *Renown*, the cruisers *Manchester*, *Sheffield*, *Newcastle* and *Berwick* and destroyers. Attacks by torpedo aircraft from the *Ark Royal*, escorted by the destroyers *Jaguar* and *Kelvin*, on *Vittorio Veneto* and *Pola* are out-manoeuvred. In an engagement of about one hour between the cruisers and battleships the Italians obtain a hit on the *Berwick* and the Italian destroyer *Lanciere*, having received a heavy hit, is taken in tow. Then Admiral Campioni breaks off the battle because he believes, on the basis of inadequate air reconnaissance, that he faces superior enemy forces.
Two attempted attacks by the Italian submarines *Dessiè* and *Tembien* in the night of 27-28 Nov on the 3rd Cruiser Sqdn sent to the Sicilian Channel to support the convoy are unsuccessful.
24 Nov-26 Dec   North Atlantic
The two last Italian submarines *Mocenigo* and *Velella* are transferred to the Atlantic. In operations between the Portuguese coast and the Azores, *Mocenigo* (Cdr Agostini) attacks the convoy OG.47 and sinks one ship of 1253 tons on 21 Dec. A gun attack on a scattered ship on 22 Dec has no great effect.
25 Nov-18 Dec   Norway
In operations off Norway the British submarine *Sunfish* attacks convoys on 25 Nov and 5 Dec and sinks the Finnish steamer *Oscar Midling* (2182 tons) from the second. The Dutch submarine *O21* operates in the Northern North Sea and the French *Rubis* off Norway.
26 Nov   Pacific
Auxiliary cruisers *Schiff 45 Komet* (Capt Eyssen) and *Schiff 36 Orion* (Cdr* Weyher) sink the British passenger ship *Rangitane* (16712 tons) NE of Auckland, New Zealand.

28 Nov   Mediterranean
The Italian 15th DD Flotilla, consisting of *Pigafetta, Da Recco, Pessagno* and *Riboty* and the attached torpedo boats *Bassini* and *Prestinari*, shell Greek positions NE of Corfu with some 1600 rounds of 12cm and 10.2cm shells.

28-29 Nov   English Channel
Second sortie by the Officer Commanding Destroyers (Capt Bey) with the destroyers *Karl Galster, Hans Lody* and *Richard Beitzen* off Plymouth. Two small ships of 424 tons are sunk and the British destroyer *Javelin* torpedoed.

30 Nov-1 Dec   Air War/Britain
Heavy German air attack on Southampton.

1 Dec   North Sea
The Norwegian passenger ship *Oslofjord* (18673 tons) and a British tanker (6990 tons) sink on German aircraft mines off the Tyne Estuary.

1 Dec   South Atlantic
The British auxiliary cruiser *Calvin Castle* stops the Brazilian steamer *Itape* off the Brazilian coast and takes off 22 German citizens.

1-11 Dec   Mediterranean
The Italian submarines *Da Procida* and *Jalea* operate SW of Corfu. *Ametista, Jantina* and *Zaffiro* are employed in the Aegean.

1-19 Dec   Central Atlantic
In a southern operation *U37* (Lt-Cdr Clausen) sinks four small ships of 6814 tons W of Spain from 1 Dec to 4 Dec, one trawler of 223 tons W of Morocco on 16 Dec and, in error, the Vichy French submarine *Sfax* and the naval tanker *Lot* (2785 tons) on 19 Dec. Because of her high expenditure of torpedoes, the boat receives orders to return.

2 Dec   North Sea
Admiral Sir C. Forbes is succeeded as Commander-in-Chief, Home Fleet, by Admiral Sir J. C. Tovey. At this time the Home Fleet has, at its disposal, the battleships *King George V, Nelson* and *Rodney*, the battlecruisers *Hood* and *Repulse* and 11 cruisers.

2-3 Dec   English Channel
Offensive mining operation 'Oskar' by the torpedo boats *Iltis* and *Jaguar* off Dover.

3 Dec   North Atlantic
Auxiliary cruiser *Schiff 41 Kormoran* (Cdr Detmers) leaves Gotenhafen on a mercantile warfare mission. Operational areas: Atlantic and Indian Ocean. The ship passes through the Denmark Strait unobserved by the enemy on 12-13 Dec.

3 Dec   Mediterranean
In an attack by Italian torpedo aircraft on Suda Bay the British cruiser *Glasgow* is badly damaged by two hits but can be brought back to Alexandria.

3-4 Dec   English Channel
Offensive mining operation 'Marianne' off Dover by the 5th TB Flotilla (Cdr Henne) consisting of the boats *Greif, Kondor, Falke* and *Seeadler*.

3-5 Dec   Red Sea
The Italian destroyers *Tigre, Leone, Manin* and *Sauro* and the submarine *Ferraris* search in vain for a British convoy.

3-11 Dec   Western Atlantic
The freighters *Idarwald* (5033 tons) and *Rhein* (6031 tons) try again to break out of Tampico. The *Idarwald* is pursued by the US destroyer *Broome* on whose reports the British cruiser *Diomede* comes up on 5 Dec. A prize crew cannot save the ship which is set on fire and sinks on 9 Dec on the Cuban South Coast. The *Rhein* is accompanied by the US destroyer *Simpson* which, with her relief, the destroyer *MacLeish*, also brings up the Dutch gunboat *Van Kinsbergen* in the Straits of Florida. The Dutch boat makes an unsuccessful effort to board. The wreck of the *Rhein*, set on fire by the crew, is sunk by the British cruiser *Caradoc* on 11 Dec.

5 Dec   South Atlantic
The German auxiliary cruiser *Schiff 10 Thor* (Capt Kähler) damages the British auxiliary cruiser *Carnarvon Castle* (20122 tons, Capt Hardy) in an engagement SE of Rio de Janeiro. A search for *Schiff 10*, started immediately by the British cruisers *Cumberland, Enterprise* and *Newcastle*, is unsuccessful.

6-7 Dec   North Atlantic
Heavy cruiser *Admiral Hipper* (Capt Meisel) passes unobserved through the Denmark Strait into the North Atlantic.

6-8 Dec   Pacific
The auxiliary cruisers *Schiff 45 Komet* (Capt Eyssen) and *Schiff 36 Orion* (Cdr* Weyher) sink, in the area of the British phosphate island of Nauru (Pacific), five ships of 25904 tons, including three

special ships for the transport of phosphates. The proposed disembarkation of a landing party of 185 men made up of the crews of both auxiliary cruisers has to be abandoned because of the unfavourable weather.

6-18 Dec Mediterranean
In operations in the Ionian Sea and off Durazzo (Albania) the British submarine *Triton* (Lt-Cdr Watkins) torpedoes one ship of 6040 tons but is sunk in the Strait of Otranto by the Italian torpedo boat *Confienza* on 18 Dec. On 6 Dec the British submarine *Regulus* is lost off Taranto, probably on a mine barrage. *Truant* (Lt-Cdr Haggard) sinks two ships of 9723 tons off Albania.

8-26 Dec North Atlantic
The U-boats *U96* and *U100* operate in the area W of the North Channel and mainly S of Rockall; and the Italian boats *Calvi*, *Emo* and *Veniero* between 15° and 20°W. On 11-12 Dec *U96* sinks four ships from the convoy HX.92 and on 18 Dec with her last torpedo hits one tanker from OB.259, But *U52* and *U100*, which are ordered to the scene, do not come up. Otherwise, the U-boats only attack stragglers and independents. *U96* (Lt-Cdr Lehmann-Willenbrock) sinks five ships of 37037 tons and torpedoes two ships of 15864 tons; *U100* (Lt-Cdr Schepke) sinks three ships of 17166 tons; *Calvi* (Cdr Caridi) one ship of 5162 tons; and *Veniero* (Cdr Petroni) one ship of 2883 tons.

9-11 Dec Mediterranean
Reorganization of the Italian Fleet. Admiral Riccardi replaces Admiral Cavagnari as Under-Secretary of State and Head of Supermarina; the former Commander of the 2nd Sqdn, Sqdn Adm Iachino, replaces Admiral Campioni as Fleet Commander. Reorganisation of the Squadrons: Flagship *Vittorio Veneto*, 5th Div (Div Adm Bruto Brivonesi): old battleships *Andrea Doria* and *Guilio Cesare* and one destroyer flotilla; 1st Div (Div Adm Cattaneo): heavy cruisers *Zara Pola*, *Gorizia*, *Fiume* and two destroyer flotillas; 3rd Div (Div Adm Sansonetti): heavy cruisers *Trieste*, *Trento*, *Bolzano* and one destroyer flotilla; 7th Div (Div Adm Casardi): light cruisers *Duca d'Aosta*, *Eugenio di Savoia*, *Montecuccoli* and two destroyer flotillas; 8th Div (Div Adm

Legnani): light cruisers *Attendolo*, *Duca degli Abruzzi*, *Garibaldi*, and one destroyer flotilla; 4th Div (Div Adm Marenco): light cruisers *Bande Nere*, *Diaz* and two destroyer flotillas. (4th Div directly under command of Supermarina).

9-17 Dec Mediterranean
A supporting force under Rear-Adm Rawlings is formed to aid the Western Desert Force in its offensive against the Italian Army in Cyrenaica. It is composed of four groups: Force A: Monitor *Terror*, gunboats *Ladybird*, *Aphis* and *Gnat*. Force B: Destroyers *Vampire*, *Vendetta*, *Voyager* and *Waterhen*. Force C: Battleships *Barham*, *Malaya*, one cruiser and seven destroyers. Force D: Carrier *Eagle*, three cruisers and three destroyers.
These units, particularly Forces A and B, carry out many shellings of Italian positions and supply routes on the coast. From 13 Dec the Italian submarines *Naiade*, *Narvalo* and *Neghelli* are employed against them. On 13 Dec *Neghelli* (Lt-Cdr Ferracuti) torpedoes the cruiser *Coventry*. On 14 Dec *Naiade* is sunk by the British destroyers *Hereward* and *Hyperion*.

10 Dec Mediterranean
OKW directive to transfer German Air Force units (X Fl.K.) to Southern Italy and Sicily.

11 Dec General Situation
Operation 'Felix' (Conquest of Gibraltar) is played down by OKW directive after an attempt to persuade Spain to enter the war has failed.

12-19 Dec North Sea
Large mining operation by German Air Force in the Thames Estuary. 12-13 Dec: 93 aircraft drop 183 mines; 13-14 Dec: 45 aircraft drop 89 mines; and another 28 are dropped up to 19 Dec. 12 ships of 20675 tons sink on these barrages up to the end of December 1940.

12-21 Dec Mediterranean
The Italian submarines *Ambra* and *Sciesa* operate SW of Corfu.

12-22 Dec Red Sea
The Italian submarine *Archimede* operates twice without result against reported ship movements in the Red Sea.

13-18 Dec North Atlantic
The Italian submarines *Bianchi* and *Brin* are transferred from Tangier to Bordeaux.

14 Dec   Mediterranean
British air attack on Naples. The heavy cruiser *Pola* is damaged.

15-16 Dec   North Sea
The German motor torpedo boat *S58* (Sub-Lt Geiger) sinks the Danish freighter *N.C. Monberg* (2301 tons) in a British convoy E of Yarmouth.

16-24 Dec   Mediterranean
Operations MC.2 (bringing a convoy through to Malta) and MC.3 (attack in the Strait of Otranto) by the Mediterranean Fleet (Adm Cunningham). While the battleship *Malaya* with three destroyers forms the close escort for the four freighters of convoy MW.5, the Fleet sets out from Alexandria on 16 Dec with the battleships *Valiant* and *Warspite*, the carrier *Illustrious*, the cruisers *Gloucester* and *York* and 11 destroyers. It joins up with the cruisers operating in the Aegean and carries out attacks with the aircraft from *Illustrious* on Italian airfields on Rhodes and Stampalia. In the night 18-19 Dec the *Valiant* and *Warspite* shell the Albanian port of Valona, while Vice-Adm Pridham-Wippell with the 7th Cruiser Sqdn (Cruisers *Ajax*, *Orion* and *Sydney* and destroyers *Janus*, *Jervis* and *Juno*) makes a sortie into the Strait of Otranto. On 20-22 Dec Admiral Cunningham enters Malta with the *Warspite*. *Malaya* proceeds westwards with three destroyers through the Sicilian Channel. Here the destroyer *Hyperion* runs on a mine off Cape Bon on 22 Dec: an attempt by the destroyer *Ilex* to take her in tow fails and the ship has to be abandoned. The force, to which two empty freighters from Malta also belong, is met S of Sardinia by Force H, comprising the battlecruiser *Renown*, the carrier *Ark Royal*, the cruiser *Sheffield* and six destroyers, which have set out from Gibraltar on 10 Dec. The carrier *Illustrious* attacks with her aircraft two convoys escorted by the Italian torpedo boats *Clio* and *Vega* on 21 Dec and sinks two steamers of 7437 tons from the second convoy.
Of the Italian submarines *Dessiè*, *Serpente* and *Bandiera*, operating in the Malta area, *Serpente* misses a destroyer of the *Malaya* force on 20 Jan.

18 Dec   Mediterranean
The Italian cruisers *Eugenio di Savoia*

and *Montecuccoli* with the destroyers *Pigafetta*, *Da Recco*, *Pessagno* and *Riboty* shell Greek positions and coastal batteries near Lukova, 30Km N of the Corfu Channel.

18 Dec   South Atlantic
The heavy cruiser *Admiral Scheer* (Capt Krancke) captures the British refrigerator ship *Duquesa* (8651 tons) in the South Atlantic. On receipt of the distress signal, which is deliberately not interfered with, three British squadrons are deployed against the cruiser: the cruisers *Dorsetshire* and *Neptune* from Freetown; the aircraft carrier *Hermes* with the cruiser *Dragon* and the auxiliary cruiser *Pretoria Castle* from St Helena; and Force K with the new aircraft carrier *Formidable* and the heavy cruiser *Norfolk* which is on the way to Freetown from Britain. The British search operations produce no results.

18-25 Dec   Mediterranean
Off the Cyrenaican coast the Italian submarines *Malachite*, *Settembrini* and *Smeraldo* operate without success against the 'in-shore fire support ships'.

18 Dec-1 Jan   Norway
The Dutch submarine *O23* operates off Korsfjord.

18 Dec-16 Jan   South Atlantic
The Vichy French submarines *Venguer*, *Monge*, *Pégase* and *L'Espoir* are transferred from Dakar to Tamatave (Madagascar).

19 Dec-18 Jan   North Atlantic
The U-boats *U95*, *U124* and *U38* operate W of the North Channel; the Italian *Bagnolini* and *Tazzoli* further to the W. They encounter only independents. *U38* (Lt-Cdr Liebe) sinks with *Tazzoli* (Cdr Raccanelli) one ship of 4980 tons and on her own one ship of 3760 tons; *U95* (Lt-Cdr Schreiber) sinks one ship of 12823 tons; *U124* (Lt Cdr Schulz) one ship of 5965 tons; *Bagnolini* (Cdr Tosoni-Pittoni) sinks one ship of 3660 tons and misses an A/S trawler *Northern Pride* on 1 Jan.

20-22 Dec   Air War/Britain
Two night attacks by the Luftwaffe with about 200 aircraft on Liverpool. In the harbour 19 merchant ships totalling 121678 tons are badly damaged and one ship of 1293 tons is sunk.

21-22 Dec   English Channel
Offensive mining operation 'S.W.a' by

the 5th TB Flotilla (Lt-Cdr Neuss) comprising the boats *Greif*, *Falke* and *Seeadler* in the Western North Sea.

21-30 Dec Mediterranean
The Italian submarines *Da Procida*, *Jalea* and *Salpa* are stationed in the Strait of Otranto against British raids. *Onice* and *Zaffiro* operate in the Aegean. *Zoea* carries out a transport mission from Taranto to Leros.

22-29 Dec Mediterranean
Greek submarines are employed against Italian supply traffic to Albania. *Papanicolis* (Lt Iatrides) unsuccessfully attacks a convoy on 22 Dec and sinks one ship of 3952 tons on 24 Dec. *Proteus* (Lt-Cdr Hazikostantis) sinks the Italian transport *Sardegna* (11452 tons) in a convoy on 29 Dec but, in a counter-attack, is rammed and sunk by the Italian torpedo boat *Antares*. The Greek submarine *Katsonis* (Sub-Lt Spanides) torpedoes on 31 Dec one small ship of 531 tons which becomes a total loss.

23-24 Dec English Channel
In an attack on the convoy FN.366 off the British South Coast by the 1st MTB Flotilla, consisting of *S26*, *S28*, *S29*, *S34*, *S56*, *S58* and *S59*, *S59* (Lt Albert Müller) sinks the Dutch freighter *Stad Maastricht* (6552 tons) and *S28* (Lt Klug) the British trawler *Pelton* (358 tons).

23-30 Dec Red Sea
The Italian submarine *Ferraris* operates off Port Sudan.

24-27 Dec North Atlantic
The German heavy cruiser *Admiral Hipper* (Capt Meisel) encounters about 700 nautical miles W of Cape Finisterre the British troop convoy WS.5A (20 ships, including five provided for the Operation 'Excess') proceeding south-

wards. The convoy is escorted by the cruisers *Berwick*, *Bonaventure* and *Dunedin* and accompanied by the carriers *Argus* and *Furious* destined for Takoradi with aircraft cargoes. On the morning of 25 Dec there is a brief engagement between the *Hipper* and the *Berwick* which receives two hits. In an attack on the convoy the transport *Empire Trooper* (13994 tons) and another ship are damaged. Because of the strong escort and the state of the *Hipper's* engines, Meisel breaks off the engagement and heads for Brest. As she withdraws, one independent (6078 tons) is sunk. On 27 Dec the cruiser arrives in Brest. On the British side, the cruiser *Naiad*, relieved by the *Berwick* on 23 Dec, is again sent to the convoy, while the cruiser *Kenya* covers the two SL convoys and the battlecruiser *Repulse* with the cruiser *Nigeria* covers the North Atlantic convoys. Force H puts to sea from Gibraltar with the battlecruiser *Renown*, the carrier *Ark Royal*, the cruiser *Sheffield* and destroyers but suffers considerable damage in a heavy storm.

27 Dec Pacific
Auxiliary cruiser *Schiff 45 Komet* (Capt Eyssen) shells the British island of Nauru (Pacific): phosphate loading equipment, oil tanks, etc., are destroyed.

28 Dec-2 Jan Arctic
First attempt by the German battleships *Gneisenau* and *Scharnhorst*, under the orders of the Fleet Commander, Admiral Lütjens, to break out into the North Atlantic to undertake mercantile warfare operations there. The operation has to be abandoned off Norway because of storm damage to *Gneisenau*.

31 Dec-7 Jan Mediterranean
The Italian submarine *Dagabur* operates off the Cyrenaican coast.

1941

1 Jan   Gibraltar/Mediterranean
Five British destroyers stop a French convoy of four ships escorted by an armed trawler off Oran, after it has previously passed through the Straits of Gibraltar. The ships are captured. The destroyer *Jaguar* fires an m.g. burst near the passenger ship *Chantilly*, which, in the cross-fire, sustains two dead and four wounded.

1-12 Jan   Mediterranean
In the Eastern Mediterranean the Italian submarines *Turchese*, *Ambra* and *Corridoni* operate in the Strait of Otranto; *Galatea* and *Tembien* off Derna; and *Beilul* and *Delfino* in the Aegean. No successes.

1-18 Jan   North Atlantic
The German U-boats *U38* and *U124* operate W of the North Channel and the Italian *Nani*, *Da Vinci* and *Glauco* W of that. In trying to attack a convoy on 7 Jan *Nani* is sunk by the British corvette *Anemone*.

1-20 Jan   Central Atlantic
In operations in the area of the Azores and Canaries the Italian submarine *Cappellini* (Cdr Todaro) sinks two ships of 14051 tons in gun engagements.

2-3 Jan   Mediterranean
British attack on Bardia which is encircled. After harassing fire from the British monitor *Terror* and several gunboats on 2 Jan, Admiral Cunningham carries out a heavy coastal shelling early on 3 Jan with the battleships *Warspite*, *Valiant* and *Barham* and seven destroyers, while aircraft from the *Illustrious* act as artillery spotters. On 5 Jan the remains of the Italian garrison capitulate.

4-5 Jan   Air War/Western Europe
54 aircraft of RAF Bomber Command attack German warships in Brest.

5-15 Jan   Mediterranean
The large British submarines of the 1st SM Flotilla (Capt Raw) stationed in Alexandria, operate, sometimes with short stays in Malta, in the Western and Central Mediterranean and against the Italian supply route between Tripoli and Benghazi. The Greek submarines operate on the Albanian-Greek coast in the Ionian Sea.

On 7 Jan the Free French submarine *Narval* is sunk off Tobruk by the Italian torpedo boat *Clio*. On 9 Jan *Pandora* (Lt-Cdr Linton) sinks two ships of 8115 tons off Sardinia and *Parthian* (Lt-Cdr Rimington) one ship of 4208 tons off Calabria. On 15 Jan *Regent* (Lt-Cdr Browne) sinks the steamer *Città di Messina* (2472 tons), accompanied by the torpedo boat *Centauro* off Benghazi. The first missions of the newly-formed 10th SM Flotilla (Cdr Simpson) with *Upright* and *Ursula*, operating from Malta, on the Trapani-Tripoli route, are unsuccessful.

6 Jan   Mediterranean
The Italian 9th DD Flotilla, consisting of *Alfieri*, *Carducci*, *Fulmine* and *Gioberti*, and the 14th TB Flotilla, comprising *Partenope*, *Pallade*, *Andromeda* and *Altair*, shell Greek positions on the front in Albania.

6-13 Jan   Mediterranean
Operation 'Excess': convoy operations to Malta and Piraeus. 6 Jan: The convoy 'Excess' (Operation MC.4) with the motor ship *Essex* (11063 tons), carrying 4000 tons of ammunition, 3000 tons of seed potatoes and 12 Hurricane fighters for Malta, and the freighters *Clan Cumming*, *Clan MacDonald* and *Empire Song* for Piraeus, set out from Gibraltar. Escort provided by Force F comprising the cruiser *Bonaventure* and the destroyers *Jaguar*, *Hereward*, *Hasty* and *Hero*. Cover as far as the Skerki Channel provided by Force H, consisting of the *Malaya* and *Renown*, the carrier *Ark Royal*, the cruiser *Sheffield* and the destroyers *Faulknor*, *Fury*, *Forester*, *Fortune* and *Firedrake* which set out on 7 Jan.

73

7 Jan: Force B (Rear-Adm Renouf) puts to sea from the Aegean with the cruisers *Gloucester* and *Southampton* (with 500 troops for Malta on board) and the destroyers *Ilex* and *Janus* which are to meet the convoy. In addition, Force A (Adm Cunningham) comprising the battleships *Valiant* and *Warspite*, the carrier *Illustrious* and the destroyers *Jervis*, *Nubian*, *Mohawk*, *Dainty*, *Greyhound*, *Griffin* and *Gallant* (and later *Juno*) puts to sea from Alexandria to cover the operation. The cruisers *Orion* and *York* with the tanker *Brambleleaf* and the corvettes *Peony*, *Gloxinia*, *Hyacinth* and *Salvia* coming from Alexandria join the cruisers *Ajax* and *Perth* (RAN) in Suda Bay to form Force D (Vice-Adm Pridham-Wippell). The convoy MW.5½ with the freighters *Breconshire* (9776 tons) and *Clan Macaulay* (10492 tons) sets out from Alexandria, escorted by Force C, comprising the AA cruiser *Calcutta* and the destroyers *Defender* and *Diamond*, joined later by the four corvettes. Force A is located in the afternoon of 7 Jan by Italian air reconnaissance. The submarines *Aradam* and *Axum* do not approach.
8.1: Force B lands the embarked troops in Malta and proceeds to sea westwards to meet the convoy 'Excess.' The Australian cruiser *Sydney* sets out with the destroyer *Stuart* in an eastward direction.
9 Jan: Force A and Force D and *Sydney* meet 210 nautical miles SE of Malta. Force H and the 'Excess' convoy are discovered by Italian reconnaissance aircraft 100 nautical miles SW of Cape Spartivento. Attacks by 10 Italian S79 bombers are not successful. In the afternoon Force H leaves the 'Excess' convoy with Force F and Force B to proceed through the Central Mediterranean and then turns off to the W. The Italian submarines *Bandiera* and *Santarosa* do not approach.
10 Jan: The Italian torpedo boats *Circe* (Cdr Caputi) and *Vega* (Cdr Fontana) attack 'Excess' with torpedoes S of Pantelleria but are repulsed. *Vega* is sunk by the fire of the cruiser *Bonaventure* and finished off by a torpedo from the destroyer *Hereward*. The Italian submarine *Settimo* misses the British ships

with a salvo of torpedoes. The destroyer *Gallant* of Force A runs on a mine and is towed to Malta by the destroyer *Mohawk*. In heavy German and Italian air attacks on Force A, Ju 87s of I/St.G. 1 (Capt Hozzel) and II/St.G. 2 (Maj Enneccerus) obtain six heavy bomb hits on the carrier *Illustrious* and one light hit on the battleship *Warspite*.
The *Illustrious* has to put into Malta badly damaged.
11 Jan: Force B leaves Malta again and then runs into new air attacks. Ju 87s of II/St.G. 2 obtain a hit on the *Gloucester* (unexploded) and damage *Southampton* so severely that she has to be abandoned in the evening. Force H reaches Gibraltar.
12 Jan: Cruisers *Orion*, *Perth* and *Gloucester* with their destroyers meet Force A, W of Crete, and another force (Rear-Adm Rawlings) which has set out from Alexandria, consisting of the battleship *Barham*, the carrier *Eagle*, the cruiser *Ajax* and destroyers. Rear-Adm Rawling's group is to carry out a raid in the Dodecanese, but abandons this plan owing to the bad weather. Between 14 Jan and 18 Jan the units of the British Mediterranean Fleet return to Alexandria.

6-29 Jan   South Atlantic
On her way through the Atlantic, the auxiliary cruiser *Schiff 41 Kormoran* (Cdr Detmers) sinks four ships of 28399 tons including an aircraft transport and the refrigerator ship *Afric Star* (11900 tons). Search operations by the heavy cruisers *Devonshire* and *Norfolk* and the auxiliary cruiser *Arawa* have no success.

7-8 Jan   English Channel
Unsuccessful sortie by German motor torpedo boats against British convoy off the Thames Estuary. Offensive mining operation 'Renate' by the torpedo boats *Kondor* and *Wolf* off Dover. On the return *Wolf* (Lt Peters†) is sunk by a mine off Dunkirk.

7-8 Jan   Mediterranean
In the night 7-8 Jan the Italian destroyers *Vivaldi*, *Malocello*, *Da Noli* and *Tarigo* and the torpedo boats *Sagittario* and *Vega* lay the mine barrages X2 and X3 each with 180 mines N of Cape Bon.

7 Jan-4 Feb   North Atlantic
On 7 Jan I/K.G. 40 with FW 200/ Condor long-range reconnaissance aircraft is put under the operational command of the Commander U-boats, the first joint operations by U-boats and air reconnaissance. *U105*, *U94*, *U96* and *U93* operate W of the North Channel and Ireland; *U106* is detached as a weather boat; and W of the German boats are the Italian *Malaspina, Marcello* and *Torelli*. A FW 200 sinks one ship on 8 Jan while on reconnaissance flight. On 11 Jan a FW 200 sights an OG convoy but the U-boats are too unfavourably placed for action and only one steamer is sunk. On 14 Jan *U105* sights an outward-bound convoy but the attempt to direct 2 FW 200s to the scene with D/F bearings fails. However, on 15-16 Jan *Torelli* approaches the convoy and sinks three ships. On 16 Jan a FW 200 sights an outward-bound convoy: two steamers are sunk with bombs. *U96, U94, U106* and *U93* are deployed but do not come up; *U96* sinks the large passenger steamers *Oropesa* and *Almeda Star* sailing on their own and *U106*, the passenger motor ship *Zealandic*. On 20 Jan FW 200s sight two homeward-bound convoys and the only U-boat in the area, *U105*, sights an outward-bound convoy; but no successes are achieved. From 21 Jan to 23 Jan the FW 200s engaged in air reconnaissance sink seven ships. On 28 Jan a large reconnaissance operation is undertaken with five machines when an outward-bound convoy is found from which each FW 200 sinks or damages two ships. Of the U-boats *U94, U103, U52, U93, U101* and *U106* engaged, *U93* sights the convoy SC.19 on 29 Jan and sinks three of its ships. Of the U-boats which are directed at once to the target *U94* and *U106* come up and each sinks one ship.
In all, the following ships, inclusive of independents, are sunk in these operations: I/K.G.40 sinks 15 ships of 57770 tons, damages two which are sunk by U-boats and also damages three of 11593 tons. *U105* (Lt-Cdr Schewe) sinks one ship of 4843 tons and sinks one ship of 6516 tons damaged from the air: *U94* (Lt-Cdr Kuppisch) sinks three

ships of 12652 tons; *U96* (Lt-Cdr Lehmann-Willenbrock) two ships of 29053 tons; *U106* (Lt-Cdr Oesten) two ships of 13540 tons; *U93* (Lt-Cdr Korth) three ships of 20283 tons and sinks one ship of 2660 tons damaged from the air; *Torelli* (Cdr* Langobardo) four ships of 17489 tons; and *Marcello* (Cdr Teppati) one ship of 1550 tons.

8-9 Jan   Mediterranean
British Wellington bombers attack Naples. The battleship *Giulio Cesare*, which is lying in harbour, springs leaks after three near-misses. Then *Cesare* and the last undamaged battleship, *Vittorio Veneto*, go to La Spezia.

9 Jan   General Situation
Final abandonment of proposed operation 'Felix' (capture of Gibraltar).

9 Jan   Mediterranean
Renewed shelling of Porto Palermo (Albania) by the Italian destroyers *Ascari, Carabiniere, Folgore* and *Fulmine*.

10-11 Jan   Air War/Britain
Heavy German air attack on Portsmouth Harbour.

11 Jan   General Situation
Hitler's directive No 22: German forces are to help in the fighting in the Mediterranean. Inter alia, it orders the establishment of a German armoured defence force for Libya and its transportation to Tripoli from about February 20th.

12 Jan   North Atlantic
A troop convoy (WS.5B) leaves Britain for North Africa; 21 passenger ships of 418000 tons with 40000 troops on board, escorted by the battleship *Ramillies*, the cruisers *Australia, Naiad* and *Phoebe* and 12 destroyers.

12-20 Jan   Mediterranean
In the Eastern Mediterranean the Italian submarine *Smeraldo* operates E of Malta; *Menotti* and *Speri* off the Strait of Otranto; *Serpente* off Derna; and *Narvalo* and *Neghelli* (Lt-Cdr Ferracuti) in the Aegean. The latter torpedoes on 19 Jan the transport *Clan Cumming* (7264 tons) in a British Piraeus convoy and is then sunk with depth charges from the escorting destroyer *Greyhound*.

12-30 Jan   Norway
Among other boats in the British 9th SM Flotilla to operate off Norway are the Dutch *O21* and *O23*.

14-15 Jan   South Atlantic
The auxiliary cruiser *Schiff 33 Pinguin* captures in the Antarctic the Norwegian whale-oil factory ships *Ole Wegger* (12201 tons), *Pelagos* (12083 tons) and *Solglimt* (12246 tons) and 11 whalers of 3417 tons. Except for three whalers all ships reach Western France in March 1941, the whale-oil factory ships with 22200 tons of whale oil on board.

15-16 Jan   Air War/Germany
76 bombers of the RAF attack Wilhelmshaven.

16 Jan   Mediterranean
Air attack by XFl.K. on Malta; the cruiser *Perth* and a freighter are damaged, and the aircraft carrier *Illustrious* is again hit several times.

16 Jan-22 Feb   North Atlantic
Unsuccessful operation by the Italian submarines *Glauco* and *Marconi* off Portugal.

17 Jan   South China Sea
As a reprisal against Thai actions against Cambodia a French naval force of the naval C-in-C Indo-China, Rear-Adm Terraux, comprising the light cruiser *Lamotte-Picquet* (Capt Béranger) and the gunboats *Dumont-d'Urville, Amiral Charner, Marne* and *Tahure*, attacks Thai warships in the roads of Koh-Chang in the Gulf of Siam. On the Thai side the small coastal defence ships *Dhonburi* and *Sri Ayuthia* and the torpedo boats *Trat, Cholbury* and *Songkhla* with, in all, eight 20.3cm, eight 8cm and nine 7.6cm guns engage the eight 15.5cm, eight 13.8cm, four 10cm, five 7.5cm and two 6.5cm guns on the French side. In a two-hour engagement the French squadron destroys, without loss to itself, *Cholbury, Dhonburi* and *Songkhla* and severely damages the remaining ships.

18 Jan   Western Atlantic
The British auxiliary cruiser *Asturias* captures the Vichy French steamer *Mendoza* (8199 tons) NE of Puerto Rico.

18-20 Jan   South Atlantic
Heavy cruiser *Admiral Scheer* (Capt Krancke) captures three British merchant ships of 18738 tons in the South Atlantic.

19 Jan   Mediterranean
In a new attack by XFl.K. on Malta further hits are secured on the carrier *Illustrious*.

19 Jan   East Africa
Indian troops take Kassala and begin an offensive in Eritrea and Abyssinia.

21-22 Jan   Mediterranean
After the shelling of Tobruk and its military installations by the British monitor *Terror*, the gunboats *Aphis* and *Ladybird* and the Australian destroyers *Stuart, Vampire* and *Voyager*, the 6th Australian Div breaks into the fortress which is occupied on 22 Jan. 25000 Italian troops are taken prisoner. In the harbour the old cruiser *San Giorgio* is scuttled.

21-31 Jan   Mediterranean
The Italian submarines *Corallo* and *Diaspro* operate N of the Tunisian coast; *Colonna* and *Settimo* in the Eastern Mediterranean E of Malta; *Jalea* and *Millelire* off the Strait of Otranto; and *Dessiè* and *Salpa* off Derna. No success.

22-30 Jan   North Atlantic
New attempt by the battleships *Gneisenau* and *Scharnhorst* to break out into the Atlantic to take part in mercantile warfare (Operation 'Berlin'). On 22 Jan they leave Kiel. The report of their passing the Belt reaches London the next day. 25-26 Jan: Home Fleet (Adm Tovey) sets out from Scapa with the battleships *Nelson* and *Rodney*, the battlecruiser *Repulse*, eight cruisers and 11 destroyers and takes up a position to intercept S of Iceland. On 27 Jan part of the Home Fleet leaves to refuel. On 28 Jan the German ships, in trying to break through S of Iceland, encounter two British cruisers of the watch line and turn away in time to the Arctic for replenishment. They are sighted briefly by the cruiser *Naiad* as they turn off but immediately after she loses contact again.

23 Jan   North Sea
The Norwegian freighters lying in Gotenburg (Sweden), *Elizabeth Bakke* (5450 tons), *John Bakke* (4718 tons), *Tai Shan* (6962 tons), *Taurus* (4767 tons) and the tanker *Ranja* (6355 tons) break through the German mine barrages in the Skagerrak under the leadership of Capt Binney and are met by cruisers of the Home Fleet. The ships only just avoid a chance meeting in the Kattegat with the German battleships setting out for the operation 'Berlin'.

23-24 Jan   English Channel
Offensive mining operation 'Weber' off the British South Coast with the destroyer *Richard Beitzen* (Cdr v. Davidson) and the torpedo boats *Iltis* (Lt-Cdr Jacobson) and *Seeadler* (Lt-Cdr Kohlauf).

23-25 Jan   Mediterranean
The aircraft carrier *Illustrious* (Capt Boyd), which has been hit several times in air attacks, gets away from Malta to Alexandria after the dockyards in Malta have done emergency repairs sufficient to allow the ship to do 24 knots again. The ship then goes to Norfolk USA for repairs.

24 Jan-2 Feb   Indian Ocean
The auxiliary cruiser *Schiff 16 Atlantis* (Capt Rogge) sinks, in the sea area of the Seychelles, one freighter and captures two other ships totalling 17329 tons. The troop transport *Strathaird* (22281 tons), which is sighted, is not attacked: the freighter *Troilus* (7422 tons) escapes.

25 Jan-18 Feb   North Atlantic
The German U-boats *U103*, *U52*, *U101*, *U48*, *U107*, and *U96* operate W of the North Channel and Ireland; *U123* is detached to the W as a weather boat; and further to the W are the Italian boats *Baracca*, *Dandolo* and *Morosini*. The latter are relieved in the middle of February by a new group consisting of *Bianchi*, *Otaria*, *Marcello* and *Barbarigo*. On 3 Feb *U107* sights the convoy OB.279, but the *U123*, *U52*, *U96* and *U103*, which are ordered to the scene, do not get there; *U107* sinks one ship from the convoy and one straggler. Up to 18 Feb the FW 200s of I/K.G.40 which are sent on reconnaissance and the U-boats attack only independents and stragglers from convoys. The following ships are sunk:
I/K.G.40 (Maj Petersen) sinks three ships of 8793 tons and damages two ships of 15489 tons; *U123* (Lt-Cdr Moehle) four ships of 22186 tons; *U103* (Cdr Schütze) three ships of 22948 tons and one ship of 10516 tons together with *U96*; *U52* (Lt-Cdr Salman) two ships of 4662 tons; *U101* (Lt-Cdr Mengersen) two ships of 10699 tons; *U48* (Lt-Cdr Schultze) two ships of 8640 tons; *U96* (Lt-Cdr Lehmann-Willenbrock) five ships of 31975 tons

and one ship of 10516 tons with *U103* and one ship of 6999 tons with K.G.40; *U107* (Lt-Cdr Hessler) four ships of 18482 tons including the ocean boarding vessel *Manistee* with the participation of *Bianchi* which does not however secure a torpedo hit. *Bianchi* (Cdr Giovannini) sinks three ships of 14705 tons and slightly damages one ship of 7603 tons with gunfire (see *U107* above; see 19-26 Feb).

26-30 Jan   Norway
Minelaying group 'Nord' (Cdr* v. Schönermark, comprising the minelayers *Tannenberg*, *Brummer*, *Königin Luise* and *Hansestadt Danzig*, carries out defensive mining operation 'Pommern' from Stavanger, escorted by the torpedo boats *T5*, *T9* and *T12*.

27 Jan-3 Feb   Mediterranean
In operations by the first four boats of the 10th SM Flotilla against the Italian Trapani-Tripoli supply line, *Upholder* (Lt-Cdr Wanklyn) sinks one ship of 3950 tons on 27-28 Jan and torpedoes one steamer of 7389 tons from a convoy. On 30 Jan *Unique*, when attacking a convoy, is herself attacked by an escorting torpedo boat *Aldebaran* with depth charges.
The minelaying submarine *Rorqual* (Lt-Cdr Dewhurst) lays a barrage off Ancona on 28 Jan. In the Gulf of Sirte *Truant* sinks one ship of 1130 tons on 3 Feb and misses a convoy.

29 Jan   General Situation
Beginning of secret Anglo-American talks in Washington on joint conduct of war in the event of American entry.

29 Jan   Mediterranean
Seven He 111s of 2/K.G.4 (Capt Kühl) drop mines in the Suez Canal.

31 Jan   General Situation
First preparatory directive drawn up by OKH for 'Barbarossa'.

31 Jan-4 Feb   Mediterranean
Unsuccessful operation by the British Gibraltar Squadron (Force H) against Sardinia. 31 Jan: Departure of the Force, consisting of the battlecruiser *Renown* (Flagship of Adm Somerville), the battleship *Malaya*, the aircraft carrier *Ark Royal*, the light cruiser *Sheffield* and ten destroyers. 2 Feb: Torpedo aircraft of the carrier unsuccessfully attack the dam at Tirso (Sardinia) against a strong defence. A

proposed attack on Genoa does not take place because of bad weather.
4 Feb: Force H returns to Gibraltar. The British Mediterranean Fleet sets out for a diversionary operation. The submarines *Corallo, Manara, Santarosa* and *Tembien*, stationed S of Sardinia and in the Malta area against a British sortie in the Central Mediterranean, do not find any targets.

1 February   North Atlantic
Heavy cruiser *Admiral Hipper* (Capt Meisel) leaves Brest for her second Atlantic operation.

1-10 February   Mediterranean
The Italian submarines *Turchese* and *Uarsciek* operate without success on the Greek/Albanian coast.

1-15 Feb   Norway
Operating off the Norwegian coast are the British *Sealion* (Cdr Bryant) of the British 9th SM Flotilla, which sinks the Norwegian coaster *Ryfylke* (1151 tons) on 5 Feb, and the Dutch *O21* and *O23* and the Free French *Minerve*.

1 Feb-15 Mar   Bay of Biscay
In operations in the Bay of Biscay *Tigris* (Lt-Cdr Bone) sinks two ships of 3704 tons and *Snapper* is lost on a mine barrage. Among others, the submarines *Unbeaten, O21* and *O23* operate in the Bay of Biscay in the course of being transferred to Gibraltar.

2 Feb   Indian Ocean
The carrier *Formidable*, which is on the way to the Mediterranean to relieve the damaged *Illustrious*, makes a raid on the harbour of Mogadishu (Italian Somaliland) together with the cruiser *Hawkins* (Force K). After mines are laid by aircraft, nine Albacore planes attack shore installations (Operation 'Breach'). At the same time the cruisers *Shropshire, Ceres* and *Colombo* blockade Kismayu.

2-3 Feb   Red Sea
Unsuccessful attack on a British convoy in the Red Sea by the Italian destroyers *Pantera, Tigre* and *Leone* based on Massawa.

3-4 Feb   Norway
Mining operation 'Rügen' by the minelaying force off the Norwegian coast. Escort provided by the 2nd TB Flotilla.

3-4 Feb   North Atlantic
The battleships *Gneisenau* (Capt Fein) *Scharnhorst* (Capt Hoffmann) pass through the Denmark Strait undetected by the enemy.

3-4 Feb   Mediterranean
Air mining operation by 2/K.G.4 against Tobruk.

3-15 Feb   Mediterranean
Not very successful activity by British submarines off the North African coast. 3.2: *Truant* (Lt-Cdr Haggard) sinks one freighter of 1130 tons from a convoy off Benghazi and on the following day unsuccessfully attacks an independent. 11-12 Feb.: *Utmost* (Lt Cayley) attacks two outward-bound convoys off Tripoli and torpedoes one steamer on 12 Feb. 15 Feb: *Upholder* (Lt-Cdr Wanklyn) unsuccessfully attacks an Italian convoy proceeding to Tripoli near Buerat.

5-6 Jan   North Sea
In a sortie by *S30, S54, S58* and *S59* of the 2nd MTB Flotilla *S30* (Lt Feldt) sinks one British freighter (501 tons) between Ipswich and Newcastle.

5-7 Feb   Mediterranean
Large Italian convoys from Naples to Tripoli with the passenger ships *Esperia* (11398 tons), *Conte Rosso* (17879 tons), *Marco Polo* (12272 tons) and *Calitea* (4013 tons). Escort provided by the destroyers *Freccia, Saetta* and *Tarigo* and from 6 Feb by the light cruiser *Giovanni delle Bande Nere*, 9-11 Feb: the convoy returns with 5000 refugees on board.

6 Feb   General Situation
Hitler issues Directive No 23: principles guiding the conduct of operations against the British war economy.

6-11 Feb   Mediterranean
Attack on Genoa by Force H (Vice-Adm Somerville). 6 Feb: The Squadron leaves in three groups. Group 1: Battlecruiser *Renown*, battleship *Malaya*, aircraft carrier *Ark Royal* and light cruiser *Sheffield*. Group 2: Destroyers *Fearless, Foxhound, Foresight, Fury, Encounter* and *Jersey*. Group 3: Destroyers *Duncan, Isis, Firedrake* and *Jupiter*. Groups 1 and 2 leave Gibraltar shortly after the convoy HG.53 on a westerly course, but they turn round in the night and pass eastwards through the Straits of Gibraltar. Group 3 carries out a submarine search E of the Straits and then joins the other two groups. 8 Feb: on receipt of a report about British carrier aircraft S of the

Balearics Supermarina thinks it is a new supply convoy for Malta, whereupon a strong Italian naval force sets out under Adm Iachino: the battleships *Vittorio Veneto, Andrea Doria* and *Giulio Cesare* and eight destroyers from La Spezia; the heavy cruisers *Trieste, Trento* and *Bolzano* and two destroyers from Messina to meet up on the morning of 9 Feb SW of Sardinia. Simultaneously, Genoa is shelled by *Renown, Malaya* and *Sheffield* with 273 15in, 782 6in and 400 4½in shells. Of 55 ships in the harbour four freighters and an old training ship are sunk, 18 others receive slight damage from splinters and near misses; 144 dead. Severe damage in the city. The damaged battleship *Caio Duilio*, which is in dock, is not hit. The defensive fire of the Italian coastal batteries is unsuccessful because of poor visibility. The Italian fleet turns N when near the Straits of Bonifacio to intercept Force H. Thick mist impedes visibility with the result that the air reconnaissance provided cannot keep contact with the withdrawing British force. In addition, the reconnaissance aircraft are misled by a French convoy of six ships proceeding to Corsica, with the result that the Italian fleet misses the enemy. The *Ark Royal* makes a raid on Livorno with four destroyers; her aircraft mine the harbour entrance of La Spezia.
11 Feb: Force H returns to Gibraltar.

7-8 Feb Mediterranean
German air attack on Malta.

8 Feb North Atlantic
The battleships *Gneisenau* and *Scharnhorst* sight the British convoy HX.106 E of Newfoundland but the Fleet Commander, Adm Lütjens, does not attack when it is established that the convoy is escorted by the battleship *Ramillies*.

8-11 Feb Mediterranean
First convoy of troops and supplies for the German Afrika Korps proceeds from Naples to Tripoli, composed of the German freighters *Ankara* (4768 tons), *Arcturus* (2596 tons) and *Alicante* (2140 tons). Escort provided by the Italian destroyer *Turbine* and the torpedo boats *Orsa, Cantore* and *Missori*. 8-10 Feb: Convoy in Palermo because of Force H. On the return an

unsuccessful attack is made by British torpedo aircraft from Malta on 14 Feb.

8-12 Feb North Atlantic
Operations against the convoys HG.53 and SLS.64. On the evening of 8 Feb *U37* (Lt-Cdr Clausen) sights HG.53 with 16 ships SW of Cape St Vincent. *U37* sinks two ships on 9 Feb and then, in accordance with orders, maintains contact and by providing bearings helps 2/K.G.40 (Capt Fliegel) to approach. Around midday on 9 Feb it attacks with five FW 200s and sinks five ships of 9201 tons. In a second approach *U37* sinks a third ship on 10 Feb. The heavy cruiser *Admiral Hipper* (Capt Meisel) is directed to the scene by the reports from the contact-keeper. But on 11 Feb she finds only one straggler from the convoy, which has been meanwhile dispersed, and sinks her. In all, nine freighters of 15218 tons are sunk out of HG.53's 16 ships. In the night 11-12 Feb *Admiral Hipper* makes contact with the convoy SLS.64, consisting of nine ships and still unescorted; on the morning of 12 Feb she sinks seven ships of 32806 tons and severely damages two more. On 15 Feb *Admiral Hipper* arrives in Brest.

9-18 Feb Mediterranean
In the Eastern Mediterranean the Italian submarines *Speri* and *Topazio* operate off the Greek-Albanian coast; *Malachite* off Cyrenaica; and *Beilul* and *Sirena* in the Aegean—without success.

10-25 Feb Indian Ocean
To support the British offensive against Italian Somaliland from Kenya the C-in-C East Indies, Vice-Adm Leatham, forms Force T with the cruiser *Shropshire* (Capt Edelsten), the carrier *Hermes*, the old cruisers *Hawkins, Capetown* and *Ceres*, and the destroyer *Kandahar*. They support the advance on land with their fire.
The German supply ship *Tannenfels* sets out from Kisimayu on 31 Jan. On 10-11 Feb eight Italian and two German merchant ships set out in an attempt to reach Mogadishu or Vichy French Diego Suarez. Three Italian ships of 16758 tons have to scuttle themselves on 12 Feb when British troops approach and occupy the town on 14 Feb with fire support from the *Shropshire*. Of the ships which set out

five Italian of 28055 tons are reported by the aircraft of the *Hermes* and are captured by the *Hawkins*; the German *Uckermark* (7021 tons) scuttles herself: the German *Askari* (590 tons) and the Italian *Pensilvania* (6861 tons) are found off Mogadishu and destroyed by bombs and gunfire. Only the Italian *Duca degli Abruzzi* (2315 tons) and *Somalia* (2699 tons) reach Diego Suarez. On 25 Feb Mogadishu is occupied.

11-17 Feb   Mediterranean
In operations by the British 10th SM Flotilla east of the Tunisian coast *Unique* misses a convoy with the torpedo boat *Missori* on 11 Feb. *Utmost* (Lt-Cdr Cayley) torpedoes one ship of 5463 tons from a convoy with the torpedo boat *Centauro*. *Upholder* misses on 16-17 Feb a convoy with the torpedo boats *Cascino* and *Pilo*. From the 1st SM Flotilla *Rover* torpedoes one ship of 6161 tons and *Triumph* (Lt-Cdr Wards) lands a commando unit on the Apulian Coast which is to destroy an important water main near Foggia.

12-13 Feb   General Situation
Mussolini and Franco meet in Bordighera and Franco and Pétain in Montpellier.

12-14 Feb   Mediterranean
Second convoy of the Afrika Korps from Naples to Tripoli with the German freighters *Adana* (4205 tons), *Aegina* (2447 tons), *Kybfels* (7764 tons) and *Ruhr* (5954 tons). Escort: the Italian destroyer *Camicia Nera* and torpedo boat *Procione*.

13 Feb-1 Mar   Red Sea
Operation 'Composition': raid on Massawa by the British carrier *Formidable* which is on the way to the Mediterranean. On 13 Feb 14 Albacore aircraft attack the harbour and destroy the Italian steamer *Moncalieri* (5723 tons). Slight damage on warships and other merchant ships. On 21 Feb there is a second raid with seven Albacores used as dive bombers but they do little damage. Because the Suez Canal is closed by German air mines *Formidable* makes another raid from Port Sudan with five Albacores on 1 Mar. Slight damage.

14 Feb-3 Mar   Indian Ocean
From 14 Feb to 17 Feb the German pocket-battleship *Admiral Scheer*, the

auxiliary cruiser *Schiff 16 Atlantis* with her prizes *Ketty Brovig* and *Speybank* and the supply ship *Tannenfels* meet some 1000 nautical miles E of Madagascar for replenishment and exchange of information. On 15 Feb the convoy WS.5B (20 troop transports, including 11 of 17000 to 27000 tons) sets out from Durban with the cruisers *Australia* and *Emerald*. On 21 Feb it is joined off Mombasa by the cruiser *Hawkins*, while *Emerald* turns off with four transports to Bombay. The *Admiral Scheer* (Capt Krancke) has, in the meantime, advanced to the area of the Seychelles. There on 20 Feb she locates two merchant ships with her aircraft, takes the *British Advocate* (6994 tons) as a prize—she arrives in the Gironde on 29 Apl—and sinks the Greek *Grigorios C.II* (2546 tons). The third ship, *Canadian Cruiser* (7178 tons), is able to transmit a distress signal before being sunk on 21 Feb. This is received by the cruiser *Glasgow*, stationed in the area, which also receives a signal from the Dutch steamer *Rantaupandjang* (2542 tons) sunk by *Scheer* on 22 Feb. When *Admiral Scheer* is sighted on 22 Feb by an aircraft from the *Glasgow*, the British C-in-C, East Indies, Vice-Adm Leatham, deploys from Mombasa the carrier *Hermes* and the cruiser *Capetown*, the cruisers *Emerald* and *Hawkins*, which are relieved by the *Enterprise*, from the convoy WS.5B and the cruiser *Shropshire* from the Somali Coast. The Australian cruiser *Canberra*, relieved on 20 Feb off Colombo by the New Zealand cruiser *Leander* whilst with the convoy US.9 (3 troop transports which left Fremantle on 12 Feb), is sent from the Maldives. Until 26 Feb the ships search in vain for the *Admiral Scheer* which turns away to the SE and reaches the South Atlantic again on 3 Mar. In the meantime, on 20-21 Feb the Italian auxiliary cruiser *Ramb I* (3667 tons) and the German supply ship *Coburg* (7400 tons) break out of Massawa. After being detached from the convoy US.9 off Bombay, the cruiser *Leander* (Capt Bevan) sights on 27 Feb W of the Maldives the *Ramb I* (Lt-Cdr Bonezzi) which, after a short engagement, explodes. 103 survivors are rescued. On 4 Mar an aircraft of the

Canberra (Capt Farncomb) sights, SE of the Seychelles, the *Coburg* with the prize tanker *Ketty Brovig* (7031 tons). Both ships scuttle themselves when approached by *Canberra* and *Leander*. The Italian colonial sloop *Eritrea* and auxiliary cruiser *Ramb II*, which set out from Massawa on 18 Feb and 22 Feb respectively, reach Kobe on 22 Mar. The motor ship *Himalaya* (6240 tons), which sets out on 1 Mar, reaches Rio de Janeiro on 4 Apl.

18 Feb Mediterranean
II/K.G.4 drops mines in the Suez Canal. There is another mining operation in the night 22-23 Feb. Because of these and other mining operations the canal has to be closed several times for a number of days. This leads to heavy delays in shipping traffic. Among other ships, the aircraft carrier *Formidable*, which is to replace the damaged *Illustrious* (see 6-13 Jan) is affected.

19 Feb North Sea
Sortie by the 1st MTB Flotilla, consisting of *S28*, *S101* and *S102*, to the Thames Estuary. *S102* (Lt Töniges) sinks the British freighter *Algarve* (1355 tons).

19-22 Feb North Atlantic
Operations against the convoy OB.287. 19 Feb: The convoy is sighted by a FW 200 of I/K.G.40 which sinks two ships of 11201 tons. The U-boats *U73*, *U107*, *U48*, *U96*, *U69*, *Bianchi*, *Marcello* and *Barbarigo* are ordered to the reported position. 20 Feb: Two FW 200s again find the convoy and damage four ships, including a large tanker, totalling 18532 tons. But, because of the inexact reports of the location, the submarines are unable to get to the convoy on this day. 21 Feb: an FW 200 damages a tanker of 6999 tons which later in the day is sunk by *U96*. The submarine operation is then broken off.
On 22 Feb an FW 200 again succeeds in finding the convoy and in hitting an already damaged steamer. Total result: two ships of 18200 tons sunk and four ships of 18694 tons damaged. On 22 Feb *Marcello* is sunk by the escorting vessels, probably by the British destroyer *Montgomery*. The destroyer *Hurricane* and the corvette *Periwinkle* attack another submarine.

19-23 Feb Mediterranean
The British Mediterranean Fleet brings the convoy MC.8 from Alexandria to Malta. At the same time there are convoys to Greece. The Italian submarine *Dagabur*, stationed SE of Malta, does not see the forces.

19 Feb-6 Mar Mediterranean
In the Eastern Mediterreanean the Italian submarines *Menotti* and *Turchese* operate off the Greek-Albanian coast; *Settimo* E of Malta; and *Ambra* off Cyrenaica, without success. The submarines *Micca* and *Zoea* bring supplies from Tobruk to Leros.

21-22 Feb Air War/Germany
RAF Bomber Command attacks Wilhelmshaven.

21-25 Feb Mediterranean
The British submarine *Regent* (Lt-Cdr Browne) torpedoes one steamer of 5609 tons in a convoy of two German steamers and the Italian destroyers *Freccia*, *Saetta* and *Turbine*. The torpedoed ship is taken in tow by *Saetta*. On the next day a convoy with two Italian steamers and the torpedo boat *Montanari* approaching from the N is attacked near Kerkennah by the British submarine *Ursula* (Lt Ward) which torpedoes one ship of 5788 tons. The second ship is later sunk off Tripoli by *Regent*. On 24-25 Feb *Unique* and *Upright* miss convoys. On the Greek-Albanian coast the Greek submarines *Nereus* (Lt-Cdr Rotas) and *Papanicolis* (Lt Iatrides) report successes.

22 Feb North Atlantic
About 500 nautical miles E of Newfoundland the battleships *Gneisenau* and *Scharnhorst* sink five merchant ships totalling 25784 from a west-bound convoy which has dispersed.

22 Feb Mediterranean
Ju 87s of I/St.G.3 damage with bomb hits the British monitor *Terror* in Benghazi harbour. She sinks off Derna on 23 Feb in the course of an attempt to tow her to Alexandria.

22-24 Feb North Atlantic
Operations against the convoy OB.288. On 22 Feb an FW 200 of I/K.G.40 sights the convoy W of Ireland and damages two ships of 11249 tons. From a favourably situated patrol line consisting of the U-boats *U73*, *U69*, *U96*, *U107*, *U552*, *U97* *Barbarigo* and

G

Bianchi, U73 establishes contact a little later. After losing contact in the evening a new patrol line, consisting of *U73, U96, U69, U123, Barbarigo* and *Bianchi,* is ordered. By day on 23 Feb *U96, U73* and *U69* approach. The convoy turns away to the N and the FW 200s fly past. At midnight on 23-24 Feb *U96, U69* and *U95* attack at short intervals and sink first one and then two ships. In the morning of 24 Feb the convoy scatters; *U95, U96, Bianchi* and *U73* each sink one ship and *U96* and *U123* each another independent. In all, 10 ships of 52875 tons are sunk. The following sinkings are made by these U-boats returning from this operation, apart from those already listed (see 25 Jan-18 Feb); *U73* (Lt-Cdr Rosenbaum) one ship of 4260 tons; *U69* (Lt-Cdr Metzler) three ships of 18576 tons; *U95* (Lt-Cdr Schreiber) five ships of 24910 tons, including two, when she is employed later as a weather boat.

22 Feb-25 Apl   Central Atlantic
Southward move and first chapter in operations of a U-boat group in the area of Freetown. In the nights from 3 Mar to 6 Mar the U-boats *U105, U106* and *U124* refuel in Las Palmas from the German tanker *Charlotte Schliemann.* From 7 Mar to 8 Mar *U105* and *U124* operate against convoy SL.67 (see entry) and then the three of them proceed in line abreast to Freetown. While *U105* and *U106* from 15 Mar to 22 Mar locate the next convoy SL.68 and pursue it (see entry), *U124* is replenished from the auxiliary cruiser *Schiff 41 Kormoran* (18 Mar), and then operates for about four weeks off Freetown, when seven ships are sunk. After the convoy operation *U105* and *U106* go for replenishment from the supply ship *Nordmark* (28 Mar) but, before they can start their operations off Freetown, they are detached, after taking further replenishment from the *Nordmark* (7 Apl) in order to go to Rio de Janeiro, to meet the German blockade-runner *Lech* and to escort her through the Pan-American Security Zone. After two weeks *U105* is relieved of this task and goes to Freetown: *U106* meets the *Lech.* These two boats only operate off Freetown with the second

wave (see 26 Apl). *U124* (Lt-Cdr Schulz) begins her return on 20 Apl, having expended all her torpedoes. Total results (inclusive of SL.67): 11 ships of 52397 tons sunk. An operation by the Italian submarine *Finzi* in the area of the Canaries (23 Mar-7 Apl) produces no result.

23-25 Feb   North Atlantic
Operations against the convoy OB.289. On 23 Feb *U552* sights the convoy and keeps contact for *U95, U97* and *U108* which are ordered to the scene. While *U552,* as a result of torpedo defects, has no success in two attacks, *U97* sinks three ships in three approaches in the night 23-24 Feb and torpedoes one tanker. *U552* maintains contact until 25 Feb, but *U95* does not come up before the convoy is dispersed. Sinkings by the U-boats, some of which remain in the operational area until March—apart from those already mentioned: *U552* (Lt-Cdr Topp) two ships of 12749 tons; *U97* (Lt-Cdr Heilmann) three ships of 16761 tons and damages one ship of 9718 tons; *U108* (Lt-Cdr Scholtz) two ships of 8078 tons. At the same time *U147* (Lt-Cdr Hardegen) and *U46* (Lt Endrass) operate between the North Minch and the Faeroes. The former sinks one ship of 4811 tons from the convoy HX.109 on 2 Mar.

24 Feb   Mediterranean
Ju 87s of I/St.G.3 sink the British destroyer *Dainty* off Tobruk.

24-26 Feb   Mediterranean
Large convoy from Naples to Tripoli with the passenger ships *Esperia, Conte Rosso, Marco Polo* and *Victoria* (13098 tons). Escort provided by the destroyers *Baleno* and *Camicia Nera,* the torpedo boat *Aldebaran* with a covering force consisting of the light cruisers *Bande Nere* and *Diaz* with the destroyers *Ascari* and *Corazziere.* The British submarine *Upright* (Lt Norman) sinks the cruiser *Diaz* (Capt Mazzola) on 25 Feb.

25 Feb   North Sea
S30 (Lt Feldt) sinks the British escort destroyer *Exmoor* off Lowestoft.

24-26 Feb   North Atlantic
Operation against the convoy OB.290. On the afternoon of 25 Feb *U47* (Lt-Cdr Prien), newly arrived in the opera-

tional area, sights the convoy but is driven off by an aircraft. She again comes up shortly before dark. In the night *U47* sinks three ships in three approaches and torpedoes a tanker. As a result of her contact reports, the boats *U73*, *U97*, *Barbarigo* and *Bianchi* are ordered to the scene and, on 26 Feb, *U99* as well; but they do not come up. With the aid of bearings *U47* leads one FW 200 of I/K.G.40 to the area at mid-day on 26 Feb, and five FW 200s in the afternoon. They sink seven ships of 36250 tons from the dispersing convoy and damage another four of 20755 tons. This is the greatest single success registered by K.G.40. A straggler is sunk by *Bianchi*. On 28 Feb *U99* misses another straggler from the convoy OB.290 which *U47* then sinks. Total result: *U47* sinks three ships of 16310 tons and damages one of 8106 tons.

25-26 Feb   English Channel
The torpedo boats *Iltis* (Lt-Cdr Jacobsen) and *Jaguar* (Lt-Cdr Hartenstein) carry out the mining operation 'Augsburg A' off Eastbourne.

25-26 Feb   Air War/West
RAF attack on Brest in which Avro Manchester bombers are used for the first time.

25-27 Feb   Mediterranean
The British destroyers *Decoy* and *Hereward* land 200 commando troops and navy personnel on the island of Castelorizo (East of Rhodes). The gunboat *Ladybird* puts a detachment of Royal Marines in the harbour. Slight Italian resistance. *Ladybird* is damaged by air attack. On the two following days the Italian destroyers *Crispi* and *Sella* and the torpedo boats *Lince* and *Lupo* are able to land reinforcements from Rhodes and with their gunfire are able with the garrison to overwhelm the British landing party. Elements get away in the night. The deployment of the submarine *Galatea* produces no result.

26-27 Feb   North Sea
In a sortie by the 1st MTB Flotilla *S28* (Lt-Cdr Klug) sinks the British freighter *Minorca* (1123 tons) off Cromer.

28 Feb   Mediterranean
Air mining sortie by 2/K.G.4 against Tobruk.

28 Feb-1 Mar   Air War/Germany
British air attack on Wilhelmshaven.

1 Mar   General Situation
Bulgaria joins the Three Power Pact.

1 Mar   Atlantic
The US Navy forms a Support Force Atlantic Fleet (Rear-Adm Bristol Jr) consisting of three destroyer flotillas and flying-boat squadrons for convoy protection in the North Atlantic: Desron 7 (Capt Kauffman): destroyers *Plunkett*, *Niblack*, *Benson*, *Gleaves*, *Mayo*, *Madison*, *Lansdale*, *Hilary P. Jones* and *Charles F. Hughes*; Desron 30 (Capt Cohen): *Dallas*, *Ellis*, *Cole*, *Bernadou*, *Dupont*, *Greer*, *Tarbell*, *Upshur* and *Lea*; Desron 31 (Capt Baker): *Macleish*, *Bainbridge*, *Overton*, *Sturtevant*, *Reuben James*, *McCormick*, *Broome*, *Simpson* and *Truxton*.

1-3 Mar   Mediterranean
Supply convoy for the Afrika Korps from Naples to Tripoli: four steamers escorted by three torpedo boats. At the same time a return convoy of five steamers with a destroyer and three torpedo boats. No losses.

1-4 Mar   Indian Ocean/Atlantic
The last Italian submarines in the Red Sea set out from Massawa for Bordeaux via the Cape of Good Hope: *Perla* (Lt-Cdr Napp), *Archimede* (Cdr Salvatori), *Guglielmotti* (Cdr Spagone) and *Galileo Ferraris* (Cdr Piomarta). *Perla* is supplied in the Indian Ocean on 29 Mar by the German auxiliary cruiser *Schiff 16 Atlantis* (Capt Rogge), the other boats in the South Atlantic on 16 Apl and 17 Apl by the Fleet tanker *Nordmark*. All four boats reach Bordeaux between 7 May and 20 May.

2-5 Mar   North Atlantic
Operations against the convoy OB.292. An FW 200 of I/K.G.40 locates the convoy OB.292 and sinks one ship of 6533 tons. A patrol line consisting of the submarines *U70*, *U108*, *U552*, *U95*, *U99*, *U47*, *Barbarigo* and *Velella* is formed for 3 Mar and 3 FW 200s are deployed. But the convoy is not found again. On 4 Mar an FW 200 sights the convoy and a new patrol line consisting of *UA*, *U70*, *U47*, *U99*, *U95*, *U108*, *U552* and *Velella* is formed for 5 Mar; but the convoy avoids the line which has been located by W/T interception.

2-17 Mar Mediterranean
The Italian submarines *Topazio* and *Uarsciek* operate on the Greek/Albanian coast and *Serpente* off the Cyrenaica.

3 Mar Norway
Operation 'Claymore': successful British raid on the Lofotens. Taking part: destroyers *Somali* (Capt Caslon), *Eskimo, Tartar, Legion* and *Bedouin*, the assault ships *Princess Beatrix* and *Queen Emma* with 500 commando troops on board. Covering forces: light cruisers *Edinburgh* and *Nigeria*. The fishery processing installations of Stamsund, Henningsvaer, Svolvaer and Brettesnes are destroyed: the patrol boat *Krebs*, three small fishery vessels and the merchant ships *Hamburg* (5470 tons), *Felix Heumann* (2468 tons), *Pasajes* (1996 tons), *Eilenau* (1404 tons), *Bernhard Schulte* (1058 tons), *Gumbinnen* (1381 tons) and *Mira* (1152 tons) are sunk. The Norwegian fishery vessel *Myrland* (321 tons) joins the British force. 215 Germans and 10 Norwegians are taken prisoner; 300 go voluntarily to Britain.

3-6 Mar Mediterranean
Supply convoy for the Afrika Korps from Naples to Tripoli: four freighters escorted by two destroyers and one torpedo boat. No losses.

5 Mar Mediterranean
The British submarine *Triumph* (Lt-Cdr Wards) sinks two ships of 1855 tons off Calabria.

5-6 Mar English Channel
Offensive mining operation 'Augsburg' by the torpedo boats *Iltis* and *Jaguar* off Eastbourne.

5-7 Mar Mediterranean
Return convoy from Tripoli to Naples: three freighters escorted by the auxiliary cruiser *Ramb III* and two torpedo boats. No losses.

5 Mar-2 Apl Mediterranean
Operation 'Lustre': transport of four British divisions from Alexandria to Greece. By 2 Apl 58000 are transported without significant loss. Air protection for the convoys provided principally by the AA cruisers, *Coventry, Calcutta* and *Carlisle*. In all, 25 ships of 115026 tons are lost in the operation, but mainly after unloading. Only seven ships in convoys. The Italian submarines *Anfitrite, Ondina, Beilul, Galatea, Malachite,* *Smeraldo, Nereide, Ascianghi, Ambra, Dagabur* and *Onice* which take their turns in the passage both sides of Crete and SE of the island have no success against the convoys. *Anfitrite* is sunk on 6 Mar by the escorting destroyer *Greyhound* when she tries to attack the convoy GA.8 E of Crete. On 30 Mar *Dagabur* attacks a British cruiser force from which *Ambra* (Lt-Cdr Arillo) sinks the cruiser *Bonaventure* on 31 Mar.

6-9 Mar North Atlantic
Operation against the convoy OB.293. On the evening of 6 Mar *U47* locates the convoy and leads *U70* and *U99* to it in the night 6-7 Mar, but she is herself temporarily driven off. *U70* (Lt-Cdr Matz) torpedoes two ships of 13916 tons in the convoy but is then sunk by the corvettes *Arbutus* and *Camellia*. Shortly after, *U99* (Lt-Cdr Kretschmer) sinks one tanker of 6568 tons and torpedoes the whaling-ship *Terje Viken* (20638 tons) which, later in the day, is finished off with further hits; but she survives as a wreck and only sinks finally on 14 Mar. In the evening of 7 Mar *UA* (Cdr Eckermann) makes contact but, after an attack which fails because of torpedo defects, she is badly damaged by depth charges from escort vessels. *U37* does not approach. In the night 7-8 Mar *U47* (Cdr Prien†) again approaches but is surprised in a heavy squall by the destroyer *Wolverine* (Cdr Rowland) and is sunk with depth charges.
During the night of 8 Mar *U74* (Lt-Cdr Kentrat) sights further to the N a homeward-bound convoy but has no success. *U99* and the Italian submarines *Emo, Mocenigo* and *Veniero*, which are ordered to the scene, do not come up on 9 Mar.

7-8 Mar North Sea
The 1st MTB Flotilla (Lt-Cdr Birnbacher) consisting of *S26, S27, S28, S29, S39, S101* and *S102* and the 3rd MTB Flotilla (Lt-Cdr Kemnade) consisting of *S31, S57, S59, S60* and *S61* attack British convoys off Cromer and Southwold. The 1st MTB Flotilla sinks five freighters of 7282 tons; the 3rd MTB Flotilla two freighters of 5852 tons, including the freighter *Boulderpool* (4805 tons) sunk by *S61* (Lt v. Gernet).

7-10 Mar   Central Atlantic
Operations against convoy SL.67. On the morning of 7 Mar the German battleships *Gneisenau* (Capt Fein) and *Scharnhorst* (Capt Hoffmann) sight the convoy some 300 nautical miles NE of the Cape Verde Islands. It is accompanied by the battleship *Malaya* and screened by the destroyers *Faulknor* and *Forester* and the corvette *Cecilia*. When he ascertains the presence of the battleship, Admiral Lütjens breaks off the attack on the convoy. On receipt of the contact report, the Commander U-boats orders *U105* (Lt-Cdr Schewe) and *U124* (Lt-Cdr Schulz), which are in the vicinity, to the scene. In the night 7-8 Mar they attack in turn and sink one ship of 5229 tons and four ships of 23259 tons respectively without, however, sighting the *Malaya* which is sailing with the convoy. *U105* is forced to submerge by a depth charge pursuit until the afternoon of 8 Mar and *U124* is driven off with the result that the battleships have to break off their operation. On 10 Mar the convoy is met by Force H.

8-12 Mar   Mediterranean
German supply convoy (four freighters, escorted by three destroyers) from Naples to Tripoli and return convoy experience no attacks.

9-10 Mar   Mediterranean
A German supply convoy for the Afrika Korps (four freighters, escorted by five destroyers and two torpedo boats), which had temporarily put in to Palermo, reaches Tripoli unmolested. Italian convoy from Trapani to Tripoli, consisting of five ships and the torpedo boat *Papa*, is attacked off the Tunisian coast by the British submarines *Utmost* (Lt-Cdr Cayley) and *Unique* (Lt Collett) which each sink one ship of 5683 and 2584 tons respectively.

10-11 Mar   Air War/Western Europe
First operation by four-engined British Handley Page Halifax bombers against Le Havre (six aircraft of No 35 Sqdn).

10-17 Mar   North Atlantic
The German U-boats *U99*, *U37*, *U74*, *U110* and *U100*, as well as the Italian submarines *Velella*, *Brin*, *Argo*, *Mocenigo*, *Emo* and *Veniero*, operate NW of the North Channel.
On the evening of 15 Mar *U110* (Lt-Cdr Lemp) sights the homeward-bound convoy HX.112 with 41 ships escorted by the 5th EG (Cdr Macintyre) consisting of the destroyers *Walker*, *Vanoc*, *Volunteer*, *Sardonyx* and *Scimitar* and the corvettes *Bluebell* and *Hydrangea*. *U99*, *U37*, *U100* and *U74* are ordered to the scene. In the night 15-16 Mar *U100* attacks twice and torpedoes one tanker of 6207 tons but is driven off towards morning. At mid-day on 16 Mar *U37* (Lt-Cdr Clausen) approaches but is driven off in the evening, whilst *U100* (Lt-Cdr Schepke) and *U110* have also to withdraw in face of the destroyers *Scimitar*, *Vanoc* and *Walker*. In the night *U99* (Lt-Cdr Kretschmer) is able to penetrate the convoy and to sink in several approaches three tankers and two steamers of 34505 tons and to torpedo one tanker of 9314 tons. Whilst *U99* withdraws, having expended her torpedoes, *U100* approaches from the stern but is located by *Vanoc* at a distance of 1000 metres with the aid of radar (first successful location with Type 286 equipment) and is rammed when she submerges. The *Vanoc*, damaged in the bows, takes the survivors screened by *Walker*. *U99* observes the two destroyers, submerges, but is located by ASDIC and is compelled to surface as a result of six depth charges from *Walker*. Six men from *U100* and Lt-Cdr Kretschmer and 39 men from *U99* are taken prisoner.
U110 follows the convoy until the next day but is not able to attack.

10-20 Mar   Norway
Among other boats, *Sturgeon*, *Sealion* and *Sunfish* of the 9th British SM Flotilla and also *Undaunted* and *Urchin* in 'working up patrols' operate off Norway. They achieve no success.

11 Mar   General Situation
The American Lease-Lend Law comes into force on its signing by President Roosevelt.

11-12 Mar   Air War/Germany
The RAF attacks Kiel and Bremerhaven.

12 Mar   North Sea
S28 (Lt-Cdr Klug) sinks the British motor ship *Trevethoe* (5257 tons) E of Orford Ness.

12-13 Mar   Air War/Germany
RAF Bomber Command attacks Hamburg and Bremen.

12-13 Mar   Mediterranean
Italian troop convoy from Naples to Tripoli, consisting of the passenger ship *Conte Rosso*, *Marco Polo* and *Victoria*. Close escort provided by three destroyers: distant escort by the heavy cruisers *Trieste*, *Trento* and *Bolzano* with three destroyers and one torpedo boat. No losses. At the same time a convoy pair for the Afrika Korps comes to Tripoli and returns to Italy without loss.

13 Mar   Air War/Britain
Heavy German air attack on Liverpool: one ship of 5644 tons sunk and seven others of 45114 tons severely damaged.

15 Mar   South-West Pacific
First troop transport convoy from Australia to New Guinea and to the Bismarck Archipelago. On 15 Mar the convoy ZK.1 sets out with two coastal steamers and the escort ship *Manoora* from Brisbane to Port Moresby and Rabaul. In April and from July to September three more convoys follow, transporting 3373 troops.

15-16 Mar   North Atlantic
The battleships *Gneisenau* (Capt Fein) and *Scharnhorst* (Capt Hoffmann) encounter in the Central North Atlantic the scattered ships of a dispersed convoy from Britain to America. *Gneisenau* sinks seven ships totalling 26693 tons and captures three tankers of 20139 tons, of which, however, only one is able to reach the Gironde on 24 Mar. At the same time *Scharnhorst* sinks six ships of 35080 tons. In rescuing the survivors of her last victim, *Gneisenau* is surprised by the British battleship *Rodney* employed in escorting the convoy HX.114; but, by skilful feinting, she is able to avoid an engagement with the slower but superior-armed opponent.

15-19 Mar   Mediterranean
In operations by the British 1st SM Flotilla, *Parthian* (Lt-Cdr Rimington) torpedoes one ship of 3141 tons on 16 Mar near Palmi; *Truant* (Lt-Cdr Haggard) penetrates the harbour of Buerat on 19 Mar but the torpedoes detonate by the pier behind the tanker *Labor*.

15-21 Mar   Central Atlantic
U-boat operations against the British convoy SL.68 off the West African coast. *U106* (Lt-Cdr Oesten) sights the convoy and leads *U105* (Lt-Cdr Schewe) to the scene. Taking turns to attack and maintain contact, the boats remain with the convoy for a week. *U105* sinks five ships of 27890 tons, *U106* two ships of 10113 tons and, without herself at first noticing it, torpedoes in the night of 19 Mar the battleship *Malaya* employed in escorting the convoy.

15-28 Mar   North Atlantic
The heavy cruiser *Admiral Hipper* (Capt Meisel) returns to Kiel from Brest. On 23 Mar she passes through the Denmark Strait unnoticed. On 28 Mar she arrives in Kiel. The cruiser's movements are unknown to the British Admiralty which, therefore, takes no special measures in the area of the Denmark Strait.

16 Mar   Mediterranean
Two He 111 torpedo aircraft of X Fl.K., in an armed reconnaissance flight, attack elements of the British Mediterranean Fleet 30 nautical miles W of Crete. They report torpedo hits on two large units—'probably battleships'. This false report has serious consequences for Italian naval operations.

16 Mar   Red Sea/East Africa
Operation 'Appearance': two Indian battalions and one Somali commando detachment are landed both sides of Berbera/Somaliland by Force D comprising the cruisers *Glasgow* (Capt Hickling) and *Caledon*, the destroyers *Kandahar* and *Kipling*, the auxiliary cruisers *Chakdina* and *Chantala*, the Indian trawlers *Netravati* and *Parvati* with two transports and *ML109*. The town is taken against only slight Italian resistance, which is broken by naval gunfire.

16 Mar-9 Apl   Mediterranean
The Italian submarines *Fisalia* and *Adua* relieve each other off the Greek-Albanian coast.

17-18 Mar   Air War/Germany
The RAF attacks Bremen and Wilhelmshaven.

17-29 Mar   North Atlantic
British operations against the German battleships reported by the *Rodney*. The Home Fleet tries to bring up the *Rodney*, from the convoy HX.114, and the *King George V*, sent to Newfoundland to cover HX.115, to the *Nelson* which is stationed with the cruiser

Nigeria and two destroyers to cover the Iceland passages, where they patrol from 17 Mar to 20 Mar. Force H sets out from Gibraltar with the *Renown*, *Ark Royal*, *Sheffield* and destroyers. On 20 Mar reconnaissance aircraft from the *Ark Royal* sight two of the tankers captured by the *Gneisenau*—*Bianca* and *San Casimiro*—which have to scuttle themselves when they come within sight of Allied ships. On the afternoon on 20 Mar a Swordfish sights the two German battleships but is only able to transmit its report after some delay with the result that an interception is no longer possible. The *Gneisenau* and *Scharnhorst* are met on 22 Mar by the torpedo boats *Iltis* and *Jaguar* and by mine destructor ships and reach Brest. Force H continues to search after contact is lost and, after brief refuelling in Gibraltar on 24 Mar, returns to the waters SW of the Bay of Biscay until 28 Mar. British air reconnaissance does not report the German battleships back in Brest before 28 Mar. Total result of mercantile warfare operation 'Berlin': 22 ships of 115622 tons sunk.

18 Mar   North Sea
Sortie by the 1st MTB Flotilla, comprising *S26*, *S29*, *S39*, *S55*, *S101* and *S102*, into the estuary of the Humber. *S102* (Lt Töniges) sinks the French freighter *Daphne II* (1970 tons).

18-19 Mar   Air War/Germany
Air attacks by the RAF on Kiel and Wilhelmshaven.

19-20 Mar   Air War/Britain
370 German bombers attack London. Heaviest raid since 29 Dec 1940.

19-24 Mar   North Atlantic
On 19 Mar an FW 200 of I/K.G.40 reports an outward-bound convoy W of Ireland to which are directed *U46*, the Italian *Brin*, *Mocenigo* and *Giuliani* (which is on the way to Gotenhafen). *U46* establishes contact and tries unsuccessfully to direct several FW 200s to the scene which, instead, find a homeward-bound convoy in the area and sink one ship of 5193 tons and damage one tanker of 8245 tons. In addition, they sight NW of the Hebrides an outward-bound convoy to which two FW 200s from Bordeaux and one from Stavanger, as well as the U-boats *U110*, *U74* and *U98*, are unsuccessfully directed for

20 Mar. At mid-day on 21 Mar *U69* sights W of Southern Ireland a homeward-bound convoy against which *U48*, *Argo* and *Mocenigo* are deployed without success. On 23 Mar *U97* sights in the area the outward-bound convoy OG.56 and sinks one tanker; on the next day *U97* and *Veniero* each sink one ship from the dispersed convoy. On the way out on 23 Mar *U551* is sunk by the British trawler *Vizalma* in the passage between Iceland and the Faeroes. Of the returning Italian submarines, *Emo* (Lt-Cdr Roselli-Lorenzini) has sunk one ship of 5759 tons and *Veniero* (Cdr Petroni) one ship of 2104 tons.

19-24 Mar   Mediterranean
With distant escort from the British Mediterranean Fleet (three battleships, one aircraft carrier and destroyers) the supply convoy MC.9 is brought to Malta without German and Italian air reconnaissance locating the forces. The Italian submarines *Malachite* and *Smeraldo*, stationed SE of Crete, do not sight the British forces.

22 Mar   Bay of Biscay
Beginning of the massive British submarine concentrations off Brest to provide against a break-out by the German battleships *Gneisenau* and *Scharnhorst*. In the following months *L27*, *Torbay*, *Tuna*, *Taku*, *L26*, *H31*, *H32*, *H33*, *H44*, *H50*, *O9* (Dutch), *O10* (Dutch), *Undaunted*, *Sokol* (Polish), *Sealion*, *Sturgeon*, *Sunfish* and *O24* (Dutch) participate.

23-31 Mar   Mediterranean
Off Valona the Greek submarine *Triton* (Lt Zepos) sinks one ship of 5451 tons in an Italian convoy accompanied by the torpedo boat *Castelfidardo*.
On 25 Mar the British minelaying submarine *Rorqual* (Lt-Cdr Dewhurst) lays a barrage near Capo Gallo W of Sicily, on which on 26 Mar two ships of 2902 tons from a convoy sink and on 28 Mar the torpedo boat *Chinotto*. *Rorqual* sinks with her torpedoes one ship of 3645 tons on 30 Mar and the Italian submarine *Capponi* on 31 Mar. On 28 Mar *Utmost* (Lt-Cdr Cayley) attacks a Naples-Tripoli convoy of five ships, escorted by the destroyers *Folgore*, *Dardo* and *Strale*; she sinks one ship of 1927 tons and torpedoes one ship of 5954 tons.

23 Mar-1 Apl   Red Sea

On 23 Mar the German-Italian steamers *Oder* (8516 tons) and *India* (6366 tons) set out from Massawa. The first is found by the British sloop *Shoreham* in the Straits of Perim and has to scuttle herself; the latter then puts in to Assab. In another attempt the *Bertrand Rickmers* (4188 tons), which sets out on 29 Mar, has to scuttle herself on 1 Apl in the presence of the destroyer *Kandahar*. The *Piave*, which sets out on 30 Mar, also goes to Assab; and the *Lichtenfels*, which puts to sea on 1 Apl, has to return.

25 Mar-5 Apl   North Atlantic

On 25 Mar the submarines *U48*, *U98*, *U69*, *U46*, *U74* and *U97* are gathered in a new concentration S of Iceland to operate with air reconnaissance on convoys, but the FW 200s of I/K.G.40 only find single ships and no convoys up to 28 Mar. They sink three ships totalling 19982 tons and damage the passenger motor ship *Staffordshire* (10683 tons). *U98* sinks an independent. On 29 Mar *U48* sights the homeward-bound convoy HX.115 with eight escort vessels and sinks two of the ships. *U98* does not approach. An FW 200 sights an outward-bound convoy which is found again on 30 Mar, but *U73* and *U97* do not come up. The convoy OB.302, sighted by *U69*, is shadowed on 29-30 Mar by *U46* and *U69*, each of which sink one ship. The attempt to direct *U73*, *U97* and *U101* also to the convoy OB.302, located on 31 Mar by two FW 200s, fails. *U46* sinks one tanker. A patrol line is formed for 2 Apl consisting of *U46*, *U98*, *U101*, *U69*, *U73*, *U97*, *U74* and *U76* against an outward-bound convoy reported by *U76* S of Iceland on 1 Apl. SC.26 runs into this patrol line in the evening. *U74* leads *U46*, *U69* and *U73* to the scene in the night and by morning they sink six ships of 33615 tons and damage the auxiliary cruiser *Worcestershire* (11402 tons)—the latter effected by *U74*. One of the partly scattered ships is sunk by day on 3 Apl by *U76*. In the evening *U94* re-establishes contact with the main body of the convoy and directs *U98* to the scene. Together they sink three more ships in the night totalling 13303 tons. On 4 Apl *U98*, *U101* and

U76 continue the operation. But only the latter fires another torpedo in the afternoon and sinks one ship. She is, however, herself sunk towards morning on 5 Apl by the destroyer *Wolverine* (Cdr Rowland) and the sloop *Scarborough*. In their operations since the HX.112 convoy the U-boats have made the following sinkings: *U110* (Lt-Cdr Lemp) damages two ships of 8675 tons; *U98* (Lt-Cdr Gysae) sinks four ships of 15588 tons; *U48* (Lt-Cdr Schultze) five ships of 27256 tons; *U97* (Lt-Cdr Heilmann) three ships of 20510 tons; *U94* (Lt-Cdr Kuppisch) two ships of 10994 tons; *U76* (Lt. v. Hippel) two ships of 7290 tons; *U74* (Lt-Cdr Kentrat) three ships of 15407 tons with *U73* (Lt-Cdr Rosenbaum) in a simultaneous attack on SC.26; *U73* also sinks one tanker of 6895 tons with *U69* (Lt-Cdr Metzler) and one ship of 4313 tons with *U46* (Lt Endrass). In addition *U46* sinks on her own one tanker of 7000 tons and *U69* one ship of 3759 tons.

26 Mar   Mediterranean

The Italian destroyers *Crispi* and *Sella*, coming from Leros, disembark six explosive boats (Lt-Cdr Faggioni) off Suda Bay (Crete). The boats penetrate unseen into the Bay, sink the Norwegian tanker *Pericles* (8324 tons) and put the British heavy cruiser *York* out of action.

26-27 Mar   North Atlantic

Pocket-battleship *Admiral Scheer* (Capt Krancke) breaks through the Denmark Strait on her way home and, unnoticed by the enemy, evades the British light cruisers *Fiji* and *Nigeria*. On 30 Mar the cruiser reaches the area off Bergen, anchors for a day in Grimstadfjord and, with destroyer escort, reaches Kiel on 1 Apl. Total result of the mercantile warfare operation: 17 ships of 113233 tons.

26-29 Mar   Mediterranean

Battle of Cape Matapan. 26 Mar: at the wish of the Germans and on the basis of a faulty appreciation of the situation (see 16 Mar), the Italian fleet puts to sea in order to attack British convoys to Greece under air cover to be provided by the German X Fl.K.

Taking part:

Battleship *Vittorio Veneto* (Capt Sparzani), as flagship of the Fleet with

Admiral Iachino on board, and the destroyers *Alpino, Bersagliere, Fuciliere* and *Granatiere* from Naples.

1st Div (Div Adm Cattaneo) comprising the heavy cruisers *Zara, Pola, Fiume* and destroyers *Gioberti, Alfieri, Oriani* and *Carducci* from Taranto.

8th Div (Div Adm Legnani) comprising the light cruisers *Duca degli Abruzzi, Garibaldi* and destroyers *Da Recco* and *Pessagno* from Brindisi.

3rd Div (Div Adm Sansonetti) comprising the heavy cruisers *Trieste, Trento, Bolzano* and destroyers *Corazziere, Carabiniere* and *Ascari* from Messina.

27 Mar: the divisions meet S of the Straits of Messina. The British cruiser squadron (Vice-Adm Pridham-Wippell) sets out as Force B: the light cruisers *Orion, Ajax, Perth* and *Gloucester* and the 2nd DD Flotilla (Capt Nicolson) comprising *Ilex, Hasty, Vendetta* and *Hereward* from Piraeus: and Force A (Adm Cunningham): the battleships *Warspite, Barham* (with the Commander 1st BB Sqdn, Rear-Adm Rawlings), *Valiant*, the aircraft carrier *Formidable* with the Commander Mediterranean Carriers (Rear-Adm Boyd) on board and the 14th DD Flotilla (Capt Mack) consisting of *Jervis, Janus, Mohawk* and *Nubian*. Detached later: Force C consisting of the 14th DD Flotilla (Capt Waller, RAN) with *Stuart, Greyhound, Griffin, Hotspur* and *Havock* from Alexandria.

Around mid-day British reconnaissance planes locate the Italian fleet. There is no sign of the German air cover. Admiral Iachino, therefore, abandons his plans to force his way into the Aegean because he can no longer count on the enemy being surprised. 28 Mar: in the morning Italian naval aircraft locate Force B. A pursuit engagement which starts between the British cruiser squadron and the 3rd Div is broken off on the orders of the Fleet Commander. The British cruisers now take up the pursuit themselves and come between the 3rd Div and *Vittorio Veneto*; but they are able, with the support of six torpedo aircraft from the *Formidable*, to break loose from the enemy. At mid-day the Italian Fleet returns and makes for Taranto. In the afternoon Swordfish torpedo aircraft from the *Formidable*

and bombers stationed on Crete attack the Italians and get a torpedo hit on both *Vittorio Veneto* and *Pola*. The battleship is able to continue on her course, but the cruiser is brought to a standstill and is rendered unmanoeuvrable. In the evening Iachino sends the remaining ships of the 1st Div to support the *Pola*. This group and Force A arrive almost simultaneously in the vicinity of *Pola*. Here the British, thanks to the radar locating of *Ajax* and *Warspite*, obtain a clearer picture of the situation than the Italians who can hardly see in the dark. In the ensuing engagement the British battleships annihilate the Italian division at short range. *Fiume* (Capt Giorgis†), *Zara* (Capt Corsi†), and the destroyers *Alfieri* and *Carducci* sink; *Oriani* gets away damaged and only *Gioberti* is not hit. The half-abandoned cruiser *Pola* (Capt Pisa), after the remaining 22 officers and 236 men have been taken off, is finished off with torpedoes and sunk by *Jervis* and *Nubian*.

29 Mar: Attacks by 16 Ju 88s of the German L.G.1 on Force A are not successful.

The Italian losses are about 3000 men, including the Division Commander, Admiral Cattaneo. British and Greek ships rescue 55 officers and 850 men; the Italian hospital ship *Gradisca* another 13 officers and 147 men.

27 Mar   General Situation
The Anglo-American staff talks in Washington lead to the drawing up of a basic strategic plan in the event of American entry into the war-the 'ABC-I Staff Agreement'.

30 Mar   General Situation
German, Italian and Danish merchant ships are seized in American harbours.

30-31 Mar   Air War/Western Europe
Unsuccessful attack by 109 RAF bombers on the battleships *Gneisenau* and *Scharnhorst*, lying in Brest.

30-31 Mar   Gibraltar/Mediterranean
A French convoy of six steamers, escorted by one destroyer, sets out from Casablanca through the Straits of Gibraltar, for North Africa and Marseilles. Because it is believed that 3000 tons of rubber are on the steamer *Bangkok*, coming from Indo-China (it has, in fact, already been unloaded

in Casablanca), Force H sends the cruiser *Sheffield* and four destroyers to seize the steamer. The French convoy is able to escape to the cover of the 15.5cm guns of the coastal battery near Nemours with the result that the destroyer *Fearless*, which has instructions to attempt to board, has to turn away.

1 Apl   English Channel
Aircraft of K.G.27 (Maj Ulbricht) attack a British convoy in the southern exit of the Bristol Channel and sink the tanker *San Conrado* (7982 tons) and *Hidlefjord* (7639 tons). Three more tankers totalling 26002 tons are severely damaged.

1-2 Apl   Mediterranean
Italian troop transport from Naples to Tripoli: passenger ships *Esperia* (11398 tons), *Conte Rosso* (17879 tons), *Marco Polo* (12272 tons) and *Victoria* (13098 tons), escorted by three destroyers and two torpedo boats. No attacks.

1-8 Apl   East Africa/Red Sea
Final battle for the Italian base of Massawa (Eritrea). After the destroyer *Leone*, which went aground on 31 Mar, is destroyed by her crew, the remaining seaworthy destroyers *Pantera*, *Tigre*, *Manin*, *Sauro* and *Battisti* go to sea on 2 Apl to attack Port Sudan. Captain Gasparini is in command of the operation. *Battisti* has soon to remain behind because of engine trouble and scuttles herself the next day off the Arabian Coast. On the same day aircraft of the British carrier *Eagle*, taking off from shore bases, attack the remaining force about 10 nautical miles off Port Sudan and sink *Manin* and *Sauro*. The two other destroyers are able to get away and scuttle themselves off the Arabian Coast. After the defenders of Massawa have beaten off some attacks, the enemy begins his big attack on 6 Apl following sea and air bombardment. This leads, two days later, to the fall of the town. The last operational motor torpedo boat *MAS 213* (Sub-Lt Valenza) torpedoes the British light cruiser *Capetown* off the harbour on 6 Apl. The motor torpedo boat is scuttled on 8 Apl with the torpedo boat *Orsini* and the motor torpedo boats *MAS 204*, *MAS 206*, *MAS 210* and *MAS 216* and many merchant ships shortly before the British enter the town. Among the latter, in addition to many small vessels, there are 11 Italian and six German ships totalling 89870 tons including the passenger ship *Colombo* (11760 tons). Apart from two Italian ships bombed beforehand, five other Italian steamers totalling 38125 tons scuttle themselves near the Island of Dalac and three others of 23765 tons in Assab on 10 Apl.

2 Apl   Pacific
The German motor ships *München* (5619 tons) and *Hermonthis* (4833 tons) scuttle themselves off Callao (Peru) to avoid capture by the Canadian auxiliary cruiser *Prince Henry*.

2-3 Apl   Mediterranean
German aircraft of X Fl.K. attack the convoys AS.23 and AFN.23 destined for Greece and sink three ships of 21155 tons including the motor ship *Northern Prince* (10917 tons).

2-5 Apl   Mediterranean
Operation 'Winch': 12 Hurricane fighters brought by the carrier *Argus* from Britain to Gibraltar are taken on board the carrier *Ark Royal* on 2 Apl. On 3 Apl with three Skua bombers they are flown off at a distance of 400 nautical miles to Malta where they all arrive safely. Escort provided by Force H comprising the battlecruiser *Renown*, cruiser *Sheffield* and destroyers *Faulknor*, *Fearless*, *Foresight*, *Fortune* and *Fury*. On 3 Apr one Cant reconnaissance aircraft is shot down by Fulmar fighters from the *Ark Royal*. The Italian submarines *Corallo*, *Santarosa* and *Turchese*, stationed N of the Tunisian coast and W of Malta, to cope with a British sortie into the Central Mediterranean, sight no ships.
Supply convoy for the German Afrika Korps from Naples to Tripoli: five freighters escorted by the Italian destroyers *Saetta* and *Turbine* and the torpedo boat *Orsa*. No attacks.

2-15 Apl   Mediterranean
The Italian submarines *Aradam* and *Onice* operate off the Cyrenaican coast.

2-18 Apl   Bay of Biscay
In the Bay of Biscay the British submarine *Tigris* sinks the tanker *Thorn* (5486 tons) off St Nazaire on 2 Apl. The submarine *Urge* (Lt Tomkinson), on the way to the Mediterranean, sinks on 18 Apl the Italian blockade-running tanker *Franco Martelli* (10535 tons), coming from Brazil.

**3-4 Apl   Air War/Western Europe/
Bay of Biscay**
RAF Bomber Command attacks the
German battleships *Gneisenau* and
Scharnhorst lying in Brest. At the same
time there are continual air mining
sorties against the approaches to Brest.
In addition to the mine barrages
(approximately 300 mines) laid at the
end of March by the minelayer *Abdiel*,
106 air mines are dropped in April.

4 Apl   Central Atlantic
The auxiliary cruiser *Schiff 10 Thor*
(Capt Kähler) sinks the British auxiliary
cruiser *Voltaire* (Capt Blackburn, 13301
tons) in a gun duel in the Central
Atlantic and rescues 197 survivors.

5-16 Apl   North Atlantic
Operation by Force H (Adm Somerville), comprising the battlecruiser
Renown, the carrier *Ark Royal*, the
cruisers *Fiji* and *Sheffield* and the destroyers *Faulknor*, *Fearless*, *Foresight*,
Fury and *Highlander* in the area W of
the Bay of Biscay to blockade the
German heavy ships in Brest.

6 Apl   Bay of Biscay
A Bristol Beaufort of No 22 Sqdn RAF
obtains a torpedo hit on the battleship
Gneisenau.

6-7 Apl   Mediterranean
11 He 111s of 2/K.G.4 (Capt Kühl)
carry out a mining action in the Bay of
Piraeus and secure a bomb hit on
the British ammunition freighter *Clan
Fraser* (7529 tons) lying in the harbour.
As a result of the explosion on the ship,
heavy damage is done to harbour
installations. Thirteen ships of 41942
tons, 60 lighters and 25 motor sailing
ships sink.

6-17 Apl   Mediterranean
Balkan campaign against Yugoslavia.
The Yugoslav Navy, which consists of
the training cruiser *Dalmacija*, the
destroyers *Dubrovnik*, *Beograd*, *Zagreb*
and *Ljubljana*, the submarines *Smeli*,
Osvetnik, *Hrabi*, and *Nebojša*, two
torpedo boats, three minesweepers and
three minelayers in Cattaro, four torpedo boats, ten motor torpedo boats,
two minesweepers and three minelayers
in Sibenik and the aircraft depot ship
Zmaj in Split, remains in harbour. In
Italian air attacks (186 bomber sorties)
the minesweeper *Malinska* and the
minelayers *Orao*, *Sokol* and *Kobac* are

damaged. On 16 Apl the submarine
Nebojša and the motor torpedo boat
Kajmakčalan and *Durmitor* (Capt Kern)
set out, break through the Strait of
Otranto, and reach Suda Bay on 22-24
Apl. On the day of the surrender (17
Apl) the *Zagreb* (Lt-Cdrs Masarat and
Spasiét) is blown up; the remaining
ships leave and are taken over by the
Italians by 25 Apl.
The Italian submarines *Salpa*, *Medusa*
and *Jalea*, detailed to guard the har-
bours, sight no targets.

6-29 Apl   Mediterranean
Balkan campaign against Greece and
the British Expeditionary Force.

7-8 Apl   Air War/Germany
RAF Bomber Command makes a heavy
air raid on Kiel.

7-30 Apl   North Atlantic
From 7 Apl to 16 Apl the U-boats
stationed SW of Iceland find hardly any
targets or convoys. *U108* (Lt-Cdr
Scholtz), ordered to watch the Denmark
Strait, sinks the auxiliary cruiser *Raj-
putana* (16444 tons) on 13 Apl. *U52*
sinks two independents. On 16 Apl an
attempt to operate against a convoy
sighted by I/K.G.40 SW of the Faeroes
and by *U96* W of Ireland fails. It is
suspected that the enemy recognizes the
U-boat concentrations and avoids them.
To obtain a better picture, a patrol line
consisting of *U65*, *U95*, *U96*, *U123* and
U552, is formed S of Iceland from 18
Apl and one consisting of *Da Vinci*,
Cappellini, *U110*, *U101*, *U73*, *Torelli*
and *Malaspina* W of Ireland, while
U147 is stationed near the Faeroes. On
22 Apl *Torelli* sights a homeward-bound
convoy but is unable to bring *U101* and
U110 to the scene; the same happens
with an outward-bound convoy on 23
Apl. Air reconnaissance with FW 200s
does not sight any convoys. On 28 Apl
U123 sights the convoy HX.121 to
which the five northern boats are
directed. When *U123* is driven off, *U96*
establishes contact and brings up *U552*
in the evening. This sinks one steamer
and torpedoes one tanker, the wreck of
which is sunk by *U201* on 2 May. *U96*
sinks two tankers. Later on 28 Apl *U65*
comes up and sinks one ship but is
herself sunk by the corvette *Gladiolus*.
The patrol lines formed on 29 Apl and
30 Apl by the remaining four boats are

avoided by the convoy which air reconnaissance also fails to find. In the S *U75* sinks the large steamer *City of Nagpur* on 29 Apl. The successes of the boats in this period are less. *U108* (Lt-Cdr Scholtz) sinks one auxiliary cruiser of 16444 tons; *U52* (Lt-Cdr Salman) two ships of 13993 tons; *U552* (Lt-Cdr Topp) three ships of 15970 tons and one ship of 8190 tons with *U201*; *U123* (Lt-Cdr Moehle) one ship of 6991 tons; *U110* (Lt-Cdr Lemp) one ship of 2471 tons; *U65* (Lt-Cdr Hoppe) one ship of 8897 tons; *U75* (Lt-Cdr Ringelmann) one ship of 10146 tons; *U95* (Lt-Cdr Schreiber) one ship of 4873 tons; *U96* (Lt-Cdr Lehmann-Willenbrock) two ships of 18408 tons; and *U147* (Lt-Cdr Hardegen) one ship of 1334 tons.

7 Apl–10 June   Western and North Atlantic
On 7 Apl the U.S. naval base in Bermuda is put into service. On 8 Apl U.S. TG 7.3 (Rear-Adm Cook) arrives to operate from here as the Central Atlantic Neutrality Patrol: carrier *Ranger*, cruisers *Tuscaloosa* and *Wichita* and the destroyers *Kearny* and *Livermoore*. On 18 Apl the boundary of the Western Hemisphere is advanced to 30°W. On 15 May TG7.3 is joined by the cruisers *Quincy* and *Vincennes*; in addition, the new destroyers of Desron 11, which are in the process of joining the fleet, are allocated to it: Leader *Sampson* (Capt Deyo) with *Eberle*, *Gwin*, *Grayson*, *Meredith*, *Monssen* and *Ericsson*, also the carrier *Wasp*.
After a directive on 7 Apl the following ships are transferred from the U.S. Pacific Fleet to the Atlantic: the carrier *Yorktown* with the destroyers *Mayrant*, *Trippe*, *Rhind*, *Mustin* and *Russell* in April. From 19 May to 23 May the following ships set out in three groups from Pearl Harbour: the battleships *Mississippi*, *Idaho* and *New Mexico* (Batdiv 3), the cruisers *Savannah*, *Brooklyn*, *Nashville* and *Philadelphia* (Crudiv 8) and the destroyers *Lang*, *Sterrett*, *Wilson*, *Winslow*, *Wainwright*, *Stack*, *Morris*, *Buck* and *Roe*; and from San Diego on 29 May the destroyers *Sims*, *Anderson*, *Hughes* and *Hammann*. They pass through the Panama Canal from 2 June to 8 June.

8–10 Apl   Mediterranean
Supply convoy for the Afrika Korps from Naples to Tripoli: five freighters escorted by three torpedo boats. At the same time a return convoy (see 2-5 Apl). No attacks.

8–14 Apl   Norway
The Norwegian destroyer *Mansfield* (Cdr Ulstrup) sails from Lerwick (Shetland) into Lopphavet (Northern Norway) and destroys a fish factory in Öksfjord on 11-12 Apl.

9–11 Apl   Mediterranean
Italian supply convoy from Naples to Tripoli: five transports escorted by one destroyer and two torpedo boats. No attacks.

9–30 Apl   North Atlantic
Unsuccessful operation by the Italian submarines *Baracca* and *Dandolo* W of Gibraltar.

10 Apl   North Atlantic
On the way to Iceland the U.S. destroyer *Niblack* (Lt-Cdr Durgin) attacks a suspected submarine contact with depth charges.

10–11 Apl   Air War/Western Europe
RAF Bomber Command, in an attack on Brest, registers four bomb hits on the *Gneisenau* lying in dock.

10–12 Apl   Mediterranean
Italian supply convoy consisting of two steamers and two tankers, escorted by the torpedo boats *Missori*, *Montanari* and *Perseo* from Palermo to Tripoli is unsuccessfully attacked by the British submarine *Upholder* off the Tunisian coast on 11 Apl. *Tetrarch* (Lt-Cdr Greenway) sinks one tanker of 2474 tons off Tripoli on 12 Apl.

10–20 Apl   Mediterranean
Units of the Mediterranean Fleet are employed to cover and support the withdrawal of the British Eighth Army in Cyrenaica between Tobruk and the Egyptian frontier. In the nights 9-10 Apl and 10-11 Apl the gunboats *Aphis* and *Gnat* shell Bomba and Gazala. On 12 Apl six destroyers, covered by the *Ajax*, *Orion* and *Perth*, make a sortie along the coast as far as Ras et Tin. On 13 Apl the destroyers *Griffin* and *Stuart* and the gunboat *Gnat* support operations near Sollum. On 15 Apl the British cruiser *Gloucester* and the destroyer *Hasty* bombard targets between Fort Capuzzo and Bardia and the gunboat *Ladybird*

bombards the airfield at Gazala. On 18 Apl *Gloucester* and *Ladybird* again shell targets near Bardia and Sollum. On 19 Apl the destroyers *Stuart, Voyager* and *Waterhen* and the AA cruiser *Coventry* set out from Alexandria with the transport *Glengyle* and carry out a commando raid against Bardia on the morning of 20 Apl. The Italian submarines *Malachite* and *Topazio* operate off the Cyrenaican coast without success.

12-13 Apl Air War/Western Europe
Renewed attacks by RAF Bomber Command on the German battleships in Brest, also on the U-boat base at Lorient and the Merignac airfield near Bordeaux, the base of I/K.G. 40 of Air Commander Atlantic (Col Harlinghausen) which is equipped with the long-range FW 200 bombers.

12-29 Apl Persian Gulf
After Rashid El-Gailani's coup in Iraq on 3-4 Apl, the convoy BM.7 (eight transports with one Indian brigade and one artillery group for Malaya), which is in Karachi, receives orders to proceed to Basra in the company of the Australian sloop *Yarra*. On the way the escort is strengthened by the sloops *Falmouth* and *Lawrence* (RIN). It is off Basra on 18 Apl where, in the meantime, the cruisers *Emerald* and *Leander* (C-in-C East Indies, Vice-Adm Leatham on board), the trawler *Seabelle* and the gunboat *Cockchafer* and 400 airborne troops have arrived. On 19 Apl the troops land. On 28 Apl a second troop convoy, BP.1, arrives, while in the Persian Gulf the carrier *Hermes* and the cruiser *Enterprise* are held on alert. On 29 Apl the troops of the second convoy land.

13-16 Apl Mediterranean
A convoy for the German Afrika Korps consisting of the freighters *Adana* (4205 tons), *Aegina* (2447 tons), *Arta* (2452 tons), *Iserlohn* (3704 tons) and *Sabaudia* (1590 tons), which is escorted by the Italian destroyers *Baleno, Lampo* and *Tarigo*, is intercepted on the evening of 16 Apl near the Island of Kerkennah by British Force K (Capt Mack), comprising the destroyers *Jervis, Nubian, Mohawk* and *Janus*. The convoy is completely destroyed. *Tarigo* (Cdr* de Cristofaro) sinks the *Mohawk* by

torpedo. On the next day seven Italian destroyers and torpedo boats, two hospital ships and sea rescue aircraft are able to save 1248 troops from the approximately 3000 embarked on the five freighters.

16-17 Apl Air War/Britain
681 German bombers attack London.

17 Apl General Situation
General Wavell receives permission from the British Government to make preparations for the withdrawal from Greece. The surrender of the Yugoslav armed forces is signed in Belgrade.

17 Apl North Sea
In an attack on a British convoy off Great Yarmouth by the 2nd MTB Flotilla (Lt Feldt), consisting of *S41, S42, S43, S55* and *S104*, two freighters of 2744 tons are sunk and a third freighter of 5673 tons is torpedoed.

17 Apl South Atlantic
The auxiliary cruiser *Schiff 16 Atlantis* (Capt Rogge) sinks the Egyptian passenger ship *Zamzam* (8299 tons) in the South Atlantic and takes the whole crew together with 138 American passengers aboard.

17 Apl Mediterranean
The British submarine *Truant* (Lt-Cdr Haggard) sinks two ships of 2753 tons and one sailing ship off the Cyrenaican coast. The submarine *Regent* (Lt-Cdr Browne) enters the Bay of Cattaro to take on board the British Minister in Yugoslavia.

18 Apl Western Atlantic
Formation of the Caribbean Patrol of the U.S. Navy: destroyers *Barney* and *Blakely*, Patron 51 with tender *Lapwing*.

18-20 Apl Mediterranean
Supply convoy from Palermo to Tripoli for the Afrika Korps (four freighters escorted by four destroyers and one torpedo boat). At the same time an Italian convoy (three freighters and two tankers escorted by five torpedo boats) from Trapani and Palermo to Tripoli.

18-23 Apl Mediterranean
Operation by the British Mediterranean Fleet (Adm Cunningham). 18 Apl; the battleships *Warspite, Barham* and *Valiant*, the aircraft carrier *Formidable* and the light cruisers *Calcutta* and *Phoebe* and destroyers leave Alexandria. The force accompanies the transport *Breconshire* (9776 tons) to Malta. On

the evening of 20 Apl the battleships with the light cruiser *Gloucester*, which has just joined the force, proceed to Tripoli, which is heavily shelled in the night 20-21 Apl. In the harbour, six freighters and one destroyer are hit and oil installations are set on fire. On the return *Valiant* is slightly damaged by a detonating mine.

23 Apl: the squadron enters Alexandria.

19 Apl Norway
The Free French submarine *Minerve* (Lt Sonneville) attacks a convoy off Stavanger and is herself then attacked with depth charges.

19-20 Apl Air War/Britain
712 German bombers attack London.

19-23 Apl Mediterranean
The Italian 7th Cruiser Div (Div Adm Casardi), consisting of the cruisers *Eugenio di Savoia*, *Duca d'Aosta*, *Montecuccoli* and *Attendolo* and the destroyers *Pigafetta*, *Zeno*, *Da Mosto*, *Da Verazzano*, *Da Recco* and *Pessagno*, lays E of Cape Bon the first part of the mine barrages S.11, S.12 and S.13 (321 mines and 492 explosive floats). The second part, consisting of 740 mines, is laid on 23-24 Apl.

20-30 Apl Mediterranean
The Italian submarines *Settembrini*, *Fisalia* and *Ondina* operate off the Cyrenaican coast and *Nereide* and *Turchese* off Alexandria.

21 Apl General Situation
Field-Marshal List receives the Greek surrender in Larissa.

21-22 Apl Air War/Britain
Heavy German air attack on Plymouth.

21-24 Apl Mediterranean
In attacks by Air Fleet 4 on shipping targets in Greek waters the old Greek battleship *Kilkis*, the destroyer *Hydra*, the torpedo boats *Thyella*, *Kios*, *Alkioni*, *Doris* and *Aigli*, three minelayers, one survey ship and 43 merchant ships, totalling altogether 63975 tons, are sunk. Supply convoy for the Afrika Korps from Naples and Palermo to Tripoli (five transports with close escort from four destroyers and distant escort from the light cruisers *Bande Nere*, *Cadorna* and two destroyers). After the convoy is located by British air reconnaissance, the destroyers *Jervis* (Capt Mack), *Jaguar*, *Janus* and *Juno* put to sea from Malta. They encounter on 23 Apl the

armed motor ship *Egeo* (3311 tons) which is sunk after a lengthy engagement. The convoy is able to evade the enemy.

23 Apl Atlantic
The auxiliary cruiser *Schiff 10 Thor* (Capt Kähler) reaches the Bay of Biscay after 322 days of raiding and arrives in Hamburg on 30 Apl. Total results: 11 merchant ships and one auxiliary cruiser, totalling 96602 tons, sunk and two more large auxiliary cruisers damaged.

24-25 Apl Air War/Germany
RAF Bomber Command attacks Kiel and Wilhelmshaven.

24-28 Apl Mediterranean
Operation 'Dunlop': Force H (Vice-Adm Somerville) comprising the battlecruiser *Renown*, the carrier *Ark Royal*, the cruisers *Fiji*, and *Sheffield*, and the 8th DD Flotilla with *Faulknor* and four destroyers, enters the Western Mediterranean in order to fly off to Malta 20 Hurricane fighters (brought to Gibraltar in the carrier *Argus*) with three Fulmar fighters from the *Ark Royal*. Because of the weather the take-off cannot take place until 27 Apl. On the same day reinforcements for the Mediterranean Fleet, consisting of the cruiser *Dido*, the minelayer *Abdiel* and the 5th DD Flotilla (Capt Lord Mountbatten) with *Kelly*, *Kashmir*, *Kipling*, *Kelvin*, *Jackal* and *Jersey* are dispatched to land reinforcements and to relieve the 14th DD Flotilla (Capt Mack). The cruiser *Gloucester* arrives in Malta on 24 Apl to reinforce Force K. On 28 Apl the reinforcements arrive. After unloading, *Dido*, *Abdiel* and the destroyers *Janus*, *Jervis* and *Nubian* and the empty transport *Breconshire* put to sea in the evening for Alexandria. The Italian submarines, stationed both sides of Malta, *Mameli*, *Manara*, *Settimo* and *Santarosa*, do not attack.

24-29 Apl Mediterranean
Operation 'Demon': evacuation from Greece by the British Fleet. In all, 50672 troops are embarked and brought to Crete and Egypt. The evacuation is carried out by Vice-Adm Pridham-Wippell with the light cruisers *Orion*, *Ajax*, *Phoebe*, *Calcutta*, *Carlisle* and *Coventry*, with destroyers *Stuart*, *Voyager*, *Vendetta*, *Waterhen*, *Vampire*,

Wryneck, Diamond, Decoy, Defender, Griffin, Hasty, Havock, Hero, Hotspur, Hereward, Isis, Nubian, Kandahar, Kingston, Kimberley, the sloops *Grimsby, Flamingo* and *Auckland,* the corvettes *Hyacinth* and *Salvia,* the assault ships *Glenearn* and *Glengyle,* 19 transports and many smaller vessels. The British army forces are mostly embarked on the open beach (near Raftina and Raftis) in Attica, at Nauplia, Monemvasia and Kalamata in the Peloponnese. The following are sunk by bombers of German VIII Fl.K.; the destroyers *Diamond* and *Wryneck* and the transports *Costa Rica* (8672 tons), *Pennland* (16381 tons), *Slamat* (11636 tons) and *Ulster Prince* (3791 tons). The Italian submarines *Settembrini, Fisalia, Ondina, Nereide* and *Turchese,* stationed between Crete and Greece, have no successes.

25 Apl-15 June   Central Atlantic
Climax of the submarine operations off Freetown. *U105* and *U106,* still belonging to the first wave, and *U107, Calvi, U103, Tazzoli, U38, UA* and *U69* (out on 5 May), which set out as the second wave from 29 Mar, operate in the area between the Canaries and Freetown. The operations of the German boats are in some cases considerably extended by fuel and torpedo replenishment from supply ships. *U105* and *U107* obtain replenishment from the supply ship *Nordmark* on 3 May: *U107* from the *Egerland* on 10 May; *U38, U103* and *U106* from the same source on 17 May and *UA* on 28 May and *U38* on 6 June. In their torpedo and gun attacks the submarines sink the following ships (inclusive of the operations against the convoys SL.67, SL.68 and SL.76): *U105* (Lt-Cdr Schewe) twelve ships of 71450 tons; *U106* (Lt-Cdr Oesten) eight ships of 44730 tons and torpedoes the battleship *Malaya*; *U107* (Lt-Cdr Hessler) 14 ships of 86699 tons—the most successful patrol of World War II; *U103* (Cdr Schütze) 12 ships of 58553 tons; *Tazzoli* (Cdr Fecia di Cossato) three ships of 17860 tons; *U38* (Lt-Cdr Liebe) eight ships of 47279 tons; *U69* (Lt-Cdr Metzler) five ships of 25544 tons and one ship of 2879 tons with a mine, as well as damaging one ship of 5445 tons.

U69 sinks, inter alia, the American steamer *Robin Moor,* in accordance with prize regulations, on 21 May, and lays seven mines each in the harbours of Lagos and Takoradi, on 25-26 May and 26-27 May respectively. *Calvi* and *UA* have no success. Owing to the loss of supply ships in connection with the operation 'Rheinübung'—it is planned to supply *U103, U107, UA* and *U69* from the tanker *Lothringen* on 18 June—the remaining boats have to return. In the process *U69* and *U103* get involved from 25 June to 27 June in the operation against the convoy SL.76 (see entry).

27 Apl   Mediterranean
German troops occupy Athens.
27 Apl   General Situation
Conclusion of an Anglo-Australian-Dutch planning conference in Singapore for the defence of the Malayan and Indonesian area with the participation of American observers.
29 Apl   North Sea
In a sortie by the 1st MTB Flotilla, consisting of *S26, S27, S29* and *S55,* in the area NW of Cromer, *S29* (Lt v. Mirbach) sinks the British freighter *Ambrose Fleming* (1555 tons).
30 Apl   General Situation
Completion of the Axis occupation of the Greek mainland including the Peloponnese.
30 Apl-1 May   Mediterranean
Supply convoy for the Afrika Korps from Messina and Augusta to Tripoli consisting of three German and two Italian steamers. Close escort provided by the Italian destroyers *Euro, Fulmine* and torpedo boats *Castore, Orione* and *Procione*; and distant escort by cruisers *Trieste, Bolzano, Eugenio di Savoia* and destroyers *Ascari, Carabiniere* and *Gioberti.* On 1 May there are many unsuccessful British air and submarine attacks. At the same time there is a return convoy consisting of four German and one Italian freighters escorted by the Italian destroyers *Folgore, Saetta, Strale* and *Turbine.* It loses two ships in two attacks by the British submarine *Upholder* (Lt-Cdr Wanklyn). Total loss, including a ship sunk on 25 Apl: 15410 tons.
30 Apl-12 May   Mediterranean
The Italian submarine *Ascianghi* oper-

ates in the area of Mersa Matruh and *Galatea* and *Sirena* in the Aegean.

1 May   Mediterranean
The Italian 7th Div (Div-Adm Casardi), consisting of the cruisers *Eugenio di Savoia*, *Duca d'Aosta* and *Attendolo* and the destroyers *Pigafetta*, *Zeno*, *Da Mosto*, *Da Verazzano*, *Da Recco* and *Pessagno*, lays N of Tripoli the mine barrage T to protect the harbour from shelling by British heavy ships (see 18-23 Apl).

1-7 May   Air War/Britain
In heavy air attacks on port installations in Liverpool 18 British merchant ships of 35605 tons are sunk and 25 others of 92964 tons are badly damaged. 69 out of 144 cargo docks are destroyed and the turnover capacity of the port is reduced to one quarter.

1-11 May   North Atlantic
U123, *U95* and *U96* are directed to an outward-bound convoy sighted by an FW 200 of I/K.G.40 on 1 May SW of the Faeroes. But neither they nor three FW 200s find it on 2 May. On 3 May *U143* sights a south-bound convoy S of the Faeroes, but *U141* and *U147* and I/K.G.40 do not come up on 3-4 May. On 4-5 May *U96* keeps contact with a homeward-bound convoy S of Iceland, but no U-boats or aircraft approach. On 6 May the Commander U-boats decides to search with the U-boats further to the SW, to forgo direct co-operation with air reconnaissance and to use the Italian submarines in their own operational areas separate from the German boats. On 6 May *U97* sinks W of the Bay of Biscay the British ocean boarding vessel *Camito* and the captured Italian tanker *Sangro*.
On 7 May an FW 200 sights the convoy HX.122 W of the Faeroes. *U95* sights the SC.29 off the North Channel and in the evening *U94* the outward-bound OB.318 south of Iceland when the 3rd EG (Cdr Baker-Cresswell) with the destroyers *Bulldog*, *Amazon*, *Broadway* and the attached auxiliary cruiser *Ranpura*, coming from Reykjavik/Hvalfjord, meets the convoy and relieves the 7th EG (Cdr Bockett-Pugh) with the destroyers *Westcott*, *Newmarket* and *Campbelltown*. But its sloop *Rochester* and the corvettes *Primrose*, *Nasturtium*, *Marigold*, *Dianthus* and *Auricula* stay

with the convoy. *U94* (Lt-Cdr Kuppisch) attacks, sinks two ships of 15901 tons and is then damaged by depth charges from the *Amazon*, *Bulldog* and *Rochester*. On 8 May the corvettes of the 3rd EG, *Aubrietia*, *Hollyhock*, *Nigella* and the trawlers *Angle*, *Daneman* and *St Apollo* come to provide escort and to relieve the corvettes of the 7th EG, which proceed to convoy HX.123. On the evening of 8 May *U110* (Lt-Cdr Lemp) makes contact with the convoy and in the morning directs *U201* (Lt Schnee) to the scene. Towards mid-day on 9 May *U110* attacks and sinks two ships of 7585 tons but is immediately forced to surface by *Aubrietia*'s depth charges and a boarding party (Lt Balme) from the *Bulldog* is able to take over the boat abandoned by the crew, before she sinks. *Broadway* is damaged in the manoeuvring by the hydroplane. Secret papers, a code machine and documents are recovered from *U110*. But the boat, which is taken in tow by *Bulldog*, sinks on 11 May on the way to Iceland. While *U110* is taken over, *U201* attacks the convoy which is still escorted by *Amazon*, *Nigella*, *Hollyhock* and *Daneman* and sinks one ship of 5802 tons and torpedoes one of 5969 tons. Damage is caused by depth charge attacks from *Nigella* and *St Apollo*. On the morning of 10 May, *U556* (Lt-Cdr Wohlfarth) attacks the convoy, which is still escorted by *Daneman* and *Hollyhock*, and torpedoes one ship. Later she sinks two more ships of 9947 tons from the convoy as it disperses.
The deployment of the Italian submarines *Cappellini* and *Torelli* against a convoy sighted by an FW 200 W of Iceland on 9 May meets with no success.

2 May   Near East
British Forces in Iraq start operations against the Iraqi Army and with it ensues an open conflict between Great Britain and the Iraqi Government of Rashid Ali El Ghailani.

2-4 May   Mediterranean
In returning from an operation by Force K (5th DD Flotilla, Capt Lord Mountbatten) the destroyers *Kelly*, *Jackal* and *Kelvin* put into harbour but the destroyer *Jersey*, which follows, runs on a mine and sinks. The result is that the cruiser *Gloucester* with the destroyers

Kashmir and Kipling go on to the W and join Force H.

4-7 May   Air War/Western Europe
93 British bombers attack the German battleships in Brest.

4-5 May   Mediterranean
Large Italian convoy to North Africa consisting of seven ships, including the motor ship Victoria (13098 tons) escorted by the destroyers Vivaldi, Da Noli, Malocello, and the torpedo boats Pegaso, Orione and Cassiopea. Distant escort provided by the cruisers Eugenio di Savoia, Duca d'Aosta and Attendolo and destroyers Pigafetta, Zeno, Da Recco, Da Mosto, Da Verazzano. On the way Pigafetta and Zeno of the covering force sink the British submarine Usk W of Sicily. British air attacks on 5 May have no success. On the return the distant escort covers a German convoy to Italy consisting of five steamers and the destroyers Euro and Fulmine and the torpedo boats Procione, Orsa, Centauro, Cigno and Perseo.

5-6 May   Mediterranean
British and Australian destroyers and sloops begin to supply the beleaguered British fortress of Tobruk in night missions. First trip made with the Australian destroyers Voyager and Waterhen. The supply missions, briefly interrupted during the Crete operation, continue until the fortress is relieved.

5-12 May   Mediterranean
Operation 'Tiger': a convoy is brought through the Mediterranean. On the evening of 5 May Force H (Vice-Adm Somerville) sets out from Gibraltar for the W with the battlecruiser Renown, the carrier Ark Royal, the cruisers Fiji and Sheffield and the destroyers Wrestler, Kashmir and Kipling, in order to meet the convoy with the 15-knot transports Clan Campbell, Clan Chattan, Clan Lamont, Empire Song and New Zealand Star and the naval reinforcements comprising the battleship Queen Elizabeth, the cruisers Naiad (Rear-Adm King) and Gloucester and the destroyers Fearless, Foresight, Fortune and Velox (the latter have gone out ahead from Gibraltar.) The groups pass through the Straits of Gibraltar in the night 5-6 May. On 6 May the destroyers Faulknor, Forester and Fury follow them, as well as the newly-arrived destroyers Harvester,

Havelock and Hesperus with the battle-cruiser Repulse, left behind because of her inadequate AA protection.

On 6 May a slow convoy of two tankers and a fast convoy of four transports set out from Alexandria for Malta. They are escorted by the AA cruisers Dido, Phoebe, Calcutta, Coventry and Carlisle as well as three destroyers and two corvettes. The operation is covered by the Mediterranean Fleet (Adm Cunningham), comprising the battleships Warspite, Barham and Valiant, the carrier Formidable, the 7th Cruiser Sqdn (Vice-Adm Pridham-Wippell) with Ajax, Orion and Perth, the fast minelayer Abdiel, the transport Breconshire and the remaining operational destroyers of the Mediterranaen Fleet (Isis, Imperial, Ilex, Havock, Hotspur, Hero, Hereward, Hasty, Greyhound, Griffin, Jervis, Janus, Juno, Jaguar, Nubian, Kandahar, Kingston, Kimberley and Nizam (RAN)). In the night 7-8 May the cruiser Ajax (Capt McCarthy) and the destroyers Imperial, Havock and Hotspur are detached. They shell the harbour of Benghazi and sink two steamers of 3463 tons to the S of it.

On 8 May both groups are located by German and Italian air reconnaissance. Several attacks by Italian S79 bomber and torpedo squadrons with CR42 fighter protection are unsuccessful: Renown and Ark Royal evade the torpedoes. Attacks by Ju 87 units with Me 110 fighter protection are intercepted by the Fulmar fighters from the Ark Royal. In the E there are air engagements between the fighters of the Formidable and the oncoming Italian and German aircraft. No damage is done to the ships. The deployment of an Italian cruiser force consisting of the Duca degli Abruzzi, Garibaldi, Bande Nere and Cadorna and five destroyers from Palermo comes too late. In the meantime Force H and the convoy with its covering forces—Queen Elizabeth, Naiad, Fiji, Gloucester, Kashmir, Kipling, Faulknor (8th DD Flotilla), Forester, Fury, Foresight, Fortune and Fearless—have separated near the Skerki Bank and proceed to Malta. In spite of the use by the 'F' Class destroyers of mine-sweeping equipment, the transport Empire Song (9228 tons) is lost on two

H

mines on 9 May and the *New Zealand Star* is damaged. The *Queen Elizabeth* is just able to avoid a torpedo attack. On the morning of 9 May the corvette *Gloxinia*, which has made a mine-free channel by the use of depth charges, escorts the two convoys from the E into the harbour of Valetta. The destroyers of the 5th DD Flotilla (Capt Lord Mountbatten) *Kelly*, *Jackal* and *Kelvin*, blockaded until then, are able to go out to the 'Tiger' convoy and meet it with the cruisers *Orion, Ajax, Perth, Dido* and *Phoebe* and escort it to the rendezvous with the Mediterranean Fleet, while the 8th DD Flotilla takes on oil in Malta and follows Force H. Bad visibility impedes German and Italian air attacks.

The Italian submarines *Santarosa* and *Settimo* W of Malta and *Corallo* off the Tunisian coast do not fire their torpedoes.

On 10 May visibility does not permit attacks by German and Italian aircraft until the afternoon. Then the *Fortune* of the 8th DD Flotilla, which is closing up on Force H, receives a heavy hit. No losses are sustained by the Mediterranean Fleet or by the convoy. In the night 10-11 May the destroyers *Kelly*, *Jackal*, *Kelvin*, *Kashmir* and *Kipling* of the 5th DD Flotilla again shell Benghazi. There is an unsuccessful night dive-bomber attack by Ju 87s of a squadron (Lt Rieger) of II/St.G.2. On 12 May the British forces reach Gibraltar and Alexandria respectively. Only 57 of 295 tanks and 10 out of 53 Hurricane fighters have been lost.

6 May   Mediterranean
Of the boats of the British 1st SM Flotilla *Taku* (Lt-Cdr Van der Byl) sinks one ship of 2322 tons off Calabria, *Truant* (Lt-Cdr Haggard) a ship of 1716 tons near Sardinia and *Triumph* unsuccessfully attacks a small convoy off Buerat and is hunted by the torpedo boat *Climene*.

6-7 May   Air War/Britain
Heavy German air raid on harbour installations in the Clyde.

7 May   Arctic
A British force, consisting of the cruisers *Edinburgh, Manchester* and *Birmingham* and four destroyers, is directed to the German weather signals put out by the German weather observation ship *München*

(*WBS-6*) (306 tons) and located by British D/F stations. On 7 May the weather observation ship is sighted. Before the abandoned ship sinks, the destroyer *Somali* goes alongside. The transmitter and code equipment have been destroyed but important documents are recovered and brought to Scapa Flow by *Nestor*. The *München* is sunk.

8 May   Indian Ocean
The British heavy cruiser *Cornwall* (Capt Manwaring) sinks the German auxiliary cruiser *Schiff 33 Pinguin* (Capt Krüder†) in an engagement near the Seychelles. 18 officers and 323 men and about 200 prisoners are lost with the German ship which, on her mission as a raider, has sunk or captured (inclusive of mine successes) a total of 32 ships amounting to 154619 tons in all. The *Cornwall* rescues three officers, 57 seamen and 22 prisoners.

8-9 May   Air War/Germany
RAF Bomber Command with 359 aircraft carries out its heaviest night attack so far on Germany. Main targets: Hamburg and Bremen which are attacked by 317 bombers.

9-29 May   Mediterranean
The Italian submarines *Atropo* and *Zoea* each carry out two transport operations with petrol and ammunition from Taranto to Derna.

10-11 May   Air War/Britain
Heavy German air raid on London (last major attack for three years). Approximately 2000 fires; five docks and 71 installations connected with the war effort, including 35 factories, destroyed or badly damaged. 110 British bombers attack Hamburg.

11 May   Mediterranean
British submarine *Rorqual* (Lt-Cdr Dewhurst) lays a mine barrage in the Gulf of Salonica.

11-14 May   Mediterranean
German-Italian supply convoy for North Africa consisting of six ships escorted by the destroyers *Aviere, Geniere, Grecale, Camicia Nera* and *Dardo* with distant escort from the cruisers *Bande Nere, Cadorna, Duca degli Abruzzi, Garibaldi*, and the destroyers *Alpino, Bersagliere, Fuciliere, Maestrale, Scirocco, Da Recco, Usodimare, Pessagno* and *Pancaldo*. This convoy, like two

returning ones, reaches its destination without incident.

In an attempt to attack a steamer escorted to Benghazi by the torpedo boat *Pleiadi*, the British submarine *Undaunted* is destroyed by depth charges in the area of Tripoli on 13 May.

11-22 May North Atlantic

After the OB.318 operation *U93*, *U94*, *U98* and *U556* are formed into a 'West' group to which are added on 13 May *U111*, *U97*, *U74* and *U109*. It proceeds to the area SSE of Cape Farewell (Greenland). In the process *U98* (Lt-Cdr Gysae) sinks on 13 May the auxiliary cruiser *Salopian* (10549 tons) which belongs to the convoy SC.30. On 19 May *U94* sights the convoy HX.126 and, before losing contact, sinks two ships; on 20 May at mid-day *U556* finds the convoy again and in two approaches sinks two ships and torpedoes one tanker. In addition, by evening *U111*, *U98* and *U94* arrive one after the other and *U93* comes up towards morning on 21 May. They each sink one ship. On 22 May *U46*, *U66*, *U557*, *U94* and *U74* also operate against the convoy. *U74* is damaged by depth charges. Only *U111* sights convoy but her one success is against an independent. Then contact is lost.

Of the boats operating with the 'West' group, the following make sinkings in the period 1-22 May (inclusive of convoys OB.318 and HX.126):

U97 (Lt-Cdr Heilmann) three ships of 17852 tons; *U556* (Lt-Cdr Wohlfarth) five ships of 23557 tons and damages two ships of 18023 tons; *U94* (Lt-Cdr Kuppisch) five ships of 31940 tons; *U110* (Lt-Cdr Lemp†) two ships of 7585 tons; *U201* (Lt Schnee) one ship of 5802 tons and damages one ship of 5969 tons; *U111* (Lt-Cdr Kleinschmidt) three ships of 15978 tons; *U98* (Lt-Cdr Gysae) two ships of 15905 tons; *U109* (Cdr Fischer) one ship of 7402 tons; and *U93* (Lt-Cdr Korth) one ship of 6235 tons.

In the eastern part of the North Atlantic I/K.G.40 sights a convoy on 11 May from which one ship of 8790 tons is sunk, but to which no U-boat comes. On 14 May a convoy is again sighted and one ship of 1843 tons is sunk. Of the Italian submarines deployed, *Bianchi*

and *Malaspina* sight the convoy but, like *Barbarigo*, *Morosini* and *Otaria*, have no success. On 19 May *Otaria* (Lt-Cdr Vocaturo) sinks one ship of 4662 tons in the convoy SL.73.

Of the U-boats operating in the area of the North Channel and the Faeroes *U96* (Lt-Cdr Lehmann-Willenbrock) sinks one ship of 2922 tons and *U138* (Lt Gramitzky) one ship of 8593 tons.

12-20 May Mediterranean

In the Eastern Mediterranean the Italian submarine *Ambra* operates SE of Malta; *Beilul* and *Salpa* NW of Alexandria; and *Onice* and *Galatea* in the Kaso Strait.

13 May Air War/Germany

Daylight attack by British bombers on Heligoland.

13-29 May Norway

Among others, the British submarine *P31/Uproar* and the French *Minerve* operate off Norway,

18 May South Atlantic

In the South Atlantic the auxiliary cruiser *Schiff 16 Atlantis* (Capt Rogge) passes unnoticed the British battleship *Nelson* and the aircraft carrier *Eagle* at a distance of only 7000 metres.

18 May Mediterranean

The British submarine *Tetrarch* (Lt-Cdr Greenway) sinks a ship of 2362 tons, escorted by the torpedo boat *Polluce*, off Benghazi.

18-27 May North Atlantic

Operation 'Rheinübung': Atlantic operation by the battleship *Bismarck* (Capt Lindemann) and the heavy cruiser *Prinz Eugen* (Capt Brinkmann) under the orders of the Fleet Commander, Adm Lütjens.

18 May: the battle squadron leaves Gotenhafen (Gdynia). To supply the squadron the escort tankers *Heide* and *Weissenburg* are stationed in the European Arctic and from France the supply ship *Spichern* and the escort tankers *Belchen, Esso Hamburg, Friedrich Breme* and *Lothringen* set out for positions in the North and Central Atlantic. In support the patrol ships *Gonzenheim* and *Kota Pinang* put to sea on 17-18 May and the weather observation ships *August Wriest, Freese,* and *Lauenberg* have taken up positions in the Arctic and Atlantic (the *München* has already been lost).

19 May: From Cape Arkona the squadron is escorted by *Sperrbrecher 13* and *Sperrbrecher 31* and the destroyers *Friedrich Eckoldt* and *Z23*. Off the Belt there is also the destroyer *Hans Lody* and an escort from the 5th MS Flotilla. On 20 May the force is reported in the Kattegat by the Swedish cruiser *Gotland*. British intelligence receives the news. On 21 May the force is discovered by British air reconnaissance when it is refuelling in Korsfjord near Bergen, but it is able to leave in the evening undetected. The submarines *Minerve* (French) and *P31*, which are sent N, cannot find the force. The commander of the Battle Cruiser Squadron, Vice-Adm Holland, puts to sea from Scapa Flow in the direction of the area S of Iceland with the battlecruiser *Hood*, the battleship *Prince of Wales* and the destroyers *Electra*, *Anthony*, *Echo*, *Icarus*, *Achates* and *Antelope*. On 22 May British air reconnaissance establishes the departure of the German ships. The British Home Fleet (Adm Tovey) then puts to sea from Scapa Flow with the battleship *King George V* (Capt Patterson), the carrier *Victorious* (Capt Bovell), the 2nd Cruiser Sqdn (Rear-Adm Curteis), comprising *Galatea*, *Aurora*, *Kenya* and *Hermione* and the available destroyers *Active*, *Punjabi*, *Nestor*, *Inglefield*, *Intrepid* and *Lance* (which returns because of damage). It is joined by the battlecruiser *Repulse* (Capt Tennant), earmarked to cover convoy WS.8B, with three Western Approaches destroyers. The light cruisers *Manchester*, *Birmingham* and *Arethusa*, five trawlers and flying-boats watch the Iceland-Faeroes passage and the heavy cruisers *Norfolk* (with the Commander 1st Cruiser Sqdn, Rear-Adm Wake-Walker) and *Suffolk* the Denmark Strait. On 23 May the German ships are sighted in the evening in the Denmark Strait by *Norfolk* (Capt Philipps) and *Suffolk* (Capt Ellis), whereupon Adm Holland's force comes up to intercept the German units south of the Denmark Strait. On the morning of 24 May there is a brief engagement between the two forces, in which the *Hood* (Capt Kerr†) is sunk in five minutes by *Bismarck* and

Prinz Eugen and the *Prince of Wales* (Capt Leach) is damaged and forced to turn away. 95 officers and 1321 men, including Vice-Adm Holland, are lost with the *Hood*. Only three seamen can be rescued. On the *Bismarck* two heavy and one light hits cause a reduction in speed and a clearly visible trail of oil. *Prinz Eugen* is undamaged. The British cruisers are able to maintain contact. The convoys HX.126, SC.31, HX.127, OB.323 and OB.324, which are particularly threatened, are ordered to make detours. The battleship *Ramillies* with HX.127; the battleship *Rodney* and the destroyers *Somali*, *Tartar* and *Mashona* (the destroyer *Eskimo* remains with the transport *Britannic*) from a force proceeding to the U.S.; and the cruiser *Edinburgh* (with the Commander of the 18th Cruiser Sqdn, Commodore Blackman) from the area W of Cape Finisterre are all deployed, while the ships of the Home Fleet try to close in. But the destroyers have to be detached because of shortage of fuel. Force H (Vice-Adm Somerville), comprising the battlecruiser *Renown* (Capt McGrigor), the carrier *Ark Royal* (Capt Maund), the cruiser *Sheffield* (Capt Larcom) and the destroyers *Faulknor*, *Foresight*, *Forester*, *Foxhound*, *Fury* and *Hesperus*, sets out from Gibraltar. The battleship *Revenge* is sent from Halifax to the convoy HX.128.
The Commander U-boats stations the 'West' group, comprising *U94*, *U43*, *U46*, *U557*, *U66* and *U93*, in a patrol line over which the *Bismarck* is to draw her pursuers on 25 May. The submarines *U73*, *U556*, *U97*, *U98*, *U74*, *U48* and *Barbarigo* are stationed in the Western part of the Bay of Biscay as a precautionary measure to meet the *Bismarck*.
24-25 May: in the night nine aircraft of the carrier *Victorious* attack the *Bismarck* and register an insignificant hit. Thanks to a brief attack by *Bismarck*, the *Prinz Eugen* is able to get away, unnoticed by the enemy, to pursue mercantile warfare on her own. Shortly after, the British cruisers, which are keeping contact by radar, lose contact when *Bismarck* turns away and makes for Brest behind the withdrawing cruisers.

25 May: *Bismarck* proceeds to the SE behind the British ships which are searching in fan formation towards the SW and she sends long W/T messages assuming that the enemy is still in contact. Bearings are at once taken on the W/T messages, although at first they are incorrect.

26 May: in the morning a Catalina flying-boat (Flying Officer Briggs) of No 209 Sqdn finds the *Bismarck* again. Force H is deployed, but its destroyers have to remain behind. Also deployed are *King George V* and *Rodney* (Capt Dalrymple-Hamilton) with the destroyers *Mashona, Somali* and *Tartar* and the cruiser *Norfolk* which follows. The destroyers *Cossack* (4th DD Flotilla, Capt Vian), *Sikh, Zulu, Maori* and *Piorun* (Polish) are withdrawn from convoy WS.8B: it continues with the cruisers *Cairo* and *Exeter* and three destroyers. The convoys OB.325 and OB.326 are re-routed and from the convoys SL.74 and SL.75, coming from the S, the cruisers *Dorsetshire* and *London*, are put on the trail, as is the battleship *Nelson* with the carrier *Eagle* from Freetown. At mid-day aircraft of the *Ark Royal* establish contact and, soon after, the cruiser *Sheffield*, which is attacked in error by the first wave of the carrier's torpedo aircraft but which is able to avoid all the torpedoes. Despite unfavourable weather, a second wave of 15 Swordfish of Nos 810, 818 and 828 Sqdns take off under Lt-Cdr Coode in the afternoon. *Bismarck* is hit twice. A torpedo hit destroys the steering gear and renders the battleship unmanoeuvrable. Shortly before, *U556* (Lt-Cdr Wohlfarth) sights Force H but, although in a certain firing position, has to let it pass because the boat is returning to her base after expending all her torpedoes.

26-27 May: in the night *Bismarck* beats off attacks by the 4th British DD Flotilla (Capt Vian), consisting of *Zulu, Sikh, Cossack, Maori* and the Polish *Piorun*.

27 May: the battleships *King George V* and *Rodney* come up in the morning and shell *Bismarck* to pieces although the latter defends herself to the last gun. The battleships then return because of fuel shortage and the cruiser *Dorsetshire*

(Capt Martin) and *Norfolk* shell the wreck and torpedo her twice. About 1035 hours the *Bismarck* sinks as the result of an internal explosion. *Dorsetshire* and *Maori* rescue 110 survivors, including two officers. *U74* and the weather observation ship *Sachsenwald* rescue another five later. Some 2100 men and the entire staff of the fleet perish. A search for survivors made by the Spanish cruiser *Canarias* finds nothing.

Attempts by the German Air Force—Air Commander Atlantic (Col Harlinghausen)—reinforced by II/K.G.1, II/K.G.54 and I/K.G.77, to help the *Bismarck*, lead to many losses on British warships. On 28 May Ju 88s of I/K.G.77 sink the British destroyer *Mashona* W of Ireland. He 111s of K.Gr.100 badly damage *Maori*.

19-21 May Mediterranean
German-Italian supply convoy from Palermo to Sicily, consisting of seven ships, escorted by the destroyers *Euro, Folgore, Fulmine, Strale* and *Turbine*. Distant escort: cruisers *Duca degli Abruzzi, Garibaldi* and destroyers *Granatiere, Alpino* and *Bersagliere*. On 19 May two ships collide in trying to avoid an attack by the British submarine *Urge* (Lt-Cdr Tomkinson) which, on the following day, sinks a single steamer of 5165 tons and on 21 May misses the *Duca degli Abruzzi*. Two returning convoys with eight ships arrive: an attack by *Upholder* fails.

19-22 May Mediterranean
Operation 'Splice': British Force H, consisting of the battlecruiser *Renown* (Vice-Adm Somerville), the carriers *Ark Royal* and *Furious*, the cruiser *Sheffield* and six destroyers, proceeds to the area S of Sardinia and flies off to Malta on 21 May 48 Hurricane fighters from the carriers, all of which arrive. The Italian submarines *Corallo* and *Diaspro*, stationed S of Sardinia, do not approach the force.

19 May-2 June Mediterranean
During the battle for Crete the Italian submarines *Tricheco, Uarsciek, Fisalia, Topazio, Adua, Dessiè, Malachite, Squalo, Smeraldo* and *Sirena* operate between Crete, Alexandria and Sollum and *Nereide* N of Crete. Their operations have no success.

20 May-1 June   Mediterranean
Operation 'Merkur': German airborne landing on Crete.
20 May: Beginning of the attacks by VIII Fl.K. (General of the Air Force von Richthofen) and airborne landings (by XI Fl.K.) in the area of Maleme, Heraklion, Canea, and Retimo against strong opposition from the British garrison. In the night 20-21 May an attack by six Italian motor torpedo boats on British Force C (Rear-Adm King), comprising the cruisers *Naiad* and *Perth* (RAN), the destroyers *Kandahar, Nubian, Kingston* and *Juno*, achieves no success. The destroyers *Jervis* (Capt Mack), *Ilex* and *Nizam* shell the airfield at Scarpanto.
21 May: In German bomber attacks the British cruiser *Ajax* is damaged and the destroyer *Juno* sunk. Both units belong to the British Mediterranean Fleet, elements of which have been at sea since 15 May in expectation of German action. It has the following units at its disposal: the battleships *Queen Elizabeth, Barham, Warspite, Valiant* the aircraft carrier *Formidable*, the cruisers *Gloucester, Fiji, Ajax, Dido, Orion, Perth, Naiad, Phoebe, Calcutta, Carlisle* the fast mine-layer *Abdiel*, the destroyers *Napier, Nizam, Kandahar, Kelvin, Kipling, Kingston, Kimberley, Kelly, Nubian, Juno, Janus, Jervis, Jackal, Isis, Imperial, Ilex, Hero, Hotspur, Hereward, Hasty, Havock, Griffin, Greyhound, Decoy, Defender, Stuart, Voyager, Vendetta, Waterhen*, the sloops *Auckland, Flamingo* and the net-layer *Protector*. In the course of the fighting all ships are involved.
21 May: Departure of first German motor sailing flotilla (Lt Oesterlin), some 20 craft, escorted by the Italian torpedo boat *Lupo* (Cdr* Mimbelli); towards midnight British Force D (Rear-Adm Glennie), consisting of the cruisers *Dido, Orion* and *Ajax* and the destroyers *Janus, Kimberley, Hasty* and *Hereward*, attacks the German convoy 18 nautical miles N of Canea and scatters it. Thanks to the courageous action of *Lupo*, only 10 motor sailing vessels are lost. Of the 2331 troops embarked only 297 are lost.
22 May: Force C (Rear-Adm King), consisting of the cruisers *Naiad, Perth, Calcutta* and *Carlisle*, as well the des-

troyers *Kandahar, Nubian* and *Kingston*, attacks the second motor sailing flotilla. As a result of the skilful action of the escorting Italian torpedo boat, *Sagittario* (Cdr* Cigala), and constant air attacks by Ju 88s of I/L.G.1 (Capt Cuno Hoffmann) and III/K.G.30, as well as by Do 17s of K.G.2 (Col Rieckhoff), the convoy loses only two craft. *Carlisle* (Capt Hampton†) and *Naiad* are damaged by bomb hits. Force C then turns away to join the powerful covering group (Rear-Adm Rawlings) which in the course of the afternoon is also the target of strong air attacks by Ju 87s of St.G. 2 (Lt-Col Dinort), Ju 88s of I/L.G.1 and II/L.G.1 (Capt Kollewe) and Me 109 fighter bombers. I/L.G.1 and a fighter bomber detachment (Lt Huy) of III/J.G.77 secure several hits on the battleship *Warspite* (Capt Crutchley); Ju 87s sink the destroyer *Greyhound*; and Ju 88s and Ju 87s the cruiser *Gloucester* (Capt Rowley†) which is lost with 45 officers and 648 members of the crew. Two single Me 109 fighter bombers of I/L.G.2 (Capt Ihlefeld) hit the cruiser *Fiji* (Capt William Powlett) so heavily in the evening that she has to be abandoned. *Kandahar* and *Kingston* rescue 523 survivors. In the air attacks *Carlisle* and *Naiad* are again hit and the battleship *Valiant* (Capt Morgan) is more lightly damaged. In the night 22-23 May *Kashmir, Kelly* and *Kipling* shell the airfield at Maleme. *Decoy* and *Hero* take the Greek king and his party on board.
23 May: I/St.G.2 (Capt Hitschhold) locates *Kashmir* and *Kelly* as they return in the evening and sinks them. *Kipling* rescues 279 survivors. Fighter bombers of III/J.G.77 (Maj v. Winterfeldt) sink in Suda Bay the boats *MTB67, MTB 213, MTB214, MTB216* and *MTB217* of the British 10th MTB Flotilla.
25 May: Vice-Adm Pridham-Wippell puts to sea from Alexandria with the battleships *Barham* and *Queen Elizabeth*, the carrier *Formidable*, and nine destroyers in order to attack the air base of III/St.G.2 (Capt Brücker) at Scarpanto.
26 May: Carrier aircraft of the *Formidable* bombard Scarpanto. On return the *Formidable* and destroyer *Nubian* are badly damaged by II/St.G.2 (Maj Enneccerus).

27 May: Ju 88s of L.G.1 damage the battleship *Barham*. Because, in the meantime, the situation on Crete has developed in a way favourable to the German invading forces, all British attempts to bring reinforcements to the island are stopped. The evacuation is begun.

28 May: On the way to the evacuation the cruiser *Ajax* and the destroyer *Imperial* are damaged by bombs. In the night 28-29 May 4700 troops are embarked in Sphakia and Heraklion: *Imperial* is abandoned when her rudder is disabled.

29 May: the destroyer *Hereward* is sunk by III/St.G.2; *Decoy* is hit and *Ajax* is again hit. The cruisers *Dido* and *Orion* (Capt Back†) are badly damaged. There are 260 dead and 280 wounded among the 1100 troops embarked on *Orion*. In the night 29-30 May another 6000 are evacuated.

30 May: The cruiser *Perth* and the destroyer *Kelvin* are damaged by L.G.1. 700 troops are evacuated in the night 30-31 May.

31 May: the destroyer *Napier* receives bomb hits. In the night 31 May-1 June Rear-Adm King makes a last effort with *Phoebe*, *Abdiel*, *Jackal*, *Kimberley* and *Hotspur* to evacuate troops from Sphakia, where there are still approximately 6000 men left behind. 4000 troops can be taken off.

1 June: the AA cruisers *Calcutta* and *Coventry*, sent out from Alexandria to meet Adm King's force, are located by two Ju 88s some 100 nautical miles N of Alexandria and *Calcutta* (Capt Leese) is sunk. *Coventry* rescues 255 survivors. 17000 troops in all are evacuated from Crete. Losses: 15743 men and, in addition, 2011 in the Navy. German losses: 6580 dead, missing and wounded.

21 May   Mediterranean
The British fast minelayer *Abdiel* lays 150 mines E of Cape Dukato. Within 24 hours the Italian destroyer *Mirabello*, the gunboat *Matteucci* and the German transports *Marburg* (7564 tons) and *Kybfels* (7764 tons) sink on this barrage.

22-25 May   Mediterranean
The British submarines *Urge* and *Upholder* each torpedo one ship of 4856 tons and 4854 tons respectively off

Tunis and Messina on 22 May and 24 May.

On 24 May an Italian troop convoy proceeds to Tripoli consisting of the passenger ships *Esperia* (11398 tons), *Conte Rosso* (17879 tons), *Marco Polo* (12272 tons) and *Victoria* (13098 tons). Close escort provided by the destroyers *Camicia Nera*, *Freccia* and torpedo boats *Procione*, *Orsa* and *Pegaso*. Distant escort: cruisers *Bolzano*, *Trieste* and destroyers *Ascari*, *Corazziere* and *Lanciere*. E of Sicily the *Conte Rosso* is sunk by the British submarine *Upholder* (Lt-Cdr Wanklyn); of the 2500 troops on board, 1680 are saved.

25 May-16 June   North Atlantic
Operation by an Italian submarine group consisting of *Argo*, *Veniero*, *Mocenigo*, *Emo*, *Marconi*, *Brin* and *Velella* against convoys W of Gibraltar. Early in the morning of 30 May *Veniero* sights the carrier *Ark Royal* from Force H returning from the hunt for the *Bismarck* and she misses one destroyer of a convoy escort. In subsequent attacks *Mocenigo* misses a tanker and *Marconi* (Lt-Cdr Pollina) sinks the British fleet tanker *Cairndale* and, later, an unmarked small Portuguese trawler, totalling 8447 tons. The submarines are heavily attacked with depth charges from the convoy escort, consisting of the corvettes *Coreopsis* and *Fleur de Lys*, and the destroyers *Faulknor*, *Forester* and *Fury* sent as reinforcements, as well as by the French corvette *Alysse*, the sloop *Bideford*, the trawler *Imperialist* and the destroyer *Wrestler* on 31 May. But they are able to evade the attacks.

On 5 June *Velella* (Lt-Cdr Terra) sights the homeward-bound convoy OG.63 and brings up *Marconi* which attacks in the night 5-6 June and observes four hits. She is followed by *Velella* which obtains two hits. Two ships of 4787 tons sink. In the afternoon of 6 June *Emo* (Cdr Roselli-Lorenzini) also attacks OG.63 and reports two unconfirmed hits. In the night 5-6 June *Veniero* (Cdr Petroni) sights the approaching HG.64 S of OG.63 and reports two unconfirmed hits. On the morning of 7 June *Brin* sights the convoy NE of Madeira, but is not able to fire. *Mocenigo* does not find the convoy.

On 12 June *Brin* (Cdr Longanesi-Cattani) sights the convoy SL.75 E of the Azores, and sinks two of its ships on 13 June totalling 7241 tons. But *Velella* and *Veniero* do not find the convoy, nor do the German U-boats *U204*, *U43*, *U73* and *U201*, stationed further to the N and known as the 'Kurfürst' group.

26 May Western Atlantic
The Dutch gunboat *Van Kinsbergen* captures E of Martinique the Vichy French steamer *Winnepeg* (8379 tons).

26-27 May Mediterranean
The Italian 13th TB Flotilla (Cdr Unger di Lowenberg), consisting of the torpedo boats *Circe*, *Calliope*, *Clio* and *Perseo*, lays the mine barrages M4 and M4A E of Malta. Italian supply convoy to Tripoli (six freighters, escorted by two destroyers and three torpedo boats with a distant escort of one cruiser and two destroyers). British aircraft from Malta attack and hit two ships.

27 May North Atlantic
The convoy HX.129 is the first British convoy from Halifax to be escorted the whole way across the Atlantic against submarines.

27 May-20 June North Atlantic
For 1 June a new 'West' group is formed from the U-boats stationed in the Western Atlantic: *U111* (replenished on 25-26 May from the tanker *Belchen* in the Davis Strait), *U43*, *U46* and *U66*. These are to be joined, after being replenished from *Belchen*, by *U557* (1-2 June) and *U93*. *Belchen* is sunk on 3 June, when replenishing *U93*, by the cruisers *Aurora* and *Kenya*. *U93* rescues 49 survivors. By 20 June the boats *U108*, *U101*, *U75*, *U48*, *U73*, *U204* (previously south of Iceland), *U553*, *U77*, *U558* and *U751* also join the 'West' group. They encounter only independents. *U557* (Lt Paulshen) sinks one ship of 7290 tons: *U46* (Lt Endrass) two of 10893 tons and damages one ship of 6207 tons; *U108* (Lt-Cdr Scholtz) six ships of 24445 tons; *U48* (Lt-Cdr Schultze) five ships of 38462 tons; *U75* (Lt-Cdr Ringelmann) one ship of 4801 tons; *U101* (Lt-Cdr Mengersen) two ships of 11644 tons; *U43* (Lt-Cdr Lüth) two ships of 7529 tons; *U204* (Lt-Cdr Kell) two ships of 7902 tons; *U553* (Lt-Cdr Thurmann) two ships of 7945 tons; *U77* (Lt-Cdr

Schonder) three ships of 11725 tons; and *U751* (Lt-Cdr Bigalk) one ship of 5370 tons. A sortie by *U111* into the area of the Belle Isle Strait and as far as Cape Race is not successful owing to mist. Off the North Channel *U147* (Lt Wetjen) sinks one ship of 2491 tons and, after torpedoing a steamer of 4996 tons in a convoy on 2 June, is sunk by the British destroyer *Wanderer* and the corvette *Periwinkle* of the escort. *U552* (Lt-Cdr Topp) sinks three ships of 24401 tons in the North Channel; and *U141* (Lt Schüler) sinks one ship of 1277 tons W of Ireland. Of the U-boats *U559* and *U79* (Lt-Cdr Kaufmann), stationed in the Denmark Strait to support the proposed break-out of the heavy cruiser *Lützow*, the latter sinks one ship of 1524 tons.

28 May General Situation
Franco-German negotiations in Paris. Agreement provides, inter alia, for support for German naval operations in the Central Atlantic from Dakar (planned from 15 July). But in view of the small German accommodation shown by Hitler the French Government returns to its policy of *attentisme* in its Note of 14 July.

30 May Mediterranean
The British submarine *Triumph* (Lt-Cdr Wards) torpedoes the Italian auxiliary cruiser *Ramb III* (3667 tons) off Benghazi. A further attack on 30-31 May on a small convoy is outmanoeuvred.

1 June North Atlantic
The US Coastguard organizes the South Greenland Patrol: four coastal guard ships operate between Cape Brewster, Cape Farewell and Upernivik.

1-13 June Mediterranean
In operations by the British 8th SM Flotilla (Gibraltar) *Clyde* (Cdr Ingram) sinks two ships of 4271 tons in the Western Mediterranean and the Dutch *O24* (Lt-Cdr De Booy) two ships of 6803 tons. In the area of Lampedusa *Unique* (Lt Collett) sinks one small ship of 736 tons. In the area of the Aegean *Parthian* (Cdr Rimington) sinks one Italian ship of 5232 tons off the Dardanelles and *Torbay* (Lt-Cdr Miers) sinks two ships and a sailing ship totalling 7114 tons and torpedoes one Rumanian passenger ship of 5700 tons.

In the area of Buerat *Taku* (Lt-Cdr van der Byl) attacks a small Italian convoy and, in a gun engagement, sinks on 5 June the Italian gunboat *Valoroso* (340 tons armed with one 7.6cm gun) and two small freighters totalling 489 tons. On 11-12 June she sinks two more ships of 2967 tons and evades the Italian torpedo boats *Pallade* and *Polluce*.

2 June   Air War/Germany
RAF Bomber Command attacks the Kaiser Wilhelm Canal.

3 June   Mediterranean
An Italian convoy (6 ships with four destroyers and a distant escort of two cruisers and four destroyers) is attacked off the Tunisian coast by British Martin Maryland bombers. The freighters *Beatrice C* (6132 tons) and *Montello* (6117 tons) are lost.

3 June   Mediterranean
The Italian 7th Div (Div Adm Casardi), comprising the cruisers *Eugenio di Savoia*, *Duca d'Aosta* and *Attendolo*, and the 4th Div (Div Adm Giovanola), comprising the cruisers *Bande Nere* and *Di Giussano*, and the destroyers *Pigafetta*, *Da Mosto*, *Da Verazzano*, *Da Recco*, *Usodimare*, *Gioberti* and *Scirocco*, lay two mine barrages NE of Tripoli against British coastal shelling. On 19 Dec the British Force K runs on to the barrages (see entry).

3-23 June   Atlantic
In connection with the operation 'Rheinübung' (see 18-25 May) units of the British Fleet begin a systematic search for the ships of the German supply organization during which German and Italian blockade-runners at sea are also lost. The process is facilitated by the capture of codes when the weather observation ship *München* (7 May) and the U-boat *U110* (10 May) are seized and later the supply ships *Gedania* and *Lothringen* (see below). This makes it possible to decode German W/T traffic for some time.
On 28 May the blockade-runner *Lech* (3290 tons), coming from Rio de Janeiro, has to scuttle herself in the South Atlantic when a British warship comes into sight. Then on 29 May the weather observation ship *August Wriedt*, and probably also the weather observation ship *Hinrich Freese*, become victims of the British search operations.

On 3 June the tanker *Belchen* (6367 tons), after replenishing *U111* and *U557* in the Davis Strait, is sunk by the British cruisers *Aurora* and *Kenya* between Greenland and Labrador. *U93* rescues the survivors.
On 4 June the tanker *Gedania* (8923 tons) is abandoned in a panic when the auxiliary warship *Marsdale* comes into sight and is captured by her (see above).
An aircraft from the carrier *Victorious*, which is proceeding to Gibraltar with the cruiser *Hermione*, sights the patrol ship *Gonzenheim* (4000 tons) north of the Azores. The latter is able to escape from the auxiliary cruiser *Esperance Bay* (14204 tons) but has to scuttle herself when the battleship *Nelson* and the cruiser *Neptune*, which are summoned to the scene, come into view. The *Neptune* torpedoes the burning wreck.
On 4 June and 5 June respectively the tankers *Esso Hamburg* (9849 tons) and *Egerland* (9798 tons) scuttle themselves in the supply area of the Freetown-Natal route when approached by the heavy cruiser *London* and the destroyer *Brilliant*.
On 6 June the blockade-runner *Elbe* (9179 tons), coming from East Asia, is sunk by aircraft from the carrier *Eagle* near the Azores.
On 8 June Force H, comprising the battlecruiser *Renown*, the carrier *Ark Royal*, the cruiser *Sheffield* and six destroyers, sets out from Gibraltar for the W to avoid the anticipated Vichy French air attacks (reprisal for the operation against Syria) and at the same time to intercept enemy supply ships and blockade runners. On 9 June the carrier *Victorious*, coming from the N, with the cruiser *Hermione*, is met. The *Sheffield* returns to Britain: on 12 June she encounters the homeward-bound *Friedrich Breme* (10397 tons) in the North Atlantic WNW of Cape Finisterre. The tanker scuttles herself. Force H arrives in Gibraltar on 11 June to carry out a new Malta operation (see 13-15 June). On 15 June the supply ship *Lothringen*, earmarked to replenish the U-boats operating off Freetown, is sighted in the Central Atlantic by an aircraft from the carrier *Eagle* and is captured by the cruiser *Dunedin*. When, at this time, the British search groups

are replenishing and Force H is operating in the Mediterranean, the patrol ship *Kota Pinang*, the supply ships *Ermland* and *Spichern*, the Italian blockade-runners *Atlanta* and *Todaro* coming from the Canaries, and the German *Regensburg* from East Asia, pass through the blockade and reach French Western ports.

On reports that ships have been sighted Force H again sets out for the Atlantic on 16 June with *Renown*, *Ark Royal*, *Hermione* and five destroyers. It is then that *U138* (Lt Gramitzky), the only U-boat deployed in the area, falls victim to the destroyers *Faulknor*, *Fearless*, *Forester*, *Foresight* and *Foxhound*, which are sent to Gibraltar on 18 June to refuel.

After another unsuccessful search Force H returns to Gibraltar on 21 June. But on the afternoon of 22 June British air reconnaissance sights the supply ship *Alstertor* (3039 tons) returning from the Indian Ocean. The auxiliary ship *Marsdale* and the destroyers *Faulknor*, *Fearless*, *Forester*, *Foxhound* and *Fury* are deployed in the search. When they come into view, the *Alstertor* has to scuttle herself on 23 June off Cape Finisterre. With the crew 78 British prisoners from the auxiliary cruiser *Atlantis* are rescued. On the return the destroyers meet the carrier *Furious*, which is proceeding to Gibraltar with the destroyers *Lance* and *Legion*, and they reach harbour again on 25 June.

In the meantime the cruiser *London* has compelled the German blockade runner *Babitonga* (4422 tons), coming from Brazil, to scuttle herself in the South Atlantic.

5-7 June Mediterranean
Operation 'Rocket': British Force H with the battlecruiser *Renown*, the carriers *Ark Royal* and *Furious* and six destroyers, leaves *Gibraltar* for the western Mediterranean and flies off on 6 June 35 Hurricane fighters which, led by Blenheim bombers from Gibraltar, reach Malta. On the return one machine makes a reconnaissance by moonlight over Mers El-Kebir in order to establish the state of the Vichy French battleship *Dunkerque* before the operation in Syria.

On the Italian side the submarines *Colonna* and *Da Procida* are stationed to counter a sortie by Force H towards Genoa; and, to the W, *Bandiera*, *Diaspro* and *Manara*, to prevent the passage through the Sicilian Channel.

6 June General Situation
Law enables the US Government to take over ships of foreign states laid up in American harbours.

7-9 June Mediterranean
Italian convoy with three troop transports and strong escort reaches Tripoli without loss.

7 June-14 July Mediterranean
British and Gaullist troops occupy Syria against strong French resistance. Sea operations under command of Vice-Adm King (15th Cruiser Sqdn). The French naval commander in Syria, Rear Adm Gouton, has at his disposal the flotilla leaders, *Guépard* (Commander: Capt Gervais de Lafond) and *Valmy*, the sloop *Elan*, the submarines *Caiman*, *Morse* and *Souffleur*, as well as some smaller units unsuitable for action. 6 June: British assault ship *Glengyle* sets out from Alexandria with destroyers *Isis* and *Hotspur*. A commando operation N of Tyre on 7-8 June is abandoned because of the swell. The operation is covered by a force consisting of the cruisers *Phoebe* (F) and *Ajax* and the destroyers *Kandahar*, *Kimberley*, *Janus* and *Jackal*.
8 June: *Kimberley* shells French positions near Tyre.
9 June: Commando party from *Glengyle* lands behind French troops to capture an important bridge. Air cover provided by the AA cruiser *Coventry*. The French submarine *Caiman* just misses *Ajax* with a torpedo. The large French destroyers *Guépard* and *Valmy* shell the forward troops of an Australian unit as they advance along the coast. In the pursuit there is an engagement off Sidon in which the British destroyer *Janus* receives five heavy hits. When the British destroyers *Jackal* (also hit), *Isis* and *Hotspur* come up, the French ships turn off and return to Beirut.
On 10 June the Australian destroyer *Stuart* and on 13 June the New Zealand cruiser *Leander* arrive as reinforcements.
14 June: unsuccessful sortie by the French destroyers which have a brief encounter with British units.

15 June: Ju 88s of II/L.G.1 (Capt Kollewe) damage the British destroyer *Isis* off Sidon and aircraft of the French 4th Naval Air Group badly damage the *Ilex* with bombs.

16 June: British torpedo aircraft of No 815 Sqdn sinks the French flotilla leader *Chevalier Paul*, employed as an ammunition transport, 50 nautical miles off the Syrian coast. *Guépard* and *Valmy* rescue the crew. The second ammunition transport, the flotilla leader *Vauquelin*, coming from Toulon, reaches Beirut but is damaged there on 17 June by British bombers.

17 June: British forces are reinforced or relieved by the cruiser *Naiad* (F) with the destroyers *Nizam*, *Jaguar* and *Kingston*.

23 June: *Guépard* tries to break through the British blockade of Beirut. In a night engagement with the cruisers *Leander* and *Naiad* and the destroyers *Jaguar*, *Kingston* and *Nizam* she receives one hit but is able to get away because of her superior speed. The British destroyers *Jervis*, *Havock*, *Hotspur* and *Decoy*, engaged in submarine hunting in the area, do not approach.

25 June: the British submarine *Parthian* (Cdr Rimington) sinks the French submarine *Souffleur* in the Bay of Djounieh.

2 July: the French 4th Naval Air Group (Lt-Cdr Hubert) attacks Haifa. The Australian cruiser *Perth* with *Naiad*, *Kandahar*, *Kingston*, *Havock* and *Griffin* shell French positions on the coast.

4 July: shelling of the coast by *Naiad*, *Ajax*, *Jackal*, *Nizam*, *Kimberley*, *Havock* and *Hasty*. Continuation of operations on 5 July, 6 July and 7 July near Damour, the last fortified position before Beirut.

4 July: Albacore torpedo aircraft of No 829 Sqdn sinks the French supply steamer *St Didier* (2778 tons) off the Anatolian coast. The second ship, which is en route with supplies for Syria, *Château Yquem* (2536 tons), is later recalled when it is clear that it is impossible to break the British blockade.

9-12 July: the French flotilla leaders *Guépard*, *Valmy* and *Vauquelin* proceed from Syria to Salonica to take on a French infantry battalion which has arrived by the land route. The force is located by British air reconnaissance 200 nautical miles off the Syrian coast and goes, in accordance with instructions, to Toulon.

12 July: Armistice in Syria after General Dentz accepts the British conditions. The submarines *Caiman* and *Morse* go to Bizerta.

14 July: Signing of an armistice agreement.

10 June   Red Sea
Operation 'Chronometer': landing of an Indian battalion in Assab, the last Italian harbour in the Red Sea, by a force (Rear-Adm Hallifax), comprising the cruiser *Dido*, the auxiliary cruiser *Chakdina*, the Indian sloops *Clive* and *Indus* and one transport.

12 June   General Situation
The US Navy calls up its non-exempted reservists.

12-13 June   North Sea
Attempt by the heavy cruiser *Lützow* (Capt Kreisch) to break out into the Atlantic to take part in mercantile warfare. Shortly before midnight on 12 June British air reconnaissance locates the cruiser with her five escort destroyers off Lindesnes. Two hours later Bristol Beaufort torpedo aircraft of No 42 Sqdn Coastal Command attack the force. Flt Sgt Loveitt secures one torpedo hit on *Lützow* amidships. With partly disabled engines and a heavy list, the cruiser returns to the Baltic and reaches Kiel on the afternoon of 14 June where she has to remain in dock until January 1942.

13-14 June   Air War/Western Europe
110 British bombers attack the German battleships in Brest.

13-15 June   Mediterranean
Operation 'Tracer': Force H with the battlecruiser *Renown*, the carriers *Ark Royal* and *Victorious* and six destroyers. On 14 June 47 Hurricane fighters are flown off to Malta S of the Balearics. 43 of them, led by four Hudson bombers, reach their destination. The Italian submarines *Corallo* and *Santarosa*, stationed S of Sardinia, do not sight the force.

14 June-11 Sept   North Atlantic
On 14 June the boundary of the Western Hemisphere is moved forward from 30° W to 26° W. The following battleships patrol in the Central North Atlantic in

7-14 day sorties in co-operation with destroyer groups: *Texas* (19-27 June and 17-25 July) and *Arkansas* (7-15 Aug and 2-11 Sept) with *Rhind* and *Mayrant*; *New Mexico* (26 June-4 July, 25 July-2 Aug and 14 Aug-23 Aug) with *Hughes* and *Russell*; *Mississippi* (3-11 July, 1-16 Aug and 27 Aug-11 Sept) with *O'Brien* and *Walke* and *Stack*, *Sterret* and *Rowan*; and *Idaho* (10-18 July) with *Morris* and *Sims*.

With the Central Atlantic Neutrality Patrol (see 7 Apl-10 June) Crudiv 7 is relieved from 15 July by Crudiv 8 comprising the cruisers *Savannah*, *Brooklyn*, *Nashville* and *Philadelphia* and from the beginning of September Desron II is withdrawn for convoy service and operations from Iceland.

On 15 June US TF 3 (Rear-Adm Ingram) with the cruisers *Memphis*, *Milwaukee*, *Cincinnati* and *Omaha* (Crudiv 2) and the destroyers *Somers*, *Winslow*, *Moffett*, *Davis* and *Jouett* begin their patrols in the Neutrality Zone, extended to 20° S from the Brazilian bases of Recife and Bahia.

17 June   Western Atlantic
The British auxiliary cruiser *Pretoria Castle* captures the Vichy French steamer *Desirade* (9645 tons) E of the Antilles.

19-21 June   General Situation
As a result of information received about German preparations to attack the Soviet Union, the People's Commissar for the Soviet Navy, Adm N.G. Kuznetsov, issues Grade 2 Alert for the subordinate fleet commanders on 19 June and Grade 1 Alert at 23.37 hours on 21 June. Strict instructions are issued to avoid any provocations which would give the Germans an excuse to attack.

19-21 June   Baltic
In the nights 18-19 June, 19-20 June and 20-21 June the German minelayers *Preussen*, *Grille*, *Skagerrak* and *Versailles*, together with six boats of the 6th MS Flotilla, under command of the Officer Commanding Minelayers Capt Bentlage, lay between Memel and Öland the mine barrages 'Wartburg I-III' (1150 EMCs and 1800 explosive floats). In the process the Soviet cruiser *Kirov* is observed in the evening of 18 June W of Libau. Finnish minelayers

lay mine barrages on 21 June near Manni and Jussarö.

19 June-11 July   Mediterranean
The British-Australian 10th DD Flotilla, comprising *Stuart*, *Vendetta*, *Waterhen*, *Voyager*, *Vampire*, *Defender*, *Decoy* and *Dainty* and the sloops *Flamingo*, *Auckland* and *Parramatta*, suffer losses in the frequent German and Italian dive bomber attacks on their supply missions between Alexandria, Mersa Matruh and the beleaguered fortress of Tobruk. On 24 June *Auckland* sinks, and on 29 June *Waterhen*, both off Bardia; and on 11 July *Defender* off Sidi Barani.

20-29 June   North Atlantic
Because it is suspected that the 'West' group is being avoided, the U-boats *U71*, *U96*, *U203*, *U79*, *U651*, *U371*, *U108*, *U553*, *U556*, *U562*, *U201*, *U751*, *U75*, *U558*, *U557*, *U77*, *U101*, *U111*, *U43*, *U559*, *U202* and *U564* are distributed in a loose formation over the Central North Atlantic.

On 20 June *U203* sights the US battleship *Texas* inside the operational area announced by Germany and shadows her for several hours. On her reporting this, orders are issued forbidding attacks on US ships even when they are in the operational area. On 23 June *U203* sights the convoy HX.133 and sinks one ship in the night 23-24 June, but then loses contact. At mid-day she comes across the approaching OB.336 from which two ships are sunk (totalling 11325 tons). On 24 June *U79* directs to the scene in turn *U71*, which is driven off, *U371* (Lt-Cdr Driver) and *U651* (Lt-Cdr Lohmeyer) which each sink one ship of 4765 tons and 5297 tons respectively. *U111* has to break off the pursuit. *U108*, *U553*, *U101*, *U77* and *U558* shadow the OB.336 without success. On 26 June *U556*, *U564* and *U201* establish contact with HX.133. *U564* (Lt Suhren) sinks two ships of 17463 tons in the night 26-27 June and torpedoes one other ship of 9467 tons. On 27 June *U556* (Lt-Cdr Wohlfarth) is sunk by the escorting corvettes *Nasturtium*, *Celandine* and *Gladiolus*. *U651*, *U79*, *U562*, and *U201* do not fire their torpedoes. On 28 June only *U651* is able to maintain contact: *U201* is driven off. Shortly after midnight on 29 June *U651* sinks one ship of 6342 tons but is then sunk by the destroyers *Malcolm*, *Scimitar*, the corvettes *Arabis*, *Violet* and the minesweeper *Speedwell*. The sighting of the convoy by a FW 200 of I/K.G.41 on 29 June does not result in any more U-boats coming to the scene. Total results: eleven ships of 57215 tons sunk and two ships damaged. On 28 June *U146* (Lt Ites), operating NW of the Hebrides, sinks one ship of 3496 tons. *U137* has no success.

21-22 June Baltic

Minelayer Group North (Cdr* v. Schönermark), comprising the minelayers *Tannenberg*, *Brummer* and *Hansestadt Danzig* and escorted by four boats of the 2nd MTB Flotilla and five boats of the 5th MMS Flotilla, lays the barrage 'Apolda' (500 EMC's and 700 explosive floats) between Fanöfjord and Dagö. The operation is carried out according to plan despite an attack by two Soviet aircraft and being sighted by destroyers and guard vessels.

At the same time the 'Cobra' Group (Cdr Dr Brill), comprising *Cobra*, *Kaiser* and *Königin Luise*, and escorted by six boats of the 1st MTB Flotilla and five minesweepers of the 5th MMS Flotilla, lays the barrage 'Corbetha' (400 EMC's and 700 explosive floats) between Kallbada-Grund and Pakerort. This force sights a Soviet battleship and a number of other vessels.

The 2nd MTB Flotilla lays 12 TMB mines in both the Soelo and Moon Sound exits ('Coburg' and 'Gotha' barrages); the 5th MTB Flotilla lays 12 TMBs in the western approach to the Irben Strait ('Eisenach') and the 3rd MTB Flotilla lays 12 TMBs in both the approaches to Libau and Windau ('Weimar' and 'Erfurt'). A few minutes after the opening of hostilities at 0300 hrs *S59* (Lt Albert Müller) and *S60* (Lt Wuppermann) sink the Latvian steamer *Gaisma* (3077 tons) off Windau. The 1st MTB Flotilla captures the Estonian steamer *Estonia* (1181 tons).

21-23 June Mediterranean

German/Italian return convoy from Tripoli is continually attacked by British aircraft based on Malta. All ships, including two damaged freighters, reach Trapani and Naples under protection of four destroyers and five torpedo boats.

22 June General Situation

Beginning of the German attack on the Soviet Union.
Strength of the Soviet Fleets:
Baltic Fleet (Vice-Adm Tributs): two battleships, two heavy cruisers, two flotilla leaders, seven old and 12 modern destroyers, seven patrol ships (torpedo boats), 65 submarines, six minelayers, 32 minesweepers, one gunboat, 48 torpedo cutters (motor torpedo boats) and 656 aircraft.
Northern Fleet (Vice-Adm Golovko): three old and five modern destroyers, seven patrol ships (including three torpedo boats), 15 submarines, two minesweepers, 15 patrol cutters, two torpedo cutters, auxiliary ships and 116 aircraft.
Black Sea Fleet (Vice-Adm Oktyabrski): one battleship, two modern, three old and one training cruiser, three flotilla leaders, five old and eight modern destroyers, two patrol ships (torpedo boats), 47 submarines, 84 torpedo cutters, 15 minesweepers and 625 aircraft.

22 June Arctic

Soviet Northern Fleet (Vice-Adm A. G. Golovko) begins operations. The submarine brigade (Capt 1st class N. I. Vinogradov) sends the submarines *K-1*, *D-3*, *Shch-421* and *Shch-401*, on operations against the German supply traffic in Söröy-Sund, to the North Cape, Nordkyn and off Syltefjord. *M-176*, *M-175*, *M-173* are stationed in defensive positions in the area of the Fisherman's Peninsula.
On orders of the People's Commissar, the submarines *Shch-403* and *Shch-404* are employed defensively off the Kola coast and the destroyers *Grozny* and *Sokrushitelny* in the entrance to the White Sea. The evacuation of women and children in transports from Murmansk to the east begins.

22 June Black Sea

The Black Sea Fleet, in accordance with plans, begins to lay out defensive mine barrages off its own bases of Sevastopol, Odessa, Kerch, Novorossisk, Tuapse and Batum. The cruisers *Krasny Kavkaz* and *Chervona Ukraina*, the flotilla leader *Kharkov*, the destroyers *Boiki*, *Besposhchadny* and *Bezu-*

prechny, the minelayer *Ostrovski* and the training cruiser *Komintern* take part off Sevastopol and the destroyer *Dzerzhinski* off Batum. In all, 3453 mines and 509 barrage protection devices are laid off Sevastopol in 1941. Aircraft of the German IV Fl.K. attack Sevastopol. Rumanian coastal batteries shell the Soviet monitors *Rostovtsev*, *Zheleznyakov* and *Zhemchuzhin*, in the Danube Estuary near Reni.

22 June   North Atlantic
U48 returns to Kiel after making her twelfth and last mission into enemy waters. On these missions under the command of Lt-Cdr Herbert Schultze (eight missions), Cdr Hans Rösing (two missions) and Lt-Cdr Heinrich Bleichrodt (two missions) she has, in all, sunk one sloop and 54 ships of 322292 tons and damaged two ships of 11024 tons. She is therefore the most successful submarine of the Second World War.

22-23 June   Baltic
Ju 88s of K.Fl. 806 drop 27 air mines in the area of Kronstadt, on which the Estonian steamer *Ruhno* (499 tons) sinks on 22 June, and they attack ships. The Soviet steamer *Luga* (2329 tons) is sunk.
The Finnish submarines *Iku Turso* (Lt-Cdr Pekkanen) and *Vetehinen* (Lt-Cdr Pakkala) lay 20 mines each on 22 June in the Gulf of Finland E of Ekholm and N of Kunda Bay respectively; and *Vesihiisi* (Lt-Cdr Kijanen) lays 20 mines N of Ekholm on 23 June (mine barrages F.4, 5, 3).
In a sortie into the area off Hangö the 3rd MTB Flotilla attacks one steamer and *S44* (Lt Opdenhoff) sinks the Soviet patrol boat *MO-238*. The 3rd MTB Flotilla lays 18 TMB mines in the Irben Strait.

22-23 June   Baltic
At 1822 hrs a force (Capt 2nd class I. G. Svyatov), comprising the cruiser *Maksim Gorki* and the destroyers *Gnevny*, *Gordy* and *Steregushchi*, leaves Ust-Dvinsk to go through the Irben Strait and take up a position off the western exit of the Gulf of Finland to cover mining operations. To carry out the mining operations (under the orders of the Commander of the Squadron, Rear-Adm D. D. Vdovichenko) the minelayers *Marti* and *Ural*, the flotilla

leaders *Leningrad* and *Minsk* and the destroyers *Karl Marks*, *Artem* and *Engels* set out from Tallinn. 3 BTShchs and some MOs and the destroyer *Smely* form the anti-mine and submarine escorts. On 23 June at 0340 hrs the covering force runs into the German 'Apolda' mine barrage in the area of the Oleg Bank; the destroyer *Gnevny* has her bow torn off by a detonating mine and sinks. *Gordy* is damaged by mines detonating in her bow paravanes. *Maksim Gorki*, as a result of hitting a mine, loses her bow up to her 60th rib. *Steregushchi* detonates two mines with her bow paravanes and is slightly damaged, but she brings the disabled cruiser to Worms. From there minesweepers and torpedo cutters bring her to Tallinn.

22-27 June   Baltic
Defence of Soviet naval base at Libau (Commandant: Capt 1st Class M.S. Klevenski) by the 67th Rifle Div (Maj-Gen Dedaev). In the harbour there are 15 submarines of the 1st SM Brigade, one destroyer, six torpedo cutters, 12 patrol cutters and one minesweeper. On 22 June the submarines *L-3*, *M-79*, *M-81* and *M-83* take up positions between Memel and Libau. The submarines *M-77*, *M-78* and *S-9* are moved with a steamer to Dünamünde and on the way *M-78* is lost off Windau from a torpedo hit from *U144*. The submarines *Kalev* and *Lembit* and the transport *Zheleznodorozhnik* with the patrol boat *MO-218* are transferred to Windau, followed by eight steamers. The minesweeper *Fugas* (Lt Gillerman) lays several barrages with 207 mines on 22-23 June, on which the minesweeper *M3134* sinks on 1 July, the submarine-chaser *UJ113* on 10 July and the minesweeper *M1706* on 22 Nov.
On 23 June the submarine *S-3* with very numerous personnel on board is transferred from Libau to Dünamünde but off Steinort, after several torpedo misses from the motor torpedo boat *S35* (Sub-Lt H. Weber), is sunk by depth charges and hand grenades. Attacks by *S27* and *S60* on the force of 12 patrol boats and one auxiliary warship, which is transferred at the same time, fail.
On 24 June the non-operational ships in

Libau, the destroyer *Lenin*, the submarines *S-1*, *M-71*, *M-80*, *Ronis* and *Spidola*, the ice-breaker *Silach* (541 tons) and the auxiliary gunboat *Tunguska* (947 tons) are scuttled. The torpedo cutter *TKA-27* is lost. On 25 June the returning *M-83* scuttles herself off Libau; the other submarines are diverted at sea to Dünamünde. In the night 25-26 June *Fugas* (see above) lays another barrage and then leaves for the N.

In the night 26-27 June the torpedo cutters *TKA-37*, *TKA-57* and *TKA-67* proceed to Dünamünde and, finally, *TKA-17* (Lt Osipov with Capt Klevenski on board) and *TKA-47*. The latter is captured off Backofen after an engagement with the 2nd MTB Flotilla. Units of the German 291st Inf Div, supported by the Naval Assault Detachment Bigler, enter Libau on 27-29 June and occupy the town.

22-30 June   Mediterranean
In British submarine operations in the Western Mediterranean *Severn* (Lt-Cdr Campbell) sinks two ships of 4192 tons and the Dutch *O23* (Lt-Cdr v. Erkel) one ship of 5317 tons. In the Central Mediterranean *Union* (Lt Galloway) and *Utmost* (Lt-Cdr Cayley) each sink one ship of 1004 tons and 4080 tons respectively. *Triumph* (Lt-Cdr Wards) sinks the Italian submarine *Salpa* off Sollum. In the middle of the year the British submarine flotillas in the Mediterranean consist of:
8th SM Flotilla (Gibraltar): *Clyde*, *Severn*, and the Dutch *O21*, *O23*, *O24* and other boats proceeding E to form the 10th and 1st SM Flotillas.
10th SM Flotilla (Malta): *Ursula*, *Utmost*, *Upright*, *Unique*, *Upholder*, *Unbeaten*, *Urge*, *Union*, *P32* and *P33*.
1st SM Flotilla (Alexandria): *Truant*, *Triumph*, *Taku*, *Tetrarch*, *Torbay*, *Regent*, *Rover*, *Otus*, *Rorqual*, *Cachalot*, *Parthian*, *Pandora* and the Greek *Katsonis*, *Papanicolis*, *Nereus*, *Triton* and *Glavkos*.
22-30 June   Baltic
The German U-boats *U140*, *U142*, *U144*, *U145* and *U149* operate W of Memel, S of Gotland, W of Windau and W of Ösel-Dagö and off the Gulf of Finland. In the night 22-23 June *U144* (Lt-Cdr v. Mittelstaedt) sinks the Soviet submarine *M-78*; on 24 June *U140*

misses a large submarine; and on 26 June *U149* (Lt-Cdr Höltring) sinks one submarine, probably *M-101*.
22-30 June   Baltic
First climax of the Soviet submarine effort. At the beginning of the war *S-4* is on the Pomeranian Coast, *S-10* in the Gulf of Danzig, *S-7* and *S-101* off Gotland for reconnaissance; and *Shch-322*, *Shch-323* and *Shch-324* in defensive positions off the Gulf of Finland and, similarly, *M-94*, *M-96*, *M-99* and *M-102* in the area Bengtskär-Utö. Of the 1st Brigade (Capt 1st class Egipko) *M-79*, *M-81* and *M-83* take up defensive positions off Libau and *L-3* (Capt 3rd Class Grishchenko) sets out for a mining operation off Memel (mines laid on 27 June). On 23 June six boats go to sea from Tallinn from the 2nd Brigade (Capt 2nd Class Orel); on 25 June there are 16 boats and on 27 June 20 boats stationed mainly in defensive positions. Apart from the boats named, some of which have come in to port, there are *S-5*, *S-6*, *S-8* and *S-102* operating from Riga and *M-89*, *M-90*, *M-95*, *M-97*, *M-98*, *Shch-309*, *Shch-310*, *Shch-311*, and *M-101* from Tallinn. On 24 June, 25 June and 28 June *S-10*, *S-4* and *L-3* make unsuccessful attacks. On 27 June the boats of the 1st Brigade, which are not yet on the way back, are recalled to Tallinn. On the return through the Irben Strait *S-7* is narrowly missed by the 3rd MTB Flotilla on 25 June. *S-10* is probably involved in an engagement on 27 June and is lost. *M-101* is probably sunk by *U149*.
22-30 June   Black Sea
First air attacks by the air force of the Soviet Black Sea Fleet on Constanza. On 22 June six SB 2s and three DB 3s of the 63rd Air Brigade (Col Khotiashvili) attack. Up to the end of the month there are 38 attacks in 285 sorties with the participation of the 2nd and 4th Air Regiments of the 62nd Fighter Brigade.
22 June-4 July   Black Sea
The German II/K.G.4, operating from Zilista, drops 120 air mines on and off Sevastopol and 50 air mines in the area of Nikolaev. On 22-23 June there sink on these mines the tug *SP-12*, the barge *Dnepr*, one floating crane and the destroyer *Bystry* which is later salvaged

and dismantled to repair damaged sister ships. The destroyer *Bditelny* is badly damaged and the flotilla leader *Kharkov* slightly damaged on 12 July.

22 June-17 July   Black Sea
Submarines of the Soviet 1st SM Brigade (Capt 1st Class P.I. Boltunov) operate from Sevastopol in defined areas off Constanza, Mangalia and Varna; some of the boats of the 2nd Brigade (Capt 1st class M.G. Solovev) operate in the area of the Danube estuary and the remainder in defensive formations off the Caucasian coast. The first wave consists of *M-33*, *M-34*, *Shch-205*, *Shch-206* and *Shch-209*. *Shch-204* does not return from a second wave at the beginning of July; she is probably sunk on one of the flanking mine barrages laid off the Rumanian coast.

23 June   Black Sea
The Soviet destroyer *Shaumyan* and the minesweeper *T-413/No 27* lay a mine barrage of 70 mines off the Kilia estuary.

23-25 June   Black Sea
On a report by the Danube Flotilla that six enemy destroyers and torpedo boats have been sighted, the flotilla leader *Kharkov* and the destroyers *Besposhchadny* and *Smyshleny* proceed to the area of Fidonisi Island but sight no enemy ships.

24-26 June   Baltic
On 24 June the Finnish submarines *Vesihiisi* and *Iku-Turso* lay 18 and 20 mines respectively E and SE of Rodskär in the Gulf of Finland. The German 2nd MTB Flotilla lays 36 TMB mines (barrage 'D 1') N of Cape Takhkona. In the night 25-26 June the German minelayer *Brummer* (Cdr Dr Tobias) lays 100 EMC mines and 50 explosive floats ('D 2') north of Moon Sound. In escorting her, boats of the 2nd and 5th MTB Flotillas run on to the Soviet barrages laid out at the beginning of the war and *S43* and *S106* sink. On returning from a minelaying operation W of the Irben Strait, the boats of the 3rd MTB Flotilla encounter the Estonian steamer *Lidaza* which is torpedoed by *S34* (Sub-Lt Lüders). *S54*, *S60* and *S61* fire torpedoes in the harbour of Windau and obtain three hits on the mole and one on a steamer.

The Finnish minelayers *Riilahti* and *Ruotsinsalmi* lay the 'Kipinola' barrage with 200 mines on the night 25-26 June. On 26 June the Finnish submarines *Vesihiisi* and *Iku-Turso* lay two more barrages of 20 and 18 mines respectively S of Stenskär and S of Suur-Tytärsaari.

24-26 June   Indian Ocean
The German auxiliary cruiser *Schiff 41 Kormoran*, coming up to mine Madras, encounters the British auxiliary cruiser *Canton* (15784 tons). *Schiff 41* is able to escape undetected, but has to abandon the proposed operation. On 26 June she sinks two freighters of 7625 tons in the Bay of Bengal.

24-27 June   Baltic
The Soviet group of light naval forces (Rear-Adm V.P. Drozd) based on Dünamünde begins with the laying-out of mine barrages in the western half of the Irben Strait. Taking part are the destroyers *Storozhevoi*, *Silny*, *Serdity*, *Strashny*, *Stoiki*, *Grozyashchi* and *Smetlivy* and, for support, the cruiser *Kirov* and minesweepers. In all, some 500 mines are laid in the nights 24-25 June and 26-27 June. In the second operation there is an engagement with the 3rd MTB Flotilla which is likewise out on a mining operation. At first *S59* (Lt Müller) and *S31* (Sub-Lt Haag) attack and obtain one hit in the bow of *Storozhevoi*. Then *S59* and *S60* (Lt Wuppermann) get hits on a vessel to the rear, possibly the submarine *S-10* which has just joined. In a third attack *S35* (Sub-Lt Weber) and *S60* probably sink the Soviet minesweeper *T-208/Shkiv*. On the barrages laid out the motor minesweeper *R205* sinks; the minesweepers *M201* and *R203* are badly damaged; and *R53*, *R63* and *R202* slightly damaged.

24 June-8 July   Black Sea
Soviet-Danube Flotilla (Rear-Adm N. O. Abramov) with the Reni group—the monitors *Rostovtsev*, *Zheleznyakov*, *Zhemchuzhin*, and four armoured cutters (BKAs)—holds up attempts by Rumanian monitors to advance down the Danube across the Pruth Estuary. From Ismailia the monitors *Udarny* and *Martynov* with 12 BKAs support small landings of units of the 25th Rifle Div on the S bank of the Kilia arm.

24 June-17 July   North Atlantic
Operations by an Italian submarine group against convoys W of Gibraltar. On 24 June *Da Vinci* (Cdr Calda) sinks one tanker of 8030 tons sailing on her own. The *Bianchi*, which is setting out to join the group, is sunk when still in the Bay of Biscay by the British submarine *Tigris* (Cdr Bone) on 5 July. On 5 July *Torelli* (Cdr de Giacomo) sights one small convoy proceeding westward to which *Da Vinci, Baracca, Malaspina* and *Morosini* are directed. Only *Torelli* is able to make an unsuccessful attack on one destroyer. On 7 July *Torelli* sights another outwardbound convoy, to which *Morosini, Da Vinci* and *Baracca*, as well as *U103*, are directed. But they do not find the convoy (possibly HG.66). From 14 July to 17 July *Morosini* (Cdr Fraternale) and *Malaspina* (Lt-Cdr Prini) each sink two ships totalling 13552 tons and 7978 tons respectively.

25-26 June   Arctic
Covered by destroyers and submarine-chasers of the Northern Fleet, the Soviet transport *Mossovet* brings troop reinforcements to the Titovka sector. German air attacks are unsuccessful.

25-27 June   Black Sea
Soviet sortie against Constanza. On the evening of 25 June the assault group (Capt 2nd Class M.F. Romanov) leaves Sevastopol with the flotilla leaders *Kharkov* and *Moskva*, followed by a covering force (Rear-Adm T. A. Novikov) comprising the cruiser *Voroshilov* and the destroyers *Smyshleny* and *Soobrazitelny*. Simultaneously with a diversionary attack by aircraft of the 63rd Naval Air Brigade the *Kharkov* and *Moskva* shell oil tanks and railway installations near Constanza on 26 June resulting in fires and the blowing up of an ammunition train. The fire is answered from a railway battery to the N and from the 28cm battery 'Tirpitz' to the S of Constanza. In avoiding the salvoes *Moskva* runs on to one of the flanking mine barrages laid before the war and sinks. As a result of a mine being detonated by the bow paravanes of *Soobrazitelny*, there is temporary damage on *Voroshilov*. The *Kharkov* becomes unmanoeuvrable for a short time because of near-miss bombs and the

two other destroyers are sent to provide help in the form of additional AA cover. The destroyers *Besposhchadny* and *Bodry*, coming from Sevastopol, meet the *Voroshilov*.

25-28 June   Arctic
The British cruiser *Nigeria* with three destroyers is directed to the weather signals from the weather observation ship *Lauenburg* (*WBS 2*) (344 tons), located by D/F. In spite of mist, it is possible to find the *Lauenburg* near Jan Mayen on 28 June after another D/F location by the destroyer *Bedouin*. She is abandoned by the crew in the fire of the British ships: the destroyer *Tartar* goes alongside at once and is able to recover valuable codes.

25-29 June   Mediterranean
Italian convoy with four large troop transports from Naples to Tripoli via Taranto. Close escort provided by four destroyers and distant escort by two cruisers and three destroyers. Slight damage sustained by the passenger ship *Esperia* in British air attacks.

26 June   Baltic
Soviet force with the minelayer *Marti* (Capt 1st Class N. I. Meshcherski) lays further parts of a mine barrage in the western part of the Gulf of Finland between Odensholm and Hangö.

26 June-1 July   Mediterranean
Operation 'Railway': Force H with the battlecruiser *Renown*, the carrier *Ark Royal*, the cruiser *Hermione* and six destroyers sets out from Gibraltar on 26 June for the area S of the Balearics where, in spite of bad weather, 22 of the Hurricane fighters, received from the *Furious*, are flown off. They all reach Malta with their Blenheim guide aircraft. Force H returns on 28 June but puts to sea on 29 June with the carrier *Furious* for a second operation. On 30 June 26 Hurricanes fly off from *Ark Royal* and nine from *Furious*; and they all reach Malta. Then a take-off accident on *Furious* makes it impossible for the remaining eight machines to fly off and Force H returns on 1 July.

27 June   Baltic
Finnish minelayers *Riilahti* and *Ruotsinsalmi* lay the 'Kulemajärvi' barrage (200 S/40s) NE of Odensholm.

27 June   Manchukuo/Western France
Blockade-runner *Regensburg* (8068 tons,

I

Capt Harder) reaches Bordeaux from Dairen.

27-28 June   Air War/Germany
British bombers attack Bremen, Cuxhaven, Emden and Wilhelmshaven.

27-30 June   Arctic
Some 150 Soviet civilian ships, boats and fishery vessels are evacuated to the White Sea from the Kola Inlet. The operation suffers no loss.

27 June-4 July   Central Atlantic
Operations against the convoy SL.76 in the area of the Cape Verde Islands. The returning *U69* (Lt-Cdr Metzler) sights the convoy as the U-boat is proceeding to Las Palmas to refuel from the German tanker *Charlotte Schliemann* and sinks two ships of 13026 tons. On the same day *U123* (Lt-Cdr Hardegen), which is outward-bound and coming from Las Palmas, establishes contact and sinks two more ships of 7642 tons. On 29 June she approaches again and sinks one steamer of 4088 tons, while the outward-bound *U66* (Cdr Zapp) sinks two scattered ships of 10031 tons and the returning *U103* (Cdr Schütze), which is in the area, sinks the Italian blockade-runner, *Ernani* 6619 tons), in error. The U-boats *UA*, *U95*, *U97* and *U98*, which are directed to SL.76 from the N, do not get to the scene.

28 June   Baltic
The Finnish submarine *Vetehinen* lays the mine barrage F6 (17 S/36s) between Suursaari and Klein Tütters.

28 June   Mediterranean
Mine barrage S.2 (442 mines and barrage protection devices) is laid in the Sicilian Channel by the Italian 7th Div (Div Adm Casardi), comprising the cruisers *Attendolo* and *Duca d'Aosta* and the destroyers *Pigafetta, Pessagno, Da Mosto, Da Verazzano* and *Da Recco*.

29 June   Baltic
The Finnish minelayers *Riilahti* and *Ruotsinsalmi* lay the 'Valkjärvi' mine barrage (200 S/40s) N of Cape Purikari.

29 June-4 July   Arctic
On 29 June the German XIX Mountain Corps (Gen Dietl) with the 2nd Mountain Div from the Petsamo area and the 3rd Mountain Div from the Yläluostari area starts to attack in the direction of Murmansk. Early on 1 July the 136th Mountain Regt has blocked with two battalions the approach to the Small Fisherman's Peninsula and forms with one battalion a bridgehead across the Titovka. To support the hard-pressed defending forces of the Soviet 14th Rifle Div, a Soviet formation (Capt 2nd Class E. M. Simonov), consisting of the destroyers *Kuibyshev* and *Uritski* and the submarine-chasers *MO-121* and *MO-123*, lands reinforcements on 30 June on the narrow neck of the Fisherman's Peninsula and shells German advance troops. Attacks by Ju 87s of IV/L.G.1. miss the Soviet ships, in particular the submarine-chaser *MO-121*. By 4 July the German Mountain Divs push the Soviet 14th and 52nd Rifle Divs back over the Litsa and form several bridgeheads. The Soviet troops are repeatedly supported by gunfire from the patrol ships *Groza* and *Smerch* from Motovski Bay.

29 June-15 July   North Atlantic
The German U-boats *U201, U562, U564, U561, U559, U557, U553, U202, U111, U108, U98, U96* and *U77* operate in a wide, loose formation in the Central Atlantic with very little success. On 29 June a convoy, probably OG.66, is sighted by I/K.G.40. On 30 June and 1 July FW 200s again report the convoy and their bearings are received by U-boats. The cryptography service also gives positions of the convoy but, of the boats directed to the scene, only *U108* comes briefly into the area and she is driven off again. *U77, U79, U96* and *U557* do not come up. On 3 July the operation is abandoned. The following sinkings of single ships are made: *U564* (Lt Suhren) one ship of 1215 tons; *U108* (Lt-Cdr Scholtz) one ship of 2486 tons; *U98* (Lt-Cdr Gysae) two ships of 10842 tons; and *U96* (Lt-Cdr Lehmann-Willenbrock) one ship of 5954 tons. *U143* operates in the North Channel without success.

30 June   South Atlantic
The British cruiser *Dunedin* captures E of St Paul the Vichy French steamer *Ville de Tamatave* (4993 tons).

30 June-2 July   Baltic
The Soviets evacuate Riga and Dünamünde. The cruiser *Kirov*, which cannot pass through the Irben Strait because of the mines, is lightened and is brought

with the destroyers *Grozyashchi, Smetlivy* and *Stoiki* through the shallow waters of the Moon Sound to Tallinn. In the move from Dünamünde to Tallinn the submarines *M-77* and *M-79* run on to German mine barrages and are damaged. *M-81* is lost on 1 July.

30 June-10 July Mediterranean
The British submarine *Torbay* (Lt-Cdr Miers) sinks in the Aegean one ship of 2933 tons and six sailing ships, as well as the Italian submarine *Jantina* (5 July). She also torpedoes one ship of 5232 tons. In the Central Mediterranean *Urge* (Lt-Cdr Tomkinson) and *Upholder* (Lt-Cdr Wanklyn) each sink one ship of 6996 tons and 5867 tons respectively.

1 July North Atlantic
Patrol Wing 7 of the US Navy starts reconnaissance over the North West Atlantic from Argentia (Newfoundland).

1-5 July Baltic
The 5th and 31st MS Flotillas make a channel in the mine barrage to Libau. In doing so, *M3134* sinks on 2 July. There are mining operations North of Cape Takhkona (1 July), E of the 'Apolda' barrage (2 July), S of 'Corbetha' and W of Soelo Sound (5 July). The minelayer *Brummer*, the 5th MMS Flotilla and the 1st, 2nd and 3rd MTB Flotillas drop in all 196 mines and 130 explosive floats.

1-19 July North Atlantic
American occupation of Iceland. On 1 July TF 19 (Rear-Adm McD. Le Breton) sets out from Argentia (Newfoundland) with the battleships *Arkansas* and *New York*, the cruisers *Brooklyn* and *Nashville* and the destroyers *Plunkett, Niblack,, Benson, Gleaves, Mayo, Charles F. Hughes, Lansdale, Hilary P. Jones* (Desron 7, Capt Kauffman) *Ellis, Bernadou, Upshur, Lea* (Desdiv 60) and *Buck*, the tanker *Salamonie* and the tug *Cherokee*. Its purpose is to land in Reykjavik on 7 July the 1st Marine Brigade (Brig-Gen Marston), embarked on the troop transports *William P. Biddle, Fuller, Heywood, Orizaba* and the freighters *Arcturus* and *Hamul*, to relieve the British forces stationed there. After the operation has been carried out according to plan, TF 19 returns to Argentia from 12 July to 19 July.

1-30 July Arctic
The Soviet submarines *M-174, Shch-422, Shch-402, Shch-401, M-172* and *D-3* operate off the Norwegian Polar Coast. On 14 July *Shch-402* (Lt-Cdr N. G. Stolbov) unsuccessfully attacks the steamer *Hanau* off Porsangerfjord and on the same day *Shch-401* (Lt-Cdr A. E. Moiseev) the submarine-chasers *UJ177* and *UJ178* off Vardö.

2-6 July Baltic
The remaining destroyers of Rear-Adm Drozd's force carry out mining operations in the Irben Strait from Moon Sound. In the process *Strashny* is badly damaged on a mine on 2 July. On 6 July *Serdity* and *Silny* encounter, when dropping mines, the German *Minenräumschiff 11* and the minesweeper *M31*: they have hurriedly to throw the remaining mines overboard and make off while firing. *Silny* is lightly hit. The two German ships reach Dünamünde undamaged after four unsuccessful air attacks.

2-27 July Mediterranean
In transport operations by the Italian submarines *Zoea* (two), *Corridoni* (two) and *Atropo* (one), 268 tons of supplies are brought to Bardia.

3-17 July Mediterranean
Of the Italian submarines *Malachite, Ametista, Settembrini* and *Dagabur* operating off the coasts of Cyrenaica and Egypt, *Malachite* is the only one to fire her torpedoes, which she does on 3 July. But she misses the cruiser *Phoebe* with two destroyers.

4 July Baltic
The Finnish submarine *Vesikko* (Lt-Cdr Aittola) sinks the Soviet steamer *Viborg* S of Someri—after unsuccessful attacks by *Saukko* and *Vetehinen*.

4 July Air War/Germany
British bombers carry out a daylight raid on Bremen.

4-6 July Baltic
The 5th German MS Flotilla creates a channel through the mine barrages from Libau to Windau. Soviet air attacks are beaten off: there is slight damage to *Sperrbrecher 6* and *11*.

4-10 July Mediterranean
The submarines *Corallo* and *Diaspro* are stationed between the Balearics and the Algerian coast to act against sorties by British Force H.

5-15 July   Arctic
First operations by the German U-boats U81 and U652 off the Kola Coast. On 6 July U652 (Lt Fraatz) sinks the Soviet patrol ship SKR-70/Voronin (558 tons) off Cape Teriberski. On 12 July the Soviet patrol ship Brilliant attacks U81 unsuccessfully off Svyatoy Nos.

5 July-6 Aug   Baltic
The Soviet submarines M-99, S-7, S-9, S-11, L-3, S-8, Shch-311, Kalev, M-90, M-94, HM-98, K-3 and S-4 operate in the Baltic from Tallinn and Soelo Sound. Kalev, L-3 and K-3 lay mine barrages near Steinort, Brüsterort and W of Bornholm. On the way M-99 is lost on a mine NW of Worms. On the return S-9 is damaged by an aircraft on 20 July off Soelo Sound and on 22 July M-94 is sunk by the U-boat U140 (Lt Hellriegel). S-11 sinks, when returning on 2 Aug, on a mine barrage off Soelo Sound, Only S-4 (Capt 3rd Class Abrosimov) reports an attack on 1 Aug.

6 July   Mediterranean
The British submarine Triumph sinks off Benghazi the Italian freighter Ninfea (607 tons) and the escorting gunboat De Lutti after a lengthy surface engagement. The submarine is also hit and has to put in to Malta.

6-8 July   Arctic
On 6 July the German 2nd and 3rd Mountain Divs start their attack across the Litsa. To support the hard-pressed Soviet 14th and 52nd Rifle Divs a landing force (Capt 1st Class V. I. Platonov) is formed, consisting of the patrol ships Groza, Musson and Tuman, the minesweepers T-890 and T-891 and the submarine-chasers MO-131, MO-132 and MO-133. It lands a naval battalion on 6 July and again on 7 July, making in all 1029 troops. Their attack leads to regrouping on the German side and to the interruption of the attack across the Litsa.

7 July   Mediterranean
Mine barrages S.31 and S.32 are laid out in the Sicilian Channel (292 mines and 444 barrage protection devices) by the Italian 7th Cruiser Div (Div-Adm Casardi), comprising the cruisers Attendolo and Duca d'Aosta, and the 4th Cruiser Div (Div Adm Giavanola), comprising the cruisers Bande Nere and

Di Giussano and the destroyers Pigafetta, Pessagno, Da Recco, Da Mosto, Da Verazzano, Maestrale, Grecale and Scirocco.

8 July   Baltic
Pernau is taken by German troops.

8-9 July   Black Sea
The Reni group of the Soviet Danube Flotilla breaks through to Ismailia with three monitors and four armoured cutters (BKA 114 sunk).

9 July   Baltic
First German convoy with six coastal motor ships and four drifters, escorted by five minesweepers leaves Libau for Riga.

9 July   Baltic
The minelayers Tannenberg (Cdr* v. Schönermark), Preussen (Cdr Barthel) Hansestadt Danzig (Cdr Schroeder) sink, on returning from Finland to Swinemünde, on a Swedish mine barrage E of the southern tip of Öland, which has been laid at German request.

9 July   Black Sea
Unsuccessful sortie by the Soviet 2nd DD Div (Flotilla leader Tashkent, destroyers Bodry, Boiki, Besposhchadny and Bezuprechny) to attack enemy shipping in the Fidonisi area.

9-11 July   Baltic
The Finnish submarines Iku-Turso (Lt-Cdr Pekkanen) and Vetehinen (Lt-Cdr Pakkala) lay mine barrages east of Ekholm.

10 July   Baltic
The 1st MTB Flotilla, comprising S28, S26, S101, S40 and S39, attacks a Soviet force in the Gulf of Finland near Ekholm. But they only encounter the Latvian steamer Rasma (3204 tons), beached after hitting a mine on 5 July on the barrage laid by the Finnish submarine Vesihiisi (Lt-Cdr Kijanen).

10 July   South Atlantic
When the British auxiliary cruiser Canton approaches, the German motor ship Hermes (7209 tons) scuttles herself NW of St Paul.

10-11 July   Baltic
The German Minenräumschiff 11 arrives with M23 off Pernau: the latter is beached after hitting a mine. UJ113 is sunk on a mine off Libau.

10-12 July   Arctic
The German 6th DD Flotilla (Capt Schulze-Hinrichs), comprising Hans Lody, Karl Galster, Hermann Schoemann,

Friedrich Eckoldt and *Richard Beitzen*, arrives in Kirkenes on 10 July and makes a sortie along the Kola Coast on 12 July. In doing so, a group of three destroyers encounters near Cape Teriberski a small Soviet convoy with the patrol ship *Passat* (Lt Okunevich) and two trawlers. *Passat* and the trawler *RT-67/ Molotov* sink and *RT-32* gets away. The other destroyers find no targets near Iokanga.

10 July-10 Aug   Central Atlantic
After the conclusion of the operation against SL.76 (27 June) *U66* and *U123* proceed to the area off Freetown but their only successes are on the way out until 10 July. Inclusive of the ships of SL.76, they sink: *U66* (Cdr Zapp) four ships of 19078 tons; and *U123* (Lt-Cdr Hardegen) five ships of 21507 tons. From 10 July to 25 July they operate without success off Freetown. *U109* is likewise unsuccessful off NW Africa from 6 July. She replenishes on 27 June from a tanker in Cadiz and then operates W of Gibraltar. From 23 July to 29 July *U93*, *U94* and *U124* proceed in line abreast to the S and are then stationed with *U123* in the area W of Morocco. With other boats they are directed on 10 Aug to the convoy HG.69 (see entry). The boats do not have any success.

11 July   Baltic
The Finnish submarine *Iko-Tursu* (Lt-Cdr Pekkanen) lays mine barrage F15 (18 mines) E of Ekholm.

11 July   Black Sea
In attempts by Soviet forces to land on the Kilia arm of the Danube estuary, the armoured cutters *BKA-111* and *BKA-134* are lost: the monitors *Zhemchuzhin*, *Rostovtsev* and *Martynov* are transferred to the Danube estuary.

11-12 July   Mediterranean
In the nightly supply missions to Tobruk the British destroyer *Defender* is badly damaged by German bombers and sinks when being towed by the destroyer *Vendetta*. The gunboat *Cricket* and sloop *Flamingo* are damaged. About 30 German aircraft attack Port Said and Ismailia on the Suez Canal in the night 11-12 July.

11-20 July   Baltic
The 5th MMS Flotilla sows mines (90) in the area N of 'Juminda' (11 July, 13 July and 20 July).

12-13 July   Baltic
The German Baltic Experimental Force proceeds from Libau to Riga with naval barges, Siebel ferries, lighters, floating gun carriers, coastal motor ships and assault boats. Cape Domesnäs is passed on 12 July with an escort from the 2nd MMS Flotilla. Ineffectual shelling from Russian coastal batteries on Svorbe. On 13 July there are attacks by Soviet motor torpedo boats under Lt Gumanenko and by aircraft. One assault ship is sunk, two larger and three small craft receive splinter damage. An attack by a Soviet destroyer formation under Rear-Adm Drozd, consisting of the destroyers *Engels*, *Gordy*, *Grozyashchi*, *Stoiki*, *Silny*, *Steregushchi* and *Serdity* and the torpedo boats *Sneg* and *Tucha*, off the Dvina estuary, has no result. Attempts by the Soviet submarine *S-102*, operating in the Gulf of Riga, to fire her torpedoes, fail because the water is too shallow.

13-16 July   Arctic
The second German attack by the reinforced 2nd Mountain Div from the widened Litsa bridgehead begins on 13 July. The Soviet defence is supported by the patrol ship *Smerch* in the bay of Litsa. On 14 July a Soviet force (Capt 1st Class V. I. Platonov), consisting of three patrol ships, three minesweepers and 10 submarine-chasers, lands the 325th Rifle Regt and a naval battalion totalling 1600 troops on the western bank of the Bay of Litsa. Their counter attack is supported by gunfire from the destroyer *Kuibyshev*, the patrol ship *Groza* and four submarine-chasers. The operation is covered towards the sea by the destroyers *Gremyashchi*, *Gromki* and *Stremitelny*. Once again the German attack comes to a standstill. On 16 July three patrol ships land another battalion in the Bay of Litsa, supported by the destroyer *Kuibyshev* and the patrol ships *Groza*, *Priliv*, *Smerch* and four submarine-chasers.

14 July   Mediterranean
Ju 88s of L.G.1 attack Suez from Crete. The troop transport *Georgic* (27751 tons) is set on fire. Total loss.

14 July   Baltic
The 1st MTB Flotilla, comprising *S28*, *S27*, *S40*, *S101* and *S26*, attacks a Soviet convoy near Ekholm without success.

14-18 July   Mediterranean
Italian supply convoys to North Africa.
From 14 July to 16 July a convoy of
five freighters, escorted by the destroyers
Malocello, Fuciliere, Alpino and the
motor torpedo boats *Procione, Pegaso*
and *Orsa*, proceeds to Tripoli. In the
area of Pantelleria the British submarine
P33 (Lt Whiteway-Wilkinson) attacks
and sinks one ship of 5293 tons.
From 16 July to 18 July the second
convoy proceeds consisting of the large
troop transports *Marco Polo, Neptunia*
and *Oceania*, escorted by the destroyers
Geniere, Gioberti, Lanciere, Oriani and
the torpedo boat *Centauro*. Distant
escort: cruisers *Bolzano, Trieste* and
destroyers *Ascari, Carabiniere* and
Corazziere. The British submarine *Unbeaten* (Lt Woodward) just misses the
Oceania.
15 July   Baltic
The boats *S54, S47, S58* and *S57* of the
3rd MTB Flotilla try, in groups, to
make a pincer attack on a Soviet destroyer in the Bay of Riga. Only one
torpedo from *S57* (Lt Erdmann) explodes near the target.
15-20 July   North Atlantic
Because of the absence of sightings, the
U-boats operating in the Central
Atlantic, *U372, U431, U401, U68,
U565, U331, U74, U126, U562, U561,
U564, U97, U98, U203* and *U95*, are
concentrated in a more compact formation. On 17 July I/K.G.40 sights an
outward-bound convoy NW of the
North Channel about which several
reports are also received from the W/T
cryptographic service. Air reconnaissance again finds the convoy on 18 July
and 19 July; but the convoy avoids the
patrol line formed on 19 July with five
boats and on 20 July with *U431, U401,
U68, U565, U331, U74, U562, U561,
U564, U97, U203, U126* and *U95*.
Only *U203* (Lt-Cdr Mützelburg) and
U95 (Lt-Cdr Schreiber) damage one
ship each of 8293 tons and 5419 tons
respectively in gun attacks on 20 July.
16 July   Baltic
Minenräumschiff 11 clears a channel
through a mine barrage newly laid by
Soviet destroyers off Dünamünde.
17 July   Mediterranean
The Italian petrol tanker *Panuco* (6212
tons) receives an air torpedo hit in the

harbour of Tripoli which makes it
partly impossible to unload the ship.
After emergency repairs she has to go
to Italy on 19 July with 6000 tons of
petrol still on board.
17-18 July   Mediterranean
The Italian submarines *Alagi* and
Diaspro are stationed N of Cape
Bougaroni against a sortie by Force H
eastwards from Gibraltar.
18 July   Baltic
Unsuccessful sortie by the 3rd MTB
Flotilla against Kübassare (Ösel). The
Soviet destroyers *Serdity* and *Steregushchi* try to attack German supply convoy
off Dünamünde. The convoy reaches
the Dvina estuary without loss. On the
return on 19 July *Serdity* is damaged by
a bomb hit (from a Ju 88 of K.Fl.Gr.
806) in Moon Sound and, after vain
attempts to salvage her, she has to be
abandoned and scuttled on 22 July.
18-19 July   Black Sea
The Soviet Danube Flotilla evacuates
the Kilia arm as part of the withdrawal
of Soviet XIV Rifle Corps from the
Danube and breaks through the Rumanian defensive positions near Peri-
prava. Off the estuary the monitors,
armoured cutters and minesweepers
are met by a detachment coming from
Odessa consisting of the cruiser *Komintern*, the gunboats *Krasnaya Armeniya*
and *Krasnaya Gruziya*, 10 torpedo cutters
and six patrol cutters as well as the destroyers *Bodry, Kharkov* and *Shaumyan*.
18-30 July   North Atlantic
German-Italian operations against Gibraltar convoys. On 18 July it is reported
that agents have observed the departure
of HG.67 from Gibraltar. The Italian
submarines *Malaspina, Morosini, Torelli,
Bagnolini* and *Barbarigo* are concentrated against the convoy which avoids
them. After *Torelli* (Cdr de Giacomo)
has sunk one single tanker of 8193 tons,
Barbarigo sights HG.67 on 22 July but
soon loses contact with the result that
the Italians and the German *U93, U94,
U124* and *U203*, which are ordered to
the scene, do not find the convoy.
Bagnolini (Cdr Chialamberto), which
has briefly sighted a homeward-bound
convoy on 19 July, attacks OG.68
on 23 July and hears three detonations which are not, however, caused
by hits.

Barbarigo (Cdr Murzi) sinks two independents of 13407 tons on 25-26 July. On 24 July the 'B' Service locates the positions of the convoys OG.69 and SL.80. *U79, U126, U331, U68, U561, U562, U564* (only briefly) and *U203* are directed to OG.69 and *U431, U565, U401, U74, U94* and *U97* to SL.80. On 25 July SL.80 is reported once and OG.69 twice by FW 200s of I/K.G.40— up to 15 boats receive the bearings from the aircraft establishing contact. On 26 July contact is not re-established with SL.80 and the operation is abandoned. On the same day *U141* (Lt Schüler) attacks off Northern Ireland the outward-bound convoy OS.1 (escorted by the 5th EG, Cdr Macintyre on the destroyer *Walker*) and sinks one ship of 5106 tons and torpedoes one more of 5133 tons. She is pursued for 20 hours with depth charges. FW 200s again establish contact twice with OG.69 and with the aid of bearings bring *U68* up in the afternoon. In addition to the seven German boats, *Barbarigo* and *Calvi* are also directed to the convoy. In the night 26-27 July *U79* (Lt-Cdr Kaufmann) and *U203* (Lt-Cdr Mützelburg) each sink one ship of 2475 tons and 1459 tons respectively. *U561, U126, U79* and *U331* have no successes. On 27 July *U371* (Lt-Cdr Driver) establishes contact with OS.1 to the west and, with interruptions, maintains contact until 30 July when two ships of 13984 tons are sunk. Two FW 200s again keep contact with OG.69 and *U68, U562* and *U126* come up; but only the last (Lt-Cdr Bauer) is able to sink two ships of 2639 tons towards midnight. In the night 27-28 July *U561* (Lt Bartels) also sinks one ship of 1884 tons. On 28 July FW 200s, *U68, U79, U561, U331* and *U126* are in temporary contact and in the evening *U203* sinks two ships of 2846 tons. An agent's report about the departure of HG.68 from Gibraltar is received. In the night 28-29 July *U331* is driven off from OG.69. A concentration with the boats *U79, U126, U66, Calvi, Bagnolini* and *Barbarigo* on 29-30 July against both convoys, OG.69 and HG.68, meets with no success. Total sinkings among OG.69: seven ships of 11303 tons.

18 July-6 Aug   Arctic
Operation by the German U-boats *U81* and *U652* off the Kola Coast. On 24 July *U652* misses the Soviet patrol ship *SKR-23* off Kildin Island.

19-31 July   Mediterranean
The Italian submarines *Axum, Squalo* and *Uarsciek* operate off the Egyptian coast.

19 July-13 Sept   North Atlantic
On 19 July the US Atlantic Fleet forms TF 1 for the defence of Iceland and to conduct convoys to and from Iceland. A Task Group consisting of the carrier *Wasp*, the cruisers *Quincy* and *Vincennes* and the destroyers *O'Brien* and *Walke*, brings *P-40* fighters to Iceland which are flown off without loss at sea and reach their destination.

Among the ships employed in convoy service to Iceland are Desron 7 (Capt Kauffman) with the destroyers *Benson, Niblack, Hilary P. Jones, Plunkett, Mayo, Madison, Gleaves, Charles F. Hughes* and *Lansdale*, from Desron 11 *Grayson, Roe, Sampson*, from Desron 30 (Capt Cohen) the destroyers *Dallas, Greer, Tarbell, Cole, Bernadou, Lea, Ellis* and *Upshur* and Desdiv 69 with the destroyers *McCormick, Sturtevant, Reuben James* and *Bainbridge*. From 6 Aug the Catalina flying-boats of Patron 73 and the Mariner flying-boats of Patron 74 operate from Reykjavik and Hvalfjord respectively.

20 July   Arctic
In an attack by Ju 88s of 5/K.G. 30 on Soviet ships in Ekaterinski Gavan in the Kola Inlet the destroyer *Stremitelny* (Capt 2nd class A. D. Vinogradov) is hit and sunk.

20-29 July   Mediterranean
On 20 July the British submarine *Union* is sunk by the Italian torpedo boat *Circe* in an attack on a convoy off Cape Bon.

On 24 July *Upright* misses a floating dock on tow near Capo dell'Armi and *Upholder* (Lt-Cdr Wanklyn) torpedoes one ship (4964 tons) east of Sicily.

On 28 July *Utmost* (Lt-Cdr Cayley) sinks one ship of 11466 tons and *Upholder* attacks near Marettimo the distant escort of an Italian return convoy from North Africa, consisting of the cruisers *Garibaldi* and *Montecuccoli* and the destroyers *Granatiere, Bersag-*

liere, Fuciliere and *Alpino.* She torpedoes the *Garibaldi.* In the Western Mediterranean *Olympus* (Lt-Cdr Dymott) sinks one ship of 747 tons and there are transport operations to Malta with submarines of the 1st SM Flotilla (see 30 June).

21 July Baltic
Finnish minelayers lay the mine barrage F.16 (85 mines and 15 explosive floats) east of the 'Valkjärvi' barrage.

21-23 July Mediterranean
The Italian motor tanker *Brarena* (6996 tons) is sunk by British aircraft when accompanied by the destroyer *Fuciliere* on the way from Palermo to Tripoli.
Supply convoy from Naples to Tripoli: five large freighters, escorted by six destroyers and one torpedo boat. On 22 July the German steamer *Preussen* (8203 tons) is hit in a British air attack and explodes.

21-27 July Mediterranean
Operation 'Substance': supply convoy from Gibraltar to Malta with the troop transport *Leinster* and the freighters *Melbourne Star, Sydney Star, City of Pretoria, Port Chalmers, Durham* and *Deucalion.* The operation is escorted by Force H (Vice-Adm Somerville), comprising the battlecruiser *Renown,* the carrier *Ark Royal,* the cruiser *Hermione,* the destroyers *Faulknor, Fearless, Foxhound, Firedrake, Foresight, Fury, Forester* and *Duncan.* They are reinforced by ships of the Home Fleet: the battleship *Nelson,* the cruisers *Arethusa, Edinburgh* and *Manchester,* the fast minelayer *Manxman* and the destroyers *Cossack, Maori, Sikh, Nestor, Lightning, Farndale, Avondale* and *Eridge.* The Mediterranean Fleet carries out a diversion in the Eastern Mediterranean. Eight submarines are stationed off Cagliari, Naples, N of Sicily and both sides of the Straits of Messina.
21 July: in setting out from Gibraltar the troop transport *Leinster* (4302 tons) goes aground and has to return.
22 July: the force is located south of the Balearics by Italian air reconnaissance. Because it is thought that aircraft are being transferred to Malta, the Italian Fleet does not set out. Of the Italian submarines *Alagi* and *Diaspro* (Lt-Cdr Dotta), stationed N of Bouga-

roni, the latter just misses the *Renown* and *Nestor* (RAN).
23 July: Italian air reconnaissance again locates the force in the area of Bône. But it is now too late for the Fleet to go into action. Italian aircraft secure hits on the cruiser *Manchester* and the destroyer *Fearless.* The latter has to be abandoned. The destroyer *Firedrake* receives a bomb hit and has to return. In the evening Force H returns to Gibraltar. The Italian submarines *Bandiera, Dessiè, Manara* and *Settimo,* stationed between Pantelleria and Malta from 23 July, do not fire their torpedoes.
24 July: the convoy continues its journey with *Edinburgh* (Rear-Adm Syfret), *Arethusa, Manxman* and destroyers. In the area of Pantelleria, the Italian motor torpedo boats *MAS 532* and *MAS 533* attack the convoy and torpedo the transport *Sydney Star* (12696 tons). On the same day the force enters Malta. From Malta seven empty ships proceed to the W, of which the tanker *Höegh Hood* (9351 tons) receives a hit from an air torpedo S of Sardinia. 25 July: Force H meets the returning cruisers and the empty convoy. They reach Gibraltar on 27 July.

22 July Baltic
Sortie by the 3rd MTB Flotilla towards the area E of Arensburg (Ösel) when the torpedo cutter *TKA-71* and one tug are sunk.

22 July South Atlantic
The British cruiser *Dunedin* captures the Vichy French steamer *Ville de Rouen* (5383 tons) E of Natal.

22-24 July Arctic
The 6th DD Flotilla, comprising *Karl Galster, Hermann Schoemann, Friedrich Eckoldt* and *Richard Beitzen,* sinks the Soviet survey ship *Meridian* in the Polar Sea between Iokanga and Teriberka.

22 July-4 Aug Arctic
British carrier raid on Kirkenes and Petsamo. 22-25 July: the ships earmarked for the operation are assembled in the Seidisfjord (Iceland). In the process the destroyer *Achates* is severely damaged on a mine.
26 July: the minelaying cruiser *Adventure,* used as a transport to Murmansk, leaves with the destroyer *Anthony.* There follows later Force P (Rear-Adm Wake-Walker), consisting of the air-

craft carriers *Furious* and *Victorious*, the heavy cruisers *Devonshire* and *Suffolk* and the destroyers *Echo, Eclipse, Escapade* and *Intrepid*.

28 July: the destroyers take on oil supplies from the cruisers and from the tanker *Black Ranger*, which is escorted by the destroyers *Icarus* and *Inglefield* and which is waiting at a rendezvous.

30 July: *Adventure* is released and the force is divided into two groups each having a carrier as its main element. The force is located by German air reconnaissance. 20 Albacore torpedo aircraft and nine Fulmar fighters take off from *Victorious* to attack the German gunnery training ship *Bremse* and other ships lying in Kirkenes. 11 torpedo aircraft and two fighters are shot down by AA fire and aircraft of 6/J.G.5. Only slight damage is sustained by the ships under attack. 18 Albacore aircraft, four Hurricane fighters and six Fulmars take off from *Furious* to attack Petsamo. Because no ships have arrived in the harbour, the force attacks land targets. One fighter and one torpedo aircraft are lost.

31 July: *Furious* hands over her operational aircraft to *Victorious* and returns because of fuel shortage. On 4 Aug three Fulmars take off from *Victorious* to attack Tromsö and one aircraft is lost. Then this force also returns.

23 July   Baltic
M3131 is sunk in clearing mines off the Dvina Estuary.

23-24 July   Arctic
The Soviet destroyers *Grozny* and *Sokrushitelny* and the minelayer *Kanin* lay a defensive barrage of 250 mines in the entrance to the White Sea.

24 July   Air War/Western Europe
Heaviest daylight attack so far by RAF with 149 bombers on the German battleships *Gneisenau* (Brest) and *Scharnhorst* (La Pallice). The latter receives five hits which cause serious damage to the ship's electric cables.

25 July   South Atlantic
The German steamer *Erlangen* (6101 tons) scuttles herself SE of the River Plate when approached by the British cruiser *Newcastle*.

25-26 July   Baltic
Aircraft of German K.G.4 drop 40 airmines east of Moon Island.

25-26 July   Mediterranean
Attempt by the Italian 10th MAS flotilla to attack the supply ships which have arrived in Malta. The frigate *Diana* with eight explosive boats and *MAS 451* and *MAS 452*, each with a human torpedo team, reach Malta, but are detected by British radar as they approach. Nevertheless, the torpedo rider, Major Tesei, the inventor of the '*Maiali*', and two explosive boats, are able to blow up the harbour boom, but, as a result of the detonation, the St Elmo bridge collapses and bars the way to the other six explosive boats. They are destroyed by coastal batteries. On the next morning fighter bombers locate the withdrawing *MAS 451* and *MAS 452* and sink them.

25-26 July   Baltic
Attacks by the Soviet Naval Air Force and a TKA group on the 2nd MMS Flotilla detailed to look for mines in the Irben Strait. On 25 July *R53* and *R63* are slightly damaged by mine detonations and on 26 July *R169* is sunk by a bomb hit. TKA attacks are unsuccessful.

26-27 July   Baltic
In a sortie by the 3rd MTB Flotilla (Lt-Cdr Kemnade) into the northern part of the Gulf of Riga the command boat *S55* and *S54* (Sub-Lt Wagner) locate a single Soviet destroyer. After an unsuccessful approach, *S54* sinks the destroyer, probably the *Smely*. *S57* and *S58* miss two minesweepers lying at anchor off Arensburg (Ösel). On (28 July the 3rd MTB Flotilla sinks the ice-breaker *Lachplesis* (253 tons) in a gun engage- ment off Arensburg.

27 July-6 Aug   Arctic
British Force K (Vice-Adm Vian), comprising the cruisers *Aurora* and *Nigeria* and the destroyers *Punjabi* and *Tartar*, leaves Scapa Flow for Spitzbergen (they arrive on 31 July) to investigate Norwegian and Russian settlements there. On the return the Norwegian weather station on Bear Island is evacuated and destroyed. A sortie against the Norwegian coast is detected in time by German air reconnaissance.

28 July   Baltic
The Soviet submarine *Shch-307* (Lt-Cdr Petrov) sinks *U144* off the Gulf of Finland.

29 July Arctic

Sortie by the 6th DD Flotilla with four destroyers (as on 22 July) towards Yugor and Kara Straits; it is abandoned in the area of Kolguev when the British carrier force is located (see 22 July-4 Aug).

29 July Mediterranean

The British submarine *Thrasher* (Lt-Cdr Cowell) arrives in Alexandria with 78 British troops who had remained hidden in Crete since the end of the fighting.

30 July Mediterranean

The Italian torpedo boat *Papa* (Lt Rosica) attacks the British submarine *Cachalot* as she proceeds on the surface with gunfire and rams her. The submarine surrenders but sinks shortly after the crew of 70 have been taken aboard.

30 July China

Japanese bombers attack the US gunboat *Tutuila* lying in Chungking.

30 July-4 Aug Mediterranean

The Italian submarine *Delfino*, operating off Mersa Matruh, is attacked by a British Sunderland flying-boat but is able to shoot it down and take four prisoners.

30 July-10 Aug North Atlantic

The U-boats which are ordered on 30 July to form a new concentration in the Central North Atlantic are directed to a convoy, detected on 1 Aug by the 'B' service: SL.81. On 2 Aug *U204* establishes contact and brings up *U559*. On 3 Aug *U204* brings up in turn *U431*, *U205*, *U558*, *U75*, *U372*, *U401*, *U565* and *U559*. An FW 200 of I/K.G.40 is shot down by a Hurricane flown off from the catapult ship *Maplin*. On 4 Aug *U558*, *U431*, *U559*, *U75*, *U83* and *U74* come up again but they are all prevented from attacking by the defence. On 3 Aug *U401* is sunk by the destroyers *Wanderer* and *St Albans* (Norwegian) and the corvette *Hydrangea* of the 7th EG. FW 200s sight the convoy on 3 Aug and 4 Aug and sink one ship of 4337 tons. *U372* (Lt-Cdr Neumann), *U204* (Lt-Cdr Kell), *U75* (Lt-Cdr Ringelmann) and *U74* (Lt-Cdr Kentrat) are not able to fire their torpedoes until the night 4-5 Aug when they do so in turn. They sink two ships, one ship, one ship and one ship respectively, totalling 23190 tons. By

day the boats are finally driven off by the air and sea escort. The U-boats *U71*, *U77*, *U96*, *U751* and *U43* are directed to a homeward-bound convoy sighted by *U565* on 4 Aug, but they have no success. On 6-7 Aug *U43*, *U71*, *U96*, *U751*, *U83*, *U75*, *U46*, *U205*, *U559*, *U204* and *U372* operate without result against the convoy HG.68 reported by the 'B' Service. Likewise from 8 Aug to 10 Aug the same boats operate against a south-bound convoy without sighting anything.

31 July-1 Aug Baltic

Aircraft of K.G.4 drop 38 LMB mines on the roads of Triigi. The 2nd MTB Flotilla lays 24 TMB mines near Dagerort.

31 July-4 Aug Mediterranean

Operation 'Style': Force X brings 1750 troops and RAF personnel and 130 tons of supplies from the disabled transport *Leinster* (see operation 'Substance') on the cruisers *Arethusa*, *Hermione*, the fast minelayer *Manxman* and two destroyers from Gibraltar to Malta. They arrive on 2 Aug, are unloaded and return. On the way the *Hermione* rams and sinks the Italian submarine *Tembien* in the area of Tunis. The other Italian submarines stationed in the Malta area, *Bandiera*, *Manara*, *Settimo* and *Zaffiro* and those positioned near Galita and Cape Bougaroni, *Serpente*, *Alagi* and *Diaspro*, do not attack. British Force H, comprising the British battlecruiser *Renown*, the battleship *Nelson*, the carrier *Ark Royal* and destroyers, operate as a covering group in the Western Mediterranean. In the night 31 July-1 Aug, the destroyers *Cossack* and *Maori* are detached to shell the harbour of Alghero (Sardinia), whose airfield is attacked early in the morning by nine Swordfish aircraft from the *Ark Royal*. After returning to Gibraltar, the battlecruiser *Renown* proceeds to Britain for an overhaul. Vice-Adm Somerville hoists his flag on the battleship *Nelson*.

1 Aug Baltic

German 1st MS Flotilla beats off near Cape Domesnös an attack by four Soviet motor torpedo boats which are covered at some distance by two Soviet destroyers. *TKA-122* is sunk.

1 Aug   General Situation
President Roosevelt forbids the export of oil and aviation spirit to countries outside British control and outside the Western Hemisphere. The substantial Japanese imports are particularly affected by the measure.

1 Aug   Black Sea
Soviet bombers attack Constanza.

1-2 Aug   Baltic
Aircraft of K.G.4 drop 15 LMBs in the area E of Moon, 22 LMBs N of Moon Island and 18 LMBs W of Worms Island.

1-20 Aug   Arctic
The German U-boats *U451* and *U566* operate off the entrance to the White Sea and the Kola Coast respectively. *U451* (Lt-Cdr Hoffmann) misses one guard boat on 7 Aug and sinks the Soviet patrol ship *Zhemchug* off Svyatoy Nos on 10 Aug.

2 Aug   Baltic
The Finnish submarine *Vesihiisi* (Lt-Cdr Kijanen) lays the mine barrage F.17 (18 mines) E of Odensholm. Unsuccessful attack by the motor torpedo boats *S55* and *S58* on the Soviet destroyer *Artem* in the Gulf of Riga.

2 Aug   General Situation
Beginning of the American Lend-Lease deliveries to the USSR.

2-3 Aug   Air War/Germany
British bombers attack Hamburg and Kiel.

2-3 Aug   Arctic
The Soviet reinforced 325th Rifle Regt, which is still on the west bank of Litsa Bay, cannot hold out against the attack of the German 136th Mountain Regt. What is left of it is evacuated on 3 Aug by ships of the Northern Fleet.

3-7 Aug   Mediterranean
In the Western Mediterranean the Dutch submarines *O21* (Lt-Cdr van Dulm) and *O24* (Lt-Cdr de Booy) sink one sailing ship and two small ships of 909 tons respectively. In the area of Rhodes the Greek submarine *Nereus* (Lt-Cdr Rotas) reports one steamer and one sailing ship sunk.

4-5 Aug   Baltic
Aircraft of K.G.4 drop 16 LMBs S of Zerel in the Irben Strait and 16 LMBs in the roads of Triigi (Kassarwik).

5-28 Aug   North Atlantic
Formation of a new U-boat group in a loose concentration SW of Iceland with *U563, U568, U129, U567, U206, U84, U501, U71, U553, U77, U43, U96, U101, U38, U73, U105, U751, U202, U82, U569* and *U652*. On 9 Aug *U206* (Lt Opitz) sinks one trawler. On 11 Aug *U501* sights an outward-bound convoy from which *U568* (Lt-Cdr Preuss) sinks the corvette *Picotee* on 12 Aug. On 12 Aug *U129* sights a west-bound convoy but *U563, U567* and *U206*, which are directed to it, find nothing up to 13 Aug. On 18 Aug *U38* (Cdr Schuch) sinks one independent of 1700 tons. Owing to lack of convoy sightings, the boats are sent eastwards on 22 Aug. The outward-bound *U452* is sunk on 25 Aug by a Catalina flying-boat of No 209 Sqdn and the trawler *Vascama*. *U570, U38, U82, U202, U652, U501, U569, U84, U567, U553,* and *U207* are unsuccessfully directed south of Iceland to the convoy HX.145 located on 27 Aug in a 'B' service report. *U570* (Lt Rahmlow) is attacked in bad weather by a Hudson bomber of No 269 Sqdn RAF (Sq-Ldr Thompson) and slightly damaged, with the result that the commander surrenders. The U-boat spends several hours on the surface with the bomber circling overhead. Supported by a Catalina of No. 209 Sqdn RAF the trawler *Northern Chief* (Lt Knight) arrives on the evening of 27 Aug, and in the morning of 28 Aug the trawler *Kingston Agathe*, the destroyers *Burwell* and *Niagara* and the trawlers *Westwater* and *Windermere*. After taking off the crew, two of the trawlers tow the boat to Iceland. On 19 Sept she is put into service as HMS *Graph* (Lt Colvin).

6 Aug   Mediterranean
British torpedo aircraft attack off the Tunisian coast a convoy (6 ships with five escorting destroyers and one torpedo boat) proceeding from Naples to Tripoli and sink the freighter *Nita* (6813 tons).

6-8 Aug   Baltic
The Soviet destroyers *Surovy* and *Statny* shell the German coastal battery 'Hainasch' in Moon Sound on 6 Aug and the battery 'Markgraf' on 8 Aug.
In the Gulf of Finland Ju 88s of K.Fl.Gr. 806 destroy the Soviet destroyer *Karl Marks* in Loksa Bay near Tallinn.

6-16 Aug   North Atlantic
U331, U126 (sinks one trawler of 172 tons on 4 Aug), *U94, U124, U79, U109, U93* and *U371* assemble in the area between Gibraltar and the Azores to operate against the convoy HG.69 whose departure is reported by agents on 9 Aug. The Italian boats *Finzi, Marconi* and *Veniero* are included in the formation. On 10 Aug *U79* sights the convoy but is driven off. On 11 Aug *U93* and *U94* establish temporary contact and *Marconi* (Lt-Cdr Pollina) misses the sloop *Deptford* and the corvette *Convolvulus* which are part of the escort. On 12 Aug *U331, Finzi* and *U123*, which is returning, and in the night of 12-13 Aug also *U124, Veniero* and *U331*, are all in turn driven off. *Marconi* continues to send contact reports with interruptions until 14 Aug when she is driven off with *Finzi*. *Marconi* destroys an independent of 2589 tons with gunfire and the wreck is finished off by a torpedo from *U126* (Lt-Cdr Bauer). A patrol line consisting of *U123, U124, U126, Marconi* and *Finzi*, has no success on 15 Aug. On 11 Aug one freighter of 2852 tons is sunk by FW200s of I/K.G.40 which have been ordered to undertake air reconnaissance and a report is sent on 12 Aug. On 16 Aug the operation has to be broken off.

6-20 Aug   Mediterranean
The Italian submarines *Zoea, Corridoni* and *Atropo* transport 192 tons of supplies and fuel to Bardia. On the way *Zoea* is attacked by aircraft.

6-30 Aug   Arctic
The Soviet submarines *Shch-421, M-175, Shch-401, Shch-402* and *K-2* (Capt 3rd class V. P. Utkin) operate off the Norwegian Polar coast. The last misses the steamers *Hans* and *Lübeck* off Tanafjord on 13 Aug. *M-173* undertakes a reconnaissance operation off Petsamo Fjord. Then *M-172* (Lt-Cdr I. I. Fisanovich), with the Div-Cdr, Capt 2nd class I. A. Kolyshkin on board, penetrates the fjord on 21 Aug but misses a ship lying alongside the pier in Liinahamari. On 22 Aug she misses the hospital ship *Alexander von Humboldt* off Petsamo Fjord.
On 11 Aug and 16 Aug respectively the British submarines *Tigris* and *Trident*,

which have been transferred to Murmansk, proceed on operations in Svaerholt and Lopphavet. *Tigris* (Cdr Bone) sinks the Norwegian coaster *Haakon Jarl* (1482 tons) on 17 Aug; *Trident* (Cdr Sladen) damages the steamer *Levante* (4769 tons) by gunfire on 19 Aug and sinks from convoys the steamer *Ostpreussen* (3030 tons) on 22 Aug and the steamers *Donau* (2931 tons) and *Bahia Laura* (8561 tons) on 30 Aug. On 25 Aug the submarines *K-21, K-22* and *K-23*, which passed through the Neva on 8 Aug, arrive in Molotovsk by way of Lake Ladoga and the White Sea Canal. They are made operational there and are transferred to Polyarnoe at the end of October.

8 Aug   Black Sea
A naval force of the North-West Command is formed under Rear-Adm D. D. Vdovichenko to support the coastal army. It consists of the cruiser *Komintern*, the destroyers *Nezamozhnik* and *Shaumyan*, the minelayer *Lukomski*, a gunboat division with the gunboats *Krasnaya Abkhaziya, Krasny Adzharistan, Krasnaya Armeniya* and *Krasnaya Gruzia*, the 2nd Torpedo Cutter Brigade (3 divisions of 12, 18 and 10 boats) and the 5th MS Div (seven auxiliary minesweepers). The force, which is based on Odessa and Ochakov, is under the command of the Commandant, Naval Base, Odessa, Rear-Adm G. V. Zhuokov.

8-12 Aug   Black Sea
Units of the Soviet Danube Flotilla support the withdrawal of troops over the Bug Estuary.

8-26 Aug   Baltic
The 'Juminda' mine barrages are laid out. The German minelayers *Cobra* (Cdr Dr Brill), *Kaiser* (Cdr Bohm) and *Königin Luise* (Lt-Cdr Wünning), supported by the 5th MMS Flotilla (Lt-Cdr Dobberstein) and the 1st MTB Flotilla (Lt-Cdr Birnbacher), lay the mine barrages D10 to D30 with, in all, 673 EMC mines and 636 explosive floats. The Finnish minelayers *Riilahti* (Sub-Lt Kivilinna) and *Ruotsinsalmi* (Lt-Cdr Arho) lay the mine barrages F.18-F.22 with a total of 696 mines and 100 explosive floats.

9-10 Aug   Arctic
Sortie by the German 6th DD Flotilla, comprising *Hans Lody, Friedrich Eckoldt*,

and *Richard Beitzen*, towards Kildin Island and the mouth of the Kola Inlet. During this the Soviet patrol ship *SKR-12/Tuman* (Sub-Lt Shestakov) is surprised and sunk after courageous resistance. The German force is shelled by coastal guns and attacked by aircraft as it withdraws. The *Richard Beitzen* is damaged by near-misses.

9-12 Aug   General Situation
President Roosevelt and Churchill meet on board the British battleship *Prince of Wales* and the heavy US cruiser *Augusta* in Argentia Bay (Newfoundland). Proclamation of the Atlantic Charter.

10-11 Aug   Baltic
Soviet convoy from Tallinn to Suursaari and Kronstadt with the transport *Vyacheslav Molotov* (7494 tons) with 3500 wounded on board, escorted by the destroyer *Steregushchi*, *BTShch* (Fugas) minesweepers and MO submarine-chasers. Minesweeper *T-201/Zaryad* is sunk after hitting a mine (possibly as early as 3 Aug); *V. Molotov* is damaged off Suursaari by a mine.
Boats of the German 2nd MTB Flotilla lay the mine barrage 'Allirahu' with 24 TMB mines in the Gulf of Riga. Boats of the 5th MS Flotilla lay the flanking mine barrages 'Pinnass I-IV' with 47 EMC mines off Cape Domesnäs.

10-23 Aug   North Atlantic
After the SL.81 operation, *U75*, *U559*, *U204*, *U83* and *U106*, *U201*, *U564* and *U552* (which have recently set out) assemble in the area W of the North Channel. On 17 Aug they are directed to convoy OG.71 reported by a FW 200 of I/K.G.40. *U201* (Lt Schnee) establishes contact late in the evening and maintains it, with several interruptions, until 19 Aug. On 18 Aug and 19 Aug Ju 88s of Air Commander Atlantic, which have taken off for operations, only find the convoy individually. Guided by reports from aircraft and *U201*, *U559* (Lt Heidtmann), *U201* and *U204* (Lt-Cdr Kell) fire their torpedoes in the night 18-19 Aug. *U204* sinks the Norwegian destroyer *Bath* (Lt-Cdr Melsom) belonging to the 5th EG and one ship of 1809 tons; *U559* and *U201* each sink one ship of 3255 tons and 1584 tons respectively. In the evening *U106* takes over contact but is

driven off. Contact is lost until the afternoon of 21 Aug but is then regained by a FW 200. However, *U201*, *U108*, *U564*, *U106* and *U552* which are directed to the scene, do not find the convoy. As a result of several aircraft reports, *U564* (Lt Suhren) establishes contact in the afternoon of 22 Aug and she brings *U201* up again. In the night 22-23 Aug *U564* sinks two ships of 1687 tons and *U201* two ships of 2761 tons. A ship (2129 tons), torpedoed by *U564*, is sunk by *U552* (Lt Topp). On the morning of 23 Aug *U564* sinks the corvette *Zinnia* belonging to the escort. Total result: two escorts and nine ships of 13225 tons.

11 Aug   North Sea
In an attack by boats of the 4th MTB Flotilla on a convoy off Dungeness *S49* (Sub-Lt Günther) sinks the British freighter *Sir Russell* (1548 tons).

11 Aug   Mediterranean
In a British air torpedo attack on ships in the harbour of Syracuse the Italian hospital ship *California* (13060 tons) sinks.

11-25 Aug   Black Sea
In submarine operations in the Black Sea, the Soviet *Shch-211* (Lt-Cdr A. D. Devyatko) disembarks agents near Varna on 11 Aug and, after an unsuccessful attack by *Shch-216*, sinks the Rumanian steamer *Peles* (5708 tons) near Cape Emine. An attack by *M-33* on the returning Rumanian submarine, *Delfinul*, off Constanza and two attacks by *Shch-210* off Varna meet with no success. *L-5* lays a mine barrage near Sulina.

12-13 Aug   Baltic
Boats of the 2nd MTB Flotilla lay the mine barrage 'Mona I' (18 TMBs) in the southern entrance to Moon Sound. Boats of the 5th MS Flotilla lay the flanking mine barrages 'Pinnas V-VI' with 28 EMC mines off Cape Domesnäs. In engagements in the Gulf of Finland motor torpedo boats of the 1st MTB Flotilla sink the Soviet motor minesweeper (Rybintsi) *R-101* and a minesweeper near Great Wrangel on 13 Aug.

12-16 Aug   Black Sea
Soviet Danube Flotilla supports withdrawal over the Lower Dnieper. It arrives in Kherson on 12 Aug. Unsuccessful operation by the Ruma-

nian submarine *Delfinul* and the MTBs *Viscolul*, *Vijelia* and *Viforul* against Soviet supplies between Sevastopol and Odessa.

12-18 Aug Mediterranean
British fast minelayers *Abdiel* and *Latona* and destroyers bring 6000 troops to the beleaguered fortress of Tobruk to relieve the battle-weary Australian units. 5000 troops are evacuated. In this operation and others from 12 Sept and 12 Oct the Australian cruiser *Hobart* and the destroyers *Napier* and *Nizam* also take part.

12-23 Aug Mediterranean
The mine barrages S.41, S.42, S.43 and S.44 are laid out on 12 Aug, 16 Aug, 19 Aug and 23 Aug in the Sicilian channel by the Italian auxiliary mine-layers (ferry ships) *Aspromonte* and *Reggio* with a total of 1125 mines. In addition, 3202 barrage protection devices are laid by the destroyers *Zeno*, *Da Verazzano*, *Pigafetta*, *Da Mosto*, *Da Noli* and *Pessagno*.

13 Aug Black Sea
The Soviet destroyers *Nezamozhnik* and *Shaumyan*, together with the gunboat *Krasny Adzharistan* and the coastal batteries Nos 412 and 726, support the counter attack of the 1st Naval Rifle Regt near Grigorevka.

13-20 Aug Black Sea
The destroyers *Shaumyan*, *Nezamozhnik*, *Frunze* and *Dzerzhinski* operate in turns in shelling Rumanian positions in the area of Odessa and Ochakov.

13 Aug-4 Sept Norway
In the British 9th SM Flotilla operating off Western Norway there are, inter alia, the French *Minerve* and *Rubis* (Lt-Cdr Rousselot), which sinks one ship of 4360 tons, the Dutch *O14* and various British submarines.

14-15 Aug Baltic
Soviet convoy from Tallinn to Suursaari-Kronstadt. The motor ship *Sibir* (3767 tons), with 2500 wounded on board, is sunk in an air attack. The minesweeper *T-202/Buy* is sunk near Suursaari on 15 Aug after hitting two mines.

14-17 Aug Black Sea
Evacuation of the Soviet naval base at Nikolaev (Rear-Adm Kuleshov). The ships on the stocks of the Marti yard, including the 45000 ton battleship

Sovetskaya Ukraina, the heavy cruiser *Ordzhonikidze*, the flotilla leaders *Perekop* and *Ochakov*, the destroyers *Opashny* and one other, the submarines *S-36*, *S-37* and *S-38* and two gunboats, are blown up. Also possibly a scarcely-begun new battlecruiser (?). The ships which are fitted out, including the cruisers *Frunze* and *Kuibyshev*, the flotilla leaders *Erevan* and *Kiev*, the destroyers *Svobodny*, *Ognevoi*, *Ozornoi*, the submarines *L-23*, *L24*, *L-25*, *S-34* and *S-35*, and the ice-breaker *Mikoyan*, are towed away. The operations are screened by the destroyers *Bodry*, *Boiki*, *Besposhchadny*, *Bezuprechny*, *Dzerzhinski*, *Frunze*, *Nezamozhnik* and *Shaumyan*.

14-19 Aug Pacific
Auxiliary cruiser *Schiff 45 Komet* (Rear-Adm Eyssen) sinks or captures three ships totalling 27178 tons in the area of the Galapagos Islands.

15 Aug South Atlantic
The German steamer *Norderney* (3667 tons) scuttles herself NE of the Amazon estuary when approached by the British cruiser *Despatch* and the auxiliary cruiser *Pretoria Castle*.

15-16 Aug Black Sea
The Soviet gunboats *Krasnaya Armeniya* and *Krasnaya Gruziya* give fire support to Soviet troops near Grigorievka and Spiridovka (Odessa).

16 Aug Baltic
Soviet convoy from Suursaari to Tallinn, led by the ice-breaker *Oktyabr*, loses several ships on the 'Juminda' mine barrage.

17 Aug Baltic
Unsuccessful attack by four Soviet TKAs on German ships off Cape Domesnäs.

18-19 Aug Baltic
In an operation in the Gulf of Riga the Soviet destroyer *Statny* runs on a mine in Moon Sound on 18 Aug and sinks. In the night 18-19 Aug the German motor torpedo boat *S58* (Lt Geiger) sinks the Soviet minesweeper *T-51/Pirmunas* lying at anchor off the southern entrance of Moon Sound.

18 Aug-8 Sept North Atlantic
The Italian submarines *Marconi*, *Finzi*, *Cappellini* and, from 23 Aug, *Calvi*, are directed from 20-24 Aug to convoy HG.70 reported to have left Gibraltar on 18 Aug. But they do not find it. Neither

is HG.71 found which sets out on 2 Sept and against which *Calvi*, *Baracca*, *Cappellini* and *Da Vinci* operate from 4 Sept to 6 Sept. On 8 Sept *Baracca*, in taking up a new patrol line, is compelled to surface W of Gibraltar by depth charges from the British destroyer *Croome* and, after a short gun engagement, she is sunk by ramming.

19 Aug Black Sea
Shelling of German-Rumanian transports near Meshchanka, Mikhailovka and Visarka in the Odessa area by the 2nd DD Division consisting of the flotilla leader *Tashkent* and the destroyers *Bodry*, *Besposhchadny* and *Bezuprechny* with 450 rounds of 13cm shells.

19-23 Aug Mediterranean
Italian supply convoy to Tripoli. On 19 Aug the British submarine *P32*, in trying to attack a convoy coming into Tripoli with four steamers and the destroyers *Freccia*, *Euro*, *Dardo* and the torpedo boats *Procione*, *Pegaso* and *Sirtori*, runs on a mine and sinks.
The submarine *Unique* (Lt-Cdr Hezlet) makes an attack 11 nautical miles N of Tripoli on a subsequent convoy comprising the troop transports *Esperia*, *Marco Polo*, *Neptunia* and *Oceania* and the destroyers *Vivaldi*, *Da Recco*, *Gioberti*, *Oriani*, *Maestrale*, *Grecale*, *Scirocco* and the torpedo boat *Dezza*. She sinks the *Esperia* (11398 tons) with three hits. Of 1170 troops, 1139 are rescued.
On 22 Aug *Upholder* (Lt-Cdr Wanklyn) sinks one ship of 3988 tons from a small convoy near Sicily, escorted by the torpedo boats *Cigno* and *Pegaso*.
On 23 Aug the submarine *P33*, in an attempted attack off Pantelleria, is sunk by the Italian torpedo boat *Partenope*.

19 Aug-10 Sept Arctic
British operations in the Arctic. On 19 Aug Force K (Rear-Adm Vian), comprising the cruisers *Aurora* and *Nigeria*, the destroyers *Icarus*, *Antelope* and *Anthony* and the troop transport *Empress of Canada*, leaves Scapa Flow for Spitzbergen in order to evacuate the Norwegian and Soviet colonies there and to destroy installations. *Empress of Canada* and *Nigeria* transport the Russian colony to Archangel and rejoin the

Aurora on 1 Sept off Barentsburg. Together with three colliers coming from Norway, one ice-breaker, one whaler, one tug and two fishing boats, the force returns to England on 3 Sept. On 21 Aug the first experimental convoy 'Dervish' (Capt Dowding) leaves Hvalfjord (Iceland) with seven merchant ships and arrives in Archangel on 31 Aug without any contact with the enemy. Escort provided by a force under Rear-Adm Wake-Walker, consisting of cruisers *Devonshire* and *Suffolk* and carrier *Victorious*. Carrier *Argus* with six destroyers flies off, just N of Kola Inlet, 24 Hurricane fighters of the 151st Fighter Wing to be stationed at Vaenga near Murmansk. 24 more aircraft are moved by steamer to Archangel, from where they are sent to Vaenga on 11 Sept. The minelaying cruiser *Adventure* brings a cargo of mines to Murmansk. On the return the covering force makes two raids with aircraft from the *Victorious* on 3 Sept and 7 Sept on German shipping in the Tromsö area. Little success.
Rear-Adm Vian makes a sortie with *Aurora* and *Nigeria* on 6-7 Sept to the Polar Coast and, in the course of it, meets a small convoy off Porsanger Fjord. The cruisers destroy the gunnery training ship *Bremse* (Cdr von Brosy-Steinberg†). The two transports *Barcelona* (3101 tons) and *Trautenfels* (6418 tons) with about 1500 troops of the 6th Mountain Div on board escape into the fjord in bad visibility. On 10 Sept the British forces arrive back in Scapa Flow.

20 Aug North Sea
In an attack by boats of the 4th MTB Flotilla on a British convoy off Cromer *S48* (Lt von Mirbach) sinks the Polish freighter *Czenstochowa* (1971 tons) and torpedoes a second of 2774 tons.

21 Aug Baltic
The 3rd wave of the ferry battalion of the Army engineers is attacked several times by Soviet aircraft after passing through the Irben Strait. Little damage is done. An unsuccessful attack is made by the Soviet destroyers *Artem* and *Surovy* in the Gulf of Riga.
On the way from Suursaari to Tallinn a Soviet convoy has losses on the 'Juminda' mine barrage.

21 Aug   Black Sea

German troops take Kherson. The Military Council of the Black Sea Fleet decides to keep the cruisers *Chervona Ukraina, Krasny Krym, Krasny Kavkaz,* the auxiliary cruiser *Mikoyan,* the flotilla leaders *Kharkov* and *Tashkent* and the destroyers *Bodry, Bezuprechny, Besposhchadny, Sposobny, Smyshleny* and *Soobrazitelny* on the alert to support the coastal army in the Odessa area.

21-22 Aug   Black Sea

The cruiser *Krasny Krym,* the destroyers *Dzerzhinski* and *Frunze* and the gunboat *Krasnaya Armeniya* shell Rumanian positions near Sverdlovka and Chebanka (east front of Odessa).

22-26 Aug   Mediterranean

Operation 'Mincemeat'. 22 Aug: Force H (Vice-Adm Somerville), consisting of the battleship *Nelson,* the carrier *Ark Royal,* the cruiser *Hermione* and five destroyers, is reported by Italian agents as it leaves Gibraltar. Intention of the force: to mine Livorno with the fast minelayer *Manxman* disguised as a large French destroyer and, simultaneously, to make a carrier attack on North Sardinia. The Italian 9th Div (Adm Iachino) sets out with the battleships *Littorio* and *Vittorio Veneto* and five destroyers and on 23 Sept east of Sardinia joins the 3rd Div coming from Messina with the heavy cruisers *Trieste, Trento, Bolzano, Gorizia* and four destroyers and other groups of 10 destroyers in all. On 24 Aug they make a sortie to the area S of Sardinia to bring to battle, within range of their own Air Force, the covering force for the suspected Malta operation. The Malta convoy is to be found by the 8th Div setting out from Palermo for the area N of Tunisia and consisting of the light cruisers *Duca degli Abruzzi, Attendolo, Montecuccoli* and five destroyers. The submarines *Alagi, Serpente, Aradam* and *Diaspro* are stationed SW of Sardinia; and the Sicilian Channel, apart from the mine barrages (see 12-23 Aug), is barred by the submarines *Squalo, Bandiera, Tricheco, Topazio, Zaffiro* and thirteen MAS boats. But the deployment is not effective. The reconnaissance aircraft flown off by the ships find nothing because Force H is

proceeding northwards to the E of the Balearics. Of the British submarines stationed between Sicily and Sardinia and off the Straits of Messina, *Upholder* reports the Italian fleet on 24 Sept. On the same day the *Manxman* lays, undetected, 70 magnetic and 70 moored mines off Livorno, while 10 Swordfish aircraft attack the airfield at Tempio in North Sardinia. The returning British force is not found by Italian reconnaissance. Adm Iachino waits in vain for the convoy and has to set out for home on 25 Aug. Before reaching harbour the cruiser *Bolzano* is torpedoed by the British submarine *Triumph* (Lt-Cdr Wood).

22-30 Aug   North Atlantic

The U-boats *U143, U83, U101, U751, U561, U557, U95* and *U141* are stationed in the area W of the North Channel. Of them *U143* (Lt Gelhaus) sinks one ship of 1418 tons in a convoy on 23 Aug. On 26 Aug *U141* (Lt Schüler) sights the outward-bound convoy OS.4 W of Ireland, but is forced to submerge by an aircraft. In the afternoon *U557* (Lt Paulshen) comes up and in the night 26-27 Aug attacks in three approaches. Four ships of 20407 tons are sunk. On 27 Aug *U557* leads *U751,* and on 28 Aug *U71* and *U558* (Lt-Cdr Krech), to the scene, the last of which sinks the motor ship *Otaio* (10298 tons). No operation is possible against convoy HG.71 located SW of Ireland by air reconnaissance on 29 Aug. *U143* sights an outward-bound convoy on 30 Aug off the North Channel but is forced to submerge. At the beginning of September *U141* sinks two fishery vessels or guard ships.

23 Aug   North Channel

German auxiliary cruiser *Schiff 36 Orion* (Cdr* Weyher) sails into the estuary of the Gironde after a raiding mission of 510 days in the Atlantic, Pacific and Indian Oceans. Successes: 10 ships of 62915 tons sunk and two more of 21125 tons in co-operation with *Schiff 45 Komet.* The ship is met by *U75* and *U205.*

23-27 Aug   Baltic

The Soviet cruiser *Kirov,* the flotilla leaders *Leningrad* and *Minsk* and several destroyers including *Gordy* support the fighting by the defenders of Tallinn.

23-28 Aug   Mediterranean
In the Gulf of Sirte the British submarine *Tetrarch* (Lt-Cdr Greenway) sinks two small ships of 808 tons. *Rorqual* (Lt Napier) lays a mine barrage on 25 Aug near Cape Skinari (Aegean) and on 28 Aug sinks with a torpedo one ship of 2747 tons escorted by the torpedo boat *Antares*. In the Central Mediterranean *Urge* (Lt-Cdr Tomkinson) torpedoes one ship of 4971 tons in a Tripoli convoy consisting of four steamers and the destroyers *Euro* and *Oriani* and the torpedo boats *Procione*, *Orsa*, *Clio* and *Pegaso*. *Unbeaten* (Lt Woodward) sinks one ship of 373 tons off Augusta.

23 Aug-17 Sept   Arctic
The German U-boats *U571*, *U752*, *U451* and *U566* operate off the Kola Coast. *U752* (Lt Schroeter) sinks the Soviet trawler *RT-44/Neva* (633 tons) on 25 Aug and torpedoes a guard ship off Svyatoy Nos on 27 Aug. *U571* (Lt-Cdr Möhlmann) torpedoes the Soviet transport *Mariya Ulyanova* (3870 tons) off Cape Teriberski on 26 Aug. On 3 Sept *U566* misses the British submarine *Trident* returning to Polyarnoe and *U451* avoids a submarine torpedo.

24-25 Aug   Baltic
Soviet convoy with ice-breaker *Oktyabr* and nine transports from Tallinn to Suuarsaari-Kronstadt. On 24 Aug the destroyer *Engels*, the minesweepers *T-209/Knecht*, *T-212/Shtag* and *T-213/Krambol* and three transports are lost on the 'Juminda' mine barrage. Two other transports are lost on 25 Aug through air attacks W of Suursaari. Among the sunken transports are probably *Daugava* (1430 tons), *Lunacharski* (3618 tons) and the tanker *Zheleznodorozhnik* (2029 tons).
The German minelayers *Brummer* and *Roland* and boats of the 3rd MTB Flotilla lay the 'Rusto' mine barrage with 170 EMCs and 30 TMBs N of Cape Ristna (Dagö).

25 Aug   Iran
Soviet and British-Indian troops move into Iran. Weak resistance by the Iranian Army is quickly broken. British naval forces carry out landing operations in Abadan, Khorramshahr and Bandar Shapur (Operation 'Countenance'). Taking part: the auxiliary cruiser *Kanimbla* (Capt Adams), sloops *Falmouth*, *Shoreham* and *Yarra* (RAN), river gunboat *Cockchafer*, corvette *Snapdragon* and some small auxiliary vessels. In Abadan *Shoreham* sinks the Iranian gunboat *Palang* (950 tons). *Yarra* seizes the gunbo ts *Chahbaaz* and *Karkass* (331 tons each) in the Karun estuary and sinks the gunboat *Babr* (950 tons) in Khorramshahr. In the defence of the naval base there the C-in-C Iranian Navy, Rear-Adm Bayendor, is killed. In Bandar Shapur the British Navy seizes the German freighters *Hohenfels* (7862 tons), *Marienfels* (7575 tons), *Sturmfels* (6288 tons) and *Wildenfels* (6224 tons), the Italian tanker *Bronte* (4769 tons) and the freighters *Barbara* (3065 tons) and *Caboto* (5225 tons); and on 27 Aug in Banda Abbas the Italian freighter *Hilda* (4901 tons). The German freighter *Weissenfels* (7861 tons) is set on fire and destroyed by her crew.

27 Aug   Baltic
Attack by four Soviet TKA's on a German coastal motor boat convoy near Cape Domesnäs. Two coastal motor boats are slightly damaged.

28-29 Aug   Baltic
Withdrawal of the Soviet Baltic Fleet and the remainder of X Rifle Corps from Tallinn to Kronstadt. After embarking the units in the night 27-28 Aug, the convoys and covering forces assemble in the course of 28 Aug in the roads of Tallinn.
1st convoy (Capt 2nd Class N. G. Bogdanov): six transports, one ice-breaker, one repair ship, one training ship, submarines *Shch-308*, *Shch-307* and *M-97*. Escort: destroyer *Surovy*, patrol ships *Ametist*, *Kasatka*, and *Saturn*, five old minesweepers, two MO-IV submarine-chasers, five patrol cutters and one tug.
2nd convoy (Capt 2nd Class N.V. Antonov): six transports, two netlayers, one survey ship and one schooner. Escort: gunboat *Moskva* patrol ship *Chapaev*, four old minesweepers, nine motor minesweepers and two MO-IV submarine-chasers. 3rd convoy (Capt 2nd Class Ya. F. Yanson): eight transports and one tanker. Escort: gunboat *Amgun*, patrol ships *Kolyvan* and *Ural*, four old minesweepers, four motor mine-sweepers and two MO-IV submarine-chasers.

K

4th convoy (Capt 3rd Class S. A. Gik-horovtsev): nine various small craft. Escort: patrol ship *Razvedchik*, gunboat *I-8*, nine motor minesweepers and two magnetic minesweepers.
Main forces (Vice-Adm V. F. Tributs): cruiser *Kirov* (F), flotilla leader *Leningrad*, destroyers *Gordy*, *Smetlivy*, *Yakov Sverdlov*, submarines *S-4*, *S-5*, *Shch-301*, *Kalev*, minesweepers *T-204*, *T-205*, *T-206*, *T-207*, *T-217*, torpedo cutters *TKA-73*, *TKA-74*, *TKA-94*, *TKA-103*, *TKA-113*, submarine-chasers *MO-112*, *MO-131*, *MO-133*, *MO-142*, *MO-202*, tender *Pikker* and ice-breaker *Suur-Töll*.
Covering detachment (Rear-Adm Yu. A. Panteleev): flotilla leader *Minsk* (F), destroyers *Skory*, *Slavny*, submarines *Shch-322*, *M-98*, *M-95*, *M-102*, minesweepers *T-210*, *T-214*, *T-215*, *T-216*, *T-218*, submarine-chasers *MO-207*, *MO-212*, *MO-213*, *MO-510*, four torpedo cutters and patrol ship *Neptun*.
Rearguard (Rear-Adm Yu. F. Rall): destroyers *Kalinin* (F), *Artem*, *Volodarski*, patrol ships *Burya*, *Sneg*, *Tsiklon*, two torpedo cutters, five MO-IV submarine-chasers and minelayer *Vaindlo*. After the departure of the ships *Burya*, *Sneg*, *Tsiklon* and *Vaindlo* lay mine barrages in the harbour and in the approaches. The old minelayer *Amur*, the steamer *Gamma* (696 tons) and three tugs are sunk as blockships. The withdrawing forces are attacked in the afternoon of 28 Aug W of the mine barrages by Ju 88s of 2/K.G. 77 and of K.Fl.Gr. 806, when the ice-breaker *Krisyanis Valdemars* (2250 tons), the transports *Skrunda* (2414 tons), *Lake Lucerne* (2317 tons), *Atis Kronvalds* (1423 tons) are sunk and the staff ship *Vironia* (2026 tons) is damaged and later sinks on mines. In breaking through the 'Juminda' mine barrages in the night 28-29 Aug, the following is sunk: the destroyers *Sverdlov*, *Skory*, *Kalinin*, *Artem*, *Volodarski*, the patrol ships *Sneg*, *Tsiklon*, *Saturn*, the minesweepers *T-214*, *T-216*, *Krab*, the submarines *Shch-301*, *S-5*, *S-6*, the gunboats *I-8*, *Amgun* (?), *Moskva* (?), the netlayers *Onega* and *Vyatka*, the torpedo cutter *TKA-103*, the submarine-chaser *MO-202*, the transports *Alev* (1446 tons), *Tobol* (2758 tons), *Yärvamaa* (1363 tons),

Everita (3251 tons), *Luga* (2329 tons), *Kumari* (237 tons), *Balkhash* (2191 tons), *Yana* (2917 tons), *Naissaar* (1839 tons), *Ergonautis* (206 tons), *Ella* (1522 tons), *Ausma* (1791 tons) and *Tanker 2* (1700 tons). Heavy damage is sustained by the flotilla leader *Minsk*, the destroyers *Gordy*, *Slavny*, the minesweeper *T-205* and other transports. On 29 Aug the remaining transports are again attacked in the area of Suursaari by the Ju 88s of 2/K.G.77 and of K.Fl.Gr. 806, after the fast warships have gone on to Kronstadt in accordance with orders. In this action the transports *Kalpaks* (2190 tons), *Vtoraya Pyatiletka* (3974 tons) and the training ship *Leningradsovet* (1270 tons), are sunk; the transports *Ivan Papanin* (3974 tons), *Saule* (1207 tons) and the repair ship *Serp i Molot* (5920 tons) are severely damaged and have to be beached near Suursaari. Only the transport *Kazakhstan*, after having disembarked 2300 of her 5000 troops on board on Steinskär, reaches Kronstadt badly damaged by bombs. A special covering and salvage force (Capt 2nd Class I. G. Svyatov) is sent out from Suursaari, consisting of 12 old minesweepers, one patrol ship division, six torpedo cutters, eight submarine-chasers, two tugs, four motor boats, two cutters and the rescue ship *Meteor*. In the following days this force rescues 12160 troops in all, including some from the islands of the Gulf of Finland.
The submarine *Shch-322*, employed in covering the operation, does not return.
28 Aug-14 Sept   North Atlantic
Operations by the U-boat 'Markgraf' group. The 'Markgraf' group is formed from *U652*, *U105*, *U432*, *U38*, *U84*, *U501*, *U43*, *U202*, *U82*, *U207*, *U569*, *U433*, *U85* and *U81* which assemble SW of Iceland. *U202* (Lt-Cdr Linder) has sunk one fishing steamer of 230 tons south of Iceland on 27 Aug.
On 4 Sept a British aircraft informs the US destroyer *Greer* (Lt-Cdr Frost with Com Desir Cdr Johnson, on board), which is on the way to Iceland, about a German U-boat located in the area. *Greer* proceeds to the position given and herself locates the submerged U-boat. The British aircraft attacks the U-boat—*U652* (Lt Fraatz)—with depth

charges. *U652* suspects that *Greer* is the attacker and tries to sink her. *Greer* takes evasive action and unsuccessfully attacks the U-boat with depth charges. On 5 Sept *U501* (Cdr Förster) sinks one independent of 2000 tons. Early on 9 Sept *U81* (Lt Guggenberger) sinks one unknown independent. In the afternoon *U85* (Lt Greger) finds the convoy SC.42 with 70 ships (Commodore Mackenzie), escorted by the Canadian 24th EG (Cdr Hibbard), comprising the destroyer *Skeena* and the corvettes *Alberni, Kenogami* and *Orillia*. A first attack by *U85* fails, but, on the basis of contact reports from *U85*, the following U-boats attack successively in the night 9-10 Sept: *U432* (Lt Schultze) sinks two ships of 10820 tons; *U81* obtains several unconfirmed hits; *U432* misses; *U652* torpedoes one tanker of 6508 tons towed by *Orillia* to Reykjavik and one freighter of 3410 tons (the wreck is sunk on 19 Sept by *U372* (Lt-Cdr Neumann)); *U432* sinks two ships of 4318 tons; *U81* one ship of 3252 tons; *U82* (Lt Rollmann) sinks one catapult ship of 7465 tons but fails to hit the *Skeena*. The fact that the three corvettes remain behind to recover the survivors facilitates the U-boats' attack. By day *U432* maintains constant contact; *U85* attacks twice and sinks one ship of 4748 tons. In the night 10-11 Sept there are again many attacks. *U82* sinks two ships of 7519 tons and 3915 tons—the latter is finished off by *U433* (Lt Ey); *U652* misses; *U207* (Lt Meyer) sinks two ships of 9739 tons; *U202* misses; *U82* sinks two ships of 7443 tons; *U207* sinks one ship of 1231 tons; and *U202, U432, U202* all miss. The Canadian corvettes *Chambly* and *Moosejaw*, coming up from the rear, surprise *U501* and sink the boat. The corvette *Kenogami* drives off *U569* with depth charges. In the night the corvettes HMCS *Wetaskiwin*, the Free French ship *Mimose*, HMS *Gladiolus* and the A/S trawler *Buttermere* arrive and, towards the morning of 11 Sept, the British 2nd EG (Cdr Banks), which is ordered to the scene from Iceland and which comprises the destroyers *Douglas, Veteran, Saladin, Skate* and *Leamington*, as well as air escort from Iceland (No 120 Sqdn RAF). *Veteran* and *Leaming-*

ton sight and sink *U207*. By day *U432* continues to maintain contact: *U652* makes an unsuccessful attack; *U202* sinks a ship of 1980 tons torpedoed in the night by *U82*; *U105* (Lt-Cdr Schewe) sinks one steamer of 1549 tons. In the night 11-12 Sept *U84* (Lt Uphoff) and *U43* (Lt-Cdr Lüth) attack unsuccessfully. By day on 12 Sept *U432, U373*, and *U433* keep contact in turn but are driven off by the strong escort. On 13 Sept *U433, U572, U552, U373* and *U575* which are still operating against the convoy, cannot find it because of poor visibility. On 14 Sept *U552* (Lt Topp) is only able to get brief contact with an escort group. The operation is broken off. Total result: 16 ships of 65409 tons sunk, one tanker of 6508 tons torpedoed.

28 Aug-24 Sept   Central Atlantic
From 28 Aug *U108, U111* and *U125* proceed in line abreast from the area W of the Azores to the area around St Paul. Only *U111* (Lt-Cdr Kleinschmidt) sinks one ship on both 10 Sept and 20 Sept totalling 14193 tons. On 24 Sept the boats are brought into the area of the Cape Verde Islands and W of Freetown in order to operate with boats of the following wave (see 21 Sept).

29-31 Aug   Baltic
A Finnish minelayer sows 24 more mines at the N end of the 'Juminda' mine barrage in the night 28-29 Aug. Boats of the 5th MMS Flotilla lay 96 mines in the nights 28-29 Aug, 29-30 Aug and 30-31 Aug between the old Finnish 'Valkjärvi' and the 'Juminda' barrage. In addition, a new barrage section of 36 EMC mines and 40 explosive floats is laid on 31 Aug on the Russian route in the 'Juminda' barrage.

30 Aug   Baltic
The ships of the squadron of the Baltic Fleet are concentrated to form an artillery support force for the Leningrad Front under Rear-Adm I. I. Gren. The first group is on the Neva consisting of the destroyers *Opytny* (provisionally completed) and *Strogi, Stroiny* and the gunboats *Zeya, Sestroretsk* and *Oka* to support the 42nd and 55th Armies SE of Leningrad. The second group is in the Leningrad area as far as the eastern part of the Sea Canal with the cruiser

Maksim Gorki which has been provisionally repaired, the cruiser *Petropavlovsk* (Capt 1st class Vanifatev) which is still being fitted out and which has two turrets capable of firing, the flotilla leader *Leningrad*, the destroyers *Svirepy Grozyashchi, Silny, Stoiki* and *Storozhevoi* (being repaired) and probably the minelayer *Marti*. The third group is in the area Kronstadt-Oranienbaum with the battleships *Oktyabrskaya Revolutsiya* (Rear-Adm M. S. Moskalenko) and *Marat* (Capt 1st Class M. G. Ivanov), the cruiser *Kirov* (Capt 1st Class M. G. Sukhoruchenko), the flotilla leader *Minsk*, the destroyers *Surovy, Gordy, Smetlivy* and *Slavny*, the destroyers *Steregushchi* and *Strashny* (which are being repaired) and the gunboat *Volga*.

1-2 Sept   Black Sea
The cruisers *Chervona Ukraina* and *Komintern* and the destroyers *Soobrazitelny, Besposhchadny, Boiki, Nezamozhnik* and *Shaumyan* are used to support the coastal army, especially near Dofinovka and Ilyichevka. Smoke screen floats are used for cover against the Rumanian coastal battery near Fontanka.

1-18 Sept   North Atlantic
The 'Kurfürst' group is formed on 1 Sept from *U77, U568, U553, U206, U567, U563* and *U96* in the area W of the North Channel and the 'Bosemüller' group from *U71, U557, U561, U95, U751, U83, U562* and *U558* W to SW of Ireland. On 1 Sept the 'Bosemüller' group is directed to an SL convoy sighted by the returning *U73*, but it finds nothing in the poor visibility. The 'Kurfürst' group is directed to OG.72 sighted by a FW 200 of I/K.G.40. On 2 Sept *U557* comes across OG.72 in the mist; *U83* sights a corvette of the escort and the convoy is also reported by air reconnaissance. In consequence, the 'Kurfürst' and 'Bosemüller' groups are combined to form 'Seewolf' and are directed to this convoy. But they find neither this convoy nor one sighted by *U98* on 3 Sept. *U567* (Lt-Cdr Fahr) sinks one independent of 3485 tons. The Italian submarines *Da Vinci, Morosini, Torelli* and *Malaspina*, operating W of Gibraltar, are driven off from convoy HG.72, which has set out on 10 Sept, by the escort—in particular, by

the destroyers *Faulknor* (S.O.E. Capt de Salis), *Avondale, Encounter, Nestor* and the sloop *Deptford*, to which are added on 12 Sept the destroyers *Boreas* and *Wild Swan* from Plymouth. On 11 Sept the 'Seewolf' is sent with the remaining boats *U69, U94, U557, U561, U565, U95* and *U98* to the area NW of the Hebrides. On 14 Sept, 15 Sept and 18 Sept convoys are sighted by air reconnaissance and also by *U565* on 14 Sept but no other boats come up and *U561* and *U95* are attacked by aircraft. Only *U98* (Lt-Cdr Gysae) is able to sink one ship of 4392 tons from the convoy SC.42 on 16 Sept.

1 Sept-7 Dec   North Atlantic
On 1 Sept the US Atlantic Fleet forms the Denmark Strait Patrol. This TG 1.5 (Rear-Adm Giffen) consists at first of the heavy cruisers *Tuscaloosa* and *Wichita* and Desdiv 22 with the destroyers *Gwin, Meredith, Grayson* and *Monssen*.
From 8 Sept to 14 Sept a convoy (Rear-Adm Munroe) with Army units (Maj-Gen Bonesteel) embarked on transports to relieve the Marine Brigade in Iceland proceeds from Argentia to Reykjavik. Escort: battleship *New Mexico*, cruiser *Vincennes*, Desron 2 (Capt Ainsworth) comprising the destroyers *Morris, Sims, Hughes, Hammann, Mustin* and *O'Brien* and from Desron 7 the destroyers *Niblack, Benson, Hilary P. Jones, Gleaves, Charles F. Hughes, Madison* and *Lansdale*, as well as the old destroyers *Simpson, MacLeish, Truxton, Overton, Reuben James* and *Bainbridge*. From the second half of September the cruisers *Tuscaloosa* and *Wichita*, the battleships *Idaho* and *Mississippi* and Desron 2 and Desdiv 22 form the White Patrol.
The battleships *New York, Arkansas, Texas, New Mexico*, the carriers *Yorktown, Ranger, Wasp, Long Island*, the cruisers *Brooklyn, Savannah, Philadelphia* and *Quincy* and destroyers from Desron 2 (see above) and Desron 8 (including *Mayrant, Rhind, Rowan, Stack* and *Sterret*) are employed in this period to cover convoys and to undertake patrol missions.

2-3 Sept   Baltic
A Finnish minelayer lays 84 new mines W of the 'Juminda' barrage. The

German minelayer *Kaiser* protects the barrage with 120 explosive floats.
In a sortie into the Koivisto narrows the Finnish motor torpedo boat *Syöksy* sinks the Soviet-Estonian steamer *Meero* (1866 tons).

3-17 Sept Arctic
Among others the Soviet submarines *K-1*, *K-2*, *Shch-422*, *M-174*, *M-176*, *M-171*, *M-173* and *M-172* operate on the Norwegian Polar Coast. *K-1* (Capt 3rd Class M. P. Avgustinovich) operates for 28 days without success in the area of Vestfjord. *K-2* (Capt 3rd Class V. P. Utkin) lays on 10 Sept the first Soviet submarine mine barrage in the Arctic off Vardö (later cleared) and attacks on 12 Sept the steamer *Lofoten* (1517 tons) with gunfire off Persfjord, but the ship gets away. On board the submarine is the Commander of the 1st SM Division, Capt 2nd Class M. I. Gadzhiev. *Shch-422* (Lt-Cdr Malyshev) achieves the first success with the sinking of the Norwegian steamer *Ottar Jarl* (1459 tons) off Tanafjord on 12 Sept. *M-172* (Lt-Cdr Fisanovich) sinks the coaster *Renöy* (287 tons) in Varangerfjord on 15 Sept. *M-173* (Lt-Cdr I. A. Kunets) disembarks 13 agents on the coast of the Varanger Peninsula. Off Breisund the British submarine *Tigris* (Cdr Bone) sinks the steamer *Richard With* (905 tons) and misses on 15 Sept and 17 Sept two convoys in Lopphavet.

4-8 Sept Norway
The pocket-battleship *Admiral Scheer* is transferred temporarily to Oslo. *B-17* bombers of No 2 Group RAF Bomber Command try unsuccessfully to attack the ship on 5 Sept and 8 Sept. She returns to Swinemünde.

5 Sept Black Sea
The Soviet cruiser *Komintern* engages the Rumanian coastal battery near Fontanka.

5-11 Sept Mediterranean
In operations in the Western Mediterranean the Dutch submarines *O21* (Lt-Cdr van Dulm) and *O24* (Lt-Cdr de Booy) sink one ship of 5738 tons and two ships of 5469 tons respectively. Off the Dardanelles the British submarine *Perseus* (Lt-Cdr Nicolay) sinks one ship of 3867 tons escorted by the torpedo boat *Sirio*. In the area of Sirte the British submarine *Thunderbolt* (Lt-Cdr Crouch)

three ships of 3191 tons from several small convoys escorted by the Italian torpedo boats *Centauro* and *Polluce*.

6-14 Sept Mediterranean
The Italian submarine *Dagabur* reconnoitres the Egyptian coast between Tobruk and Port Said and *Topazio* (Cdr Berengan) sinks one ship of 691 tons on the Syrian coast.

7 Sept North Sea
In an attack by the 4th TB Flotilla (Lt-Cdr Bätge), comprising *S48*, *S49*, *S50*, *S52* and *S107*, on a British convoy off the Norfolk coast, two freighters of 1914 tons are sunk.

7 Sept Black Sea
The Soviet flotilla leader *Kharkov* with the destroyers *Boiki* and *Sposobny* brings the C-in-C Black Sea Fleet, Vice-Adm F. S. Oktyabrski, to Odessa for inspections and conferences. During their stay the ships, together with the destroyer *Dzerzhinski*, shell Rumanian positions. The destroyer *Sposobny* is damaged by a near-miss bomb in the second engine compartment.

7-8 Sept Baltic
On 7 Sept the cruiser *Maksim Gorki* fires from the Leningrad merchant harbour and the battleship *Marat* from the Sea Canal on attacking outposts of the German 18th Army S of Leningrad. On 8 Sept the gunboat *Krasnoe Znamya* supports from Cape Shepelev the right wing of the Soviet 8th Army in the Oranienbaum cauldron and the battleship *Oktyabrskaya Revolutsiya* and the cruiser *Kirov* shell German assembly areas near Krasnoe Selo and Peterhof.
Boats of the German 5th MTB Flotilla lay a barrage of 48 EMC mines NE of Seiskari and the 1st MTB Flotilla protects it with 40 explosive floats. On the next day, on the way to another mining operation, the motor minesweeper *R58* hits a mine and is towed to harbour badly damaged.

8 Sept-Nov Baltic
In transport operations from Suursaari to Hangö submarines of the Baltic Fleet are used. *P-1* (17 Sept), *L-2* and *Kalev* are lost through mines.

8-14 Sept Mediterranean
Operation 'Status' 8-10 Sept: the *Ark Royal* proceeds with the cruiser *Hermione* and six destroyers to the area

S of the Balearics and flies off 14 Hurricane fighters. In a second sortie the battleship *Nelson* and another destroyer take part. On 13 Sept the carriers *Ark Royal* and *Furious* fly off another 45 Hurricane fighters to Malta. The Italian submarines *Alagi* and *Serpente*, stationed N of the Algerian coast, do not approach. The concentration of the submarines *Axum*, *Adua*, *Aradam* and *Settembrini* near Cape Bon is ineffective.

8-19 Sept   Arctic
New attack by the German XIX Mountain Corps across the Litsa has to be broken off after initial, small ground gains against the tough defence of the Soviet 14th Army.

10 Sept   Manchukuo/Western France
The blockade-runner *Anneliese Essberger* (5173 tons, Capt Bahl) arrives in Bordeaux from Dairen.

10-13 Sept   General Situation
Military exercise by the Japanese Navy under the command of the C-in-C of the Combined Fleet, Adm Yamamoto.

10-15 Sept   Arctic
The Soviet 1st DD Div of the Northern Fleet, consisting of the destroyers *Gremyashchi*, *Gromki*, *Grozny* and *Sokrushitelny*, lays two mine barrages in the area of the Fisherman's Peninsula using the mines brought to Murmansk by the British minelaying cruiser *Adventure*.

11 Sept   Baltic
In the night the 5th MMS Flotilla lays a barrage of 36 EMC mines east of Suursaari and the 1st MTB Flotilla 40 explosive floats.

11 Sept   General Situation
President Roosevelt announces, as an answer to the *Greer* incident (see 28 Aug-14 Sept 1941), the so-called 'shoot on sight' order against all ships of the Axis Powers which dare to sail into seas 'the protection of which is necessary for American defense'.

11-12 Sept   Arctic
The Soviet torpedo cutters *TKA-11* (Lt-Cdr G. K. Svetlov) and *TKA-12* (Sub-Lt A. O. Shabalin) attack a German convoy for the first time off Petsamofjord. The convoy is escorted by the patrol vessel *NT05/Togo* (ex-Norwegian minesweeper *Otra*). No hit.

11-12 Sept   Black Sea
The Soviet cruiser *Krasny Kavkaz* shells off Odessa Rumanian positions near Ilinka and Krasny Pereselnets. On 12 Sept she is attacked several times by German aircraft without suffering any damage.

12-18 Sept   Baltic
The Soviet submarine *M-77* occupies a position near Someri, *M-99* near Tallinn and *M-98* and *M-102* near Helsinki as a defence against German-Finnish operations. *M-97* (Lt-Cdr A. I. Mylnikov) makes an unsuccessful attack on 17 Sept.

12-22 Sept   Mediterranean
The British fast minelayers *Abdiel* and *Latona* and some destroyers transport 6300 troops and 2100 tons of supplies to Tobruk and bring 6000 Australians back to Alexandria.

13-14 Sept   Air War/Western Europe
Heavy attack by RAF Bomber Command on the German battleships in Brest.

13 Sept-5 Oct   Baltic
Ösel Island captured. 13-14 Sept: Feint operations 'Nordwind' with the Finnish Armoured Ship Division (Capt Rahola): the coastal defence vessels *Ilmarinen* (Cdr* Göransson) and *Väinämöinen* (Cdr* Koivisto) escorted by a patrol boat force (Lt-Cdr Peuranheimo) with *VMV1*, *VMV14*, *VMV15* and *VMV 16*, the German minelayer *Brummer* (Cdr Dr Tobias), five boats of the 3rd Patrol Boat Flotilla, two ocean tugs, eight smaller craft and the Finnish ice-breakers *Tarmo* and *Yääkarhu*; and 'Westwind' with the torpedo boats *T11*, *T2*, *T5*, *T8*, the 2nd and 3rd MTB Flotillas and 9 smaller craft against the western side of the island. A third operation, 'Südwind', consisting of three groups with approximately 50 small craft, is directed against the south coast from Riga to distract the Soviet garrison. *Ilmarinen* sinks with 13 officers and 258 men after being hit by a drifting mine. The patrol boats rescue 132 survivors. 14 Sept: landing by the first wave of the 61st Inf Div on Moon Island. 16 Sept: formation of a bridgehead on Dagö. 16-17 Sept: shelling of Soviet defenders forced back on the Sworbe Peninsula by the light cruisers *Emden* (Capt

Mirow) and *Leipzig* (Capt Stichling) with *T-7*, *T-8* and *T-11*. Unsuccessful attack by four Soviet motor torpedo boats. Soviet submarine *Shch-317* fails to hit the *Leipzig*.

14 Sept Baltic
In the Helsinki dockyards the German motor minesweepers *R60*, *R61* and *R62* are destroyed by sabotage and two tugs are damaged.

14-15 Sept Arctic
Soviet torpedo cutters *TKA-13* (Sub-Lt Polyakov) and *TKA-15* (Lt P. I. Chapilin) attack the Norwegian coaster *Mittnattsol* on the route Petsamo-Kirkenes and sink her.

15-16 Sept Air War/Germany
Attacks by RAF Bomber Command on Hamburg, Bremen, Cuxhaven and Wilhelmshaven.

15-18 Sept Baltic
After the break-through by the German Army units into Kronstadt Bay near Peterhof German Army coastal batteries shell the Soviet warships. On 16 Sept the *Marat* and *Petropavlovsk* receive the first 15cm hits without, however, much effect. On 18 Sept the *Maksim Gorki* is lightly hit and the *Petropavlovsk* severely.

15-29 Sept Black Sea
In Soviet submarine operations the submarine *M-34* misses the Italian steamer *Tampico* off Varna. *Shch-211* (Lt-Cdr A. D. Devyatko) sinks the Italian tanker *Superga* (6154 tons) S of Varna on 29 Sept. *Shch-206* is lost on a flanking mine barrage off Sulina. *L-4* (Capt 3rd Class E. P. Polyakov) lays a mine barrage in the area of Varna and *L-5* (Lt-Cdr A. S. Zhdanov) a barrage near Ochakov. On 10 Oct the Rumanian minelayer *Regele Carol I* (2369 tons) and on 15 Sept the Bulgarian steamer *Khipka* (2304 tons) sink on the first and on 24-25 Oct the escort ship *Theresia Wallner* and the tugs *Brüsterort* and *Drossel* on the second.

15 Sept-2 Oct North Atlantic
Operations by the U-boat 'Brandenburg' group in the area SE of Greenland. On the way to assembling in a patrol line SE of Cape Farewell *U94* (Lt Ites) sinks three stragglers of 14447 tons from the convoy ON.14. From 18-19 Sept *U74*, *U94*, *U575*, *U372*, *U373*,

U552, *U69*, *U562* and *U572* take up their positions. As early as 18 Sept *U74* (Lt-Cdr Kentrat) sights the convoy SC. 44 consisting of 66 ships escorted by one destroyer and four corvettes. Owing to radio interference, no planned operation is possible; in addition to *U74*, only *U373*, *U94*, *U552* and *U562* operate. In the night 18-19 Sept *U74* attacks for the first time and, in the following night, she sinks one ship of 6956 tons and the corvette *Levis*. *U552* (Lt-Cdr Topp) sinks two ships of 12361 tons and, in the second approach, torpedoes one tanker of 6325 tons which is finished off in daylight by *U69* (Lt-Cdr Zahn). Further attacks by *U74* and *U562* (Lt Hamm) fail, but the latter sinks one independent of 1590 tons on 22 Sept. The remaining 'Brandenburg' boats, *U94*, *U372*, *U562*, *U431*, *U564*, *U575*, *U69*, *U373* and *U572*, are ordered to proceed to a new patrol line SE of Cape Farewell. After some boats have started to return, the formation is further dispersed on 26 Sept. On 30 Sept-1 Oct *U372* shadows a convoy without success. On 2 Oct *U94* sinks the tanker *San Florentino* (12842 tons); *U562* the catapult ship *Empire Wave* (7463 tons); *U575* (Lt-Cdr Heydemann) and *U431* (Lt-Cdr Dommes), each one ship of 4652 tons and 3198 tons respectively.

16-18 Sept Mediterranean
Large Italian convoy consisting of the troop transports *Vulcania*, *Oceania* and *Neptunia*, escorted by the destroyers *Da Recco*, *Da Noli*, *Pessagno*, *Usodimare* and *Gioberti*, from Taranto to Tripoli. Early on 17 Sept British air reconnaissance locates the ships E of Calabria. The British submarines *Upright*, *Upholder* and *Unbeaten* are deployed in a patrol line NE of Tripoli and *Ursula* off the harbour. *Upholder* (Lt-Cdr Wanklyn) led to the scene by *Unbeaten* (Lt Woodward), sinks the *Neptunia* (19475 tons) and *Oceania* (19507 tons). *Upright* (Lt Wraith) is driven off by the destroyers; a salvo from *Ursula* (Lt-Cdr Hezlet) against the *Vulcania* is evaded. 6500 men are rescued and 384 drown.

16-21 Sept Black Sea
The Russian 157th Rifle Div is transported from Novorossisk to Odessa in five groups each with two to three transports,

escorted by the cruisers *Chervona Ukraina, Komintern, Krasny Krym*, and the destroyers *Bodry, Boiki, Besposhchadny, Bezuprechny, Sposobny, Soobrazitelny* and *Frunze*. On 17 Sept German bombers and torpedo aircraft attack the group comprising the transports *Abkhaziya, Dnepr* and *Gruziya* and escorted by the cruiser *Chervona Ukraina* and the destroyers *Bezuprechny, Boiki* and *Nezamozhnik* but the convoy reaches Odessa without loss.

16 Sept-5 Oct   North Atlantic/ Mediterranean
The first group of German U-boats proceeds to the Mediterranean: 'Goeben' consisting of *U371, U559, U97, U331, U75* and *U79*. Between 24 Sept and 5 Oct they pass through the Straits of Gibraltar and go to the Eastern Mediterranean.

17 Sept   North Sea
The boats *S50, S51* and *S52* of the 4th MTB Flotilla sink the freighter *Teddington* (4762 tons) in a British convoy E of Cromer and torpedo one ship of 5389 tons.

17 Sept   Baltic
Swedish destroyers *Göteborg, Klas Horn* and *Klas Uggla* are severely damaged by an explosion. *Klas Uggla* has to be broken up.

17-19 Sept   Black Sea
The destroyer *Dzerzhinski* and the cruiser *Voroshilov* shell, on 17 Sept and 19 Sept respectively, German troops on the coast near Alexeevka, Khorli and Skadovsk (Odessa).

17-25 Sept   Baltic
The 'Juminda' mine barrages are reinforced against a possible break-out by the Soviet Baltic Fleet towards Sweden in the event of the fall of Leningrad. On 17 Sept the minelayers *Cobra* and *Kaiser* lay barrages near Cape Purikari (36 EMCs and 100 explosive floats) and W of 'Juminda' (136 EMCs and 200 explosive floats). On 21 Sept *Kaiser* lays another barrage (86 EMCs and 100 explosive floats) N of 'Juminda' and on 22 Sept *Cobra* a barrage near Kallbadagrund (126 EMCs and 100 explosive floats). On 25 Sept the minelayer *Königin Luise* (Lt-Cdr Wünning) lays a further barrage (86 EMCs) but is lost, when returning, on a mine barrage laid by Soviet torpedo cutters off Helsinki.

17 Sept-31 Dec   North Atlantic
US Navy TF 4 (Rear-Adm Bristol) takes over from Argentia (Newfoundland) and Hvalfjord (Iceland) the escorting of the HX and ON convoys on the North Atlantic route in the area between Newfoundland and Iceland. The slow SC and ONS convoys in the same area are escorted by the Canadian Newfoundland Escort Force (Rear Adm Murray). East of approximately 22°W the British Escort Groups take over.
On 17 Sept TG 4.1.1 (Capt Deyo), comprising the destroyers *Ericsson, Eberle, Upshur, Ellis* and *Dallas*, escorts the convoy HX.150 (Commodore: Rear-Adm Manners RN) consisting of 50 ships and hands it over to a British Escort Group on 25 Sept. On 23 Sept there follows the convoy HX.151 with a group under Capt Thebaud consisting of the destroyers *Plunkett, Livermoore, Kearny, Decatur* and *Greer* while on 24 Sept the group under Capt Kirtland consisting of *Madison, Gleaves, Lansdale, Charles P. Hughes* and *Simpson* relieves the British group with the convoy ON.18 S of Iceland. On 30 Sept this is followed by the group with ON.20 under Cdr Webb, comprising *Benson, Hilary P. Jones, Niblack, Reuben James* and *Tarbell*.
Apart from those mentioned, the following US destroyers take part in the convoy operations up to the end of the year: *Mayo, Nicholson, Buck, Ludlow, Swanson, Edison, Bernadou, Lea, Sturtevant, Badger, Leary, Bainbridge, McCormick, Cole* and the coastguard cutters *Campbell, Hamilton, Ingham* and *Spencer*. The composition of the groups varies.

18-27 Sept   Mediterranean
In British submarine operations *Triumph* (Lt-Cdr Woods) sinks one ship of 2373 tons and torpedoes two others of 15573 tons in the Adriatic. *Tetrarch* (Lt-Cdr Greenway) sinks one ship of 2499 tons from a Piraeus-Candia convoy in the Aegean escorted by the torpedo boats *Sella* and *Libra*. *Upright* (Lt Wraith) sinks the Italian torpedo boat *Albatros* off Sicily and the Dutch submarine *O21* (Lt-Cdr van Dulm) sinks one sailing ship in the Western Mediterranean.

18-28 Sept   North Atlantic

Operations on the Gibraltar convoy route. On 20 Sept the outward-bound *U124* (Lt-Cdr Mohr) reports the convoy OG.74 SW of Ireland. It consists of 27 ships, the ocean boarding vessel *Corinthian* and an Escort Group (Lt-Cdr White) with one sloop and five corvettes. For the first time there is an escort carrier, *Audacity* (Cdr Mackendrick), with the convoy. The only U-boat in the area, the outward-bound *U201* (Lt Schnee), is directed to it but is forced to submerge by a Martlet aircraft, the sloop *Deptford* and the corvette *Arbutus*. *U124* continues to keep contact and sinks two ships of 4225 tons in the night 20-21 Sept. On 21 Sept one FW 200 of I/K.G.40 sinks the rescue ship *Walmer Castle* (906 tons) which has stayed behind; another FW 200 is shot down by a Martlet fighter. While the main group continues its journey with the corvette *Pentstemon*, the *Deptford* and the corvette *Marigold* turn back to support a scattered group of four steamers with which *U124* and *U201* are in contact. *U201* sinks three of them totalling 4467 tons in the night 21-22 Sept. After losing contact, the two boats are directed to the oncoming convoy HG.73. The Italian submarines *Torelli*, *Morosini* and *Da Vinci*, which are stationed in the waiting areas W of Gibraltar, are directed towards this convoy for 18 Sept. The convoy which set out in the afternoon of 17 Sept consists of 25 ships (Commodore: Rear-Adm Creighton), the catapult ship *Springbank* and an escort of one destroyer, two sloops and eight corvettes. *Malaspina* is probably sunk from an unknown cause on the way out after 7 Sept.

On 19 Sept *U371*, which is on the way to the Mediterranean, *Morosini* and *Torelli* successively establish brief contact. On the evening of 20 Sept *Torelli* again establishes contact but is damaged by depth charges from the British destroyer *Vimy* in the night 21-22 Sept. On 23 Sept *Da Vinci* maintains contact for some time. On 24 Sept an FW 200, in contact with the convoy, is driven off by the Fulmar fighter of the *Springbank*. In the night 24-25 Sept *U124* first comes up and sinks one ship of 2922 tons,

then *U203* also comes up. In the night 25-26 Sept *U203* (Lt-Cdr Mützelburg) sinks three ships of 7658 tons including that of the convoy Commodore (who is rescued by the corvette *Periwinkle*); and *U124* sinks two ships of 2702 tons. Aircraft in contact bring up *U124*, *U203* and *U205* by day on 26 Sept; in the night *U124* sinks one ship of 1810 tons and *U201* two ships of 7623 tons, including the *Springbank*. On 27 Sept *U203*, *U205* and aircraft keep contact, but *U205* is bombed by British air escort taking off from Cornwall and is damaged. In the evening of 27 Sept *U201* sinks one more ship of 3103 tons SW of Ireland. On 28 Sept the operation has to be broken off because all the operational U-boats have expended their torpedoes. Total result with OG.74: six ships of 9598 tons sunk; and with HG.73: nine ships of 25818 tons.

19 Sept   Black Sea

Soviet monitor *Udarny* sunk by German aircraft near Tendra Island.

19-20 Sept   Air War/Germany

Attack by RAF Bomber Command on Stettin.

20 Sept   Mediterranean

The Italian submarine *Scirè* (Cdr Prince Borghese) penetrates the Bay of Gibraltar by night and launches three human torpedo teams which sink a freighter of 2444 tons in the roads and naval base and severely damage the motor ship *Durham* (10893 tons). In addition, the naval tanker *Denbydale* (8145 tons) sinks.

20 Sept-21 Oct   Baltic

The Soviet Submarines *Shch-317*, *Shch-319* and *Shch-320* (Lt-Cdr I. M. Vishnevski) set out for operations in the Baltic. The last is said to have sunk the steamer *Holland* (991 tons) off the Gulf of Danzig on 26 Sept. *Shch-319* does not return. *S-7* (Capt 3rd Class S. P. Lisin) operates off the Swedish coast and sinks one ship of 343 tons which, however, is salvaged.

21-22 Sept   Black Sea

Soviet landing near Grigorevka. Aim: to land the 3rd Naval Rifle Regt behind the 13th and 15th Rumanian Inf Divs to facilitate the attack by the 157th and 421st Rifle Divs designed to remove the Rumanian coastal batteries near Fontanka and Dofinovka. On 21 Sept the cruisers *Krasny Kavkaz* and *Krasny Krym* take one and two battalions respectively of the 3rd Marine Rifle Regt on board in Sevastopol and set out, escorted by the destroyers *Besposhchadny*, *Bezuprechny* and *Boiki* under the orders of the Commander of the Cruiser Brigade, Capt 1st Class S. G. Gorshkov. They are preceded by the destroyer *Frunze* with the Commander of the Squadron, Rear-Adm L. A. Vladimirski, on board, who is to coordinate the landing operation with the forces coming from Odessa—the gunboat *Krasnaya Gruziya*, one tug, 22 cutters, and 10 barges with which to disembark the troops. In the afternoon of 21.9 *Frunze*, while en route, turns off to help the gunboat *Krasnaya Armeniya* which has been attacked by Ju 87s of St.G.77 off the Tendra Peninsula. Both ships are sunk by the Stukas together with the tug *OP-8* which is summoned to the scene. In spite of this loss, the disembarkation and landing succeeds in the night 21-22 Sept and the heights near Fontanka and Dofinovka are re-taken. On 22 Sept Ju 87s of St.G.77 attack the destroyers *Besposhchadny*, *Bezuprechny* and *Boiki*, which are still cruising off the coast to give fire support to the troops already landed. *Bezuprechny* is damaged by a near-miss; *Besposhchadny* receives heavy hits in the bow and is towed into Odessa, stern first, by the tug *SP-14*. The destroyer *Soobrazitelny* takes over the escort.

21-24 Sept Baltic
Attacks by the I and III Gruppen of St.G.2 (Lt-Col Dinort) on ships of the Soviet Baltic Fleet. On 21 Sept a Ju 87 of III/St.G.2 under Lt Rudel hits the battleship *Marat* with a 1000Kg bomb. With demolished bow, the *Marat* settles on the bottom off the harbour mole of Kronstadt; but the 30.5cm turrets C and D, and later also, B, are again made operational. In the dive-bombing attack on the cruiser *Kirov* in Kronstadt harbour, the Ju 87 of the Commander of III/St.G.2, Capt Steen, is hit by AA fire and falls into the sea near the ship which is damaged by the explosion. In the area of the Sea Canal *Oktyabrskaya Revolutsiya* evades many attacks but is hit by six medium bombs. The destroyer *Steregushchi* capsizes

after a direct hit (she is later salvaged), the destroyers *Gordy*, *Grozyashchi*, *Silny*, the submarine depot ship *Smolny* and the submarine *Shch-306* are damaged. On 23 Sept the cruiser *Maksim Gorki* is again damaged in Leningrad and the *Kirov* and the destroyer *Grozyashchi* off Kronstadt. The submarine *P-2* is destroyed in the dockyards; and in the harbour the flotilla leader *Minsk* sinks after a direct hit (she is later salvaged). The patrol ship *Taifun* is destroyed; and the submarine *Shch-302* damaged.

21-28 Sept. Mediterranean
The Italian submarine *Ascianghi* (Lt-Cdr di Derio) sinks one ship of 389 tons off the coast of Palestine and *Fisalia* is sunk by the British corvette *Hyacinth* off Haifa on 28 Sept.
The Italian submarines *Malachite* and *Tricheco* operate North of Cyrenaica.

21 Sept-5 Nov Central Atlantic
Of the U-boats proceeding in line abreast to a southern operation, *U107* (Cdr Hessler) sights the convoy SL.87 with 11 ships, escorted by the sloops *Bideford* and *Gorleston*, the corvette *Gardenia* and the Free French sloop *Commandant Duboc*. On the evening of 21 Sept *U68* (Cdr Merten) comes up and, after an unsuccessful attack, sinks one ship of 5302 tons. *U107* makes two unsuccessful approaches. On 22 Sept *U103* (Lt-Cdr Winter) also comes up and, after a miss by *U68* on an escort, sinks two ships of 10594 tons in the night. *U68* misses an isolated tanker. The convoy divides into two groups. From the first *U67* (Lt-Cdr Müller-Stöckheim) sinks one ship of 3753 tons by day on 23 Sept and *U107* sinks three out of four ships totalling 13641 tons from the second on the morning of 24 Sept. Total result: seven ships of 33290 tons sunk. At the end of this operation *U66*, *U103*, *U107* and *U125* head for the area W of Freetown; *U108* for the line Cape Verde Islands-St Paul; and *U68* for Ascension and St Helena. *U111*, which is to provide *U67* and *U68* with supplies in Tarafal Bay in the Cape Verde Islands, is surprised by a British submarine on 27-28 Sept, but the torpedoes explode prematurely. *U67* and *U111* return and *U111* gets involved on 4 Oct near Madeira in an engagement with the British A/S trawler, *Lady*

Shirley, and is lost. Of the remaining U-boats only *U66* (Cdr Zapp) sinks a tanker of 7052 tons. On 16 Oct *U66*, *U103*, *U107* and *U125* start the delayed return in line abreast without, however, finding more targets. *U126* (Lt-Cdr Bauer), new to the operational area, sinks one ship en route and two ships on 19-20 Oct off Freetown totalling 16905 tons, including the US steamer *Lehigh*. She continues operations with *U68* in the South Atlantic (see 12 Oct).

22 Sept Baltic
In an attack by the Finnish motor torpedo boats *Vinha* and *Syöksy* on the harbour of Suursaari, the latter (Chief Petty Officer Ovaskainen) sinks the incoming minesweeper *T-41/Kirov* (400 tons).

22-23 Sept Mediterranean
The mine barrages M6 and M6A are laid out SE of Malta by the Italian 12th DD Flotilla (Capt Melodia), consisting of the destroyers *Corazziere, Ascari, Carabiniere* and *Lanciere*. Escort: the destroyers *Aviere* and *Camicia Nera*.

22-27 Sept Arctic
The British cruiser *London* brings an Anglo-American delegation with Lord Beaverbrook and Averell Harriman from Scapa Flow to Archangel for the purpose of a meeting with the Soviet Government in Moscow.

23-29 Sept Baltic
The German 'Baltic Fleet' (Vice-Adm Ciliax) is transferred to the Aaland Sea to prevent a possible break-out by the Soviet Fleet into the Baltic. Northern Group: the battleships *Tirpitz* (Capt Topp), *Admiral Scheer* (Capt Meendsen-Bohlken), the cruisers *Köln* (Capt Hüffmeier), *Nürnberg* (Capt von Studnitz), the destroyers *Z25, Z26, Z27* and torpedo boats *T2, T5, T7, T8, T11* and some motor torpedo boats in the Aaland Sea. Southern Group: the cruisers *Emden* (Capt Mirow), *Leipzig* (Capt Stichling), and motor torpedo boats in Libau. 23 Sept: the Fleet leaves Swinemünde. 24 Sept: after heavy air attacks on the Soviet warships (see 21-24 Sept) *Tirpitz, Admiral Scheer* and two torpedo boats are recalled and three torpedo boats join the Southern Group. 29 Sept: the remaining units return to Gotenhafen.
Against the expected entry of these ships into the Gulf of Finland, the Soviet Baltic Fleet Command concentrates the Soviet submarines *M-95, M-98, S-4, Shch-303, Shch-311* and *Lembit* in the western part of the Gulf of Finland; *L-3* remains in the area W of Suursaari. In the eastern part of the Gulf of Finland near Suursaari the minelayer *Marti* lays a barrage on 24 Sept to cover Kronstadt Bay.

23 Sept-11 Oct Arctic
In submarine operations off the Norwegian Polar Coast the British submarine *Trident* (Cdr Sladen) misses the steamer *Weser* off Rolvsöy on 23 Sept and the hospital ship *Birka* on 30 Sept. On 27 Sept the submarine-chaser *UJ1201* is sunk in a convoy. The Soviet submarine *D-3* (Lt-Cdr F. V. Konstantinov with the Commander of the 2nd SM Division, Capt 2nd class I. A. Kolyshkin, on board) attacks ships and convoys off Tanafjord on 26 Sept, 27 Sept, 30 Sept and 1 Oct and 11 Oct. But the torpedoes miss or explode on the cliffs. On 26 Sept. the Soviet submarine *M-174* (Lt-Cdr N. E. Egorov) and on 2 Oct *M-171* (Lt-Cdr V. G. Starikov) penetrate Petsamofjord as far as Liinahamaari, but the torpedoes which are fired damage only the pier. In a similar attempt to penetrate Bökfjord (Kirkenes) *M-176* runs into a net on 30 Sept and has to return. On 3 Oct and 8 Oct *M-176* and *M-175* miss ships in Varangerfjord. On 25 Sept the submarines *K-3, S-101* and *S-102* arrive in Molotovsk from the Baltic having come via the White Sea Canal. They are transferred in Nov to Polyarnoe. *L-20* and *L-22*, which are not yet ready for operations, remain at present in the White Sea.

24 Sept General Situation
Fifteen governments of Allied countries, including the USSR, endorse the aims of the Atlantic Charter.

24-30 Sept Mediterranean
Operation 'Halberd': supply convoy from Gibraltar to Malta consisting of the transports *Breconshire, Clan Macdonald, Clan Ferguson, Ajax, Imperial Star, City of Lincoln, Rowallan Castle, Dunedin Star* and *City of Calcutta*. Close escort for the convoy is provided by Group II (Vice-Adm Curteis) comprising the battleships *Prince of Wales* and *Rodney*, the cruisers *Kenya* (10th

Cruiser Sqdn), *Edinburgh* (18th Cruiser Sqdn), *Sheffield* and *Euryalus* and destroyers *Duncan* (13th DD Flotilla), *Gurkha, Legion, Lance, Lively, Oribi, Isaac Sweeres* (Dutch), *Piorun* (Polish), *Garland* (Polish), *Fury, Farndale* and *Heythrop.* Covering Group (I) Force H (Vice-Adm Somerville) with battleship *Nelson,* carrier *Ark Royal,* cruiser *Hermione,* destroyers *Cossack* (4th DD Flotilla), *Zulu, Foresight, Forester, Laforey* (19th DD Flotilla) and *Lightning.* The tanker *Brown Ranger* is sent on ahead with the corvette *Fleur de Lys* to refuel the destroyers.

On 26 Sept Italian air reconnaissance locates parts of the British forces S of the Balearics. The submarines *Adua, Dandolo* and *Turchese* are stationed N of Cape Ferrat, *Axum, Serpente, Aradam* and *Diaspro* N of Cape Bougaroni and *Squalo, Bandiera* and *Delfino* N of Cape de Fer, and *Narvalo* near Cape Bon. Motor torpedo boats near Pantelleria. In the evening the Italian Fleet (Adm Iachino), comprising the battleships *Littorio, Vittorio Veneto,* the heavy cruisers *Trento, Trieste, Gorizia,* the light cruisers *Attendolo, Duca degli Abruzzi,* and 14 destroyers, sets out for the area SE of Sardinia, so as to be able to attack from there the British forces (whose strength is under-estimated) within range of Italian air escort. Other Italian units cannot put to sea because of shortage of oil. 27 Sept: neither side is able to form a clear picture of the situation from reports from reconnaissance aircraft. Italian torpedo aircraft torpedo the British battleship *Nelson* S of Sardinia. Admiral Curteis and Admiral Iachino cruise between Sardinia and the Skerki Bank keeping an even distance between each other and start the return journey in the evening. The transports separate in the area of the Skerki Bank on the evening of 27 Sept and go on to Malta with Force X (five cruisers and destroyers *Cossack, Zulu, Laforey, Oribi, Heythrop, Farndale,* as well as the *Forester, Foresight* and *Fury* which are equipped as minesweepers). In the evening they lose the *Imperial Star* (12427 tons) to Italian torpedo aircraft in the area of Cape Bon. Motor torpedo boats are unable to find the convoy in the night 27-28 Sept. 28 Sept: *Hermione*

shells Pantelleria without effect. On 29 Sept *Diaspro* and *Serpente* and on 30 Sept *Adua* unsuccessfully attack the returning British forces off the Algerian coast. *Adua* is sunk by the British destroyers *Gurkha* and *Legion.* During the operation four unescorted empty transports proceed from Malta to Gibraltar.

Of the Allied submarines *Utmost, Upright, Urge, Sokol* (Polish), *Trusty, Upholder* stationed N of Sicily, only *Utmost* is able to attack the three homeward-bound Italian heavy cruisers— unsuccessfully. *Unbeaten* and *Ursula,* stationed S of the Straits of Messina, and *O21* (Dutch) stationed off Cagliari, sight no ships.

27 Sept   General Situation
The first 14 Liberty Ships are launched in American yards. Another 312 merchant ships of this type amounting to 2200000 tons have already been ordered.
27 Sept-5 Oct   Arctic
The German U-boats *U132* and *U576* operate in the entrance to the White Sea. On 18 Oct *U132* (Lt-Cdr Vogelsang) attacks a small coastal convoy near Cape Gorodetski and sinks the steamer *Argun* (3487 tons) and later an unknown ship.
28 Sept-9 Oct   Arctic
The British convoy QP.1 with 14 merchant ships, accompanied by the cruiser *London,* returns from Archangel to Scapa Flow.
29-30 Sept   Air War/Germany
Air attacks by RAF Bomber Command on Stettin and Hamburg (repeated in the night 30 Sept-1 Oct).
29 Sept-1 Oct   Black Sea
Owing to the unfavourable situation of the 51st Army, which is defending the approaches to the Crimea, the Military Council of the Black Sea Fleet proposes to the Stavka on 29 Sept that the coastal army should be evacuated from Odessa and moved to the Crimea. On 30 Sept the Stavka agrees to this proposal and on 1 Oct the Deputy People's Commissar of the Navy, Vice-Adm E. I. Levchenko, arrives in Odessa in order to work out evacuation plans with the Military Council of the Odessa Defence District.
29 Sept-11 Oct   Arctic
British convoy PQ.1 with ten merchant ships, escorted by the cruiser *Suffolk* and

two destroyers, proceeds from Hvalfjord to Archangel without contact with the enemy.

1-4 Oct   Norway
The Norwegian torpedo boat *Draug* tows the Norwegian *MTB56* from Scapa Flow to a point 120 nautical miles off the Norwegian coast. In the night 3-4 Oct *MTB56* (Sub-Lt Danielsen) attacks a German convoy in Korsfjord consisting of *M1101*, *V 5505/Seeteufel* and the Norwegian tanker *Borgny* (3015 tons) which is sunk by a torpedo hit. *MTB56* is met by *Draug* and towed back.

2-8 Oct   Mediterranean
On 2 Oct the British submarine *Perseus* (Lt-Cdr Nicolay) sinks one ship of 2086 tons off Benghazi belonging to a convoy from Naples with the torpedo boats *Calliope* and *Pegaso*. In the Aegean *Tetrarch* (Lt-Cdr Greenway) sinks one ship of 3751 tons in a convoy with the torpedo boats *Monzambano*, *Calatafimi* and *Aldebaran*; *Talisman* (Lt-Cdr Willmott) one other ship of 8194 tons. *Rorqual* (Lt Napier) lays a mine barrage (8 Oct) in the Gulf of Athens on which the Italian torpedo boats *Aldebaran* and *Altair* sink on 20-21 Oct. *Thunderbolt* (Lt-Cdr Crouch) sinks a small sailing ship. In the Western Mediterranean the Dutch submarine *O21* (Lt-Cdr van Dulm) sinks one ship of 1369 tons.

2-14 Oct   North Atlantic
Operation by the 'Breslau' group against convoy OG.75. On 2 Oct two FW 200s of I/K.G.40 successively sight the convoy W of the North Channel with 25 steamers and nine escort vessels. On 3 Oct and 4 Oct the convoy is located by air reconnaissance but the outward-bound U-boats *U71*, *U83*, *U206* and *U563*, the homeward-bound *U204* and the *U564*, released from escorting the outward-bound blockade-runner *Rio Grande*, all of which are directed to the convoy, do not come up. On 5 Oct, 6 Oct and 7 Oct the air reconnaissance which is provided finds only a small steamer of 744 tons. This is sunk. Only on 8 Oct does an FW 200 report the convoy in the area of Cape Finisterre. *U83* comes up by day and *U71* briefly in the night: but on 9 Oct contact is again lost in bad weather. A single tanker of 9158 tons is probably sunk by *U204* (Lt-Cdr

Kell). On 10 Oct an FW 200 again reports the convoy, but the U-boats fall astern because the speed of the convoy is under-estimated. *U83* (Lt Kraus) sinks a large floating crane and on 12 Oct a Portuguese steamer of 2044 tons in accordance with prize regulations. *U563*, which again gets near the convoy on 12 Oct, is forced to submerge by an aircraft, and *U206* (Lt Opitz) sinks the corvette *Fleur de Lys* off the Straits of Gibraltar just before she comes into harbour. *U204* and *U564* put into Cadiz at night to take on fuel from a German tanker.

3 Oct   North Atlantic/Bay of Biscay
The U-boat supply ship *Kota Pinang*, which is proceeding with *U129* to the South Atlantic, is sunk W of Cape Finisterre by the British cruiser *Kenya* with gunfire. The U-boat rescues 119 survivors and hands them over to a Spanish naval tug on 6 Oct.

3-6 Oct   Black Sea
Evacuation of the Soviet 157th Rifle Div from Odessa to Sevastopol in several convoys comprising the transports *Armeniya*, *Kotovski*, *Bolshevik*, *Zhan Zhores*, *Volga*, *Belostok* and the tankers *Moskva* and *Sergo* (3 Oct); the transports *Egurtsa*, *Uralets* and the tug *SP-14* with lighter (4 Oct); and the transports *Abkhaziya*, *Dnepr*, *Kalinin* the patrol ships *SKR-113/Bug* and *SKR-114/Dnestr*, the gunboat *Krasny Adzharistan*, the minesweepers *TShch-38/Raikomvod*, *TShch-39/Doroteya* and *TShch-41/Khenkin* (5 Oct). Escort and cover provided by the cruisers *Chervona Ukraina*, *Krasny Kavkaz*, *Krasny Krym* and the destroyers *Bodry*, *Boiki*, *Nezamozhnik*, *Shaumyan* and *Dzerzhinski*.

4-25 Oct   Mediterranean
The first group of German U-boats operates on the British supply routes between Alexandria and Tobruk. *U-559* (Lt-Cdr Heidtmann) misses supply steamers on 4 Oct and 10 Oct and an escort vessel and three A-lighters on 18 Oct. *U331* (Lt von Tiesenhausen) damages *A18* in a gun engagement with three A-lighters on 10 Oct: *U-75* (Lt-Cdr Ringelmann) sinks the lighters *A2* and *A7* on 12 Oct and misses a destroyer on 25 Oct. *U97* (Lt-Cdr Heilmann) sinks two transports of 1966 tons from a supply convoy on 17 Oct and sinks a

steamer on 23 Oct. *U79* (Lt-Cdr Kaufmann) sinks an A-lighter on 18 Oct and torpedoes the gunboat *Gnat* on 21 Oct which has to be beached in Bardia as a total loss. *U371* (Lt-Cdr Driver) is damaged by depth charges on 20 Oct.

5-6 Oct   Arctic
Under Lt-Cdr S. G. Korshunevich the Soviet torpedo cutters *TKA-12, TKA-14* and *TKA-15* attack ships between Kirkenes and Petsamo and *TKA-12* (Sub-Lt A. O. Shabalin) sinks the Norwegian cutter *Björnungen* (163 tons).

5-11 Oct   Arctic
Operation by the Home Fleet against the Norwegian coast. On 8 Oct aircraft of the carrier *Victorious* carry out a raid on shipping in the area of Vestfjord. Two steamers are hit.

6 Oct and 8 Oct   Mediterranean
German bombers sink two freighters of 8861 tons off Suez.

7-16 Oct   Black Sea
Flanking mine barrages are laid out to protect Axis Sea traffic off the Bulgarian coast. Participating: the Rumanian minelayers *Dacia, Regele Carol I, Amiral Murgescu* (Cdr Niculescu, German adviser Cdr von Davidson). Escort provided by Rumanian torpedo boats *Naluca, Sborul, Smeul,* gunboats *Dumitrescu* and *Ghigulescu* and, for a time, by the Bulgarian torpedo boats *Smeli, Derzky* and *Khabri* and, in the approach and the departure, also by Rumanian destroyers. Four mine barrages and one partial barrage are laid. Shortly after setting out from Varna on 10 Oct *Regele Carol I* sinks with 150 mines on board on a Soviet submarine mine barrage.

8 Oct   Black Sea
German troops occupy Mariupol on the Sea of Azov.

8-10 Oct   Black Sea
Evacuation of heavy equipment and weapons, rear services, party organisations and labour force from Odessa to Sevastopol in the transports *Chekhov, Kalinin,* the tanker *Moskva,* the minelayer *Syzran,* the minesweeper *TShch-32/Zemlyak,* escorted by the cruiser *Komintern,* the destroyer *Shaumyan* and three SKA patrol cutters (8 Oct) and the transports *Armeniya* and *Sergo* on 9 Oct.

10 Oct-10 Nov   Baltic
In an operation E of the Swedish coast the Soviet submarine *Shch-323* (Capt 3rd Class Ivantsev) unsuccessfully attacks the German cruiser *Köln* as she sets out on 13 Oct N of Dagö. From 15 Oct to 5 Nov the submarine makes seven attacks on merchant ships: but she sinks only the steamer *Baltenland* (3724 tons).

10-18 Oct   North Atlantic
From 10 Oct a new patrol line is formed SE of Cape Farewell consisting of *U374, U573, U208* and *U109* and nine more boats are on the way. Of these *U502* (Lt-Cdr v. Rosenstiel) sinks the whale-oil factory ship *Svend Foyn* (14795 tons) on 7 Oct: and *U558* (Lt-Cdr Krech) sinks the freighter *Vancouver Island* (9472 tons) on 15 Oct. In the night 14-15 Oct *U553* (Lt-Cdr Thurmann) sights SC.48 still comprising 39 ships (11 stragglers) after a storm and escorted by the corvettes HMCS *Wetaskiwin,* HMS *Gladiolus,* the Free French ship *Mimose* and HMCS *Baddeck.* She sinks two ships of 5937 tons at once and, on her report, first the oncoming *U568, U432, U558* and *U502,* and then the *U77, U751, U73* and *U101* lying further to the E, are directed to the convoy. At mid-day *U553* is driven off by an additional destroyer HMCS *Columbia,* which avoids a torpedo salvo. *U568* (Lt-Cdr Preuss) takes over contact, sinks one ship of 6023 tons and is driven off by the *Gladiolus* in the evening. In the morning of 16 Oct *U502* and *U568* again establish contact but are driven off when the escort is reinforced by a US Escort Group (Capt Thebaud) ordered up from convoy ON.24. It consists of the destroyers *Plunkett, Livermoore, Kearny* and *Decatur,* as well as the destroyer HMS *Broadwater* and the Free French corvette *Alysse* arriving from Reykjavik. In the afternoon of 16 Oct *U553, U568, U558, U502* and *U432* establish contact in turn. *Livermoore* attacks *U553* with depth charges. In the night 16-17 Oct the U-boats attack and make the following sinkings: *U553* probably the missing corvette *Gladiolus; U558* one tanker and two freighters of 17516 tons in two approaches. *U432* (Lt Schultze) sinks three ships of 18244 tons in two approaches. *U568* torpedoes the US des-

troyer *Kearny* mistaken for a British destroyer; *U553* narrowly misses the *Plunkett*. After the corvettes HMS *Veronica* and HMCS *Pictou* arrive, having been ordered away from another convoy in the night, a British Escort Group, consisting of the destroyers *Highlander, Bulldog, Amazon, Richmond* and *Georgetown*, relieves the remaining destroyers on the morning of 17 Oct. In the meantime the *Greer* has taken the disabled *Kearny* to Hvalfjord. Air escort from the US Navy Squadrons VP-73 and VP-74 from Iceland drives the U-boats off. Of the four newly-arrived U-boats, *U101* (Lt-Cdr Mengersen) sinks the destroyer *Broadwater* in the night 17-18 Oct. By day the operation is broken off.

10-26 Oct   Mediterranean
The Italian submarines *Saint Bon, Cagni* (large new boats) and *Atropo* transport 354 tons of fuel and supplies from Taranto to Bardia in spite of various air attacks.

11-12 Oct   Air War/Germany
RAF Bomber Command attacks Emden

12 Oct   North Sea
Attack by the 2nd MTB Flotilla (Lt-Cdr Feldt), comprising *S41, S47, S53, S62, S104* and *S105*, on a British convoy North of Cromer. The British freighter *Chevington* (1537 tons) and the Norwegian freighter *Roy* (1768 tons) are sunk.

12-13 Oct   Air War/Germany
RAF Bomber Command attacks Bremen.

12-13 Oct   Mediterranean
Proposed Italian mining operation 'B' to protect Benghazi with the cruisers *Duca d'Aosta, Eugenio di Savoia, Montecuccoli* and the destroyers *Vivaldi, Malocello, Pigafetta, Da Verazzano, Aviere* and *Camicia Nera* is abandoned because reconnaissance reports that the British Mediterranean Fleet has set out.

12-21 Oct   Baltic
12-13 Oct: capture of Dagö. Feint operation 'Westfalen' with the cruiser *Köln* (Capt Hüffmeier), the torpedo boats *T2, T5, T7, T8* and seven minesweeping boats of the 1st and 2nd MS Flotillas near Cape Ristna and 'Ostpreussen' with the 2nd MMS Flotilla against the East Coast near the Kertel battery. In this way the Soviet forces are

misled and tied down. A landing is made with craft of the experimental force on the South Coast. Support from the 5th MS Flotilla against Soviet coastal batteries.
14 Oct *Köln* again shells Cape Ristna. 16-21 Oct: the Soviets evacuate part of the island garrison to Odensholm and Hangö. 21 Oct: end of Soviet resistance at Cape Takhkona. In all, 3388 prisoners are taken.

12-26 Oct   Mediterranean
The fast British minelayers *Abdiel* and *Latona* transport 7100 troops and supplies to Tobruk to relieve 7900 Australians. On the last journey *Latona* (2650 tons) is destroyed by Ju 87s of St.G.3 (Lt-Col Sigel) off Bardia in the night 25-26 Oct. Among the escorting destroyers *Hero* is damaged by a near-miss.

12 Oct-20 Nov   South Atlantic
U68 (Cdr Merten) operates in the area of Ascension from 12 Oct to 18 Oct and on 22 Oct sinks the British naval tanker *Darkdale* (8145 tons) in the roads of St Helena, and then, on the way to the Walfish Bay area, sinks another two steamers of 10250 tons. On 13 Nov she meets S of St Helena the German auxiliary cruiser *Schiff 16 Atlantis* (Capt Rogge) for replenishment. *U126* (Lt-Cdr Bauer), which on 13 Nov sinks one steamer of 6961 tons off the Guinea coast, is to be replenished from *Schiff 16* on 22 Nov (see entry). The U-boats *U124* and *U129*, which set out from Western France with the supply ship *Python*, go off into their operational areas after refuelling from the supply ship on 20 Nov SW of the Cape Verde Islands. *UA* operates off Freetown from 9 Nov.

13-16 Oct   Black Sea
On 13 Oct the Military Council of the Black Sea Fleet gives approval for the early evacuation, requested by the Odessa Defence District, to take place on the night 15-16 Oct. On 14 Oct the transports *Ukraina, Gruzit, Abkhaziya, Armenia, Kotovski, Zhan Zhores, Vostok, Kalinin, Bolshevik, Kursk, Chapaev,* the minelayers *Lukomski, Syzran* and the survey ships *Chernomorets* and *Tsenit* arrive. The warships assemble are the cruisers *Chervona Ukraina* and *Krasny Kavkaz,* the destroyers *Smyshleny, Bodry,*

Nezamozhnik and *Shaumyan*, the patrol ships *SKR-102/Petrash*, *SKR-113/Bug* and *SKR-114/Dnestr*, the fast minesweepers *T-404/Shchit*, *T-405/Vzryvatel*, *T-406/Iskatel* and *T-408/Yakor*, the auxiliary minesweeper *T-39/Doroteya* and many patrol boats, tugs and other base craft. On 14 Oct *Gruziya* receives a hit in a German air attack. During a heavy bombardment by guns and warships combined with simulated attacks, the forces of the coastal army begin quickly to withdraw from their positions to the harbour at 1900 hrs on 15 Oct. From 2300 hrs until 0300 hrs on 16 Oct some 35000 men of the 421st and 95th Rifle Divs and of the 2nd Cavalry Div are embarked and the transports proceed to the roads. Towards 0600 hrs the cruisers and destroyers, which have taken the rear guard and defence battalions on board, put out to sea. The patrol ship *SKR-101/Kuban* takes 1200 men from demolition parties and rear guard on board. At 0900 hours the last patrol boat departs and the minesweeper *T-405/Vzryvatel* lays magnetic ground mines in the harbour and approach. The evacuation is accomplished in one night without any enemy counteraction. Not before the afternoon of 16 Oct do German aircraft begin to attack the evacuation transports. But only the transport *Bolshevik* (1412 tons) is sunk; all the other ships, including the damaged *Gruziya*, reach Sevastopol.

During the embarkation the destroyers *Bodry* and *Smyshleny* lay a mine barrage in the area of Ilyichevka. Part of it, consisting of 32 mines, is cleared on 21 Oct by boats of the German Danube Flotilla. The Hungarian steamer *Ungvar* (Commander of the German Danube Flotilla, Cdr Petzel†) and the Rumanian motor torpedo boats *Viforul* and *Vijelia* on 9 Nov, and the German steamer *Cordelia* (1357 tons) and the Rumanian steamer *Cavarna* (3495 tons) on 2 Dec, run on to another part of it and are lost.

14 Oct Mediterranean
A Commando unit (Lt-Col Keyes†), landed from the British submarines *Talisman* and *Torbay*, makes an unsuccessful raid on the headquarters of the German C-in-C in North Africa, General Rommel.

14-19 Oct Mediterranean
British Force H (Vice-Adm Somerville), consisting of the battleship *Rodney*, the carrier *Ark Royal*, the cruiser *Hermione* and seven destroyers, proceeds eastwards and on 18 Oct flies off 11 Albacores and two Swordfish torpedo bombers to Malta from the carrier when 450 nautical miles away. At the same time Force K (Capt Agnew) goes with the cruisers *Aurora*, *Penelope* and the destroyers *Lance* and *Lively* to Malta where it arrives on 21 Oct. On the news that Force H has set out, apart from the Italian submarines *Bandiera* and *Aradam* already stationed near Galita and Cape Bougaroni, a patrol line is concentrated from 17 Oct. with *Turchese*, *Serpente*, *Diaspro* and *Alagi* N of Cape de Fer, *Narvalo* and *Squalo* near Cape Bon, *Settembrini* and *Delfino* near Pantelleria. But they do not sight any ships.

14-20 Oct Arctic
Off the Norwegian Polar Coast there operate, inter alia, the British submarine *Tigris* and the Soviet *K-1*, *Shch-402*, *Shch-401*, *M-172* and *M-174*. *K-1* (Capt 3rd Class M. P. Avgustinovich) lays a mine barrage in Breisund. *Tigris* misses a convoy in Svaerholthavet on 14 Oct and, after a short stay in Polyarnoe, begins the return trip to England on 20 Oct. *Shch-402* (Lt-Cdr N. G. Stolbov) sinks the Norwegian coaster *Vesteraalen* (682 tons) on 17 Oct in Söröysund.

15-22 Oct Mediterranean
The Italian submarines *Dagabur*, *Topazio* and *Zaffiro* operate off Mersin Bay E of Cyprus and W of Haifa and *Uarsciek* off Cyrenaica.

16 Oct-13 Nov North Atlantic
U573, *U374*, *U208* and *U109*, which did not take part in the operations against SC.48, are sent from 16 Oct as the 'Mordbrenner' group to reconnoitre in the area off the Strait of Belle Isle but they find hardly any traffic and have no success. From 28 Oct they proceed to the area SW of Newfoundland and from 31 Oct they are directed to the ON convoy shadowed by the 'Reissewolf' group since 27 Oct. *U374* (Lt von Fischel) sinks one independent of 5120 tons and sights the convoy SC.52 on 1 Nov (see entry). The other three

boats start the return on 3 Nov after
U208 (Lt Schlieper) has sunk one more
independent of 3872 tons on 2 Nov.

17-29 Oct   North Atlantic
Operation by the 'Breslau' group against
convoy HG.74. From 17 Oct *U206*,
U563 and *U564* are stationed near
Cape Trafalgar for the expected depar-
ture of convoy HG.74 from Gibraltar.
U204, *U71* and *U83* are stationed near
Cape Spartel; and further W the Italian
boats *Archimede*, *Ferraris* and *Marconi*.
On 19 Oct *U206* (Lt Cdr Opitz) and
U204 (Lt-Cdr Kell) each sink one ship
of 3081 tons and 9158 tons respectively.
But the latter is then sunk in the U-boat
search undertaken by the sloop
Rochester and the corvette *Mallow*.
U71 (Lt-Cdr Flachsenberg) misses a
destroyer. HG.74 only sets out on the
afternoon of 22 Oct and is reported
shortly after midnight on 23 Oct by *U71*.
Two attacks by *U206* and *U564* (Lt
Suhren) fail but the boats are able to
maintain contact in spite of the strong
escort (13 sloops and corvettes). In the
night 23-24 Oct *U563* (Lt Bargsten)
sinks one ship of 1352 tons and torpedoes the destroyer *Cossack* which sinks
on 26 Oct. *U564* sinks two ships of
5846 tons. The lost contact is regained
in the afternoon of 24 Oct by I/K.G.40
and in the evening by *U71*. On 25 Oct
U71, *U83*, *U206* and *Archimede* are
driven off partly by aircraft and partly
by the naval escort. *Ferraris* springs a
leak in an oil tank as a result of bombing
by a Catalina flying-boat; Lt-Cdr Flores
remains on top when the destroyer
Lamerton approaches and sinks the boat
after a long gun duel. In the night 25-26
Oct *U83* and *U563* come up and *U83*
(Lt Kraus) torpedoes the catapult ship
Ariguani (6746 tons). By day *U71* and
U564 maintain contact, but the attacks
by *U563* and *U564* in the night 26·27
Oct have no success. At this period
Marconi must have been lost from an
unknown cause. *U564* and *U563* maintain contact until 28 Oct and bring up
the returning *U432* (Lt Schultze) which
sinks one more ship of 1574 tons. On 29
Oct the three boats, having fired all their
torpedoes, begin the return journey.

17-30 Oct   Arctic
Convoy PQ.2 proceeds with six ships
from Scapa Flow to Archangel.

18 Oct   Black Sea
German troops occupy Taganrog.

18-27 Oct.   Black Sea
Soviet submarines make a number of
unsuccessful attacks off the Dnieper
estuary, Bugaz, Sulina, Constanza and
Burgas. Off Cape Kaliakra *Shch-212*
(Lt-Cdr I. K. Burnashev) runs on a mine
of a flanking barrage and is only brought
into harbour with great difficulty. *M-35*
(Lt-Cdr M. V. Greshilov) misses the
solitary submarine-chaser *Schiff 19/
Lola* off Sulina on 27 Oct.

18-30 Oct   Mediterranean
In operations in the Central Mediterranean the British submarine *Ursula*
(Lt-Cdr Hezlet) torpedoes (18 Oct) one
ship of 4459 tons near Lampedusa which
is in a convoy of five steamers with the
destroyers *Folgore*, *Fulmine*, *Usodimare*,
Gioberti, *Da Recco*, *Sebenico* and the
torpedo boat *Calliope*. On 22 Oct *Urge*
(Lt-Cdr Tomkinson) misses one ship and
on the next day torpedoes one other ship
of 5996 tons, which is sunk by *Utmost*
(Lt-Cdr Cayley) on 28 Oct. On the
Petrasso-Brindisi route *Truant* (Lt.Cdr
Haggard) sinks two ships of 5570 tons,
including one in a convoy and torpedoes
one more ship of 1589 tons. *Triumph*
(Lt-Cdr Woods) sinks one ship of 6703
tons in the Aegean and *Thrasher* (Lt
Mackenzie) one ship of 384 tons off
Benghazi.
Rorqual (Lt Napier) lays a mine barrage
off Sardinia on 21-22 Oct.

19 Oct-1 Nov   North Atlantic
After the conclusion of the SC.48 operation *U568*, *U502*, *U432*, *U77*, *U751*,
U73 and *U101* form the 'Reissewolf'
group in the Central North Atlantic.
The formation is twice deferred on 25-
26 Oct because of 'B' Service reports
about an ON convoy. On 27 Oct the
outward-bound *U74* (Lt-Cdr Kentrat)
sights the ON convoy to which 'Reissewolf' is directed. *U106* (Lt Rasch),
which is also outward-bound, sinks an
unidentified independent. On 28 Oct,
29 Oct and 30 Oct *U568*, *U77*, *U73*,
U751 and *U106* successively maintain
brief contact, and *U77* and *U74* more
than once, but they are not able to
attack. Because of the fuel situation
U568, *U751*, *U77* and *U502* have to
break off and they join the 'Stosstrupp'
group. Only *U73*, *U74* and *U106* con-

L

tinue to shadow: the last torpedoes the US Navy tanker *Salinas* (8246 tons) on 31 Oct. The boats of the 'Mordbrenner' group, which are directed to the scene, do not approach the convoy and the fruitless searches are broken off on 1 Nov. *U74* has maintained contact for over 1600 nautical miles. From the newly-arrived U-boats in the operational area, *U569*, *U123*, *U38*, *U82*, *U202*, *U84*, *U203*, *U93* and *U85*, the 'Schlagetot' group is formed W of Ireland. On 20 Oct *U84* (Lt Uphoff) sights a group of fast vessels and attacks them unsuccessfully on 21 Oct. *U123* (Lt-Cdr Hardegen) comes up and torpedoes the British auxiliary cruiser *Aurania* (13984 tons). In the afternoon *U123* sights convoy SL.39 to which the group is directed. In the evening *U203* and *U82* (Lt Rollmann) come up and the latter sinks two ships of 9317 tons. On 22 Oct the convoy is located by German air reconnaissance, but the U-boats *U85*, *U202* and *U203* are driven off and the operation has to be broken off on 23 Oct. The group is sent to a new patrol line SE of Greenland and *U123* is sent to reconnoitre off the Strait of Belle Isle. From 1 Nov the boats are directed to SC.52 and form the 'Raubritter' group.

10-21 Oct   Air War/Germany
RAF Bomber Command attacks Wilhelmshaven, Bremen and Emden.

20 Oct-15 Nov   Baltic
In operations by Soviet submarines *L-3* (Capt 3rd Class P. D. Grishchenko) lays a mine barrage at the end of Oct in the area of the Gulf of Danzig and *Lembit* (Lt A. M. Matiyasevich) off Koivisto Sound. *S-4* operates on the Tallinn-Helsinki route and misses the transport *Hohenhörn* on 21 Oct; *S-7* disembarks agents in Narva Bay; and *S-8*, when setting out, runs on a mine W of Suursaari and sinks.

21-25 Oct   Black Sea
Creation of a mine-free passage from the Kilia estuary to the Dnieper estuary by the Danube Flotilla (Cdr Petzel), comprising the depot ship *Theresia Wallner*, three river minesweepers and three Rumanian auxiliary minesweepers. 21 Oct: a passage is made through a mine barrage near Ilyichevka S of Odessa,

23 Oct: Ochakov reached. 24 Oct: journey continued to Kherson. 25 Oct: the lower course of the Dnieper is checked. On 24 Oct the tug *Drossel* runs on a barrage laid by a Soviet submarine. On 25 Oct *Theresia Wallner* and a second tug, *Brüsterort*, are lost on the same barrage.

23-27 Oct   Baltic
A Soviet force of three fast minesweepers and two submarine-chasers (Capt 3rd Class V. P. Likholetov) proceeds from Kronstadt to Hangö. *T-203/Patron* is lost on a mine when she sets out on 25 Oct. The remaining vessels go with 499 troops and the equipment of a Rifle Brigade to Oranienbaum.

24 Oct-2 Nov   Mediterranean
The Italian submarines *Alagi*, *Axum*, *Diaspro* and *Santarosa* are concentrated off the Algerian-Tunisian coast to operate against British traffic expected between Gibraltar and Malta.

25 Oct-2 Dec   Atlantic/Indian Ocean
On 25 Oct Force G (Adm Phillips) sets out from the Clyde for East Asia with the battleship *Prince of Wales* and the destroyers *Electra* and *Express*. On 5 Nov the ships arrive in Freetown, on 16 Nov in Simonstown and on 28 Nov in Colombo, where they are joined by the battlecruiser *Repulse* from the Atlantic and the destroyers *Encounter* and *Jupiter* from the Mediterranean. On 2 Dec the Force arrives in Singapore.

26-27 Oct   Air War/Germany
RAF Bombers attack Hamburg.

29-31 Oct   Black Sea
After the German break-through near Ishun on the Perekop Isthmus (26 Oct), the main Fleet base at Sevastopol is put in a state of defence. Vice-Adm F. S. Oktyabrski becomes the Commander of the Sevastopol Defence District (S.O.R.). The German advance drives the 51st Army on to the Kerch Peninsula and the Coastal Army to the Yaila Mountains and passes the 7th Naval Infantry Brigade stationed on the W coast.

On 29-30 Oct the cruiser *Krasny Kavkaz* transports the 8th Naval Infantry Brigade from Novorossisk to Sevastopol and there the 16th, 17th, 18th and 19th Naval Inf Bns are formed out of ships' crews.

By decision of the Military Council, the battleship *Parizhskaya Kommuna*, the cruiser *Molotov*, the flotilla leader *Tashkent* and the destroyer *Soobrazitelny* leave Sevastopol and are brought to Caucasian ports. An air attack on the force has no result. There remain in Sevastopol the cruisers *Chervona Ukraina* and *Krasny Krym*, the destroyers *Bodry, Nezamozhnik* and *Shaumyan* forming an artillery support unit under the Chief of Staff of the Squadron, Capt 1st Class V. A. Andreev. In addition, there are added on 31 Oct the cruiser *Krasny Kavkaz* and the destroyers *Dzerzhinski* and *Zheleznyakov*. Of the ships still being repaired, the destroyers *Bditelny* and *Boiki* are also allotted to the artillery support force.

On 31 Oct the destroyer *Bodry* shells German forward tank units in the area of Nikolaevka. In an attack by Ju 87s, Stukas, of St.G.77 50 men, including the commander, are wounded by aircraft gun fire.

30 Oct   North Atlantic
New outward-bound boats receive orders on 30 Oct to form the 'Stosstrupp' group E of the Newfoundland Bank: they are *U571, U577, U133, U567, U552* and *U96*. While still on the way, *U552* (Lt-Cdr Topp) sights on the morning of 31 Oct in the Central North Atlantic convoy HX.156 with a US Escort Group (Cdr Webb) comprising five destroyers. *U552* attacks at once and sinks the destroyer *Reuben James*. *U552* is driven off in the afternoon but *U567* (Lt-Cdr Endrass) comes up. The boats continually take turns in maintaining contact up to 3 Nov, but two attacks in the morning of 1 Nov fail. In looking for HX.156 *U96* (Lt-Cdr Lehmann-Willenbrock) encounters the convoy OS.10 on 31 Oct and sinks one ship of 5998 tons. The returning and outward-bound *U568, U502, U77, U571* and *Barbarigo* are directed to it, and because *U96* is in contact, also *U572, U201, U98, U373, U103, U107* and *U66* from 1 Nov. Air reconnaissance again reports the convoy on 2. Nov. *U98* comes up briefly; then contact is lost and is also not re-established by air reconnaissance on 4 Nov.

31 Oct-1 Nov   Air War/Germany
Air attacks by RAF Bomber Command on Hamburg and Bremen.

31 Oct-4 Nov   Baltic
First evacuation convoy leaves Kronstadt on 31 Oct under the Commander of the Squadron of the Baltic Fleet, Vice-Adm V. P. Drozd, and goes on 1 Nov from Suursaari to Hangö. Taking part are the destroyers *Slavny* and *Stoiki*, the fast minelayer *Marti* (Capt 1st Class N. I. Meshcherski), the minesweepers *T-207/Shpil, T-210/Gak, T-215 T-217* and five MO-IV submarine-chasers. On the return 16 mines explode in the ships' bow paravanes and *Marti* and *T-210* are damaged. There are 4230 men on board. The submarines *S-9* and *Shch-324* are stationed in the western entrance to the Gulf of Finland and *S-7* off Tallinn to cover the operation.

1-2 Nov   Mediterranean
The British submarine *Utmost* (Lt-Cdr Cayley) sinks the Italian freighters *Balilla* (2469 tons) and *Marigola* (5996 tons) in surface engagements in the Mediterranean.

1-7 Nov   Indian Ocean
British naval forces (heavy cruiser *Devonshire*, light cruiser *Colombo* and auxiliary cruisers *Carnarvon Castle* and *Carthage* capture a French convoy coming from Madagascar off South Africa. It consists of the freighter *Bangkok* (8056 tons), *Commandant Dorise* (5529 tons), the passenger ships *Compiègne* (9986 tons), *Cap Touraine* (8009 tons) and *Cap Padaran* (8009 tons). The only escort vessel for the convoy, the sloop *D'Iberville*, is able to withdraw unmolested. As a reprisal, the French Admiralty orders the submarines *Le Glorieux* and *Le Héros*, which are en route to Madagascar, to attack British ships on the way. *Le Héros* sinks the Norwegian freighter *Thode Fagelund* (5757 tons) on 17 Nov.

1-9 Nov   Black Sea
The cruisers *Krasny Krym, Krasny Kavkaz, Chervona Ukraina*, the flotilla leader *Kharkov*, the destroyers *Bodry, Boiki, Bditelny, Bezuprechny, Nezamozhnik, Shaumyan* and *Zheleznyakov* evacuate troops which are cut off and dispersed from the Tendra Peninsula and from the Crimean ports of Chernomorsk, Yalta, Evpatoria and Feodosia and transport them to Sevastopol. By 9 Nov 8000 troops have arrived by this means. The cruisers mentioned above

also transport 15000 troops from the Caucasus ports to Sevastopol. The flotilla leader *Tashkent* and the destroyers *Sposobny*, *Smyshleny* and *Soobrazitelny*, as well as the patrol ships *Shtorm* and *Shkval*, escort the supply convoys between Caucasus ports and Sevastopol.

1-11 Nov North Atlantic
The 'Störtebecker' group, consisting of *U96*, *U98*, *U69*, *U201*, *U103*, *U107*, *U373* and *U572*, is concentrated for 5 Nov W of Spain to operate against convoy HG.75 which leaves Gibraltar on 1 Nov but is not located by four FW 200s of I/K.G.40 sent out to reconnoitre nor is it reported on 6 Nov by six aircraft and a patrol line. From 7 Nov the 'Störtebecker' group—without *U103* and *U107*—is directed to convoy SL.91 located by the 'B' Service. But up to 11 Nov it is not found either by the air reconnaissance sent out or the U-boats.

1-16 Nov North Atlantic
The U-boats *U123*, *U569*, *U38*, *U82*, *U202*, *U84*, *U203*, *U93*, *U85*, *U74* and *U106* are deployed as the new 'Raubritter' group against convoy SC.52 sighted on 1 Nov by *U374* (Lt Fischel) near Newfoundland. *U374* keeps contact and brings up on 3 Nov first *U123* and later also *U38*, *U569*, *U82* and *U202*. On 3 Nov *U202* (Lt-Cdr Linder) sinks three ships of 8440 tons in two approaches; *U203* (Lt-Cdr Mützelburg) two ships of 10456 tons; and *U569* (Lt Hinsch) one ship of 3439 tons. The operation is much impeded by radio interference and mist. Contact is lost on 3 Nov and is not re-established on 4 Nov. For 8 Nov *U123*, *U38*, *U577*, *U106*, *U571*, *U133*, *U82* and *U85* form a new concentration as the 'Raubritter' Group SE of Greenland. From 12 Nov to 15 Nov the boats are deployed against convoy ONS.33 located by the 'B' Service; but they do not find it and begin the return. *U577*, *U571*, *U85* and *U133* operate, still unsuccessfully, against the convoy OS.11 on 16 Nov. On the return *U74* (Lt-Cdr Kentrat) sinks one ship of 8532 tons.

2 Nov Black Sea
In an attack by three Ju 88s of K.G.51 the Soviet cruiser *Voroshilov* (Capt 1st Class F. S. Markov) receives two bomb hits. The cruiser is towed to Poti, where

she remains for repairs until February 1942.

2-5 Nov Baltic
Second evacuation convoy sets out for Hangö under Capt 2nd Class V. N. Narykov from Kronstadt on 2 Nov and Suursaari on 3 Nov. Participating: the destroyers *Smetlivy* and *Surovy*, minesweepers *T-205/Gafel*, *T-206/Verp*, *T-207/Shpil*, *T-211/Rym*, four MO-IV submarine-chasers, four TKAs. During the stay in Hangö, while loading, *Smetlivy* receives one hit from Finnish artillery. On the evening of 4 Nov the convoy leaves Hangö. *Smetlivy* (Capt 2nd Class V. I. Maslov†) runs on two mines in the channel through the 'Corbetha' mine barrage and sinks. *T-205* returns to Hangö with 350 survivors. The remainder of the force reaches Suursaari with 1200 men from Hangö.

2-8 Nov Mediterranean
The fast British minelayer *Abdiel* and destroyers in several missions relieve the Cyprus garrison by transporting 14000 troops to and from Alexandria.

The Italian submarine *Dandolo* (Lt-Cdr Auconi) torpedoes the French tanker *Tarn* (4220 tons) off Algiers on 4 Nov in a sortie towards the Straits of Gibraltar and on 8 Nov she sinks the Spanish steamer *Castillo Oropesa* (6600 tons) off Melilla.

2-12 Nov Arctic
Off the Norwegian Polar Coast the Soviet submarine *K-22* operates in Vestfjord and *Shch-421* (Lt-Cdr N. A. Lunin) in Lopphavet (three unsuccessful attacks on 2 Nov, 10 Nov and 11 Nov). *K-21* (Capt 3rd Class A. A. Zhukov) lays mine barrages in Söröysund and off Hammerfest. On the latter steamer *Bessheim* (1774 tons) sinks on 21 Nov. An attack on a convoy misses the patrol boat *Nordwind* on 12 Nov. The British submarine *Trident* (Cdr Sladen) sinks the submarine-chaser *UJ1213* on 3 Nov in Svaerholthavet and the steamer *Flottbek* (1930 tons) on 7 Nov from convoys. The Soviet submarine *K-23* (Capt 3rd Class I. S. Potapov) lays a mine barrage in Bökfjord (Kirkenes) on which the minesweeper *M22* runs on 5 Nov and is seriously damaged. In addition, Soviet submarines *M-172* and *S-102* are among others at sea.

2-17 Nov Arctic
The British convoy QP.2 with 12 merchant ships returns to Kirkwall from Archangel without contact with the enemy.

2-18 Nov Black Sea
In operations near the Bulgarian-Turkish frontier the Soviet submarine *Shch-214* (Lt-Cdr V. Ya. Vlasov) sinks on 2 Nov and on 5 Nov the Turkish sailing ship *Karaltepe* and the Italian tanker *Torcello* (3336 tons) and *Shch-215* (Lt-Cdr G. P. Apostolov) the Turkish freighter *Yenice* (300 tons) on 18 Nov. On 11 Nov and 14 Nov respectively the Soviet submarines *Shch-211* and *S-34* are lost on flanking mine barrages off Cape Schabla and Sozopol.

3 Nov Baltic
The German minelayer *Kaiser* (Cdr Bohm) lays a new barrage with 150 EMC mines on the Russian route W of 'Juminda'.

3 Nov Western Atlantic
The British aircraft carrier *Indomitable* is damaged off Kingston (Jamaica) when she runs aground.

3-10 Nov Mediterranean
The British submarines *Proteus* and *Olympus* and the Greek *Glavkos* (Cdr Aslanoglu) each torpedo one ship of 4958 tons, 1049 tons and 2392 tons respectively in the Aegean. *Proteus* also sinks one ship of 1773 tons off Milos.

5 Nov Arctic
Adm Tovey with the Home Fleet—the battleship *King George V*, the carrier *Victorious*, three heavy and two light cruisers—and an American battle squadron (Rear-Adm Giffen) with the battleships *Idaho* and *Mississippi* and the cruisers *Tuscaloosa* and *Wichita* take up covering positions S of Iceland and in the Denmark Strait respectively to counter the expected break-out of the German battleship *Tirpitz* into the Atlantic.

5-20 Nov North Atlantic/ Mediterranean
U205, *U81*, *U433* and *U565* set out from France for the Mediterranean as the 'Arnauld' group. They pass through the Straits of Gibraltar between 11 Nov and 16 Nov and operate at first E of Gibraltar. Early on 13 Nov, and in the afternoon of that day, *U205* (Lt-Cdr Reschke) and *U81* (Lt-Cdr Guggen-

berger) are respectively able to fire their torpedoes at British Force H reported on 12 Nov by Italian air reconnaissance. The latter torpedoes the carrier *Ark Royal* (see 10-14 Nov). On 16 Nov *U433* (Lt-Cdr Ey) tries to attack a convoy setting out eastwards but is then herself sunk by the corvette *Marigold*. From 18 Nov the boats move off to the Eastern Mediterranean.

6 Nov South Atlantic
The US cruiser *Omaha* (Capt Chandler) captures off the Brazilian coast the German blockade-runner *Odenwald* (5098 tons, Capt Loehr), disguised as a US freighter.

6 Nov Western France/Japan
The blockade-runner *Rio Grande* (6062 tons, Capt von Allwörden) arrives in Osaka from Bordeaux.

8-9 Nov Mediterranean
British Force K—cruisers *Aurora* (Capt Agnew) and *Penelope* (Capt Nicholl) and destroyers *Lance* and *Lively*—attacks shortly after midnight a large Italian supply convoy for North Africa located the day before by a Maryland Bomber of No 69 Sqdn RAF. It sinks all seven transports: *Duisburg* (7389 tons), *San Marco* (3113 tons), *Maria* (6339 tons), *Sagitta* (5153 tons), *Rina Corrado* (5180 tons), the tankers *Conte di Misurata* (5014 tons) and *Minatitlan* (7599 tons) and *Fulmine*, one of six escorting destroyers. Two other destroyers, *Euro* and *Grecale* of the close escort, are damaged. Force K is able, with the help of radar, to manoeuvre itself unnoticed into a favourable position to attack and destroy the convoy without the Italian covering force (heavy cruisers *Trento* (Capt Parmigiano) and *Trieste* (Capt Rouselle) and the 13th DD Flotilla (Capt Capponi), comprising *Granatiere*, *Fuciliere*, *Bersagliere* and *Alpino*), which has no radar, being able to intervene effectively. The next morning the British submarine *Upholder* (Lt-Cdr Wanklyn) torpedoes the destroyer *Libeccio* engaged in recovering the survivors which sinks shortly afterwards when being towed by the damaged *Euro*. The destroyers *Maestrale*, *Euro*, *Oriani*, *Alpino*, *Fuciliere* and *Bersagliere* rescue in all 704 survivors of the sunken ships. The Italian submarines *Beilul*, *Corallo*, *Delfino* and *Settembrini* sta-

tioned to protect the convoy, do not fire their torpedoes.

9 Nov Black Sea

The cruiser *Molotov* (Capt 1st Class Yu. K. Zinovev) shells German troop concentrations in the area Feodosia—Cape Chauda to support the hard-pressed units of the 51st Army. An attack by torpedo aircraft and bombers on 10 Nov off Tuapse is beaten off.

9-10 Nov Air War/Germany

Attacks by RAF on Hamburg, Cuxhaven and Emden.

9-12 Nov Baltic

Third evacuation convoy to Hangö under Rear-Adm M.S. Moskalenko leaves Kronstadt on 9 Nov and Suursaari on 10 Nov. Participants: the flotilla leader *Leningrad*, the destroyer *Stoiki*, the minelayer *Ural* (Capt 2nd Class I. G. Karpov), the transport *Andrei Zhdanov* (Capt 1st Class N. I. Meshcherski), the minesweepers *T-201/Zaryad*, *T-211/Rym*, *T-215*, *T-217*, *T-218* and 4 MO-IV submarine-chasers. On the way out on the evening of 10 Nov *T-217* and *T-218* collide in poor visibility and have to return. Because of the weather, the force turns back to Suursaari on the morning of 11 Nov and sets out again in the evening of the same day. In the night *Leningrad* (Capt 3rd Class G. M. Gorbachev) is brought to a standstill after two near-misses from mines and then returns with two minesweepers and the *Zhdanov* which, however, runs on a mine and sinks. On the morning of 12 Nov the remainder of the force turns round and goes back to Suursaari.

9-28 Nov Arctic

British Convoy PQ.3 with eight merchant ships proceeds from Hvalfjord to Archangel without contact with the enemy. One ship returns because of damage from ice.

The convoy PQ.4 (eight merchant ships) follows on 17 Nov and arrives with the PQ.3.

10-12 Nov Black Sea

The Soviet cruisers *Chervona Ukraina* (Capt 2nd Class N. E. Basisty) and *Krasny Krym* (Capt 2nd class A. I. Zubkov) and the destroyers *Nezamozhnik* and *Shaumyan* support with their guns the defence against German attacks on the N and E front of the Sevastopol fortress. At mid-day on 12

Nov forces of the IV German Fl.K attack the ships. Ju 87s of I/St.G.77 (Capt Orthofer) obtain three bomb hits on the *Chervona Ukraina* which, in spite of measures to save her, slowly fills with water and sinks on the bottom. The guns are later dismantled and taken ashore. In these attacks the destroyer *Sovershenny*, lying in the south dock of the navy yard waiting to be fitted out, and the destroyer *Besposhchadny*, having only left dock on 11 Nov after repairs to the damage sustained on 22 Sept, are heavily hit. The latter is towed on 17 Nov by the destroyer *Shaumyan* to Poti for repairs.

10-14 Nov Mediterranean

Operation 'Perpetual': British Force H (Vice-Adm Somerville) proceeds from Gibraltar to the Western Mediterranean with the battleship *Malaya*, the carriers *Argus* and *Ark Royal*, the light cruiser *Hermione* and seven destroyers including *Laforey*, *Legion*, *Sikh* and the Dutch *Isaac Sweers*. On the afternoon of 12 Nov seven Blenheim bombers, flown off as escort planes from Gibraltar, arrive in Malta and 37 Hurricane fighters are flown off from the carriers, 34 of which arrive in Malta. On the return early on 13 Nov *U205* (Lt-Cdr Reschke) first attacks the force with a salvo of three torpedoes, one of which explodes in the wake of the *Legion*. Although six radar-equipped Swordfish are flown off, neither *U81* nor *U205* are found. At mid-day *U81* (Lt-Cdr Guggenberger) torpedoes the *Ark Royal* (Capt Maund) with one torpedo from a salvo of four. The carrier sinks on tow the next day after the crew has been rescued (one life lost), only 25 nautical miles from Gibraltar. The Italian submarines *Aradam*, *Squalo*, *Turchese*, *Bandiera*, *Onice* and *Narvalo* are stationed too far to the east.

10 Nov-27 Dec Atlantic/Indian Ocean

On 10 Nov the convoy WS.12 puts to sea from Halifax to proceed to the Near East via the Cape of Good Hope. It has more than 20000 British troops on board the US troop transports *Wakefield*, *Mount Vernon*, *West Point*, *Leonard Wood*, *Joseph T. Dickman* and *Orizaba* with the tanker *Cimarron*. Escort: TG 14.4 (Rear-Adm Cook) with the carrier *Ranger*, the cruisers

Quincy and *Vincennes* and the destroyers (Capt Kinkaid) *Wainwright, Moffet, McDougal, Winslow, Mayrant, Trippe, Rhind* and *Rowan.* At 17° S *Ranger* returns to Trinidad with *Rhind* and *Trippe.* The convoy is ordered to Bombay instead of Basra. It arrives in Capetown on 9 Dec and then sets out with the British cruiser *Dorsetshire* and arrives in Bombay on 27 Dec. *Mount Vernon* goes direct to Singapore.

11-22 Nov   North Atlantic
From 5 Nov the 'Störtebecker' group, consisting of *U552, U567, U98, U96, U572, U69, U373, U201* and *U77* operates against the convoy OS.11 which has been located by the 'B' Service. The air reconnaissance with six machines provided for 16 Nov is unsuccessful; nor is the convoy found by the patrol line, reinforced by *U332* and *U402*, on 17 Nov and 18 Nov. On 19 Nov the boats are formed in three loose lines to meet an expected OG convoy: the 'Gödecke' group with *U98, U69, U201* and *U572*; the 'Benecke' group with *U332, U402, U96* and *U552*; and the 'Störtebecker' group with *U85, U133, U571* and *U577*. From 22 Nov the developments in the Mediterranean necessitate the sending of all U-boats to the Mediterranean or to the area W of Gibraltar.

11-28 Nov   Arctic
The German U-boats *U578* and *U752* operate in the entrance to the White Sea. On 15 Nov *U752* (Lt Schroeter) attacks a small convoy near Cape Gorodetski and torpedoes a timber freighter and an escort ship. On 27 Nov the Soviet patrol ship *Briz* attacks *U578* near Kanin Nos and slightly damages her by ramming.

12-13 Nov   Baltic
The Finnish minelayers *Riilahti* and *Ruotsinsalmi* lay a new barrage with 141 EMC mines NW of 'Juminda'.

12 Nov-7 Dec   Arctic
Soviet MO-IV submarine-chasers, operating from the bays of the Fisherman's Peninsula, lay 34, 20 and 14 mines off Petsamo, Kirkenes and Vardö in several operations.

13 Nov   General Situation
Change in the American Neutrality Law: it allows American merchant ships to enter the war zone and provides for the arming of merchant ships (it comes into force on 18 Nov).

13-25 Nov   Baltic
Fourth evacuation convoy to Hangö under Capt 2nd class V. N. Narykov sets out from Suursaari on 13 Nov. Participating: the destroyers *Gordy* and *Surovy,* the minelayer *Ural,* minesweepers *T-206/Verp, T-207/Shpil, T-211/Rym, T-215* and four MO-IV submarine-chasers. In the night 13-14 Nov the submarine-chaser *MO-301,* the minesweeper *T-206* and the destroyer *Surovy* (Capt 3rd Class M. T. Ustinov) run on mines of the newly laid Finnish barrage and sink. On the evening of 14 Nov *Gordy* (Capt 3rd Class E. B. Efet) runs on mines of the 'Corbetha' barrage and also sinks. Only *T-215, Ural* and three submarine-chasers reach Hangö on 14 Nov. Because of the losses, the movements of the larger ships are temporarily halted. Only after some small convoys have made the passage does the force return, reinforced by *T-205/Gafel, T-217 T-218* and three submarine-chasers. On 25 Nov it lands 4588 men in Kronstadt.

13-26 Nov   Mediterranean
The Italian submarines *Atropo, Saint Bon, Cagni* and *Millo* carry out transport operations from Taranto to Bardia.

13 Nov-1 Dec   North Atlantic
The U-boats *U431, U402, U332* and *U105,* which were stationed in the area of the Denmark Strait from 4 Nov to 10 Nov in anticipation of the intended sortie of the battleship *Tirpitz,* are sent from 13 Nov to the area of Cape Race. *U332* and *U402* join the 'Störtebecker' group and *U43* and *U575* go as replacements to the 'Steuben' group. From 23 Nov the boats are recalled to the area W of Gibraltar. On the way there *U43* (Lt-Cdr Lüth) sights a WS troop convoy on 28 Nov to which the boats *U105, U372, U434, U575* and *U574* are directed. On both 29 Nov and 30 Nov *U43* sinks one ship: together they total 10437 tons. The other boats partly reach the convoy by 1 Dec but they cannot achieve any success. On 2 Dec *U43* sinks, in addition, the US tanker *Astral* (7541 tons), sailing on her own.

14-15 Nov   Mediterranean
Italian torpedo aircraft sink off the Tunisian coast the British transports *Empire Defender* (5649 tons) and *Empire*

Pelican (6463 tons) which try to break through from Gibraltar to Malta.

14-18 Nov Mediterranean
Successful attempts by the Italians to bring supplies to North Africa with small fast convoys and warships. Both on 16 Nov and 18 Nov two ships reach Benghazi.

15-24 Nov Mediterranean
Unsuccessful sortie by the Italian submarine *Ascianghi* to the Palestine coast.

15 Nov-1 Dec Black Sea
Strong elements of the Soviet Black Sea Fleet, including the battleship *Parizhskaya Kommuna*, the cruisers *Krasny Kavkaz*, *Krasny Krym*, the destroyers *Besposhchadny*, *Boiki*, *Smyshleny*, *Soobrazitelny*, *Zheleznyakov* and others, support the defenders of Sevastopol with their gunfire on 15 Nov, 23 Nov, 25 Nov, 28 Nov, 29 Nov and 1 Dec.

15 Nov-11 Dec Baltic
The Soviet submarines *S-9* and *Shch-309* operate in the western part of the Gulf of Finland. *M-103* is probably lost in the same area.

16 Nov Black Sea
Capture of Kerch. With it the whole of the Crimea, with the exception of Sevastopol, is in the hands of the German 11th Army.

17-21 Nov North Atlantic
After the U-boats *U561* (Lt Bartels) and *U652* have served as an escort for the homeward-bound auxiliary cruiser *Schiff 45 Komet*, *U561* sinks two stragglers from the convoy SC.53 totalling 8514 tons.

17-24 Nov Arctic
In submarine operations off the Norwegian Polar Coast the Soviet *M-171* (Lt-Cdr V. G. Starikov) unsuccessfully attacks a tanker. The British submarines *Sealion* (Lt-Cdr Colvin) and *Seawolf* (Lt Raikes), recently transferred to the Arctic, respectively sink the tanker *Vesco* (331 tons) on 18 Nov in Svaerholthavet and, after an unsuccessful firing on 22 Nov, the steamer *Bahia* (4117 tons) on 24 Nov off Syltefjord. In addition, *M-172* and *Shch-403* are among the submarines at sea.

17 Nov-2 Dec Black Sea
A counter-attack by the Soviet 9th and 37th Armies against the flank of the German 1st Panzer Army advancing on Rostov begins on 17 Nov. German

forward troops actually take Rostov on 21 Nov, but have to evacuate it again on 24 Nov because of the threatening situation in the rear. The 1st Panzer Army withdraws to the Mius sector by 2 Dec.

18-27 Nov Mediterranean
The British 8th Army (Gen Cunningham) starts a counter-offensive in North Africa on 18 Nov to relieve Tobruk—(Operation 'Crusader'). On 21 Nov the Tobruk garrison breaks out to the E to meet the advancing 8th Army. To supply Tobruk the Australian sloops *Parramatta* and *Yarra* bring a slow convoy to the fortress (18-23 Nov). To relieve the shortage of ammunition the *Parramatta* and the destroyer *Avondale* escort the ammunition transport *Hanne* (1360 tons) to Tobruk. *U559* (Lt-Cdr Heidtmann) sinks the *Parramatta* near Tobruk on 27 Nov.

18 Nov-7 Dec Pacific
The Japanese SM flotillas 1 (Rear-Adm Sato) and 2 (Rear-Adm Yamazaki) leave Yokosuka on 18-19 Nov for the waters round Hawaii. *I-26* (Cdr*M. Yokota) reconnoitres the Aleutian island of Kiska on 25 Nov, Dutch Harbor with her aircraft on 27-28 Nov and Adak and Kodiak on 30 Nov. *I-10* (Cdr *Kayahara) reconnoitres with her aircraft over Suva (Samoa) on 29 Nov, and by periscope off Pago-Pago on 4 Dec.
From 3 Dec *I-9*, *I-15*, *I-17*, *I-25* form a patrol line north of Oahu; *I-7* is stationed N of Oahu with *I-1*, *I-2*, *I-3* W and *I-4*, *I-5*, *I-6* E of Oahu. The 3rd SM Flotilla (Rear-Adm Miwa), coming from Kwajalein, consisting of *I-8*, *I-68*, *I-69*, *I-70*, *I-71*, *I-72*, *I-73*, *I-74* and *I-75*, takes up positions in a semicircle S of Oahu.
In the night 6-7 Dec the midget submarine transports *I-16*, *I-18*, *I-20*, *I-22*, *I-24* put out their midget submarines. One of them is sunk in the night by the destroyer *Ward* (Lt-Cdr Outerbridge) off the harbour (first shot in the Pacific War), two are sunk penetrating the harbour and two are sunk in the harbour before they are able to fire. On the return *I-16* and *I-22* shell Johnston on 16 Dec.

19 Nov Indian Ocean
The Australian light cruiser *Sydney* (Capt Burnett†) encounters the German

auxiliary cruiser *Schiff 41 Kormoran* (Cdr*Detmers) about 170 nautical miles W of Shark Bay (Western Australia). Detmers is able to prolong the signal exchanges until the *Sydney* has approached within 900 metres and come alongside the German ship. The latter has no choice but to drop the disguise and to open fire with all her guns. The *Sydney* is badly hit by the first salvoes and receives a torpedo hit in the bow. *Sydney* disappears from view on fire and is never seen again. *Schiff 41* has also to be abandoned when a fire caused by burning oil cannot be extinguished because the auxiliary engines are out of action.
The majority of the crew reaches the Australian coast and is taken aboard Allied ships. Total result of the auxiliary cruiser's activities: 11 merchant ships of 68274 tons sunk.

19 Nov   Bay of Biscay
The British submarine *Rorqual* (Lt Napier) lays a mine barrage off La Rochelle. A French trawler of 600 tons is lost on it.

19-20 Nov   North Sea
Attack by the 2nd MTB Flotilla with four boats on a British convoy off Great Yarmouth. *S104* (Lt Regensburg) sinks the British naval tanker *War Mehtar* (5502 tons); *S105* the freighter *Aruba* (1159 tons); and *S41* the freighter *Waldinge* (2462 tons). *S41* (Lt Popp) is damaged in a collision in an engagement with the convoy escort and, on the return, has to be abandoned while on tow.

19-25 Nov   Baltic
After the losses on 14 Nov several small Soviet convoys proceed from Suursaari to Hangö and back.
On 19-20 Nov Capt 3rd class D. M. Belkov goes to Hangö with the netlayer *Azimut*, the patrol ship *Virsaitis*, the minesweepers *T-58*, *T-35*, *T-42* and *Klyuz*. On the return on 21-22 Nov *Azimut* and *T-35/Menzhinski* are lost on mines.
On 20-21 Nov the minesweepers *T-205*, *T-217* and *T-218* go to Hangö; the transport *No 548/Minna* and two submarine-chasers have to turn back. The minesweepers return with the fourth convoy.
On 21-22 Nov the transport *No 10* goes with five motor minesweepers to Hangö.

On 22-23 Nov Lt-Cdr G. S. Dus goes with the transport *No 548/Minna*, the patrol ship *Korall*, the minesweeper *Udarnik* and two submarine-chasers to Hangö.
On 23-24 Nov Capt 3rd class Belkov follows with *T-42*, *Klyuz*, *Virsaitis*, and two submarine-chasers. On 24 Nov the force, comprising *No. 548/Minna*, *Klyuz*, *Udarnik*, and *Virsaitis*, starts the return journey. *Klyuz* is lost on mines and *Udarnik* is slightly damaged. In all, 4424 men, 18 tanks, 720 tons of rations and 250 tons of ammunition are evacuated by these convoys.

19-28 Nov   Mediterranean
In operations in the Western Mediterranean the Dutch submarine *O21* (Lt-Cdr van Dulm) sinks two sailing ships and the U-boat *U95*.
On 19 Nov the Polish submarine *Sokol* (Cdr Karnicki) attacks the harbour of Navarino and damages the destroyer *Aviere*.
Thrasher (Lt Mackenzie) sinks one ship of 3510 tons from a Patrasso/Brindisi convoy. In the Aegean *Triumph* (Lt-Cdr Woods) sinks one ship of 632 tons.

20-22 Nov   Mediterranean
The critical supply situation of the German/Italian Army forces the Italian Fleet to make further efforts to bring through supply transports. 21 Nov: two convoys each with two transports set out, escorted by seven destroyers and torpedo boats and the 3rd Div (Div-Adm Parona) comprising the heavy cruisers *Gorizia*, *Trento* and *Trieste*.
21 Nov: British air reconnaissance and a submarine locate the convoys. As it passes through the Straits of Messina, the 8th Div (Div-Adm Lombardi), comprising the light cruisers *Duca degli Abruzzi* and *Garibaldi* join the covering group. From both Taranto and Brindisi two further transports set out; in addition, from Brindisi, the cruiser *Cadorna* as a fuel transport. A ship from the Taranto convoy has to return because of engine trouble; the other three and *Cadorna* reach Benghazi on 22 Nov.
The rest of the force is attacked shortly before midnight on 21-22 Nov by the British submarine *Utmost* (Lt-Cdr Cayley). The *Trieste* (Capt Rouselle) receives a torpedo hit and only reaches Messina with difficulty. A little later the

force is attacked by British aircraft from Malta and the *Duca degli Abruzzi* (Capt Zannoni) is hit by an air torpedo. Meanwhile, the 'B' service has learnt of the departure of the British Force K from Malta but the Italian submarines *Delfino*, *Squalo*, *Tricheco*, *Settembrini* and *Corallo*, stationed E of Malta as a cover, do not sight it. The 3rd Div receives orders to put into Taranto with the transports. *Garibaldi* and the destroyers *Vivaldi*, *Da Noli*, *Granatiere*, *Fuciliere*, *Alpino*, *Corazziere*, *Carabiniere*, *Turbine* and the torpedo boat *Perseo* take over the task of escorting the badly damaged *Duca degli Abruzzi*. The Mediterranean Fleet, which has put to sea to support Force K, returns.

21 Nov-15 Dec   Arctic
The Soviet submarines *K-3* (Capt 3rd Class K. I. Malofeev, with the Commander 1st SM Division, Capt 2nd Class M. I. Gadzhiev, on board) and *K-23* (Capt 3rd Class I. S. Potapov) set out on 21 Nov and lay mine barrages on 26-27 Nov off Hammerfest and in Kvaenangenfjord respectively. The Norwegian coasters *Ingar Nielsen* and *Kong Ring* (1994 tons) run onto the second barrage mentioned on 26 Dec and have to be beached. The submarine-chaser *UJ1110* is possibly lost on the first on 9 July 1942. On 26 Nov *K-23* unsuccessfully attacks a minesweeper and on 3 Dec *K-3* attacks a convoy with the steamer *Altkirch* off Rolvsöy. The submarine-chasers *UJ1403*, *UJ1416* and *UJ1708* attack the submarine with depth charges. Capt 2nd Class Gadzhiev orders the submarine to surface because of the resulting damage and in a gun engagement gets a direct hit on *UJ1708* (470 tons) which sinks. The two other submarine-chasers, which are only armed with 2cm AA guns, have to withdraw in face of the superior-armed submarine (two 10cm and two 4.5cm guns), which escapes. Off Porsangerfjord *D-3* (Lt-Cdr N. A. Bibeev, with the Commander 2nd SM Division, Capt 2nd Class I. A. Kolyshkin, on board) attacks steamers on 26 Nov, 5 Dec and 6 Dec, but the torpedoes explode on the cliffs. Off Tanafjord the British submarine *Sealion* (Lt-Cdr Colvin) sinks the small Norwegian steamer *Island* (638 tons); the Soviet *M-171* misses a

tanker in Varangerfjord; *M-174* lands agents on the Varanger coast; and *M-176* operates without result. *K-22* (Capt 3rd Class V. N. Kotelnikov) which sets out on 6 Dec with the Commander of the Submarine Brigade, Capt 1st Class N. I. Vinogradov, lays a mine barrage in Rolvsöy Sound on 9 Dec, attacks a Norwegian cutter with gunfire, (which, however, escapes) and sinks a convoy of vessels in tow on 11 Dec near Mylingen.

22 Nov-30 Nov   South Atlantic
On 22 Nov the German auxiliary cruiser *Schiff 16 Atlantis* (Capt Rogge) is surprised by the British heavy cruiser *Devonshire* (Capt Oliver) N of Ascension when she is replenishing *U126* (Lt-Cdr Bauer). She has to scuttle herself. *U126* submerges near *Schiff 16* under the impression that the cruiser will approach closer. After the sinking of the auxiliary cruiser and the departure of the *Devonshire*, she tows the crew in their boats and takes the wounded below until on 24 Nov they can be handed over to the submarine supply ship *Python* which is summoned to the scene.
On her way to support *U126*, *U124* (Lt-Cdr Mohr) encounters the British cruiser *Dunedin* proceeding on her own and sinks her. For the period 30 Nov-4 Dec it is proposed to supply a U-boat group consisting of *U68*, *UA*, *U129* and *U124* 780 nautical miles south of St Helena for an operation off Cape Town. On the way *U124* sinks the American steamer *Sagadahoc* (6275 tons) on 3 Dec (cf. 1 Dec).

22 Nov-3 Dec   North Atlantic/ Mediterranean
The situation in North Africa necessitates the transfer of more German U-boats to the Mediterranean and the concentration of the remaining boats in the Gibraltar area. *U431* and *U95*, which are proceeding to the Atlantic, are ordered to the Mediterranean and pass through the Straits of Gibraltar on 24 Nov and 26 Nov respectively. *U95* (Lt-Cdr Schreiber) is sunk on 28 Nov by the Dutch submarine *O21* (Lt-Cdr van Dulm). After taking supplies in Spanish harbours, *U557* and *U562* first take up their positions in the Western Mediterranean from 27-29 Nov and then from 2 Dec proceed with *U431* to the Eastern

Mediterranean. Of the boats supplied from German tankers in Cadiz, *U562* passes through the Straits of Gibraltar on 28 Nov and remains just E of there until 7 Dec. *U96* and *U558* are located on 1 Dec and 3 Dec respectively with ASV radar by the Swordfish aircraft of No 812 Sqdn of the *Ark Royal* operating from the airfield at Gibraltar. They are damaged by bombs and have to return. On 2 Dec *U562* (Lt Hamm) and *U557* (Lt-Cdr Paulshen) each sink one ship of 4274 tons and 4033 tons respectively.

23-25 Nov   Mediterranean
Further attempts by the Italian Navy to bring small convoys through to North Africa. The ship movements are detected by British air reconnaissance whereupon Force K, comprising the cruisers *Aurora* (Capt Agnew) and *Penelope* and the destroyers *Lance* and *Lively*, sets out from Malta. But it is reported that the Italian submarine *Settembrini* and all convoys receive orders to put into the nearest harbour. A convoy (two freighters and two torpedo boats) from the Aegean, and destined for Benghazi, does not receive the orders and is attacked by Force K 100 nautical miles W of Crete. The two German transports *Maritza* (2910 tons) and *Procida* (1842 tons) are sunk by *Penelope* and *Lively*, although the Commander of the escort (Cdr* Mimbelli), comprising the torpedo boats *Cassiopea* and *Lupo*, does everything to prevent their fate.
At Churchill's insistence, Admiral Cunningham has gone to sea with the bulk of the Mediterranean Fleet— battleships *Queen Elizabeth*, *Barham*, *Valiant* and eight destroyers (Force A) and Rear-Adm Rawlings with the cruisers *Ajax*, *Neptune*, *Naiad*, *Euryalus* and *Galatea* and four destroyers (Force B) as support for Force K. At this time the Italian submarines *Beilul*, *Dagabur*, and *Zaffiro* are operating as escorts off the Cyrenaican coast and the German U-boats *U79*, *U331* and *U559* on the supply route to Tobruk. The British troop transport *Glenroy* (9809 tons) receives an air torpedo hit on 23 Nov and is beached near Tobruk. On 25 Nov *U331* (Lt von Tiesenhausen) penetrates the screen of the battleship force of the Mediterranean Fleet north of Bardia and, at short range, obtains three hits

from a salvo of four torpedoes on the *Barham* which capsizes and explodes. The destroyers *Jervis*, *Jackal*, *Nizam* (RAN) and *Hotspur* rescue the Commander of the 1st Battle Squadron, Vice-Adm Pridham-Wippell, and 450 survivors. The ship's Commander, Capt Cooke, and 861 men perish.

23 Nov-2 Dec   Baltic
The Soviet gunboat *Laine* evacuates in the nights 22-23 Nov, 24-25 Nov and 28-29 Nov 165, 70 and 206 men respectively from the island of Odensholm (Capt Verbizki) to Hangö. In the night 1-2 Dec she takes 543 men on board and brings them direct to Suursaari. The last demolition parties (17 men) are brought by torpedo cutters to Suursaari.

24 Nov   Arctic
A British force (Rear-Adm Burrough), consisting of the cruiser *Kenya* and the destroyers *Bedouin* and *Intrepid* and the attached Soviet destroyers *Gremyashchi* and *Gromki*, searches unsuccessfully for German ships on the Norwegian Polar Coast between Nordkyn and Vardö and shells Vardö.

24 Nov   North Sea
Attack by the 4th MTB Flotilla (Lt-Cdr Bätge) comprising *S50*, *S51*, *S52*, *S109* and *S110*, on British convoy E of Orford Ness. *S109* (Sub-Lt Bosse) sinks the British tanker *Virgilia* (5723 tons) and *S52* (Lt Karl Müller) sinks the Dutch freighter *Groenlo* (1984 tons). *S51* torpedoes the freighter *Blairnevis* (4155 tons).

25 Nov   Pacific
The US Navy introduces compulsory convoys for merchant ships in the Pacific.

25 Nov   General Situation
President Roosevelt decides to break off negotiations with Japan and hands the Japanese Ambassador, through Secretary of State Hull, on 26 Nov a 10-point note which is unacceptable to Japan. A breach between the two states has, therefore, become inevitable.

25 Nov-30 Nov   Black Sea
The tankers *Avanesov*, *Tuapse*, *Sakhalin* and the ice-breaker *Mikoyan* (former auxiliary cruiser) leave Batum on 25 Nov, escorted by the flotilla leader *Tashkent* (Rear-Adm L. A. Vladimirski) and the destroyers *Soobrazitelny* and *Sposobny* for the Bosphorus which they enter on 28 Nov when the warships

return. On the subsequent journey to the Far East *Avanesov* is sunk on 19 Dec by *U652* (Lt-Cdr Fraatz) off the Turkish coast near Cape Baba.

25 Nov   North Atlantic
After the withdrawal of all fully operational U-boats to the Gibraltar area, there remain, for the time being, in the North Atlantic, the U-boats which have small reserves of fuel: *U69*, *U201* and *U402*. They form the 'Letzte Ritter' group. They are directed to convoy OG.77 which sets out on 26 Nov and is located by air reconnaissance on 28 Nov but which is not found again on 29 Nov, 30 Nov and 1 Dec.

26 Nov   Pacific
The Japanese Striking Force, which is to attack Pearl Harbour and which is assembled in Hittokappu Bay, sets out. The Commander is the Officer Commanding the 1st Naval Air Fleet, Vice-Adm Nagumo, comprising the aircraft carrier Sqdns 1, 2 and 5 (*Akagi, Kaga; Hiryu, Soryu; Shokaku, Zuikaku;* with a total of 423 aircraft). Escort provided by the 1st DD Flotilla: light cruiser *Abukuma* (Rear-Adm Omori), destroyers *Tanikaze, Urakaze, Isokaze, Hamakaze, Kasumi, Arare, Kagero, Shiranuhi* and *Akigumo*. Support force (Vice-Adm Mikawa): 3rd BB Sqdn with the battleships *Hiei* and *Kirishima* and the 8th Cruiser Sqdn comprising the heavy cruisers *Chikuma* and *Tone*. In addition, the submarines *I-19, I-21* and *I-23* and eight tankers and supply ships as well as a destroyer force (Capt Konishi) consisting of *Akebono* and *Ushio*, intended for the shelling of Midway Island, belong to the group. The force proceeds eleven days under conditions of complete radio silence, at first on easterly courses in storm and mist, then to the SE and better weather.

27 Nov   General Situation
'War Warning' to the overseas commanders of the US armed forces.

27-29 Nov   Mediterranean
Rear-Adm Rawlings moves from Alexandria to Malta with the cruisers *Ajax* (Capt McCarthy) and *Neptune* and the destroyers *Kimberley* and *Kingston* to reinforce Force K. On the first part of the journey they are accompanied by the cruisers *Naiad* (Rear-Adm Vian) and *Euryalus* and two destroyers.

The Italian submarines *Delfino* and *Squalo*, which are stationed SE of Sicily to cover Italian operations, and *Alagi* and *Aradam*, stationed on the Tunisian coast, sight no targets. SE of Malta *Tricheco* unsuccessfully attacks the advancing cruiser force.

27 Nov-12 Dec   Arctic
The British convoy QP.3 with 10 merchant ships proceeds from Archangel to Seidisfjord (Iceland) without contact with the enemy. Two ships have to return because of storm damage.
The British convoy PQ.5 with seven merchant ships goes from Hvalfjord to Archangel without contact with the enemy.

28-29 Nov   Black Sea
The battleship *Parizhskaya Kommuna* (Capt 1st Class Kravchenko) and the destroyer *Smyshleny* from Cape Feolent shell German and Rumanian positions S of Sevastopol: 146 rounds of 305mm, 120 rounds of 130mm and 299 rounds of 120mm. On 29 Nov the cruiser *Krasny Kavkaz* (Capt 2nd Class A. M. Gushchin) and the destroyer *Zheleznyakov* shell German positions near Kutschuk.

28 Nov-7 Dec   Mediterranean
The German U-boats *U81, U205* and *U565* arrive from 28 Nov in the operational area between Alexandria and Tobruk from the Western Mediterranean and reinforce *U79, U331* and *U559*. Their attacks on supply ships, sailing ships, destroyers and warship formations, including one on 6 Dec by *U79* (Lt-Cdr Kaufmann) on the battleship *Queen Elizabeth*, are unsuccessful. On 6-7 Dec the transport *Chakdina* (3033 tons) is lost by a torpedo hit (possibly from *U81*) and *Chantala* (3129 tons) on a mine off Tobruk. Both are engaged in the Tobruk supply traffic. The sloop *Flamingo* is damaged by bomb hits.

28 Nov-31 Dec   Mediterranean
Major deployment of Italian submarines as supply transports: to Bardia (13 transports), Derna (2), Benghazi (4) and Tripoli (2). The following boats participate: *Millo* (3), *Menotti* (2), *Cagni* (2), *Settimo* (1), *Caracciolo* (1), *Saint Bon* (2), *Mocenigo* (2), *Dandolo* (2), *Otaria* (1), *Bragadino* (1), *Veniero* (1) and *Emo* (1). On 11 Dec *Caracciolo* is encountered on the return by the

British destroyer *Farndale* and sunk. The submarines transport, in all, 1757.6 tons of material and fuel.

29 Nov North Sea
In an attack by the 4th MTB Flotilla on a British convoy NW of Cromer *S51* (Lt Hans-Jürgen Meyer) sinks the freighter *Cormarsh* (2848 tons); *S52* (Lt Karl Müller) the *Empire Newcomen* (2840 tons); and *S64* (Lt Wilcke) the tanker *Asperity* (699 tons).

29 Nov-2 Dec Mediterranean
New Italian convoy operations to North Africa. From Brindisi the freighters *Capo Faro* (3476 tons) and *Iseo* (2366 tons) set out with the torpedo boat *Procione*; from Taranto the motor ship *Sebastiano Venier* (6311 tons) with the destroyer *Da Verazzano*; from Navarino the tanker *Volturno* (3363 tons) with two destroyers; and from Argostoli the passenger ship *Adriatico* (1976 tons). All ships are destined for Benghazi. From Trapani to Tripoli there set out the motor tanker *Iridio Mantovani* (10540 tons) and the destroyer *Da Mosto* and, in addition, two covering groups: the 7th Div (Div-Adm de Courten) comprising the light cruisers *Attendolo*, *Duca d'Aosta*, *Montecuccoli*, the destroyers *Aviere*, *Camicia Nera*, *Geniere* and the battleship *Caio Duilio* (Div Adm Giovanola), the cruiser *Garibaldi* and the destroyers *Granatiere*, *Alpino*, *Bersagliere*, *Fuciliere*, *Corazziere* and *Carabiniere*. The Italian movements are again detected by British air reconnaissance. *Volturno* again receives bomb hits and has to return. 30 Nov: Force K, comprising *Aurora*, *Penelope*, *Ajax*, *Neptune* and the destroyers *Lively*, *Kimberley* and *Kingston* leave Malta, whereupon the Italian cruisers join the *Venier* convoy which is the most threatened. The *Duilio* group is held up by engine trouble on *Garibaldi* and cannot arrive on time. Supermarina therefore orders the other cruisers to avoid the superior Force K and the convoys to go off eastwards. Bombers from Malta sink the *Capo Faro*, and the *Iseo* has to return to Argostoli after a bomb hit. In the night 30 Nov-1 Dec Force K sinks the solitary *Adriatico* but *Venier* is able to avoid it and reaches Benghazi on 2 Dec. About 70 nautical miles N of Tripoli *Mantovani* is hit

by an air torpedo and, some hours later, is sunk by bombs. *Da Mosto* (Cdr dell'Anno) sights the advancing British cruiser *Penelope*, while rescuing the survivors from the large tanker, and attacks her with torpedoes. But she is destroyed by the fire of the British ships and sinks.

29 Nov-4 Dec Baltic
Evacuation of the rest of the Hangö garrison (Lt-Gen S. I. Kabanov). On 29 Nov Vice-Adm V. P. Drozd leaves Kronstadt with the destroyers *Slavny*, *Stoiki*, the transports *Josif Stalin*, the minesweepers *T-205/Gafel*, *T-207/Shpil*, *T-111/Rym*, *T-215*, *T-217*, *T-218* (Capt 2nd Class N. A. Mamontov), seven submarine-chasers and four torpedo-cutters. On the way to Suursaari the ice-breaker *Oktyabr* is lost in an air attack. The force arrives in Hangö on 30 Nov. On 30 Nov-1 Dec another force proceeds to Hangö under Lt-Cdr P. B. Shevtsov with the transport *No 539/Maya*, the minesweeper *T-210/Gak*, the gunboat *Volga*, the *Udarnik* and *Virsaitis*, the submarine-chasers *MO-405* and *MO-406*. An attempted attack by the Finnish gunboats *Hämeenmaa* and *Uusimaa* with two boats of the 3rd Patrol Boat Flotilla and four other patrol boats is unsuccessful. On 2 Dec the Soviet troops leave and are embarked. In the evening Lt-Cdr Shevtsov leaves first with his force strengthened by the gunboat *Laine* and four tugs. *Virsaitis* is lost on the way on a mine and *Maya* and *Volga* are damaged. In the late evening Vice-Adm Drozd follows with the minesweepers *T-205*, *T-207*, *T-211*, *T-215*, *T-217*, *T-218*, *J. Stalin*, *Slavny*, *Stoiki* and submarine protection consisting of seven submarine-chasers and four torpedo cutters. The remaining demolition parties and command staffs are taken on board fourteen other torpedo cutters. On 3 Dec the force runs onto the 'Corbetha' mine barrage; *T-211*, *T-215* and *T-218* lose their minesweeping equipment on explosive floats. *J. Stalin* (7500 tons) drifts into the barrage and is hit by four mines in succession. The last causes the magazine to explode bringing about heavy loss of life (some 4000 men?). 650 men are recovered by *T-217*,

160 by *T-205* (damaged on a mine), 120 by *T-207*, 500 by *T-211* and *T-215* and 400 by the submarine-chasers *MO-106*, *MO-210*, *MO-307* and *MO-407*. About 2000 men remain on the drifting wreck. Capt 2nd Class Svyatov sets out from Suursaari with the destroyer *Svirepy* and the rescue ship *Neptun*, but has to return when *T-207* loses her minesweeping equipment. A second attempt to set out on 4 Dec with four minesweepers is abandoned on orders of the Fleet Command because, in the meantime, German patrol boats of the 3rd Patrol Boat Flotilla have taken the wreck of *J. Stalin* in tow. Only a half of the last 12000 men reach Suursaari. From there the ships are brought to Kronstadt with the help of the ice-breaker *Ermak*.

30 Nov   North Sea
The auxiliary cruiser *Schiff 45 Komet* (Rear-Adm Eyssen) comes into Hamburg after 516 days in enemy waters. Results: 6 ships of 31005 tons sunk and two other ships totalling 21125 tons in co-operation with the auxiliary cruiser *Schiff 36 Orion*.

30 Nov   Indian Ocean
The Free French destroyer *Léopard* (Cdr*Evenou) occupies the island of Reunion after an engagement with the Vichy French battery at Point des Galets and breaking the local resistance.

30 Nov-18 Dec   Black Sea
In Soviet submarine operations off the Rumanian-Bulgarian coast *M-34* and *M-59* are lost on flanking mine barrages and the submarine *M-54* as a result of a depth charge attack following an unsuccessful assault on the Rumanian destroyer *Regele Ferdinand I*. *Shch-205* (Lt-Cdr T. D. Sukhomlinov) runs on a flanking barrage on 4 Dec near Varna and only reaches Sevastopol with difficulty. Near Cape Emine the Rumanian steamer *Oituz* (2686 tons) is probably damaged by *M-58* (Lt-Cdr N. V. Eliseev) which is also lost on a mine.

1 Dec   Western France/Japan
The blockade-runner *Portland* (7132 tons, Capt Tünemann) reaches Osaka from Bordeaux.

1-3 Dec   Black Sea
The destroyer *Boiki* shells assembly positions near Kalych Kiap on 1 Dec; the destroyer *Zheleznyakov* the area E

of Inkerman from Severnaya Bay on 1 Dec and 2 Dec; and the cruiser *Krasny Krym* the area of Balaklava on 1 Dec. On 3 Dec the cruiser *Krasny Kavkaz* brings 1000 troops, shells German positions from Severnaya Bay and returns to Novorossisk with 600 wounded. On the way the Balaklava area is shelled.

1-7 Dec   Arctic
The British cruiser *Kent* brings the British Foreign Secretary, Eden, from Scapa Flow to Murmansk, from where he travels to Moscow to a conference with Stalin.

1-12 Dec   Pacific
The US submarines *Tambor* and *Triton* are stationed off Wake and *Argonaut* and *Trout* off Midway for reconnaissance purposes.

1-13 Dec   Mediterranean
New Italian convoy operations to North Africa: greatly impeded by stormy weather. 9-10 Dec: the light cruiser *Luigi Cadorna* brings petrol to Benghazi and returns with 900 prisoners of war on board. 9-12: the British submarine *Porpoise* (Cdr Pizey) sinks the motor ship *Sebastiano Venier* (6311 tons) which is returning from Benghazi with 2000 prisoners of war. In spite of bad weather, the hospital ship *Arno* is able to rescue 1800 of those on board. 11 Dec: the cruiser *Cadorna* again brings petrol to Benghazi. The British submarine *Talisman* (Lt-Cdr Willmott) sinks the Italian motor ship *Calitea* (4013 tons) S of Cape Matapan. 13 Dec the 4th Div (Div-Adm Toscano), comprising the cruiser *Da Barbiano* (Capt Rodocannacchi) and *Di Giussano* (Capt Marabotto), has set out as petrol transports with the torpedo boat *Cigno* from Palermo but have turned back shortly after passing Cape Bon when located by British air reconnaissance. On the return both cruisers are sunk by torpedoes from the British destroyers *Sikh* (Cdr Stokes) *Legion* and *Maori* and by the Dutch *Isaac Sweers*, proceeding from Gibraltar to Alexandria Div-Adm Toscano and over 900 members of the crews of both cruisers perish. *Cigno* is able to get away.

1-29 Dec   South Atlantic
The British heavy cruiser *Dorsetshire* (Capt Agar) surprises the German

U-boat supply ship *Python* (Lt-Cdr Lueders) when providing *UA* (Cdr Eckermann) and *U68* (Cdr Merten) with oil at 27° 53' S, 03° 55' W. Both U-boats submerge at once and *UA* attacks the cruiser with five torpedoes which, however, miss. With that the fate of the *Python* is sealed. When the *Dorsetshire* fires a salvo to halt her, the crew of the *Python* leaves the ship which sinks after being blown up. The crews of *Schiff 16* (see 22 Nov) and *Python*, in all 414 men, are towed on the following days in boats and floats, first by *UA* and *U68*, and then on 3 Dec *U129* (Lt-Cdr Clausen) comes up and takes the entire *Python* crew on board. On 5 Dec *U124* (Lt-Cdr Mohr) also comes up. Between 14 Dec and 18 Dec the Italian submarines *Torelli* (Cdr Giacomo), *Tazzoli* (Cdr Fecia di Cossato), *Finzi* (Cdr *Giudice*) and *Calvi* (Cdr Olivieri) take a part of the crew of *Schiff 16* and bring them to St Nazaire, where the crews of the two German ships are landed between 23 Dec and 29 Dec.

2 Dec   Indian Ocean
British battleship *Prince of Wales* and battlecruiser *Repulse* and four destroyers arrive in Singapore.

2 Dec   Southern Asia
The submarines of the Dutch East Indies Fleet, which are ready for operations, take up their positions: *K-XII*, *O16* on the east coast of the Malayan peninsula; *K-XI*, *K-XIII*, *O19* in the Karimata Strait; and *K-XIV*, *K-XV*, *K-XVI* and *K-XVII* off Kuching.

2-5 Dec   Mediterranean
The Italian submarine *Ametista* operates S of Crete.

4-11 Dec   Mediterranean
In operations in the area of the Peloponnese the British submarine *Trusty* (Lt-Cdr Batstone) sinks one ship of 3586 tons (4 Dec); *Talisman* (Lt-Cdr Willmott) sinks one ship of 4013 tons in a Brindisi-Benghazi convoy on 11 Dec; and *Truant* (Lt-Cdr Haggard) torpedoes on the same day the torpedo boat *Alcione* which is beached. The British submarine *Perseus* is probably lost on a mine in this area.

4-7 Dec   Southern Asia
On the morning of 4 Dec the Japanese Malaya landing group sets out from Samah (Hainan) with 18 transports; on

board: 26640 troops of the 5th Inf Div (Lt-Gen Matsui) and the 56th Inf Regt of the 18th Inf Div. Escort: 3rd DD Flotilla with the cruiser *Sendai* and the destroyers of the 12th DD Div (*Murakumo, Shinonome, Shirakumo, Usugumo*), the 19th (*Isonami, Uranami, Shikinami, Ayanami*) and the 20th (*Amagiri, Asagiri* and *Yugiri*). Vice-Adm Ozawa's flagship, the heavy cruiser *Chokai*, accompanies the convoy with the destroyer *Sagiri*.
At the same time the 7th Cruiser Sqdn (Rear-Adm Kurita), comprising the heavy cruisers *Kumano, Mikuma, Mogami* and *Suzuya*, and the 11th DD Div (destroyers *Fubuki, Hatsuyuki* and *Shirayuki*), set out as a covering force. On 4 Dec Vice-Adm Kondo puts to sea from the Pescadores with the 1st Div of the 4th Cruiser Sqdn, comprising the heavy cruisers *Atago* and *Takao*, and the 2nd Div of the 3rd BB Sqdn with the battleships *Haruna* and *Kongo*, as a distant escort force for the Malaya and Luzon landings. The plan is to take up a position in the South China Sea. The heavy ships are screened by the destroyers of the 4th DD Div (*Arashi, Hagikaze, Maikaze* and *Nowake*), the 2nd Group of the 6th DD Div *Ikazuchi* and *Inazuma* and the 8th DD Div (*Asashio, Oshio, Michishio* and *Arashio*). On 5 Dec the convoy is joined by the minesweepers (Sokaitei)*W2, 3* and *4* from Camranh Bay and by the minesweepers (Sokaitei) *W1, 5* and *6*, a submarine-chaser division, the mine layer *Hatsutaka* and two transports from the Poulo Condore Islands. In the afternoon the Southern Expeditionary Fleet sets out from Saigon with the cruiser *Kashii* and four transports and the frigate *Shimushu* with three transports carrying units of the 143rd Inf Regt of the 55th Div. They join the convoy S of Cape Camao on 6 Dec. In this area the Japanese forces are, in part, located and reported by British air reconnaissance on 6 Dec, but contact is lost owing to bad weather. A Catalina flying-boat of the RAF is shot down by Japanese fighters at mid-day on 7 Dec (in point of time the first military action in the 'Greater East Asian War').
To cover the operation the submarines *I-121* and *I-122* have laid barrages each

containing 42 mines off the NE exits from Singapore in the night 6-7 Dec. The auxiliary minelayer *Tatsumiya Maru* lays a barrage of 456 mines between the islands of Tioman and Anamba. And, N of that, the submarines *I-54* and *I-55* take up positions NE of Kuantan and *I-53* N of Anamba. In the area of Trengganu *I-57*, *I-58*, *I-62*, *I-64* and *I-66* form a patrol line; and *I-57* is stationed NE of Redang. At mid-day on 7 Dec the convoy divides up into its attack groups. From the Southern Expeditionary Fleet one transport proceeds to Prachuab, two to Jumbhorn, one with the *Kashii* to Bandon and three with the *Shimushu* to Nakhorn to block the Kra Isthmus. The main force of 17 transports, the 20th and 12th DD Divs, four minesweepers, the submarine-chaser division and nine assault vessels proceeds to Singora and Patani, while the *Sendai* with the 19th DD Div, the minesweepers *Sokaitei W2* and *3*, submarine-chasers and three transports go to Khota Bharu. The flagship *Chokai* and the *Sagiri* join the Kurita group S of Cape Camao.

6-15 Dec   Southern Asia
Operation by the Japanese South Philippines Force from Palau. On 6 Dec a force consisting of the 5th Cruiser Sqdn (Rear-Adm Takagi) with *Haguro*, *Myoko* and *Nachi*, the 4th Carrier Sqdn with the *Ryujo* and the destroyer *Shiokaze* and the 2nd DD Flotilla with the cruiser *Jintsu*, the 15th DD Div (*Kuroshio*, *Oyashio*, *Hayashio* and *Natsushio*) and the 16th DD Div (*Hatsukaze*, *Amatsukaze*, *Yukikaze* and *Tokitsukaze*) sets out from Palau. While the cruisers take up a covering position W of Mindanao, *Ryujo* flies off 13 bombers with 9 fighters to make a raid on Davao on the morning of 8 Dec. At the same time the 15th DD Div enters the Gulf of Davao and the remainder of the 2nd DD Flotilla provides a rendezvous off the approach.
On the same day (8 Dec) an assault force (Rear-Adm Kubo) sets out from Palau with the cruiser *Nagara*, the 22nd DD Div (*Umikaze*, *Yamakaze*, *Kawakaze* and *Suzukaze*), the 11th Carrier Sqdn with the seaplane carriers *Chitose* and *Mizuho*, the minelayers *Itsukushima* and *Yaeyama* (17th ML Div) and seven

transports. On the way to the NW it joins up on 9 Dec and 10 Dec with Takagi's force. In the night 10-11 Dec Rear-Adm Kobayashi with the minelayer *Itsukushima*, escorted by the destroyers *Kuroshio* and *Oyashio*, lays 300 mines in the San Bernardino Strait, and the minelayer *Yaeyama* with the cruiser *Jintsu* and the destroyers *Hayashio* and *Natsushio* 133 mines in the Surigao Strait. The destroyers frustrate with depth charges an attack by the American submarine *S39*. In the night 11-12 Dec the assault force (Attack Force 4) lands a batallion of 2500 men of the 16th Inf Div near Legaspi.

6-16 Dec   Mediterranean
The U-boats *U431* and *U557* arrive in the operational area between Alexandria and Tobruk from the Western Mediterranean. *U431* misses on 6 Dec and 10 Dec one destroyer and one steamer and torpedoes on 13 Dec the water tanker *Myriel* (3560 tons). *U557* is rammed and sunk in error by the Italian torpedo boat *Orione* in the Aegean on her return to Salamina.

6-23 Dec   North Atlantic
More German U-boats are transferred to the Mediterranean. After *U206*, which was to be transferred to the Mediterranean, has been sunk in the Bay of Biscay on 30 Nov by a Whitley bomber of No 502 Sqdn RAF, *U208*, *U372* and *U375*, which are operating W of Gibraltar, are detached on 6 Dec for transfer to the Eastern Mediterranean; and *U568*, *U374*, *U573* and *U453* follow on 7 Dec. *U372*, *U375* and *U453* pass through the Straits of Gibraltar on 9 Dec and *U568*, *U374* and *U208* on 11 Dec. In the process *U374* (Lt von Fischel) sinks the British A/S trawlers *Rosabelle* and *Lady Shirley* and *U208* is sunk by the British corvette *Bluebell*.
On 13 Dec *U453* (Lt-Cdr von Schlippenbach) sinks one Spanish ship of 4202 tons E of Gibraltar. After several attempts *U573* (Lt-Cdr Heinsohn) breaks through the Straits of Gibraltar on 21 Dec and sinks one ship of 5289 tons. On 11 Dec *U74*, *U77*, *U569*, *U83* and *U432* receive orders to proceed to the Eastern Mediterranean. They pass through the Straits of Gibraltar on 16-17 Dec but *U432* and *U569* are damaged

Top: Summer, 1941: The end of the first phase of the U-boat war in the Atlantic. The increasing strength of Allied escort groups forced the U-boats to seek easier targets on the Gibraltar-Freetown routes. Coastal Command aircraft now covered these routes and there was a lull in the battle, with few successes scored by either side. The picture shows a typical Atlantic convoy taken from an escorting aircraft of Coastal Command.   *[IWM*

Above: Destruction and humanity side by side! A corvette armed with depth charges about to rescue the survivors of a ship sunk by a U-boat.   *[BFZ*

Above: Dec 10, 1941: The Royal Navy suffers a severe blow when Japanese aircraft sink the battleship *Prince of Wales* and battle cruiser *Repulse*. A destroyer rescues survivors from amidships on the starboard side of the battleship. *[IWM*

Below: April 4-9, 1942: Japanese carrier raids in the Indian Ocean. Warned of the impending attack, the Eastern Fleet of the Royal Navy leaves its base in Ceylon for the open sea. On April 5 Japanese aircraft find the cruisers *Dorsetshire* and *Cornwall*, and sink them both. *[IWM*

Below: The Japanese continue their raids in the Indian Ocean and on April 9 locate a British force withdrawing south along the coast. They sink the carrier *Hermes*, a destroyer, a corvette and two tankers. *[IWM*

Above: May 8, 1942: Japanese advances in the South Pacific lead to the battle of the Coral Sea. On May 7 American forces sink a Japanese carrier, and on the following day the two opposing forces attack each other in strength. The American carrier *Lexington* is severely damaged and has to be abandoned. *[Official USN*

Below: May 8, 1942: During the battle of the Coral Sea the Japanese carrier *Shokaku* received three hits, and is shown frantically weaving to avoid the attacks of the American aircraft. *[Official USN*

Below: June 4, 1942: At the end of May the Japanese began preparatory moves for their proposed landing on the island of Midway. These moves led to a **great** carrier battle in which four Japanese carriers were sunk. The carrier *Hiryu* was the last of the carriers to be sunk at Midway. *[S. Fukui*

Top: 1942: The Battle of the Atlantic reaches a crucial stage with U-boats sinking merchant ships faster than replacement construction can be delivered. An American Liberty ship sinks after a U-boat attack. The Liberty ships were a standard construction. *[BFZ*

Above: March, 1942: Early in 1942 Type IX-C U-boats gathered to attack tankers off the East Coast of America. One of the tankers sunk by *U124.* *[BFZ*

Above: March 27, 1942: A British Commando force carries out a successful raid on the giant dock at St. Nazaire. The only dock capable of holding the Tirpitz is rendered useless when the charge of explosive in the bows of the destroyer *Campbeltown* wrecks the dock gates and gear.   *[IWM*

Below: Aug 19, 1942: A British force carries out a landing at Dieppe on the coast of France. Although a disaster, much was learnt from the raid and put to good use in 1944 when the Allies landed in Normandy. Landing craft approach Dieppe under cover of a smoke screen.   *[IWM*

Above: Aug 19, 1942: Three Churchill tanks and LCT 5 lying on "White" beach west of the promenade at Dieppe.   *[BFZ*

Above: Feb 12, 1942: The Kriegsmarine carries out a brilliant operation when the battleships *Gneisenau* and *Scharnhorst*, and the heavy cruiser *Prinz Eugen* escape from Brest up the English Channel to Germany.

[Bundesarchiv

Below: Feb 21-23, 1942: Following opera-tion "Rheinubung", in which both the *Scharnhorst* and *Gneisenau* suffered mine damage, the *Prinz Eugen* and *Admiral Scheer* are transferred to Norway. On Feb 23, off Trondheim, the submarine *Trident* torpedoes the *Prinz Eugen*, which, with temporary repairs to her stern, returns to Germany on May 16.

[IWM

Above: Dec 7, 1941: The Japanese carry out a devastating surprise attack on the American Fleet in Pearl Harbour. The illustration shows Ford Island early on in the attack, with water rising from the torpedo hit on the battleship *Oklahoma* (centre). In the left foreground smoke is rising from bomb hits on the *Raleigh* and *Utah*. [*Official USN*

Below: Dec 7, 1941: The fiercely burning wreck of the battleship *West Virginia*, with the *Tennessee* behind, in Pearl Harbour. [*Official USN*

Above: Dec 29-30, 1941: Units of the Black Sea Fleet provide gunfire support for troops ashore. The battleship *Parizhskaya Kommuna* providing support for Russian defenders of Sevastopol and for the Soviet landing operations against German positions on the Kerch Peninsula. *[Novosti Press*

Nov 1941-June 1942: Cruisers and destroyers of the Russian Black Sea Fleet transport men and supplies to the beleaguered fortress of Sevastopol. June 27, 1942, destroyer leader *Tashkent* transports 1000 men *(above and below)*, and evacuates 2300 under numerous attacks by air and surface forces. After suffering severe damage during her return, *Tashkent* finally sinks on the bottom of the harbour at Novorossijsk on July 2. *[Novosti Press*

by Swordfish aircraft and have to return. Of the boats ordered into the Eastern Mediterranean on 18-19 Dec *U451* is sunk by Swordfish aircraft and *U202* is damaged and compelled to return. *U133* and *U577* come through on 23 Dec and 21 Dec respectively.

7 Dec Pacific
Japanese attack on Pearl Harbour: the Japanese Force (see 26 Nov for its composition) reaches the take-off point N of Oahu and flies off the first wave (Cdr *Fuchida) at 0600 hrs. It consists of 50 high-level bombers, 40 torpedo bombers, 51 dive bombers and 43 fighters. Shortly after, the second wave takes off with 54 high-level bombers, 81 dive bombers and 36 fighters. In a surprise strike they knock out the American air defence and sink the battleships *Arizona* (flagship Rear-Adm Kidd†, Capt van Valkenburgh†) with 47 officers and 1056 men; *California* (flagship Vice-Adm Pye, Capt Bunkley) with six officers and 92 men; *Nevada; Oklahoma* (Capt Bode) with 20 officers and 395 men; *West Virginia* (Capt Bennion†) with two officers and 103 men; the minelayer *Oglala* and the target ship *Utah*. In part heavily damaged are the battleships *Maryland* (Capt Godwin); *Pennsylvania* (Capt Cooke) and *Tennessee* (Capt Reordan); the light cruisers *Helena, Honolula, Raleigh;* the flying-boat tender *Curtiss,* the destroyers *Cassin, Downes, Shaw* and the repair ship *Vestal.* 92 naval and 96 army aircraft are destroyed. Losses in personnel: 2403 dead and 1178 wounded. The Japanese lose five torpedo bombers, 15 dive-bombers, 9 fighters with 55 men and five midget submarines.
Among the ships undamaged are: the heavy cruisers *New Orleans* and *San Francisco;* the light cruisers *Detroit, Phoenix* and *St Louis*; the destroyers *Selfridge, Case, Tucker, Reid, Conyngham, Monaghan, Farragut, Dale, Aylwin, Phelps, MacDonough, Worden, Dewey, Hull, Henley, Patterson, Ralph Talbot, Jarvis, Mugford, Helm, Cummings, Blue, Bagley,* and *Schley*; the destroyer-minelayers *Preble, Pruitt, Sicard* and *Tracy*; the fast minesweepers *Ramsay, Gamble, Montgomery, Trever, Breese, Zane, Perry* and *Wasmuth*; the submarines *Cachalot, Narwhal, Gudgeon, Dolphin*

and *Tautog* and numerous other auxiliary ships.
There are at sea in the area of Oahu the cruiser *Minneapolis,* the destroyer *Litchfield* and the submarines *Thresher, Plunger, Pollack* and *Pompano.* En route to Midway is TF 11 (Rear-Adm Newton) with the carrier *Lexington,* whose mission has been to bring aircraft of the Marine Corps to Midway, and the cruisers *Astoria, Chicago* and *Portland* and the destroyers *Porter, Flusser, Drayton, Lamson* and *Mahan.* The submarine *Trout* is stationed near Midway. The Japanese destroyers *Akebono* and *Ushio* are not, however, impeded in their shelling of Midway.
TF 8 (Vice-Adm Halsey), which set out from Pearl Harbour on 24 Nov with the carrier *Enterprise,* the cruisers *Chester, Northampton* and *Salt Lake City,* and the destroyers *Balch, Gridley, Craven, McCall, Maury, Dunlap, Fanning, Benham* and *Ellett,* is returning to Oahu after flying off aircraft to Wake on 4 Dec. The aircraft from *Enterprise* run into the Japanese attack as they arrive over Ford Island.

7-10 Dec Mediterranean
The sloops *Flamingo* and *Yarra* escort the last supply convoy to Tobruk. In an air attack on 7 Dec the *Flamingo* is rendered unmanoeuvrable as a result of several near-misses and has to be taken in tow by *Yarra.* The Australian cruiser *Hobart,* which is escorting the transport *Breconshire* on her way back from Malta is summoned to the scene and provides cover. On 8 Dec the British 8th Army re-establishes land communications with the beleaguered garrison in Tobruk. Units of the British Mediterranean Fleet and transports have brought during the siege of Tobruk from 12 Apl, 32667 troops and 33946 tons of supplies to the garrison and evacuated 34115 troops, 7516 wounded and 7097 prisoners. In the process, two destroyers, three sloops, seven submarine-chasers and mine-sweepers, one gunboat, one minelaying cruiser, seven supply ships and six A-lighters have been sunk; and seven destroyers, one sloop, 11 submarine-chasers and minesweepers, three gunboats, three A-lighters, one schooner, one troop transport and six merchant ships have been damaged.

M

7-12 Dec   Southern Asia

Attack by the Japanese North Philippines Force on North Luzon. At first light on 8 Dec 192 aircraft of the 21st and 23rd Naval Air Flotillas of the 11th Air Fleet (Vice-Adm Tsukahara) attack from Formosa the US air bases at Clark and Iba Fields and destroy 12 B-17 bombers and 30 fighters, while losing seven of their own number. Aircraft of the 5th Army Air Division attack from Formosa, Tuguegarao and Baguio. A surprise force (Rear-Adm Hirose), which set out from Takao (Formosa) on 7 Dec, comprising the destroyer *Yamagumo*, the torpedo boats *Chidori*, *Hatsukari*, *Manadzuru* and *Tomodzuru*, two minesweepers, two gunboats, two patrol boats, nine submarine-chasers and two transports, lands on the morning of 8 Dec an assault group on the island of Bataan, where an immediate start is made in establishing an airfield. A second force (Rear-Adm Hara), with the cruiser *Natori*, the destroyers *Fumitsuki*, *Satsuki*, *Nagatsuki*, *Minatsuki*, *Harukaze* and *Hatakaze*, three minesweepers, nine submarine-chasers and six transports, sets out on 7 Dec from Mako (Pescadores) and lands 2000 troops of an advanced detachment of the 14th Army near Aparri on the N coast of Luzon early on 10 Dec. In an attack by P-40 fighters and B-17 bombers of the US Far East Air Force, the minesweeper (Sokaitei) *W19* is hit and has to be beached. A third force (Rear-Adm Nishimura), comprising the cruiser *Naka*, the destroyers *Murasame*, *Yudachi*, *Harusame*, *Samidare* (2nd DD Div); *Asagumo*, *Minegumo* and *Natsugumo* (4th DD Div), six minesweepers, nine submarine-chasers and six transports, which has also set out from Mako, tries on 10 Dec to land some 2000 troops near Padan on the NW tip of Luzon. But it has to abandon the plan because of the weather. The minesweeper (Sokaitei) *W10* is lost as a result of action by US aircraft and two transports are damaged. On 11 Dec a landing further S near Vingan succeeds.

The operation is covered by the Commander of the 3rd Fleet, Vice-Adm Takahashi, with the cruisers *Ashigara*, *Kuma* and *Maya*, the destroyers *Asakaze* and *Matsukaze* and the aircraft depot ships *Sanuki Maru* and *Sanyo Maru*. The latter is hit on 14 Dec by an unexploded torpedo from the US submarine *Seawolf*. After successfully carrying out the landings, the air units of the 11th Naval Air Fleet and the 5th Army Air Division make new heavy attacks on the US air bases on Luzon (12 Dec) and eliminate the US Far East Air Force. What is left withdraws to Mindanao and Australia.

7-13 Dec   Black Sea

Five transports and the cruisers *Krasny Kavkaz* and *Krasny Krym*, the flotilla leader *Kharkov* and the destroyers *Bodry* and *Nezamozhnik* transport the 388th Rifle Div (10582 troops) from Novorossisk and Tuapse to Sevastopol.

7-18 Dec   Pacific

The Japanese 3rd SM Flotilla operates in the area S of Hawaii. On 8 Dec *I-68* and *I-69* are attacked with depth charges S of Pearl Harbour. On 10 Dec an aircraft of the US carrier *Enterprise* sinks *I-70*. *I-75* (Cdr*Inoue) and *I-72* (Cdr Togami) each sink one ship of 3253 tons and 5113 tons respectively. On the return, on 22 Dec, *I-68* shells Johnston and *I-71* and *I-72* Palmyra.

7-27 Dec   Pacific

In the pursuit of a US carrier sighted by a submarine the Japanese 1st SM Flotilla makes a sortie on 10 Dec to the US West Coast and takes up positions between Vancouver and Los Angeles. On the way and in the operational area the submarines sink and damage the following ships: *I-26* (Cdr*M. Yokota) sinks one ship of 2140 tons; *I-10* (Cdr*Kayahara) sinks one ship of 4473 tons; *I-9* (Cdr* Fujii) sinks one ship of 5645 tons; *I-17* (Cdr*Nishino) sinks one ship of 6912 tons and damages one ship of 7038 tons; *I-23* (Cdr*Shibata) damages two ships of 8890 tons; *I-19* (Cdr*Narahara) damages two ships of 16458 tons; *I-21* (Cdr*Matsumura) sinks one ship of 8272 tons and damages one ship of 6418 tons; and *I-25* (Cdr*Tabata) damages one ship of 8684 tons. On 27 Dec the boats start the return journey. *I-19* reconnoitres over Pearl Harbour with her aircraft on 8 Jan 42.

7 Dec-31 Jan   Pacific

The submarine cruisers of the Japanese 2nd SM Flotilla operate in the area S of Hawaii. Many ships are sighted but only *I-4* (Cdr*Nakagawa) sinks one ship of 4858 tons. On 17 Dec the command boat *I-7* reconnoitres over Pearl Harbour with her aircraft. *I-1* shells the island of Hilo on 30-31 Dec. On 11 Jan *I-6* (Cdr*Inaba) torpedoes the US carrier *Saratoga*.

8 Dec China
Japanese Army and Navy units, supported by the old armoured cruiser *Izumo*, occupy the international settlement in Shanghai. The British gunboat *Peterel* sinks after a short engagement and the US gunboat *Wake* surrenders. In addition, the Japanese seize 13 British, US and Panamanian merchant ships totalling 15586 tons and four other ships of 18744 tons, including the US freighter *President Harrison* (10509 tons) on the Wangpo.

8-10 Dec Pacific
After several air attacks, in which the US minesweeper *Penguin* is sunk, transports with BF 5 (7th GB Div, 15th MS Div, 59th and 60th SC Divs) land parts of the South Sea Detachment of the Army and some 700 naval assault troops on Guam. The operation is under the command of Rear-Adm Goto, who supports the action with the 6th Cruiser Sqdn, comprising *Aoba, Kinugasa, Kako* and *Furutaka* and the destroyers *Kikuzuki, Uzuki* and *Yuzuki*. The American garrison is overwhelmed after a brief resistance.

8-10 Dec Central Pacific
The 19th ML Division of the Japanese 4th Fleet (Vice-Adm Inoue) with the minelayers *Okinoshima, Tokiwa* and *Tsugaru* and two transports proceeds from Kwajalein and makes landings on the Gilbert Islands of Tarawa and Makin (Butaritari) on 9 Dec and 10 Dec.

8-11 Dec Mediterranean
The British destroyers *Jervis* (Capt Mack), *Jackal* and *Javelin*, supported by the light cruisers *Naiad* (Rear-Adm Vian), *Euryalus, Galatea* and the destroyers *Griffin* and *Hotspur*, make a sortie against German and Italian supply traffic to North Africa and shell Derna. Italian torpedo aircraft severely damage the *Jackal* with air torpedoes.

8-12 Dec South Asia
The Japanese transports of the Malaya Force (see 4-7 Dec), which have arrived on the evening of 7 Dec off their assault

areas, begin in the night 7-8 Dec the first landings of the Pacific War. In the N they are impeded by the sea swell but encounter no resistance from the Thai forces; in the S they meet resistance at Kota Bharu. In attacks by British aircraft one transport of 9749 tons is destroyed and the two others are damaged.

In the afternoon of 8 Dec Force Z (Adm Phillips) sets out from Singapore with the battleship *Prince of Wales*, the battlecruiser *Repulse* and the destroyers *Electra, Express, Tenedos* and *Vampire* to attack the Japanese invasion fleet. After passing E of the Anamba Islands the Force is reported in the afternoon of 9 Dec by the most easterly submarine *I-65* of the patrol line. Because of the inaccuracy of the position given, the air reconnaissance which is provided, and the submarines operating on the report, do not find the targets. The British Force Z, after dismissing the destroyer *Tenedos*, proceeds northwards in order to attack the invasion fleet in the morning at Kota Bharu. But, as a result of a new and false reconnaissance report, it turns away to the SW on the evening of 9 Dec to attack a Japanese landing near Kuantan on the morning of 10 Dec.

On the Japanese side Vice-Adm Kondo, who with his force (cruisers *Atago* and *Takao*, battleships *Haruna* and *Kongo* and destroyers *Arashi, Hagikaze, Nowake, Maikaze, Ikazuchi, Inazuma, Asashio, Oshio, Michishio* and *Arashio*) is proceeding S from Poulo Condore, orders Rear-Adm Kurita in the night to join him with the cruisers *Kumano, Mikuma, Mogami* and *Suzuya*, and the destroyers *Fubuki, Hatsuyuki, Shirayuki* and Vice-Adm Ozawa with the cruiser *Chokai*, the destroyer *Sagiri*. From the assault area the cruiser *Sendai* with the destroyers *Asagiri, Murakumo, Shinonome, Shirakumo, Usugumo, Amagiri* and *Yugiri; Ayanami, Isonami, Shikinami* and *Uranami*, receive orders to close up, as do the cruisers *Kinu* and *Yura* stationed between Poulo Condore and Kurita.

During its advance to Kuantan British Force Z is sighted shortly after midnight by the Japanese submarine *I-58* (Lt-Cdr Kitamura), is unsuccessfully attacked with torpedoes and shadowed for five and a half hours. Air reconnaissance by ten aircraft of the 22nd Naval Air Flotilla (Rear-Adm Matsunaga), provided as a result of the submarine's reports, finds Force Z and leads 27 bombers and 61 torpedo aircraft from the flotilla (which have already taken off) to the scene. They sink the *Repulse* (Capt Tennant) and *Prince of Wales* (Capt Leach†, Adm Phillips†) in perfectly co-ordinated torpedo and bomb attacks. The destroyers rescue 1285 and 796 members of the crews of the two ships.

8-13 Dec   Central Pacific
First Japanese attack on Wake. The 6th DD Flotilla (Rear-Adm Kajioka) sets out to sea from Kwajalein with the cruiser *Yubari* and the destroyers *Hayate*, *Oite* (29th DD Div), *Mutsuki*, *Yayoi*, *Mochizuki* and *Kisaragi* (30th DD Div), the fast transports *P32* and *P33* and two transports with naval assault troops on board. Shore-based air formations attack Wake from Kwajalein on 8 Dec, 9 Dec and 10 Dec. The operation is supported by the cruisers *Tatsuta* and *Tenryu* (18th Cruiser Sqdn) and the submarines *Ro-60* and *Ro-61* off Wake.
In the night 10-11 Dec the invasion force arrives off Wake but the attempted landing, which is supported by the cruisers and destroyers, is repulsed by the island's garrison (450 marines under Maj Devereux) and an air squadron. The destroyers *Hayate* and *Kisaragi* are lost as a result of the shelling by the American coastal batteries. On 13 Dec the remainder of the force returns to Kwajalein.

8-15 Dec   South Asia
The minelaying submarines of the 6th Flotilla (Rear-Adm Kono) lay barrages on 8-9 Dec: *I-121* (Cdr Yendo) and *I-122* (Cdr Utsuki) off Singapore, *I-123* (Cdr Ueno) off Balabac, *I-124* (Cdr Kishigami) off Manila. One ship is lost on the Manila barrage and *I-124* sinks another ship with a torpedo, making 3404 tons sunk in all.

8-23 Dec   Arctic
The British convoy PQ.6 with seven ships proceeds from Hvalfjord to Murmansk without contact with the enemy. Two ships remain there on 20 Dec; the other five go on with a Soviet

ice-breaker but on 23 Dec they get stuck in the ice in Molotovsk and have to spend the winter there.

8-31 Dec   South West Pacific
The submarines of the US Asiatic Fleet are stationed from 8 Dec to 9 Dec partly in defensive positions round the Philippines, e.g. *Seal* near Vingan, *S-36*, *Saury* and *Seawolf* near the San Bernardino Strait, and partly in offensive positions, e.g. *S-38*, *S-37*, *S-41* near Mindoro; *Sculpin* E of Luzon; *S-39*, *S-40*, *Tarpon*, *Shark*, *Sailfish*, and *Stingray* off Lingayen Gulf; *Perch* and *Permit* W of Luzon; *Searaven* and *Sturgeon* near Formosa; *Pike*, *Snapper* and *Sword*; *fish* near Hainan; *Spearfish* off Camranh-*Sargo* in the Gulf of Siam and *Skipjack* near Palau. The operations of the boats, which make numerous attacks on Japanese ships and formations, are very restricted by torpedo failures (depth keeping and magnetic fusing). (see German Norwegian operation). Only *Swordfish* (Cdr Smith) sinks one ship of 8663 tons; *Seal* (Lt-Cdr Hurd) one ship of 850 tons; and *S-38* (Lt Chappell) one ship of 5445 tons off Lingayen Gulf.

9 Dec   Arctic
On the way to Kirkenes the German U-boat *U134* (Lt-Cdr Schendel) sinks in error the German steamer *Steinbek* (2184 tons) off Tanafjord.

10 Dec   North Atlantic
U130 (Cdr Kals), on the way out from Norway to France, meets an eastward-bound convoy W of Ireland and sinks three ships of 14971 tons.

10 Dec   Japan/Western France
The German blockade-runner *Burgenland* (7320 tons, Capt Schütz) reaches Bordeaux from Kobe.

11 Dec   General Situation
Declaration of war on America by Germany and Italy.

11-14 Dec   Pacific
The first US submarines *Gudgeon*, *Plunger* and *Pollack* leave Pearl Harbour for operations in Japanese home waters.

12 Dec   South Asia
The Allied ships left in Singapore, the British cruisers *Danae*, *Dragon* and *Durban*, the British destroyers *Encounter*, *Stronghold*, and *Tenedos*, the Dutch cruiser *Java* with the destroyer *Evertsen*, the Australian minesweepers *Burnie*, *Bendigo*, *Goulburn* and *Maryboroug*

are employed on escort duties between Singapore and Sunda Strait. They are joined on 8 Dec by the British destroyers *Scout* and *Thanet* which have broken out of Hong Kong and by the destroyers *Electra*, *Express* and *Jupiter*, which have returned from the operation with Force Z and the Australian *Vampire*.

13 Dec South Asia
British forces evacuate Kowloon, the suburb of Hong Kong on the Chinese mainland, before the attack by the Japanese 38th Inf Div.

13-19 Dec Mediterranean
Italian convoy operation M41 to North Africa. The intention is to bring eight transports in three convoys with seven destroyers and two torpedo boats to Benghazi covered by the whole operational part of the Italian Fleet comprising four battleships, five cruisers and eighteen destroyers. Of the British submarines *Unbeaten*, *Utmost* and *Upright* (Lt Wraith) stationed off the Gulf of Taranto, the last sinks the motor ships *Fabio Filzi* and *Carlo del Greco* (each 6836 tons) on the morning of 13 Dec as they proceed with the destroyers *Da Recco* and *Usodimare* to the Taranto assembly point.
On the afternoon of 13 Dec the motor ships *Monginevro*, *Napoli* and *Vettor Pisani* put to sea with three destroyers and the German freighter *Ankara* with two destroyers as two groups. In addition, two freighters put to sea with two destroyers from Argostoli. From Taranto there set out as close covering forces Sqdn Adm Bergamini with the battleship *Duilio*, the cruisers *Garibaldi*, *Gorizia* and *Montecuccoli* and three destroyers and Div Adm De Courten with the battleship *Doria*, the cruisers *Duca d'Aosta* (F) and *Attendolo* and three destroyers. Two groups of destroyers follow (one of three and one of four): the latter is to join the distant covering force from Naples to which belong the battleships *Littorio* and *Vittorio Veneto* and four destroyers under Adm Iachino. When British submarines report the movements of Italian forces in the Ionian Sea, Rear-Adm Vian puts to sea on the evening of 13 Dec with the cruisers *Euryalus*, *Galatea* and *Naiad* and destroyers

(Force B) in order to attack the Italian convoys, after joining up with Force K consisting of the cruisers *Aurora*, *Neptune* and *Penelope* and destroyers. On the evening of 14 Dec the British submarine *Urge* (Lt-Cdr Tomkinson), stationed off the Straits of Messina, torpedoes the *Vittorio Veneto*. The latter reaches Taranto, but the Italian operation is then abandoned and the convoys and covering forces return. In the process the two freighters of the Argostoli convoy, *Capo Orsam* and *Iseo* (accompanied by the destroyers *Stralè* and *Turbine*), collide and drop out. British Force K, against which the Italian submarines *Santarosa*, *Narvalo*, *Squalo*, *Veniero* and *Topazio* are stationed E of Malta, remains in Malta. Force B is recalled. The Italian boats *Ascianghi*, *Dagabur* and *Galatea* stationed S of Crete, are too far N. The last misses the returning British submarine *Talisman*. On 15 Dec the German U-boat *U557* (Lt-Cdr Paulshen) sinks off Alexandria the cruiser *Galatea* (Capt Sims†) from the returning Force B.
British convoy operation to Malta: on 15 Dec British force B (Rear-Adm Vian) with the cruisers *Naiad*, *Euryalus*, *Carlisle* and the destroyers *Jervis*, *Kimberley*, *Kingston*, *Kipling*, *Nizam* (*RAN*), *Havock*, *Hasty* and *Decoy* sets out to bring the transport *Breconshire* (9776 tons) from Alexandria to Malta. On 16 Dec Force K (Capt Agnew) sets out to sea from Malta with the cruisers *Aurora* and *Penelope* and the destroyers *Lance* and *Lively*, as well as the destroyer division (Capt Stokes), comprising *Sikh*, *Legion*, *Maori* and *Isaac Sweers* (Dutch) to meet the transport on 17 Dec. The cruiser *Neptune* is to follow with the destroyers *Jaguar* and *Kandahar*. Italian convoy operation M42: on the afternoon of 16 Dec a convoy sets out from Taranto with the motor ships *Monginevro*, *Napoli* and *Vettor Pisani*, escorted by the destroyers *Vivaldi*, *Da Noli*, *Da Recco*, *Malocello*, *Pessagno* and *Zeno* and a second with the freighter *Ankara*, the destroyer *Saetta* and the torpedo boat *Pegaso*. Adm Bergamini provides a close covering force with the battleship *Duilio*, the cruisers (7th Div, Div Adm de Courten) *Duca d'Aosta*, *Attendolo* and *Montecuccoli* and the

destroyers *Ascari, Aviere* and *Camicia Nera.* The distant covering force, which sets out at the same time, is formed by Adm Iachino with the battleships *Doria, Cesare* and *Littorio,* the heavy cruisers (3rd Div, Div-Adm Parona) *Gorizia* and *Trento* and the destroyers *Granatiere, Bersagliere, Alpino, Fuciliere,Corazziere, Carabiniere, Usodimare, Maestrale, Oriani,* and *Gioberti.* First battle of Sirte. On 17 Dec British forces B and K join up. Italian air attacks are unsuccessful. As a result of reports from his reconnaissance aircraft, Adm Iachino turns towards the British force and is in engagement with it shortly after dark. No results are achieved on either side because both forces try to cover their convoys without knowing about the worthwhile targets on the other side.

18 Dec: Rear-Adm Vian returns to Alexandria and *Breconshire* arrives in Malta with Force K. The Italian convoy then continues its journey to Tripoli. Off Tripoli Force K with the cruisers *Aurora, Neptune* and *Penelope* and the destroyers *Havock, Kandahar, Lance,* and *Lively* is directed to the convoy but soon runs into the Italian mine barrage 'T' (see 3 June 41). *Neptune* (Capt O'Connor†) sinks after hitting four mines with about 550 members of the crew. Only one survivor can be rescued. *Kandahar* also has to be abandoned after hitting a mine. *Aurora* (Capt Agnew) is severely and *Penelope* (Capt Nicholl) lightly damaged. In the night 18-19 Dec the Vian force returns to Alexandria and is unsuccessfully attacked by *U371* (Lt-Cdr Driver). Through the harbour boom gap opened for the ships to come in three Italian human torpedo teams (Lt-Cdr Durand de la Penne with Sgt-Maj Bianchi, Capt Marceglia with L/Cpl Schergat and Capt Martellotta with Sgt-Maj Marino),, launched from the Italian submarine *Scirè* (Cdr *Borghese), enter the harbour and get their explosive charges under the battleships *Queen Elizabeth* (Capt Barry) and *Valiant* (Capt Morgan) and the Norwegian tanker *Sagona* (7554 tons). All ships come to rest on the bottom badly damaged. The destroyer *Jervis,* lying alongside the *Sagona,* is also damaged.

13-26 Dec   South Asia
Landing by the second wave of the Malaya Force. On 13 Dec the second wave sets out from Camranh Bay with the bulk of the 5th Inf Div and the supporting troops of the Japanese 25th Army (Gen Yamashita) on 39 transports. It is accompanied by the cruiser *Kashii,* the frigate *Shimushu,* the minesweeper *W4* and the 3rd DD Flotilla with the cruiser *Sendai* and the destroyers *Isonami, Uranami, Shikinami, Ayanami* (19th DD Div), *Arashi, Hagikaze, Maikaze, Nowake* (4th DD Div), *Amagiri, Asagiri* and *Yugiri* (20th DD Div). Vice-Adm Ozawa provides a covering force with the heavy cruiser *Chokai* and the light cruiser *Kinu,* to which are added the 2nd Div of the 7th Cruiser Sqdn (*Mikuma* and *Mogami*) and the destroyers *Hatsuyuki* and *Shirayuki* from Poulo Condore on 14 Dec. They take up a covering position NE of Kuantan by 17 Dec. In the night 16-17 Dec the submarines *I-58, I-57, I-56* (which has sunk one ship on 11 Dec) and *I-55* take up a patrol line N of the Anamba Islands and *I-53* and *I-54* W of Natoma Island. In the night 16-17 Dec one transport arrives off Bandon, two off Nakhorn, 31 with the aircraft depot ship *Sagara Maru* flying air cover, the minesweeper *W2* and the 11th SC Div off Singora and Patani and five off Kota Bharu. Dutch submarines are deployed from Singapore against the Japanese landings. *K-XII* (Lt-Cdr Coumou) sinks a transport off Kota Bharu on 12 Dec and a tanker on 13 Dec totalling 5464 tons. *O16* (Lt-Cdr Bussemaker) torpedoes four transports of 34435 tons off Patani on 16 Dec but is lost on a British minefield when returning to Singapore. *O20* is sunk on 20 Dec by the Japanese destroyer *Uranami* and *K-XVII* on 24 Dec by other Japanese destroyers in the landing area. Off Camranh Bay the American submarines *Sargo* and *Swordfish* attempt several attacks on 14 Dec but only the latter sinks one ship of 8663 tons. Japanese landing on Borneo: simultaneously with the Malaya convoy a convoy sets out for Miri (North Borneo) on 13 Dec from Camranh Bay. It consists of 10 transports with the 124th Inf Regt (16th Inf Div) and the 2nd

Yokosuka Special Landing Force. Escort for the convoy: the cruiser *Yura* (Rear-Adm Hashimoto) with the destroyers of the 12th DD Div (*Murakumo, Shinonome, Shirakumo* and *Usugumo*), the submarine-chaser *Ch7* and the aircraft depot ship *Kamikawa Maru.* Support force: Rear-Adm Kurita with the cruisers *Kumano, Suzuya* and the destroyers *Fubuki* and *Sagiri.* Distant covering force for the Malaya and Borneo operations NE of Natoma Island from 15 Dec to 17 Dec: Vice-Adm Kondo with the heavy cruisers *Atago* and *Takao* the battleships *Haruna* and *Kongo* and the destroyers *Ikazuchi, Inazuma, Asashio, Oshio, Michishio* and *Arashio.* To provide cover westwards the submarines *I-62, I-64, I-65* and *I-66* are stationed in the passage between Natoma Island and NW Borneo.

Before daylight on 16 Dec the troops are landed at Miri, Seria and Lutong in N Borneo where the oilfields are set on fire by the withdrawing Dutch and British forces. On 17 Dec the destroyer *Shinonome* is sunk by the Dutch flying boat X-32 with a torpedo and X-33 damages a transport.

On 22 Dec six of the transports leave again with two battalions re-embarked in order to land these troops in Kuching (Sarawak) on 23 Dec. The convoy is accompanied by the cruiser *Yura*, the destroyers *Murakumo, Shirakumo, Usugumo*, the minesweepers (Sokaitei), *W3* and *W6* and the *Kamikawa Maru.* The cruisers *Kinu, Kumano* and *Suzuya* with the destroyers *Fubuki* and *Sagiri* form the covering force. W of it the 2nd Div of the 7th Cruiser Sqdn (*Mikuma* and *Mogami*) cruises with the attached destroyer *Hatsuyuki.* The approaching convoy is attacked by the Dutch submarine *K-XIV* (Lt-Cdr Van Well Groeneveld). Two transports of 14729 tons sink and two more of 27678 tons are damaged. In the night 23-24 Dec *K-XVI* (Lt-Cdr Jarman) sinks the destroyer *Sagiri* but is herself sunk on the return by the Japanese submarine *I-66* (Cdr Yoshitome.) Dutch Martin bombers sink on 26 Dec the Japanese minesweeper (Sokaitei) *W6* and one transport of 2827 tons.

14-17 Dec South Asia
On 14 Dec 'Gull Force' puts to sea from Port Darwin with 1090 Australian troops on board three Dutch freighters. Escort: Australian cruiser *Adelaide* and minesweeper *Ballarat.* On 17 Dec the troops are landed in Ambon. On 16-17 Dec 650 Dutch and Australian troops (Sparrow 'Force') are brought from Koepang to Dili in Portuguese Timor by the Dutch coastal defence ship *Soerabaja* with one transport.

14-23 Dec North Atlantic
Operation by the 'Seeräuber' group against the convoy HG.76. On 14 Dec the convoy of 32 ships (Commodore Fitzmaurice) sets out, escorted by the 36th EG (Cdr Walker) consisting of the sloops *Deptford* and *Stork* and the corvettes *Rhododendron, Marigold, Convolvulus, Pentstemon, Gardenia, Samphire* and *Vetch.* Support Group consisting of the escort destroyers *Blankney, Exmoor* and *Stanley,* as well as the escort carrier *Audacity* (Cdr MacKendrick). At the same time a U-boat hunter group from Force H, comprising the destroyers *Croome, Gurkha, Foxhound* and *Nestor* (RAN), sets out. The last sinks *U127* (Lt-Cdr Hansmann) with depth charges on 15 Dec. In addition, a Near East convoy of four ships goes to sea escorted by one destroyer and three corvettes. Following agents reports the 'Seeräuber' group, comprising *U434, U131, U67, U108* and *U107,* is directed to the scene. *U108* (Lt-Cdr Scholtz) sinks an independent Portuguese ship of 4751 tons. Shortly before midnight on 14-15 Dec *U74,* which is on the way to the Mediterranean sights the Near East convoy from which *U77* (Lt-Cdr Schonder) sinks one ship of 4972 tons in the night. On 15 Dec air reconnaissance has no success while the convoy goes S along the Moroccan coast. On 16 Dec an FW 200 of I/K.G. 40 sights HG.76 at mid-day. But *U67* and *U108,* which approach the area, are driven off. Likewise *U131* is driven off in the night. *U574* is ordered to the area. On 17 Dec the convoy is sighted by *U107, U108* and *U131* (Cdr Baumann). The last, after several air attacks and the shooting down of a Swordfish from the *Audacity,* is unable to submerge and has to scuttle herself when *Stork, Blankney, Exmoor* and *Stanley* approach. *U434* (Lt-Cdr Heyda)

which has had contact since the evening of 17 Dec, is detected in the morning of 18 Dec and forced to surface by depth charges from the destroyers *Blankney* and *Stanley* and the crew has to abandon the boat. Two of the FW 200s keeping contact with the convoy are shot down by Martlet fighters from the *Audacity*. In the evening *Pentstemon* forces *U107* to submerge and *U67*, after a miss, is driven off by *Convolvulus*. Towards morning on 19 Dec *U574* (Lt Gengelbach) establishes contact and sinks the destroyer *Stanley* shadowing her but is rammed by Cdr Walker in a counter-attack by *Stork* and sinks. *U108*, in the meantime, shells one ship of 2809 tons out of the convoy. Martlets of the *Audacity* shoot down in the afternoon two FW 200s keeping contact, but *U107* (Lt-Cdr Gelhaus) is able to maintain contact and, in the course of 20 Dec and 21 Dec, to bring up *U108*, *U67* and *U567*, *U751* and *U71* (newly deployed since 20 Dec). *U67* is driven off by an aircraft and other U-boats by depth charges from *Marigold* and *Samphire*. In the night 21-22 Dec *U567* (Lt-Cdr Endrass) and *U751* (Lt-Cdr Bigalk) attack in quick succession and respectively sink one freighter of 3324 tons and the carrier *Audacity*. *U567* then falls victim to a depth charge attack by the *Deptford*. *U67* (Lt-Cdr Müller-Stöckheim) just misses a catapult ship in the convoy. On 22 Dec *U71*, *U125* (which is on the way to America) and, early on 23 Dec, *U751* are in contact but they are driven off by the corvette *Vetch* and the destroyers *Vanquisher* and *Witch* which have come up as reinforcements.

14-23 Dec   Central Pacific
Second battle for Wake. American attempt to relieve the island.
On 14 Dec TF 11 (Rear Adm Brown) sets out from Pearl Harbour with the carrier *Lexington*, the cruisers *Chicago*, *Indianapolis* and *Portland* and the destroyers of Desron 1 comprising *Phelps*, *Dewey*, *Hull*, *MacDonough*, *Worden* (Desdiv 1), *Aylwin*, *Dale*, *Drayton* (Desdiv 2) and the tanker *Neosho* in order to carry out a diversionary raid on Jaluit. On 16 Dec TF 14 (Rear-Adm Fletcher) follows with the carrier *Saratoga* (Rear-Adm

Fitch with 18 Buffalo fighters for Wake), the cruisers *Minneapolis* (F), *Astoria* and *San Francisco* and the destroyers of Desron 4 comprising *Selfridge*, *Henley*, *Blue*, *Helm* (Desdiv 7), *Jarvis*, *Mugford*, *Patterson* and *Ralph Talbot* (Desdiv 8) with the aircraft depot ship *Tangier* (with supplies for Wake) and the tanker *Neches*. To support the operation and for cover from Hawaii TF 8 (Vice-Adm Halsey) sets out from Pearl Harbour on 20 Dec with the carrier *Enterprise*, the cruisers *Northampton* (Rear-Adm Spruance), *Chester* and *Salt Lake City* and the destroyers of Desron 6 *Balch*, *Craven*, *Gridley*, *McCall*, *Maury* (Desdiv 11), *Fanning*, *Dunlap*, *Benham* and *Ellet* (Desdiv 12) for the area between Midway and Johnston. On 20 Dec TF 11 is turned away to the N to support the Wake operation and the raid on Jaluit is abandoned.
Japanese attack on Wake. On 20 Dec Rear-Adm Kajioka's Force again sets out from Kwajalein with the cruisers *Tatsuta*, *Tenryu*, *Yubari*, the destroyers *Asanagi*, *Oite*, *Yunagi* (29th DD Div), *Mochizuki*, *Mutsuki* and *Yayoi* (30th DD Div) with the fast transports *P32* and *P33*, three transports, one minelayer and one aircraft tender to attack Wake. Suport force: 6th Cruiser Sqdn (Rear-Adm Goto) comprising the cruisers *Aoba*, *Furutaka*, *Kinugasa*, and *Kako* and the 23rd DD Div with *Kikuzuki*, *Uzuki* and *Yuzuki* from Truk. A force from the returning 1st Air Fleet under Rear-Adm Abe, comprising the carriers *Hiryu* and *Soryu*, the heavy-cruisers *Chikuma* and *Tone* and the destroyers *Tanikaze* and *Urakaze*, is detached to support the operation. After shore-based aircraft have made attacks on Wake on 12 Dec, 14 Dec, 15 Dec, 16 Dec, 17 Dec and 19 Dec, 48 and 39 aircraft from the Japanese carriers make attacks on the island on 21 Dec and 22 Dec respectively. On 22 Dec some 2000 troops from the 2nd Maizuru Special Landing Force are able to land on the island. By 23 Dec they have captured the island with support from the ships. The two fast transports *P32* and *P33* are sunk by the American defensive fire.
Because of the difficulty in refuelling at sea, the US Task Forces do not arrive

in time and they are recalled on 23 Dec. On the same day Wake surrenders.

15-28 Dec   South West Pacific
On 15 Dec the Australian cruisers *Canberra* and *Perth* leave Sydney to meet, with the New Zealand cruiser *Achilles*, the American cruiser *Pensacola* (which has set out with eight transports for the Philippines from San Francisco on 21 Nov) and to bring her to Brisbane. At the same time the New Zealand cruiser *Leander* and the large Free French destroyer *Le Triomphant* escort reinforcements from New Zealand to the Fiji Islands and from Sydney to New Caledonia respectively.
On 28 Dec convoy ZK.5 with three large transports (4250 troops and 10000 tons of supplies) sets out from Brisbane for Port Moresby, escorted by the cruisers *Achilles*, *Australia*, *Canberra* and *Perth*, while *Pensacola* proceeds to Darwin with seven of her transports. On 28 Dec US TF 5, comprising the cruiser *Houston*, and the destroyers *Alden*, *Edsall* and *Whipple*, bring three important supply ships of the Asiatic Fleet from Surabaya to Port Darwin.

15-29 Dec   Arctic
The Soviet submarines *M-172*, *M-174*, *S-101*, *S-102*, *Shch-403* and *Shch-404*, operate off the Norwegian Polar Coast. On 18 Dec there is an indecisive engagement between a submarine (*S-101*?) and the submarine-chaser *UJ1214* off Kvaenangenfjord. On 22 Dec *Shch-403* (Lt-Cdr S. I. Kovalenko) misses the coaster *Ingöy* off Porsangerfjord and on 21 Dec *M-174* (Lt-Cdr N. E. Egorov) sinks the steamer *Emshörn* (4301 tons) off Vardö.

16-20 Dec   South Asia
Japanese landing on Mindanao. The Japanese South Philippines Force sets out from Palau on 16 Dec with the minelayer *Shirataka* and 14 transports with some 5000 troops of the 56th independent mixed Brigade. Escort: 2nd DD Flotilla (Rear-Adm Tanaka) with the cruiser *Jintsu* and destroyers *Kuroshio*, *Oyashio*, *Hayashio*, *Natsushio* (15th Div), *Amatsukaze* and *Hatsukaze* (16th Div). Covering force (Rear-Adm Tagaki) with the 5th Cruiser Sqdn comprising *Myoko* (F), *Haguro* and *Nachi*, the carrier *Ryujo* with the destroyer *Shiokaze* and the seaplane carrier *Chitose*. In the night

19-20 Dec the Japanese land their troops on both sides of Davao against slight resistance, occupy the town and establish a seaplane base on 20 Dec. At the beginning of January 1942 the 21s Naval Air Flotilla is transferred to Davao.

16-30 Dec   Bay of Biscay
All available Allied submarines are stationed in the area W of Brest because it is feared that the heavy German ships in Brest are about to leave (see 22 Mar). Boats include the Free French *Junon*. In these operations *H31* is lost, probably on a mine.

16-31 Dec   Mediterranean
In the nights 15-26 Dec, 21-22 Dec, 22-23 Dec and 30-31 Dec the German 3rd MTB Flotilla (Lt-Cdr Kemnade), comprising the boats *S-55*, *S-35*, *S-61*, *S-31* and *S-34*, carries out the first mining operations off Valetta/Malta: MT 1-4. 73 TMA mines are laid.

17 Dec   Arctic
In a sortie to the Kola coast the German 8th DD Flotilla (Capt Pönitz), comprising *Z23*, *Z24*, *Z25* and *Z27*, encounter about 14 nautical miles N of Cape Gorodetski the British minesweepers *Hazard* and *Speedy* which have come out to meet the convoy PQ.6. They are taken in error for Russian destroyers of the 'G'-class. *Speedy* receives four hits; *Hazard* is undamaged. The British heavy cruiser *Kent* puts to sea with two Soviet destroyers from the Kola Inlet to intercept the German force but has no success.

17 Dec   General Situation
Adm Chester W. Nimitz relieves Adm Husband E. Kimmel as C-in-C US Pacific Fleet. Adm Pye assumes command until the arrival of the new C-in-C.

17-24 Dec   South Asia
Japanese landing in Lingayen Gulf and in Lamon Bay (Luzon). On 17 Dec the 3rd Attack Force (Rear-Adm Hirose), consisting of the 2nd BF with the destroyer *Yamagumo*, the torpedo boats *Chidori*, *Hatsukari*, *Manazuru*, *Tomozuru* and eight smaller and auxiliary warships as well as 21 transports, sets out from Keelung (Formosa). On 18 Dec there follow from Takao (Formosa) the 1st Force (Rear-Adm Hara) with the cruisers *Natori*, the destroyers *Fumitsuki*, *Satsuki*, *Nagatsuki*, *Minatsuki*, *Haru-*

kaze and *Hatakaze*, two minesweepers and auxiliary warships and 27 transports; and the 2nd Force (Rear-Adm Nishimura) with the cruiser *Naka*, the destroyers *Murasame, Yudachi, Harusame, Samidare, Asagumo, Minegumo* and *Natsugumo*, five minesweepers, six submarine-chasers and 28 transports. In the night 21-22 Dec Forces 1 and 2 arrive, and in the following night Force 3, off Lingayen Gulf where they land, with the reinforced 48th Inf Div, the bulk of the 14th Army (Lt-Gen Homma) on the NE side of the bay. Air support for the landing is provided from the advanced fighter bases won on 8-10 Dec and from Formosa with units of Naval Air Flotillas 21 and 23, as well as from the 5th Army Air Division. To cover the operation Vice-Adm Takahashi takes up a position 250 nautical miles W of Luzon with the heavy cruisers *Ashigara* and *Maya* and the light cruiser *Kuma*. Vice-Adm Kondo stands by to provide a heavy covering force in the western part of the South China Sea (simultaneously to assist the Borneo operation) with the heavy cruisers *Atago* and *Takao* and the battleships *Haruna* and *Kongo*.

The C-in-C Asiatic Fleet, Adm Hart, deploys against the invasion the US submarines *S38, S40, Stingray, Saury* and *Salmon*. *S-38* (Lt Chappell) sinks the converted minelayer *Hayo Maru* (5446 tons) and *Seal* (Lt-Cdr Hurd) one ship of 836 tons. All other attacks fail because of torpedo defects.

On 24 Dec a 4th Attack Force (Rear-Adm Kubo), comprising the cruiser *Nagara*, the destroyers *Yamakaze, Suzukaze, Kawakaze, Umikaze* (24th DD Div), *Tokitsukaze* and *Yukikaze* (16th Div) and smaller units of the 1st BF with 24 transports, which have set out from Amami O shima (Ryukyu Islands) on 17 Dec, lands some 7000 troops on the 16th Inf Div in Lamon Bay on the SE side of Luzon.

18-25 Dec   South Asia
Final battle for Hong Kong. The Japanese 38th Inf Div has, by 25 Dec, driven the defenders into a small area of the western part of the island with the result that they have to capitulate. In the harbour the Japanese capture 26 more or less damaged British, Soviet,

Panamanian and Norwegian merchant ships totalling 52604 tons. During the fighting there sink, or there are scuttled before the capitulation, the British destroyer *Thracian*, the minelayer *Redstart*, the gunboats *Cicala, Moth, Robin,* and *Tern*, the motor torpedo boats *MTB7, MTB8, MTB9, MTB10, MTB11, MTB12, MTB26, MTB27* and four auxiliary ships.

18-27 Dec   Baltic
The attempt by the large Soviet submarine *K-51* to reach the Baltic from Kronstadt and to operate for three months there has to be abandoned because of the ice W of Lavansaari.

18-28 Dec   Mediterranean
The German U-boats coming from Salamis, *U371, U559, U562, U79* and *U75*, as well as the U-boats newly transferred from the W, *U652, U374, U568, U74, U77, U83, U573, U577* and *U133*, operate off the coast of Egypt and Cyrenaica. Of them *U371* (Lt-Cdr Driver) misses a cruiser of Force B off Alexandria on 18 Dec and a destroyer force on 20 Dec. In attacks on a convoy on 23 Dec *U559* (Lt-Cdr Heidtmann) sinks one ship of 3059 tons and with *U562* misses escort vessels, among which *Hasty* and *Hotspur* sink *U79* with depth charges. On 24 Dec *U568* (Lt-Cdr Preuss) sinks the corvette *Salvia* from a convoy escort and *U562* misses one ship. On 26 Dec *U559* sinks one more ship of 2486 tons. In an attack on a convoy on 28 Dec *U559* and *U652* miss their targets: *U75* (Lt-Cdr Ringelmann) sinks one ship of 1587 tons and is then sunk by the destroyer *Kipling*.

18-29 Dec   South Asia
The Japanese 6th SM Flotilla, comprising *I-123, I-124, I-121* and *I-122* operates in the area W of Mindanao. *I-123* lays a mine barrage off Surabaya.

18 Dec-1 Feb   Pacific
First reconnaissance operations by US submarines: *Dolphin* on Arno, Maloelap, Wotje, Kwajalein and Jaluit; and *Pompano* keeps watch on Wake, Ujelang, Ponape, Rongelau, and Bikini.

19-20 Dec   Black Sea
The Soviet cruisers *Krasny Kavkaz* and *Krasny Krym*, the flotilla leader *Kharkov* and the destroyers *Bodry* and *Nezamozhnik* transport the 79th Naval Infantry Brigade (3500 men) to Sevastopol.

19-24 Dec   Mediterranean
The Italian submarines *Axum* and *Turchese* are stationed near Cape Bougaroni and *Alagi* and *Aradam* E of that to counter an expected operation by Force H.
20 Dec-16 Jan   Arctic
British convoy QP.4 with eleven merchant ships leaves Archangel for Seidisfjord; two other ships remain in Murmansk.
21-27 Dec   Black Sea
In operations to bring the 345th Rifle Div (10600 men) and ammunition transports to Sevastopol the following ships of the Squadron shell German positions and assembly areas on the Sevastopol front: 21 Dec *Krasny Krym, Kharkov, Bodry*. 22 Dec: *Krasny Kavkaz, Krasny Krym, Tashkent, Kharkov, Bodry, Smyshleny, Nezamozhnik*—1,938 rounds fired. 23 Dec: *Smyshleny, Tashkent*. 24 Dec: *Boiki, Smyshleny, Tashkent*. 25 Dec: *Tashkent, Smyshleny, Boiki, Bezuprechny*. 26 Dec: *Bezuprechny*. 27 Dec: *Smyshleny, Tashkent*. From 23 Dec to 27 Dec 1299 rounds are fired. On 22 Dec the cruisers *Krasny Kavkaz* and *Krasny Krym*, the flotilla leader *Kharkov* and the destroyer *Bodry* are withdrawn in preparation for the Kerch-Feodosia landing.
22 Dec   Mediterranean
The British submarine *Umbra* sinks one ship of 1010 tons from a convoy off Misurata (Tripolitania).
22-25 Dec   South Asia
Part of the Japanese South Philippines Force, comprising nine transports with a part of the 56th Brigade on board, proceeds from Davao to Jolo and lands there on 24 Dec. On 25 Dec the island is captured. Escort for the operation provided by Rear-Adm Tanaka with the cruiser *Jintsu*, the 15th DD Div (see 17 Dec), the carrier *Ryujo* with the destroyer *Shiokaze* and the seaplane carrier *Chitose*.
At the beginning of Jan 1942 the 23rd Naval Air Flotilla is stationed in Jolo.
22-29 Dec   Mediterranean
The British cruiser *Dido* with the destroyers *Gurkha* and *Nestor* sets out from Gibraltar for the E and reaches Malta on 24 Dec. From there the ships proceed with the convoy ME.8, which consists of returning empty ships, to

Alexandria, where they arrive on 29 Dec.
22 Dec-1 Jan   Arctic
British raid on the Lofotens: operation 'Anklet'. On 22 Dec Rear-Adm Hamilton sets out from Scapa Flow with the cruiser *Arethusa*, the destroyers *Somali, Ashanti, Bedouin, Eskimo*, the escort destroyers *Wheatland, Lamerton, Krakowiak* (Polish), *Kujawiak* (Polish), the Norwegian corvettes *Acanthus* and *Eglantine*, the minesweepers *Speedwell, Harrier, Halcyon*, the landing ships *Prince Albert, Princess Charlotte* (Belgian), the tankers *Black Ranger, Grey Ranger*, the auxiliary ships *Gudrun Maersk* (Danish), *Scott*, and the tug *Jaunty*. The force is led into Vestfjord on 26 Dec by the marker submarine *Sealion* (*Princess Charlotte* returns with *Wheatland* because of disablement). *Prince Albert* with *Lamerton, Eglantine* and *Acanthus* land 260 commando troops to destroy the fish-oil factory in Moskenesöy and the wireless station in Tind. *Bedouin* destroys the Napp wireless station on Flakstadöy on the N side. *Arethusa, Somali, Ashanti* and *Eskimo* penetrate into Vestfjord in a search for ships. The Norwegian coasters *Kong Harald* and *Nordland* (1125 tons and 725 tons respectively) are captured, the German patrol boat *V5904/Geier* (145 tons) is sunk by *Ashanti* after the crew has been taken off. In German air attacks *Arethusa* is damaged by near-misses; the operation is broken off and on 28 Dec the return journey is begun. Operation 'Archery'. On 24 Dec Rear-Adm Burrough sets out from Scapa Flow with the cruiser *Kenya*, the destroyers *Offa, Onslow, Oribi*, the escort destroyer *Chiddingfold* and the landing ships *Prince Charles* and *Prince Leopold*. The force is piloted into Vaagsfjord by the marker submarine *Tuna* on 27 Dec. Commandos, numbering 585 men, are landed in five groups in the area of Vaagsö and Maalöy and they destroy the local fish-processing and telecommunication installations. In Maalöy Sound *Onslow* and *Oribi* sink the patrol boat *V5108/Föhn* (207 tons) and drive the freighters *Reimar Edzard Fritzen* (2935 tons), *Norma* (2258 tons), *Eismeer* (1003 tons) and a little later the *Anita L. M. Russ* (1712 tons) on to the beach. Near Vaagsöy *Offa* and *Chiddingfold*

sink the patrol boat *V5102/Donner* (223 tons) and the freighter *Anhalt* (5870 tons). *Kenya* receives several hits in an engagement with the Rugsundöy coastal battery. Attacks by some German aircraft on 27 Dec and 28 Dec meet with no success. On 1 Jan 42 the Allied forces arrive back in Scapa Flow and bring with them 266 and 77 Norwegian volunteers respectively.

23 Dec   Mediterranean
Axis troops evacuate Benghazi.

24 Dec   Western Atlantic
Vice-Adm Muselier with the Free French corvettes *Mimose*, *Alysse* and *Aconit* and the large submarine *Surcouf* occupies the islands of St Pierre and Miquelon off Newfoundland which have been loyal to Vichy France.

24 Dec-2 Jan   Indian Ocean
The British convoy BM.9A (troop transports *Devonshire*, *Ethiopia*, *Lancashire*, *Rajula* and *Varsova*), escorted by the Australian cruiser *Hobart*, proceeds from Colombo to Singapore.

25 Dec-25 Jan   Arctic
First deployment of a German U-boat group 'Ulan' comprising *U134*, *U454* and *U584* in the passage S of Bear Island against British Murmansk convoys. Attacks on the convoys PQ.7A and PQ.8 (see entry).

26-31 Dec   Black Sea
Soviet landing on the Kerch Peninsula. On 26 Dec formations of the Azov Flotilla (Rear-Adm S. G. Gorshkov) from Temryuk and Kuchugury land the 244th Rifle Div and the 83rd Naval Infantry Brigade of the 51st Army (Lt-Gen Lvov) on the north coast of the Kerch Peninsula; simultaneously units of the Kerch base (Rear-Adm Frolov) from Taman land the 302nd Rifle Div on both sides of Kerch with the object of pinning the forces of the German XLII Corps to the coast in the N and E. Of the five groups of the Azov Flotilla at first only groups 1 and 2 reach land near Cape Zyuk and Group 4 near Cape Khroni because of bad weather and enemy resistance. Groups 3 and 5 are later brought to these assault areas. By 29 Dec 5870 men and nine tanks are landed from lighters, fishing cutters and patrol boats with support from the gunboats *Dnestr* and *Don* but are forced on the defensive until

29 Dec by the German 72nd Inf Regt. Adm Frolov's forces (three groups with eight TKAs, 41 fishing cutters, three towed convoys of barges) are able to land 2175 men at four points near Kamysh-Burun on 26 Dec and, in spite of the bad weather, to bring up 9050 men by 29 Dec and to hold the bridgehead against the attacks of the 42nd Inf Regt. The landing of Group B (Rear-Adm N. O. Abramov) with the 122nd and 143rd Rifle Brigades from Anapa near Cape Opok on 27 Dec has to be postponed because of the stormy weather. The troops land on 29 Dec near Kamysh-Burun. The support group consists of the gunboats *Krasny Adzharistan*, *Krasnaya Gruziya*, the patrol ship *Shtorm*, a TKA detachment and patrol boats.

On 29 Dec the main landing of the 44th Army (Maj-Gen Pervukhin) is effected by the squadron (Capt 1st Class Basisty) in Feodosia with the object of cutting off the German forces on the Kerch Peninsula from the rear and encircling them and, by advancing into the Crimea, to relieve beleaguered Sevastopol. In the night 28-29 Dec 300 naval infantry are at first landed from an advance party of 12 patrol boats and two motor minesweepers (Lt-Cdr A. P. Ivanov). They occupy the moles and the lighthouse. Shortly after, the support force (Capt 1st Class V. A. Andreev) begins to disembark some 4200 troops. The cruiser *Krasny Krym* anchors 300 metres from the mole; the *Krasny Kavkaz* lies alongside the mole; the destroyers *Zheleznyakov*, *Shaumyan* and *Nezamozhnik* go into the harbour after being led to it by the marker submarines *M-51* and *Shch-201*. During the day on 29 Dec the ships support the disembarked troops with their guns against what is, at first, weak German and Rumanian defence. On the news of the landing in Feodosia the Commander of the German troops on the Kerch Peninsula, Lt-Gen Count Sponeck, orders, on his own responsibility, the 46th Inf Div to withdraw quickly from Kerch to form a defensive position in the west. In the following days a new defence line is constructed with troops which are quickly brought up by the commander of the 11th Army, Col-Gen von Manstein. But the current attack on

Sevastopol has to stop. In the night 29-30 Dec the transport detachment (Capt 2nd Class N. A. Zaruba) with the 63rd Rifle Div (11270 troops) on the transports, *Kuban, Azov, Shakhter, Zyryanin, Krasny Profintern, Tashkent, Nogin, Zhan Zhores* and *Serov* arrives with the escort group (Capt 3rd Class N. P. Negoda) comprising the destroyers *Bodry* and *Boiki*. And in the following night the 2nd Transport Detachment (Capt 2nd Class A. M. Filipov) with the 157th Rifle Div (6395 troops) on the transports *Kalinin, Kursk, Dmitrov, Fabritsius* and *Krasnogvardeets* arrives with the escort group (Capt 2nd Class M. F. Romanov) comprising the destroyers *Soobrazitelny* and *Sposobny*. In the roads of Feodosia *Krasny Kavkaz* receives 17 hits, *Krasny Krym* 11, *Shaumyan* and *Zhelezynakov* four each and *Nezamozhnik* one from artillery and mortar fire. The patrol boat *SKA-063* sinks and also the minesweeper *T-402/Minrep* after an air attack.

28 Dec   South West Pacific
The convoy ZK.5 with 4250 Australian troops and 10000 tons of supplies on board the transports *Aquitania, Herstein* and *Sarpedon* puts to sea from Sydney for Port Moresby. It is escorted by the cruisers *Achilles, Australia, Canberra* and *Perth*. The US cruiser *Pensacola* proceeds to sea with a convoy of seven ships from Brisbane to Port Darwin. On the same day the US cruiser *Houston* and the destroyers *Alden, Edsall* and *Whipple* and three auxiliary ships arrive in Port Darwin from Surabaya.

29 Dec-30 Dec   Black Sea
The battleship *Parizhskaya Kommuna* arrives in Sevastopol having been met on the evening of 27 Dec by the flotilla leader *Tashkent* and the destroyer *Smyshleny* off Poti. She is followed by the cruiser *Molotov* with the destroyer *Bezuprechny*. The ships support with their gunfire the defence against German attacks in the areas of Belbek, Kamyshly and Verkhne on 29 Dec and 30 Dec. When they return the battleship takes 1025 wounded on board and the cruiser 600.

30 Dec   Mediterranean
In the area of the Peloponnese the British submarine *Thorn* (Lt-Cdr Norfolk) sinks one ship of 3032 tons and the

Proteus torpedoes another of 2480 tons.

31 Dec   Black Sea
The Soviet submarine *Shch-214* (Lt-Cdr Vlasov) sinks the Turkish sailing ship *Kaynakdere* on the Turkish-Bulgarian frontier.

31 Dec   Mediterranean
Bombardment of Bardia with the participation of the destroyers of the 7th DD Flotilla, including the Australian *Napier* (F), *Nestor* and *Nizam*.

31 Dec-10 Jan   South Asia
On 31 Dec a convoy sets out from Formosa with the third wave of the Japanese 25th Army for Malaya on 56 transports. Escort provided by the 5th DD Flotilla with the cruiser *Natori* and destroyers *Asakaze, Harukaze, Hatakaze Matsukaze* (5th DD Div), *Satsuki, Minazuki, Fumitsuki, Nagatsuki* (22nd DD Div), and *Asashio, Oshio, Michishio,* and *Arashio* (8th DD Div), the cruiser *Kashii*, the frigate *Shimushu* and destroyers *Ayanami* and *Isonami*. The heavy cruiser *Maya* with the destroyers *Ikazuchi* and *Inazuma* operates as a covering force until 2. Jan in the South China Sea. On 3 Jan the *Arashi* and *Hagikaze* from the 4th DD Div and the *Fubuki* take the place of the two first destroyers of the 8th DD Div. The cruiser *Kashii*, the *Shimushu* and *Ayanami, Isonami,* and *Fubuki* with 11 transports proceed off Cape Camao to Bangkok to unload supplies for the Guards Division. The remainder go to Patani and Singora where on 8 Jan 45 transports arrive. From 5 Jan to 10 Jan the 1st Div of the 7th Cruiser Sqdn operates as a covering force with *Kumano* and *Suzuya* and the destroyers *Hatsuyuki* and *Shirayuki* SW of Saigon. From 8 Jan to 10 Jan elements of the 18th Inf Div are transferred from Canton to Camranh Bay in a convoy of 11 transports. Escort for the convoy is provided by the cruiser *Sendai* with destroyers *Amagiri, Asagiri, Yugiri* (20th DD Div) and *Shikinami*. The US submarine *Stingray* (Lr-Cdr Moore) sinks one ship of 5100 tons from the convoy as it comes in.
During these operations small battle groups of the Japanese 16th Inf Div proceed from Miri in Sarawak in small vessels to Labuan in Brunei Bay (1 Jan) and Jesselton/North Norneo (8 Jan).

1942

1 Jan   General Situation
United Nations Pact. 26 nations declare in Washington that they will not conclude a separate peace with Germany and Japan. The principles of the Atlantic Charter are accepted.

1-5 Jan   Black Sea
The Soviet cruiser *Molotov*, the flotilla leader *Tashkent* and the transports *Abkhaziya* and *Belostok* bring elements of the 386th Rifle Div from Novorossisk to Sevastopol. Before the return on 2 Jan *Molotov* and *Tashkent* with the destroyers *Bezuprechny* and *Smyshleny* repeatedly shell German positions near Sevastopol. *Smyshleny* brings the transport *Pestel* with 690 reserve troops and 185 tons of ammunition to Sevastopol on 3 Jan. Supplies for the 44th Army are brought on 1 Jan by the destroyer *Sposobny* with the transport *Kalinin* from Novorossisk and by the cruisers *Komintern* and *Krasny Krym* from Tuapse to Feodosia. On 2 Jan the destroyers *Boiki* and *Shaumyan* follow with the minesweeper *T-401/Tral* and five transports from Novorossisk. On 3 Jan the cruiser *Krasny Kavkaz* with the 224th AA Div (22 8.5cm AA guns) on board, *Krasny Krym* and the destroyers *Soobrazitelny* and *Sposobny* shell land targets near Feodosia before they return. On the return *Krasny Kavkaz* is attacked on 4 Jan off Tuapse by six Ju 87s of St.G.77 and badly damaged by four near-misses by the stern (her repairs continue until October 1942).
From 3 Jan to 5 Jan the destroyers *Boiki* and *Soobrazitelny* accompany the transports *Kuban* and *Krasnogvardeets* to the Bosphorus.

1-18 Jan   Mediterranean
In British submarine operations in the Central Mediterranean *Upholder* (Lt-Cdr Wanklyn) sinks the Italian submarine *St Bon* which is being used as a petrol transport; *Unbeaten* (Lt Woodward) the German *U374;* and *P35/Umbra* (Lt Maydon) a small ship of 301 tons. On the western side of

Cephalonia *Thunderbolt* (Lt-Cdr Crouch) sinks a caique of 32 tons and *Proteus* and *Thrasher* (Lt Mackenzie) each sink one ship of 5413 tons and 5016 tons respectively near Cape Ducato. *Porpoise* (Cdr Pizey) lays a barrage of 50 mines off Crete on 11 Jan and sinks one ship of 2471 tons with a torpedo. *Triumph* is lost through unknown causes (mine?) off Milos and in Malta *P31/Uproar* is damaged in an air attack on 14 Jan.

2 Jan   Arctic
U134 (Lt-Cdr Schendel) sinks in the Arctic the British freighter *Waziristan* (5135 tons) belonging to the Murmansk convoy PQ.7A (two ships, PQ.7B nine ships).

3 Jan   General Situation
Formation of the Allied ABDA Command (American, British, Dutch, Australian) under General Wavell in the Dutch East Indies.

3-6 Jan   Mediterranean
Italian operation M.43. Three Italian supply convoys set out on 3 Jan: three transports with the destroyers *Vivaldi, Da Recco, Usodimare, Bersagliere* and *Fuciliere* from Messina; two transports with the torpedo boats *Orsa, Aretusa, Castore* and *Antares* from Taranto; and one transport with the destroyer *Freccia* and the torpedo boat *Procione* from Messina. The convoys join up on 4 Jan. A close escort force (Div-Adm Bergamini), comprising the battleship *Duilio*, the cruisers *Garibaldi, Montecuccoli, Duca d'Aosta* and *Attendolo* and the destroyers *Maestrale, Gioberti, Oriani, Scirocco* and *Malocello*, is added and a distant covering force (Adm Iachino), consisting of the battleships *Littorio, Doria* and *Cesare*, the cruisers *Gorizia* and *Trento* and the destroyers *Carabiniere, Alpino, Pigafetta, Da Noli, Ascari, Aviere, Geniere* and *Camicia Nera*, sets out. The operation is covered E of Malta by the submarines *Pisani, Onice, Dandolo, Alagi, Aradam, Tricheco* and *Axum* and between Crete and Cyrenaica by *Beilul, Dessiè, Galatea* and *Zaffiro*. Although the convoy is

sighted by the British submarine *P34/Ultimatum* and the covering force by *Unique* and aircraft, this does not lead to successful attacks. On 5 Jan the transports arrive in Tripoli. The *Littorio* force returns on 5 Jan and the *Duilio* force on 6 Jan to Taranto.

4-9 Jan   Dutch East Indies
Of the Japanese 4th SM Flotilla (Rear-Adm Yoshitome) *I-57* (Cdr Nakashima) sinks one ship of 3077 tons and *I-56* (Cdr Ohashi) three ships of 7957 tons and torpedoes two more ships of 5065 tons S of Java. In the Java Sea *I-58* (Cdr Kitamura) sinks one ship of 2380 tons, while *I-55*, like *Ro-33* and *Ro-34* has no success in the area of the Anambas Islands.

4-18 Jan   Pacific
Off the Japanese East Coast the US submarine *Gudgeon* (Lt-Cdr Grenfell) sinks one ship of 2225 tons, *Plunger* (Lt-Cdr White) one ship of 4702 tons and *Pollack* (Lt-Cdr Mosely) sinks two ships of 7612 tons and damages one ship of 2700 tons.

5-8 Jan   Black Sea
Soviet offensive to relieve Sevastopol. In the night 4-5 Jan a Soviet force (Capt 2nd class Buslaev), consisting of the minesweeper *T-405/Vrzyvatel*, the tug *SP-14* and seven SKA cutters, lands a naval infantry battalion in Evpatoria where at the same time partisan units have assembled. The *Vrzyvatel* is damaged in an air attack, goes aground and is lost. In the night 5-6 Jan a second force, consisting of the destroyer *Smyshleny*, the minesweeper *T-408/Yakor* and four SKAs, lands another battalion. A third wave with the flotilla leader *Tashkent*, the *Yakor* and two SKAs is not able to land on the evening of 6 Jan because of the defensive fire. The main body of the disembarked troops is destroyed by the German defenders (which includes Reconnaissance Detachment 22, Lt-Col von Boddien). 203 prisoners are brought in. The remainder embark on the evening of 6 Jan. The cruiser *Molotov*, which comes to Sevastopol with supplies on 5 Jan, and the *Tashkent* support with their gunfire Soviet attacks on the north front of the fortress on 5 Jan, 6 Jan and 7 Jan. The battleship *Parizhskaya Kommuna* (Commander of the Squad-

ron, Rear-Adm Vladimirski, on board) and the destroyer *Boiki* shell German positions near Stary Krym (Feodosia) in the night 5-6 Jan. Simultaneously the destroyer *Sposobny* with the patrol cutter *SKA-0111* lands 218 men of the 226th Mountain Regt near Sudak. On the return *Sposobny* evades attacks by Ju 88s off Feodosia. In the night 7-8 Jan the destroyer *Boiki* lands a battalion (450 men) in Dvuyakornoy Bay W of Feodosia instead of in Feodosia because of the danger of air attack. The *Sposobny*, which has set out to land a second battalion, is badly damaged by ground mines off Cape Myskhako and is towed to Novorossisk by the destroyer *Nezamozhnik*.

5-9 Jan   Mediterranean
British supply operation MF.2 to Malta. On 5 Jan the transport *Glengyle* sets out from Alexandria with Force B (Rear-Adm Vian), comprising the cruisers *Dido*, *Euryalus*, *Naiad*, the destroyers *Gurkha*, *Sikh*, *Kipling*, *Kingston* and *Foxhound*. On 6 Jan the empty transport *Breconshire* puts to sea from Malta with Force C, consisting of the destroyers *Lance*, *Lively*, *Jaguar* and *Havock*. On 7 Jan the two forces meet: they exchange the transports and the destroyers *Sikh* and *Havock* and arrive in Malta and Alexandria respectively on 8-9 Jan. The Italian submarines (see 3-6 Jan) do not approach.

5-15 Jan   Arctic
Of the Soviet submarines operating off the Norwegian Polar Coast, *K-23* (Capt 3rd Class Potapov) lays a mine barrage on 5 Jan W of Nordkyn on which a Norwegian coaster of 327 tons sinks on 30 Jan. Attacks by *Shch-401* and *Shch-404* have no success. *S-102* (Capt 3rd Class Gorodnichi) attacks a convoy NW of Vardö on 14 Jan and sinks the steamer *Türkheim* (1904 tons). The escorting submarine-chasers *UJ1205*, *UJ1403* and the patrol boat *V5903* drop 198 depth charges, but the submarine escapes.

7-13 Jan   Dutch East Indies
Japanese landing on Tarakan. On 7-8 Jan the units of the Central Force (Vice-Adm Hirose) with the 2nd BF as an advance party set out from Davao (Mindanao) and Jolo. It comprises the minelayers *Imizu Maru*, *Itsukushima*

Left: Mar 9, 1942: German forces attempt to attack convoy PQ.12 in the Arctic. The *Tirpitz* manoeuvres violently to avoid torpedoes from Albacore aircraft of the *Victorious.* [*IWM*

Below: March-April, 1942: Three German destroyers attempt to attack convoy PQ.13 on March 29. In the confused melee a salvo from the cruiser *Trinidad* renders *Z26* unmanoeuvrable. The crew are rescued by *Z24* and *Z25.* [*BFZ*

Bottom: June-July, 1942: PQ.17 sails, and due to the threat of a German surface attack in superior strength, is ordered to scatter. The close covering force, including the cruisers *Wichita* (US) and *London* (RN) is forced to leave the merchant ships to their fate. [*IWM*

Above: Sept 12-18, 1942: Operation against convoy PQ.18 in the Arctic. Following the disaster to PQ.17 this convoy is provided with close support cover consisting of the cruiser *Scylla* and 16 destroyers. Above: the *Fury* and *Ashanti* are followed by 'Tribal' and 'M' class destroyers. *[BFZ*

Above: Sept 14, 1942: In air attacks on PQ.18 by K.G. 30 the ammunition ship *Mary Luckenback* is hit and explodes.
[BFZ

Above: Dec 30, 1942: A German force attacks convoy JW.51B in the Arctic. The attack is foiled by the destroyer escort, but the *Onslow* suffers heavy damage in the action. *[IWM*

Left: Oct 1942: Aircraft from the two American Task Forces attack the Japanese fleet and obtain hits on the carriers *Zuiho* and *Shokaku* and the cruiser *Chikuma*. The *Tone* (left) manages to avoid the bombs and torpedoes of American planes.

[*Official USN*

Below: Nov 1942: Eleven Japanese transports following behind the Main Fleet carry troops needed to maintain pressure on American Forces on Guadalcanal. The transports are attacked at sea and lose seven of their number. The four remaining vessels head for Guadalcanal where they are beached on Nov 14-15. They are destroyed the following day by American air attacks. [*Official USN*

Oct, 1942: The bitter battle for Guadalcanal reaches its height. The Japanese and American fleets clash at the battle of Santa Cruz. Aircraft from the four Japanese carriers attack US TF.61 (*above*), obtaining two hits on the carrier *Enterprise* (left) and damaging the new battleship *South Dakota* (right). US TF.17 is not so lucky. The carrier *Hornet* is hit by four bombs, two torpedoes, and two crashing aircraft, and has to be abandoned. (*below*) US destroyers fail to sink the carrier, which is later sunk when Japanese destroyers arrive on the scene. *[Official USN*

Above: July 16, 1942: Minelayer *Welshman* disguised as a French destroyer of the *Lynx* class, takes urgently needed supplies to Malta. A tarpaulin alters the line of the focsle, and the black paint the line of the deck. Black caps identical to those in use in the French navy are added to the funnels. *[IWM*

Below: Aug, 1942: Yet another attempt is made to relieve Malta. The convoy is heavily escorted by units of the Mediterranean Fleet, including the carrier *Indomitable*, which is severely damaged by bombs. *[IWM*

Below: Aug 13, 1942: Italian surface forces sailing to attack the Pedestal convoy to Malta are forced to return due to insufficient air cover. On their return the submarine *Unbroken* torpedoes the cruisers *Attendolo* and *Bolzano* near the Aeolian Islands. *[BFZ*

Above: Nov 8, 1942: The Allies carry out a major landing in North Africa. This creates major logistic problems and entails the movement of many convoys. The picture above shows one of the major troop convoys for Operation Torch, en route for Gibraltar. *[IWM*

Left: Nov 1942: Operation Torch. The landings in North Africa meet strong resistance from the Vichy French. At Oran, the sloops *Walney* and *Hartland* fail to prevent the French warships scuttling themselves and both vessels are sunk at point blank range by French destroyers. The *Hartland* suffers heavy casualties. *[IWM*

Nov 27, 1942: As German troops occupy Toulon the French navy scuttles its warships there (*top*). From left to right the vessels are *Strasbourg*, *Colbert*, *Algerie* and *Marseillaise*. The *Colbert* (*above*) was completely wrecked. [*BFZ*

Above: March, 1942: Convoy MW.10 sails with supplies for. Malta. Italian forces sortie to attack the convoy, and the second battle of Sirte ensues. The cruiser *Cleopatra* (shown ahead laying a smoke screen during the action) received a 15cm hit, and the *Euryalus* (with guns trained and firing) splinter damage.   [*IWM*

Below: May, 1942: British and Free French Forces land on the island of Madagascar. Above: the carriers *Illustrious, Indomitable,* battleship *Ramillies,* cruiser *Hermione* and troop transports anchor in the harbour of Diego Sauraez.   [*IWM*

Below: June, 1942: Two convoys sail from either end of the Mediterranean in a desperate attempt to relieve Malta. Convoy MW.11 from Alexandria bears the brunt of the air attacks, the cruiser *Cleopatra* proving invaluable with her heavy armament of ten 5.25-inch guns.   [*IWM*

and *Wakataka*, the submarine-chasers (Kusentai) *Ch10, 11, 12*, the minesweepers (Sokaitei) *W13, W14, W15, W16* (17th MS Division), *W17* and *W18* (30th MS Division), the fast assault boats (Ishokaitei) *P36, P37, P38* and *P39* and a convoy of sixteen transports with the 56th Regimental Combat Group and the 2nd Kure Special Landing Force on board. As escort it has the 4th DD Flotilla (Rear-Adm Nishimura) with the cruiser *Naka* and the destroyers *Yudachi, Harusame, Samidare* and *Murasame* (2nd DD Div), *Asagumo, Minegumo* and *Natsugumo* (9th DD Div). Air escort is provided by the 23rd Naval Air Flotilla (Jolo) and seaplanes from the depot ships *Sanuki Maru* and *Sanyo Maru*. On 10 Jan the invasion fleet arrives off Tarakan. In the night 10-11 Jan the landing succeeds in the face of slight resistance, after the Dutch defenders have set the oil wells on fire. *W13* and *W14* are lost in engagements with coastal batteries and on mine barrages. On 16 Jan the airfield is operational. The *Asagumo* is put out of action when she goes aground.
Japanese landing near Menado and Kema (Celebes). On 9 Jan the Eastern Force (Rear-Adm Kubo) puts to sea from Davao with the 1st BF. It consists of the cruiser *Nagara*, the minelayer *Aotaka*, the freighter *Tsukushi Maru*, the fast transports (Ishokaitei) *P1, P2, P34*, the minesweepers (Sokaitei) *W7, W8, W9, W11, W12* (21st MS Div) and the submarine-chasers (Kusentai) *Ch1, Ch3* with six transports (the 1st Sasebo Special Landing Force on board). Escort: the 2nd DD Flotilla (Rear-Adm Tanaka) with the cruiser *Jintsu* and the destroyers *Kuroshio, Oyashio, Natsushio, Hayashio* (15th DD Div), *Yukikaze, Tokitsukaze, Amatsukaze* and *Hatsukaze* (16th DD Div). Air escort provided by the 21st Naval Air Flotilla from Davao and seaplanes from the 11th Carrier Sqdn, consisting of the seaplane carriers *Chitose* and *Mizuho* (Rear-Adm Fujita). On 11 Jan 334 men of the Yokosuka Naval Air Landing Force are dropped by parachute near Menado: there follows a landing from the sea near Menado and Kema. Slight resistance. Both operations are covered to the

N

S by the 5th SM Flotilla comprising *I-59, I-60, I-62, I-64, I-65* and *I-66*, to the N by Rear-Adm Takagi with the heavy cruisers *Haguro* and *Nachi* (*Myoko* is damaged on 4 Jan in an air attack in Davao) and the destroyers *Inazuma* and *Ikazuchi* in the Celebes sea.

8 Jan-12 Feb Western Atlantic
A first wave of 12 Type VII-C boats ('Ziethen' group) arrives one after the other in the area of the Newfoundland Bank and operates singly as far S as Nova Scotia. Many ships are sunk. *U135* (Lt-Cdr Praetorius) sinks one ship of 9626 tons; *U87* (Lt-Cdr Berger) two ships of 16324 tons), including one on 31 Dec while en route; *U552* (Lt-Cdr Topp) two ships of 6722 tons; *U86* (Lt-Cdr Schug) one ship of 4271 tons and damages one ship of 8627 tons; *U203* (Lt-Cdr Mützelburg) three ships of 2341 tons and damages one ship of 888 tons; *U582* (Lt-Cdr Schulte) one ship of 5189 tons; *U654* (Lt Forster) the Free French corvette *Alysse; U701* (Lt-Cdr Degen) one ship of 3657 tons; *U333* (Lt-Cdr Cremer) three ships of 14045 tons; *U553* (Lt-Cdr Thurmann) two ships of 16366 tons; and *U754* (Lt-Cdr Oestermann) four ships of 11386 tons. *U84* (Lt Uphoff) returns without success.

9-17 Jan Mediterranean
In operations against British supplies for Tobruk *U77* (Lt-Cdr Schonder) torpedoes on 12 Jan the British destroyer *Kimberley* which has to be towed to Alexandria with a blown-off stern. *U133* (Lt-Cdr Hesse) sinks the British destroyer *Gurkha* (*II*) on 17 Jan. *U205* has no success and *U577* is sunk by an aircraft.

9-20 Jan Pacific
The Japanese 3rd SM Div with *I-16, I-20, I-22* and *I-24* and the 2nd SM Flotilla still operating in the area of Hawaii with *I-7, I-1, I-2, I-3, I-4, I-5* and *I-6* (Cdr* Inaba) are directed to US TF 14 with the carrier *Saratoga* which has been reported by the Japanese submarine *I-18. I-6* torpedoes the carrier on 11 Jan. On the return *I-18* and *I-24* shell Midway without success.
9 Jan-3 Feb Indian Ocean
I-65 (Lt-Cdr Harada) and *I-66* (Cdr Yoshitome) of the Japanese 5th SM

Flotilla operate at first in the Java Sea and later off Rangoon. They sink two and three ships of 6105 and 10530 tons respectively. *I-59* (Cdr Yoshimatsu) sinks W of Sumatra one ship of 4184 tons and one further unidentified ship in Sabang. In proceeding through the Sunda Strait, *I-60* is sunk by the British destroyer *Jupiter*. In the Bay of Bengal *I-64* (Cdr Ogawa) sinks four ships of 16244 tons and damages one ship of 391 tons. *I-62* (Lt-Cdr Kinashi) torpedoes two tankers of 16865 tons.

10 Jan   Arctic
U584 (Lt-Cdr Deecke) sinks the Soviet submarine *M-175* NW of the Fisherman's Peninsula.

10 Jan   South Asia
In Allied submarine operations the US submarine *Pickerel* (Lt-Cdr Bacon) sinks one ship of 2929 tons off Davao. The Dutch *O19* (Lt-Cdr Knoops) torpedoes two ships of 9417 tons in the Gulf of Siam. The US submarines *Stingray* (Lt-Cdr Moore) and *Sculpin* (Lt-Cdr Chappell) each torpedo one ship of 5167 tons and 3817 tons respectively off Hainan and off Lamon Bay.

10-18 Jan   South Asia
Japanese forces are transferred in the South China Sea. The heavy covering force under Vice-Adm Kondo which has returned to the Pescadores on 11 Jan is transferred to Palau by 16 Jan. It comprises the heavy cruisers *Atago*, *Maya* and *Takao* (4th Cruiser Sqdn), the battleships *Haruna* and *Kongo* (3rd BB Sqdn) and the destroyers *Arashi*, *Hagikaze*, *Maikaze*, *Nowake* (4th DD Div) and *Akatsuki* and *Hibiki* (6th DD Div). The 2nd Carrier Sqdn (Rear-Adm Yamaguchi) arrives there from Kure on 17 Jan with the carriers *Hiryu* and *Soryu*, the cruiser *Tone* and the destroyers *Tanikaze* and *Urakaze*.
From 12 Jan to 18 Jan the 8th DD Div, consisting of the destroyers *Asashio*, *Oshio*, *Michishio* and *Arashio*, is transferred from Hong Kong to Davao. While light craft transport elements of the Japanese 16th Inf Div from Brunei and Jesselton to Sandakan (North Borneo) on 17 Jan the Western Force under Vice-Adm Ozawa cruises in the South China Sea from Camranh Bay from 16 Jan to 19 Jan. It consists of the flagship, the heavy cruiser *Chokai*, the

7th Cruiser Sqdn (Rear-Adm Kurita) with the heavy cruisers *Kumano*, *Suzuya*, *Mikuma* and *Mogami*, the 4th Carrier Sqdn (Rear-Adm Kakuta) with the carrier *Ryujo* and destroyer *Shikinami*, the 3rd DD Flotilla with the cruiser *Sendai* and the destroyers *Fubuki*, *Hatsuyuki*, *Shirayuki* (11th DD Div), *Murakumo*, *Shirakumo*, *Usugumo* (12th Div) *Ayanami*, *Isonami*, *Uranami* (19th DD Div), *Amagiri*, *Asagiri* and *Yugiri* (20th DD Div) and the light cruisers *Kinu* and *Yura*.

11-16 Jan   North Atlantic
The three German U-boats *U71*, *U93* and *U571* operating off Gibraltar and the Azores ('Seydlitz' group) try to attack convoy HG.78 but are driven off by the Escort Group, whose leading destroyer *Hesperus* sinks *U93* on 15 Jan.

11 Jan-7 Feb   Western Atlantic
The first five U-boats to arrive off the American East Coast open the attack on American coastal shipping (operation 'Paukenschlag'). *U123* (Lt-Cdr Hardegen) sinks nine ships of 53173 tons and torpedoes one ship; *U130* (Cdr Kals) sinks six ships of 36993 tons and torpedoes one ship of 6986 tons; *U66* (Cdr Zapp) sinks five ships of 33456 tons; *U109* (Lt-Cdr Bleichrodt) sinks five ships of 33733 tons; and *U125* (Lt-Cdr Folkers) sinks one ship of 5666 tons.

12 Jan   Black Sea
The Soviet battleship *Parizhskaya Kommuna*, escorted by the destroyers *Bodry* and *Zheleznyakov*, shells German positions near Isyumovki and Stary Krym.

12-14 Jan   North Atlantic
U43 (Lt-Cdr Lüth), which is returning home from France, sinks a straggler from the convoy HX.168 in the North Atlantic and in a heavy storm three ships from the convoy ON.55 totalling 21307 tons.

12-25 Jan   South Asia
The Japanese 6th SM Flotilla lays mine barrages: *I-121* and *I-122* in the Clarence Strait on 12 Jan and 16 Jan respectively and *I-123* in the Bundas Strait. In a mining operation off Port Darwin *I-124* is sunk on 20 Jan by the US destroyer *Edsall* and the Australian minesweepers *Deloraine*, *Lithgow* and *Katoomba*.

13 Jan Arctic
The German 8th DD Flotilla (Capt Pönitz), comprising Z25, Z23 and Z24, lays four barrages with 100 EMC mines in the western channel of the White Sea near Cape Kachovski.

13-24 Jan Arctic
Allied convoy QP.5 leaves with four ships from Murmansk for Reykjavik.

14-25 Jan North Atlantic
12 of the Type VII U-boats setting out from Germany, ('Schlei' group) are halted, on Hitler's instructions, in the area W of the Hebrides and Faeroes, so as to be ready, if necessary, to repel an invasion of Norway. The operation leads to no result. Only U588 (Lt-Cdr Vogel) reports the sinking of a so-far unidentified ship. On 24 Jan the U-boats receive orders to continue their journey to France.

14-25 Jan South West Pacific
Japanese landings at Rabaul and Kavieng. On 14 Jan the 19th ML Div (Rear-Adm Shima) sets out from Guam for Rabaul with the minelayers Okinoshima, Tenyo Maru and Tsugaru, the destroyers Mochizuki and Mutsuki (30th DD Div), the auxiliary gunboats Kongo Maru and Nikkai Maru and Army transports with the 144th Inf Regt of the South Sea Detachment. On 17 Jan Rear-Adm Kajioka comes out from Truk to meet the force with the cruiser Yubari, the destroyers Asanagi, Oite, Yunagi (29th DD Div) and Yayoi (30th DD Div) and one auxiliary ship and two transports with elements of the Maizuru Naval Landing Force and the aircraft depot ship Hijirigawa Maru. To cover and support the operation 1st Carrier Air Fleet (Vice-Adm Nagumo) with the carriers Akagi, Kaga (1st Carrier Sqdn), Shokaku and Zuikaku (5th Carrier Sqdn), the battleships Hiyei and Kirishima (1/3rd BB Sqdn), the cruiser Chikuma (8th Cruiser Sqdn) and the 1st DD Flotilla with the cruiser Abukuma and the destroyers Isokaze, Hamakaze, Kasumi, Arare, Kagero, Shiranuhi and Akigumo puts to sea from Truk on 17 Jan for the area N of New Ireland. On 18 Jan the 6th Cruiser Sqdn (Rear-Adm Goto) follows with the cruisers Aoba, Kinugasa, Kako and Furutaka and on 20 Jan the invasion force for Kavieng with the

18th Cruiser Sqdn (Rear-Adm Matsuyama) with the cruisers Tatsuta and Tenryu, the destroyers Kikuzuki, Uzuki and Yuzuki (23rd DD Div) and, on several transports, the rest of the Maizuru and the Kashima Naval Landing Forces.

On 20 Jan the carrier force makes a heavy attack on Rabaul. While the 1st Carrier Sqdn remains in the area N of New Ireland, the 5th Carrier Sqdn proceeds with the Chikuma and three destroyers on 21 Jan into the Bismarck Sea where the 6th Cruiser Sqdn is also taking up a covering position for the landings. The 7th SM Flotilla (Flagship Jingei, Rear-Adm Onishi) takes up a patrol line in the area off St George's Channel to cover the Rabaul operation with the submarines Ro-61, Ro-62, Ro-63, Ro-64, Ro-65, Ro-67 and Ro-68. After the destroyers have been refuelled on 21 Jan, and with air support from the carriers, the assault forces arrive off their targets on the evening of 22 Jan and land their troops in the night 22-23 Jan. By 24 Jan they have occupied all key points and have begun to establish airfields.

The covering forces start the return journey on 23 Jan and reach Truk again on 25 Jan.

14 Jan-2 Feb Indian Ocean
The British carrier Indomitable proceeds with the Australian destroyers Napier, Nestor and Nizam from Port Sudan on 14 Jan to the area S of Java via Addu Atoll (21 Jan) and Cocos Islands (25 Jan for refuelling). The purpose is to fly off 48 Hurricane fighters on 27-28 Jan to reinforce the air defence of Java. The force arrives in Trincomalee (Ceylon) on 2 Feb.

15 Jan Mediterranean
The German 3rd TB Flotilla (Lt-Cdr Kemnade) lays the barrage MT 5 E of Valetta (Malta) with 24 TMA mines, four protection and eight explosive floats.

15-16 Jan Black Sea
Soviet landing force (Capt 1st Class Andreev), comprising the cruiser Krasny Krym, the gunboat Krasny Adzharistan and six SKA patrol cutters, lands the bulk of the 226th Mountain Regt in Sudak; the destroyers Shaumyan and Soobrazitelny land diversionary groups at three other coastal points numberin

in all 750 men. Covering fire is provided by the covering force (Rear-Adm Vladimirski) consisting of the battleships *Parizhskaya Kommuna* and destroyers *Bezuprechny* and *Zheleznyakov*. As a diversion the destroyer *Smyshleny* simultaneously shells Evpatoria. The destroyer *Boiki* brings supplies to Sevastopol.

16-20 Jan Mediterranean
British supply operation MF.3 to Malta. On 16 Jan there set out from Alexandria the convoys MW.8A (the transports *Ajax* and *Thermopylae* with the AA cruiser *Carlisle* and destroyers *Arrow*, *Griffin*, *Hasty* and *Hero*) and MW.8B (the transports *City of Calcutta* and *Clan Fergusson* with destroyers *Gurkha*, *Isaac Sweers*, *Legion* and *Maori*) which later join up. They are followed by the covering group, Force B (Rear-Adm Vian), with the cruisers *Naiad*, *Dido*, *Euryalus* and the destroyers *Kelvin*, *Kipling*, *Havock*, *Foxhound* and *Hotspur*. On 17 Jan the German U-boat *U133* (Cdr Hesse) torpedoes the *Gurkha*. *Isaac Sweers* tows the sinking ship out of the burning oil and rescues the crew. On 18 Jan the *Thermopylae*, because of engine trouble, has to be sent to Benghazi with the *Carlisle*, *Foxhound* and *Hotspur*. They are harassed by air attacks on 19 Jan as they continue their journey. The convoy is met on 18 Jan by Force K, coming from Malta with the cruiser *Penelope* and the destroyers *Sikh*, *Zulu*, *Lance*, *Lively* and *Jaguar*, and brought to Malta on 19 Jan. After exchanging the destroyers *Legion* and *Moari* for *Jaguar*, Force B returns to Alexandria on 20 Jan.

16 Jan-4 Feb North Atlantic
The outward-bound *U402* and *U581* locate a troop transport convoy from which *U402* (Lt-Cdr S. Freiherr von Forstner) torpedoes the *Llangibby Castle* (12053 tons) which is brought into Punta Delgada. When news is received that the repaired ship is about to sail, *U402*, *U572* and *U581* which are operating between Gibraltar and the Azores, are directed to her (1-4 Feb), but they have no success. The British destroyer *Westcott*, belonging to the escort, sinks *U581* on 2 Feb. Of the Italian submarines operating at this time in the area of the Azores,

Bagnolini and *Barbarigo*, the latter sinks on 23 Jan the Spanish steamer *Navemar* (5473 tons), which is returning empty after a journey with Jewish refugees from Cadiz to New York.

17 Jan Arctic
For the first time a U-boat group ('Ulan'), consisting of *U134*, *U454* and *U584*, operates against an Arctic convoy. After the torpedoing of the Soviet minesweeper *T-68* from a Soviet coastal convoy, *U454* (Lt-Cdr Hackländer) attacks in several approaches the convoy PQ.8 (eight steamers). She torpedoes the convoy commodore's ship, *Harmatris* (5395 tons), and sinks the destroyer *Matabele*. The C-in-C Home Fleet sends Rear-Adm Burrough with the cruiser *Nigeria* to Murmansk to persuade the Command of the Soviet Northern Fleet to take a larger part in bringing in the convoys.

18 Jan Black Sea
Troops of the German 11th Army recapture Feodosia.

19 Jan-5 Feb Arctic
On 19 Jan on the Norwegian Polar Coast the Soviet submarines *K-23* (Capt 3rd Class Potapov) and *K-22* (Capt 3rd Class Kotelnikov with Div Commander, Capt 2nd Class Gadzhiev, on board) attack the fishing harbours of Svaerholthavet (Porsangerfjord) and Berlevaag (Tanafjord) and each sink with their guns one small ship of 506 tons and 106 tons respectively. Three attacks by *Shch-422* (Lt-Cdr Malyshev with the Div Cdr, Capt 2nd Class Kolyshkin, on board) are unsuccessful; similarly one by *M-171* (Lt-Cdr Starikov). *Shch-421* (Lt-Cdr Lunin) sinks, after two abortive attacks, the steamer *Konsul Schulte* (2975 tons) from a convoy in Porsangerfjord on 5 Feb.

20 Jan Dutch East Indies
Formation of the 'China Force' (Commodore Collins) for convoy duties between Singapore, Sunda Strait and Java, consisting of the cruisers *Danae*, *Dragon*, *Durban*, the destroyers *Jupiter*, *Encounter*, *Express*, *Electra*, *Stronghold* and *Vampire* (RAN) and the sloops *Jumna* (RIN) and *Yarra* (RAN).

20-26 Jan South Asia
On 20 Jan a Japanese convoy of 11 transports with the 18th Inf Div on

board sets out from Camranh Bay for Singora and Patani. The convoy is escorted by the destroyers *Amagiri*, *Asagiri*, *Fubuki* and *Yugiri*. The troops are disembarked on 24 Jan. From there two transports, escorted by the above destroyers, proceed to Kuantan and disembark troops there on 26 Jan. From 25 Jan support is also provided by the cruiser *Sendai* and destroyers *Hatsuyuki* and *Shirayuki*, coming from Poulo Condore, as well as by the 1st MS Div, comprising the minesweepers (Sokaitei) *W1*, *W2*, *W3*, *W4*, *W5* and the 11th A/S Div, consisting of the submarine-chasers (Kusentai) *Ch7*, *Ch8* and *Ch9*. To cover the operation, the cruisers *Kumano*, *Suzuya* and *Yura* with the destroyers *Ayanami* and *Isonami* cruise NW of Natoma. Further off, the carrier *Ryujo* provides air cover with the destroyer *Shikinami*. The cruisers *Mikuma* and *Mogami*, which also set out originally, proceed on 22 Jan to Saigon with the destroyer *Uranami*. After an unsuccessful attack by 68 British aircraft from Singapore (13 planes lost), the destroyers *Thanet* (RN) and *Vampire* (RAN) are deployed in the night 26-27 Jan to attack the Japanese transports reported off Endau. *Vampire* misses with her three torpedoes *W4* and *Shirayuki; Thanet* sinks in an engagement with *Yugiri*, *W1*, *Sendai*, *Fubuki* and *Asagiri*.

20 Jan-20 Feb   Pacific

Operation by the Japanese 3rd SM Flotilla (Rear-Adm Miwa) in the Pacific. The Command Boat *I-8* (Cdr* Emi) reconnoitres the American West Coast between San Francisco and Seattle; *I-71* (Cdr Kawasaki) and *I-72* (Cdr Togami) operate in the area of Hawaii. The latter sinks the Fleet tanker *Neches* (7383 tons). *I-73* (Cdr* Isobe) shells Midway on 25 Jan, sinks a small transport of 244 tons near Oahu and is herself sunk on 29 Jan by the US destroyers *Jarvis* and *Long*. *I-69* (Cdr Watanabe) shells Midway on 8 Feb and 10 Feb. *I-74* (Cdr* Ikezawa) and *I-75* (Cdr Inoue) operate without success in the area of the Aleutians.

21-25 Jan   Dutch East Indies

Japanese landing at Kendari (Celebes). On 21 Jan the Eastern Force (Rear-Adm Kubo) sets out from Bangka Roads

near Menado with the 1st BF (the cruiser *Nagara*, the minelayer *Aotaka*, the freighter *Tsukushi Maru*, the fast transports *P1*, *P2* and *P34*, the minesweepers *W7*, *W8*, *W9*, *W11*, *W12*, the submarine-chasers *Ch1*, *Ch2* and *Ch3* and six transports (with the 1st Sasebo Special Landing Force on board). It is escorted by the destroyers of the 15th and 16th DD Divs: *Kuroshio*, *Oyashio*, *Hatsushio*, *Hayashio*, *Yukikaze*, *Tokitsukaze*, *Amatsukaze* and *Hatsukaze*. The purpose is to land at Kendari on 24 Jan which they do without encountering strong resistance. Air escort and support is provided by the 23rd Naval Air Flotilla and the 11th Carrier Sqdn with the seaplane carriers *Chitose* and *Mizuho*.

On 24 Jan one transport of 4124 tons is sunk by the US submarine *Swordfish* (Lt-Cdr Smith) and another of 8035 tons is damaged. The 21st DD Div arrives off Kendari on 25 Jan as a reinforcement and consists of the destroyers *Nenohi*, *Hatsushimo*, *Wakaba* and *Hatsuharu*. The last is damaged in an attack by US bombers.

To cover the operation the submarines *I-59*, *I-60*, *I-62*, *I-64*, *I-65* and *I-66* form a patrol line in the Ambon Sea. In the Celebes Sea Rear-Adm Takagi cruises with the heavy cruisers *Haguro* and *Nachi* and the destroyers *Akebono* (a replacement for the *Inazuma*, damaged when she goes aground) and *Ikazuchi*. The Allied base at Ambon, after a heavy attack on 24-25 Jan by the 23rd Naval Air Flotilla, is repeatedly attacked by the aircraft of a carrier force (Rear-Adm Yamaguchi), consisting of the carriers *Hiryu* and *Soryu*, the cruiser *Tone*, the destroyers *Tanikaze* and *Urakaze*, which is operating in the Banda Sea. As additional covering groups there operate E of Mindanao the battleship *Haruna* with the heavy cruiser *Maya* and the destroyers *Akatsuki* and *Hibiki* and S of Palau the heavy cruisers *Atago* and *Takao*, the battleship *Kongo* and the destroyers *Arashi*, *Hagikaze*, *Maikaze* and *Nowake*.

21-27 Jan   Dutch East Indies

Japanese landing at Balikpapan (Borneo). On 21 Jan the Central Force sets out from Tarakan with 13 transports. Close escort: the fast assault boats (APD) *P36, P37, P38,* the minesweepers *W15, W16, W17, W18* and the submarine-chasers *Ch10, Ch11,* and *Ch12.* Covering force: Rear-Adm Nishimura with the cruiser *Naka* and destroyers *Yudachi, Harusame, Samidare, Murasame, Natsugumo, Minegumo, Yamakaze* and *Suzukaze.* Advance detachment: one transport with destroyers *Kawakaze* and *Umikaze.* Allied air reconnaissance locates the force and in the Makassar Strait the American submarines *S40, Pickerel, Porpoise, Saury, Spearfish,* and *Sturgeon,* as well as the Dutch *K-XIV* and *K-XVIII,* are deployed against it. Allied TF 5 (Rear-Adm Glassford, USN), comprising the cruisers *Boise* and *Marblehead* and the destroyers *John D. Ford, Parrott, Paul Jones* and *Pope,* is directed to it from Koepang Bay, but the *Boise* drops out in Sape Strait when she goes aground and *Marblehead,* because of engine trouble, can only take up a position to meet the destroyers.

On the evening of 23 Jan the Japanese invasion force arrives off Balikpapan with the 56th RCT on board. In the meantime it has also been reported by *Sturgeon* which has made an abortive attack due to torpedo failures. Before the bulk of the embarked troops can be landed, the four US destroyers (Cdr Talbot) arrive in the night 23-24 Jan. This happens immediately after the Dutch submarine *K-XVIII* (Lt-Cdr van Well Groeneveld), having missed the *Naka,* has sunk the transport *Tsuruga Maru* (6988 tons) and therefore diverted the Japanese destroyers to sea in a submarine hunt. With the oilfields ablaze in the background, the destroyers can easily recognize the transports lying at anchor, but in several approaches at short ranges, when 48 torpedoes are fired against initially little resistance, they are only able to sink the three transports *Kuretake Maru* (5175 tons), the *Sumanoura Maru* (3519 tons), and the *Tatsukami Maru* (7064 tons) and *P37* and to damage two other ships. The *Naka* and the Japanese destroyers *Minegumo* and *Natsugumo* which come up first are not able to catch the US destroyers as they withdraw. On the morning of 24 Jan the Japanese troops are landed and they

occupy Balikpapan. On 25 Jan the aircraft depot ships *Sanuki Maru* and *Sanyo Maru* arrive, followed on 26 Jan by reinforcements consisting of the minelayers *Imizu Maru, Itsukushima* and *Wakataka* and transports. The *Sanuki Maru* (9246 tons) is lost in an air attack on 26 Jan. On 28 Jan the Japanese 23rd Naval Air Flotilla has Balikpapan in operation.

21 Jan-19 Feb   Western Atlantic
A second wave of eight type VII U-boats makes the following sinkings in the area between the Newfoundland Bank and Nova Scotia: *U85* (Lt Greger) one ship of 5408 tons; *U82* (Lt-Cdr Rollmann) two ships of 18117 tons and the destroyer *Belmont*; *U566* (Lt-Cdr Borchert) one ship of 4181 tons; *U751* (Lt-Cdr Bigalk) two ships of 11487 tons and damages one ship of 8096 tons; *U98* (Lt-Cdr Gysae) one ship of 5298 tons; *U564* (Lt-Cdr Suhren) one ship of 11410 tons and torpedoes one ship of 6195 tons; and *U576* (Lt-Cdr Heinicke) one ship of 6946 tons. *U575* (Lt-Cdr Heydemann), which was held up by special duties, returns without success. Two operational ventures against escorted convoys are not successful. *U564,* which had gone furthest to the S, takes on fuel supplies from *U107* on 16 Feb for the return.

21 Jan-6 Mar   Western Atlantic
A second wave of five Type IX U-boats operates off the US East Coast. *U103* (Lt-Cdr Winter) sinks four ships of 26539 tons; *U106* (Lt-Cdr Rasch) five ships of 42139 tons; *U107* (Lt-Cdr Gelhaus) two ships of 10850 tons; *U108* (Cdr Scholtz) five ships of 20082 tons; and *U128* (Lt-Cdr Heyse) three ships of 27312 tons.

22 Jan   Black Sea
The cruiser *Molotov* and the destroyers *Boiki* and *Smyshleny* are damaged in a storm in Tuapse.

22-24 Jan   Central Pacific
US TF 11 (Rear-Adm Brown) sets out from Pearl Harbour on 22 Jan to make a raid on Wake. It consists of the carrier *Lexington,* the cruisers *Minneapolis, Indianapolis, Pensacola* and *San Francisco* and Desron 1 comprising the destroyers *Phelps, Dewey, MacDonough, Hull, Aylwin, Dale, Clark, Patterson, Bagley* and *Drayton.* When

on 23 Jan the Japanese submarine *I-72* (Cdr Togami) sinks the escort tanker *Neches* (7383 tons), the sortie has to be abandoned because it cannot be carried out without the destroyers being refuelled.

22-25 Jan   Mediterranean
Italian supply operation T.18 to Tripoli. On 22 Jan five transports set out from Taranto and Messina and join up under the escort of the destroyers *Vivaldi, Malocello, Da Noli, Aviere, Camicia Nera, Geniere* and the torpedo boats *Orsa* and *Castore.* A close escort force (Div-Adm De Courten), comprising the cruisers *Duca d'Aosta, Attendolo* and *Montecuccoli* and the destroyers *Alpino, Bersagliere, Carabiniere* and *Fuciliere,* also joins it. Further away, a distant covering force (Div-Adm Bergamini) is at sea, comprising the battleship *Duilio* and the destroyers *Pigafetta, Oriani, Scirocco* and *Ascari.* In spite of air escort from German Ju 88s, British torpedo aircraft from Malta sink the transport *Victoria* (13098 tons) NE of Tripoli on 24 Jan. The convoy and the covering forces arrive respectively in Tripoli on 24 Jan and Taranto on 25 Jan.

23-24 Jan   Black Sea
Soviet landing force (Capt 1st Class Andreev), comprising the cruiser *Krasny Krym,* the destroyer *Shaumyan,* the minesweeper *T-412/Arseni Rasskin* and six SKA patrol cutters, lands 1576 troops of the 544th Rifle Regt in Sudak. Fire support from the destroyers *Bezuprechny* and *Soobrazitelny.* The cruiser *Komintern* brings supplies to Sevastopol.

23 Jan-11 Feb   Dutch East Indies
In Allied submarine operations the US submarine *Sturgeon* (Lt-Cdr Wright) torpedoes two ships of 15803 tons which are beached; *Seadragon* (Lt-Cdr Ferrall) torpedoes three ships 19689 tons, one of which sinks. On 11 Feb *Shark* is sunk by the Japanese destroyer *Amatsukaze* off Menado.

24-28 Jan   Mediterranean
British supply operation MF.4 to Malta. On 24 Jan the transport *Breconshire* sets out from Alexandria with Force B (Rear-Adm Vian), consisting of the cruisers *Naiad, Euryalus, Dido* and *Carlisle* and the destroyers *Griffin, Kelvin, Kipling, Arrow, Kingston, Jaguar,*

Hasty and *Isaac Sweers* (Dutch). On 25 Jan Force K—the cruiser *Penelope* (Capt Nicholl), destroyers *Zulu, Lance, Legion, Lively* and *Maori*—puts to sea from Malta with the empty transports *Glengyle* and *Rowallan Castle.* On 26 Jan the two convoys meet. The covering forces exchange the destroyers *Kingston* and *Lance* and the transports and return to Malta on 27 Jan and Alexandria on 28 Jan respectively. Attempted air attacks lead to no result.

24 Jan-2 Feb   Arctic
Allied convoy QP.6 proceeds with six ships from Murmansk to Britain.

25 Jan-7 Feb   Central Pacific
US carrier raid on Marshall and Gilbert Islands. On 25 Jan TF 8 (Vice-Adm Halsey) and TF 17 (Vice-Adm Fletcher) join up off Samoa to proceed northwards. When the submarine *Dolphin* reports the light defence of the Marshall Islands, Halsey deploys his Task Force on 27 Jan in three groups to attack on 1 Feb. TG.8.5, comprising the carrier *Enterprise* and the destroyers *Ralph Talbot, Blue* and *McCall,* carries out raids in two waves on the islands of Wotje, Maloelap and Kwajalein with a total of 18 torpedo aircraft and 46 dive bombers. Six of its aircraft are lost. The Japanese minelayer *Tokiwa,* the cruiser *Katori* and five auxiliary and transport ships are damaged: only one small auxiliary gunboat sinks. In counter-attacks by Japanese aircraft the *Enterprise* is slightly damaged. TG.8.1 (Rear-Adm Spruance), comprising the cruisers *Northampton* and *Salt Lake City* and the destroyer *Dunlap,* shells Wotje; and TG.8.3 (Capt Shock), comprising the cruiser *Chester* and the destroyers *Balch* and *Maury,* shells the island of Taroa in the Maloelap Atoll. The *Chester* is slightly damaged. TF 17, comprising the carrier *Yorktown,* the cruisers *Louisville* and *St Louis,* the destroyers *Hughes, Mahan, Russell, Sims* and *Walke,* carries out raids on Jaluit, Mili and Makin with 37 aircraft in all, losing six. The tankers *Platte* and *Sabine* refuel the ships.
As a counter-move against the US raid, the submarine cruisers *I-9, I-15, I-17, I-25, I-19, I-23* (sustains slight damage in an attack) and *I-26* are deployed from Kwajalein, and *I-71* and *I-72* from the

boats stationed in the area of Hawaii, but they do not approach. The 1st Carrier Air Fleet (Vice-Adm Nagumo) puts to sea from Truk with the carriers *Akagi, Kaga, Shokaku, Zuikaku,* the battleships *Hiyei* and *Kirishima,* the cruisers *Abukuma* and *Chikuma* and destroyers (see 14-25 Jan); but it is recalled on 4 Feb. The *Shokaku* and *Zuikaku* are ordered to home waters to stand on the alert for possible US raids; the remainder of the force arrives in Palau on 8 Feb.

26 Jan-3 Feb Mediterranean
In British submarine operations in the Central Mediterranean *P34/Ultimatum* (Lt Harrison) and *P35/Umbra* (Lt Maydon) each sink one ship of 3320 tons and 6142 tons respectively. In the Adriatic *Thorn* (Lt-Cdr Norfolk) sinks one ship of 4583 tons and the Italian submarine *Medusa;* and *Thunderbolt* (Lt-Cdr Crouch) sinks two ships of 5156 tons W of Greece.

26 Jan-26 Mar North Atlantic
On Hitler's orders six U-boats remain temporarily stationed in the area W of the Hebrides and Faeroes (see 14-24 Jan). In Feb *U653, U213, U136, U591, U455, U352* and *U752* participate and in Mar *U135, U553, U87, U753, U701, U569* and *U593.* Occasionally convoys are located, eg ONS.63 on 4 Feb near the Rockall Bank against which *U136, U213* and *U591* operate. Only *U136* (Lt-Cdr Zimmermann) is able to attack. She sinks the British corvette *Arbutus* on 5 Feb and misses a destroyer of the escort on 7 Feb. On 10 Feb *U591* (Lt-Cdr Zetzsche) sights the convoy SC.67 (21 ships and an escort of the Canadian corvettes *Spikenard, Dauphin, Louisbourg, Chilliwack, Shediac* and *Pictou*). She sinks one ship of 4028 tons and brings up *U136* which sinks the *Spikenard* on 11 Feb. On 22 Feb *U154* (Cdr Kölle), which is on the way to France, reports convoy HX.175 (26 ships and the US destroyers *Decatur, Leary* and *Simpson.*) On the morning of 23 Jan she makes four approaches and on the morning of 24 Jan two, but 14 torpedoes miss because of a failure in the range equipment. One destroyer and one steamer and, in the second case, several ships are missed by *U136* and *U752,* which are directed

to the scene, because of the ships' defensive manoeuvring. In individual operations *U569* (Lt Hinsch) sinks one ship of 984 tons and *U701* (Lt-Cdr Degen) three ships of 1253 tons and one unidentified vessel.

27 Jan-3 Feb Dutch East Indies
Japanese landing on Ambon. On 27 Jan five transports set out from Davao with one Japanese infantry regiment, escorted by the destroyers *Arashio* and *Michishio* (8th DD Div) and the submarine-chasers *Ch1* and *Ch2.* On 28 Jan Rear-Adm Tanaka, coming from Menado, with the cruiser *Jintsu,* the destroyers *Hatsushio* and *Hayashio* (2/15th DD Div), *Yukikaze, Tokitsukaze, Amatsukaze,* and *Hatsukaze* (16th DD Div) and six transports with a Kure Naval Landing Force, joins it. On 29 Jan Rear-Adm Fujita comes from Kendari with the seaplane carriers *Chitose* and *Mizuho,* the destroyers *Kuroshio* and *Oyashio* (1/15th DD Div), the minesweepers *W7, W8, W9, W11, W12,* the assault boats (ex-torpedo boats) *P34* and *P39.* The operation is covered in the Celebes Sea by Vice-Adm Takagi with the cruisers *Haguro* and *Nachi* and the destroyers *Akebono* and *Ikazuchi.* Whilst Rear-Adm Tanaka takes up a covering position in the SW with the *Jintsu, Tokitsukaze* and *Yukikaze,* six transports with *Amatsukaze, Hatsukaze, W9* and *W11* land troops in the N on 31 Jan. 15th DD Div makes a demonstration in the W and the remaining ships land the army units in the S of the island of Ambon. By 2 Feb the island is occupied despite resistance by a Dutch/Australian battle group. *W9* sinks on mines laid by the Dutch minelayer *Gouden Leeuw* at the end of Dec, and *W11* and *W12* are damaged.

27 Jan- 20 Feb South Asia
The US submarines *Seawolf, Seadragon, Sargo, Trout, Swordfish, Permit* and others are used for transport operations to Corregidor. The supplying by submarines is continued until the island falls on 8 May.

28 Jan-9 Feb Black Sea
In the night 28-29 Jan the Soviet destroyer *Bezuprechny* shells German positions near Feodosia. The Soviet flotilla leaders *Kharkov* and *Tashkent* transport supplies to Sevastopol from

31 Jan to 2 Feb and from 3 Feb to 4 Feb in co-operation with *Bezuprechny*. Before returning, they repeatedly shell land targets on the fronts near Sevastopol and on 4 Feb also near Feodosia. *Kharkov* carries out a further operation from 7 Feb to 9 Feb.

29 Jan   North Atlantic
U132 (Lt-Cdr Vogelsang), in an attack on a convoy, sinks the US coastguard cutter *Alexander Hamilton* off Reykjavik.

29 Jan-4 Feb   Mediterranean
The German U-boats *U431*, *U375*, *U73* and *U561*, despite many attacks, operate without success against British supply traffic to Tobruk.

31 Jan-3 Feb   North Atlantic
On 31 Jan the outward-bound *U105* (Cdr Schuch) encounters the convoy SL.93 W of the Bay of Biscay and sinks the sloop *Culver* from the escort, the first ship to be equipped with automatic HF/DF. *U105* has to turn back damaged.
On 31 Jan *U82* (Lt-Cdr Rollmann) sights an NA convoy consisting of two transports and two destroyers and sinks the British destroyer *Belmont*. *U556*, *U86* and *U575*, which are in the area, cannot come up by 3 Feb because of the high speed of the convoy.

31 Jan-6 Mar   South West Pacific
On 31 Jan TF 11 (Rear-Adm Brown) sets out from Pearl Habour with the carrier *Lexington*, the cruisers *Indianapolis*, *Minneapolis*, *Pensocola*, *San Francisco* and Desron 1 with the destroyers *Phelps*, *Clark*, *Patterson*, *Dewey*, *MacDonough*, *Hull*, *Aylwin*, *Dale*, *Bagley* and *Drayton* to cover the journey of two convoys from the Panama Canal into the SW Pacific. They consist of six transports with 4500 troops and supplies for Bora Bora, escorted by the cruisers *Concord* and *Trenton* with two destroyers; and eight transports with 20000 troops for Christmas, Canton and Nouméa. After completing this assignment, TF 11 is allocated to the ANZAC forces (Vice-Adm Leary, USN).
From 17 Feb TF 11 proceeds to the NW from the area of the New Hebrides in order to carry out a heavy carrier raid on Rabaul. But the force is reported on 20 Feb some 300 nautical miles ENE of Rabaul by Japanese four-engined flying-

boats (Emily)—two are shot down by the fighter cover. An attack by two squadrons each with nine carrier aircraft of the Japanese 25th Naval Air Flotilla from Rabaul is intercepted by the *Lexington*'s fighter cover: Lt O'Hare alone shoots down five planes. Rear-Adm Brown abandons the plan to attack and makes for the rendezvous with the tanker *Platte* on 23 Feb. She is accompanied by the ANZAC Force (Rear Adm Crace, RAN), comprising the cruisers *Achilles* (RNZN), *Australia* (RAN), *Chicago* (USN) and *Leander* (RNZN), and the destroyers *Flusser* and *Perkin*. (USN). The combined forces make a sortie into the Coral Sea from 27 Feb to 4 Mar and join up with the newly-arrived TF 17 on 6 Mar near the New Hebrides.

1-10 Feb   Arctic
Allied convoys PQ.9 and PQ.10 with ten ships leave Reykjavik together for Murmansk. Escort: destroyers *Faulknor* and *Intrepid* with several trawlers. Cover provided by cruiser *Nigeria*.

3-6 Feb   Dutch East Indies
On 3 Feb 26 bombers of the Japanese 23rd Naval Air Flotilla, based on Kendari, make an attack on Soerabaya for the first time with fighter protection. Following a reconaissance report by an Allied aircraft about the concentration of a Japanese landing force off Balikpapan ABDAFLOAT, Adm Hart, orders an Allied Force under the Dutch Rear-Adm Doorman to make a sortie towards the Makassar Strait. It sets out from Madoera in the night 3-4 Feb with the cruisers *De Ruyter* (F, Dutch), *Houston*, *Marblehead* (US), *Tromp* (Dutch) and the destroyers *Barker*, *Bulmer*, *Edwards*, *Stewart* (US), *Banckert*, *Piet Hein* and *Van Ghent* (Dutch). The force is sighted on the morning of 4 Feb north of Bali by a Japanese formation of 37 bombers with fighter protection as it flies to Soerabaya and it is attacked. The *Marblehead* (Capt Robinson) is badly damaged by hits and many near-misses and only reaches Tjilatjap by steering her with propellers. The *Houston* loses her third 8in turret. The other ships are unharmed despite near misses but they turn back and reach port on 5-6 Feb.
The US submarine *Salmon* (Lt Mc-

Kinney) torpedoes the Japanese destroyer *Suzukaze* off Kendari on 4 Feb.

4-18 Feb   Dutch East Indies
Of the Japanese 4th SM Flotilla *I-55* (Cdr Nakajima) sinks two ships of 6456 tons in the area of Makassar and the Java Sea and two more sinkings are unconfirmed. *I-56* (Cdr Ohashi) sinks one ship of 979 tons and one other unidentified vessel in Sunda Strait.

5-7 Feb   Dutch East Indies
To cover a Dutch reinforcement mission with two transports, escorted by the cruiser *Java* from Batavia to Palembang, a British force comprising the cruiser *Exeter* and the destroyers *Encounter* and *Jupiter*, strengthened by the Australian cruiser *Hobart*, makes a sortie from Sunda Strait through Banka Strait. On the return the force is unsuccessfully attacked NW of Sunda Strait by the Japanese submarine *Ro-34* (Lt-Cdr Ota). *Ro-34* (Lt-Cdr Ota) misses a Dutch destroyer.
At this time the cruisers *Canberra*, *Cornwall*, *Danae*, *Dragon* and *Durban*, the destroyer *Electra* and the sloops *Sutlej* and *Yarra* operate in convoy service between Ceylon and Sunda Strait.

5-15 Feb   Mediterranean
In British submarine operations *Upholder* (Lt-Cdr Wanklyn) sinks one ship of 2710 tons E of Sardinia; *Una* (Lt Norman) one ship of 8106 tons off Cotrone; and *P38* (Lt Hemingway) one ship of 4116 tons in a convoy escorted by the Italian destroyer *Premuda* and the torpedo boat *Polluce* off the Tunisian coast. In an attempt to attack a convoy off Cephalonia *Proteus* is damaged by the Italian torpedo boat *Sagittario*. On 13 Feb *Tempest* is forced to surface in the Gulf of Taranto by the Italian torpedo boat *Circe* (Cdr Palmas) and sinks when an attempt is made to take her in tow.

6 Feb   North Atlantic
The U-boat *U82*, which is on her way from the US coast, encounters the convoy OS.18 and is sunk by depth charges from the sloop *Rochester* and the corvette *Tamarisk*.

6-9 Feb   Dutch East Indies
Japanese landing near Makassar (Celebes). On 6 Feb Rear-Adm Kubo sets out from Kendari with the cruiser *Nagara*, three fast assault boats and two submarine-chasers of the 1st BF and six transports with the Sasebo Special Landing Force on board. Escort: minesweepers *W7* and *W8*, destroyers *Asashio*, *Oshio*, *Michishio*, *Arashio* (8th DD Div), *Kuroshio*, *Oyashio*, *Hayashio*, *Natsushio* (15th DD Div), *Hatsushimo*, *Nenohi* and *Wakaba* (21st DD Div). On 8 Feb the force arrives off Makassar, where the US submarine *S37* (Lt Dempsey) sinks the destroyers *Natsushio*. In addition, the destroyer *Kawakaze*, *Umikaze* (1/24th DD Div), *Minegumo* and *Natsugumo* (9th DD Div) and the minesweepers *W15*, *W16*, *W17* and *W18* under Rear-Adm Hirose come from Balikpapan to support the landing. Air escort for the operation is provided by the 11th Carrier Sqdn (Rear-Adm Fujita) with the seaplane-carriers *Chitose* and *Mizuho* and the depot ship *Sanyo Maru*. A covering force is provided (by Vice-Adm Takagi) with the cruisers *Haguro* and *Nachi* and the destroyers *Akebono* and *Ikazuchi*. The landing succeeds against slight resistance. A sortie made by the Dutch Rear-Adm Doorman with the cruisers *De Ruyter*, *Tromp* and two destroyers is abandoned on 8 Feb shortly after they set out.

6-23 Feb   Arctic
Allied convoy PQ.11 with 13 ships leaves Loch Ewe for Murmansk.

7-8 Feb   Mediterranean
The British destroyers *Lively* and *Zulu* sink two small Italian independents of 816 tons in a sortie W of Sicily.

7-15 Feb   South Asia
Final battle for Singapore. In the night 7-8 Feb a battle group of the Japanese Guards Div lands on the island of Ubin in the eastern part of the Johore Strait.
On 8 Feb the artillery of the 25th Army begins to shell Singapore, while bombers of the 3rd Air Division simultaneously attack the British positions. In the night of 9 Feb the Japanese 5th and 18th Inf Divs cross the Johore Strait and they are followed on the next night by the Guards Div from Johore-Bharu. Supported by two armoured regiments, the Japanese force the British back in to the city of Singapore by 15 Feb. On the evening of the same day Lt-Gen Percival, who is responsible for the

defence, surrenders to the Commander of the 25th Army, Lt-Gen Yamashita.

8-9 Feb   North Atlantic
U85 and U654 (Lt Forster) attack the convoy ONS.61 off Newfoundland. U654 sinks the Free French corvette Alysse.

8 Feb-8 Mar   Pacific
Japanese submarines I-9, I-17 and I-23 operate from 8 Feb to 15 Feb S of Oahu. I-17 (Cdr*Nishino) then proceeds to the American West Coast. On 20 Feb she observes San Diego; on 23-24 Feb she shells Elwood in California; and on 1 Mar she unsuccessfully attacks the tanker William H. Berg (8298 tons) off San Francisco. I-23 disappears after 14 Feb. I-9 (Cdr*Fujii) reconnoitres over Pearl Harbour with her aircraft on 24 Feb. On 26 Feb I-15, I-19 and I-26, after being equipped as flying-boat suppliers, set out from Kwajalein to the French Frigate Shoals and supply there on 3-4 Mar two four-engined flying-boats on their flight from Wotje to attack Pearl Harbour. The bombs miss. On 7 Mar I-15 (Cdr*Ishikawa) sights US TF 8 with the carrier Enterprise returning from the raid on Marcus, but the other boats do not come up.

9 Feb   Mediterranean
German bombers badly damage the British destroyer Farndale W of Mersa Matruh.

9 Feb   Western Atlantic
The US troop transport Lafayette (ex-Normandie), 83423 tons, is burnt out and capsizes in New York Harbour.

9-11 Feb   Mediterranean
The British cruiser Cleopatra is transferred with the destroyer Fortune from Gibraltar to Malta.

9-17 Feb   Dutch East Indies
Japanese landings near Palembang. On 9 Feb an advance detachment of the Japanese 38th Inf Div on board eight transports sets out from Camranh Bay. It is escorted by Rear-Adm Hashimoto with the cruiser Sendai and the destroyers Fubuki, Amagiri, Yugiri and Asagiri, the minesweepers W1, W2, W3, W4, W5 and the submarine-chasers Ch7 and Ch8. On 10 Feb Vice-Adm Ozawa follows with the covering group of the Western Force, comprising the cruisers Chokai, Kumano, Mikuma,

Mogami, Suzuya, the destroyers Uranami, Isonami, Ayanami, the cruiser Yura and the carrier Ryujo with the destroyer Shikinami. On 11 Feb the bulk of the 229th Inf Regt and one battalion of the 230th Inf Regt put to sea on board 13 smaller transports. Escorts: the cruiser Kashii (Capt Kojima), the frigate Shimushu, the destroyers Shirayuki, Hatsuyuki, Murakumo. Shirakumo and the submarine-chaser Ch9.
The Dutch submarines K-XI, K-XII, K-XIII and K-XIV, which have been stationed both sides of the Anambas against such operations, do not approach. On 11 Feb an Allied reconnaissance aircraft sights the invasion fleet. At this point many small craft as well as 13 larger merchant ships, the transports Empire Star and Gorgon, the auxiliary ship Kedah and the British cruiser Durban and the destroyers Jupiter and Stronghold, loaded with refugees from Singapore, now threatened from the mainland, are proceeding to Sumatra and Java. On 11-12 Feb two auxiliary ships, 12 steamers and a convoy with six large tankers, coming from Palembang, join the convoys. They are accompanied by the Australian minesweeping corvettes Wollongong, Bendigo, Toowoomba and Ballarat.
Carrier aircraft from the Ryujo and shore-based bombers with fighter protection from the Genzan Air Corps are deployed by the Japanese against shipping concentrations. On 13 Feb the large tankers Manvantara (8237 tons) and Merula (8277 tons), the steamer Subadar (5424 tons) and many smaller ships fall victim. The transport Anglo-Indian (5609 tons), the Empire Star (12656 tons), and the tanker Seirstad (9916 tons) are badly damaged. From the Japanese submarines of the 4th Flotilla deployed against the evacuations and as cover, I-55 (Lt-Cdr Nakajima) sinks the ammunition transport Derrymore (4799 tons) north of Sunda Strait and I-56 (Lt-Cdr Ohashi) torpedoes a ship from the convoys JS.1 and SJ.1 escorted by the cruisers Exeter, Hobart and Java, the destroyer Electra and the sloop Jumna S of Sunda Strait.
While in the night 13-14 Feb the Japanese advance detachment enters the Banka Strait, an Allied Striking Force

(Rear-Adm Doorman), comprising the cruisers *De Ruyter, Java, Tromp* (Dutch), *Exeter* (British) and *Hobart* (Australian) and the destroyers *Banckert, Kortenaer, Piet Hein, Van Ghent* (Dutch), *Barker, Bulmer, John D. Edwards, Parrott, Pillsbury* and *Stewart* (US), puts to sea from Batavia to attack. It is located on the morning of 14 Feb by Japanese air reconnaissance and throughout the day attacked by carrier aircraft from the *Ryujo* and shore-based aircraft S of Banka Island, without significant hits being obtained. Only the *Barker* and *Bulmer* drop out because of numerous near-misses. The *Van Ghent* is lost on the way out when she goes aground.

Because of the threat from the Allied squadron, Adm Ozawa orders the advance detachment to anchor off Muntok (Banka) and the main body to withdraw to the NE. At the same time he tries with all his operational ships to close in on the Allied squadron which, however, gets away. But many of the smaller evacuation transports fall victim to his ships and aircraft.

Early on 14 Feb Japanese transport aircraft land 460 parachute troops to capture the airfield N of Palembang and the refinery and oil fields of Pladjoe to the E of it. Against tough resistance the Japanese can only just hold on with their remaining forces. Air attacks by 36 Hudson and Blenheim bombers with 22 Hurricane fighters on the invasion force off Muntok on 14 Feb sink the transport *Inabasan Maru* (989 tons) and hold up the advance of the Japanese assault boats on the Moesie River on the way to Palembang on 15 Feb. After the Allied Striking Force has gone away, the main Japanese force arrives and lands with the result that Palembang has to be evacuated on 16 Feb.

9-20 Feb   Indian Ocean
Off Ceylon the Japanese submarines *I-65* (Lt-Cdr Harada) and *I-66* (Cdr Yoshitome) sink two ships of 9960 tons (and probably one more unknown ship) and one ship of 2076 tons respectively.

9-28 Feb   Pacific
Off the east coast of Japan the US submarine *Trout* (Lt-Cdr Fenno) sinks three ships of 9542 tons; *Triton* (Lt-Cdr Lent) sinks three ships of 8638 tons;

and *Cuttlefish* (Lt-Cdr Hottel) damages one ship of 6515 tons.

10 Feb-20 Mar   Western Atlantic
A third wave of 15 U-boats operates singly in the area between Newfoundland and Cape Hatteras, including the six boats which participate in the operation against the convoy ONS.67 (21-25 Feb). The following are the successes achieved solely on the American East Coast: *U432* (Lt-Cdr Schultze) sinks five ships of 24987 tons; *U504* (Cdr Poske) four ships of 26561 tons; *U96* (Cdr Lehmann-Willenbrock) five ships of 25464 tons; *U69* (Lt-Cdr Zahn) has no success; *U578* (Cdr Rehwinkel) two ships of 10540 tons and the destroyer *Jacob Jones;* *U653* (Lt-Cdr Feiler) one ship of 1582 tons; *U656* (Lt-Cdr Kröning) is lost on 1 Mar, having achieved no success; *U404* (Lt-Cdr v. Bülow) four ships of 22653 tons; *U94* (Lt Ites) four ships of 14442 tons; *U558* (Lt-Cdr Krech) has successes only with convoy ONS.67; *U587* (Lt-Cdr Borcherdt) two ships of 6619 tons; *U155* (Lt-Cdr Piening) one ship of 7874 tons; *U158* (Lt-Cdr Rostin) three ships of 21202 tons and torpedoes one ship of 7118 tons.

10-25 Feb   Mediterranean
The German U-boats *U652, U83, U81* and *U559*, despite many attacks, operate without success against British supply traffic for Tobruk.

11 Feb   Western Atlantic
American troops occupy Curaçao and Aruba (Dutch West Indies).

12 Feb   English Channel
Operation 'Cerberus'. After several weeks of mine-sweeping work by the 1st, 2nd, 4th, 5th and 12th MS Flotillas and the 2nd, 3rd and 4th MMS Flotillas in the Channel and in the southern North Sea, in which *M1208* is lost in the night 10-11 Feb off Barfleur, the battleships *Scharnhorst* (Capt Hoffmann with the Commander Battleships, Vice-Adm Ciliax on board), the *Gneisenau* (Capt Fein) and the heavy cruiser *Prinz Eugen* (Capt Brinkmann) set out from Brest on the night of 11-12 Feb. Escort provided by the destroyers *Z29* (with the Officer Commanding Destroyers, Rear-Adm Bey, on board), *Richard Beitzen* (with the Commander 5th DD Flotilla, Capt Berger, on board),

Z25, *Paul Jacobi*, *Friedrich Ihn* and *Hermann Schoemann*. Later the 2nd TB Flotilla (Cdr Erdmann), comprising *T2*, *T4*, *T5*, *T11* and *T12* from Le Havre and the 3rd TB Flotilla (Cdr Wilcke), comprising *T13*, *T15*, *T16* and *T17*, from Dunkirk, join the force. In addition, the 5th TB Flotilla (Cdr* Schmidt), consisting of *Seeadler*, *Falke*, *Kondor*, *Iltis* and *Jaguar*, joins them in the area of Cape Gris Nez. Beyond this, units of Commander Naval Defence Forces West and, later, Commander Naval Forces North and the MTB Flotillas 2 (Lt-Cdr Feldt), 4 (Lt-Cdr Bätge) and 6 (Lt-Cdr Obermaier) form part of the Force's escort. Air Fleet 3 (Field Marshal Sperrle) makes 176 heavy bombers and fighter aircraft available (chiefly J.G. 2 and 26 and later J.G. 1) for air protection, of which at least 16 machines are able to fly constantly over the naval force. The German force is first discovered in the area of Le Touquet and unsuccessfully shelled by British coastal batteries. From Dover five MTBs (Cdr Pumphrey) and from Ramsgate three MTBs (Lt-Cdr Long) put to sea. Their torpedo attacks are unsuccessful. Three boats are damaged. The Swordfish Sqdn No 825 (Cdr Esmonde†) which is on the spot, attacks the German ships in the area of Gravelines; all six torpedo aircraft are shot down. Many bombers and torpedo aircraft which are later sent in fail to find their targets. They sink the patrol ship *V1302* and damage the torpedo boats *T13* and *Jaguar*. Finally, a destroyer force from Harwich (21st DD Flotilla, Capt Pizey), comprising *Campbell* and *Vivacious*, and, under command, the 16th DD Flotilla (Capt Wright), comprising *Worcester*, *Whitshed* and *Walpole*, succeeds in approaching the German force; but these destroyer attacks also fail in the heavy defensive fire. *Worcester* is set on fire and reaches harbour with difficulty. On the way *Scharnhorst* hits two mines and *Gneisenau* one; but they are able to reach Wilhelmshaven and the Elbe estuary respectively under their own steam.

12 Feb South West Pacific

Formation of the Anzac Squadron (Rear-Adm Crace), consisting of the cruisers *Australia* (Australian), *Chicago* (US), *Achilles* and *Leander* (New Zealand) and the destroyers *Lamson* and *Perkins* (US) in Suva (Fiji).

12-16 Feb Mediterranean

British supply operation MF.5 to Malta. On 12 Dec the convoys MW.9A (transports *Clan Campbell* and *Clan Chattan*, escorted by the cruiser *Carlisle*, the destroyers *Lance*, *Heythrop*, *Avon Vale* and *Eridge*) and MW.9B (transport *Rowallan Castle*, escorted by the destroyers *Beaufort*, *Dulverton*, *Hurworth* and *Southwold*) set out from Alexandria with a small interval between them. They are followed by the covering group Force B (Rear-Adm Vian), comprising the cruisers *Naiad*, *Dido* and *Euryalus* and the destroyers *Jervis*, *Kipling*, *Kelvin*, *Jaguar*, *Griffin*, *Havock*, *Hasty* and *Arrow*. In a German air attack on Malta the destroyer *Maori* is sunk by bomb hits. On 13 Feb Force K, consisting of the cruiser *Penelope* and destroyers *Zulu*, *Sikh*, *Legion*, *Lively*, *Fortune* and *Decoy*, puts to sea from Malta with convoy ME.10 (the transports *Ajax*, *Breconshire*, *Clan Fergusson* and *City of Calcutta*). On 13 Feb German and Italian air reconnaissance locates the west-bound forces and the *Clan Campbell* (7255 tons) has to put into Tobruk after being hit by a bomb. Shortly before the convoys MW.9 and ME.10 join up on 14 Feb, the first is again attacked by German bombers: the *Clan Chattan* (7262 tons) is so badly hit that she has to be scuttled. After the convoys have joined up, the *Rowallan Castle* (7798 tons) also sinks after bomb hits. The covering forces, after exchanging the destroyer *Lance* for the *Decoy* and *Fortune*, start the return journey. Div-Adm Bergamini sets out to sea to search for the British forces from Taranto with the battleship *Duilio*, the cruisers *Duca d'Aosta*, *Montecuccoli* and the destroyers *Folgore*, *Fulmine*, *Saetta*, *Alpino*, *Carabiniere*, *Fuciliere* and *Bersagliere* and Div-Adm Parona from Messina with the heavy cruisers *Gorizia* and *Trento* and the destroyers *Aviere*, *Geniere*, *Camicia Nera* and *Ascari*. But the search produces no results on 15 Feb. Force K, with *Penelope*, *Lance* and *Legion*, reaches Malta on this day and *Zulu*, *Sikh* and

Lively proceed with Force B to Alexandria where they arrive on 16 Feb. The British submarine *P36* (Lt Edmonds) torpedoes the destroyer *Carabiniere* from the returning Italian forces off Taranto; but she is taken in tow.

12-22 Feb   Arctic

The Allied convoy QP.7 proceeds with eight ships from Murmansk to Seidisfjord, escorted by the destroyers *Faulknor* and *Intrepid*. Cover is provided by the cruiser *Nigeria*.

13-14 Feb   Black Sea

On 13 Feb and 14 Feb respectively the Soviet cruisers *Komintern* and *Krasny Krym*, accompanied by the destroyers *Dzerzhinski* and *Shaumyan* bring 2109 reserve troops to Sevastopol.

14 Feb-10 Mar   Central Pacific

US carrier raids on Wake and Marcus. On 14 Feb TF 8 (Vice-Adm Halsey) sets out from Pearl Harbour with the carrier *Enterprise*, the cruisers *Northhampton* (Rear-Adm Spruance) and *Salt Lake City* and Desron 6, comprising the destroyers *Balch, Maury, Craven, Dunlap, Blue* and *Ralph Talbot* and the escort tanker *Sabine*. On 24 Feb 36 bombers, accompanied by six fighters, make a raid on Wake (one plane lost); then the island is shelled by *Northampton, Salt Lake City, Balch* and *Maury*. On 4 Mar the *Enterprise* makes a similar raid on the island of Marcus, lying further to the W (one plane lost). TF 17 (Vice-Adm Fletcher), which sets out on 16 Feb to make a raid on Eniwetok Atoll (Carolines) and which consists of the carrier *Yorktown*, the cruisers *Astoria* and *Louisville*, the destroyers *Sims, Hughes, Walke, Russell, Anderson* and *Hammann* and the escort tanker *Guadeloupe*, has to be recalled to undertake very urgent convoy covering duties on the route to the SW Pacific. From 17 Feb it proceeds via the Phoenix Islands (21-28 Feb) to the New Hebrides, where on 6 Mar it joins up with TF 11.

15-24 Feb   Dutch East Indies

Japanese attacks on Port Darwin, Timor and Bali.

To counter the growing threat to Timor an Allied convoy of four transports, escorted by the US cruiser *Houston*, the US destroyer *Peary* and the Australian sloops *Swan* and *Warrego*, tries on 15 Feb to bring reinforcements from Port Darwin to Timor. After an air attack by 36 Japanese naval bombers from Kendari (Celebes) on the force on 16 Feb, it is recalled and arrives back in Port Darwin on 17 Feb. The Dutch Vice-Adm Helfrich, who is appointed ABDAFLOAT in place of the US Adm Hart on 16 Feb, takes those ships which are still operational and are being used to cover the evacuation from Southern Sumatra in the area of the Sunda Strait to the E. The *Houston* is ordered to proceed at high speed to Tjilatjap to join Rear-Adm Doorman's forces.

Japanese carrier raid on Port Darwin. On 15 Feb the 1st Carrier Air Fleet (Vice-Adm Nagumo) sets out from Palau with the carriers *Akagi, Kaga* (1st Carrier Sqdn), *Hiryu* and *Soryu* (2nd Carrier Sqdn), the battleships *Kirishima* and *Hiyei* (1/3rd BB Sqdn), the heavy cruisers *Chikuma* and *Tone* (8th Cruiser Sqdn) and the 1st DD Flotilla with the cruiser *Abukuma* and the destroyers *Urakaze, Isokaze, Tanikaze, Hamakaze* (17th DD Div), *Kasumi, Arare, Kagero, Shiranuhi* (18th DD Div) and *Akigumo*. It proceeds westwards past Halmahera and Ambon into the Banda Sea. There, early on 19 Feb it flies off 71 dive-bombers and 81 torpedo bombers with 36 fighters to attack the North Australian harbour of Port Darwin. The US destroyer *Peary* and seven large transports and merchant ships of 43429 tons are destroyed and, in addition, four small defence and harbour craft. The Australian sloop *Swan*, the US aircraft tender *William B. Preston* and six large transports and merchant ships are damaged. On 21 Feb the Japanese force returns to Kendari (Celebes). On the same day Vice-Adm Kondo, who sets out from Palau on 18 Feb, arrives there with the Japanese Main Force. He has in his force the heavy cruisers *Atago, Maya* and *Takao* (4th Cruiser Sqdn), the battleships *Haruna* and *Kongo* (2/3rd BB Sqdn) and the destroyers *Nowake, Hagikaze, Maikaze, Arashi* (4th DD Div), *Akatsuki* and *Hibiki* (1/6th DD Div).

Landing on Bali/battle in the Bandoeng Strait. On 17 Feb a Japanese advance detachment sets out from Makassar, comprising the transports *Sagami Maru*

(7189 tons) and *Sasago Maru* (8260 tons) with one battalion of the 48th Inf Div on board, escorted by the destroyers *Oshio, Asashio, Michishio* and *Arashio* (8th DD Div). North of Bali Rear-Adm Kubo, with the cruiser *Nagara* and the destroyers *Wakaba, Hatsushimo* and *Nenohi* (21st DD Div), acts as a covering force. The invasion force arrives on the evening of 18 Feb and lands the troops early on 19 Feb without resistance. In an air attack by Dutch planes both transports are slightly damaged. Torpedo attacks by the submarine *Seawolf* (US) and *Truant* (British) fail as a result of defects and misses.

When air reconnaissance reports the force, the Dutch Rear-Adm Doorman sets out on the evening of 18 Feb from Tjilatjap (South Java) with the cruisers *De Ruyter* and *Java* and the destroyers *Kortenaer, Piet Hein* (Dutch), *Ford* and *Pope* (US) to attack the invasion fleet. In addition, the Dutch cruiser *Tromp* sets out from Soerabaya with the US destroyers *Stewart, Parrott, John D. Edwards* and *Pillsbury*. Rear-Adm Doorman's force, which arrives first in the late evening of 19 Feb after the withdrawal of the remaining Japanese ships in the Bandoeng Strait, only encounters the *Sasago Maru* which is hit several times by the guns of the *Java*. The *Asashio* and *Oshio* sink the *Piet Hein* in a confused engagement. Shortly after midnight on 20 Feb the second Allied force attacks but all 20 torpedoes fired by the US destroyers miss. In the gun engagement the *Stewart* and *Tromp*, as well as the *Oshio*, sustain damage. One hour later the Japanese destroyers *Asashio* and *Michishio*, which are recalled, again find the withdrawing Allied force. In a fierce engagement the *Michishio* is shelled and becomes unmanoeuvrable and the *Tromp* receives heavy hits from the *Arashio*. Five Dutch motor torpedo boats, directed to the Japanese force, do not find their targets.

In attacks by shore-based Japanese naval air units the Dutch destroyer *Van Nes* is destroyed on 18 Feb in the Sunda Straight and the coastal defence ship *Soerabaja* and the submarine *K-XII* in Soerabaya.

Japanese landing on Timor. On 17 Feb the seaplane-carrier *Mizuho* sets out from Kendari with a submarine-chaser for the Flores Sea to reconnoitre for the Timor and Port Darwin operations. On the same day nine transports with the 228th Inf Regt and the 3rd Yokosuka Special Air Landing Force put to sea from Ambon, escorted by Rear-Adm Tanaka with the cruiser *Jintsu* and the destroyers *Yukikaze, Tokitsukaze, Amatsukaze, Hatsukaze* (16th DD Div), *Kuroshio, Oyashio, Hayashio* (15th DD Div) and *Umikaze*. On 18 Feb a second force of five transports follows, escorted by the destroyers *Kawakaze* and *Yamakaze* (1/24th DD Div), the minesweepers *W7, W8*, the fast transports *P1, P2, P34* and submarine-chasers. Rear-Adm Takagi provides cover for the operation in the Timor Sea with the heavy cruisers *Haguro* and *Nachi* (5th Cruiser Sqdn) and the destroyers *Akebono* and *Ikazuchi*. Early on 20 Feb the landings succeed in Dili (Portuguese Timor) and Koepang (Dutch Timor). An attack by the US submarine *Pike* on the minesweeper *W7* fails. On 24 Feb all key points in Timor are occupied and the Japanese forces return to Makassar, Ambon and Kendari.

15 Feb-3 Mar   Arctic
Off Tanafjord on 15 Feb the Soviet submarine *S-101* (Capt 3rd Class Vekke with the Div Commander, Capt 3rd Class Khomyakov, on board) sinks the Norwegian steamer *Mimona* (1147 tons) from a convoy. On the way to laying out the first flanking mine barrages to protect German supplies from Soviet submarine attacks the minelayer *Brummer* (Cdr* Dr Tobias) sights in the mist off Porsangerfjord on 18 Feb the surfaced Soviet submarine *Shch-403* (Lt-Cdr Kovalenko) which narrowly evades being rammed by the minelayer but is then lightly rammed by *M1503* (Sub-Lt Abel). The Commander is rescued from the sinking conning tower of the submarine. But the crew saves the submarine and brings her back to Murmansk. On 19 Feb *M-171* (Lt-Cdr Starikov) attacks a convoy, misses two steamers and is attacked by depth charges from the submarine-chasers *UJ1205* and *UJ1214*. The *Shch-402*

(Capt 3rd Class Stolbov), which has come into Porsangerfjord as a relief, sinks the patrol boat *NM01-Vandale* on 27 Feb, misses a convoy on 1 Mar and is severely damaged by the submarine-chasers *UJ1102* and *UJ1105* on 3 Mar. Because the submarine-chasers withdraw with the minesweeping ship *Paris*, the *K-21* (Capt 3rd Class Lunin), which is sent to give help, is able to meet the disabled *Shch-402* and bring her to Polyarnoe.

16 Feb-18 Mar   Western Atlantic
Operation 'Neuland': simultaneous attack on the oil terminal ports at Aruba (*U156*), Curaçao (*U67*) and Maracaibo/Venezuela (*U502*) on 16 Feb. On 19 Feb *U161* enters Port of Spain (Trinidad) and on 10 Mar Port Castries (St Lucia) and torpedoes ships lying along the pier. *U129* operates on the Guiana coast and the other boats, after their attacks, in the Caribbean. Their total successes: *U67* (Lt-Cdr Müller-Stöckheim) sinks one ship of 8436 tons and damages two ships of 12210 tons; *U156* (Cdr Hartenstein) sinks five ships of 22723 tons and damages two ships of 10769 tons; *U502* (Lt-Cdr von Rosenstiel) sinks five ships of 25232 tons, damages one ship of 9002 tons and has one more certain but unidentified success; *U129* (Lt-Cdr Clausen) sinks seven ships of 25613 tons; *U161* (Lt-Cdr Achilles) sinks four ships of 26903 tons and the US coastal guard ship *Acacia* and torpedoes four ships of 30511 tons in harbour.

17 Feb-23 Mar   Pacific
Reconnaissance operation by the Japanese submarine *I-25* (Cdr* Tagami) in the South Pacific. With her aircraft (Chief Petty Officer Fujita) she reconnoitres over Sydney (17 Feb), Melbourne (26 Feb), Hobart (1 Mar), Wellington (8 Mar), Suva/Samoa (19 Mar) and, with periscope, Pago Pago (23 Mar).

17-24 Feb   Dutch East Indies
Japanese forces prepare to attack Java. Eastern Force: from 17 Feb to 18 Feb light escort forces are transferred from Jolo to Balikpapan. From 19 Feb to 22 Feb the main body with the 48th Inf Div on 41 transports proceeds from Jolo to Balikpapan. Escort provided by the 4th DD Flotilla (Rear-Adm Nishimura—see 25 Feb-9 Mar for

composition of forces). On 21 Feb they are reported by a US submarine. In Balikpapan the 56th Regimental Combat Group is embarked.
Western Force: on 8 Feb Vice-Adm Ozawa puts to sea from Camranh Bay with the main force—HQ 16th Army, the 2nd Inf Div and the 230th Inf Regt of the 38th Inf Div—on board 56 transports. Escort: the 5th DD Flotilla (Rear-Adm Hara). On 21 Feb the 3rd DD Flotilla (Rear-Adm Hashimoto) and the 1st MS Div come up from the Anamba Islands. On 22 Feb the invasion, fixed for 26 Feb, is postponed for two days when Allied naval forces are sighted by Japanese air reconnaissance. The Western Force cruises in the area of the Anamba Islands (Flagship cruiser *Chokai*, the destroyer *Ayanami* out of action on going ashore) and the Eastern Force off Balikpapan. On 24 Feb the Western Force is reported by the US submarine *Saury*.

18 Feb   Western Atlantic
The large French submarine *Surcouf* (2880/4300 tons) sinks near the Antilles after collision with an American freighter.

20 Feb-24 Mar   Western Atlantic
Four Italian submarines ('Da Vinci' group) operate E of the Antilles and make the following sinkings: *Torelli* (Cdr de Giacomo) two ships of 16469 tons; *Finzi* (Cdr Giudice) three ships of 21496 tons; *Tazzoli* (Cdr Fecia di Cossato) six ships of 29198 tons; and *Morosini* (Cdr Fraternale) three ships of 22048 tons.

21-23 Feb   Norway
The pocket-battleship *Admiral Scheer* and heavy cruisers *Prinz Eugen*, escorted by the destroyers *Z25*, *Hermann Schoemann* and *Friedrich Ihn*, are transferred from Brunsbüttelkoog to Norway. British reconnaissance aircraft locate the ships in the southern North Sea, but an aircraft, maintaining contact, is shot down by fighters. Of the British aircraft which are then deployed only one bomber finds the force. It drops its bombs near *Prinz Eugen* and is shot down by the ships AA guns. 22 Feb: British reconnaissance aircraft again locate the force as it enters and anchors in Grimstadfjord, from where it sets out again on the same evening. 23 Feb: from a British submarine

group (four boats), stationed off Trondheim, the *Trident* (Cdr Sladen) approaches the force in the morning and gets a heavy torpedo hit on the stern of *Prinz Eugen*. An attempt by the British Home Fleet (Adm Tovey) with the aircraft carrier *Victorious*, the heavy cruiser *Berwick* and four destroyers—and the battleship *King George V* as cover—to intercept the German ships on their way N fails. The British force had put to sea to attack German shipping off Tromsö.

21-23 Feb   Mediterranean

Italian operation K.7 with two convoys from Messina and Corfu to Tripoli. One convoy of three ships escorted by the destroyers *Vivaldi*, *Malocello*, *Premuda*, *Zeno*, *Strale* and the torpedo boat *Pallade;* and one convoy of three ships escorted by the destroyers *Pigafetta*, *Pessagno*, *Usodimare*, *Maestrale*, *Scirocco* and the torpedo boat *Circe*. Distant cover: cruisers *Bande Nere*, *Gorizia*, *Trento*, destroyers *Alpino*, *Da Noli*, *Oriani* and battleship *Duilio* with destroyers *Ascari*, *Aviere*, *Camicia Nera* and *Geniere*. Air attacks are repelled on 22 Feb by German fighter protection. An attempted attack by the British submarine *P38* ends with the sinking of the boat by *Circe* and *Usodimare*.

21-25 Feb   North Atlantic

U155 (Lt-Cdr Piening) locates on 21 Feb, some 600 nautical miles NE of Cape Race, the convoy ON.67 which consists of 36 ships and is escorted by a US Escort Group (Cdr Murdaugh), comprising the destroyers *Edison*, *Nicholson*, *Lea*, *Bernadou* and the Canadian corvette HMCS *Algoma*. For the first time contact signals are located by the rescue ship *Toward* fitted with a short wave D/F ('Huff-Duff'). But *U155* is able to evade the search by *Lea*, which is not yet equipped with radar, and in the night 21-22 Feb sinks two ships of 9783 tons. On the basis of her reports, the outward-bound U-boats *U587*, *U558*, *U94*, *U588* and *U158* are directed to the convoy. On the morning of 24 Feb *U558* (Lt-Cdr Krech), in three approaches, torpedoes four ships of 27508 tons of which two sink at once and the other two later. *U158* (Lt-Cdr Rostin) torpedoes two stray tankers of which one (8032 tons) sinks

and the other (8146 tons) is taken in tow. *U587* (Lt-Cdr Borcherdt) torpedoes one tanker of 9432 tons which *U558* later finishes off.

22 Feb   Black Sea

Soviet cruiser *Krasny Krym* and destroyer *Boiki* bring supplies to Sevastopol and shell land targets.

22 Feb-1 Mar   Indian Ocean

In operations against the evacuation from Java the Japanese submarines sinks twelve ships south of the Dutch East Indies Archipelago. *I-58* (Cdr Kitamura) sink two ships of 10117 tons and torpedoes one other of 6735 tons; *I-53* (Cdr Nakamura) sinks three ships of 11002 tons; *I-54* (Cdr Kobayashi) one ship of 8806 tons; *I-7* (Cdr* Koizumi) one ship of 3271 tons; *I-1* (Cdr* Ankyu) one ship of 8667 tons; *I-2* (Cdr* Inada) one ship of 4360 tons; *I-3* (Cdr* Tonozuka) one unknown, medium-sized ship; *I-4* (Cdr* Nakagawa) one ship of 1693 tons; *I-59* (Cdr Yoshimatsu) one ship of 1035 tons. *I-121* operates in the Timor Sea, *I-122* in the Arafura Sea and *Ro-33* and *Ro-34* S of Java without success. *I-123* lays a mine barrage in the Torres Strait.

23 Feb   South Asia

General MacArthur, the C-in-C on the Philippines, receives orders from President Roosevelt to proceed to Australia and to take over the command of Allied forces there. General Wainwright becomes the new C-in-C on the Philippines.

24 Feb   Black Sea

In operations against German and Rumanian shipping between the Bosphorus and Constanza the Soviet submarine *Shch-213* (Lt-Cdr Isaev) sinks just N of the Bosphorus the Bulgarian steamer *Struma* sailing under the Panamanian flag with 764 Jewish refugees on board of whom only one is saved. The ship had set out from Constanza on 12 Dec with 769 refugees and had arrived in the Bosphorus on 16 Dec. The landing of the refugees and the continued journey of the ship were forbidden by the Turkish authorities because the British mandatory government in Palestine did not grant immigration visas. Only five refugees were allowed on land. On 24 Feb the Turkish authorities forced the ship to put to sea in the Black Sea.

o

25 Feb-9 Mar   Dutch East Indies

Japanese invasion of Java.

On 25 Feb the Japanese forces start their advance from the assembly areas. The Western Force consists of 56 transports, escorted by the 5th DD Flotilla (Rear-Adm Hara) comprising the cruiser *Natori* and the destroyers *Asakaze, Harukaze, Hatakaze, Matsukaze* (5th DD Div), *Satsuki, Minatsuki, Fumitsuki, Nagatsuki* (22nd DD Div) and the 3rd DD Flotilla (Rear-Adm Hashimoto) comprising the cruiser *Sendai* and the destroyers *Fubuki, Hatsuyuki, Shirayuki* (11th DD Div), *Murakumo* and *Shirakumo* (12th DD Div) and other units of the 9th BF including the cruiser *Yura* and the minelayer *Shirataka*, the minesweepers *W1, W2, W3, W4* (1st MS Div) and submarine-chasers. Cover is provided by the 7th Cruiser Sqn (Rear-Adm Kurita, also in overall command) with cruisers *Kumano, Mikuma, Mogami* and *Suzuya* and destroyers *Isonami, Shikinami* and *Uranami* (19th DD Div). Air support from the 4th Carrier Sqn (Rear-Adm Kakuta) with carrier *Ryujo*, the 22nd Carrier Sqn with seaplane-carrier *Chiyoda* and depot ship *Kamikawa Maru* and destroyers *Amagiri, Asagiri* and *Yugiri* (20th DD Div).

The Eastern Force consists of 41 transports, escorted by the 4th DD Flotilla (Rear-Adm Nishimura) comprising the cruiser *Naka* and destroyers *Asagumo, Minegumo, Natsugumo* (9th DD Div), *Murasame, Harusame, Samidare, Yudachi* (2nd DD Div) and *Umikaze;* in addition, units of the 2nd BF including the cruiser *Kinu*, the minelayer *Wakataka*, the minesweepers *W15, W16*, submarine-chasers *Ch4, Ch5, Ch6, Ch16, Ch17* and *Ch18*. The 2nd DD Flotilla (Rear-Adm Tanaka), comprising the cruiser *Jintsu* and the destroyers *Yukikaze, Tokitsukaze, Amatsukaze* and *Hatsukaze* (16th DD Div), sets out from Koepang (Timor) on 24 Feb and joins the force. The 5th Cruiser Sqn (Rear-Adm Takagi), comprising the cruisers *Haguro* and *Nachi* and the destroyers *Sazanami, Ushio* (1/7th DD Div), *Kawakaze* and *Yamakaze* (from the 24th DD Div), operates in the eastern part of the Java Sea as a covering force. In addition, the Com-

mander of the 3rd Fleet (Vice-Adm Takahashi) comes up from Kendari (Celebes) with the 16th Cruiser Sqn, the cruisers *Ashigara* and *Myoko* and the destroyers *Akebono* and *Inazuma*. Apart from shore-based aircraft, air escort is provided by the 24th Carrier Sqn with the seaplane-carrier *Mizuho* and the depot ship *Sanyo Maru*.

On 25 Feb the 1st Carrier Air Fleet (Vice-Adm Nagumo) sets out from Kendari (Celebes) through the Sape Strait to the area S of Java. It consists of the carriers *Akagi* and *Kaga* (1st Carrier Sqn), *Hiryu* and *Soryu* (2nd Carrier Sqn), the battleships *Hiyei* and *Kirishima* (1/3rd BB Sqn), the heavy cruisers *Chikuma* and *Tone* (8th Cruiser Sqn) and the 1st DD Flotilla comprising the cruiser *Abukuma* and the destroyers *Tanikaze, Isokaze, Hamakaze, Urakaze* (17th DD Div), *Shiranuhi, Kasumi, Ariake* and *Yugure* (18th DD Div) and six tankers. It is followed by the main force under Vice-Adm Kondo with the cruisers *Atago, Maya* and *Takao* (4th Cruiser Sqn), the battleships *Haruna* and *Kongo* (2/3rd BB Sqn) and the destroyers *Arashi, Hayashio* and *Nowake* (4th DD Div).

Of the Allied submarines *S37, S38, S39, Perch, Seal, Saury, Sailfish* (US), *K-XIV, K-XV, K-X* and *O19* (Dutch) stationed in anticipation of Japanese movements, *S38* and *Seal* report elements of the Eastern Force on 24-25 Feb and *Saury* elements of the Western Force, but they do not attack. Further reports are received from air reconnaissance. The Allied Naval Commander, Vice-Adm Helfrich, then orders up the British cruiser *Exeter*, which is on escort duties with the destroyers *Electra, Encounter* and *Jupiter*, from Batavia to Soerabaya to reinforce Rear-Adm Doorman's battle squadron as well as the Australian cruiser *Perth*, the US cruiser *Houston* and the destroyers *Paul Jones, Alden* and *John D. Ford*. The old British cruisers *Danae* and *Dragon* are ordered to Tandjok Priok (Batavia) with the destroyers *Scout* and *Tenedos* and also the Australian cruiser *Hobart* which cannot be refuelled in time.

When Japanese air reconnaissance reports the Allied shipping movements off Java, the Japanese invasion forces are again halted on 26 Feb and forced to retire. A sortie made by the Allied Western Force (Capt Howden) with the cruisers *Danae, Dragon, Hobart* and destroyers *Scout* and *Tenedos* from Batavia to the area of Banka and Biliton on 26-27 Feb finds nothing. But attacks by Japanese aircraft from the *Ryujo, Chiyoda* and *Kamikawa Maru* are also unsuccessful. A sortie by the Eastern Force (Rear-Adm Doorman) with the cruisers *De Ruyter, Java, Houston, Exeter, Perth* and nine destroyers (see below) from Soerabaya against Japanese forces reported by reconnaissance in the night 26-27 Feb. likewise leads to no result, as does a US air attack on the Japanese Eastern Force. Battle of the Java Sea. Directly after returning to harbour at mid-day on 27 Feb Doorman receives new reports and sets out again at once. He sends out the British destroyers *Electra, Encounter* and *Jupiter* ahead and to the port side the Dutch destroyers *Kortenaer* and *Witte de With,* in line the cruisers *De Ruyter, Exeter, Houston* and *Java,* followed by the US destroyers *Alden, John D. Edwards, John D. Ford* and *Paul Jones.* As a result of air recon-naissance reports from aircraft from the Japanese ships, the advancing eastern convoy is turned away to the W with the destroyers *Natsugumo* and *Umikaze* early in the afternoon when W of Bawean Island. The covering forces proceed at high speed to meet the Allied force. Shortly after 1600hrs Rear-Adm Takagi opens fire with the cruisers *Haguro* and *Nachi* at a range of 26km. In the east the *Jintsu* with the destroyers *Yukikaze, Tokitsu-kaze, Amatsukaze* and *Hatsukaze,* fol-lowed by *Ushio, Sazanami, Yamakaze* and *Kawakaze* and in the W the *Naka* with *Murasame, Samidare, Harukaze, Yudachi, Asagumo* and *Minegumo* ap-proach to make torpedo attacks. Of the 34 and 86 torpedoes fired, only one hits the *Kortenaer* which sinks. A heavy shell hit compels the *Exeter* to turn away. Escorted by the *Witte de With,* she proceeds to Soerabaya whilst Doorman orders the British destroyers

to attack in order to cover this man-oeuvre. In poor visibility caused by smoke screens the destroyers become involved in engagements at short range with the *Naka's* destroyers, in which *Electra* is sunk. Before Takagi breaks off this phase of the battle because of the proximity of suspected Dutch mine barrages, the *Perth* obtains a heavy hit on the *Asagumo.* An attack by four US destroyers fails as do 24 Japanese torpedoes. After reforming his force with four cruisers and six destroyers Doorman makes a sortie to the NW, when there is another brief engagement with the *Haguro* and *Nachi* and four torpedoes miss from the *Jintsu* before contact is lost. Owing to fuel shortage, Doorman has to dismiss the four US destroyers and, off the coast when proceeding westwards, *Jupiter* is lost following an explosion— either on a mine from the field laid by the Dutch minelayer *Gouden Leeuw* or from a torpedo by the US submarine *S38.* The *Encounter* shortly afterwards remains behind to rescue the survivors of the *Kortenaer* and goes to Soerabaya. At the same time Doorman makes an-other sortie to the N with his four cruisers, in the course of which there is an engagement in the night 27-28 Feb with the cruisers *Haguro* and *Nachi.* They respectively fire four and eight torpedoes and hit and sink the *De Ruyter* (Cdr Lacomblé) and *Java.* The two remaining cruisers, *Houston* and *Perth,* get away to Batavia. A sortie by the Western Force, which has just been joined by the Dutch destroyer *Evertsen,* leads to no result in the night 27-28 Feb. The force then goes through the Sunda Strait; only *Evertsen* returns to Batavia. On the Japanese side *Asagumo* and *Minegumo* are damaged. Of the surviving Allied ships, the US destroyers *Alden, John D. Edwards, John D. Ford* and *Paul Jones* proceed early in the morning of 28 Feb from Soerabaya through the Bali Strait to Australia which they reach after a short, indecisive engagement with three Japanese ships. On the afternoon of 28 Feb the cruisers *Houston* and *Perth,* followed later by the *Evertsen,* put to sea from Batavia/ Tandjok and the *Exeter* with the destroyers *Encounter* and *Pope* (US) from Soerabaya, in order to reach Tjilatjap through the Sunda Straits. In the meantime the Japanese invasion forces have resumed their advance. In the evening the Eastern Force (41 transports), covered by the 2nd and 4th DD Flotillas (see above), reaches the area of Kragan some 100 nautical miles W of Soerabaya and, in spite of Allied air attacks, in which the cruiser *Kinu* and one transport are damaged, begins to disembark troops. To the N Rear-Adm Takagi cruises to provide cover with the cruisers *Haguro* and *Nachi* and the destroyers *Kawakaze* and *Yamakaze* and, further to the NW, Vice-Adm Takahashi with the cruisers *Ashigara* and *Myoko* and the destroyers *Akebono* and *Inazuma*. S of Borneo the *Exeter* (Capt Gordon) with her destroyers comes between both forces and is sunk on 1 Mar with the *Encounter* by gunfire and torpedoes from the *Inazuma*. The *Pope* at first gets away but is then rendered unmanoeuvrable by six dive bombers from the *Ryujo* and sunk by gunfire. Some 800 survivors are rescued by the Japanese.

Battle of the Sunda Strait. The Japanese Western Force (56 transports) divides up early on 28 Feb. Two smaller groups (each consisting of about 10 transports) land troops in the night 28 Feb-1 Mar. The first comprises the cruiser *Yura* and the 22nd DD Div (see above) and lands near Anjer Lor on the NW extremity of Java in the entrance to the Sunda Strait and the second consists of the *Sendai* and the 20th DD Div and lands near Semarang in Central Java. The main force arrives in Banten Bay N of Serang in NW Java on the evening of 28 Feb and begins to disembark. Shortly after midnight the destroyer *Fubuki* which is providing a screen to the NE sights the Allied cruisers *Houston* (Capt Rooks) and *Perth* (Capt Waller) approaching from Batavia. Taking advantage of the mutual surprise, the two cruisers try to attack the Japanese invasion fleet. The transports *Horai Maru* (9192 tons) and *Sakura Maru* (7167 tons) sink; the minesweeper *W2* and the destroyer *Harukaze*, which comes up from the S,

are damaged. After a torpedo attack by the *Fubuki* the covering forces, summoned from the W, attack: they consist of the destroyers *Asakaze* and *Hatakaze*, the cruiser *Natori* with the destroyers *Hatsuyuki* and *Shirayuki*, the minelayer *Shirataka* and, finally, from the N, the covering group with the cruisers *Mikuma* and *Mogami* and the destroyer *Shikinami*. In the fierce gun and torpedo duels the *Houston* and *Perth* sink and on the Japanese side the *Shikinami* and *Shirakumo* suffer damage. 368 survivors are rescued from the Allied cruisers. The Dutch destroyer *Evertsen*, which is behind the two cruisers, runs into the Japanese forces, is set on fire by shelling and has to be beached in the Sunda Strait.

Operations in the Indian Ocean S of Java. When the US aircraft depot ship *Langley* is sunk on 27 Feb by Japanese bombers of the 21st and 23rd Naval Air Flotillas as she brings fighter planes to Java after the attack on Java begins, the remaining Allied ships try to get away. The cruisers *Danae*, *Dragon* and *Hobart* with the destroyers *Scout* and *Tenedos* set out from the Sunda Strait for Colombo on 28 Feb and, on the way, take on board refugees in Padang. Some of the ships which set out on 28 Feb-2 Mar from Tjilatjap, however, run into the operations being carried out by the Japanese Task Forces under Vice-Adms Nagumo and Kondo from the S of Java to the S of Christmas Island. On 1 Mar the battleships *Hiyei* and *Kirishima*, supported by the cruisers *Chikuma* and *Tone*, sink the US destroyer *Edsall* and aircraft from the carrier *Soryu* sink the tanker *Pecos* (14800 tons). Five merchant ships are sunk and one is captured. On 2 Mar the cruiser *Maya* with the destroyers *Arashi* and *Nowake* sink the British destroyer *Stronghold* in a one-hour engagement and the cruisers *Atago* and *Takao* the US destroyer *Pillsbury*. One merchant ship is sunk and one captured. On 3 Mar units of Kondo's force sink the US gunboat *Asheville*. On 4 Mar the last-named Japanese cruisers and destroyers sink a whole convoy with the Australian sloop *Yarra*, the minesweeper *MMS51*, the auxiliary ship *Anking* and the tanker

Francol; one more ship is captured. On 5 Mar the carriers of the Nagumo force, *Akagi, Hiryu, Kaga* and *Soryu*, make a raid on Tjilatjap which is already being demolished and evacuated: two merchant ships are destroyed and 15 more are scuttled or blown up. On 7 Mar the *Hiyei* and *Kirishima*, with the destroyers *Tanikaze, Isokaze, Hamakaze* and *Urakaze*, shell Christmas Island and sink one merchant ship. Further successes are obtained by the Japanese submarines deployed from 22 Feb (see entry). Of the Allied ships, apart from merchantmen, the Indian sloop *Jumna* escapes to Colombo; in addition, the US destroyers *Parrott* and *Whipple*, the gunboats *Isabel* and *Tulsa*, the Australian minesweepers of the 21st MS Division *Maryborough, Toowoomba, Ballarat, Bendigo, Goulburn, Burnie* and *Wollongong*. Likewise, the Allied troop transports and convoys proceeding 400 to 800 nautical miles W to S of Christmas Island are not caught by the Japanese Forces, e.g. the convoy MS.5 handed over by US cruiser *Phoenix* to the British *Enterprise;* the troop transport *Mount Vernon* (with 4668 troops on board) proceeding on her own to Australia; and the convoy SU.1 with 12 transports and 10,090 troops on board, escorted by the battleship *Royal Sovereign*, the cruiser *Cornwall*, the destroyers *Express, Nizam* and *Vampire*, the corvette *Hollyhock* and the Australian auxiliary cruiser *Manoora*. Allied submarines: during the fighting for Java the US submarine *Seal* misses a cruiser of the Japanese Eastern Force on 1 Mar; *Sailfish* (Lt-Cdr Voge) sinks one ship of 6440 tons; *Perch* is sunk by the destroyers *Amatsukaze* and *Hatsukaze* when she tries to attack the advancing Japanese eastern invasion force. *Seawolf* torpedoes one ship of 4466 tons. The Japanese naval tanker *Tsurumi*, belonging to the Western Force, is torpedoed by the US submarine *S39* (Lt-Cdr Coe) and the Dutch submarine *K-XV* (Lt-Cdr V. Boetzelaer). In Soerabaya the nonoperational submarines *K-XII, K-XVIII* and *K-IX*, the US destroyer *Stewart* and many other warships and merchant ships are blown up.

On 9 Mar the Allied forces on Java capitulate: 60000 prisoners.

25 Feb-21 April   Central Atlantic
Off the West African coast the submarine *Da Vinci* (Cdr Longanesi-Cattani) sinks four ships of 19997 tons; *U68* (Cdr Merten) seven ships of 39350 tons; and *U505* (Lt-Cdr Loewe) four ships of 25041 tons.

26-27 Feb   Air War/Germany
In an attack by RAF Bomber Command on Kiel the battleship *Gneisenau* receives a heavy bomb hit in the bows. The passenger ship *Monte Sarmiento* (13625 tons), lying alongside, is burnt out. *Gneisenau* remains in Kiel unfit for operations until 4 Apr and is then brought to Gotenhafen to be lengthened and equipped with 38cm guns. The work is however suspended at the beginning of 1943 and the ship is laid up.

26-28 Feb   Black Sea
In support of an offensive by the Soviet 44th Army on the Kerch Peninsula, units of the Squadron (Rear-Adm Vladimirski) of the Black Sea Fleet shell positions and troop concentrations W and N of Feodosia: the flotilla leader *Tashkent* and destroyers *Bditelny* and *Boiki* in the night 25-26 Feb; the battleship *Parizhskaya Kommuna*, the cruiser *Molotov* and the destroyers *Bezuprechny* and *Smyshleny* in the nights 26-27 Feb and 27-28 Feb. The cruiser *Krasny Krym* supports the defenders of Sevastopol on 26 Feb and 28 Feb and on 27 Feb she shells with the flotilla leaders *Kharkov* and *Tashkent* and the destroyers *Boiki, Shaumyan* and *Zheleznyakov* the harbours on the South Coast of the Crimea as a diversionary move. In all, 1590 rounds—10.2cm to 30.5cm—are fired.

27-28 Apl   Air War/Germany
RAF Bomber Command attacks Kiel and Wilhelmshaven.

27-28 Feb   Mediterranean
An attempt by Force H (Vice-Adm Syfret), comprising the battleship *Malaya*, the carriers *Argus* and *Eagle*, the cruiser *Hermione* and the destroyers *Laforey, Lightning, Active, Anthony, Duncan, Whitehall, Wishart, Blankney* and *Croome*, to fly off fighter aircraft for Malta S of the Balearics has to be broken off because of trouble with the supplementary tanks of the aircraft.

27 Feb-5 Mar   Mediterranean

In British submarine operations *Upholder* (Lt-Cdr Wanklyn) sinks a steamer of 5584 tons escorted by the destroyer *Strale* off Tripoli. *Torbay* (Cdr Miers) torpedoes two ships of 6455 tons off Corfu. E of Tunisia *Unbeaten* (Lt-Cdr Woodward) and *P31/Uproar* (Lt Kershaw) each sink one ship of 5417 tons and 5081 tons respectively.

1-30 Mar   Pacific

In operations by US submarines off Japan, in the East China Sea and in the area of the Mandate Islands *Narwhal* (Lt-Cdr Wilkins) sinks one ship of 1243 tons; *Pollack* (Lt-Cdr Mosely) one ship of 1134 tons; *Gar* (Lt-Cdr McGregor) one ship of 1520 tons; *Grayback* (Lt-Cdr Saunders) one ship of 3291 tons; *Gudgeon* (Lt-Cdr Grenfell) one ship of 6526 tons. *Tuna* (Lt-Cdr De Tar) damages one ship; *Grenadier* one ship of 4550 tons; and *Tambor* (Lt-Cdr Murphy) one ship of 6334 tons. *Grampus* (Lt-Cdr Hutchinson) sinks one ship of 8632 tons near Truk.

2-23 Mar   Western Atlantic

On the American East Coast *U332* (Lt-Cdr Liebe) sinks four ships of 25125 tons; *U124* (Lt-Cdr Mohr) seven ships of 42048 tons and torpedoes three ships of 26167 tons. *U503* (Lt-Cdr Gericke) is sunk on 15 Mar by an aircraft belonging to the escort of convoy ON.72.

3 Mar   Mediterranean

16 Wellington bombers from Malta attack Palermo. In the harbour the ammunition ship *Cuma* (8260 tons) explodes after being hit and four other steamers, four auxiliary ships and five destroyers and torpedo boats are damaged.

5-13 Mar   Arctic

Operations in connection with the convoys PQ.12 (16 ships) and QP.8 (15 ships) which set out on 1 Mar from Reykjavik and the Kola Inlet respectively. On 5 Mar a FW 200 locates the PQ.12 about 70 nautical miles S of Jan Mayen. *U134*, *U377*, *U403* and *U584* then form a patrol line. On 6 Mar the battleship *Tirpitz* (Capt Topp with Vice-Adm Ciliax) and the destroyers *Friedrich Ihn*, *Hermann Schoemann* and *Z25* set out to sea from Trondheim in an attempt to attack the convoy. One of the five British submarines stationed there, *Seawolf* (Lt Raikes), reports that the force is setting out. In the meantime the covering force (Vice-Adm Curteis), consisting of the battleships *Duke of York* and *Renown*, the cruiser *Kenya* and the destroyers *Faulknor*, *Eskimo*, *Punjabi*, *Fury*, *Echo* and *Eclipse* and the main body of the Home Fleet (Adm Tovey), comprising the battleship *King George V*, the carrier *Victorious*, the cruiser *Berwick* and the destroyers *Onslow*, *Ashanti*, *Intrepid*, *Icarus*, *Lookout* and *Bedouin*, join up. The *Kenya* is detached as close escort to PQ.12. The cruiser *Sheffield*, which has come out to relieve the *Berwick* (left behind with engine trouble), is damaged on a mine and has to return. In the prevailing poor visibility the Home Fleet does not find the *Tirpitz*. The German ships just miss the convoy QP.8, escorted only by two minesweepers and two corvettes, and the destroyers only find a straggler, the Soviet freighter *Izhora* (2815 tons), which *Friedrich Ihn* sinks. On 9 Mar *Tirpitz* is unsuccessfully attacked off Vestfjord by 12 Albacore torpedo aircraft from the *Victorious*, escorted by *Faulknor*, *Eskimo*, *Bedouin* and *Tartar*, and two aircraft are shot down. An attempt by three Ju 88s to attack the British carrier on 9 Mar is unsuccessful.

The *Tirpitz* enters Narvik. On 11-12 Mar the destroyers *Faulknor*, *Fury*, *Intrepid*, *Icarus*, *Bedouin*, *Eskimo*, *Tartar* and *Punjabi* try to intercept the expected *Tirpitz* off Bodö. But the battleship is transferred again to Trondheim on 12-13 Mar.

The Soviet submarines *D-3*, *K-21*, *K-23*, *S-102* and *Shch-422*, which were stationed to cover the convoys S of the convoy routes, proceed to the Norwegian Polar Coast on the conclusion of the operation on 13 Mar. Here *D-3* (Capt 3rd Class Bibeev) misses on 14 Mar the German minelayer *Brummer*, which is on the way to laying out a flanking mine barrage, and *M1504*. She is attacked with depth charges by the submarine-chaser *UJ1109*. The Soviet submarines *M-171* and *M173* make unsuccessful attacks in Varangerfjord.

5-18 Mar   South Pacific

Elements of the Japanese 4th Fleet (Vice-Adm Inoue)—transports, minelayers, minesweepers and other small craft—which set out from Rabaul on 5 Mar land a battalion of the South Sea Detachment of the Army in Salamaua and a naval landing unit in Lae in Huon Gulf on 8 Mar. Escort and support for the landings is provided by the 6th DD Flotilla with the cruiser *Yubari* and the destroyers *Oite, Asanagi, Yunagi, Mutsuki, Yayoi* and *Mochizuki*, as well as the 24th Naval Air Flotilla with the depot ship *Kiyokawa Maru*. Covering force: the 6th Cruiser Sqdn, comprising the cruisers *Aoba, Kinugasa, Kako* and *Furutaka* and the 18th Cruiser Sqdn with the light cruisers *Tatsuta* and *Tenryu* investigate Buka N of Bougainville on 8 Mar.

From 7 Mar to 12 Mar convoy ZK.7, escorted by the US cruisers *Honolulu* and *New Orleans* and the destroyer *Mugford*, transports the US American Div from Melbourne to Noumea. TF 11 (Rear-Adm Brown), consisting of the carrier *Lexington*, the cruisers *Indianapolis, Minneapolis, Pensacola, San Francisco* and the destroyers (Desron 1) *Phelps, Clark, Patterson, Dewey, MacDonough, Hull, Aylwin, Dale, Bagley* and *Drayton*, joins TF 17 (Rear-Adm Fletcher) which comprises the carrier *Yorktown* and the destroyers *Russell* and *Walke* (on 6 Mar), to make a raid on Japanese landing points from S of the Papuan Peninsula. On 10 Apl the two carriers fly off 104 aircraft which attack the harbours over the Owen Stanley Mountains: the transport *Yokohama Maru* (6143 tons) is sunk and the cruiser *Yubari*, the minelayer *Tsugaru*, the destroyers *Asanagi* and *Yunagi*, two transports and two auxiliary ships are damaged. The transport *Tenryu Maru* (6843 tons) has to be beached after being hit.

The Anzac Force (Rear-Adm Crace), comprising the cruisers *Australia* (RAN) and *Chicago* and the destroyers *Lamson* and *Perkins*, as well as the cruisers *Astoria* and *Louisville* and the destroyers *Anderson, Hammann, Hughes* and *Sims* detached from TF 17, operates as a covering group SE of Papua. From 16 Mar to 18 Mar the Australian auxiliary cruiser *Westralia* brings one battalion of the US Americal Div from Noumea to Efate (New Hebrides). Escort provided by the New Zealand cruisers *Achilles* and *Leander*.

6-8 Mar   Mediterranean

British Force H (Vice-Adm Syfret) flies off 15 Spitfire fighters for Malta from the carriers *Argus* and *Eagle* S of the Balearics. They arrive there together with seven Blenheim bombers from Gibraltar. Escort: battleship *Malaya*, cruiser *Hermione*, destroyers *Laforey, Lightning, Active, Anthony, Whitehall, Wishart, Blankney, Exmoor* and *Croome*. Italian submarine *Brin* reports Force H on 6 Mar and 8 Mar.

6-8 Mar   Indian Ocean

Because of the advance made by the Japanese 33rd Inf Div on Rangoon from the N, reinforcement convoys for the Allied defenders have to turn back on 6 Mar. On 7 Mar Rangoon is evacuated on the orders of Gen Alexander. Light craft evacuate 3500 troops with cover from the US destroyer *Allen* and the Indian sloop *Hindustan*. The last demolition parties are taken aboard the freighter *Heinrich Jensen*. On 8 Mar the Japanese enter Rangoon.

6-20 Mar   Black Sea

Soviet supply transports to Sevastopol: on 6-7 Mar with the cruiser *Komintern;* on 11-12 Mar with the cruiser *Krasny Krym* and destroyers *Shaumyan* and *Svobodny* and the transport *Lvov*—several air attacks beaten off; on 12-13 Mar with the destroyer *Dzerzhinski*—shelling of land targets; on 13-14 Mar with the cruiser *Molotov* and destroyers *Bditelny* and *Boiki*—shelling of land targets near Feodosia and Sevastopol; on 15-16 Mar with the destroyers *Bditelny* and *Svobodny*—shelling of land targets; from 18 Mar to 20 Mar with the cruiser *Krasny Krym*, the destroyer *Nezamozhnik* and the tankers *Peredovik* and *Sergo* and the destroyers *Bditelny* and the transport *Abkhaziya* respectively —several air attacks beaten off and some shelling of land targets.

7-18 Mar   Mediterranean

Italian supply operation V.5 to North Africa. From 7 Mar to 9 Mar three Italian convoys with four transports, escorted by the destroyers *Pigafetta, Da Noli, Bersagliere, Vivaldi, Fuciliere* and the torpedo boats *Aretusa* and *Castore*, set out from Brindisi, Messina and Naples for Tripoli. Covering force: Div-Adm De Courten with cruisers *Eugenio di Savoia, Garibaldi, Montecuccoli* and destroyers *Ascari, Aviere, Geniere, Oriani* and *Scirocco*. A return convoy with four transports puts to sea from Tripoli on 8 Mar, escorted by the destroyer *Strale* and the torpedo boats *Cigno* and *Procione*, which are joined by *Pigafetta* and *Scirocco* on 9 Mar. On 9 Mar a second convoy with two steamers and one tug with the destroyers *Bersagliere, Da Noli*, and the torpedo boats *Castore* and *Pallade* follows. Another operation 'Sirio' with two transports (a close escort of six destroyers and one torpedo boat and a distant escort of one cruiser and two destroyers) is also undertaken without loss. Italian submarines *Corallo, Millo, Veniero, Uarsciek* and *Onice* are in covering positions E of Malta.

In British submarine operations in the Central Mediterranean *P34/Ultimatum* (Lt Harrison), *Unbeaten* (Lt-Cdr Woodward) and *Upholder* (Lt-Cdr Wanklyn) sink the Italian submarines *Guglielmotti, Millo* and *Tricheco*. *Una* (Lt Norman) sinks one sailing ship (248 tons) in a gun duel.

As a result of a false report about the torpedoing of an Italian cruiser British Force B (Rear-Adm Vian) sets out from Alexandria on 9 Mar with the cruisers *Naiad, Dido, Euryalus* and the destroyers *Jervis, Kipling, Kelvin, Lively, Sikh, Zulu, Hasty, Havock* and *Hero* to intercept the ship and to meet the cruiser *Cleopatra* and the destroyer *Kingston* coming from Malta. Italian torpedo aircraft and German bombers attack the force unsuccessfully. 11 Mar: *U565* (Lt Jebsen) sinks Vian's flagship, *Naiad* (Capt Grantham), from the returning force N of Sollum. All except 82 of the crew are rescued.

8-12 Mar   Indian Ocean
Japanese landing in Northern Sumatra. On 8 Mar a Japanese force, comprising the cruiser *Kashii* (flagship of the 1st Southern Expeditionary Fleet), the cruiser *Yura*, the destroyers *Shirakumo, Yugiri, Asagiri, Amagiri, Uranami, Isonami* and *Ayanami* and transports, sets out from Singapore to land troops on

12 Mar in Sabang and Iri in Northern Sumatra. Cover for the operation is provided by Vice-Adm Ozawa with the cruisers *Chokai, Kumano, Suzuya, Mikuma, Mogami* and the destroyers *Hatsuyuki, Fubuki, Shirakumo* and *Murakumo* and by the aircraft depot ship *Soya Maru* in the area of the Nicobars.

10-24 Mar   Indian Ocean
On the Indian East Coast *I-62* (Lt-Cdr Kinashi) and *I-64* (Cdr Ogawa) sink two ships and one ship respectively of 1100 tons and 1513 tons. *I-62* also torpedoes three larger ships but of them only one tanker of 8012 tons is identified.

11 Mar   English Channel
In an attack by boats of the German 2nd MTB Flotilla on a British convoy in the Channel *S70* (Lt Klose) sinks one freighter of 951 tons.

11-26 Mar   Mediterranean
In operations against the British supply traffic for Tobruk *U83* (Lt-Cdr Kraus) torpedoes one ship of 2590 tons; *U652* (Lt-Cdr Fraatz) sinks on 20 Mar the destroyer *Jaguar* and the tanker *Slavol* (2623 tons) from a convoy; *U371, U559, U568* and the Italian *Onice* miss their targets. *U133* is lost on one of her own mines. Of the Italian submarines, *Ametista* and *Galatea* off Palestine, the latter sinks one sailing vessel. In the Western Mediterranean the Italian submarine *Mocenigo* (Lt-Cdr Monechi) sinks a Vichy French ship of 1518 tons.

12-13 Mar   South Africa
The German auxiliary minelayer *Schiff 53 Doggerbank* (Lt-Cdr Schneidewind) lays 60 mines off Cape Town and 15 off Cape Agulhas on which one freighter of 4534 tons sinks and two others of 13015 tons are damaged.

13-14 Mar-24 Apl   English Channel
The German auxiliary cruiser *Schiff 28 Michel* (Cdr* v. Ruckteschell) passes through the Channel, escorted by the 5th Torpedo Boat Flotilla (Cdr* Schmidt) comprising *Seeadler, Iltis, Jaguar, Falke* and *Kondor* and nine minesweepers. In fierce engagements with British MTBs, motor gunboats and destroyers the destroyers *Fernie* and *Walpole* are damaged without German loss. *Schiff 28* reaches Le Havre on 14 Mar, St Malo on 15 Mar

and La Pallice on 17 Mar, from where she sets out for the Atlantic on 20 Mar.

14-15 Mar-24 Apl   English Channel
In mining operations by German motor torpedo boats in the Channel and off the British South East coast *S53* is lost on a mine. *S104* (Lt Roeder) sinks the British destroyer *Vortigern* on 15 Mar. On her return *S111* is badly damaged in an engagement with motor gunboats *MGB87*, *MGB88* and *MGB91* and sinks when being towed away.

14 Mar   Western Atlantic
The 11 U-boats of a fourth wave which arrive successively sink many ships off the US East Coast in individual operations. *U373* (Lt Loeser) sinks two ships of 9867 tons; *U71* (Lt-Cdr Flachsenberg) five ships of 38894 tons; *U202* (Lt-Cdr Linder) one ship of 5249 tons and torpedoes one ship of 8882 tons; *U160* (Lt Lassen) five ships of 36731 tons and torpedoes one ship of 6837 tons; *U105* (Cdr Schuch) two ships of 18005 tons; *U123* (Lt-Cdr Hardegen) eight ships of 39917 tons and torpedoes three ships of 24310 tons; *U552* (Lt-Cdr Topp) seven ships of 45731 tons; *U754* (Lt-Cdr Oestermann) seven ships of 31578 tons and damages one tug of 490 tons; *U203* (Lt-Cdr Mützelburg) two ships of 14232 tons and torpedoes two ships of 16164 tons; *U571* (Lt-Cdr Möhlmann) three ships of 24319 tons; and *U572* (Lt-Cdr Hirsacker) two ships of 9532 tons and torpedoes one ship of 6207 tons.

15 Mar   Mediterranean
The British cruisers *Dido* and *Euryalus* and six destroyers shell Rhodes.

15-19 Mar   Mediterranean
The German 3rd MTB Flotilla (Lt-Cdr Kemnade) lays in four nights E and W of Valetta/Malta the barrages MT 6-9 with 48 TMA and 45 UMB mines, 18 protection floats and 54 explosive floats.

18-20 Mar   North Atlantic
U507 (Cdr Schacht), which is on the way to France, sights the convoy ONS.76 (28 ships) but cannot maintain contact until *U506*, *U593* and *U753*, which are ordered to the scene, arrive. An attack made on 19 Feb at too great range is not successful.

19-20 Mar   Norway
The heavy cruiser *Admiral Hipper* (Capt Meisel) moves to Trondheim with the destroyers *Z24*, *Z26*, *Z30* and the torpedo boats *T15*, *T16* and *T17*.

19-25 Mar   Indian Ocean
Japanese transport Fleet brings troops of the Japanese 56th Inf Div from Singapore to Rangoon from 19 Mar to 25 Mar. In these operations Japanese detachments establish seaplane bases and emergency fleet bases at Pukhet on 21 Mar and Mergui on 23 Mar. On 20 Mar a force sets out from Penang with a battalion of the 18th Inf Div which on 23 Mar occupies Port Blair in the Andaman Islands. Apart from transports the flag cruiser *Kashii* of the 1st Southern Expeditionary Fleet and the 9th and 12th Special BF are employed on these operations. The operations are escorted and covered by the Malaya Force (Vice-Adm Ozawa), comprising the cruisers *Chokai*, *Kumano*, *Suzuya*, *Mikuma*, *Mogami*, the carrier *Ryujo*, the light cruisers *Sendai* and *Yura* and 11 destroyers (see 8-12 Mar).

20-26 Mar   Mediterranean
Second battle of Sirte. 20 Mar: the British 5th DD Flotilla, comprising *Southwold*, *Beaufort*, *Dulverton*, *Hurworth*, *Avon Vale*, *Eridge* and *Heythrop*, sets out from Alexandria for Tobruk on a submarine-hunting operation. N of Sollum *U652* (Lt Fraatz) sinks the *Heythrop*.
Supply convoy MW.10 for Malta sets out from Alexandria: transports *Breconshire* (9776 tons), *Clan Campbell* (7255 tons), *Pampas* (5415 tons) and *Talabot* (6798 tons). Escort: AA cruiser *Carlisle* and the 22nd DD Flotilla consisting of *Sikh*, *Zulu*, *Lively*, *Hero*, *Havock* and *Hasty*. Covering force: Rear-Adm Vian with the cruisers *Cleopatra*, *Dido*, *Euryalus* and the 14th DD Flotilla consisting of *Jervis*, *Kelvin*, *Kingston* and *Kipling*. Six British submarines take up flanking positions in the Gulf of Taranto and off Messina. 21 Mar: Force H (Composition as on 6 Mar) puts to sea from Gibraltar to fly in more Spitfire fighters to Malta. The Italian submarines *Mocenigo* and *Dandolo* sight the force and *Mocenigo* attacks without success the *Argus*.
The Italian submarines *Onice* and *Platino* report MW.10. To deal with it Supermarina sends out from Messina Div-Adm Parona with the cruisers

Bande Nere, Gorizia, Trento and destroyers *Alpino, Bersagliere, Fuciliere* and *Lanciere* and from Taranto the battleship *Littorio* (Adm Iachino) with the destroyers *Ascari, Aviere, Grecale, Oriani*, followed later by *Geniere* and *Scirocco*. In addition, the submarines *Perla, Acciaio, Galatea, U73, U205* and *U431* are deployed and bombers and torpedo aircraft of the German II Fl.K. and the Italian 4th Air Fleet act together. The British submarine *P36* reports the *Littorio* force. The cruiser *Penelope* and the destroyer *Legion* set out from Malta to escort MW.10 and they join it on 22 Mar. At 1424hrs the Italian Messina force sights the British covering force and tries in vain to entice it on to the *Littorio*. At 1618hrs *Littorio* has come up in a strong freshening wind and deteriorating visibility and tries to get between the convoy and Malta. Rough seas and skilful operating by Adm Vian in the use of smoke impede the Italian gunnery to such an extent that only *Havock* and *Kingston* are severely damaged by near-hits or direct hits by the 38cm shells. *Cleopatra* receives a hit from a 15cm shell whilst on *Euryalus* and *Lively* only slight splinter damage is sustained. Torpedo attacks by destroyers on both sides are unsuccessful. At 1858 hrs *Iachino* breaks off the engagement as darkness begins to fall. MW.10 resumes its course to Malta. On the return the Italian force loses *Lanciere* and *Scirocco* in the storm. The cruiser *Trento* has to break off her attempts to help because of severe storm damage. Almost all other Italian and British ships suffer more or less heavy storm damage on the return.

The evasive movements in the engagement result in MW.10 only arriving off Malta after daybreak on 23 Mar. There the ships are attacked by bombers of the II Fl.K. *Clan Campbell* sinks; *Breconshire* is badly damaged and beached and later capsizes when attempts are made to salvage her after further hits; *Southwold* sinks on a mine barrage. 24 Mar: *Legion* is beached after a near-miss and is destroyed on 26 Mar. On the same day *Pampas* and *Talabot* also sink after bomb hits, so that only 5000 tons of the 25900 tons of cargo come ashore. The covering force reaches Alexandria

on 24 Mar after the already badly-damaged *Kingston* has received a bomb hit on 23 Mar.

25 Mar: *Carlisle, Hurworth, Dulverton, Eridge* and *Beaufort* set out from Malta and reach Alexandria on 27 Mar without incident.

20-30 Mar Mediterranean
British Force H (Vice-Adm Syfret), comprising the battleship *Malaya*, the carriers *Argus* and *Eagle*, the cruiser *Hermione* and destroyers *Laforey, Duncan, Active, Anthony, Whitehall, Wishart, Blankney, Exmoor* and *Croome*, sets out from Gibraltar on 20 Mar to make a new attempt to fly aircraft into Malta. But the force has to break off the attempt and return on 23 Mar. The operation is repeated from 27 Mar to 30 Mar with the same force and sixteen Spitfire fighters reach Malta.

29 Mar: The cruiser *Aurora*, repaired after hitting a mine in December 1941, proceeds with *Avon Vale* from Malta to Gibraltar. On the way the ships are sighted by the Italian submarine *Narvalo* and unsuccessfully attacked by torpedo aircraft S of Sardinia. The Italian submarines *Aradam, Santarosa* and *Turchese* report no contacts.

21-22 Mar Black Sea
The Soviet battleship *Parizhskaya Kommuna* (Rear-Adm Vladimirski), together with the flotilla leader *Tashkent* and the destroyers *Boiki* and *Zheleznyakov*, shell land targets in the area of Feodosia in the nights 20-21 Mar and 21-22 Mar. After returning on 23 Mar the battleship goes into the dockyard at Poti to change her heavy guns and for repairs.

23 Mar-beginning of Apl
                              Western Atlantic
First use of U-boat decoys (Q ships) off the American East Coast fails. The USS *Asterion* and *Eagle*, disguised respectively as a freighter and a fishing steamer, sight no U-boats. The *Atik* (Lt-Cdr Hicks) is attacked by *U123* (Lt-Cdr Hardegen) on 26 Mar and sunk after a violent gun duel.

23 Mar-9 Apl South Atlantic
The German auxiliary cruiser *Schiff 10 Thor* (Capt Gumprich) sinks five ships totalling 23626 tons.

29 Mar-22 Apl Atlantic
Preparatory naval movements for Allied operation 'Ironclad' (Madagascar). On

23 Mar a convoy leaves Britain with troops of the British 5th Inf Div earmarked for the operation. On 25 Mar US TF 39 (Rear-Adm Wilcox†—lost overboard in a storm, then Rear-Adm Giffen) sets out from Casco Bay (USA) for Scapa Flow with the battleship *Washington*, the carrier *Wasp*, the heavy cruisers *Tuscaloosa* and *Wichita* and Desron 8 with the destroyers *Wainwright, Lang, Sterett, Wilson, Plunkett, Madison, Livermoore* and *Ellyson*. Its role is to relieve units of the Home Fleet as a replacement for Force H earmarked for 'Ironclad'. The US force is met on 3 Apl by the British cruiser *Edinburgh* and four destroyers and reaches Scapa Flow on 5 Apl. The 'Ironclad' convoy joins Force H (Rear-Adm Syfret), comprising the battleship *Malaya*, the cruiser *Hermione* and destroyers and the carrier *Illustrious* with destroyers in Freetown on 6 Apl. On 9 Apl the entire force sets out. On 19 Apl the warships put in to Cape Town; the *Malaya* then returns and the other ships arrive in Durban on 22 Apl.

24-25 Mar   North Atlantic
The newly-replenished *U203* (Lt-Cdr Mützelburg) sights the convoy ON.77 and directs the returning *U94* (Lt Ites) to it; the latter torpedoes a tanker of 8022 tons.

24 Mar-3 Apl   North Atlantic
The U-boat *UA* (Cdr Cohausz), which is equipped as a supply boat, carries out for the first time the refuelling of *U84* and *U203*, which are proceeding to the American coast, and of the returning *U202*.

24 Mar-9 Apl   Arctic
Operations in connection with the convoys QP.9 and PQ.13. QP.9 (19 ships), which leaves the Kola Inlet on 21 Mar, passes, without incident, the concentration of the German U-boats *U209, U376, U378* and *U655*. The last is sunk on 24 Mar after being rammed by the escorting minesweeper *Sharpshooter*. Vice-Adm Curteis with the battleships *Duke of York* and *Renown*, the carrier *Victorious*, the cruiser *Nigeria* and destroyers acts as a covering force NE of Iceland. From 24 Mar to 27 Mar PQ.13 (19 ships with an escort consisting of the cruiser *Trinidad*, the destroyers *Eclipse* and *Fury*, the A/S

trawlers *Blackfly* and *Paynter* and three Norwegian M/S whalers *Silja, Sulla* and *Sumba* being transferred to the Soviet Northern Fleet) is scattered in a heavy storm. On the morning of 27 Mar a BV 138 of 2/K.Fl.Gr 406 sights ships of PQ.13. Then on 28 Mar the U-boats *U435, U436, U454, U456, U585* and *U589* and the 8th DD Flotilla (Capt Pönitz) comprising *Z26, Z24* and *Z25* are ordered to it. Ju 88s of III/K.G. 30 sink the scattered freighters *Raceland* (4815 tons) and *Empire Ranger* (7007 tons). On 29 Mar the British destroyer *Oribi* and the Soviet *Gremyashchi* and *Sokrushitelny* arrive from the Kola Inlet. Of the 8th DD Flotilla *Z26* (Cdr. v. Berger) sinks the scattered freighter *Bateau* (4687 tons) and then the three destroyers encounter the *Trinidad* running ahead of the convoy with *Fury*. In confused engagements impeded by a heavy snowstorm the *Trinidad* renders *Z26* unmanoeuvrable but is hit by one of her own torpedoes despatched to finish the destroyer off. In the melee *Z24* and *Z25* rescue 96 men from the sinking *Z26*, hit the *Eclipse* heavily and escape following a short exchange with the *Oribi* and *Sokrushitelny*. *U585* (Lt-Cdr Lohse) is sunk by *Fury* as she tries to attack the disabled *Trinidad*. On 30 Mar the British 6th MS Flotilla (Cdr Jay), comprising *Harrier, Gossamer, Speedwell* and *Hussar*, which sets out from Murmansk on 28 Mar, reaches the convoy. *U209* (Lt-Cdr Brodda) and *U456* (Lt-Cdr Teichert) miss ships of the convoy groups. *U376* (Lt-Cdr Marks) and *U435* (Lt-Cdr Strelow) sink the stragglers *Induna* (5086 tons) and *Effingham* (6421 tons). On 1 Apl *U436* (Lt-Cdr Seibicke) sinks a single ship, probably the missing *Sulla*, and *U589* (Lt-Cdr Horrer) misses a destroyer. The Soviet submarines *K-21, K-22, Shch-404* and *Shch-421*, which were formed in a flanking concentration S of the convoy as a screen against surface attacks, leave for the Polar Coast on 1 Apl, where *Shch-404* (Capt 2nd Class Ivanov) sinks the steamer *Michael* (2318 tons) off Tanafjord. In Svaerholthavet *K-22* misses a minesweeping force consisting of *M1505, M1506* and *M1508* on 3 Apl. Further attacks by *K-21*, *Shch-404* and *Shch-421* and by *M-171* deployed in Varangerfjord, are unsuccessful. Shortly after the German Minelayer Group 'Nord' (Capt Schönermark), consisting of the minelayers *Ulm*, *Brummer* and *Cobra*, has laid a flanking mine barrage to protect German traffic in Svaerhollthavet the Soviet submarine *Shch-421* (Lt-Cdr Vidyaev with the Div Cdr, Capt 2nd Class Kolyshkin, on board) runs on this barrage, is badly damaged and is sunk by *K-22* after the crew has been taken off.

25-26 Mar   Black Sea
The Soviet Flotilla leader *Kharkov* and destroyer *Svobodny* bring supplies to Sevastopol on 25 Mar. The destroyers *Bditelny* and *Boiki* shell German positions on the edge of the fortress on 26 Mar.

25 Mar–12 Apl   South Atlantic
The Italian submarine *Calvi* (Cdr Olivieri) sinks five ships of 29031 tons off the Brazilian NE coast.

26 Mar-8 Apl   Baltic
The Finnish group P, consisting of three infantry battalions of the 18th Inf Div, advances on skis over the ice from Kotka to Suursaari and, helped by a snowstorm, overwhelms the Soviet defenders, the remainder of whom withdraw to Suur-Tytärsaari. Finnish units, and German ones coming over the ice from the S, destroy the Soviet garrison of this island on 3-4 Apl. A Soviet relief sortie on 5 Apl and 7-8 Apl, consisting of a total of 10 battalions, is driven off.

26 Mar-11 Apl   Indian Ocean
Japanese raid on Ceylon. On 26 Mar the Japanese 1st Carrier Fleet (Vice-Adm Nagumo) sets out from Staring Bay (South Celebes). It comprises the carriers *Akagi* (1st Carrier Sqdn), *Hiryu* (Rear-Adm Yamaguchi, 2nd Carrier Sqdn), *Soryu*, *Zuikaku* (Rear-Adm Hara, 5th Carrier Sqdn), *Shokaku*, the battleships *Kongo* (3rd BB Sqdn, Rear-Adm Mikawa), *Haruna*, *Hiyei*, *Kirishima*, the heavy cruisers *Tone* (8th Cruiser Sqdn, Rear-Adm Abe) and *Chikuma* and the 1st DD Flotilla (Rear-Adm Omori) with the cruiser *Abukuma* and the destroyers *Urakaze*, *Tanikaze*, *Isokaze*, *Hamakaze* (17th DD Div), *Kasumi*, *Arare*, *Kagero*,

Shiranuhi (18th DD Div) and *Akigumo*. The force proceeds W of Timor to the area S of Java where it is replenished by a tanker force from 1 Apl. The 1st SM Flotilla with *I-7*, *I-2*, *I-3*, *I-4*, *I-5* and *I-6* leaves Penang from 27 Mar to take up covering positions W of India. Adm Somerville who took over command as C-in-C Eastern Fleet on 27 Mar, receives reports on 29 Mar of an impending Japanese attack on Ceylon. He concentrates his available naval forces in two groups S of Ceylon by 31 Mar: Force A (fast group) flagship battleship *Warspite*, carriers (Rear-Adm Boyd) *Indomitable* and *Formidable*, the cruisers *Cornwall*, *Dorsetshire*, *Emerald*, *Enterprise*, the destroyers *Napier* (RAN), *Nestor* (RAN), *Paladin*, *Panther*, *Hotspur* and *Foxhound*; Force B (Vice-Adm Willis): battleships *Resolution*, *Ramillies*, *Royal Sovereign* and *Revenge*, carrier *Hermes*, cruisers *Caledon*, *Dragon*, *Jacob van Heemskerck* (Dutch), destroyers *Griffin*, *Norman* (RAN), *Arrow*, *Vampire* (RAN), *Decoy*, *Fortune*, *Scout*, *Isaac Sweers* (Dutch). The Eastern Fleet cruises S of Ceylon without sighting the enemy until the evening of 2 Apl and then proceeds to Addu Atoll for replenishment (arrives 4 Apl). The *Cornwall* and *Dorsetshire* are detached to Colombo and the *Hermes* and *Vampire* to Trincomalee. On 1 Apl the Japanese destroyer *Ayanami* proceeds from Penang to Port Blair (arrives on 4 Apl) with the transport *Tatekawa Maru* and reinforcements for the Andaman Islands. On the same day the Malaya Force (Vice-Adm Ozawa) with the heavy cruisers *Chokai* and *Kumano* (7th Cruiser Sqdn, Rear-Adm Kurita), *Mikuma*, *Mogami*, *Suzuya*, the carrier *Ryujo* (4th Carrier Sqdn, Rear-Adm Kakuta), the light cruisers *Yura* and the destroyers *Fubuki*, *Shirayuki*, *Hatsuyuki* and *Murakumo* (11th DD Div), sets out to sea from Mergui to make a raid in the Bay of Bengal. On 3-4 Apl the force waits S of the Andamans and in the process exchanges the 11th DD Div, which goes to Port Blair, for the 20th DD Div, comprising *Amagiri*, *Asagiri*, *Shirakumo* and *Yugiri*.
On 2 Apl a Japanese convoy with 46 transports puts to sea from Singapore

for Rangoon with the 18th Inf Div on board. It is escorted by the cruiser *Kashii* and the destroyers *Hatakaze* and *Shikinami* and the submarine-chaser *Ch8*. On 4 Apl *Kashii* and *Shikinami* tuin away and are replaced by an escort force from Penang consisting of the minelayer *Hatsutaka* and the destroyers *Asakaze, Harukaze* and *Matsukaze* (5th DD Div). The convoy arrives in Rangoon on 7 Apl without incident.

On the evening of 4 Apl the 3rd DD Flotilla comprising the cruiser *Sendai* and the destroyers *Fubuki, Hatsuyuki, Murakumo, Shirayuki* (11th DD Div), *Isonami, Uranami* and *Ayanami* (19th DD Div), leaves Port Blair to take up a covering position W of the Andamans until 8 Apl.

The Japanese Carrier Fleet, advancing from the S, is reported on the afternoon of 4 Apl by one of the six British Catalina flying-boats stationed in Ceylon before it is shot down by the fighter cover. Then all operational ships leave the harbour of Colombo, including the cruisers *Cornwall* and *Dorsetshire* which receive orders to join up with Force A. The latter, after hurried refuelling, sets out from Addu Atoll shortly after midnight on 5 Apl. Force B follows in the morning.

Early on 5 Apl a Catalina again reports the Japanese Carrier Fleet. At the same time Nagumo flies off 53 high-level and 38 dive-bombers with 36 fighters 300 nautical miles SE of Ceylon to attack Colombo. In heavy air engagements the Japanese fighters shoot down 19 out of 42 Hurricane and Fulmar fighters and six Swordfish torpedo aircraft, whilst losing seven of their own. The attack causes heavy damage. The auxiliary cruiser *Hector* (11198 tons) and the destroyer *Tenedos* sink in the harbour. At mid-day a reconnaissance plane from the *Tone* sights the British cruisers *Cornwall* (Capt Manwaring) and *Dorsetshire* (Capt Agar). 53 dive-bombers under Lt-Cdr Egusa, which are immediately flown off from the Japanese carriers, sink the ships with many hits. 1122 men from a total of 1546 are later rescued by the *Enterprise* and two destroyers. Although the distance between British Force A and the Japanese Carrier Fleet on the afternoon of 5 Apl is at times no more than 200 nautical miles, the Japanese reconnaissance aircraft do not find the British forces and Adm Somerville is able to keep out of the Japanese range during the day. From 5 Apl to 8 Apl the Japanese Carrier Fleet withdraws to the SE. On the evening of 5 Apl Vice-Adm Ozawa divides his force in order to attack shipping off the Indian Coast. on 6 Apl. A Northern Group (Rear-Adm Kurita) with the cruisers *Kumano Suzuya* and the destroyer *Shirakumo* sinks nine ships off Puri (Orissa); a Central Group (Vice-Adm Ozawa) with *Chokai, Yura, Asagiri* and *Yugiri* sinks four ships; and a Southern Group (Capt Sakiyama) with the cruisers *Mikuma* and *Mogami* and the destroyer *Amagiri* sinks three ships and damages two more. The carrier *Ryujo*, operating with the Central Group, carries out raids with her aircraft on Vizagapatam and Cocanada and sinks three ships and damages one more. In all, 92000 tons of shipping are sunk.

On 8 Apl a Catalina flying-boat again reports the advancing Japanese Carrier Fleet but, in the meantime, Adm Somerville has returned with his two battle squadrons to Addu Atoll. The ships in Trincomalee receive orders to withdraw to the S. Early on 9 Apl 91 Japanese high-level bombers and dive-bombers with 38 fighters attack Trincomalee. Nine of the 23 British Hurricane and Fulmar fighters which are sent up to defend the harbour are shot down. The Japanese fighter escort over the carriers intercepts a force of nine Blenheim bombers and shoots five down. Only a few near-misses are obtained. Japanese reconnaissance aircraft again locate the British ships withdrawing southwards along the coast. 80 dive-bombers with fighter escort destroy the *Hermes* (Capt Onslow†), the destroyer *Vampire*, the corvette *Hollyhock* and two tankers. The Japanese forces, which, apart from the above-mentioned warships, have sunk, in all, 23 merchant ships of 112312 tons, start the return journey. Adm Ozawa, reinforced by the 3rd DD Flotilla, passes through the Straits of Malacca on 9-10 Apl, followed by Vice-Adm Nagumo on 12-13 Apl.

Of the British formations Force A proceeds on 9 Apl to Bombay and Force B to Kilindini on the East African coast.

Of the Japanese submarines operating W of India in the Maldive and Laccadive passages and W of Ceylon *I-6* (Cdr* Inaba) sinks two ships of 11321 tons and two sailing ships; *I-7* (Cdr* Koizumi) one ship of 9415 tons; *I-5* (Cdr* Utsuki) one ship of 6617 tons and one sailing ship; *I-3* (Cdr* Tonozuka) one ship of 5051 tons and torpedoes one ship of 4872 tons; and *I-2* (Cdr* Inaba) one unknown ship.

27 Mar   North Atlantic
U587 (Lt-Cdr Borcherdt), which is returning from the American East Coast, hears and sights the fast troop transport convoy WS.17. Her contact report is located by HF/DF. The escort destroyer *Leamington*, which is sent to the scene, at first goes past her but, on her return, sights the U-boat which has just sent off a second report and is now sunk by the destroyers *Aldenham*, *Grove*, *Leamington* and *Volunteer*. First success with shipboard HF/DF

27-28 Mar   Bay of Biscay
British raid on St Nazaire with the object of destroying the giant drydock capable of taking the *Tirpitz*. The following ships are deployed: the destroyer *Campbelltown* (Lt-Cdr Beattie), *MGB314*, *MTB74* and 16 motor launches with, in all, crews of 353 and 268 Commandos (Lt-Col Newman). They are to be supported and met by the destroyers *Atherstone*, *Tynedale*, *Cleveland* and *Brocklesby*. *Campbelltown*, in spite of strong defensive fire which takes heavy toll, particularly of the small craft of the force as they approach, succeeds in ramming the dock gate and setting the time fuses for the explosive charge. The Commandos are unable to overcome the defence and are wiped out. When the 5th TB Flotilla (strength as on 13-14 Mar) intervenes from the sea, only four launches are able to break through to the destroyers waiting to meet them and to reach Plymouth.

27 Mar-9 Apl   Mediterranean
The German U-boats *U205*, *U431* and *U453* (Lt-Cdr Freiherr v. Schlippenbach) operate against British Tobruk supply traffic. *U453* torpedoes the hospital ship *Somersetshire* (9716 tons) not recognized as such.

28 Mar-1 Apl   South Asia
The US submarine *Sturgeon* (Lt-Cdr Wright) sinks one ship of 842 tons off Makassar. In several attacks on a Japanese landing force off Christmas Island on 31 Mar and 1 Apl the US submarine *Seawolf* (Lt-Cdr Warder) torpedoes the Japanese cruiser *Naka*. The British *Truant* (Lt-Cdr Haggard) sinks two ships of 11719 tons off Penang.

29 Mar-5 Apl   Black Sea
The Soviet flotilla leader *Tashkent* and destroyer *Shaumyan* bring supplies to Sevastopol on 29 Mar and the destroyers *Bditelny* and *Soobrazitelny* shell land targets. On 2 Apl the flotilla leader *Kharkov* and the destroyer *Svobodny*, and on 5 Apl the destroyer *Boiki*, arrive in Sevastopol with supplies.

29 Mar-5 Apl   Mediterranean
The British submarine *Proteus* sinks on 29 Mar off Brindisi one ship from a convoy of seven ships, escorted by the destroyer *Sebenico* and the torpedo boats *Bassini*, *Castelfidardo* and *Mosto* and on 31 Mar a second ship escorted by the destroyer *Strale*. Together they amount to 11688 tons. On 1 Apl *Urge* (Cdr Tomkinson) sinks the Italian cruiser *Bande Nere* off Stromboli.

From 2 Apl to 4 Apl three Italian convoys (operation 'Lupo') proceed to Tripoli without incident. They consist of six ships escorted by seven destroyers and two torpedo boats. Distant escort: cruiser *Eugenio di Savoia* and two destroyers.

On 5 Apl the British submarine *Una* (Lt Norman) sinks one ship of 5335 tons off Calabria.

30 Mar   Norway
33 Halifaxes of No 4 Group RAF Bomber Command unsuccessfully attack the battleship *Tirpitz* lying in Föttenfjord off Trondheim. Five aircraft are shot down.

April 1942   Mediterranean
The British Admiralty allows Italy to fetch colonists from East Africa in the passenger ships *Vulcania* (24469 tons), *Saturnia* (24470 tons), *Duilio* (23635 tons) and *Giulio Cesare* (21900 tons). The 7 arrive back in Italy in July 1942.

1 Apl Norway

11 Norwegian merchant ships try to break through the Kattegat and Skagerrak from Göteborg to England. Only two ships reach their goal. The whaling depot ship *Skytteren* (12358 tons), the tankers *Buccaneer* (6222 tons) and *Storsten* (5343 tons) and two smaller freighters (totalling 2752 tons) are either sunk by German warships or scuttle themselves. German bombers destroy the tanker *Rigmor* (6305 tons) and damage the tanker *Newton* (10324 tons). The remaining three ships return to Göteborg.

1-11 Apl Mediterranean

Heavy air attacks by II Fl.K. (Gen Loerzer) and Italian formations on Malta. In them the British destroyers *Lance*, *Gallant*, *Kingston*, the minesweeper *Abingdon*, the submarines *P36*, *Glavkos*, *Pandora*, the naval tanker *Plumleaf* (5916 tons) and several smaller ships are sunk. The cruiser *Penelope* is damaged. In the middle of the month the remaining boats of the British 10th SM Flotilla have to leave Malta. In April 1942 comes the climax of the air attacks on Malta. German bombers fly 4082 day and 256 night sorties against the island.

2-25 Apl Central Pacific

US raid on Tokyo. On 2 Apl the carrier *Hornet*, escorted by the cruisers *Nashville* and *Vincennes* and the destroyers *Grayson*, *Gwin*, *Meredith* and *Monssen* (Desdiv 22) and the tanker *Cimarron*, sets out from San Francisco. On 8 Apl Vice-Adm Halsey with the carrier *Enterprise*, the cruisers *Northampton* (Rear-Adm Spruance), *Salt Lake City* and the destroyers *Balch* (Desron 6), *Benham*, *Ellet* and *Fanning* (Desdiv 12) and the tanker *Sabine* put to sea from Pearl Harbour. The two groups join up to form TF 16 on 13 Apl. On the way they are located early on 18 Apl by the Japanese picket boat line stationed 700 nautical miles E of Japan; two boats are sunk by aircraft of the *Enterprise* and two others are damaged; one is captured by *Nashville*. Halsey decides to fly off the 16 B-25 bombers (Lt-Col Doolittle) embarked on the *Hornet* to make a daylight attack on Tokyo when still 668 nautical miles away. The damage done in Tokyo (13 aircraft),

Nagoya (two aircraft) and Kobe (one aircraft) is slight. Apart from one bomber which makes an emergency landing near Vladivostok, all aircraft are lost making forced landings in China. The crews of two are taken prisoner.

On the basis of the picket boats' reports the Japanese 1st Carrier Fleet (Vice-Adm Nagumo), comprising five carriers, four battleships, two heavy and one light cruiser and nine destroyers (see 26 Mar-11 Apl), which is in the area E of Formosa on its return to Japan from the raid on Ceylon, is put on the trail. But it has to abandon the sortie on 22 Apl as hopeless. Likewise, the submarines *I-21*, *I-22*, *I-24*, *I-27*, *I-28* and *I-29*, which are E of the Bonin Islands on their way from Japan to Truk, and the 3rd SM Flotilla, comprising *I-8*, *I-74*, *I-75*, *I-68*, *I-69*, *I-71* and *I-72*, do not get to TF 16 which withdraws at high speed and reaches Pearl Harbour on 25 Apl.

3 Apl Arctic

German bombers sink in Murmansk the British freighter *Empire Starlight* (6850 tons) and *New Westminster City* (4747 tons) belonging to PQ.13.

4-24 Apl Western Atlantic

U154 (Cdr Kölle) sinks five ships of 28715 tons in the Greater Antilles.

4-30 Apl Baltic

The German IFl.K. (Gen Förster) attacks the large units of the Baltic Fleet in Leningrad to prevent their deployment after the ice thaw.

Operation 'Eisstoss': on 4 Apl 62 Ju 87s of St.G.1 (Lt-Col Hagen) with III/St.G.1, I and II/St.G.2 and 33 Ju 88s of K.G.1 (Maj-Gen Angerstein) attack the ships and 37 He 111s of K.G.4 (Col Rath) attack the AA positions with fighter protection from J.G.54 (Maj Trautloft) comprising 59 Me109s. In the night 4-5 Apl 31 He 111s of K.G.4 again attack the ships. The battleship *Oktyabrskaya Revolutsiya* receives four hits; the cruiser *Maksim Gorki* seven medium calibre hits; the cruisers *Kirov* and *Petropavlovsk* and the destroyer *Silny* one serious hit each; and the destroyer *Grozyashchi,,* the minelayer *Marti* and the training ship *Svir* less serious hits.

Operation 'Götz von Berlichingen': in

the continuation of the attacks on 24 Apl, 25 Apl and 30 Apl, one hit, *inter alia*, is scored on *Kirov*. In all, IFIK. flies 596 sorties against Leningrad in Apl and Air Fleet 1 in the same period a total of 9047 sorties in support of Army Group North. 29 aircraft are lost.

5 Apl Mediterranean
The British destroyer *Havock*, in attempting to break through from Malta to Gibraltar, goes aground near Kelibia and is destroyed there by a torpedo from the Italian submarine *Aradam*.

7-19 Apl Mediterranean
In British submarine operations *Turbulent* (Cdr Linton) sinks two ships of 5677 tons off Brindisi; *Thrasher* (Lt-Cdr Mackenzie) two ships of 2326 tons on the Cyrenaican coast from a convoy escorted by the torpedo boats *Pallade* and *Perseo* and four German motor minesweepers; and *Torbay* (Cdr Miers) two ships of 1434 tons off Corfu and Taranto. Off Sfax *P35/Umbra* (Lt Maydon) sinks a ship of 4219 tons which is setting out and has just been met by the torpedo boat *Castore*.

8-25 Apl Arctic
Operations against the convoys PQ.14 and QP.10. On 8 Apl the PQ.14 sets out from Iceland with 24 ships, escorted by five destroyers, four corvettes, two minesweepers and four A/S trawlers. Close escort: cruisers *Edinburgh* (Rear-Adm Bonham-Carter), *Norfolk* and two destroyers. Near Jan Mayen the convoy runs into pack-ice: 16 ships and two minesweepers have to return after being damaged by ice. On 10 Apl the QP.10 sets out from the Kola Inlet with 16 ships, escorted by the cruiser *Liverpool*, the destroyers *Oribi*, *Punjabi*, *Marne*, *Fury*, *Eclipse*, the minesweeper *Speedwell* and the A/S trawlers *Blackfly* and *Paynter*. Between Iceland and Norway a covering force operates, comprising the battleships *Duke of York*, *King George V*, the carrier *Victorious*, the cruisers *Kent* and *Nigeria* and eight destroyers. On 11 Apl the Soviet Air Force attacks the German airfield at Kirkenes with little success. Ju 88s of III/K.G.30 sink the freighter *Empire Cowper* (7164 tons) from QP.10. In the night 12-13 Apl *U435* (Lt-Cdr

Strelow) misses the *Punjabi* and sinks in turn the freighters *El Occidente* (6008 tons) and *Kiev* (5823 tons). Towards morning an attack by *U209* fails and Ju 88s of III/K.G.30 sink the freighter *Harpalion* (5486 tons). German air reconnaissance locates the PQ.14 but isolated air attacks on the convoy from 15 Apl to 17 Apl fail and the escort of QP.10 (Cdr McBeath on *Oribi*) counters attacks by the U-boats *U376*, *U377* and *U456*. *U376* narrowly misses the *Edinburgh* on 17 Apl. E of Bear Island. *U403* (Lt-Cdr Clausen) sinks the freighter *Empire Howard* (6985 tons) from the convoy PQ.14 and the convoy Commodore Rees is lost. Attempts by the German 8th DD Flotilla to find the two convoys fail in the prevailing bad weather. Seven freighters arrive in Murmansk and 11 in Iceland. The Soviet submarines, including *K-21*, *S-101* and *Shch-401*, which were stationed as a flank screen, go to the Polar Coast. On 19 Apl the German minesweepers *M154* and *M251* prevent an attack by *Shch-401* (Capt 3rd Class Moiseev) on a convoy off Tanafjord. *Shch-401* sinks the steamer *Stensaas* (1359 tons) from another convoy on 24 Apl and is then attacked with depth charges from the submarine-chasers *UJ1101* and *UJ1110*. After that the boat is missing but it is possible she was sunk in error by two Soviet torpedo cutters on her return on 25 Apl.

8 Apl-11 May Western Atlantic
Twelve U-boats arrive one after the other off the American East Coast as the fifth wave. In individual operations they sink many ships. *U84* (Lt Uphoff) sinks two ships of 8240 tons; *U654* (Lt Forster) three ships of 17755 tons; *U85* (Lt Greger) one ship of 4904 tons; *U575* (Lt-Cdr Heydemann) one ship of 6887 tons; *U201* (Lt-Cdr Schnee) three ships of 15313 tons and torpedoes one ship of 7417 tons; *U576* (Lt-Cdr Heinicke) two ships of 6441 tons; *U109* (Lt-Cdr Bleichrodt) three ships of 12099 tons and torpedoes one ship of 6548 tons; *U136* (Lt-Cdr Zimmermann) three ships of 12707 tons and torpedoes one ship of 8955 tons; *U402* (Lt-Cdr Freiherr von Forstner) three ships of 11135 tons; *U752* (Lt-Cdr Schroeter)

three ships of 15506 tons. Attacks made by *U86* (Lt-Cdr Schug) and *U582* (Lt-Cdr Schulte) fail. *U84* is sunk on 14 Apl by the US destroyer *Roper*.

9-15 Apl   Black Sea
In German air attacks on Novorossisk and Tuapse the cruiser *Voroshilov* and the destroyers *Nezamozhnik* and *Sposobny* are damaged. 30 dead. On 10 Apl the flotilla leader *Kharkov* and the destroyer *Svobodny* bring supplies to Sevastopol. On 13 Apl the destroyers *Boiki* and *Nezamozhnik* follow, while *Bditelny* and *Soobrazitelny* shell land targets. *Nezamozhnik* carries out another supply journey on 15 Apl.

10 Apl-4 June   Pacific
US submarines sink the following ships off Japan: *Thresher* (Lt-Cdr Anderson) one ship of 3039 tons; *Trout* (Lt-Cdr Fenno) two ships of 7138 tons and damages one ship of 16801 tons; *Drum* (Lt-Cdr Rice) the seaplane-carrier *Mizuho* and two ships of 7736 tons; *Grenadier* (Lt-Cdr Lent) two ships of 19218 tons; *Silversides* (Lt-Cdr Burlingame) damages two ships of 10421 tons; *Tuna* (Lt-Cdr de Tar) sinks one ship of 805 tons and damages one ship of 8469 tons; *Pollack* (Lt-Cdr Mosely) sinks two guard boats of 123 tons; *Pompano* (Lt-Cdr Parks) sinks two ships of 8784 tons. Near Truk *Greenling* (Lt-Cdr Bruton) sinks two ships of 9921 tons; *Tautog* (Lt-Cdr Willingham) two ships of 9928 tons and the submarine *I-28;* and *Triton* (Lt-Cdr Kirkpatrick) three ships of 14208 tons.

10 Apl-9 June   South Asia
Elements of the Japanese South-West Area Fleet land army units on the West and East coast of Cebu on 10 Apl. By 14 Apl they have broken the resistance of the American forces. 4160 troops are landed on 16 Apl near Ho Ho on Panay and two days later near San José (Panay). By 20 Apl this island is also occupied.
4852 troops are embarked on 26 Apl in Cebu to be landed on 29 Apl in Cotabato and Parang (Mindanao). On 3 May further Japanese forces from Panay are landed in Macajalar Bay on Mindanao. After General Wainwright on Corregidor has officially offered the capitulation of the American Forces on the Philippines many of the remaining

battle groups are dissolved in order to carry out partisan warfare with the Filipinos.
The Japanese land on Leyte and Samar —from Panay on 21 May and from Cebu on 25 May.

11-13 Apl   Mediterranean
The Italian destroyers *Vivaldi* and *Malocello* lay in two nights SW of Marettimo (Western Sicily) the barrages S51 and S52, each with 180 EMC mines. The German 3rd MTB Flotilla (Lt-Cdr Kemnade) lays in three nights E of Malta the barrages MT10–12 with 8 EMF and 72 UMB mines as well as 16 protection floats and 48 explosive floats.

12 Apl-19 May   Western Atlantic
In the Caribbean and near Trinidad *U130* (Cdr Kals) sinks two ships of 13092 tons and *U66* (Cdr Zapp) six ships of 43956 tons and torpedoes one ship of 12502 tons. On 19 Apl *U130* shells the oil installations of Curaçao.

12 Apl-28 May   Arctic
Intensive deployment of the Soviet 3rd SM Division (Capt 3rd Class Morosov) against convoy traffic on both sides of the Varanger Peninsula. In up to five operations *M-171* (Lt-Cdr Starikov) makes four attacks and torpedoes the steamer *Curityba* (4,969 tons); *M-172* (Lt-Cdr Fisanovich) five attacks with no success; *M-173* (Lt-Cdr Terekhin) three attacks and sinks the steamer *Blankenese* (3263 tons); *M176* (Lt-Cdr Bondarevich) five attacks with no success. The submarines avoid the depth charge pursuits by the German submarine-chasers e.g. *M-172* on 15 May after an eight-hour pursuit in which *UJ1104* and *UJ1108* drop depth charges, but then have to turn away when under fire from the Soviet coastal batteries on the Fisherman's Peninsula.

13-26 Apl   Mediterranean
From 13 Apl to 16 Apl the U-boats *U562* (Lt Hamm), *U331* (Lt-Cdr v. Tiesenhausen), *U81* (Lt-Cdr Guggenberger) and *U561* (Lt-Cdr Bartels) lay mine barrages off Famagusta (Cyprus) —two ships of 238 tons sunk; and off Beirut, Haifa and Port Said—two ships of 11754 tons sunk and one ship of 4043 tons damaged. Later *U331* sinks three sailing ships; and *U81* one tanker of

P

6018 tons and nine sailing ships. *U97* has no success off Tobruk.

14 Apl North Atlantic
After disembarking agents in Iceland (8 Apl) and a still unconfirmed attack on a small ship on 11 Apl, *U252* (Lt-Cdr Lerchen) encounters in the night 13-14 Apl the convoy OG.82 which is escorted by the 36th EG (Cdr Walker). It is located by the corvette *Vetch* with radar at a distance of 7,000 metres (first successful locating with the 10cm radar type 271), which evades a torpedo salvo and, together with the command boat, the sloop *Stork*, sinks the boat by gunfire and depth charges.

14 Apl Mediterranean
In an attempt to attack an Italian convoy off Tripoli, Britain's most successful submarine *Upholder* (Lt-Cdr Wanklyn†) is sunk by the Italian torpedo boat *Pegaso* on her 24th mission against the enemy.

14-26 Apl Mediterranean
Operation 'Calendar': Anglo-American Force W (Commodore Daniel) sets out from Greenock on 14 Apl with the British battlecruiser *Renown*, the US carrier *Wasp* and the destroyers *Inglefield*, *Echo*, *Partridge* and *Ithuriel* (British) and *Lang* and *Madison* (US). It is reinforced off Gibraltar on 19 Apl by the British cruisers *Cairo* and *Charybdis* and flies off 47 British Spitfire fighters for Malta on 20 Apl. 46 of them arrive. Force W returns to Scapa Flow on 26 Apl. The Italian submarines *Brin*, *Veniero*, *Argo* and *Velella* operate S of the Balearics, but only *Velella* attacks a destroyer which is missed.

16 Apl South Africa
Schiff 53 Doggerbank (Lt-Cdr Schneidewind) drops 80 EMC mines in five sections off Cape Agulhas (South Africa). The British freighter *Soudan* (6,677 tons) sinks, and the depot ship *Hecla* (10850 tons) is damaged, on the barrages.

17-26 Apl South West Pacific
The US submarine *Tambor* (Lt-Cdr Murphy) sinks one ship of 394 tons off Kavieng; *Spearfish* (Lt-Cdr Dempsey) one ship of 5402 tons and torpedoes two other ships of 13990 tons off Lingayen Gulf; and *Pickerel* (Lt-Cdr

Bacon) torpedoes one ship of 9347 tons off Ambon.

18-19 Apl Mediterranean
The Italian destroyers *Malocello* and *Vivaldi* lay S of Malta the barrage M5 consisting of 156 mines. The laying out of the barrage M7 planned for the following night SE of Malta has to be abandoned because the mine-laying formation is prematurely sighted.

19-22 Apl South Atlantic
The German auxiliary cruiser *Schiff 28 Michel* (Cdr* von Ruckteschell) sinks two tankers of 16152 tons in the South Atlantic.

20 Apl Norway
NW of Namsos the British submarine *Trident* (Cdr Sladen) sinks one ship of 5386 tons.

20 Apl Black Sea
After the thawing of the ice German and Rumanian convoy traffic begins between Constanza and Ochakov. The merchant ships used are *Zar Ferdinand* (1994 tons), *Kolozsvar* (1200 tons), *Kassa* (1022 tons), *Danubius* (1489 tons), *Oituz* (2686 tons), *Sulina* (3495 tons), *Tisza* (961 tons), *Budapest* (485 tons), *Carpati* (4336 tons), *Salzburg* (1742 tons), *Arkadia* (1756 tons), *Ardeal* (5695 tons), *Suceava* (6876 tons) and *Le Progrès* (311 tons). Escort provided by the Danube Flotilla and Rumanian warships (destroyers *Marasesti*, *Maresti*, *Regina Maria*, the torpedo boat *Smeul* and gunboat *Dumitrescu*). The Soviet destroyers *Bditelny* and *Soobrazitelny* bring supplies to Sevastopol.

20-28 Apl Mediterranean
The German 3rd MTB Flotilla (Lt-Cdr Kemnade) lays W and NE of Valetta and E of Malta the mine barrages MT13 to 18 with 19 UMB and 84 EMC mines, 36 protection floats and 108 explosive floats.

20 Apl-9 May South Pacific
The Japanese submarines *Ro-33* and *Ro-34* each undertake two patrol operations off Port Moresby.

20 Apl-14 June North Atlantic
First rota with 11 regularly established ocean escort groups for the Allied North Atlantic convoys HX, SC, ON and ONS from WESTOMP (Western Ocean Meeting Point) to EASTOMP (Eastern Ocean Meeting Point).
HX.186 leaves Halifax on 20 Apl with

21 ships. EG B7 with destroyers HMS *Churchill, Firedrake,* corvettes HMS *Dianella, Kingcup, Loosestrife* and the Free French *Roselys.*
SC.81 leaves Halifax on 23 Apl with 70 ships. EG B2 with destroyers HMS *Hesperus, Piorun* (Polish), corvettes HMS *Clematis, Gentian, Sweetbriar* and *Vervain.*
HX.187 leaves Halifax on 27 Apl with 26 ships. EG B1 with destroyers HMS *Hurricane, Rockingham,* corvettes HMS *Anchusa, Dahlia* and *Monkshood.*
SC.82 leaves Halifax on 30 Apl with 32 ships. EG B4 with destroyers HMS *Highlander, Winchelsea,* corvettes HMS *Anemone, Asphodel* and *Pennywort.*
HX.188 leaves Halifax on 3 May with 28 ships. EG B3 with destroyers *Harvester,* corvettes HMS *Mignonette, Narcissus,* Free French *Lobelia* and *Renoncule.*
SC.83 leaves Halifax on 7 May with 63 ships. EG B6 with destroyer HMS *Viscount,* corvettes *Acanthus* (Norwegian), *Eglantine, Potentilla* and *Rose.*
HX.189 leaves Halifax on 10 May with 21 ships. EG C1 with destroyers HMCS *Assiniboine, St Croix,* corvettes HMCS *Buctouche, Chambly,* HMS *Dianthus, Nasturtium,* Free French *Mimose* and *Aconit.*
SC.84 leaves Halifax on 14 May with 46 ships. EG C2 with destroyers HMS *Broadway,* corvettes HMCS *Brandon, Drumheller, Dunvegan, Morden* and HMS *Polyanthus.*
HX.190 leaves Halifax on 17 May with 18 ships. EG A3 with US Coastguard cutters *Campbell, Ingham,* corvettes HMCS *Rosthern, Agassiz, Mayflower* and *Collingwood.*
HX.191 leaves Halifax on 24 May with 26 ships. EG C3 with destroyers HMCS *Saguenay, Skeena,* corvettes HMCS *Westaskiwin, Sackville, Galt* and *Camrose.*
SC.85 leaves Halifax on 29 May with 62 ships. EG C4 with destroyers HMCS *Ottawa, St Francis,* corvettes HMCS *Lethbridge, Prescott, Eyebright* and *Arvida* arrives in Britain on 14 June.
These ocean escort groups meet an ON or ONS convoy at EASTOMP and return with it to WESTOMP. Between the convoy journeys they take on supplies in St John's (Newfoundland) and

Londonderry (Northern Ireland). In later operations the composition of the escort groups changes depending on the availability of the vessels.

23 Apl–4 May Mediterranean
In operations against the British Tobruk supply traffic *U565* (Lt-Cdr Franken) sinks one ship of 1301 tons and *U372* misses two guard ships. E of Gibraltar *U573* is lost on 1 May as a result of action by a Hudson of No 233 Sqdn RAF and *U74* is lost on 2 May as a result of action by the British destroyers *Wishart* and *Wrestler* with air support. The Italian submarine *Corallo* (Cdr Andreani) sinks two sailing vessels off the Tunisian coast.

23 Apl–5 May North Atlantic
The first U-boat tanker *U459* (Lt-Cdr von Wilamowitz-Moellendorf) refuels 14 outgoing and homeward-bound U-boats 500 nautical miles NE of Bermuda.

24 Apl–24 May Western Atlantic
Between the Bahamas and the Greater Antilles (*U108*), in the Gulf of Mexico (*U506* and *U507*), off Cuba and Yucatan (*U125*) and off Guiana (*U162*), *U108* (Cdr Scholtz) sinks five ships of 31340 tons; *U506* (Lt-Cdr Würdemann) eight ships of 39906 tons and damages three ships of 23354 tons; *U507* (Cdr Schacht) sinks nine ships of 44782 tons; *U125* (Lt-Cdr Folkers) nine ships of 47055 tons and *U162* (Cdr* Wattenberg) nine ships of 47181 tons.

25 Apl Baltic
Beginning of the transfer of German forces to the Gulf of Finland for the summer of 1942. Taking part are: Officer Commanding Minesweepers East, Capt Böhmer; the 3rd MS Flotilla (seven minesweepers Type 35); the 1st MMS Flotilla (one tender and nine R-boats); the 17th MS Flotilla (5 converted trawlers—only until May 1942); the 18th MS Flotilla (7 converted trawlers); the 12th SC Flotilla (10 converted trawlers and whalers); 3rd Patrol Boat Flotilla (11 converted trawlers); the 31st MS Flotilla (one R-boat, 13 converted fishing drifters); the 34th MS Flotilla (14 converted fishing drifters); the 27th Landing Flotilla (5 large gun carriers, 15 minelaying barges and nine transport barges); two minesweeping depot ships

(each with 16 sweeper long-boats); one mine destructor ship and the minelayers *Kaiser* and *Roland*. In addition, auxiliary vessels and the coastal defence flotilla Ostland.

25 Apl-8 May   Indian Ocean

Operation 'Ironclad': British landing near Diego Suarez (Madagascar). On 25 Apl the slow convoy Y with two special landing ships, six supply transports, one fleet tanker and one hospital ship sets out from Durban, escorted by the cruiser *Devonshire* and three destroyers, the 14th MS Flotilla and the 3rd EG. On 28 Apl the fast convoy Z with five attack transports and three troop transports follows with the covering force (Rear-Adm Syfret) with the battleship *Ramillies*, the carrier *Illustrious*, the cruiser *Hermione* and six destroyers. On 3 May the convoys and reinforcements detached from the Eastern Fleet, comprising the carrier *Indomitable* (Rear-Adm Boyd) and two destroyers, join up. From there the invasion fleet (Capt Oliver) reaches the area NW of the island. It comprises the *Devonshire*, the destroyers *Anthony*, *Laforey*, *Lightning* and *Pakenham*, the corvettes *Freesia*, *Auricula*, *Nigella*, *Fritillary*, *Genista*, *Cyclamen* and *Jasmine* and the minesweepers *Cromer*, *Poole*, *Romney*, *Cromarty* and *Thyme*, as well as the transports. The covering force operates with the *Ramillies*, the carriers *Illustrious* and *Indomitable* and the destroyers *Active*, *Duncan*, *Javelin*, *Lookout*, *Inconstant*, *Paladin* and *Panther* further off. The *Hermione* carries out a diversionary sortie.

5 May: Attack by British carrier aircraft on the French airfields and ships. The auxiliary cruiser *Bougainville* is sunk. The submarine *Bévéziers* is destroyed by depth charges. The British landing in Courrier Bay, where the corvette *Auricula* runs on a mine, takes place without resistance; but the further advance of the British landing troops is held up on 5 May and 6 May by the French defenders. The landing of British marine commandos by the destroyer *Anthony* and the capture of important central installations lead, however, to the rapid collapse of French resistance. The gunboat *D'Entrecasteaux* which has supported the defenders with

her guns, has to be beached after being hit by bombs. 7 May: the French submarine *Le Héros* is sunk by a corvette and aircraft of the *Illustrious* when attempting to attack the British main force.

8 May: the submarine *Monge* unsuccessfully attacks the British carrier *Indomitable* and is then sunk by the destroyers *Active* and *Panther*. The French submarine *Le Glorieux* and the gunboat *D'Iberville* escape to South Madagascar and, later, from there to Toulon.

26 Apl-1 May   Black Sea

On 26 Apl the Soviet cruiser *Krasny Krym* and the destroyers *Bditelny* and *Boiki* with 3487 relief troops and the transport *Serov*, escorted by the destroyers *Soobrazitelny* and *Zheleznyakov*, and carrying equipment and ammunition, arrive in Sevastopol. On 28 Apl *Krasny Krym*, *Bditelny* and *Soobrazitelny* with 2000 relief troops for Sevastopol have to return because of an air attack: they reach Sevastopol on 29 Apl, when the flotilla leader *Tashkent* takes the place of *Bditelny*. On 1 May the flotilla leader *Kharkov* brings supplies to Sevastopol and shells land targets.

26 Apl-12 May   Arctic

Operations against the convoys PQ.15 and QP.11. On 26 Apl PQ.15 sets out from Iceland with 50 ships, escorted by the destroyers *Somali*, *Matchless*, *Boadicea*, *Venomous*, *Badsworth* and *St Albans*, four minesweepers, four A/S trawlers, the AA ship *Ulster Queen* and the catapult ship *Empire Morn*. Senior officer of the escort: Capt Crombie on the minesweeper *Bramble*. Close support: cruisers *Nigeria* (Rear-Adm Burrough), *London* and two destroyers. Covering force between Iceland and Norway: battleships HMS *King George V* (Adm Tovey), USS *Washington* (Rear-Adm Giffen), carrier HMS *Victorious*, cruisers USS *Tuscaloosa*, *Wichita*, HMS *Kenya* and four British and four US destroyers. On 28 Apl QP.11 sets out from Murmansk with 13 ships, escorted by the destroyers *Bulldog* (Cdr Richmond), *Amazon*, *Beagle*, *Beverley*, four corvettes and one A/S trawler. Close escort: the cruiser *Edinburgh* (Rear-Adm Bonham-Carter), the destroyers *Foresight*, *For-*

ester and, until 29 Apl, one British minesweeper and the Soviet destroyers *Kuibyshev* and *Sokrushitelny*. Flanking concentration of four British submarines and the Soviet submarines *D-3, K-2, K-22* and *K-23* against German surface ships. German U-boats assembled: *U88, U251, U405, U436, U456, U589* and *U703*. On 29 Apl German air reconnaissance and U-boats establish contact with QP.11. On 30 Apl *U88* misses the convoy and *U436* (Lt-Cdr Seibicke) misses the *Edinburgh* ahead of the convoy, but the cruiser is later hit with two torpedoes by *U456* (Lt-Cdr Teichert). The German destroyers *Hermann Schoemann* (Capt Schulze-Hinrichs), *Z24* and *Z25* are deployed against QP.11. But they are impeded by ice and are repeatedly driven off by the four British destroyers and the corvette *Snowflake*. They are only able to sink the Soviet freighter *Tsiolkovski* (2847 tons) and to damage the *Amazon*. They operate against the disabled *Edinburgh* where, in the meantime, the Soviet patrol ship *Rubin*, one tug and the British minesweepers *Harrier, Niger, Gossamer* and *Hussar* have arrived. In the attack on 1 May *Hermann Schoemann* is badly hit by the *Edinburgh* (Capt Faulknor). In heavy engagements impeded by a snow shower and a smoke screen *Z24* (Cdr Saltzwedel) and *Z25* (Cdr* Peters) badly damage the *Forester* (Lt-Cdr Huddart†) and *Foresight* (Cdr Salter) and hit the *Edinburgh* with another torpedo with the result that she has to be abandoned and sunk by a torpedo from *Foresight*. *Z24* and later *U88* rescue the majority of the crew from the *Hermann Schoemann*. In attacks on QP.11 *U589* misses one steamer and *U251* one destroyer. With the PQ.15 the Norwegian destroyer *St Albans* and the minesweeper *Seagull* sink the Polish submarine *P551/Jastrzab* which has wandered from her position in the flanking concentration. In the case of the covering force, *King George V* runs into the destroyer *Punjabi*, whose exploding depth charges damage the battleship as she sinks, with the result that the battleship has to be relieved by the *Duke of York* (Vice-Adm Curteis). Attacks by German torpedo

aircraft and bombers on QP.11 are unsuccessful. On 2 May torpedo aircraft of I/K.G.26 sink the British freighters *Botavon* (5848 tons, convoy Commodore Capt Anchor†) and *Cape Corso* (3807 tons) and damage the *Jutland* (6153 tons) which is sunk on 3 May by *U251* (Lt-Cdr Timm). 22 ships of PQ.15 arrive in Murmansk on 5 May and 12 ships of QP.11 in Iceland on 7 May. After the operations the Soviet submarines go to the Polar Coast, where *D-3* and *K-2* attack several convoys without success. On 12 May *K-23* (Capt 3rd Class Potapov with Capt 2nd Class Gadzhiev on board) misses off Nordkyn a convoy with two steamers, the patrol boats *V6106, V6107, V6108* and the submarine-chaser group *UJ1101, UJ1109* and *UJ1110* from which the submarine tries to escape with her superior speed on the surface. She is forced to submerge by an aircraft called to the scene and is sunk by the submarine-chasers in a group depth charge attack.

26 Apl-23 May Western Atlantic
13 U-boats arrive in turn on the American East Coast and in Canadian coastal waters and they operate individually against the still largely unorganized coastal traffic. The following ships are sunk by this sixth wave: *U564* (Lt-Cdr Suhren) sinks four ships of 24390 tons and torpedoes two ships of 13245 tons; *U333* (Lt-Cdr Cremer) sinks three ships of 13596 tons and torpedoes one ship of 8327 tons; *U455* (Lt-Cdr Giessler) sinks one ship of 6994 tons; *U553* (Lt-Cdr Thurmann) three ships of 16995 tons; *U588* (Lt-Cdr Vogel) four ships of 13975 tons and torpedoes one ship of 7460 tons; *U593* (Lt-Cdr Kelbling) sinks one ship of 8426 tons and torpedoes one ship of 4853 tons; *U653* (Lt-Cdr Feiler) sinks one ship of 6225 tons; *U135* (Lt-Cdr Praetorius) one ship of 7127 tons; *U432* (Lt-Cdr H. O. Schultze) five ships of 6110 tons and torpedoes one ship of 7073 tons. *U352* (Lt-Cdr Rathke) is lost on 9 May after an unsuccessful attack on the US coastguard cutter *Icarus* which then counter-attacks. *U98* and *U566* return without success. *U213* (Lt-von Varendorff) lays an unsuccessful mine barrage near St Johns on 14 May.

27-28 Apl   Norway

Thirty-one Halifax and 12 Lancaster bombers attack without result the German battleship *Tirpitz* lying off Trondheim. Five aircraft are shot down. Another attack on the following night by 23 Halifax and 11 Lancaster bombers is also unsuccessful. Two aircraft are lost.

1 May   South Atlantic

The British turbine ship *Menelaus* (10307 tons, Capt J. H. Blyth) escapes in the South Atlantic from an attack by the auxiliary cruiser *Schiff 28 Michel* (Cdr* von Ruckteschell) and her motor torpedo boat.

2-9 May   Mediterranean

In British submarine operations *Proteus* torpedoes one ship of 3682 tons off the Albanian coast. Two attacks on 2 May and 7 May on Italian convoys off Benghazi are repelled by the escort ships *Cantore* and *Vivaldi* and *Turbine* respectively. On a supply journey to Malta *Olympus* sinks on one of the mines laid by the German 3rd MTB Flotilla. *Upright* (Lt Wraith) attacks a towed convoy with a dock off Calabria.

3-8 May   South Pacific

Carrier air battle in the Coral Sea. The Japanese plan is to make an amphibious landing near Port Moresby (New Guinea) on 10 May and to establish an air base on the South Solomons Island of Tulagi. Overall command: Vice-Adm Inoue.

The Tulagi Force (Rear-Adm Shima) comprises the minelayer *Okinoshima*, the destroyers *Kikutsuki* and *Yuzuki*, eight auxiliary minesweepers, some smaller vessels and one transport with parts of the 3rd Kure Special Landing Force.

The Port Moresby Force (Rear-Adm Kajioka) comprises the cruiser *Yubari*, the minelayer *Tsugaru*, the destroyers *Oite*, *Asanagi*, *Uzuki*, *Mutsuki*, *Mochitsuki* and *Yayoi*, some smaller units and 11 transports with the bulk of the 3rd Kure Special Landing Force and the South Sea Detachment (Maj-Gen Horii). The Support Force (Rear-Adm Marumo) comprises the cruisers *Tatsuta* and *Tenryu*, one aircraft depot ship and three gunboats. Covering Force (Rear-Adm Goto): the cruisers *Aoba*, *Furutaka*, *Kako* and *Kinugasa*, the aircraft

carrier *Shoho* and the destroyer *Sazanami*. Carrier Force (Rear-Adm Hara): *Shokaku* and *Zuikaku*, escorted by Vice-Adm Takagi with the cruisers *Haguro* and *Myoko* and the destroyers *Ushio*, *Akebono*, *Ariake*, *Yugure*, *Shiratsuyu* and *Shigure* and a tanker.

US TF 17 (Rear-Adm Fletcher), comprising the carrier *Yorktown*, the cruisers (Rear-Adm Smith), *Astoria*, *Chester* and *Portland* and the destroyers *Morris*, *Anderson*, *Hammann* and *Russell*, has joined up with TF 11 (Rear-Adm Fitch) on 1 May. The latter consists of the carrier *Lexington*, the cruisers (Rear-Adm Kinkaid) *Minneapolis* and *New Orleans* and the destroyers *Phelps*, *Dewey*, *Farragut*, *Aylwin* and *Monaghan*. A support force (Rear-Adm Crace)—TF 44—comprises the Australian cruisers *Australia* and *Hobart* and the US cruiser *Chicago* and destroyers *Perkins* and *Walke*; it operates to the SW and joins up on 4 May. Tanker Force: *Neosho* and *Tippecanoe* and destroyers *Sims* and *Worden*. Submarines: *S37*, *S38*, *S39*, *S40*, *S41*, *S42*, *S43*, *S44*, *S45*, *S46* and *S47*.

3 May: Japanese landing on Tulagi.

4 May: 99 carrier aircraft from the *Yorktown* attack the Japanese Tulagi Force and sink the destroyer *Kikutsuki* and three minesweepers and damage four other ships.

5 May: The US carriers and cruisers refuel and then make a sortie in the direction of the expected Japanese landing fleet for Port Moresby. Simultaneously, the Japanese Carrier Force enters the Coral Sea from the E. On 6 May both forces look for each other in vain in poor visibility, although at times they are only 70 nautical miles apart.

7 May: 93 US carrier aircraft attack the Japanese covering force and Japanese aircraft attack the US supply force. The Japanese carrier *Shoho* (Capt Izawa†), the US tanker *Neosho* and destroyer *Sims* are sunk. The Japanese destroyer *Sazanami* rescues 100 survivors from the carrier. 8 May: In the morning the two carrier forces sight each other and fly off their aircraft (90 Japanese and 78 American) to attack. *Shokaku* receives three bomb hits while the *Lexington* (Capt F. C. Sherman) has

to be abandoned after bomb and torpedo hits. *Yorktown* is damaged. The Japanese abandon the Port Moresby landing, although they have achieved a tactical success. Thus the American fleet achieves its strategic aim.

3-15 May   Mediterranean
Operation 'Bowery'. The Anglo-American force W (Commodore Daniel), comprising the battlecruiser *Renown*, the US carrier *Wasp*, the British cruiser *Charybdis* and the destroyers *Lang*, *Sterett* (US), *Echo* and *Intrepid* (RN), sets out from Scapa Flow on 3 May. In the night 7-8 May it joins up with the British carrier *Eagle* coming from Gibraltar with the destroyers *Partridge*, *Ithuriel*, *Antelope*, *Wishart*, *Wrestler*, *Westcott*, *Vidette*, *Georgetown* and *Salisbury*. On 9 May it flies off 47 and 17 Spitfires respectively from both carriers. Three of them are lost; the remainder reach Malta. Force W returns to Scapa Flow on 16.5. During the operation the fast minelayer *Welshman* sets out from Gibraltar on 8 May with important supplies and reaches Malta on 10 May. After unloading she puts to sea at once and arrives in Gibraltar on 12 May.

3 May-20 June   South Pacific
B Group of the Japanese 8th SM Flotilla (Capt Sasaki) operates in the South Pacific. From 5 May to 11 May *I-22*, *I-24*, *I-27* and *I-28* form a patrol line to cover the Port Moresby operation against US carrier forces. After the battle of the Coral Sea they return to Truk to take on board the midget submarines. In the process *I-28* is sunk by the US submarine *Tautog* (Lt-Cdr Willingham) S of Truk. *I-21* (Cdr* Matsumura) reconnoitres in the area of New Caledonia and sinks two ships of 11821 tons. On 19-20 May her aircraft reconnoitres Suva (Fiji) and on 23-24 May Auckland. *I-29* (Cdr* Izu) scours the Australian coast, damages one ship of 5135 tons and reconnoitres Sydney with her aircraft on 22-23 May. After renewed air reconnaissance over Sydney on 29 May *I-22*, *I-24* and *I-27* put out their midget submarines on 31 May, some of which penetrate the bay of Sydney. But they only sink the accommodation ship *Kuttabul* there and just miss the cruiser *Chicago*. After

an unsuccessful search for the midget submarines *I-21* shells Newcastle and *I-24* (Cdr*Hanabusa) Sydney on 8 June. While *I-22* carries out a periscope reconnaissance of Wellington, Auckland and Suva and *I-29* makes a sortie towards Brisbane, *I-21* pursues mercantile warfare off Newcastle, *I-24* off Sydney and *I-27* (Cdr* Yoshimura) off Tasmania. In the course of this *I-21* sinks one ship of 5527 tons; *I-24* one ship of 4312 tons and lightly damages three ships of 15844 tons; and *I-27* sinks one ship of 3353 tons and damages one ship of 4239 tons.

4 May   General Situation
OKW directive to capture Malta (Operation 'Herkules').

4-5 May   Black Sea
German positions on the SE coast of the Crimea are shelled by night by the Soviet flotilla leader *Kharkov* and destroyers *Bditelny*, *Bezuprechny* and *Smyshleny*.

5 May-22 June   Western Atlantic
A wave of seven U-boats proceeds singly from Cape Hatteras to the Straits of Florida and to the area of the Greater Antilles, Cuba, Yucatan and the Eastern Caribbean. In their operations they sink many ships. *U106* (Lt-Cdr Rasch) sinks five ships of 29154 tons and damages one ship of 4639 tons; *U753* (Cdr von Mannstein) sinks two ships of 13769 tons and damages two of 6908 tons; *U751* (Lt-Cdr Bigalk) sinks two ships of 4555 tons; *U558* (Lt-Cdr Krech) six ships of 16380 tons and damages one ship of 7061 tons; *U103* (Lt-Cdr Winter) sinks nine ships of 42169 tons; and *U107* (Lt-Cdr Gelhaus) six ships of 26983 tons.

6-19 May   South West Pacific
In operations in the South China Sea the US submarine *Skipjack* (Lt-Cdr Coe) sinks three ships of 12848 tons; *Swordfish* (Lt-Cdr Smith) one ship of 5307 tons; and *Pickerel* (Lt-Cdr Bacon) torpedoes one ship of 5973 tons. In the South Pacific *S42* (Lt Kirk) sinks the Japanese minelayer *Okinoshima* and *S44* (Lt Moore) one ship of 5644 tons.

7-17 May   Mediterranean
The German 3rd MTB Flotilla (Lt-Cdr Kemnade) lays NE of, and off, Valetta, as well as E of Malta, the barrages MT19-24 with 108 FMC mines,

16 protection floats and 46 explosive floats.

7 May-28 June   Western Atlantic
In individual operations in the area of the Caribean *U69* (Lt Gräf) sinks four ships of 12030 tons and one unidentified tug; *U155* (Lt-Cdr Piening) seven ships of 33086 tons; *U502* (Lt-Cdr von Rosenstiel) seven ships of 36894 tons; *U156* (Cdr Hartenstein) eleven ships of 44086 tons and torpedoes the US destroyer *Blakeley* and one ship of 8042 tons.

7 May-2 July   Black Sea
77 missions in all by submarines of the Soviet Black Sea Fleet to supply Sevastopol. From 7 May *D-4* (five), *L-4* (seven); from 15 May *L-5* (six), *L-23* (seven); from 30 May *S-31* (five), *S-32* (seven); from the beginning of June *D-5* (three), *L-24* (four); from the middle of June *Shch-205* (two), *Shch-208* (two), *Shch-209* (two), *Shch-212* (two), *Shch-213* (two), *Shch-214* (one), *A-2* (two), *A-4* (three), *M-31* (three), *M-32* (one), *M-33* (three), *M-52* (one), *M-60* (one), *M-112* (two), *M-117* (two) and *M-118* (three). In these missions the following boats are lost: *Shch-212* by a petrol explosion; *Shch-208* when hit by a torpedo from the Italian midget submarine *CB-2* on 18 June; *Shch-214* when hit by a torpedo from the Italian *MAS571* on 19 June; and *S-32* by a bomb hit on 26 June.

8-16 May   Black Sea
The German 11th Army (Col-Gen von Manstein) attacks the Soviet Crimean Front on the Kerch Peninsula consisting of the 47th, 51st and 44th Armies, breaks through the front in the S and destroys the main body of the Soviet forces W of Kerch. The remainder escape by sea from Kerch to the Taman Peninsula. From 10 May to 16 May the Soviet cruiser *Voroshilov*, the flotilla leaders *Kharkov* and *Tashkent* and the destroyers *Bditelny* and *Soobrazitelny* intervene in the fighting from the S but with little success.
On 9 May the two destroyers escort the transport *Serov* to Sevastopol and on 12 May they themselves bring further supplies. From 12 May to 14 May the cruiser *Krasny Krym* and the destroyers *Dzerzhinski* and *Nezamozhnik* bring 2250 relief troops to Sevastopol. On

14 May *Dzerzhinski* runs on an air ground mine and sinks, whilst *Nezamozhnik* shells land targets.

9-10 May   Norway
The pocket-battleship *Admiral Scheer* is transferred from Trondheim to Narvik with the fleet tanker *Dithmarschen* and the torpedo boats *T5* and *T7*.

9-15 May   Baltic
The German minelayers *Kaiser* and *Roland* lay out the mine barrages 'Nashorn 1-5" between Porkkala and Naissaari. They are later supplemented by nine more sections. 1915 mines are laid in all.

10 May   South Atlantic
The US carrier *Ranger* flies off 40 P-40 fighters for Accra off the Gold Coast. They are transferred from there via Africa and the Near East to India.

11 May   Mediterranean
The British destroyers *Jervis* (Capt Poland), *Jackal*, *Kipling* and *Lively* make a sortie from Alexandria against a German-Italian convoy reported to be on the way to Benghazi. In the process the force is located by German reconnaissance aircraft S of Crete and returns in accordance with orders. In the afternoon the destroyers are attacked by 14 Ju 88s of I/L.G.1 (Capt Helbig) from Heraklion (Crete) when *Lively* sinks. An attack by II/L.G.1 (Capt Kollewe) from Eleusis, near Athens, is unsuccessful. In a second attack by I/L.G.1 at sunset *Kipling* and *Jackal* (sunk on 12 May) are destroyed. Only *Jervis* is able to escape after rescuing 630 survivors.

11-14 May   North Atlantic
The outward-bound U-boats *U126*, *U161* and *U128* (Lt-Cdr Heyse) which sinks one ship of 3491 tons, operate against the convoy SL.109, located by chance.

11 May-21 June   North Atlantic
First attempt to carry out a planned group operation 'Hecht' in the North Atlantic with *U124*, *U94*, *U569*, *U406*, *U96* and *U590*. On the way to their patrol line *U569* (Lt-Cdr Hinsch) sights on 11 May the convoy ONS.92 (41 ships, escort: US coastguard cutters *Campbell*, *Ingham*, Canadian corvettes *Algoma*, *Arvida*, *Bittersweet* and *Shediac*). In the night 11-12 May *U124* (Lt-Cdr Mohr) fires torpedoes in

two approaches and sinks four ships of 21784 tons; *U569* possibly gets one hit on a disabled ship; and *U94* (Lt Ites) sinks one ship of 5630 tons. In the next night *U406* (Lt Dieterichs) misses a corvette as a result of torpedo failure; *U94* sinks two ships of 8870 tons in two approaches. Then contact is lost in bad weather. On the afternoon of 20 May *U406* sights the convoy ONS.94 but she is driven off after four hours by a destroyer and aircraft and the other boats do not come up in the mist of the Newfoundland Bank. After being supplied from *U116* (Cdr von Schmidt) from 25 May to 27 May the boats of the 'Hecht' group again take up a patrol line in the area of the Newfoundland Bank. On 1 June *U590* (Lt-Cdr Müller-Edzards) sights the convoy ONS.96 in a heavy westerly storm and on on a moonlit night. Because of the weather and the proximity to Newfoundland the operation is broken off on 2 June. On the evening of 8 June *U124* sights the convoy ONS.100 (37 ships, Escort Group C.1, comprising the Canadian destroyers *Assiniboine* and *St Croix*, Canadian corvettes *Buctouche*, *Chambly*, the British *Dianthus* and *Nasturtium* and the French *Aconit* and *Mimose*). *U124* sinks the *Mimose* in the first attack. On 9 June all six U-boats of the 'Hecht' group establish contact, but *U96*, *U406* and *U590* remain behind because of diesel trouble. *U94* sinks two ships of 11002 tons in the night 9-10 June. Contact is lost in the mist. On 11 June *U96* (Lt Hellriegel) again sights the convoy. *U94* and *U569* are held up by a straggler (4458 tons) which they sink in several approaches. On the morning of 12 June *U124* again comes up and sinks one ship of 4093 tons. On the morning of 16 June *U94* sights the convoy ONS.102 (48 ships, Escort Group A.3. (Cdr Heinemann, USN), comprising the US coastguard cutters *Campbell*, *Ingham*, the destroyers USS *Leary*, HMCS *Restigouche* and the Canadian corvettes *Collingwood*, *Rosthern*, *Mayflower* and *Agassiz*). The contact signals from *U94*, *U406*, *U96*, *U124* and *U569* are located by *Restigouche*, which is equipped with HF/DF, and the escorts drive the U-boats off. *U94* and *U590* are damaged by depth charges. *U406* misses the *Leary* with five torpedoes on the morning of 17 June. After breaking off the operation on 18 June *U124* meets the convoy again and sinks one ship of 5627 tons in an underwater attack. By 21 June the 'Hecht' group has begun the return journey. In all, 12 ships of 61464 tons and one corvette have been sunk without loss.

12-19 May English Channel
The German auxiliary cruiser *Schiff 23 Stier* (Cdr* Gerlach) breaks through the Channel. 12 May: she leaves Rotterdam, escorted by the 5th TB Flotilla (Cdr* M. Schmidt) comprising *Kondor*, *Falke*, *Iltis* and *Seeadler* and 16 motor minesweepers. In the early hours of 13 May, after shelling from British coastal batteries in the Straits of Dover, there is an attack by British MTBs. *Iltis* (Lt-Cdr W. Jacobsen†) and *Seeadler* (Lt-Cdr Strecker) sink after torpedo hits with heavy loss of personnel. The British force loses *MTB220*. The auxiliary cruiser continues her journey in the following nights by small stages without further contact with the enemy. 19 May: she enters the Gironde Estuary. From here the ship breaks out into the Atlantic undetected on 10-21 May.

13-15 May Arctic
The British cruiser *Trinidad* (Capt Saunders), having received emergency repairs after being hit by a torpedo on 29 Mar, sets out from Murmansk with the destroyers *Somali*, *Matchless*, *Foresight* and *Forester*. W of Bear Island there is a force of cruisers—*Nigeria* (Rear-Adm Burrough), *Kent*, *Liverpool*, *Norfolk*—and four destroyers to meet them. Of the promised Soviet long-range fighter cover up to 200 nautical miles from the coast, only a few aircraft arrive. On 14 May the force is located by German reconnaissance about 100 nautical miles from the coast. There follow several unsuccessful attacks by torpedo aircraft of I/K.G.26 and bombers of III/K.G.30. Then a Ju 88 of III/K.G.30 hits the cruiser in a dive-bombing attack. The ship is set on fire. On 15 May the fire can no longer be brought under control with the result that the *Trinidad* has to be sunk by *Matchless*. The Home Fleet sets out from Scapa Flow to cover the returning ships.

13 May-2 June   Mediterranean

In operations against the British Tobruk supply traffic *U431* (Lt-Cdr Dommes) sinks one ship of 4216 tons; *U83* misses a convoy; *U81*, *U205* and *U565* are unsuccessful. *U568* (Lt-Cdr Preuss) is sunk on 28 May off Sollum after a 15-hour pursuit by the British destroyers *Hero*, *Hurworth* and *Eridge*. On 2 June *U652* is so badly damaged by aircraft that *U81* has to sink the boat by torpedo after taking off the crew. Operations by the Italian submarines *Galatea*, *Nereide*, *Asteria*, *Platino* and *Beilul* off the Cyrenaican coast are unsuccessful.

14 May   Western Atlantic

The pro-Vichy French warships (aircraft carrier *Béarn* and the cruisers *Emile Bertin* and *Jeanne d'Arc*) which have been stationed in Martinique and Guadeloupe since June 1940 are demilitarized under American pressure.

14-19 May   Western Atlantic

Introduction of through-convoy traffic on the American East Coast. On 14 May the first convoy proceeds from Hampton Roads to Key West (NK), on 15 May from Key West to Hampton Roads (KN); on 19 May the first feeder convoy from New York to Halifax (BX). The grouping of the ships in convoys leads to a sharp decline in the number of merchant ships being sighted by U-boats.

14-31 May   Mediterranean

In operations against the Italian supply traffic to Benghazi the British submarine *Turbulent* (Cdr Linton) attacks convoys with destroyer and torpedo boat escort on 14 May, 18 May, 20 May, 24 May, 25 May and 29 May. Three ships of 5799 tons and the destroyer *Pessagno* are sunk. Off Bari *Thrasher* (Lt-Cdr Mackenzie) sinks one ship of 1160 tons and on 30-31 May *Proteus* sinks two ships of 8407 tons from two convoys.

15 May   Arctic

Ju 87s of I/St.G.5 attack Murmansk. The Soviet submarine *Shch-403* and the US freighter *Yaka* (6187 tons) are badly damaged.

16-20 May   Norway

On 16 May the heavy cruiser *Prinz Eugen* (Capt Brinkmann), which has received emergency repairs after being hit by a torpedo on 23 Feb, leaves Trondheim with the destroyers *Z25*

and *Paul Jacobi* and the torpedo boats *T11* and *T12* on transfer to Kiel (operation 'Zauberflöte'). On 17 May 12 Beauforts, six Blenheims and four Beaufighters of No 42 Torpedo Bomber Sqdn RAF (Wing-Cdr Williams) attack without success. Three aircraft are lost to AA fire and Me 109s of III/J.G.1. Attacks by 30 more aircraft are intercepted by Me 109s which shoot down another four aircraft while losing a total of three. On 18 May *Prinz Eugen* arrives in Kiel. From 18 May to 20 May the heavy cruiser *Lützow* (Capt Stange) moves in stages with *T15* from Kiel to Trondheim via Kristiansand.

16-25 May   Black Sea

Soviet supply transports to Sevastopol and some shelling of land targets. On 16 May the destroyer *Bditelny;* on 17 May the cruiser *Krasny Krym* and flotilla leader *Tashkent;* on 19 May the flotilla leader *Kharkov;* on 21 May the destroyer *Svobodny;* on 22 May *Krasny Krym*, *Tashkent* and destroyers *Nezamozhnik* and *Zheleznyakov;* on 23 May the destroyer *Boiki;* on 24 May the destroyer *Bezuprechny;* and 25 May *Krasny Krym* and *Tashkent*.

17-20 May   Mediterranean

British force H sets out from Gibraltar with the carriers *Argus* and *Eagle*, the cruiser *Charybdis* and the destroyers *Partridge*, *Ithuriel*, *Antelope*, *Wishart*, *Westcott*, *Wrestler* and *Vidette* on 17 May. It flies off 17 Spitfire fighters on 18 May all of which arrive in Malta. But six Albacore torpedo aircraft have to turn back. Force H returns to Gibraltar on 20 May. Of the Italian submarines *Mocenigo*, *Otaria* and *Dessiè*, only *Mocenigo* fires a salvo of three torpedoes on a cruiser without success.

18 May-11 June   Black Sea

In Soviet submarine operations *Shch-205* (Lt-Cdr Sukhomlinov) sinks the small Turkish steamers *Duatape* and *Safak* of 628 tons off the Turkish-Bulgarian frontier. *Shch-214* (Capt 3rd Class Vlasov) sinks three small Turkish schooners. In the bay of Odessa *A-3* (Lt-Cdr Tsurikov) sinks the Rumanian transport *Sulina* (3495 tons) and *A5* (Lt Kukuy) torpedoes the Rumanian transport *Ardeal* (5695 tons), which is beached.

20 May-30 June   Western Atlantic
In the Gulf of Mexico, off Cuba and Yucatan, *U-158* (Lt-Cdr Rostin) sinks 12 ships of 62536 tons; and *U504* (Cdr Poske) six ships of 19418 tons. On the return *U158* is lost in the area of Bermuda, after being located by HF/DF, as a result of an attack by an American Mariner flying-boat of VP-74.

21 May   North Atlantic
U159 (Lt-Cdr Witte) attacks the convoy OS.28 and sinks two ships from it of 9175 tons. Then the boat continues her journey out to the Caribbean.

21-25 May   Baltic
The German minelayers *Kaiser* (Cdr Bohm) and *Roland* (Capt von Kutzleben), the 3rd MS Flotilla (Cdr* Knuth) and the 27th Landing Flotilla (Capt Masberg) lay out the mine barrages 'Seeigel 1-8' SE of Suursaari with 2522 mines. They are later extended to 41 sections with 5779 mines, 1450 protection floats and 200 explosive floats.

21 May-27 June   North Pacific
Reconnaissance operation by the Japanese 1st SM Flotilla (Rear-Adm Yamazaki) in the area of the Aleutians. With their aircraft *I-9* (Cdr* Fujii) reconnoitres Kiska and Amchitka on 25 May and Kiska on 26 May; *I-26* (Cdr* Yokota) Kodiak on 24 May, Sitkinak on 26 May and Seattle on 1 June; *I-25* (Cdr* Tagami) Kodiak on 27 May. *I-19* (Cdr* Narahara) is surprised when flying off her aircraft near Bogorlov Island on 27 May and is damaged by depth charges: she reconnoitres Dutch Harbour by periscope on 4 June. In June *I-25* operates in the area of Seattle, torpedoes one ship of 7100 tons and shells Port Stevens (Oregon) on 24 June. *I-26* sinks one ship of 3286 tons and shells Port Estevan (Vancouver) on 20 June.

23-27 May   Western Atlantic
Because of the absence of sightings (the result of the through-convoy traffic) the six U-boats operating off the American coast are concentrated in a new formation 'Pfadfinder' away from the coast in which two newly-arrived boats participate. But the formation has no success and the boats are sent back to the coast.

24-25 May   Norway
The heavy cruiser *Lützow* is moved with the tanker *Dithmarschen* and *T-7* from Trondheim to Narvik and joins the pocket-battleship *Admiral Scheer* which was transferred from Trondheim to Narvik on 9-10 May.

25 May   Arctic
The Soviet submarine *S-101* (Capt 3rd Class Vekke) is attacked for 22 hours off Tanafjord by the submarine-chasers *UJ1102*, *UJ1105*, *UJ1108* and *UJ1109* with depth charges but is able to escape with severe damage.

25 May-8 July   Western Atlantic
After the attack on SL.109 three U-boats proceed to the area of the Brazilian North Coast but they find little traffic there and then go into the Caribbean. They make the following sinkings: *U126* (Lt-Cdr Bauer) seven ships of 41708 tons and damages one ship of 7104 tons; *U128* (Lt-Cdr Heyse) sinks four ships of 32129 tons; *U161* (Lt-Cdr Achilles) three ships of 14201 tons and torpedoes one ship of 3305 tons in the harbour of Santa Lucia.

25 May-1 June   Arctic
Operations against the Allied convoys QP.12 and PQ.16. The QP.12 (15 ships, one of which turns back) sets out from the Kola Inlet on 21 May but is not engaged. An aircraft keeping contact is shot down on 25 May by the Hurricane fighter of the catapult ship *Empire Morn* sailing in the convoy. 14 ships arrive in Reykjavik on 29 May. The PQ.16 (35 ships and the AA ship *Alynbank*), which sets out from Reykjavik on 21 May with the minesweeper *Hazard* and the A/S trawlers *St Elstan*, *Lady Madelaine*, *Northern Spray* and (only until 23 May) *Retriever*, is met early on 25 May by the Escort Group consisting of the destroyers *Ashanti* (Cdr Onslow), *Martin*, *Achates*, *Volunteer* and *Garland* (Polish) and the corvettes *Honeysuckle*, *Starwort*, *Hyderabad* (RIN) and *Roselys* (French). A little later the close escort force, consisting of the cruisers *Nigeria* (Rear-Adm Burrough), *Kent*, *Liverpool*, *Norfolk* and the destroyers *Onslow*, *Oribi*, and *Marne*, takes up positions with the convoy. The Home Fleet cruises as a covering force between Iceland and Norway.

Two British submarines sail with PQ.16 to operate against German surface ships and five British and three Soviet submarines form a flanking screen. On 25 May German air reconnaissance locates the PQ.16 which has evaded a German U-boat formation. In two air attacks by III/K.G.26 (air torpedoes) and III/K.G.30 with 19 He 111s and six Ju 88s two bombers are lost through massive AA fire and one torpedo aircraft falls victim to the Hurricane of the catapult ship *Empire Lawrence* travelling with the convoy. The freighter *Carlton* (5127 tons) is damaged by near-misses and towed back to Iceland by *Northern Spray*. In the night 25-26 May *U703* (Lt-Cdr Bielfeld) sinks the freighter *Syros* (1691 tons). On 26 May the close escort force leaves the convoy because of the U-boat danger. But *U436* misses a steamer and a corvette and *U591* the *Ashanti*. Weak air attacks have no success. SE of Bear Island seven He 111s of I/K.G.26 and 111 Ju 88s of K.G.30 attack in several waves on 27 May and, while losing three of their number, sink the freighters *Alamar*, *Mormacsul*, *Empire Lawrence* and *Empire Purcell* with bombers and the *Lowther Castle* by torpedo, making in all 30796 tons. The *Stari Bolshevik*, *Ocean Voice* (convoy Commodore Capt Gale), *Empire Baffin*, *City of Joliet* and the destroyer *Garland* are damaged. On 28 May the *City of Joliet* (6167 tons) has to be abandoned. The Soviet destroyers *Grozny*, *Kuibyshev* and *Sokrushitelny* reinforce the escort. Because of poor visibility there are only a few unsuccessful single attacks by German bombers. In the night 28-29 May *U586* attacks the convoy unsuccessfully and by day the attacks of K.G.30 achieve nothing. The British minesweepers *Bramble*, *Seagull*, *Harrier*, *Niger*, *Gossamer*, and *Hussar* come out from the Kola Inlet to the convoy and six steamers are detached for Archangel with the *Alynbank*, *Martin* and two minesweepers. On 30 May bombers of K.G.30 attack both parts of the convoy but are driven off by the AA fire and Soviet fighters. In air combats over the convoy the most successful pilot of the Soviet Northern Fleet, Lt-Col Safonov is killed. On 31 May the Murmansk

part of the convoy arrives and on 1 June the Archangel part. Total convoy losses: 43205 tons with a cargo of 32400 tons including 147 tanks, 77 aircraft and 770 vehicles.

25 May-2 June   Central Pacific

Preparatory movements for the Midway operation.

The Japanese plan is, after making a diversionary sortie against the Aleutians (see 21 May), to carry out an air attack and an invasion of Midway with all available units of the Combined Fleet (Adm Yamamoto) and then to seek a decisive battle with the American Fleet as it approaches to relieve the island.

American naval W/T Intelligence learns of the operation from the radio picture and Cdr Rochefort in Hawaii is able to identify its target as Midway so that counter-measures are promptly set in train.

On 25 May the 2nd Carrier Force (Rear-Adm Kakuta) sets out from Ominato (Hokkaido) with the carriers *Junyo* and *Ryujo* (4th Carrier Sqdn), the heavy cruisers *Maya* and *Takao* (2/4th Cruiser Sqdn), the destroyers *Akebono*, *Sazanami* and *Ushio* (7th DD Div) and the tanker *Teiyo Maru* to carry out a diversionary raid on Dutch Harbour (Aleutians).

On 26 May US TF 16 (see below) arrives in Pearl Harbour, having been recalled from the South Pacific. On 27 May TF17 follows with the damaged carrier *Yorktown* which is repaired in 48 hours.

On 26 May the Japanese 1st Carrier Fleet (Vice-Adm Nagumo) sets out from Hashirajima Bay (Inland Sea) to attack Midway. It comprises the carriers *Akagi*, *Kaga* (1st Carrier Sqdn), *Hiryu* and *Soryu* (2nd Carrier Sqdn, Rear-Adm Yamaguchi), the battleships *Haruna* and *Kirishima* (2/3rd BB Sqdn), the heavy cruisers *Chikuma* and *Tone* (8th Cruiser Sqdn, Rear-Adm Abe), the 10th DD Flotilla (Rear-Adm Kimura) with the light cruiser *Nagara* and the destroyers *Nowake*, *Arashi*, *Hagikaze*, *Maikaze* (4th DD Div), *Kazegumo*, *Makigumo*, *Yugumo* (10th DD Div), *Urakaze*, *Isokaze*, *Tanikaze* and *Hamakaze* (17th DD Div) and five tankers with the destroyer *Akigumo*.

On 27 May the Japanese forces earmarked for the operation against the

Aleutians set out from Ominato. They consist of the Attu/Adak Force (Rear-Adm Omori) with the light cruiser *Abukuma*, the destroyers *Wakaba*, *Nenohi*, *Hatsuharu* and *Hatsushimo* (21st DD Div) with one auxiliary minelayer and one transport with 1200 army troops; the Kiska Force (Capt Ohno) with the light cruisers *Kiso* and *Tama* and the auxiliary cruiser *Asaka Maru* (21st Cruiser Sqdn), the destroyers *Akatsuki*, *Hibiki* and *Hokaze* (6th DD Div), two transports with 1250 troops and three auxiliary minesweepers; and the covering force (Vice-Adm Hosogaya) comprising the heavy cruiser *Nachi*, the destroyers *Ikazuchi* and *Inazuma*, two tankers and three freighters.

On 27 May the Japanese invasion fleet earmarked for Midway puts to sea from Saipan (Marianas). It comprises 12 transports with 5000 army and naval landing troops, one tanker, the fast assault boats *P1*, *P2* and *P34* escorted by the 2nd DD Flotilla (Rear-Adm Tanaka), consisting of the light cruiser *Jintsu*, the destroyers *Kuroshio*, *Oyashio* (15th DD Div), *Yukikaze*, *Amatsukaze*, *Tokitsukaze*, *Hatsukaze* (16 DD Div), *Shiranuhi*, *Kasumi*, *Arare* and *Kagero* (18th DD Div); a seaplane force (Rear-Adm Fujita) with the seaplane carrier *Chitose*, the depot ship *Kamikawa Maru* (11th Carrier Sqdn), the destroyer *Hayashio* and the APD *P35;* a minesweeping force with four minesweepers, the submarine-chasers *Ch16*, *Ch17*, *Ch18*, one supply ship and two freighters. At the same time the 7th Cruiser Sqdn (Rear-Adm Kurita) puts to sea from Guam as a covering force with the heavy cruisers *Kumano*, *Suzuya*, *Mikuma* and *Mogami*, the destroyers *Arashio* and *Asashio* (8th DD Div) and one tanker.

On 28 May the main force of the invasion fleet (Vice-Adm Kondo) puts to sea from Hashirajima Bay with the heavy cruisers *Atago*, *Chokai* (4th Cruiser Sqdn), *Haguro*, *Myoko* (5th Cruiser Sqdn, Vice -Adm Takagi), the battleships *Hiyei* and *Kongo* (3rd BB Sqdn, Rear-Adm Mikawa) and the 4th DD Flotilla (Rear-Adm Nishimura) with the light cruiser *Yura* and the destroyers *Murasame*, *Harusame*, *Samidare*, *Yudachi* (2nd DD Div), *Asagumo*,

Minegumo and *Natsugumo* (9th DD Div) and the carrier *Zuiho* with the destroyer *Mikazuki*. In addition, the bulk of the fleet puts to sea. This consists of the Midway Support Group (Adm Yamamoto) with the battleships *Yamato*, *Nagato* and *Mutsu* (1st BB Sqdn), the carrier *Hosho* with the destroyer *Yukaze*, the seaplane carrier *Chiyoda*, (*Mizuho* is sunk) used as a midget submarine transport, the 3rd DD Flotilla (Rear-Adm Hashimoto) with the light cruiser *Sendai* and the destroyers *Fubuki*, *Hatsuyuki*, *Murakumo*, *Shirayuki* (11th DD Div), *Isonami*, *Uranami*, *Shikinami*, *Ayanami* (12th DD Div) and two tankers; the Aleutian Support Group (Vice-Adm Takasu) with the battleships *Fuso*, *Hyuga*, *Ise* and *Yamashiro* (2nd BB Sqdn) the light cruisers *Kitakami* and *Oi* (9th Cruiser Sqdn, Rear-Adm Kishi) and the destroyers *Asagiri*, *Yugiri*, *Shirakumo*, *Amagiri* (20th DD Div), *Umikaze*, *Yamakaze*, *Kawakaze*, *Suzukaze* (24th DD Div), *Ariake*, *Shigure*, *Shiratsuyu*, *Yugure* (27th DD Div) and two tankers.

On the US side TF 16 (Rear-Adm Spruance) puts to sea from Pearl Harbour on 28 May with the carriers *Enterprise* and *Hornet*, the heavy cruisers (Rear-Adm Kinkaid) *Minneapolis*, *New Orleans*, *Northampton*, *Pensacola*, *Vincennes*, the AA cruiser *Atlanta* and the destroyers (Desron 1) *Phelps*, *Worden*, *Monaghan*, *Aylwin*, *Balch*, *Conyngham*, *Benham*, *Ellet* and *Maury* and the tanker force comprising *Cimarron* and *Platte* with the destroyers *Dewey* and *Monssen*. On 28 May TF 17 (Rear-Adm Fletcher) follows with the repaired carrier *Yorktown*, the cruisers (Rear-Adm Smith) *Astoria* and *Portland* and the destroyers (Desron 2) *Hammann*, *Hughes*, *Morris*, *Anderson*, *Russell* and *Gwin*. On 2 June the Task Forces meet. From the Central Pacific forces the cruisers *Louisville*, *St Louis*, *Indianapolis* and *Honolulu* and nine more destroyers are sent to join TF 8 (Rear-Adm Theobald) formed in the Aleutians area on 21 May with the cruiser *Nashville* and five destroyers. They join up on 3 June S of the Aleutian island of Kodiak.

From the US West Coast Rear-Adm

Anderson puts to sea from San Francisco on 31 May with the battleships *Colorado* and *Maryland* and three destroyers; Rear-Adm Fitch sets out from San Diego on 1 June with the carrier *Saratoga*.

25 May-21 June South West Pacific
In operations in the South China Sea the US submarine *Salmon* (Lt-Cdr McKinney) sinks the repair ship *Asahi* (old battleship of 11441 tons) and one ship of 4382 tons; *Permit* (Lt Chapple) one ship of 4472 tons; *Seal* (Lt-Cdr Hurd) and *Swordfish* (Lt-Cdr Smith) together one ship of 1946 tons and the latter one more ship of 4585 tons alone; and *Seawolf* (Lt-Cdr Warder) one ship of 1206 tons.
In the South Pacific *S44* (Lt Moore) sinks one ship of 2626 tons. Off Penang the British submarine *Trusty* (Lt Cdr King) sinks two ships of 12853 tons.

27 May-7 June Black Sea
Soviet supply transports to Sevastopol. On 27-28 May Rear-Adm Basisty with the cruiser *Voroshilov* (Capt 1st class Markov) and the destroyers *Soobrazitelny* (Capt 3rd Class Vorkov) and *Svobodny* (Lt-Cdr Sevchenko) brings the 9th Naval Infantry Brigade (3017 men and 340 tons of supplies) from Batumi to Sevastopol. On the way out and back air attacks by He 111s are out-manoeuvred. *Svobodny* shells land targets. On 28 May the destroyer *Bezuprechny* (Lt-Cdr Burnyak), on 30 May *Bezuprechny* and *Svobodny*, on 1 June *Svobodny* and on 2 June *Tashkent* and *Bezuprechny* bring supplies and from time to time shell land targets. On 3 June the cruiser *Krasny Krym* (Capt 2nd Class Zubkov) with *Soobrazitelny* and *Svobodny* brings 1759 relief troops and evacuates 1998 wounded and 275 civilians. On 5 June and 6 June the flotilla leaders *Kharkov* (Capt 3rd Class Melnikov) and *Tashkent* (Capt 3rd Class Eroshenko) put in to Sevastopol with *Bezuprechny* in spite of bomb and torpedo attacks. On 7 June the destroyer *Nezamozhnik* (Lt-Cdr Bobrovnikov) brings supplies.

27 May-26 June Western Atlantic
Nine U-boats of the 'Pfadfinder' group operate in changing positions off the American East Coast against ships increasingly travelling in convoys. They make the following sinkings: *U404* (Lt-Cdr von Bülow) seven ships of 31051 tons: *U578* (Cdr Rehwinkel) two ships of 13095 tons. And of the boats still left of the sixth wave *U135* (Lt-Cdr Praetorius) sinks one ship of 4549 tons; *U566* (Lt-Cdr Borchert) one ship of 8967 tons; *U653* (Lt-Cdr Feiler) the flying boat tender *Gannet; U553, U432* and *U213* return without success, and *U455* sinks a ship of 6914 tons on the return journey.

29 May-6 June Baltic
First operation by the Soviet submarine *M-97* (Lt-Cdr Dyakov) to reconnoitre the German 'Seeigel' mine barrage.

30 May-15 June Pacific
From 30 May the Japanese submarines *I-174, I-175, I-169* and *I-171* take up positions off Oahu; *I-121* and *I-123* go as flying-boat suppliers to the French Frigate Shoals and *I-122* to Lisianski Island. *I-168* operates in the Midway area on 1 June. From 4 June the boats *I-156, I-157, I-158, I-159, I-162, I-165* and *I-166* (*I-164* is sunk on the way out by the US submarine *Triton* —Lt-Cdr Kirkpatrick) take up patrol lines as Group B and *I-174, I-175, I-169, I-171, I-121, I-122* and *I-123* as Group C between Oahu and Midway against advancing US carrier forces but they sight no targets.
The submarines of the US Pacific Fleet (Rear-Adm Lockwood) are concentrated against the Japanese operation against Midway as established by W/T Intelligence. *Gudgeon, Grouper, Nautilus, Grenadier, Grayling, Gateo, Trout, Dolphin, Tambor, Flying Fish* and *Cachalot* against a landing NW of the island; *Narwhal, Plunger, Trigger* NE of Midway; *Finback, Growler, Pike* and *Tarpon* N of Oahu. *Cuttlefish* is stationed 700 nautical miles W of Midway for reconnaissance and the returning *Greenling, Drum, Pollack, Tuna, Pompano* and *Porpoise* are appropriately deployed.

30 May-26 July Indian Ocean
A-Group of the Japanese 8th SM Flotilla (Rear-Adm Ishizaki) operates in the area of Madagascar. The *I-30* (Cdr* Endo), which set out on 20 Apl with two auxiliary cruisers, after refuelling from the *Aikoku Maru* on

25 Apl, reconnoitres Aden on 7 May with her aircraft in a search for the British Eastern Fleet, followed by Djibouti on 8 May, Zanzibar and Dar-es-Salaam on 19 May and Mombasa on 20 May by periscope. The *I-10*, *I-16*, *I-18* and *I-20*, which set out from Penang on 29-30 Apl, refuel from the *Hokoku Maru* on 5 May. *I-10* reconnoitres over Durban with her aircraft on 20 May and on the following days observes East London, Port Elizabeth and Simonstown. After finding British Naval forces in Diego Suarez, *I-10* reconnoitres with her aircraft over the bay in the night 29-30 May; *I-16* and *I-20* put out their midget submarines which in the night of 30-31 May torpedo the battleship *Ramillies* and the tanker *British Loyalty* (6993 tons). The midget submarine from *I-18* falls out with motor trouble. In two more flights the aircraft of *I-10* tries to establish the result of the attack. While *I-30* again reconnoitres Durban, the other four submarines go from 5 June to 12 June to carry out mercantile warfare in the Mozambique Channel. After being refuelled from the auxiliary cruisers, *I-30* proceeds to Western France (she arrives in Lorient on 5 Aug); the other submarines operate again from 28 June to 9 July against merchant ships on the African coast and off Madagascar. On the return *I-10* reconnoitres Réunion and Mauritius with her aircraft on 15 July and 16 July; *I-16* and *I-18* carry out periscope observations of Mahé (Seychelles), the Rodriguez Islands and Diego Garcia. On 10 Aug *I-16* is the last boat to return to Penang. They have made the following sinkings: *I-10* (Cdr* Kayahara) eight ships of 34536 tons; *I-16* (Cdr* K. Yamada) four ships of 17727 tons; *I-18* (Cdr Otani) three ships of 11304 tons; *I-20* (Cdr* T. Yamada) seven ships of 35501 tons; and the auxiliary cruisers three ships of 21051 tons.

1 June   Arctic
Ju 87s of I/St.G.5. sink the British freighter *Empire Starlight* (6850 tons) in Murmansk. In the course of the month German aircraft repeatedly drop mines in the Kola Inlet, on which the American freighter *Steel Worker* (5686 tons)

sinks on 3 June and the steamer *Alcoa Cadet* (4823 tons) on 21 June.

1 June-24 July   Western Atlantic
In operations in the area of the Greater Antilles, in the Gulf of Mexico and in the Gulf of Campeche *U157* (Cdr Henne) sinks one ship of 6401 tons; *U129* (Lt-Cdr Witt) 11 ships of 41571 tons; and *U67* (Lt-Cdr Müller-Stöckheim) six ships of 30015 tons and damages two ships of 14831 tons. *U157* is sunk off Cuba on 13 June by the US Coastguard cutter *Thetis*.

2-4 June   Mediterranean
Operation 'Style'. British Force H, comprising the carrier *Eagle*, the cruiser *Charybdis* and the destroyers *Ithuriel*, *Antelope*, *Wishart*, *Wrestler* and *Westcott*, sails from Gibraltar on 2 June and flies off 31 Spitfire fighters on 3 June S of the Balearics. 27 of them reach Malta. Force H returns on 4 June to Gibraltar. The Italian submarines *Brin* and *Malachite* off Algiers sight nothing. Off Tunisia *Corallo* (Cdr Andreani) sinks one sailing vessel.

3-7 June   Pacific
Battle of Midway. 3 June: attack by the diversionary force (Rear-Adm Kakuta) with the carriers *Junyo* and *Ryujo* on Dutch Harbour has little effect because it is anticipated. The diversion, therefore, fails. In the morning American air reconnaissance locates parts of the Japanese invasion force (Vice-Adm Kondo) with a total of two battleships, one aircraft carrier, eight heavy and two light cruisers, 21 destroyers, two aircraft depot ships, six tankers, 20 transports and seven small escort vessels. In the afternoon 9 B 17s attack the transports unsuccessfully; in the night four Catalinas get a torpedo hit on the tanker *Akebono Maru*.
4 June: In the morning an attack on Midway by 108 aircraft of the Japanese carrier force (Vice-Adm Nagumo), comprising the carriers *Akagi*, *Kaga*, *Hiryu*, *Soryu*, the battleships *Haruna* and *Kirishima*, the heavy cruisers *Chikuma* and *Tone*, the light cruiser *Nagara* and the destroyers *Nowake*, *Arashi*, *Hagikaze*, *Maikaze*, *Kazegumo*, *Yugumo*, *Makigumo*, *Urakaze*, *Isokaze*, *Tanikaze* and *Hamakaze*. Thanks to prompt radar reporting, there are no aircraft on the ground. In air combat

the American fighters are wiped out, but only limited damage is sustained on the ground. Simultaneously attacks are made on the Japanese carrier force by US aircraft based on Midway (4 B 26s with torpedoes, six Avengers with torpedoes, 27 dive bombers and 15 B 17s): they lose 17 aircraft and secure no hit. Japanese air reconnaissance locates parts of the US carrier forces, which are advancing to the attack (Rear-Adms Fletcher and Spruance) and which comprise the carriers *Enterprise, Hornet* and *Yorktown*, the cruisers *Astoria, Portland, New Orleans, Minneapolis, Vincennes, Northampton, Pensacola, Atlanta* and destroyers *Hammann, Hughes, Morris, Anderson, Russell, Gwin, Phelps, Worden, Monaghan, Aylwin, Balch, Conyngham, Benham, Ellet* and *Maury*. As a result of confusing reports, Nagumo decides too late to deploy his aircraft against this carrier force. The US carrier aircraft (156 machines), however, divide themselves up as they approach. The torpedo squadrons from *Enterprise, Hornet* and *Yorktown* reach the Japanese carriers successively and without fighter protection: 35 of the 41 aircraft are shot down by Japanese fighters and AA fire. They secure no hits and all the squadron leaders (Lt-Cdrs Lindsey, Massey and Waldron) are killed. Simultaneously, after a wide detour, the dive bombers of the *Enterprise* and the dive bombers of the *Yorktown* (which flew off later) under Lt-Cdrs McClusky and Leslie respectively reach the Japanese carriers whose defence is still busy dealing with the torpedo aircraft. Within five minutes *Akagi* (Capt Aoki†), *Kaga* (Capt Akada†) and *Soryu* (Capt Yanagimoto†) are hit by 2-4 bombs which detonate between the aircraft on deck ready for take-off and cause serious fires and explosions. The three carriers sink later in the day or in the night. At mid-day and in the afternoon *Hiryu* flies off her aircraft in two waves (Lt-Cdr Tomonaga). They obtain two torpedo and three bomb hits on the *Yorktown*. In the late afternoon air groups from *Enterprise* and *Hornet* concentrate their attacks on the *Hiryu* (Capt Kaku†, Rear-Adm Yamaguchi†, Cdr of the 2nd Carrier Sqdn) which,

likewise, is set on fire and has to be abandoned in the morning.
In the night 4-5 June Adm Yamamoto, who with the bulk of his forces, is far to the NW (two groups with a total of seven battleships, one carrier, three light cruisers, 21 destroyers and two midget submarine-carriers), has to break off the operation. In a sortie by four cruisers against Midway, *Mikuma* and *Mogami* collide in avoiding the US submarine *Tambor* with the result that the sortie is abandoned.
5 June: the Japanese Fleet concentrates NW of Midway for the return. US carriers take up the pursuit but are unable to catch the Japanese when they attack in the afternoon.
The destroyer *Tanikaze*, which arrives independently, escapes the attack of 58 dive bombers. Attacks by B 17 bombers on the damaged cruisers *Mikuma* and *Mogami* have no result. The Japanese submarine *I-168* shells Midway.
5 June: the US carriers *Enterprise* and *Yorktown* attack in three waves the damaged cruisers: *Mikuma* (Capt Sakiyama) finally sinks, while *Mogami* (Capt Sato) escapes, badly damaged, with the destroyers *Arashio* and *Asashio*.
7 June: *I-168* (Cdr Tanabe) sinks the damaged *Yorktown* (Capt Buckmaster) and the destroyer *Hammann* lying alongside. A sortie by a fast task force of the Japanese against the US carriers finds nothing because, in the meantime, the latter have started the journey to their supply ships. During the battle of Midway, Japanese troops land on the Aleutian Islands of Attu and Kiska, and lose 3500 dead and 253 aircraft; the US Navy loses 307 men and 150 aircraft.
3 June-2 Aug Western Atlantic
In operations in the area of the Caribbean *U68* (Cdr Merten) sinks seven ships of 50898 tons; *U159* (Lt-Cdr Witte) eight ships of 41197 tons and two unidentified sailing ships; and *U172* (Lt-Cdr Emmermann) ten ships of 40745 tons.
4-6 June Central Atlantic
The German auxiliary cruiser *Schiff 23 Stier* (Capt Gerlach) sinks the British freighter *Gemstone* (4986 tons) and the Panamanian turbine tanker *Stanvac Calcutta* (10170 tons) in the Central Atlantic.

4-16 June   Mediterranean
In operations against the British Tobruk supply traffic *U431* (Lt-Cdr Dommes) sinks one ship of 2073 tons and *U77* (Lt-Cdr Schonder) the British destroyer *Grove* on 12 June. *U331*, *U453* and *U205* have no success. Off Alexandria *U559* (Lt-Cdr Heidtmann) sinks one ship of 4681 tons and torpedoes one ship of 5917 tons. *U81* misses a target. Off the Palestine coast *U83* (Lt-Cdr Kraus) sinks five and *U97* (Lt Bürgel) two small vessels. The Italian submarines *Ondina*, *Sirena*, *Galatea* and *Beilul* have no success.

8-10 June   Mediterranean
British Force H, comprising the carrier *Eagle*, the cruisers *Cairo* and *Charybdis* and the destroyers *Partridge*, *Ithuriel*, *Antelope*, *Wishart*, *Wrestler* and *Westcott*, flies off 32 Spitfire fighters for Malta from S of the Belearics on 9 June. They all arrive.

8-30 June   Black Sea
Major attack by the German 11th Army (Col-Gen von Manstein) on the Soviet fortress of Sevastopol with strong support from the heaviest artillery and the VIII Fl. K. (Col-Gen von Richthofen). The Soviet Black Sea Fleet (Vice-Adm Oktyabrski) is fully committed to supplying the fortress and taking off the wounded. Air Force units of the Air Commander South, and from 10 June Italian small battle units (Cdr* Mimbelli) and from 17 June the German 1st MTB Flotilla (Lt-Cdr Birnbacher), are deployed against Soviet shipping traffic.
10 June: The Soviet destroyers *Bditelny* and *Svobodny* escort with two minesweepers and three patrol cutters the transport *Abkhaziya* to Sevastopol. On the way there is an attack by the Italian *MAS573* and destroyers shell land targets. There is a German air attack while unloading and *Abkhaziya* (4727 tons), the minesweeper *T-413* and *Svobodny* are sunk by Ju 88s in the Southern Bay.
12 June: The cruiser *Molotov* (Capt 1st Class Romanov) and the destroyer *Bditelny* bring 3300 men of the 138th Rifle Brigade to Sevastopol and shell land targets. Air attacks are outmanoeuvred. The return journey is made shortly after the departure of the

German motor torpedo boats *S28*, *S72* and *S102*. The Italian midget submarine *CB3* misses.
13 June: The transport *Gruziya* (4857 tons) is attacked by Italian motor boats in the night on the way to Sevastopol. In the morning she is sunk by the mine pier in Sevastopol in an air attack.
15-16 June: the *Molotov* and *Bezuprechny* bring 3855 troops as relief, shell land targets and evacuate 3000 wounded and civilians. Located by air reconnaissance, motor torpedo boats, MAS boats and midget submarines cannot approach.
18 June: The flotilla leader *Kharkov* is rendered unmanoeuvrable by near-misses from German bombers when proceeding to Sevastopol. She is towed away by Rear-Adm Vladimirski in *Tashkent*.
19 June: attacks by the German motor torpedo boats *S27*, *S72* and *S102* (Lt-Cdr Töniges), of which the last sinks an evacuation transport.
20 June: the *Bditelny*, *Bezuprechny* and the patrol ship *Shkval* bring 845 men and 293 tons of ammunition into the southern bay of Sevastopol.
23 June: the *Tashkent* and *Bezuprechny* bring supplies into Kamyshov Bay. On the way there are unsuccessful torpedo attacks by the German motor torpedo boats *S28*, *S72* and *S102*.
24 June: the *Bditelny* and *Bezuprechny* bring supplies to Sevastopol. Unsuccessful attacks are made by the motor torpedo boats *S27*, *S28*, *S40*, *S72* and *S102*.
25 June: the *Tashkent* and *Bditelny* bring supplies to Sevastopol. Unsuccessful attack by *S28* and *S40*.
26 June: the *Bezuprechny* brings supplies to Sevastopol. On the return she is sunk S of the Crimea by Ju 88s of the Air Commander South.
27 June: the *Tashkent* (Capt 3rd Class Eroshenko) brings 944 relief troops to Sevastopol and evacuates 2300 wounded and civilians. There are many air attacks on the return and many leaks caused by splinters from near-misses and aircraft fire: 1900 tons of water in the ship. The destroyer *Bditelny* with seven TKAs and the rescue ship *Jupiter* set out from Novorossisk to help; the Squadron Commander, Rear-Adm Vladimirski, is on one of the TKAs.

Q

The *Soobrazitelny* takes on 1975 wounded and *Bditelny* tows the *Tashkent* to Novorossisk where she sinks on the bottom.

10-15 June Pacific

Reinforcement and reorganization of the US Pacific Fleet. On 10 June the carrier *Wasp*, returning from the Home Fleet Force with the destroyers *Lang*, *Sterett*, *Stack*, and *Wilson* (Desdiv 15), the heavy cruiser *Quincy* and the new ships, the battleship *North Carolina* and destroyers *Farenholt*, *Aaron Ward*, *Laffey* and *Buchanan* (Desdiv 23) pass through the Panama Canal.

On 15 June the new organization comes into force: TF 1 (Vice Adm-Pye): the old battleships *Pennsylvania*, *Colorado*, *Maryland*, *Tennessee*, *Idaho*, *Mississippi* and *New Mexico* with eight to 10 destroyers in San Francisco up to 1 Aug, then Pearl Harbour.

TF 8 (Rear-Adm Theobald): the cruisers *Louisville*, *Indianapolis*, *Nashville*, *Honolulu*, and *St Louis*, the destroyers *Reid*, *Case*, *Gridley*, *McCall* and *Elliot* (DMS) in the Aleutians.

TF 11 (Rear-Adm Fitch): the carrier *Saratoga*, cruisers *Astoria*, *Minneapolis*, and *New Orleans*, destroyers (Desron 1) *Phelps*, *Farragut*, *MacDonough*, *Worden*, *Dale*, *Dewey* and *Hull* on the way to Hawaii.

TF 16 (Rear-Adm Fletcher): the carrier *Enterprise*, cruisers *Portland*, *Chester* and *Atlanta*, destroyers (Desron 6) *Balch*, *Maury*, *Benham*, *Ellet*, *Gwin*, *Grayson* and *Monssen* in Pearl Harbour.

TF 17 (Rear-Adm Mitscher): the carrier *Hornet*, cruisers *Northampton*, *Salt Lake City*, *Pensacola* and *San Diego*, destroyers (Desron 2) *Morris*, *Hughes*, *Anderson*, *Russell*, *O'Brien*, *Walke* and *Mustin* in Pearl Harbour.

TF 18: (Rear-Adm Noyes): the carrier *Wasp*, battleship *North Carolina*, cruisers *Quincy*, *Vincennes*, *San Francisco*, *San Juan* and destroyers of Desdivs 15 and 23 (see above) in San Diego.

TF 44 (Rear-Adm Crutchley, RN): the cruisers *Australia*, *Canberra*, *Hobart* (RAN) and *Chicago*, destroyers (Desron 4) *Selfridge*, *Patterson*, *Ralph Talbot*, *Mugford*, *Jarvis*, *Blue*, *Helm*, *Henley* and *Bagley* in Australian and New Zealand waters.

Other ships do convoy service between the USA, Hawaii, South Sea and Australia.

11-16 June North Atlantic

The departure of the convoy HG.84 (23 ships, escort: 36th EG (Cdr Walker) comprising the sloop *Stork* and the corvettes *Convolvulus*, *Gardenia* and *Marigold*) is reported by agents on 9 June. I/K.G.40 is ordered to reconnoitre: an FW 200 reports the convoy on 11 June and escapes from the Hurricane of the catapult ship *Empire Moon*. The outward-bound U-boats *U132*, *U89*, *U552*, *U84*, *U437*, *U575*, *U134* and *U571* are ordered to operate as the 'Endrass' group for 14 June. On the afternoon of 14 June and FW 200 sights the convoy and first leads *U552* (Lt-Cdr Topp) to it and then *U89* and *U132* which are, however, driven off by *Stork*, *Gardenia* and *Marigold*. As *Stork* must soon follow the convoy again, *U552* is able to operate on the reports of *U437* which has, in the meantime, come up but then been driven off by *Convolvulus*. In the night 14-15 June she sinks first three and then two ships in two approaches totalling 15858 tons. By day on 15 June *U71*, *U84* and *U575* are driven off by the air escort. In the night *Stork*, *Marigold* and *Convolvulus* drive off *U84*, *U71*, and *U552*. *U575* (Lt-Cdr Heydemann) misses the convoy with five torpedoes fired at great range. Although on the morning of 16 June *U571* and two FW 200s establish contact, the operation is broken off because of the weather (wind and sea Force 0 with good visibility). The Support Group sent to support the escort, consisting of the British destroyers *Beagle*, *Wild Swan*, the frigate *Spey* and the Polish Hunt class destroyer *Krakowiak*, is attacked in the evening of 17 June by a squadron of K.Fl.Gr. 106, which sinks *Wild Swan*.

11 June-19 July Western Atlantic

German U-boats lay mines off the American East Coast: *U87* (Lt-Cdr Berger) near the Ambrose lightship off Boston (no success), but later sinks two ships of 14298 tons; *U373* (Lt-Loeser) off Delaware—sinks one tug of 396 tons and later fails with two torpedo attacks; *U701* (Lt-Cdr Degen) off Chesapeake Bay, on which one A/S trawler and one ship totalling 7565 tons are sunk and the destroyer *Bainbridge* and two tankers of 22852 tons are damaged. Then, the harbour defence boat *YP-389* is sunk by gunfire, one tanker of 14054 tons is sunk by torpedo and two ships of 14241 tons are damaged. *U701* is sunk by a USAAF bomber on 7 July. *U584* (Lt-Cdr Deecke) and *U202* (Lt-Cdr Linder) disembark agents on the American East Coast and then *U202* sinks two ships of 10725 tons. *U332* (Lt-Cdr Liebe) sinks two ships of 10738 tons in a torpedo operation off the American East Coast.

12-16 June Mediterranean
Double convoy operation 'Harpoon' and 'Vigorous' from Gibraltar and Alexandria to supply Malta.
Western convoy (Force X): the freighters *Troilus*, *Burdwan*, *Chant*, *Tanimbar*, *Orari* and the tanker *Kentucky* with an escort provided by the AA cruiser *Cairo* (Capt Hardy), the destroyers *Bedouin*, *Marne*, *Matchless*, *Ithuriel*, *Partridge*, *Blankney*, *Middleton*, *Badsworth* and *Kujawiak* (Polish), the minesweepers *Hebe*, *Speedy*, *Rye*, *Hythe* and six motor gunboats. Covering force (Force W): the battleship *Malaya*, aircraft carriers *Argus* and *Eagle*, cruisers *Kenya* (Vice-Adm Curteis), *Charybdis*, *Liverpool*, destroyers *Onslow*, *Icarus*, *Escapade*, *Wishart*, *Westcott*, *Wrestler*, *Vidette* and *Antelope*. Tanker force (Force Y): tanker *Brown Ranger* with corvette *Coltsfoot* and one other corvette. The fast minelayer *Welshman*, with supplies on board, operates with Force X.
On signs of a British operation two Italian submarine groups, *Malachite*, *Zaffiro*, *Velella*, *Bronzo* and *Emo* and *Uarsciek*, *Giada*, *Acciaio*, *Otario* and *Alagi* are stationed N of the Algerian coast; a third group, consisting of *Corallo*, *Dessiè*, *Onice*, *Ascianghi* and *Aradam*, in the area Malta—Lampedusa; and a fourth group, consisting of *Axum*, *Platino*, *Micca*, *Zoea* and *Atropo*, in the Ionian Sea. *Galatea*, *Sirena* and the German *U77*, *U81*, *U205*, *U431*, *U453* and *U559* operate further to the E.
12 June: the Western convoy passes through the Straits of Gibraltar and is met by Force W. German reconnais-

sance aircraft locate the convoy S of the Balearics.
The Eastern convoy MW.11 (Commodore Rear-Adm England) sets out from Alexandria, Port Said and Haifa with the freighters *City of Pretoria*, *City of Calcutta*, *Bhutan*, *Potaro*, *Bulkoil*, *Rembrandt*, *Aagtekerk*, *City of Edinburgh*, *City of Lincoln*, *Elizabeth Bakke* and *Ajax*, the dummy battleship *Centurion* and the rescue ships *Antwerp* and *Malines*. With the convoy as close escort are the corvettes *Delphinium*, *Primula*, *Erica*, *Snapdragon* and the minesweepers *Boston* and *Seaham*; in addition, the 2nd DD Flotilla with *Fortune*, *Griffin*, *Hotspur* and the 5th DD Flotilla with *Dulverton*, *Exmoor*, *Croome*, *Eridge*, *Airedale*, *Beaufort*, *Hurworth*, *Tetcott* and *Aldenham*, Covering Force (Rear-Adm Vian) provided by the 15th Cruiser Sqdn with *Cleopatra*, *Dido*, *Hermione*, *Euryalus*, *Arethusa* and *Coventry*, the 4th Cruiser Sqdn (Rear-Adm Tennant) with *Birmingham* and *Newcastle*, the 7th DD Flotilla with *Napier*, *Nestor*, *Nizam* and *Norman* (RAN), the 14th DD Flotilla with *Jervis*, *Kelvin* and *Javelin*, the 12th DD Flotilla with *Pakenham*, *Paladin* and *Inconstant* and the 22nd DD Flotilla with *Sikh*, *Zulu*, *Hasty* and *Hero*. Four MTBs towed by merchant ships have to return because of the stormy weather. *MTB259* is lost on the way back to Alexandria.
The British submarines *Proteus*, *Thorn*, *Taku*, *Thrasher*, *Porpoise*, *Una*, *P31*, *P34* and *P35* are stationed off Taranto and S of the Straits of Messina and *P211*, *P42*, *P43* and *P46* between Sicily and Sardinia.
The convoy MW.11 is located by German air reconnaissance on 12 June and attacked S of Crete by Ju 87s of I/K.G.54 (Maj Linke). The transport *City of Calcutta* (8063 tons) is damaged and has to put in to Tobruk.
13 June: German and Italian air reconnaissance again locate the western convoy but Italian torpedo aircraft from Sardinia cannot find it. The 7th Italian Div (Cruisers *Eugenio di Savoia* and *Montecuccoli* and the destroyers *Oriani*, *Ascari* and *Gioberti*) goes to sea from Cagliari to attack the convoy in the area of Cape Bon, but puts in to

Palermo after being reported by two British submarines. The British forces join up N of Mersa Matruh. In the night 13-14 June a raid is made on the airfield of Maleme (Crete) used by the German LG.1 by a British commando party landed from the Greek submarines *Papanicolis* and *Triton*. The Italian submarines *Giada* and *Uarsciek* attack the western convoy unsuccessfully.

14 June: In the morning there are attacks by Italian torpedo aircraft (Savoia S79s) on the western convoy: the *Tanimbar* (8619 tons) is sunk; the *Liverpool*, after a hit in the engine room, has to be towed back to Gibraltar. Other attacks by German and Italian bombers are unsuccessful. Force W turns off to the W. The 7th Italian Div (Div-Adm da Zara), reinforced by the destroyers *Vivaldi*, *Malocello* and *Premuda* (two others—*Zeno* and *Gioberti*—have to return because of engine trouble), sets out from Palermo to attack. The freighter *Aagtekerk* (6811 tons) from the Eastern convoy has to be sent off to Tobruk, escorted by the corvettes *Erica* and *Primula*, because of engine trouble. This group is attacked a few nautical miles from the harbour by approximately 40 Ju 87s and Ju 88s: *Aagtekerk* is sunk and *Primula* is damaged. In the afternoon Ju 88s of LG.1 from Crete attack the main convoy and sink the freighter *Bhutan* (6104 tons) and damage the *Potaro* (5410 tons). In the evening the German 3rd MTB Flotilla (Lt Wuppermann), comprising *S54*, *S55*, *S56*, *S58*, *S59* and *S60*, operates from Derna against the Eastern convoy. *S56* (Lt Wuppermann) torpedoes the British cruiser *Newcastle; S55* (Lt Horst Weber) sinks the destroyer *Hasty*. The Italian Fleet sets out with the battleships *Littorio* (Adm Iachino) and *Vittorio Veneto* (9th Div, Div-Adm Fioravanzo), the heavy cruisers *Gorizia* and *Trieste* (3rd Div, Div-Adm Parona), the light cruisers *Garibaldi* (the Commander 8th Div, Div-Adm de Courten) and *Duca d'Aosta* and 12 destroyers (*Legionario*, *Folgore*, *Freccia*, *Saetta* [7th Flotilla] *Alpino*, *Bersagliere*, *Pigafetta*, *Mitragliere* [13th Flotilla], *Aviere*, *Geniere*, *Camicia Nera*, *Corazziere* [11th Flotilla]) **15 June**: the Italian 7th Div attacks the

Western convoy and sinks the British destroyer *Bedouin* and badly damages the *Partridge*, but cannot penetrate the strong convoy escort and is driven off. Simultaneously, the German St. G. 3 (Lt-Col Siegel) attacks: the freighters *Burdwan* (5601 tons) and *Chant* (5601 tons) and the tanker *Kentucky* (9308 tons) are so badly damaged that they have later to be abandoned. Further losses are avoided by the AA fire of the escort vessels and by the fast minelayer *Welshman* which joins the convoy. But the convoy runs into a newly-laid minefield off Malta: the destroyer *Kujawiak* is sunk and *Badsworth*, *Matchless*, *Hebe* and *Orari* (10350 tons) are damaged. In the night and early morning British torpedo aircraft from Malta attack the Italian fleet. *Trento* (Capt Esposito) is torpedoed by a Beaufort of No 217 Sqdn and later sunk by the British submarine *Umbra* (Lt Maydon). In the morning an American Liberator bomber gets a hit on *Littorio*. In the afternoon Ju 87s of St.G.3 hit the British cruiser *Birmingham*, sink the destroyer *Airedale* and damage the *Nestor* so badly that she sinks on the following day. As the Italian Fleet at first continues its sortie, the British convoy turns away and then the Italians also start to return to Taranto. In the process five Wellington torpedo aircraft of No 38 Sqdn find the force again. Pilot-Officer O. L. Hawes gets a torpedo hit on *Littorio*.

16 June: *U205* (Lt-Cdr Reschke) sinks S of Crete the cruiser *Hermione* from the returning British Eastern Force. *Cairo*, *Welshman*, *Marne*, *Ithuriel*, *Blankney* and *Middleton* start the return journey from Malta to Gibraltar.

12-19 June Baltic
The Soviet submarines *M-95*, *S-4*, *Shch-304*, *Shch-317* and *Shch-320*, break through the 'Seeigel' mine barrage from Lavansaari. They set out at one-day intervals supported by sorties by Soviet torpedo cutters and patrol boats and by operations of the Soviet naval air force against the mine barrage guard. In the night 12-13 June there is an engagement off Suursaari between the Finnish minelayers *Ruotsinsalmi* and *Riilahti*, the gunboats *Hämeenmaa* and *Uusimaa* and three VMV boats

(patrol boats) and Soviet minesweeper vessels (Capt Pakholchuk) which try to bring the submarines through the barrages. In the following days there are more engagements. On 15 June *M-95* is lost on a mine E of Suursaari.

14 June-4 July   Indian Ocean
The German auxiliary cruiser *Schiff 10 Thor* (Capt Gumprich) sinks the Dutch tanker *Olivia* (6307 tons) in the Indian Ocean and captures the Norwegian tankers *Herborg* (7892 tons) and *Madrono* (5894 tons). Both later reach Japan.

15 June-5 Aug   Baltic
Finnish minelayers lay in the second half of June the mine barrages 'Rukajärvi A-C' (559 mines) N of Suursaari. Later these are extended to 18 sections with 1326 mines and 221 protection floats. Of the Soviet submarines of the first wave which broke into the Baltic, *Shch-303* and *Shch-304* operate in the area of Porkkala-Utö; *Shch-317* and *Shch*-406 on the Swedish coast; *S-4* and *Shch-320* on the Baltic Coast and near Rixhöft; and *S-7* first on the Swedish and then on the Baltic Coast. They make the following sinkings: *Shch-304* (Capt 3rd Class Ya.P Afanasev), misses the minelayer *Kaiser; Shch-317* (Lt-Cdr Mokhov) sinks four ships of 8283 tons and misses one ship; *Shch-320* (Capt 3rd Class Vishnevski) sinks one ship of 676 tons and misses two; *S-4* (Capt 3rd Class Abrosimov) has two misses; *Shch-406* (Capt 3rd Class Osipov) damages one ship of 545 tons and misses four ships; *Shch-303* (Capt 3rd Class Travkin) damages one ship of 7891 tons and misses one ship; *S-7* (Capt 3rd Class Lisin) sinks four ships of 9164 tons and misses one ship. Amongst the sunken ships are three Swedish.

17 June-20 July   North Pacific
Deployment of the Japanese 2nd SM Flotilla (Rear-Adm Ichioka) in the area of the Aleutians with *I-1, I-2, I-3, I-4, I-7* and later (until 15 Aug) also *I-6*. Only *I-7* (Cdr* Koizumi) sinks one ship of 2722 tons.

18 June   English Channel
During an attack on a German convoy (two ships with an escort of one torpedo boat flotilla) by the destroyer *Albrighton* and gunboats *SGB6, SGB7*

and *SGB8*, one German transport and *SGB7* are sunk.

20-21 June   Mediterranean
On 20 June Tobruk is taken by the German Afrika Korps. Operation by the 3rd MTB Flotilla (Lt-Cdr Kemnade) consisting of *S36, S54, S55, S56, S58* and *S59* from Derna against British ships fleeing from Tobruk. 21 June: in an engagement the South African auxiliary minesweeper *Parktown* (250 tons) is sunk and *S58* (Lt Geigert†) badly damaged. In addition, one motor yacht and six LCs and two motor launches are sunk or captured. *S55* (Lt Weber) captures *LCT150* (296 tons).

20 June-6 July   Mediterranean
U561 (Lt Schomburg) lays a mine barrage off Port Said (20 June). *U97* (Lt Bürgel) sinks three ships of 3974 tons off the Palestine coast; *U372* (Lt-Cdr Neumann) sinks the British submarine depot ship *Medway* (14600 tons) off Port Said on 30 June; *U375* (Lt-Cdr Könenkamp) sinks one ship of 1376 tons. *U77* and *U562* have no success. The Italian submarines *Atropo, Micca, Zoea* and *Corridoni* transport fuel to Cyrenaican ports.

20 June-19 July   Western Atlantic
The last seven U-boats deployed on the American East Coast find no more worth-while targets apart from convoys. After the loss of two boats (*U215* and *U576*) the rest receive orders on 19 July to leave the coast. *U402* starts the return journey without achieving any success and *U89, U132, U458* and *U754* go to the area SE of Nova Scotia.

20 June-28 July   Arctic
Convoy operation QP.13 and PQ.17 in the Arctic.
On 26 June 12 ships of QP.13 set out from Archangel and on 27 June 23 ships of QP.13 set out from Murmansk. Escort for the whole convoy: five destroyers, three corvettes, one AA ship, three minesweepers, two trawlers and one submarine. Convoy PQ.17 (Commodore Dowding) leaves Reykjavik with 36 ships, one fleet tanker and three rescue ships: three ships return because they run aground or suffer damage from ice. Close escort: Cdr Broome with destroyers *Keppel* (F), *Offa, Fury, Leamington, Ledbury* and *Wilton*, corvettes *Lotus, Poppy, Dianella* and *La*

Malouine, minesweepers Britomart, Halcyon and Salamander, and trawlers Lord Austin, Ayrshire, Northern Gem and Lord Middleton, AA ships Palomares, Pozarica, and submarines P614 and P615.
28-29 June: distant covering force (Adm Tovey), comprising battleships Duke of York and Washington, carrier Victorious, cruisers Cumberland and Nigeria and nine (later 14) destroyers, leaves Scapa Flow for area between Iceland and Bear Island.
30 June: convoy QP.13 is located in the Barents Sea by German air reconnaissance but is not pursued because the target of the German operation is convoy PQ.17. Close covering force (Rear-Adm Hamilton), consisting of cruisers London, Norfolk, Tuscaloosa and Wichita and destroyers Somali, Rowan and Wainwright leaves Seidisfjord (Iceland) for position N of PQ.17.
1 July: German 'B' Service locates PQ.17 which is also sighted in the morning by U255 (Lt-Cdr Reche) and U408 (Lt-Cdr von Hymmen) about 60 nautical miles E of Jan Mayen. U334 (Lt Siemon) and U456 (Lt-Cdr Teichert) are directed to it at once and U251 (Lt-Cdr Timm), U355 (Lt-Cdr La Baume), U657 (Lt Göllnitz), U88 (Lt-Cdr Bohmann), U457 (Cdr Brandenburg) and U376 (Lt-Cdr Marks) form a patrol line further to the E as the 'Eisteufel' group. PQ.17 and distant covering force are located by German air reconnaissance in the afternoon.
2 July: German air reconnaissance and U88 locate QP.13, but there is no additional operation since the target is PQ.17, which passes QP.13 in the afternoon. The sighting of both convoys and the mistaken reporting of the close covering force as the distant escort by German air reconnaissance leads to confusion. U456 keeps contact with PQ.17 and U457, U657, U376 and U255 are partly driven off in attacks. In the afternoon Force I (Adm Schniewind), comprising the battleship Tirpitz, the cruiser Admiral Hipper, the destroyers Karl Galster, Friedrich Ihn, Hans Lody, Theodor Riedel and torpedo boats T7 and T15, leaves Trondheim for Northern Norway as a base for the operation 'Rösselsprung'. In the after-

noon an attack by seven He 115s of 1/K.Fl.Gr.906 has no success.
3 July: Force II (Vice-Adm Kummetz), comprising the pocket-battleships Lützow, Admiral Scheer, the destroyers Z24, Z27, Z28, Z29, Z30 and Richard Beitzen, proceeds from Narvik to Altafjord to join up with Force I which has arrived there together with the destroyers Erich Steinbrinck and Friedrich Eckoldt. But Lützow, Hans Lody, Karl Galster and Theodor Riedel are put out of action by going aground in Grimsöystraumen. Air contact is lost in poor visibility. U88 attacks destroyers unsuccessfully and U456, U255, U657, U703 (Lt-Cdr Bielfeld) and U334 generally establish only brief contact. British air reconnaissance establishes the departure of the German surface forces northwards. The British submarines P212/Sahib, Sturgeon, Minerve (FFN), P45/Unrivalled, P54/Unshaken and Ursula, Tribune, Seawolf and Trident are stationed in two lines S of Bear Island to cover the convoy. In addition, there are the Soviet submarines D-3, K-22, K-21, Shch-402 and Shch-403. Inter alia, M-176 is off Varangerfjord. In these operations D-3 and M-176 are probably lost on German flanking mine barrages. The cruiser Manchester and the destroyer Eclipse come from Spitzbergen to join the distant covering force.
4 July: a single He 115 torpedo aircraft of 1/K. Fl. Gr.906 obtains hits on steamer Christopher Newport (7191 tons), which is later finished off and sunk by the British submarine P614 and U457. U88, U225 and U334 are in temporary contact with the convoy and U457 with the cruiser force. Two attacks by U88 fail. The Germans are unclear about the position of the British heavy forces with the result that the Fleet receives no order to sail. In the evening a squadron of K.G. 30 attacks without success. Torpedo aircraft of I/K.G. 26 (Capt Eicke) sink the freighter Navarino (4841 tons); the freighter William Hooper (7177) tons is damaged and finished off by U334; and the Soviet tanker Azerbaidzhan (6114 tons) is torpedoed. Of 25 attacking He 111s three are shot down. In the evening the First Sea Lord (Adm Pound), expecting

a German surface attack in superior strength, orders the cruiser force and the destroyers of the escort to turn back to the W and has the convoy scattered.
5 July: German air reconnaissance and U-boats report the breaking up of the convoy and the departure of the cruisers westwards. Then *Tirpitz* (Capt Karl Topp), *Admiral Hipper* (Capt Meisel), *Admiral Scheer* (Capt Meendsen-Bohlken), seven destroyers and two torpedo boats put to sea. Off Ingöy the Soviet submarine *K-21* (Capt 2nd Class Lunin) makes an unsuccessful attack on *Tirpitz*. In the course of the day all three Gruppen (Capts Kahl, Stoffregen and Herrman) of K.G. 30 (Maj Bloedorn) attack the transports of the convoy as they sail singly or in groups and sink the freighters *Washington* (5564 tons), *Bolton Castle* (5203 tons), *Pan Kraft* (5644 tons), *Peter Kerr* (6476 tons), *Fairfield City* (5686 tons) and the rescue ship *Zaafaran* (1559 tons) and damage *Paulus Potter* (7168 tons), *Earlston* (7195 tons—finished off by *U334*), *Empire Byron* (6645 tons—finished off by *U703*) and the fleet tanker *Aldersdale*. *U88* sinks *Carlton* (5127 tons) and *Daniel Morgan* (7177 tons), *U456* the *Honomu* (6977 tons) and *U703* the *River Afton* (5479 tons). A Catalina flying boat of No 210 Sqdn RAF and the British submarine *Unshaken* sight and report the German naval force. After the early and intercepted report by the submarines and the aircraft the C-in-C of the Navy, in accordance with the Führer's directive not to take risks, orders the naval operation to be broken off. The destruction of the remaining ships in the convoy is to be left to U-boats and aircraft. Convoy QP.13 runs into one of its own minefields in the Denmark Strait in the mist and storms and loses the minesweeper *Niger* and the steamers *Heffron*, *Hybert*, *John Randolph*, *Massmar* and *Rodina* totalling 30909 tons.
6 July: the German naval force arrives in the Kaa-fjord. The British cruiser force joins up with the distant covering force. Aircraft of K.G. 30 sink the tanker *Pan Atlantik* (5411 tons), *U255* the *John Witherspoon* (7191 tons).
7 July: of the U-boats deployed to hunt the single ships *U255* sinks the *Alcoa*

Ranger (5116 tons), *U355* the *Hartlebury* (5082 tons) and *U457* the abandoned tanker wreck *Aldersdale* (8402 tons). Five ships and some escort vessels of the convoy arrive in the Matochkin Strait.
8 July: *U255* sinks the steamer *Olopana* (6069 tons) off Novaya Zemlya. Commodore Dowding forms a convoy in the Matochkin Strait consisting of five steamers, three minesweepers, three corvettes and three trawlers, the AA ships *Palomares* and *Pozarica* and the rescue ship *Zamalek* and this proceeds southwards along the West Coast of Novaya Zemlya and the ice barrier. The Soviet destroyers *Gremyashchi* and *Grozny* reinforce the escort.
9 July: part of the convoy, comprising the rescue ship *Rathlin* and the motor tanker *Donbass* and steamer *Bellingham*, arrives in Archangel. *U255* establishes contact with the rest of the convoy against which *U457*, *U703*, *U376* and *U251* operate.
10 July: in attacks by II/K.G. 30 against the rest of the convoy off the entrance to the White Sea the steamer *Hoosier* (5060 tons) and *El Capitan* (5255 tons) are damaged and then finished off by *U376* and *U251* respectively. The steamer *Samuel Chase* is damaged by bomb hits.
11 July: the rest of the convoy, comprising *Zamalek*, the steamers *Ocean Freedom* and *Samuel Chase*, arrives in Archangel. Another group of ships with the trawler *Ayrshire* arrives in the Matochkin Strait.
12 July: *U376* attacks trawler off Kanin Noss without success.
13 July: from the homeward-bound U-boats *U255* sinks the abandoned wreck of the steamer *Paulus Potter*.
15 July: German U-boats put into harbour.
16 July: Commodore Dowding sets out with the corvettes *Poppy*, *Lotus* and *La Malouine*, accompanied by the Soviet destroyer *Gremyashchi*, to fetch the ships anchored off the coast of Novaya Zemlya.
20-24 July: the second remnant of the convoy comprising the above-named escort vessels and the steamers *Benjamin Harrison*, *Silver Sword*, *Troubadour*, *Ironclad* and *Azerbaidzhan*, led by the

Soviet ice-breaker *Murman* (Commodore Dowding) and the trawler *Kerov*, proceeds from the Matochkin Strait to Archangel. The steamer *Empire Tide* is met on the way in Moller Bay. 28 July: the steamer *Winston Salem*, which was temporarily beached, is the last straggler to arrive in Molotovsk. Total losses sustained by PQ.17: 24 ships of 143977 tons. German losses: five aircraft in 202 sorties. Sunk by U-boats: nine ships of 56611 tons; by the Luftwaffe eight ships of 40376 tons. In addition, seven ships of 46982 tons, damaged by air attack, are finished off by U-boat torpedoes. 3350 vehicles, 430 tanks, 210 aircraft and 99316 tons of other war equipment are lost.

20 June-4 Aug Western Atlantic
Of the U-boats operating in the area of Cuba, the Gulf of Mexico and off the Greater Antilles *U84* (Lt-Cdr Uphoff) sinks three ships of 14206 tons and torpedoes one ship of 7176 tons; *U154* (Cdr Kölle) sinks one ship of 2160 tons and one unidentified ship; *U571* (Lt-Cdr Möhlmann) sinks three ships of 18980 tons and torpedoes one ship of 11394 tons; *U134* and *U437* have no success with their attacks.
Of the U-boats operating in the area of Trinidad, in the Caribbean and off Panama *U153* (Cdr Reichmann) sinks three ships of 16166 tons; *U203* (Lt-Cdr Mützelburg) sinks five ships of 32985 tons; *U505* (Lt-Cdr Loewe) sinks three ships of 12748 tons; and *U575* (Lt-Cdr Heydemann) sinks four ships of 8274 tons and torpedoes one ship of 12910 tons. *U153*, after an unsuccessful attack on a netlayer off the Panama Canal, is forced to submerge by the submarine-chaser *PC458* and is jointly damaged by USN and USAAF aircraft. Later she is sunk on 13 July by the destroyer *Lansdowne* (Lt-Cdr Smedburg).

23 June Baltic
Soviet motor minesweepers enter the 'Seeigel' mine barrage while torpedo cutters attack German submarine-chasers W of Suursaari in order to bring the submarine *Shch-406* through the barrages.

23-29 June Mediterranean
In the Gulf of Sirte on 23 June and 24 June the British submarines *Thrasher* (Lt-Cdr Mackenzie) and *Turbulent* (Cdr

Linton) attack an Italian convoy of three ships, escorted by the torpedo boat *Perseo* on the way from Tripoli to Benghazi, and each sink one ship of 1480 tons and 1085 tons respectively. On 29 June *Thrasher* also sinks the Italian fast sloop *Diana*.

24 June Arctic
The I/St. G.5 (Ju 87s) sinks the British minesweeper *Gossamer* in the Kola Inlet.

24-27 June Black Sea
Strong flanking mine barrages to protect Odessa Bay against Soviet submarines are laid out by the Rumanian minelayers *Amiral Murgescu* and *Dacia* with an escort from the destroyers *Regele Ferdinand*, *Regina Maria*, *Marasesti*, the gunboats *Dumitrescu*, *Ghigulescu*, *Stihi*, the torpedo boat *Smeul* and motor minesweepers of the Danube Flotilla. In Aug/Sept the Soviet submarines *M-33* and *M-60* are lost on these barrages.

25 June-9 July Pacific
In the area of Truk the US submarine *Grouper* (Lt-Cdr Duke) torpedoes the Japanese whale factory-ship *Tonan Maru No 2* (19262 tons); *Thresher* (Lt-Cdr Millican) sinks one ship of 4836 tons. *Plunger* (Lt-Cdr White) sinks two ships of 6259 tons off Japan.

26 June Western Atlantic
Germany announces the extension of the blockade area to the American East Coast.

28 June-27 July South West Pacific
In operations in the South China Sea the US submarine *Sturgeon* (Lt-Cdr Nimitz) sinks one ship of 7266 tons; *Sailfish* (Lt-Cdr Voge) one ship of 8811 tons; *Seadragon* (Lt-Cdr Ferrall) three ships of 15637 tons. *Spearfish* (Lt-Cdr Dempsey) torpedoes one ship of 9626 tons. *Stingray* (Lt-Cdr Lamb) sinks one ship of 1292 tons E of the Philippines and *S37* one ship of 2775 tons off Rabaul. In the Malacca Straits the British submarine *Trusty* (Lt-Cdr King) torpedoes one ship of 3019 tons.

29-30 June North Atlantic
On the way to the American coast *U458* (Lt-Cdr Diggins) and *U754* (Lt-Cdr Oestermann) each sink an independent of 2714 tons and 12435 tons respectively in the North Atlantic.

30 June Black Sea
The Soviet Command gives orders to

evacuate Sevastopol. But the evacuation can only be carried out on a small scale with small units and submarines before the last attempts at resistance are wiped out.

30 June-15 July   Baltic
Soviet minesweeper forces and torpedo cutters support the return of the submarine *Shch-304* (30 June) and the break-out of *S-7* and *Shch-303* through the mine barrages (4 July and 8 July). The returning *Shch-317* (with the Div Cdr, Capt 3rd Class Egorov, on board) is attacked repeatedly from 12 July to 15 July by Finnish and German submarine-chasers between the 'Nashorn' and 'Seeigel' mine barrages and is lost. Many mines detonate as the vessels break through.

1 July   Black Sea
The German *Sperrbrecher 191* sinks on a Soviet mine barrage on the route Odessa-Ochakov.

1-20 July   South Pacific
Forces are assembled for the operation 'Watchtower' (landing on Guadalcanal).
On 1 July a convoy consisting of six transports with the last additional troops of the Marine Corps, sets out from San Diego, accompanied by the newly-formed TF 18 (see 10-15 June). On 7 July TF 11 and 16 put to sea from Pearl Harbour to join up with the other forces in the area of the Fiji Islands on 20 July.

2 July   Black Sea
Air attack by I/K.G.100 (Capt Heise) on Novorossisk. The wreck of the Soviet flotilla leader *Tashkent* is destroyed; the destroyer *Bditelny* is sunk and the training cruiser *Komintern* damaged.

3 July   Western Atlantic
U215 (Lt-Cdr Hoeckner) sinks one ship of 7191 tons from a convoy S of Nova Scotia and is then destroyed by the escort.

5-30 July   North Pacific
The US submarine *Growler* (Lt-Cdr Gilmore) sinks off Kiska the Japanese destroyer *Arare* and torpedoes the destroyers *Kasumi* and *Shiranui*. The destroyer *Nenohi* is sunk by the submarine *Triton* (Lt Cdr-Kirkpatrick) and *Finback* misses another. On 15 July *Grunion* (Lt-Cdr Abele) sinks the

Japanese submarine-chasers *Kusentai Ch25* and *Ch27*; the submarine is lost on 30 July.

6 July   Black Sea
II/K.G.26 sinks a Soviet submarine-chaser S of the Crimea.

6-20 July   Western Atlantic
U132 (Lt-Cdr Vogelsang), which has penetrated the Gulf of St Lawrence, sinks three ships of 10249 tons from the convoy QS.15 on 6 July and one ship of 4367 tons from another QS convoy on 20 July.

7-11 July   Baltic
After a preparatory air attack some 30 Soviet craft, chiefly torpedo cutters (TKAs) and patrol boats (MOs), attack in the night 7-8 July the island of Someri in the inner Gulf of Finland which is occupied by weak Finnish forces. At first they are able to land some 80 men and to take the base of Itäpää and later to bring up some reinforcements. But the Finnish defenders hold out until the Finnish gunboats *Hämeenmaa* and *Uusimaa* and the patrol boats *VMV8, VMV9, VMV10, VMV12* and *VMV17* and the motor torpedo boat *Vasama* come up before dawn. Together with the coastal guns the latter sink the Soviet *TKA83, TKA113* and *TKA-123*. Simultaneously with the arrival of Soviet reinforcements, which are landed by MO cutters, the Finnish gunboat *Turunmaa* with eight motor boats brings a Finnish company whose counter attack is supported by the fire of the German minesweeper *M18* as well as of the Finnish minelayers *Riilahti* and *Ruotsinsalmi*, the German minesweeper *M37*, the auxiliary gunboat *SAT27/Ostsee* and the motor minesweeper tender *Nettelbeck* which arrive in the afternoon. They also prevent a Soviet gunboat, two patrol ships and several Fugas minesweepers from effectively intervening. By midday on 9 July the Soviet forces which landed are defeated: 149 men surrender and 126 dead are counted. At sea the Soviets, in gun engagements with the German and Finnish ships on 9 July, also lose *TKA101, TKA31* and *TKA72*. The gunboat *Kama* sinks after being hit by a bomb from the Finnish aircraft Le. R4. The Soviets continue their efforts to establish

contact with the forces landed up to 11 July.

9 July English Channel
The German 2nd MTB Flotilla (Lt-Cdr Feldt), comprising *S48*, *S50*, *S63*, *S67*, *S70*, *S104* and *S109*, attacks a British convoy off Lyme Bay. *S67* (Lt-Cdr Zymalkowski) sinks the British tanker *Pomella* (6766 tons), the other boats the trawler *Manor* and four freighters totalling 5426 tons.

9-23 July Mediterranean
U561 (Lt Schomburg) lays another mine barrage off Port Said. *U562* (Lt Hamm) torpedoes one ship of 3359 tons and *U375* (Lt-Cdr Könenkamp) sinks a watch ship off Famagusta. Off the Syrian coast the Italian submarine *Perla* misses a large transport and *Alagi* (Lt-Cdr Puccini) sinks one Turkish ship of 3723 tons. *Ondina*, *Nereide* and *Asteria* have no success.

10 July-10 Sept Western Atlantic
In the area of Trinidad and to the SE of it, *U160* (Lt Lassen) sinks six ships of 29281 tons and *U66* (Lt-Cdr Markworth) nine ships of 48896 tons. *U66* lays mines on 20 July off Port Castries (St Lucia) on which one US coastguard cutter and the British *MTB339* and *MTB342* are damaged. *U160* also torpedoes the Norwegian tanker *Havsten* (6161 tons) which is later sunk by the Italian submarine *Tazzoli* (Cdr Fecia di Cossato).

11-15 July Central Atlantic
From the 'Hai' group proceeding S the U-tanker *U116* (Cdr von Schmidt) locates the convoy OS.33 (41 ships), after a part (six ships) has been detached for South America. In a simultaneous attack by *U116* and *U201* (Lt-Cdr Schnee) one ship of 7093 tons is sunk and *U582* (Lt-Cdr Schulte) sinks one ship of 8826 tons. *U136* (Lt-Cdr Zimmermann) is sunk by the frigate *Spey* and sloop *Pelican* and the Free French destroyer *Léopard*. *U572* (Lt-Cdr Hirsacker) and *U752* (Lt-Cdr Schroeter) keep contact with the main convoy, with interruptions, until the evening of 13 July. *U582* sinks a straggler of 7524 tons on 15 July. In shadowing the western part of the convoy, *U116* sinks one ship of 4284 tons and *U201* two ships of 11965 tons.

11 July-21 Sept Western Atlantic
U166 lays a mine barrage on 25 July off the estuary of the Mississippi which remains undetected. In the Gulf of Mexico *U166* (Lt Kuhlmann) sinks four ships of 7593 tons and *U171* (Lt-Cdr Pfeffer) three ships of 17641 tons. Operations by *U173* (Cdr* Beucke) off the Greater Antilles and by *U509* (Cdr Wolff) in the Gulf of Mexico have no success. *U166* is sunk by a US coastguard aircraft off the Mississippi estuary on 1 Aug. *U171* is lost (9 Oct) on a mine off Lorient.

12-15 July Mediterranean
The British submarine *P.211/Safari* (Cdr Bryant) sinks one ship and damages one ship totalling 2094 tons off the coast of Sardinia.

13-27 July North Atlantic
Resumption of the convoy operations on the North Atlantic route by the U-boat 'Wolf' group (*U454*, *U704*, *U597*, *U71*, *U552*, *U43*, *U379*, *U86*, *U90* and from 25 July also *U607*). On 13 July *U71* (Lt Rodler von Roithberg) sights the convoy ON.111 (EG B.6) S of Iceland but, as a result of an obscure report, the boats search in the wrong direction. *U704* and *U552* are driven off by the escort on 14 July. The group proceeds to the SW without sighting anything until 23 July and is directed to ON.113 which is identified by the 'B' Service. *U552* (Cdr Topp) locates it on 24 July according to plan. The convoy consists of 33 ships and is escorted by the Canadian EG C.2 whose destroyer *St Croix* sinks *U90* (Lt-Cdr Öldorp) with depth charges as she keeps contact. In the first night only *U552* attacks: she sinks one ship of 5136 tons and torpedoes one tanker of 8093 tons. In poor visibility and bad weather only a few boats get near the convoy on 25 July. Attacks by *U43* and *U597* in the night fail; only *U607* (Lt-Cdr Mengersen) torpedoes one ship of 6942 tons which is later sunk by *U704* (Lt-Cdr Kessler). On 26 July the contact is lost and a search on 27 July yields no results. The 'Wolf' group splits up and goes to the supply boat *U461* (29-30 July).

13 July-7 Aug South Pacific
Of the Japanese 3rd SM Flotilla (Rear-Adm Kono) *I-11*, *I-174* and

I-175 operate off Sydney, *I-169* off New Caledonia and *I-171* off Fiji. They make the following sinkings: *I-11* (Cdr* Hichiji) three ships of 15301 tons and lightly damages one ship; *I-175* (Cdr Uno) sinks two ships of 3023 tons and damages one ship of 3279 tons; and *I-169* (Cdr* Watanabe) sinks one ship of 9227 tons.

14 July Pacific
Reorganization of the Japanese Combined Fleet as a result of Midway. Combined Fleet (Adm Yamamoto), comprising the battleship *Yamato*, the escort carriers *Taiyo* and *Unyo*, the seaplane carriers *Chiyoda* and *Nisshin* and the destroyers *Akebono*, *Ushio* and *Sazanami* (7th Destroyer Div).
1st Fleet (Adm Yamamoto), comprising the battleships *Nagato*, *Mutsu*, *Fuso* and *Yamashiro* (2nd BB Sqdn, Vice-Adm Takasu) and from 5 Aug the *Musashi* and *Yamato* (1st BB Sqdn); the cruisers *Kitakami* and *Oi* (9th Cruiser Sqdn), *Abukuma* (1st DD Flotilla, Rear-Adm Omori), the destroyers *Akatsuki*, *Ikazuchi* and *Inazuma* (6th DD Div—detached to the Aleutians), *Hatsuharu*, *Hatsushimo* and *Wakaba* (21st DD Div—detached to the Aleutians); the cruiser *Sendai* (3rd DD Flotilla, Rear-Adm Hashimoto) with the destroyers *Fubuki*, *Hatsuyuki*, *Murakumo* and *Shirayuki* (11th DD Div), *Ayanami*, *Isonami*, *Shikinami* and *Uranami*, (19th DD Div), *Amagiri*, *Asagiri*, *Shirakumo* and *Yugiri* (20th DD Div).
2nd Fleet (Vice-Adm Kondo), comprising the heavy cruisers *Atago*, *Maya* and *Takao* (4th Cruiser Sqdn), *Haguro* and *Myoko* (5th Cruiser Sqdn, Vice-Adm Takagi), the battleships *Haruna* and *Kongo* (3rd BB Sqdn, Rear-Adm Kurita) and the 2nd DD Flotilla (Rear-Adm Tanaka) with the cruiser *Jintsu* and destroyers *Kagero*, *Kuroshio*, *Oyashio* and *Hayashio* (15th DD Div), *Umikaze*, *Kawakaze* and *Suzukaze* (24th DD Div) and the 4th DD Flotilla (Rear-Adm Takama) with the cruiser *Yura* and destroyers *Murasame*, *Yudachi*, *Harusame* and *Samidare* (2nd DD Div), *Asagumo*, *Minegumo* and *Natsugumo* (9th DD Div), *Ariake*, *Yugure*, *Shiratsuyu* and *Shigure* (27th DD Div). Also under command: the 11th Carrier Sqdn with the seaplane carriers and

tenders *Chitose*, *Kamikawa Maru* and *Kamikaze Maru*.
3rd Fleet (Vice-Adm Nagumo) comprising the carriers *Shokaku*, *Zuikaku* and *Zuiho* (1st Carrier Sqdn), *Ryujo*, *Junyo* and *Hiyo* (from 31 July) (2nd Carrier Sqdn, Rear-Adm Kakuta), battleships *Hiyei* and *Kirishima* (11th BB Sqdn, Rear-Adm Abe), the heavy cruisers *Kumano* and *Suzuya* (7th Cruiser Sqdn, Rear-Adm Nishimura), *Chikuma* and *Tone* (8th Cruiser Sqdn, Rear-Adm T. Hara) and the 10th DD Flotilla (Rear-Adm Kimura) with the cruiser *Nagara* and the destroyers *Arashi*, *Hagikaze*, *Maikaze* and *Nowake* (4th DD Div), *Akigumo*, *Yugumo*, *Makigumo* and *Kazegumo* (10th DD Div), *Hatsukaze*, *Yukikaze*, *Amatsukaze* and *Tokitsukaze* (16th DD Div), *Urakaze*, *Isokaze*, *Tanikaze* and *Hamakaze* (17th DD Div.)
4th Fleet (Vice-Adm Inouye) in Truk with the cruiser *Kashima* as flagship, the minelayer *Tokiwa*, the 2nd ES with the cruiser *Yubari* and the destroyers *Yuzuki*, *Oite*, *Asanagi* and *Yunagi* (29th DD Div), two auxiliary gunboats and the 4th, 5th and 6th BF with light vessels and auxiliary ships in the Mandate territories.
5th Fleet (Vice-Adm Hosogaya) with the heavy cruiser *Nachi*, the cruisers *Kiso* and *Tama*, the destroyers *Oboro*, *Usugumo*, *Hokaze* and *Shiokaze* with further units detached from the 1st Fleet, three auxiliary cruisers, three picket boat divisions and the 7th BF in the area of the Kuriles and Aleutians. In addition, the 7th SM Flotilla.
6th Fleet (Vice-Adm Komatsu) with the cruiser *Katori* and the 1st, 2nd, 3rd and 8th SM Flotillas.
8th Fleet (Vice-Adm Mikawa) with the heavy cruisers *Chokai* (F), *Aoba*, *Kinugasa*, *Furutaka* and *Kako* (6th Cruiser Sqdn, Rear-Adm Goto), the light cruisers *Tatsuta* and *Tenryu* (18th Cruiser Sqdn, Rear-Adm Matsuyama), the destroyers *Mutsuki*, *Yayoi*, *Mochizuki* and *Uzuki* (30th DD Div), the minelayers *Shirataka* and *Tsugaru* and light vessels of the 8th BF and the 6th SM Flotilla.

14-19 July Mediterranean
Operation 'Pinpoint'. Part of British Force H leaves Gibraltar with the

carrier *Eagle*, the cruisers *Cairo* and *Charybdis* and five destroyers to fly off 31 Spitfire fighters for Malta S of the Balearics. The Italian submarines *Emo*, and *Otaria* sight nothing. The fast minelayer *Welshman* with supplies continues the journey to Malta. On the way there are unsuccessful attacks by 28 Italian bombers and 16 Ju 87s and by the submarine *Axum*. The British ship arrives in Malta on 16 July and returns on 18-19 July. Italian attempts to intercept her with surface forces, submarines (*Cobalto, Dessiè, Velella, Malachite, Dagabur* and *Bronzo* off Cape Bon) and aircraft fail. The British submarines *Parthian, Regent, Rorqual, Porpoise* and *Cachalot* bring supplies to Malta. The Italian submarines *Bragadino, Sciesa, Toti, Santarosa, Atropo, Narvalo, Micca, Zoea* and *Corridonei* transport 1105 tons of supplies to North Africa (15 missions).

15 July   Western Atlantic
U576 (Lt-Cdr Heinicke), which has previously torpedoed a tanker of 11147 tons, attacks a convoy on the American East Coast and sinks two ships of 10373 tons. She is then attacked by an aircraft, rammed by the steamer *Unicoi* in the convoy and is lost.

15 July-23 Aug   Central Atlantic
After the operation against OS.33 the 'Hai' group proceeds in line abreast to the Freetown area. The following additional sinkings are made (some of the boats have in the meantime taken oil from *U116*): *U201* (Lt-Cdr Schnee) the A/S trawler *Laertes* and two ships totalling 21963 tons; *U572* (Lt-Cdr Hirsacker) one ship of 5281 tons; *U752* (Lt-Cdr Schroeter) four ships of 21624 tons; and *U582* (Lt-Cdr Schulte) two ships of 14294 tons.

15 July-14 Oct   Arctic
Operation EON.18. A Soviet destroyer force is transferred by the Northern seaway from the Pacific to the Arctic. On 15 July the flotilla leader *Baku* and the destroyers *Razumny, Raz-yarenny* and *Revnostny* leave Vladivostok. The last collides on 18 July with the freighter *Terney* in the Tatar Sound and has to remain behind. The other ships go through the Kurile Passage on 22 July and put into Petropavlovsk on 26 July. They pass through the Bering Strait

on 30 July and reach Tiksi on 14 Aug accompanied by the ice-breaker *Mikoyan*. On 19 Aug the journey is continued; on 24 Sept Dikson is reached and on 9 Oct the Yugor Strait. On 14 Oct the ships are met by the Northern Fleet off the Kola Inlet.

16 July   South Atlantic
The German auxiliary cruiser *Schiff 28* (Capt Ruckteschell) sinks the US tanker *William F. Humphrey* (7983 tons) in the South Atlantic.

16 July   Black Sea
In an air attack on Poti the Soviet cruiser *Komintern* receives such heavy hits that she has to have her armament dismantled. The destroyer *Bodry* is badly damaged. A large ship has a near-miss.

17-20 July   Central Atlantic
The returning *U202* (Lt-Cdr Linder) sights the convoy OS.34 (35 ships) but is driven off in the night 17-18 July by a corvette. On the morning of 18 July the returning *U126* (Lt-Cdr Bauer), which has expended her torpedoes, sights the convoy and brings up the outward-bound *U564* (Lt-Cdr Suhren), *U108* (Cdr Scholtz) and *U654* (Lt Forster), which, even during darkness, are repeatedly forced to submerge by aircraft. In the night 18-19 July *U564* sinks two ships of 11096 tons and *U108*, after an unsuccessful attack, is attacked with depth charges. At mid-day on 19 July *U108* and *U126* are finally driven off and on 20 July after a fruitless search, the operation is stopped. The outward-bound boats continue their journey to the Caribbean.

19 July   South Atlantic
The US carrier *Ranger* flies off 60 P.40 fighters of the USAAF for Accra off the Gold Coast. From there they are transferred across Africa to the Near East and India and Burma.

20 July   Indian Ocean
The German auxiliary cruiser *Schiff 10 Thor* (Capt Gumprich) sinks the British freighter *Indus* (5187 tons) in the Indian Ocean.

20-22 July   English Channel
The 3rd TB Flotilla (Cdr Wilcke), comprising *T13, T4, T10* and *T14*, carries out two defensive mining operations, 'Rhein' and 'Stein', in the Channel.

20-22 July Mediterranean
Operation 'Insect'. British Force H with the carrier *Eagle*, the cruisers *Cairo* and *Charybdis* and five destroyers proceeds to the area S of the Balearics from Gibraltar and flies off 28 Spitfire fighters for Malta. On 20 July the Italian submarine *Dandolo* misses the *Eagle* with four torpedoes. *Platino* sights nothing.

20-24 July Arctic
The British destroyers *Blankney*, *Marne*, *Martin* and *Middleton* proceed to Murmansk with supplies and ammunition for escort vessels of the convoy QP.14.

20 July-5 Aug Western Atlantic
The four U-boats withdrawn from the American East Coast operate SE of Nova Scotia. Here *U89* (Lt-Cdr Lohmann) sinks one sailing ship of 54 tons; *U754* (Lt-Cdr Oestermann) one fishery vessel of 260 tons; and *U458* (Lt-Cdr Diggins) one ship of 4870 tons. On 29 July *U132* (Lt-Cdr Vogelsang) sights the convoy ON.113 and sinks one ship of 6734 tons from it on 30 July. *U458* and *U754* are not able to attack; the latter is sunk on 31 July by an RCAF aircraft.

20 July-7 Aug South Pacific
A Japanese force with three transports escorted by the light cruisers *Tatsuta* and *Tenryu* (18th Cruiser Sqdn), the destroyers *Asanagi*, *Uzuki* and *Yuzuki*, the minelayer *Tsugaru* and submarine-chasers and other light vessels, sets out from Rabaul on 20 July. It lands in the afternoon of 21 July naval landing troops and units of the South Sea Detachment of the Army near Buna (New Guinea) which are to advance over land in the direction of Port Moresby. Allied air attacks on 22 July damage the transport *Ayatosan Maru* (9788 tons) and the *Uzuki*, but all the ships get back to Rabaul by 24 July. On 26 July and 29-30 July the Japanese bring more troops to Buna with these ships and also the destroyer *Yunagi*. On 29 July a transport, the *Kotoku Maru* (6701 tons) is lost in an air attack. On 30 July Vice-Adm Mikawa arrives in Rabaul on the cruiser *Chokai* as the new Commander of the 8th Fleet. On 31 July another Japanese convoy for Buna, comprising *Tsugaru*, one

transport and submarine-chasers, has to return because of air attacks. A convoy, which sets out on 5 Aug with three transports, the *Tatsuta*, *Uzuki* and *Yuzuki*, is recalled on 7 Aug when news is received of the Allied landing on Guadalcanal.

22 July-19 Aug North Atlantic
On 22 July the outward-bound *U609* (Lt Rudloff) sights a UR convoy and shadows it with *U254* (Lt-Cdr Gilardone) to the neighbourhood of Reykjavik. Then the boats are stationed in the area W of Iceland but attempts to attack US Task Groups on 28 July and 1 Aug fail. On 2 Aug *U609* sinks one ship of 1218 tons. In the area of the Faeroes the outward-bound *U605* (Lt-Cdr Schütze) sinks one trawler of 239 tons on 3 Aug.

24-25 July Mediterranean
After an attack by the British submarine *Unbeaten* (Lt-Cdr Woodward), British torpedo aircraft and bombers sink near Argostoli the Italian transport *Vettor Pisani* (6339 tons), escorted by the torpedo boats *Antares*, *Calliope* and *Orsa*. On 26 July the British submarine *Thrasher* is damaged off Port Said by the attack of a British Swordfish aircraft.

24 July-17 Aug Pacific
Off the South Kuriles the US submarine *Narwhal* (Lt-Cdr Wilkins) sinks five ships of 6019 tons and torpedoes two other ships of 6904 tons. Off Japan *Silversides* (Lt-Cdr Burlingame) sinks one ship of 5811 tons; off Truk *Greenling* (Lt-Cdr Bruton) sinks two ships of 17228 tons, *Gudgeon* (Lt-Cdr Stovall) one ship of 4853 tons and torpedoes two tankers of 20040 tons; and off Wotje *Tambor* sinks one ship of 891 tons.

26 July-1 Aug Arctic
In the search for the remaining ships of PQ.17 sighted by German reconnaissance off the West Coast of Novaya Zemlaya *U601* (Lt-Cdr Grau) shells on 26 July the Soviet Polar station Karmakuly, destroys two aircraft and sinks the steamer *Krestyanin* (2513 tons) off the Kostin Strait on 1 Aug.

26 July-10 Sept Western Atlantic
In the area SE of Trinidad *U108* (Cdr Scholtz) sinks three ships of 17495 tons; *U155* (Lt-Cdr Piening) 10 ships

of 43892 tons; and *U510* (Cdr Neitzel) two ships of 10256 tons and torpedoes one ship of 8016 tons.

27-28 July Baltic
The returning Soviet submarine *S-4* is damaged by a mine on the 'Seeigel' barrage: the Commander (Capt 3rd Class Abrosimov) is blown overboard but the boat reaches Lavansaari. On 28 July the minesweeper *T-58* is damaged by a German coastal battery when the *Shch-320* is transferred to Kronstadt.

27 July-11 Sept South West Pacific
In the Malacca Straits the Dutch submarine *O23* (Lt-Cdr Valkenburg) sinks two ships of 12333 tons and torpedoes one ship of 729 tons. In the South China Sea the US submarine *Saury* (Lt-Cdr Mewhinney) sinks one ship of 8606 tons and torpedoes one ship of 9024 tons; and *Seal* (Lt-Cdr Hurd) and *Skipjack* (Lt-Cdr Coe) each torpedo one ship of 7260 tons and 6500 tons respectively and *Seawolf* (Lt-Cdr Warder) sinks two ships of 4462 tons. Off Bougainville *Tautog* (Lt-Cdr Willingham) sinks one ship of 5627 tons.

29 July-3 Aug North Atlantic
The outward-bound *U210* (Lt-Cdr Lemcke) sights in the North Atlantic the convoy ON.115 (41 ships and the Canadian EG C.3 including the destroyers *Saguenay* and *Skeena* and corvettes *Agassiz*, *Sackville* and *Wetaskiwin*, in addition there is the destroyer HMCS *Hamilton*). The escort repeatedly drives off on 30 July and 31 July the U-boats which make contact—*U164*, *U210*, *U511*, *U553* and *U217*. *U588* is sunk by depth charges from *Skeena* and *Wetaskiwin*. On 1 Aug a patrol line 'Pirat' is formed with *U210*, *U217*, *U553*, *U511* and *U164* which the replenished 'Wolf' boats *U607*, *U454*, *U704*, *U597*, *U71*, *U552* and *U43* join on 2 Aug. On 2 Aug *U552* (Cdr Topp) sights the convoy and brings up *U71*, *U704*, *U217*, *U597* and *U553*. *U552* torpedoes two ships, one of 10627 tons and another of 7176 tons: the latter is sunk by *U607* (Lt-Cdr Mengersen). *U553* (Cdr Thurmann) sinks one ship of 9419 tons. Further attacks by *U71*, *U217* and *U552* on the convoy and by *U597* on a straggler fail. On 3 Aug the opera-

tion has to be broken off in the mist.

30 July-9 Aug Mediterranean
In operations off the Palestine coast *U77* (Lt-Cdr Schonder) sinks nine sailing ships and *U565* (Lt-Cdr Franken) one sailing ship. *U372* is found and sunk by a British patrol consisting of the destroyers *Zulu*, *Sikh*, *Croome* and *Tetcott* with air support. In attempting to launch torpedo riders to attack the port of Haifa the Italian submarine *Scirè* is sunk by the British A/S trawler *Islay*.

31 July North Atlantic
The outward-bound *U213* (Lt von Varendorff†) encounters a convoy W of the Bay of Biscay and is sunk by the sloops *Erne*, *Rochester* and *Sandwich*, belonging to the escort.

31 July-6 Aug South Pacific
Preparations for the operation 'Watchtower' (landing on Guadalcanal). After final landing exercises the South Pacific Amphibious Force—TF 62 (Rear-Adm Turner)—advances from the area of the Fiji Islands. It consists of the convoy (TG 62.1) divided into six sections, comprising 19 troop and supply transports, four fast transports, the TG 62.2 (Rear-Adm Crutchley) with the cruisers *Australia*, *Canberra*, *Hobart* (RAN) and *Chicago* and the destroyers (Desron 4) *Selfridge*, *Patterson*, *Ralph Talbot*, *Mugford*, *Jarvis*, *Blue*, *Helm*, *Henley* and *Bagley*, the Fire Support Groups 62.3 (Capt Riefkohl) with the cruisers *Vincennes*, *Quincy* and *Astoria* and the destroyers *Dewey*, *Ellet*, *Hull* and *Wilson* and 62.4 (Rear-Adm Scott) with the cruiser *San Juan* and the destroyers *Buchanan* and *Monssen* and also the Minesweeper Force 62.5 with five fast minesweepers.
Cover is provided by the Air Support Force—TF 61 (Vice-Adm Fletcher, Air Operations Rear-Adm Noyes) with the units 1 (Fletcher), comprising the the carrier *Saratoga*, the cruisers *Minneapolis* and *New Orleans*, the destroyers *Phelps*, *Farragut*, *Worden*, *MacDonough* and *Dale*; 2 (Rear-Adm Kinkaid) with the carrier *Enterprise*, the battleship *North Carolina*, the cruisers *Portland* (Rear-Adm Tisdale) and *Atlanta*, the destroyers *Balch*, *Maury*, *Gwin*, *Benham* and *Grayson;* 3 (Noyes) with the

carrier *Wasp*, the cruisers *San Francisco* and *Salt Lake City*, the destroyers *Lang*, *Sterett*, *Aaron Ward*, *Stack*, *Laffey* and *Farenholt*. The Tanker Force consists of the fleet tankers *Platte*, *Cimarron*, *Kaskaskia*, *Sabine* and *Kanawha*. For preparatory air action and support the shore-based aircraft in TF 63 (Rear-Adm McCain) are assembled. To cover the operation the submarines (TF 42, Capt Christie) *S38*, *S39*, *S41*, *S43*, *S44* and *S46* are deployed from Brisbane in the area of Kavieng and Rabaul and the submarines *Drum* and *Greenling* from the Pacific Fleet in the area of Truk. Overall command of the operation is in the hands of Vice-Adm Ghormley (at Nouméa). Protected by a weather front, the advance is un-detected by the enemy until 6 Aug.

31 July-12 Aug   South Pacific
From Rabaul *Ro-34* (Cdr Morinaga) and *Ro-33* (Cdr Kuriyama) of the Japanese 7th SM Flotilla (Rear-Adm Yoshitomi) operate in the area of the Gulf of Papua. They torpedo one transport of 8424 tons and sink one fishery vessel of 300 tons respectively. After the US landing on Guadalcanal *I-121*, *I-122*, *I-123*, *Ro-33* and *Ro-34* are ordered to Indispensable Strait.

1 Aug   Black Sea
Soviet TKAs sink the store ferry *F334* by torpedo in the Bay of Ivan Baba.

1-2 Aug   English Channel
The German 3rd TB Flotilla (Cdr Wilcke), comprising *T13*, *T10* and *T14*, lays defensive mine barrage 'Masuren' in the Channel.

1 Aug-16 Sept   Western Atlantic
In individual operations in the Caribbean the following sinkings take place (apart from convoy operations—see entry): *U164* (Cdr Fechner) one ship of 1745 tons; *U217* (Lt Reichenbach) one sailing ship of 75 tons; *U558* (Lt-Cdr Krech) one ship of 2606 tons. *U511* and *U94* have no individual successes.

1-10 Aug   Indian Ocean
Operation 'Stab'. Force A of the British Eastern Fleet (Vice-Adm Somerville) which was transferred from Kilindini (East Africa) to Colombo at the end of July and which comprises the battleship *Warspite*, the carriers *Formidable* and *Illustrious*, the 4th

Cruiser Sqdn and destroyers, simulates an intended invasion of the Andamans to divert the attention of the Japanese from the operation 'Watchtower' (landing on Guadalcanal). It employs three decoy convoys on the East Coast of India and in the Bay of Bengal.

2 Aug   North Atlantic
Beginning of the troop transports from the USA to England and Northern Ireland with the large passenger ships *Queen Elizabeth* (83673 tons), *Queen Mary* (81235 tons), *Pasteur* (29253 tons), *Empress of Scotland* (26313 tons), *Wakefield* (24289 tons), *Mariposa* (18017 tons) and others.

2-3 Aug   Black Sea
The Commander of the Soviet Cruiser Brigade, Rear-Adm N.E. Basisty, goes to sea on 2 Aug with the cruiser *Molotov* and the flotilla leader *Kharkov* and shells targets in the Bay of Feodosia in the night 2-3 Aug. The submarine *M-62* is sent in as a marker. On the return there are attacks by German torpedo aircraft and the Italian motor torpedo boats *MAS568* and *MAS573*. The cruiser *Molotov* receives a torpedo hit in the bows and 20 metres of the ship are blown off.

3-7 Aug   Mediterranean
On the Libyan coast the British submarine *Thorn* (Lt-Cdr Norfolk) sinks on 3 Aug the Italian transport *Monviso* (5322 tons), already slightly damaged by air torpedo on 28 July, when escorted by the destroyers *Alpino* and *Corazziere*. After two unsuccessful attacks on a tanker escorted by the destroyers *Turbine* and *Graecale*, *Thorn* is sunk on 7 Aug by the Italian torpedo boat *Pegaso*. *Turbulent* (Lt-Cdr Linton) destroys on 6 Aug the wreck of the destroyer *Strale* which went ashore on 21 June near Cape Bon. In the Aegean the Greek submarine *Nereus* sinks two small ships. The British *Proteus* sinks the German steamer *Wachtfels* (8467 tons) on 7 Aug.

3-11 Aug   North Atlantic
After the ON.115 operation the U-boats *U210*, *U607*, *U454*, *U704*, *U597*, *U71*, *U379* and *U593* form the 'Steinbrinck' group E of the Newfoundland Bank. After the sighting of an ON convoy by *U704* (Lt-Cdr Kessler), which is not shadowed, *U593* (Lt-Cdr Kelbling)

reports on 5 Aug the convoy SC.94 (36 ships, the Canadian EG C.1 with the destroyer *Assiniboine*, the corvettes *Chilliwack* and *Orillia* and the British *Primrose*, *Nasturtium* and *Dianthus*). *U593* at once attacks and sinks one ship of 3616 tons from an isolated group, but is driven off with *U595* by *Nasturtium* and *Orillia*. On 6 Aug *U595* is damaged by gunfire and depth charges from *Chilliwack* and *Primrose* and *U454* by depth charges from *Dianthus*: they have to break off. *U210* (Lt-Cdr Lemcke) is forced to surface by *Assiniboine* and in a gun duel at close range is sunk by ramming. Apart from *U595*, the outward-bound *U176*, *U660*, *U256*, *U174*, *U438* and *U705* also operate on SC.94 from 7 Aug. On the afternoon of 7 Aug *U607* (Lt-Cdr Mengersen) misses a group of stragglers and in the night 7-8 Aug *U704*, and in the morning of 8 Aug *U660* (Lt Baur), miss the convoy. At mid-day attempts by *U597* and *U605* to attack stragglers fail. On the afternoon of 8 Aug *U176* (Lt-Cdr Dierksen) and *U379* (Lt-Cdr Kettner) attack almost simultaneously and sink three ships and two ships respectively of 16687 tons and 8910 tons. Three other undamaged ships are abandoned in a panic, one of which (3201 tons) is later finished off by *U176*. An attack by *U704* fails. On the evening of 8 Aug the British destroyer *Broke* (Lt-Cdr Layard) joins the convoy and, later in the night, also the Polish destroyer *Blyskawica*, but *Dianthus*, which has sunk *U379* with depth charges and by ramming, drops out. All escorts, apart from *Primrose*, remain behind in the night fighting U-boats. *Broke* is just missed by torpedoes from *U595* (Lt-Cdr Quaet Faslem). All attempts at attack are thwarted; only *U607* is able to fire—unsuccessfully— and then keeps contact. In spite of the deployment of air protection with Liberators of No. 120 Sqdn RAF from Northern Ireland on the afternoon of 9 Aug, *U254*, *U174*, *U704*, *U256* in the afternoon and evening and *U597* in the morning of 10 Aug are able to fire, but no hits are scored. The fact that some escorts remain behind to deal with the located U-boats makes it possible for *U438* (Lt-Cdr Franzius) and *U660* to make a simultaneous attack at mid-day They sink three ships of 16074 tons and one of 4439 tons respectively.

3-12 Aug Norway
In operations off the Norwegian Coast the British submarine *P213/Saracen* (Lt Lumby) sinks the German *U335* on 3 Aug and *P54/Unshaken* (Lt Oxborrow) and *Sturgeon* (Lt Wingfield) each sinks one ship of 2890 tons and 3335 tons respectively on 12 Aug.

3-26 Aug Western Atlantic
On the American East Coast *U98* (Cdr Schulze) lays a mine barrage on 8 Aug off Jacksonville, which is swept without loss. S of Cape Hatteras this boat, like the *U86* (Lt-Cdr Schug), which, because of damage, is at the time cruising away from the coast, has no success.

4 Aug Black Sea
Beginning of German supply operations by sea in the Sea of Azov.

4-24 Aug Arctic
In operations by Soviet submarines *Shch-403* (Capt 3rd Class Shuyski) unsuccessfully attacks two convoys near Vardö and is attacked on 11 Aug with 110 depth charges from the submarine-chasers *UJ1104*, *UJ1108* and *UJ1101*. On 14 Aug the Commander, Capt 3rd Class Stolbov, and 17 men are killed in an internal explosion on *Shch-402;* the rest of the crew bring the damaged boat from Tanafjord to Polyarnoe. In Lopphavet *K-21* unsuccessfully attacks a German minelaying force on 19 Aug. On 22-23 Aug *Shch-422* (Lt-Cdr Vidyaev) misses two convoys in Varangerfjord. After an attack on a convoy of three steamers, *V6105* and the submarine-chasers *UJ1101*, *UJ1108* and *UJ1112* on 24 Aug, the last sinks a submarine, probably *M-173.*

5-23 Aug Black Sea
In Soviet submarine operations *Shch-205* (Capt 3rd Class Sukhomlinov) attacks convoys off the Bosphorus and *M-118* (Lt-Cdr Savin), *M-62* (Lt-Cdr Malyshev), *M-111* (Lt-Cdr Josseliani) and *M-36* (Lt-Cdr Komarov) in the Bay of Odessa and off the Rumanian Coast. But only *M-36* sinks the German tug *Ankara*. *M-33* is lost on a flanking mine barrage.

6-10 Aug Baltic
Soviet ground attack air formations attack the German minesweepers and submarine-chasers stationed in the A/S

positions W of the 'Seeigel' mine barrages, and Soviet motor minesweepers penetrate the 'Seeigel' barrages on 6 Aug in order to meet the returning submarines *Shch-303* and *Shch-406*. In pursuing one of the boats between Suur- and Pien-Tytärsaari *UJ1211* runs on an old Soviet mine barrage and sinks. On 11 Aug *S-7* arrives in Lavansaari.

7 Aug Black Sea
The Soviet cruiser *Krasny Krym* and the destroyer *Nezamozhnik* evacuate 2895 men and 100 tons of supplies from Novorossisk to Batum.

7-9 Aug South Pacific
Operation 'Watchtower': US landing on Guadalcanal. 7 Aug: after preparatory fire from aircraft of the carriers *Enterprise*, *Saratoga* and *Wasp* and from the guns of the cruisers and destroyers of the Support Force, the Amphibious Force (Rear-Adm Turner) lands the reinforced 1st Marine Div from 15 transports on the North side of Guadalcanal and parts of the division from four transports and four fast transports on Tulagi. The nearly completed Japanese airfield on Guadalcanal is seized and there is stiff resistance on Tulagi. In the afternoon two attacks by 27 bombers and 16 dive bombers of the Japanese 25th Flotilla are intercepted by fighters from the *Enterprise* and *Saratoga:* 12 US and 16 Japanese aircraft are shot down and the US destroyer *Mugford* is slightly damaged. The Japanese 8th Fleet (Vice-Adm Mikawa), comprising five heavy and two light cruisers and one destroyer, sets out from Rabaul: it is sighted by the US submarine *S38*. 8 Aug: Attack by 26 Japanese torpedo aircraft; 17 are shot down by AA fire and fighters, but the US destroyer *Jarvis* is sunk. In the following attack by dive bombers and fighter bombers a crashing aircraft hits the US transport *G. F. Elliott* (8378 tons) which catches fire and later has to be abandoned. *S38* (Lt-Cdr Munson) sinks the Japanese supply transport *Meiyo Maru* (5628 tons) S of Rabaul. Reconnaissance reports from Australian aircraft about the Japanese cruiser force are tardily transmitted. 9 Aug: by night the Japanese force, comprising the cruisers *Chokai*, *Aoba*,

Kinugasa, *Furutaka*, *Kako*, *Tenryu* and *Yubari* and the destroyer *Yunagi*, enters the narrows between Savo Island and Guadalcanal and passes the US radar picket destroyers *Blue* and *R. Talbot* undetected. There the Southern covering force, comprising the cruisers *Canberra* (RAN) and *Chicago* and the destroyers *Bagley* and *Patterson*, is surprised. The *Canberra* (Capt Getting†) is set on fire and reduced to a wreck; the *Chicago* is damaged by torpedo hits; and the *Patterson* by gunfire. Then Mikawa, thanks to serious deficiencies in the Allied command organisation, is also able to surprise the Northern covering force, comprising the cruisers *Vincennes*, *Quincy* and *Astoria* and the destroyers *Helm* and *Wilson*, and to destroy the cruisers with concentrated torpedo salvoes and gunfire. *Quincy* (Capt S. N. Moore), *Vincennes* (Capt Riefkohl) sink at once; *Astoria* (Capt Greenman) and *Canberra* have to be abandoned in the morning. On the Japanese side only *Chokai* and *Kinugasa* suffer slight damage The northern picket destroyer *R. Talbot* is badly hit by the retiring Japanese. As a result of the obscure situation and the faulty command, the cruisers *Australia* (RAN), *Hobart* (RAN) and *San Juan* and seven destroyers, which are stationed in the area, are not deployed. The carrier force (Vice-Adm Fletcher), operating S of Guadalcanal, after 48 hours of operations, has turned away on the evening of 8 Aug from fear of torpedo aircraft and submarines, and can no longer catch the retiring Japanese. Adm Turner decides to withdraw with his remaining warships and transports. The 1st Marine Div (Maj-Gen Vandergrift) is left on its own. 10 Aug: from the returning Japanese force the US submarine *S44* (Lt-Cdr Moore) sinks the cruiser *Kako* off Kavieng. Allied losses: 1270 dead and 709 wounded.

7 Aug-8 Oct Central Atlantic
Off West Africa *U109* (Lt-Cdr Bleichrodt) sinks five ships of 35601 tons; *U125* (Lt-Cdr Folkers) six ships of 25416 tons and *U506* (Lt-Cdr Würdemann) five ships of 28023 tons.

9 Aug South Atlantic
The auxiliary cruiser *Schiff 23/Stier* (Cdr Gerlach) sinks the British freighter

R

Dalhousie (7072 tons) in the South Atlantic.

9-11 Aug   Black Sea
The Soviet cruiser *Krasny Krym* and the destroyer *Nezamozhnik* evacuate 2000 men from Novorossisk to Batum. The German *S102* (Lt-Cdr Töniges) sinks a Soviet steamer off Tuapse on 10 Aug; on 11 Aug she makes an unsuccessful attack with *S28* (Lt-Cdr Künzel) on tankers between Novorossisk and Tuapse.

10-15 Aug   Mediterranean
Operation 'Pedestal'. 10 Aug: in anticipation of a large supply convoy for Malta Supermarina stations the submarines *Brin, Dagabur, Giada, Uarsciek, Volframio, U73* and *U331* between Algiers and the Balearics. In the area N of Tunisia and off Cape Bon another submarine group is formed with *Granito, Emo, Otaria, Dandolo, Avorio, Cobalto, Alagi, Ascianghi, Axum, Bronzo* and *Dessié* and W of Malta *Asteria*. The British convoy, consisting of 13 transports and one tanker, escorted by Rear-Adm Burrough with the cruisers *Nigeria, Kenya, Manchester* and *Cairo*, destroyers *Ashanti, Intrepid, Icarus, Foresight, Fury, Pathfinder, Penn, Derwent, Bramham, Bicester* and *Ledbury*, passes through the Straits of Gibraltar together with the covering force (Vice-Adm Syfret), consisting of the battleships *Nelson* and *Rodney*, carriers *Victorious* (Rear-Adm Lyster), *Indomitable, Eagle* and *Furious*, the cruisers *Phoebe, Sirius* and *Charybdis* and the destroyers *Laforey, Lightning, Lookout, Quentin, Eskimo, Tartar, Ithuriel, Antelope, Wishart, Vansittart, Westcott, Wrestler, Zetland* and *Wilton*. An empty convoy, consisting of the transports *Orari* and *Troilus*, accompanied by the destroyers *Badsworth* and *Matchless*, sets out from Malta. There is a brief engagement with the Italian destroyer *Malocello* near Cape Bon which is laying a mine barrage there. 11 Aug: there is an unsuccessful attack by the Italian submarine *Uarsciek* on carriers of the covering force. The 24 British destroyers and cruiser *Cairo* take on fuel from the supply force, consisting of the tankers *Brown Ranger* and *Derwentdale*. German and Italian air reconnaissance locates the British

forces. *Furious* flies off S of the Balearics 37 Spitfire fighters for Malta and is then met by the reserve destroyers *Keppel, Malcolm, Venomous, Wolverine* and *Wrestler* for the return journey to Gibraltar. *U73* (Lt-Cdr Rosenbaum) sinks with a salvo of four torpedoes the carrier *Eagle* (Capt L. D. Mackintosh) with 260 of the crew. Ten British Beaufighter aircraft attack Italian air bases in Sardinia. In the evening an attack by 36 German Ju 88s and He 111s is frustrated by fighter and AA defence. 12 Aug: in attempting to attack the returning *Furious* the Italian submarine *Dagabur* is rammed and sunk by the destroyer *Wolverine* (Lt-Cdr Gretton). The Italian submarine *Giada* is bombed and damaged by a Sunderland flying boat. In the morning there is an unsuccessful attack by 19 Ju 88s in which six planes are lost. At mid-day there are attacks by 10 S 84, eight G 42 and 33 S 79 bombers and 10 S 84 torpedo aircraft of the Italian Air Force and 37 German Ju 88s with fighter protection. The transport *Deucalion* is damaged and left behind with the destroyer *Bramham*. Two Italian Re 2001 fighter bombers attack the carrier *Victorious* with armour-piercing bombs but they rebound from the armoured flight deck. In the afternoon the submarines are repeatedly driven off by the destroyers *Tartar, Zetland* and *Pathfinder. Emo* fires a salvo of four on the destroyer *Lookout; Cobalto* is rammed by the destroyer *Ithuriel* which is herself badly damaged. In the late afternoon there is an attack by 29 Ju 87s of St. G. 3 with fighter protection:—they score three heavy hits on the carrier *Indomitable* which is then no longer able to operate aircraft—and by 14 S 79 torpedo aircraft which torpedo the destroyer *Foresight* with the result that she later has to be sunk by *Tartar*. The covering force turns away to the W. In the evening the submarines *Dessié* and *Axum* (Lt-Cdr Ferrini) attack in turn: each gets one hit on the cruisers *Cairo* and *Nigeria* and the tanker *Ohio. Cairo* has to be abandoned and *Nigeria* starts the return journey with the destroyers *Bicester, Derwent* and *Wilton*. There follows an attack by 30 Ju 88s with bombs to which the transports *Empire*

Hope (12688 tons) and *Glenorchy* 8982 tons) fall victim and by seven He 111s with torpedoes which cause the *Brisbane Star* (12791 tons) to stop. In an attack by the Italian submarine *Alagi* (Lt-Cdr Puccini) the cruiser *Kenya* and the transport *Clan Ferguson* are torpedoed and damaged. Shortly before midnight the submarine *Bronzo* (Lt-Cdr Buldrini) sinks the wreck of the *Empire Hope*. 13 Aug: in 15 successive motor torpedo attacks in four hours *Ms16* (Cdr Manuti) and *Ms22* (Lt Mezzadra) score hits on the cruiser *Manchester* which is later abandoned; *Ms31* (Lt-Cdr Calvani) on the wreck of the *Glenorchy* which sinks; *S30* Lt Weber), *S36* (Lt Brauns), *MAS554* Lt Calcagno) and *MAS557* (Sub-Lt Cafiero) on the transports *Rochester Castle*, *Santa Elisa* (8379 tons), *Almeria Lykes* (7773 tons) and *Wairangi* (12436 tons), the last three of which sink at once. The attacks by *S59*, *Ms26*, *Ms25*, *Ms23*, *MAS552*, *MAS564* and *MAS 553* are not successful. In the night the cruiser *Charybdis* and the destroyers *Eskimo* and *Somali* reach the convoy as reinforcements. The two destroyers are sent off to the *Manchester* and then start the return journey after taking on the survivors. In the morning there are continuous air attacks: six He 111s have no success; 12 Ju 88s sink the transport *Waimarama* (12843 tons); eight Italian Ju 87s score hits on the transports *Dorset*, *Port Chalmers* and the tanker *Ohio;* 20 Ju 88s and Ju 87s again hit *Ohio*, *Rochester Castle* and *Dorset* with bombs; and five S 79 torpedo aircraft have no success. In the evening 14 Ju 87s sink the damaged *Dorset* (10624 tons). The minesweepers *Hebe*, *Speedy*, *Hythe* and *Rye* from Malta meet the convoy with seven motor minesweepers and accompany the remaining transports *Melbourne Star*, *Port Chalmers* and *Rochester Castle* to Malta. Later, the badly damaged *Ohio* arrives accompanied by the destroyers *Penn*, *Ledbury* and *Bramham*. The *Brisbane Star* which remains temporarily behind near Sousse follows on 14 Aug. The intervention of the Italian surface ships, the cruisers *Gorizia*, *Trieste*, *Bolzano*, *Eugenio di Savoia*, *Montecuccoli* and *Attendolo* and 11

destroyers, (*Aviere*, *Geniere*, *Camicia Nera*, *Legionario*, *Ascari*, *Corsaro*, *Grecale*, *Maestrale*, *Gioberti*, *Oriani* and *Fuciliere*), planned for 13 Aug, has to be abandoned because insufficient air escort is available. On the return the British submarine *Unbroken* (Lt Mars) torpedoes the cruisers *Attendolo* and *Bolzano* near the Aeolian Islands. 14 Aug: on the return the British escort forces, comprising the cruisers *Kenya* and *Charybdis* and the destroyers *Ashanti*, *Intrepid*, *Icarus*, *Fury* and *Pathfinder*, are successively attacked by *MAS556*, the submarine *Granito*, 26 Ju 88s, 13 Ju 87s, 15 S 84s and 20 S 79s without result. In the afternoon the force joins the covering group which has returned to meet it N of Algiers. An attack by *U73* on the damaged *Nigeria* and four destroyers is unsuccessful. By 15 Aug all ships have reached Gibraltar.

10 Aug-1 Sept   Western Atlantic
The U-boats *U658*, *U598*, *U600*, *U553* and *U163* operate in the area of the Greater Antilles. Only *U600* (Lt-Cdr Zurmühlen) sinks a sailing ship of 130 tons. Otherwise the boats only attack convoys. On 13 Aug they attack the WAT.13, on 13-14 Aug TAW.12 and on 17-18 Aug TAW.13 and PG.6 (see entry).

11-21 Aug   Baltic
The first part of the second wave of Soviet submarines, *L-3*, *M-96*, *M-97* (sunk on the 'Seeigel' barrage on 14 Aug), *Shch-407*, *Shch-309* and *Lembit*, break through the mine barrages of the Gulf of Finland. On the way to Lavansaari *Shch-405* sinks on an old Soviet barrage near Seiskari. The operation is supported by Soviet ground attack aircraft which sink the German motor minesweeper *R106* on 16 Aug. The Soviet submarines are brought into the mine barrages by sweeper cutters and are at first covered by *MO* patrol cutters. Torpedo cutters attack the German-Finnish guard forces W of the barrages: in one such operation the submarine-chaser *UJ1216* is sunk.

11-22 Aug   South Pacific
When news is received of the American landing on Guadalcanal elements of the Combined Fleet are moved on 11 Aug from the Inland Sea to Truk. They

include Adm Yamamoto with the flagship of the Fleet, the battleship *Yamato*, the escort carrier *Taiyo* and the destroyers *Akebono*, *Sazanami* and *Ushio;* the 2nd Fleet (Vice-Adm Kondo); and the 3rd Fleet (Vice-Adm Nagumo). (For composition see 14 July 1942). The 2nd DD Flotilla (Rear-Adm Tanaka) with the cruiser *Jintsu* and the destroyers *Kagero*, *Hagikaze*, *Maikaze*, *Urakaze*, *Isokaze* and *Hamakaze* is put under the command of the 8th Fleet in Rabaul.

On 16 Aug Capt Sato puts to sea from Truk with the above six destroyers and 916 men of the Ichiki Detachment of the Army on board. He lands them in the night 18-19 Aug E of the US bridgehead on Guadalcanal. But the force is annihilated when it attacks the positions of the much under-estimated 1st US Marine Div. The remainder of the Ichiki detachment with supplies follows on 16 Aug with two transports, escorted by the *Jintsu* and the APDs *P34* and *P35* which are then joined by the destroyers *Umikaze*, *Kawakaze* and *Suzukaze*. They are followed by the fast convoys with the transport *Kinryu Maru* and the APDs *P1* and *P2* which have the 5th Yokosuka special Landing Force on board. This is to be landed on 21 Aug.

The three ships of the 17th DD Div return to Rabaul but the *Kagero*, *Hagikaze* and *Maikaze* (4th DD Div), which remain behind, are attacked on 19 Aug by B17 bombers coming from Espiritu Santo. *Hagikaze* is damaged by bomb hits and has to return with *Maikaze*.

On 20 Aug the US escort carrier *Long Island* flies off S of Guadalcanal the first 31 US Marine Corps fighters for Henderson Airfield. When the *Kagero* reports attacks by carrier air-craft and air reconnaissance reports a US carrier force, the Japanese landing force is temporarily turned away, so that the elements of the 2nd and 3rd Fleets, which have in the meantime put to sea, can come up to support the landing now postponed until 23 Aug. The *Kagero* withdraws.

On 21-22 Aug the US transports *Alhena* and *Fomalhaut* with the de-stroyers *Blue*, *Helm* and *Henley* bring supplies to Guadalcanal. In screening the unloading *Blue* is torpedoed in Savo Sound by the Japanese destroyer *Kawakaze* which comes up from a reconnaissance sortie S of Guadalcanal to relieve the *Kagero*. She has to be abandoned on the following day.

11 Aug-3 Sept Western Atlantic
After refuelling from *U463* (Cdr Wolf-bauer), *U564* (Lt-Cdr Suhren) and *U654* (Lt Forster) arrive in the Carib-bean with *U162* (Cdr* Wattenberg) *U654* falls victim on 22 Aug to a USAAF aircraft off the Panama Canal Of the two other boats, after the opera-tion against the convoy TAW(S) on 19 Aug, *U162* sinks three ships of 24759 tons and *U564* one ship of 8176 tons. *U162* is sunk on 3 Sept S of Barbados after an unsuccessful attack on the British destroyer *Pathfinder* by the latter and the destroyers *Quentin* and *Vimy*.

11-30 Aug Arctic
To prepare the German operation against the Siberian sea route *U255* (Lt-Cdr Reche) reconnoitres Spitz-bergen together with a BV 138 flying boat equipped with additional fuel tanks and *U435* (Lt-Cdr Strelow) disembarks there the weather observa-tion detachment 'Knospe' (11-17 Aug). Operation 'Wunderland': on 16 Aug the pocket-battleship *Admiral Scheer* (Capt Meendsen-Bohlken) sets out from Narvik to the Barents Sea and, following ice reconnaissance by *U601* (Lt-Cdr Grau) and *U251* (Lt-Cdr Timm), passes Cape Zhelania on 19 Aug and proceeds eastwards through the Kara Sea. The ship's aircraft reports parts of three ship convoys with the ice-breakers *Krassin* and *Lenin* on 20 Aug near the island of Krakovka and on 23 Aug in the Vilkitski Strait. Mist and ice prevent an approach. On 25 Aug *Scheer* encounters NW of the Norden-skjöld Archipelago the Soviet ice-breaker *Sibiryakov* (Capt Kacharev) which is sunk after a courageous defence. On 27 Aug *Scheer* attacks the main base of Dikson and badly damages the shore installations and the patrol ship *SKR-19/Dezhnev* and the steamer *Revolutsioner*. On 30 Aug *Scheer* returns to Narvik. Of the two U-boats operating in the Kara Sea, *U601* sinks

ne ship E of Dikson on 24 Aug; and of he boats stationed W of Novaya Zemlya *U209* (Lt-Cdr Brodda) sinks the ugs *Nord* and *Komsomolets* with the ighters *B-III* and *P-IV* W of the Yugor trait on 17 Aug and *U456* (Lt-Cdr Teichert) tries in vain to torpedo the ce-breaker *SKR-18/Fedor Litke* off Belusha on 20 Aug. *U255* and *U209* hell the wireless stations at Cape Zhelania and Khodovarikha on 25 Aug nd 28 Aug respectively.

From 13 Aug to 23 Aug the US cruiser *Tuscaloosa* with the destroyers *Rodman*, *Emmons* and *Onslaught* (British) proeeds to Murmansk with ground personnel, supplies and torpedoes for two quadrons of Hampden bombers of RAF Bomber Command which are being transferred to Northern Russia. They are met by the British destroyers *Marne* and *Martin* off Kola. Operation 'Zar'. The German minelayer *Ulm* (Lt-Cdr Biet) is to lay mines in the rea N of Cape Zhelania after the return f the *Scheer*. After unloading, the *Tuscaloosa*, *Emmons* and *Rodman* set ut from Murmansk to return to Scapa Flow on 24 Aug. *Marne*, *Martin* and *Onslaught* are detached to make a ortie to the Norwegian Polar Coast. n the course of this sortie they encounter the *Ulm* on 25 Aug S of Bear sland and sink her.

Of the simultaneously planned mining perations 'Peter' with *U589* (Lt-Cdr Horrer) off the Matochkin Strait and Paul' with *U591* off the Yugor Strait nly 'Peter' can be carried out (28 Aug). The Soviet patrol ship *SKR-23/Musson* s lost on it.

2 Aug   Western Atlantic
U508 (Lt-Cdr Staats), which operates off Cuba from the end of July to 18 Aug, ttacks a Key West-Havana convoy nd sinks two ships of 2710 tons.

2 Aug   Mediterranean
The Italian destroyer *Malocello* (Cdr* Tona) lays the mine barrage St.1 with 04 mines in two sections off Cape Son. Escort provided by the torpedo boat *Climene*. *Malocello* meets British Force Y—destroyers *Matchless*, *Badsworth* and transports *Troilus* and *Orari*— n the way from Malta to Gibraltar, each thinking the other to be Vichy French.

12-13 Aug   Black Sea
The Soviet cruiser *Krasny Krym* and the destroyer *Nezamozhnik* evacuate a regiment of the 32nd Guards Rifle Div from Novorossisk to Batum.

12-18 Aug   Mediterranean
The British submarine *Porpoise* (Cdr Bennington) lays a mine barrage on 12 Aug on the Cyrenaican coast on which the Italian torpedo boat *Cantore* is lost on 22 Aug. In attacks on 12 Aug on a steamer escorted by the torpedo boat *Montanari* and on 16 Aug on a convoy with the destroyers *Mitragliere*, *Bersagliere* and the torpedo boats *Calliope* and *Castore*, *Porpoise* sinks two ships of 10623 tons. In a further attack on 19 Aug the submarine is assailed by depth charges from the torpedo boats *Lince* and *Sagittario*. On 17 Aug *Turbulent* (Cdr Linton) torpedoes near Navarino the transport *Nino Bixio* (7137 tons), escorted by the destroyers *Da Recco* and *Saetta* and the torpedo boats *Castore*, *Orione* and *Polluce*. The transport has 2000 prisoners on board of whom 336 perish.
Near Pantelleria *P-44/United* (Lt Roxburgh) torpedoes the transport *Rosolino Pilo* (8326 tons) escorted by the destroyers *Maestrale* and *Gioberti*. The transport is later sunk by torpedo aircraft from Malta. Off Sardinia *P211/Safari* (Cdr Bryant) sinks two ships of 5075 tons.

12-19 Aug   South Pacific
Japanese reinforcement convoys from Rabaul to Buna. On 12-13 Aug three transports with the cruiser *Tatsuta*, the destroyers *Yunagi* and *Yuzuki* and submarine-chasers land the Nankai Detachment. On 16-17 Aug the same force bring elements of the South Sea Detachment of the Army and of the 25th Naval Air Flotilla ashore. On 19 Aug a third convoy, comprising two transports, suffers slight damage from US air attacks. The Japanese make air attacks on Milne Bay to cover the operations.

13-14 Aug   Western Atlantic
In the Windward Passage *U658* (Lt-Cdr Senkel) sights two convoys meeting each other. From convoy WAT.13 (Escort Commander on the British destroyer *Havelock*) she sinks one ship of 1311 tons, but then operates on the

northward-bound TAW.12 (47 ships, escort: Lt-Cdr Fitzgerald (RN) on the destroyer HMS *Churchill* with the trawler HMS *Ruby*, the US coastguard cutter *Lemaire*, the corvette HMCS *Agassiz*, the submarine-chasers USS *PC475* and *PC505* and the minesweeper *YMS50*). From this convoy *U600* (Lt-Cdr Zurmühlen) sinks two ships of 9552 tons on 14 Aug. Despite reinforcement of the escort by the new US destroyers *Fletcher* and *O'Bannon*, *U598* (Lt-Cdr Holtorf) is able to sink two more ships of 9295 tons on 14 Aug and to torpedo one tanker of 6197 tons.

13-27 Aug   North Atlantic
On 13 Aug the following U-boats (coming from the SC.94 operation as well as new outward-bound boats), *U755*, *U438*, *U705*, *U373*, *U660*, *U569*, *U596*, *U176*, *U256*, *U174*, *U605* and later *U135* and *U432*, take up a new patrol line 'Lohs'. On 15 Aug *U256* (Lt-Cdr Loewe) sights the convoy SC.95 (27 ships, EG A.3), but contact is soon lost because an ON convoy had been expected. Attacks by *U256* and *U605* fail. *U705* (Lt-Cdr Horn) sinks one ship of 3279 tons. On 16 Aug *U596* (Lt-Cdr Jahn) sinks a straggler of 4966 tons. On 22 Aug *U135* (Lt-Cdr Praetorius) sights by chance the convoy ONS.122 routed by C-in-C Western Approaches S of the 'Lohs' group. It includes 36 ships and has with it EG B.6 with the destroyer HMS *Viscount*, the Norwegian corvettes *Potentilla*, *Montbretia*, *Eglantine* and *Acanthus* and the rescue ship *Stockport*. *U135* and *U660*, which are in contact, are located by the HF/DF equipment of *Stockport* and *Viscount* on 23 Aug and 24 Aug are driven off. In rainy weather nine U-boats come into the area of the convoy in the night 24-25 Aug. *U605* (Lt-Cdr Schütze) sinks two ships of 8180 tons and is then damaged by depth charges from the *Eglantine*. *U176* (Lt-Cdr Dierksen) and *U438* (Lt-Cdr Franzius), which shortly after attack simultaneously, each sinks one ship of 7454 tons and 1598 tons respectively. Mist impedes the operation and causes contact to be lost. *U256*, which has suffered damage in a depth charge attack by *Potentilla* and *Viscount*, is heavily bombed on 2 Sept in the Bay of Biscay when she

returns and has to be out of action for more than one year. *U705* is sunk in the Bay of Biscay on 3 Sept. The 'Lohs' group proceeds southwards to refuel from *U174* (3 boats) and *U462* (6 boats).

14 Aug   South Atlantic
The auxiliary cruiser *Schiff 281 Michel* sinks the British freighter *Arabistan* (5874 tons) in the South Atlantic.

14 Aug-28 Sept   Baltic
Of the Soviet submarines of the second wave which have broken through the German mine barrages *L-3* (Capt 3rd Class Grishchenko) sinks the steamer *C. F. Liljevalch* (5492 tons) from a Swedish convoy W of Gotland and lays a mine barrage on 23 Aug off the Bay of Pomerania, on which one ship of 5798 tons probably sinks. Further torpedo attacks have no success. Of the remaining boats *M-96* (Lt-Cdr Marinesko) operates near Porkkala (one miss); *Shch-407* (Capt 3rd Class Afanasev) on the Baltic Coast (one miss); *Shch-309* and *Shch-308* in the Aaland Sea; *S-13* in the Gulf of Bothnia; and *Lembit* off Utö. *Shch-309* (Capt 3rd Class Kabo) sinks one ship of 695 tons and misses two; *Shch-308* (Capt 3rd Class Kostylev) sinks one ship of 1467 tons and misses two; *S-13* (Lt-Cdr Malanchenko) sinks two ships of 3704 tons and misses one; *Lembit* (Capt 3rd Class Matiyasevich) damages one ship of 2302 tons and misses two.

15 Aug   South Pacific
The US fast transports *Colhoun, Gregory, Little* and *McKean* bring supplies for the first time to Guadalcanal.

15 Aug-26 Sept   Indian Ocean
In the Arabian Sea the Japanese submarine *I-29* (Cdr* Izu) reconnoitres with her aircraft over the Seychelles on 19 Aug and then up to 22 Sept sinks four ships of 23303 tons. *I-27* cruises without success off East Africa and *I-162* in the Bay of Bengal. In the area of Ceylon *I-165* (Cdr Torisu) sinks one ship of 5237 tons and *I-166* has no success.

16 Aug   English Channel
The German 10th MMS Flotilla lays a flanking mine barrage off Calais and is attacked by the British *MGB330*, *MGB331*, *MGB609*, *MGB6* and *MGB10*. All boats are heavily damaged

but *MGB330* sinks the German motor minesweeper *R184* by ramming.

16-17 Aug   Black Sea
The Soviet cruiser *Krasny Krym* and destroyer *Nezamozhnik* evacuate 1850 men and 60 tons of supplies from Novorossisk to Batum.

16-18 Aug   Mediterranean
Operation 'Baritone'. British Force H, comprising the carrier *Furious*, the cruiser *Charybdis* and 12 destroyers sets out from Gibraltar for the area S of the Balearics and flies off 32 Spitfire fighters to Malta. All except three land safely. The British submarines *Otus*, *Rorqual* and *Clyde* bring aviation petrol, torpedoes and ammunition to Malta. The Italian submarines *Alagi*, *Ascianghi*, *Asteria*, *Avorio*, *Bronzo* and *Porfido* report no contacts.

16-20 Aug   Central Atlantic
U653 (Lt-Cdr Feiler) of the 'Blücher' group, which is assembling to proceed to Freetown, reports the convoy SL.118. *U566*, *U214*, *U406*, *U594*, *U333* and *U590* are directed to it. On 17 Aug *U566* (Lt Remus) sinks one ship of 6607 tons; *U214* (Lt-Cdr G. Reeder) sinks two ships of 13840 tons on 18 Aug and torpedoes the auxiliary cruiser *Cheshire* belonging to the escort. The U-boats are driven off by the air escort provided by Liberator bombers from Cornwall on 18 Aug and *U653* is damaged. On 19 Aug only *U406* (Lt-Cdr Dieterichs) is able to attack and sinks one ship of 7452 tons. *U333* (Lt-Cdr Cremer) is damaged by depth charges from a corvette. The operation is broken off when contact is lost.

17 Aug   Mediterranean
U83 (Lt-Cdr Kraus) sinks a British transport (5875 tons) off Port Said.

17 Aug   Pacific
The 2nd Raider Battalion, landed by the US submarines *Argonaut* and *Nautilus*, carries out a raid on the Gilbert Island of Makin.

17-20 Aug   Western Atlantic
On 17 Aug *U658* (Lt-Cdr Senkel) sights S of Cuba the convoy PG.6 (23 ships, escort: the US destroyers *Goff* and *Tattnall*, the submarine-chasers *SC497* and *SC530*) and sinks two ships of 10835 tons and torpedoes one ship of 6466 tons. On that evening the convoy PG.6 joins up with the convoy TAW.13

off Guantanamo and then consists of 36 ships with the destroyers USS *Breckinridge* and *Goff*, the corvettes HMS *Pimpernel* and USS *Spry*, the submarine-chasers USS *PC431*, *PC460*, *PY20* and later the *Tattnall* and *SC530*. From the combined convoy *U553* (Cdr Thurmann) sinks three ships of 16980 tons in two approaches. *U163* (Cdr Engelmann) shadows the convoy into the Yucatan Strait but is unable to attack.

18-21 Aug   Western Atlantic
Off Trinidad *U564* (Lt-Cdr Suhren) sights the convoy TAW(S) with 15 ships escorted by the corvettes HMS *Clarkia*, USS *Courage*, the US coastguard cutters *Antietam* and *Marion* and the submarine-chasers USS *PC482*, *PC492*, *SC504* and *SC514*. After an attack by *U162* (Cdr* Wattenberg) on 19 Aug in the area of Grenada (one ship of 5722 tons sunk), *U564* attacks and sinks two ships of 12909 tons. Further attempts to attack are frustrated.

19 Aug   English Channel
Operation 'Jubilee': British raid on Dieppe. Landing of 6100 men, in all, of the 4th and 6th Brigades of the 2nd Canadian Div (Maj-Gen Roberts) and the 3rd and 4th Commandos of the Royal Navy with tanks and strong air support both sides of Dieppe. Transported on the infantry landing ships *Prins Albert*, *Princess Beatrix*, *Invicta*, *Queen Emma*, *Princess Astrid*, *Glengyle*, *Prince Charles*, *Prince Leopold* and *Duke of Wellington*. Cover from the destroyers *Calpe*, *Garth*, *Berkeley*, *Albrighton*, *Bleasdale*, *Brocklesby*, *Slazak* (Polish) and *Fernie*, the minesweeper *Alresford* and the gunboat *Locust* and many SGBs, MGBs, MTBs, etc. In all 252 ships, including landing craft. In approaching, the eastern landing group encounters a German coastal convoy in the dark and in the engagement the landing craft of the group are scattered, the leading boat *SGB5* is set on fire and the German *UJ1404* is sunk. Inf Regt 71 (Lt-Col Bartel) of the 302nd Inf Div, coastal artillery and fighter bombers of the Air Commanders 2 and 3 (Cols Huth and Ibel) are deployed against the forces which have gone ashore. By mid-day the remnants of the raiding party begin to re-embark having

sustained heavy losses. Thanks to fighter bombers of 10/J.G.2 (Lt Fritz Schröter) and of 10/J.G.26 (Lt Paul Keller) the destroyer *Berkeley* is sunk and *Calpe* damaged. *Brocklesby* and *Fernie* are hit by gunfire and, in addition, 33 landing craft and small vessels, 106 aircraft and all 30 tanks are lost. Losses in personnel are 4350 including 1179 dead and 2190 taken prisoner. German losses are 48 aircraft and 591 men, including 311 dead and missing.

20 Aug-10 Oct Western Atlantic
From 20 Aug to 31 Aug *U165*, *U513* and *U517* operate off the Belle Isle Strait when *U517* (Lt-Cdr Hartwig) sights on 27 Aug the convoy SG.6F with the transport *Chatham* (5649 tons) and the US coastguard cutter *Mojave* and sinks the *Chatham*. On 28 Aug *U165* (Cdr Hoffmann) attacks the following convoy SG.6S (five steamers and the US coastguard cutters *Algonquin* and *Mohawk*) and sinks one steamer of 3304 tons and torpedoes one of 7252 tons. The wreck of the first is finished off by *U517*. On 31 Aug both boats enter the St Lawrence River and there *U517* attacks on 3 Sept the convoy QS.32, out-manoeuvres the Canadian corvette *Weyburn* and sinks one ship of 1781 tons. On 6 Sept *U517* sights the convoy QS.33 escorted by two corvettes, two motor minesweepers and the yacht *Raccoon*. Whilst the corvette HMCS *Arrowhead* follows the U-boat, *U165* sinks one ship of 4729 tons and two hours later the *Raccoon* (358 tons) which has stayed behind to save the crew. On 7 Sept *U517* sinks three ships of 10742 tons from the convoy. On 11 Sept *U517* attacks the corvette *Charlottetown* steaming on her own with the minesweeper *Clayoquot* and sinks the first. On 15 Sept *U517* sinks two ships of 4907 tons from the homeward-bound convoy SQ.36 (escort: one British destroyer, two Canadian corvettes and motor minesweepers) and brings up *U165* which sinks two ships of 10292 tons on the morning of 16 Sept and torpedoes one of 4570 tons. *U165* then starts the homeward journey. *U517* has no success in two further attacks on convoys in the Gulf of St Lawrence.

U513 (Cdr Rüggeberg) in the meantime continues to operate in the waters around Newfoundland, enters the roads of St John's on 5 Sept and sinks two ships of 12789 tons and torpedoes another of 7174 tons on 29 Sept.

U165 is probably lost on a British mine off her own base.

21 Aug-17 Sept Pacific
Off North East Honshu the US submarine *Guardfish* (Lt-Cdr Klakring) sinks five ships of 14093 tons and two fishery vessels. Off Japan *Cuttlefish* (Lt-Cdr Hottel) torpedoes one ship of 6534 tons and near Formosa *Haddock* (Lt-Cdr Taylor) sinks two ships of 8585 tons, *Growler* (Lt-Cdr Gilmore) the naval transport *Kashino* (10360 tons), three steamers and one patrol boat of 11007 tons, *Grouper* (Lt-Cdr McGregor) two ships of 11123 tons, including the transport *Lisbon Maru* with 1800 British prisoners of whom only a few are rescued.

23-26 Aug Central Pacific
A Japanese force, consisting of the cruiser *Yubari*, the destroyers *Yuzuki*, *Oite*, *Asanagi* and *Yunagi* and other auxiliary ships, shells the island of Nauru on 23 Aug, which is then occupied. On 26 Aug the same force occupies Ocean Island.

23-31 Aug South Pacific
Sea and air battle E of the Solomons. The Japanese plan (Operation KA) is to land 1500 men on Guadalcanal under cover of the Combined Fleet. 23 Aug: two Japanese forces are to intercept the US carrier groups E of the Solomons after they have been diverted by a special force. The main body (Vice-Adm Kondo) comprises the cruisers *Atago*, *Takao*, *Maya*, *Myoko*, *Haguro*, *Yura* and destroyers *Asagumo*, *Yama-gumo*, *Kuroshio*, *Oyashio* and *Hayashio* and a support force with the battleship *Mutsu*, the seaplane carrier *Chitose* and the destroyers *Natsugumo*, *Murasame*, *Harusame* and *Samidare*. The carrier force (Vice-Adm Nagumo) comprises the carriers *Shokaku* and *Zuikaku* and destroyers *Akigumo*, *Yugumo*, *Maki-gumo*, *Kazegumo*, *Shikinami* and *Ura-nami* and a covering force with the battle-ships *Hiyei* and *Kirishima*, the cruisers *Kumano*, *Suzuya*, *Chikuma* and *Nagara* and destroyers *Akizuki*, *Hatsukaze*, *Maikaze*, *Nowake*, *Tanikaze* and *Yuki-*

kaze. The diversionary force (Rear-Adm Hara) comprises the cruiser *Tone*, the carrier *Ryujo* and destroyers *Amatsukaze* and *Tokitsukaze.* US carrier groups of TF 61 (Vice-Adm Fletcher): 61.1 the carrier *Saratoga*, the cruisers *Australia* (Rear-Adm Crutchley), *Hobart*, *Minneapolis* and *New Orleans* and destroyers *Phelps*, *Farragut*, *Worden*, *MacDonough* and *Dale;* 61.2 (Rear-Adm Kinkaid) the carrier *Enterprise*, the battleship *North Carolina*, the cruisers *Portland* (Rear-Adm Tisdale) and *Atlanta*, destroyers *Balch*, *Benham*, *Maury*, *Ellet*, *Grayson* and *Monssen;* 61.3 (Rear-Adm Noyes) the carrier *Wasp*, the cruisers *San Juan* (Rear-Adm Scott) *San Francisco* and *Salt Lake City*, destroyers *Farenholt*, *Aaron Ward*, *Buchanan*, *Lang*, *Stack*, *Sterett* and *Selfridge.*
In the cover of the operations of the Japanese forces mentioned against the US carrier groups, the Japanese landing force (Rear-Adm Tanaka) with the cruiser *Jintsu*, the destroyers *Suzukaze*, *Umikaze* and *Uzuki*, the APDs *P1*, *P2*, *P34* and *P35* and three transports, is to land the troops on Guadalcanal after the island has been shelled in the night 23-24 Aug by the destroyers *Kagero*, *Isokaze*, *Kawakaze*, *Mutsuki* and *Yayoi*, whilst the cruisers *Chokai*, *Aoba*, *Kinugasa* and *Furutaka* take up a covering position in the NW.
Simultaneously the submarines *I-121*, *I-123* and *Ro-34* occupy the approaches to Guadalcanal (*I-121* is damaged by carrier aircraft in the process). From the 3rd SM Flotilla *I-11*, *I-174* and *I-175* take up a patrol line W of the Solomons and the 1st SM Flotilla (Rear-Adm Yamazaki), comprising *I-9*, *I-15*, *I-17*, *I-19*, *I-26* and *I-31*, E of Santa Cruz.
23 Aug: US air reconnaissance from Ndeni locates the Japanese landing force. The attack force from *Saratoga* flies off and, after unsuccessful attempts, lands on Henderson Field. TG 61.3, because of fuel shortage, has to retire to the S for replenishment.
In the night 23-24 Aug the Japanese destroyer *Kagero* shells Henderson airfield with little result. *Saratoga's* aircraft return to the carrier in the morning.

24 Aug: US air reconnaissance locates the *Ryujo* force. The *Saratoga* flies off her attack force which sinks the *Ryujo* with bombs and torpedoes and damages the *Tone*. In the meantime Japanese air reconnaissance sights the US carrier groups. The *Shokaku* and *Zuikaku* fly off their attack forces. They secure three hits on the *Enterprise* in spite of strong US fighter cover over the carriers. The *Enterprise's* attack force does not find the enemy. The aircraft of the *Saratoga* damage the seaplane carrier *Chitose*.
In the night 24-25 Aug the Japanese destroyers *Isokaze*, *Kagero*, *Kawakaze*, *Mutsuki* and *Yayoi* shell Henderson Airfield and then join the Tanaka force. This is attacked on the morning of 25 Aug by US Marine Corps aircraft from Henderson Field: the *Mutsuki* and *Kinryu Maru* are sunk and the *Jintsu* damaged.
The Japanese break off the operation without seeking a decision.
Of the Japanese submarines *I-17* (Cdr* Nishino) is damaged on 27 Aug by an aircraft from the *Wasp.* On 30 Aug the aircraft from *I-19* (Cdr* Narahara) reconnoitres over Santa Cruz and on 31 Aug *I-26* (Cdr* Yokota) attacks TG 61.1 and torpedoes the *Saratoga.*
The Japanese 2nd DD Flotilla continues supply transports to Guadalcanal. On 26 Aug the destroyers *Suzukaze*, *Umikaze* and *Isokaze* set out with 390 men from Shortland but are recalled on 27 Aug in order to land them jointly with the newly-arrived 20th DD Div (Capt Arita) which has elements of the Kawaguchi Detachment from Borneo on board. Owing to inadequate co-ordination, the 20th DD Div is attacked by US Marine Corps dive bombers N of Guadalcanal when on its own on 28 Aug. They sink the *Asagiri*, damage the *Shirakumo* and *Yugiri* severely and the *Amagiri* slightly. On 28 Aug the *Umikaze*, *Kawakaze*, *Suzukaze* and *Isokaze* (Capt Murakami), which have returned, again set out, followed by *Fubuki*, *Hatsuyuki* and *Murakumo* and land their troops near Cape Taivu in the night 28-29 Aug. Japanese aircraft sink the APD *Colhoun* from a small US supply force comprising one transport and the APD *Little* and

Colhoun. In the night 29-30 Aug *Yudachi, P1* and *P34* land troops. In the night 31 Aug-1 Sept 1000 men of the Kawaguchi Detachment are landed from the destroyers *Kagero, Fubuki, Hatsuyuki, Murakumo, Umikaze, Kawakaze, Suzukaze* and *Amagiri.*

In trying to attack a US reinforcement convoy the Japanese submarine *I-123* is sunk on 29 Aug by the US destroyer-minesweeper *Gamble.*

24 Aug-11 Sept South Pacific
Battle for Milne Bay. In the night 24-25 Aug seven Japanese assault boats from Buna land 1318 men of the 5th Sasebo Special Landing Force on Goodenough Island off the Papuan Peninsula. In the night 25-26 Aug two transports land 1171 men of the 5th Kure and 5th Sasebo Special Landing Forces in the eastern part of Milne Bay at the southern extremity of the Papuan Peninsula. Escort is provided by Rear-Adm Matsuyama with the cruisers *Tatsuta* and *Tenryu* and by the destroyers *Tanikaze, Urakaze, Hamakaze* and the submarine-chasers *Ch22* and *Ch24.* On 27 Aug 775 men of the 3rd Kure Special Landing Force arrive on the destroyers *Arashi, Murakumo* and *Yayoi* and three submarine-chasers, escorted by Matsuyama's force. After initial successes, the Japanese forces are unable to overcome the strong resistance put up by Australian and American units. A Japanese cruiser sortie on 29 Aug cannot prevent them being repulsed. On 31 Aug the C-in-C of the 17th Army, Lt-Gen Hyakutake, orders the army operations to be concentrated against Guadalcanal and Milne Bay to be evacuated. Whilst the Australian destroyer *Arunta* and the sloop *Swan* bring reinforcements from Port Moresby into Milne Bay and *Arunta* sinks the Japanese submarine *Ro-33* after the torpedoing of a ship of 3310 tons, the Japanese cruisers and destroyers evacuate troops which had been landed. In the process *Tenryu* and the destroyer *Arashi* sink an Allied transport on 5 Sept. TF 44 (Rear-Adm Crutchley), which comprises the cruisers *Australia, Hobart* and *Phoenix* and the destroyers *Selfridge, Bagley, Henley, Helm* and *Patterson* and which sets out from Brisbane on 7 Sept to support the

operations, is not able on 11 Sept to intercept the Japanese destroyers *Isokaze* and *Yayoi,* which have come up to help the evacuation of the Trobriand Islands. But the latter falls a victim to the two US air attacks.

24 Aug-14 Oct Indian Ocean
The Japanese *I-30* (Cdr* Endo) proceeds from Lorient as the first transport submarine to Penang without incident. She arrives there on 9 Sept but on her further journey she is lost with her cargo on a mine off Singapore on 14 Oct.

25 Aug Western Atlantic
U558 (Lt-Cdr Krech) and *U164* (Cdr Fechner) each sink a straggler of 1987 tons and 3780 tons respectively from the convoy WAT.15 in the Caribbean.

25-29 Aug Central Atlantic
The convoy SL.119 is located by *U214* (Lt-Cdr G. Reeder) of the 'Iltis' group which is proceeding southwards. The other three U-boats, *U566, U406* and *U107,* are directed to the convoy and also the favourably situated four boats of the 'Eisbär' group, *U68, U156, U172* and *U504,* which are proceeding to South Africa. On 26 Aug *U156* (Cdr Hartenstein) sinks a straggler (5941 tons). On orders from the Skl the 'Eisbär' group continues its journey. *U566* (Lt Remus) sinks two ships of 14085 tons on 28 Aug and is then damaged by a depth charge pursuit. *U107* is driven off. On 29 Aug the other boats have to turn away.

26 Aug-15 Sept Mediterranean
In the Eastern Mediterranean *U375* (Lt-Cdr Könenkamp) destroys two ships of 6846 tons and two sailing ships. *U205, U371* and *U331* have no success.

27 Aug Western Atlantic
In the Windward Passage the convoy TAW.15 (21 ships, escort: destroyer USS *Lea* (Cdr Walsh), the minelayer *Jan van Brakel,* corvettes HMCS *Halifax, Oakville* and *Snowberry* and one PC and three SC submarine-chasers) is sighted by *U94* (Lt-Cdr Ites). The U-boat is damaged by depth charges dropped from a US Catalina flying-boat and three times rammed by the corvette *Oakville* and sunk. In the meantime *U511* (Lt-Cdr Steinhoff) attacks the convoy, sinks two ships of

21999 tons and torpedoes a third ship of 8773 tons.

27 Aug   North Atlantic
From the outward-bound boats the 'Vorwärts' group is formed on 27 Aug on the eastern side of the North Atlantic. To it belong the *U609*, coming from Iceland and *U407*, *U91*, *U411*, *U92*, *U659*, *U756*, *U409*, *U211* and *U604* (Lt-Cdr Höltring), which has been stationed since 15 Aug in a waiting area and has sunk one ship of 7906 tons there. On 31 Aug *U609* (Lt Rudloff) sights the convoy SC.97 (58 ships, EG C.2) in the N of the patrol line. She attacks immediately and sinks two ships of 10228 tons but is then driven off. On the morning of 1 Sept there are six U-boats in the neighbourhood of the convoy, but attacks by *U604* and *U756* fail. By day the U-boats are driven off by Catalina flying boats of USN VP.73 from Iceland which sink *U756* (Lt-Cdr Harney). In the night 1-2 Sept only *U91* is able to attack—unsuccessfully. By day the operation has to be broken off because of the strong air escort.

27 Aug-5 Sept   Mediterranean
The British submarine *P35/Umbra* (Lt-Cdr Maydon) sinks near Cape Spada the transport *Manfredo Campiero* (5463 tons) which is proceeding to Tobruk, accompanied by the destroyer *Da Recco* and the torpedo boats *Climene* and *Polluce*. *Rorqual* (Lt-Cdr Napier) lays a mine barrage near Corfu on 30 Aug and sinks by torpedo one ship of 5311 tons. On 4 Sept a convoy from Piraeus to Tobruk with the torpedo boats *Castore*, *Lupo* and *Polluce* is attacked by torpedo aircraft and the British submarine *Thrasher* (Lt-Cdr Mackenzie); the latter sinks one ship of 1589 tons and the aircraft one more steamer and the *Polluce*. Off the Cyrenaican coast the British submarine *Traveller* (Lt-Cdr St John) sinks a ship of 1245 tons escorted by the torpedo boat *Montanari*.

28 Aug-11 Oct   Pacific
The Japanese submarine *I-25* (Cdr* Tagami) carries out a reconnaissance operation to the American West Coast, and on 28-29 Aug and 9-10 Sept her aircraft drops incendiary bombs in the forests of Oregon. At the beginning of October the boat sinks two ships of 13691 tons and on 11 Oct attacks with her last torpedo the Soviet submarines *L-15* and *L-16* which are proceeding from Dutch Harbour to San Francisco. She sinks the latter.

29 Aug-24 Sept   North Atlantic
After the operation against convoy SL.119 *U107*, *U214*, *U406*, *U590*, *U87* and *U333* assemble W of Lisbon. Only *U107* (Lt-Cdr Gelhaus) sinks two ships of 8565 tons. On 8 Sept the boats proceed in line abreast to the area of the Cape Verde Islands, but they find no targets. From 25 Sept to 27 Sept they are refuelled from *U460* (Lt-Cdr Schnoor) and four boats then occupy operational areas off Freetown.

30 Aug-25 Sept   North Pacific
On the news of a US landing on the Aleutian island of Adak the Japanese submarines *Ro-61*, *Ro-62* and *Ro-64* are directed there. *Ro-61* (Lt-Cdr Tokutomi) torpedoes on 30 Aug the aircraft tender *Casco* but is sunk on 31 Aug by the US destroyer *Reid*. In the following weeks the submarines *Ro-62*, *Ro-63*, *Ro-64*, *Ro-68* and, from the middle of September, *Ro-62*, *Ro-65* and *Ro-67* operate in turns in the area of the Aleutians.

31 Aug   Black Sea
Off Novorossisk *S102* (Lt-Cdr Töniges) sinks a tanker and *S28* (Lt-Cdr Künzel) the Soviet freighter *Zhan-Tomp* (1988 tons).

31 Aug-14 Sept   North Atlantic
From the 'Stier' group, formed from outward-bound boats during the SC.97 operation and the boats coming from the SC.97 operation a new 'Vorwärts' group is formed from 4 Sept consisting of *U96*, *U594*, *U608*, *U380*, *U404*, *U584*, *U211*, *U218*, *U407*, *U91*, *U411*, *U92* and *U659*. On the evening of 5 Sept *U584* (Lt-Cdr Deecke) reports the convoy ON.127 (32 ships, EG C.4 with the Canadian destroyers *St Croix* (Lt-Cdr Dobson), *Ottawa* and corvettes *Amherst*, *Arvida*, *Sherbrooke* and HMS *Celandine*). Contact is lost in the night and is only regained at mid-day on 10 Sept. *U96* (Lt Hellriegel) sinks two ships of 10554 tons in an underwater attack and torpedoes one more ship of 12190 tons. In the night 10-11 Sept successive attacks are made; *U659*

(Lt-Cdr Stock)-torpedoes one ship of 8029 tons, later sunk by *U584;* by *U404* (Lt-Cdr Bülow)-torpedoes one ship of 7147 tons; by *U608* (Lt Struckmeier)-misses; by *U218* (Lt-Cdr Becker) torpedoes one ship of 7361 tons; by *U92* (Lt Oelrich)-misses; and by *U594* (Lt Mumm)-misses. The escort is greatly impeded by the failure of all radar equipment. By day on 11 Sept *U96* sinks one trawler of 415 tons with gunfire in the area of the convoy. In the night 11-12 Sept there attack successively *U584*-sinks one ship of 4885 tons; *U380* (Lt-Cdr Röther) misses; *U211* (Lt-Cdr Hauser) torpedoes two ships of 20646 tons, both later finished off by *U608; U92* misses the *Ottawa;* and *U404* torpedoes one ship of 9272 tons. The escort, which has damaged *U659* on 11 Sept, is able to drive off the U-boats throughout the day on 12 Sept, but in the darkness they come up again. The attacks by *U407* (Lt Brüller) and *U594* in the night 12-13 Sept fail. By day one straggler of 6131 tons falls victim to *U594*. Air escort sent from Newfoundland drives some of the U-boats off. In the night 13-14 Sept *U91* (Lt-Cdr Walkerling) sinks the destroyer *Ottawa* (Lt-Cdr Rutherford) in two attacks. *U92* misses the convoy and *U411* (Lt Litterscheid) one corvette. Because of the proximity of air bases in Newfoundland the operation has to be ended on 14 Sept: the only case in 1942-43 when all the U-boats deployed against a North Atlantic convoy fire their torpedoes.

1-9 Sept Black Sea
Battle for the Taman Peninsula. The break-through of the Rumanian Cavalry Div to Anapa on 31 Aug has prevented parts of the Soviet 47th Army from withdrawing from the Taman Peninsula into which the Rumanian 5th and 6th Cavalry Divs penetrate. On 2 Sept the German 46th Inf Div is landed on the N and W side of the Taman Peninsula (operation 'Blücher') in 24 MFPs (naval store ferries) of the 1st Landing Flotilla (Lt-Cdr Giele), Siebel ferries, engineers' landing and assault boats under the protection of the 3rd MMS Flotilla (Cdr Hölzerkopf) and the Luftwaffe. The Rumanian 3rd Div follows. From 2 Sept to 5 Sept Soviet warships and transports, under the commander of the Azov Flotilla (Rear-Adm S. G. Gorshkov), including the patrol ship *Shtorm* and the gunboats *Oktyabr* and *Rostov-Don* evacuate the bulk of the Army and naval forces from the South Coast of the Taman Peninsula to Novorossisk. In the nights of 2 Sept, 3 Sept and 5 Sept the 1st MTB Flotilla (Lt-Cdr Christiansen), comprising *S102* (Lt-Cdr Töniges), *S28* (Lt-Cdr Künzel), *S27* (Lt-Cdr Büchting) and *S72* (Lt Schneider), attacks the loading points and reports 19 successes. *S27* is sunk by her own torpedo. Battle for Novorossisk, which is defended against the attack of the German V Army Corps (125th, 73rd and 9th Inf Divs) by the Soviet 77th Rifle Div and the 14th, 142nd, 83rd and 2nd Naval Infantry Brigades under Rear-Adm Kholostyakov. Despite fire support for the defenders from the Soviet flotilla leader *Kharkov* (Capt 2nd Class Melnikov) and the destroyer *Soobrazitelny* (Capt 3rd Class Vorkov) on 1 Sept, 2 Sept and 4 Sept, German units enter the outskirts of Novorossisk on 5 Sept, capture the centre of the city on 6 Sept and occupy the harbour area on 9 Sept. The elements of the Soviet forces driven to the W are evacuated to Gelendzhik by sea.

1-9 Sept South Pacific
Continuation of Japanese attempts to supply and reinforce Guadalcanal. In this the following units are deployed as fast transports: the aircraft depot ships *Akitsushima* and *Nisshin,* the minelayer *Tsugaru* and the 3rd DD Flotilla (Rear-Adm Hashimoto) with the cruiser *Sendai* and the destroyers *Isonami, Uranami, Shikinami* and *Ayanami* (19th DD Div), *Fubuki, Hatsuyuki* and *Murakumo* (11th DD Div), and *Amagiri* (from 20th DD Div) and the 4th DD Flotilla (Rear-Adm Takama) with the cruiser *Yura* and the destroyers *Yudachi, Harusame, Murasame* and *Samidare* (2nd DD Div), *Akatsuki, Ikazuchi* and *Inazuma* (6th DD Div), *Ariake, Yugure, Shiratsuyu* and *Shigure* (27th DD Div) and also the 34th DD Div with *Akikaze, Hakaze* and *Tachikaze.*
In attacks by US B17 bombers the *Akitsushima* and *Akikaze* are slightly

damaged on 1 Sept and the *Tsugaru* on 3 Sept. In the nights 4-5 Sept the 4th DD Flotilla brings the last elements of the Kawaguchi Detachment to Guadalcanal. Off Lunga Point the covering force, consisting of the destroyers *Yudachi*, *Hatsuyuki* and *Murakumo*, encounters the patrolling US APDs *Gregory* and *Little* and sinks them after a brief engagement.

On 7 Sept the US APDs *McKean* and *Manley* land 600 men from Tulagi on Guadalcanal E of the Japanese landing area near Cape Taivu. They make a sortie in the rear of the Kawaguchi Detachment which is preparing for an attack on 12 Sept and by their raid upset the Japanese preparations. At the same time the transports *Bellatrix* and *Fuller* land supplies near Lunga Point. Japanese bombers from Rabaul are deployed without success against the transports on 8 Sept. In addition, the 3rd DD Flotilla with *Sendai* and eight destroyers sets out but is unable to find the transports in the night 8-9 Sept and, instead, shells *Tulagi*.

From the 1st Japanese SM Flotilla (see 23-31 Aug), operating further E of the Solomons, *I-9* reconnoitres over Nouméa with her aircraft on 4 Sept. On 6 Sept *I-11* (Cdr* Hichiji, command boat of the 3rd Flotilla) attacks US TF 18 (Rear-Adm Murray) (see 9-23 Sept) which has arrived to relieve the *Saratoga* group and just misses the flagship, the carrier *Hornet*, whose aircraft are covering supply transports to Guadalcanal (see above). On 8 Sept *I-31* shells the island of Graciosa.

1 Sept-25 Oct   Western Atlantic
After unsuccessful mining operations off Chesapeake Bay (10 Sept) and off Charleston (18 Sept) *U69* (Lt Gräf) and *U455* (Lt-Cdr Giessler) operate S of Novia Scotia and near Cape Race, as well as in the Gulf of St Lawrence, where *U69* after several misses sinks two ships of 4597 tons. *U455* returns without success.

SE of Trinidad the U-boats sink the following independent ships: *U175* (Lt-Cdr Bruns) nine ships of 33426 tons; *U512* (Lt-Cdr Wolfgang Schultze) two ships of 14585 tons; and *U514* (Lt-Cdr Auffermann) five ships of 17354

tons and torpedoes one ship of 5458 tons; *U515* (Lt-Cdr Henke) nine ships of 46782 tons; *U516* (Cdr Wiebe) five ships of 29357 tons. In addition, *U512* and *U515* jointly sink one ship of 6034 tons. On 2 Oct *U512* is sunk by a B18A bomber of the USAAF from Trinidad.

4-8 Sept   Arctic
Offensive mining operation with the destroyers *Richard Beitzen*, *Z29* and *Z30* off the Kara Strait.

5-8 Sept   Baltic
Break-out of the last part of the second wave of Soviet submarines, *S-13*, *Shch-308* and *Shch-323* through the mine barrages. The last runs on a mine and returns to Lavansaari with severe damage. The *L-3*, which is returning from the Baltic, is met by patrol and minesweeping cutters.

6-25 Sept   North Atlantic
The boats of the 'Lohs' group—*U755*, *U373*, *U569*, *U596*, *U176*, *U135* and *U432*—having refuelled from *U462* (Lt Vowe) form a new patrol line on 6 Sept on the western side of the North Atlantic. On 9 Sept *U755* (Lt-Cdr Göing) sinks the US weather observation ship *Muskeget* (1827 tons). From 13 Sept the boats *U410*, *U599* and *U259* also join the 'Lohs' group. Following a decoded course instruction, the group locates on 18 Sept the convoy SC.100 (24 ships, EG A.3 (Cdr Heineman US) with the US Coast Guard cutters *Campbell* and *Spencer*, and, among others, the Canadian corvettes *Rosthern*, *Trillium* and *Dauphin*). As a result of a skilful, evasive movement, the submarine in contact is shaken off on 18 Sept. On 19 Sept only individual boats get close to the convoy in deteriorating weather, mist and rain. To find the convoy again, the 'Pfeil' group, stationed to the SE and comprising *U615*, *U258*, *U221*, *U617*, *U216*, *U356*, *U595* and *U607*, is deployed. *U569* and *U373* miss escort vessels when they try to approach on 20 Sept. *U596* (Lt-Cdr Jahn) sinks one ship of 5676 tons. The storm prevents both sides on 21 Sept from using their weapons and the operation is broken off on 22 Sept but on 23 Sept the favourably stationed boats are directed to RB.1 located by the 'Vorwärts' group whilst

others follow SC.100. *U617* (Lt-Cdr Brandi) sinks one ship from the convoy in the night 22-23 Sept and two stragglers on the following day totalling 14787 tons and *U432* (Lt-Cdr H. O. Schultze) one ship of 5868 tons. Attacks by *U258*, *U221* and *U755* fail. On 25 Sept the pursuit of SC.100 has to be finally broken off.

7-28 Sept Black Sea
Soviet submarines operate off the Bosphorus, off Burgas, off Constanza, in the Bay of Odessa, off Sevastopol, and off the Kerch Peninsula. *L-4* (Capt 3rd Class Polyakov) and *L-5* (Lt-Cdr Zhdanov) lay mine barrages near Sulina and off Sevastopol. *M-35*, *M-111* and *S-31*, among others, make unsuccessful attacks.

8-11 Sept Black Sea
The Soviet cruiser *Krasny Krym*, the flotilla leader *Kharkov*, the destroyers *Soobrazitelny* and *Zheleznyakov* and the patrol ship *Shtorm* bring elements of the 137th and 145th Rifle Regts and the 3rd Naval Infantry Brigade with supplies from Poti to Tuapse and Gelendzhik.

9-10 Sept Mediterranean
British torpedo aircraft sink the Italian hospital ship *Arno* (8024 tons) N of Tobruk.

9-23 Sept South Pacific
Both sides carry out naval operations to reinforce their positions on Guadalcanal. On 9 Sept there set out from Truk the Japanese 2nd Fleet (Vice-Adm Kondo), comprising the heavy cruisers *Atago*, *Takao*, *Maya*, *Myoko* and *Haguro*, the battleships *Haruna* and *Kongo* and the 2nd DD Flotilla (Rear-Adm Tanaka) with the destroyers *Hayashio*, *Kagero*, *Kuroshio* and *Oyashio* (15th DD Div) and *Asagumo*, *Minegumo* and *Natsugumo* (9th DD Div); and the 3rd Fleet (Vice-Adm Nagumo), comprising the carriers *Shokaku*, *Zuiho* and *Zuikaku*, the cruisers *Kumano*, *Suzuya* and *Chikuma*, the battleships *Hiyei* and *Kirishima* and the 10th DD Flotilla with the cruiser *Nagara* and the destroyers *Arashi*, *Nowake*, *Maikaze*, *Akigumo*, *Yugumo*, *Makigumo*, *Kazegumo*, *Hatsukaze*, *Yukikaze*, *Amatsukaze* and *Tokitsukaze*. Their purpose is to escort and cover against US naval forces and reinforce-

ments new troop movements carried out by the 3rd and 4th DD Flotillas from Rabaul (see 1-9 Sept) and to cover the attack on Guadalcanal planned for 12 Sept by the Kawaguchi Detachment which has already been landed. But the attack by the Kawaguchi Detachment fails. The Japanese forces which make a sortie on 13 Sept as far as Ndeni do not find targets and withdraw to the N for supplies.

After US TF 18 (Rear-Adm Noyes), comprising the carrier *Wasp*, the cruisers *San Francisco* (Rear-Adm Scott), *Salt Lake City*, *San Juan* and *Juneau* and the destroyers (Desron 12) *Farenholt*, *Aaron Ward*, *Buchanan*, *Laffey*, *Lansdowne* and *Lardner*, has flown off on 12 Sept from S of Guadalcanal aircraft to reinforce the US marine Corps air strength on Henderson Field, it joins up S of the Solomons on 14 Sept with TF 17 (Rear-Adm Murray). The latter comprises the carrier *Hornet*, the battleship *North Carolina*, the cruisers *Northampton*, *Pensacola* and *San Diego* and the destroyers (Desron 2) *Morris*, *Anderson*, *Hughes*, *Mustin*, *O'Brien*, *Russell* and *Barton*. Their function is to cover a convoy which sets out on the same day from Espiritu Santo with six transports (7th US Marine Corps Regt) and cruiser and destroyer escort for Guadalcanal (TF 65, Rear-Adm Turner.)

On 14 Sept US B17 bombers attack the Japanese forces and slightly damage the *Myoko*. When many reports are received about the Japanese forces the US convoy turns back temporarily. The US carrier groups run into the Japanese submarine concentration of the 1st Flotilla (see 23 Aug-1 Sept) on 15 Sept. *I-19* (Cdr Narahara) fires a salvo of six of her 'Long-Lance' torpedoes. Three hit the *Wasp* (Capt Sherman), one just misses the *Lansdowne*, which later has to finish off the abandoned *Wasp* with torpedoes, and two more torpedoes reach TF 17 some 5 nautical miles away and hit the *North Carolina* and *O'Brien*. The latter sinks on 19 Oct on the way back to the US. *I-15*, stationed in the vicinity, observes the successful attack but is not herself able to fire.

After replenishing from 15 Sept to 17 Sept, the Japanese 2nd and 3rd Fleets make another sortie to the S, but they are recalled on 20 Sept and arrive back in Truk on 23 Sept. When no further air reconnaissance reports are received, Adm Turner orders the convoy to turn back to Guadalcanal on 16 Sept. On 18 Sept the transports supported by the cruisers *Minneapolis*, *Boise* and *Leander* (RNZN) and the destroyers *Phelps*, *Farragut*, *Worden*, *MacDonough*, *Dale*, *Grayson* and *Monssen* land their troops near Lunga Point.

10 Sept   English Channel
A British Force comprising *MTB234*, *MTB230*, *MGB91*, *MGB82* and *MGB84* attacks a German convoy off Texel and damages two ships.

10-27 Sept   Mediterranean
In British submarine operations *Una* misses a convoy W of Crete on 10 Sept. On 12 Sept *P212/Sahib* (Lt Bromage) sinks one sailing ship of 24 tons near Marettimo. On 17 Sept two small independents of 419 tons fall victim to *P-44/United* (Lt Roxburgh) off Sliten, while *Talisman* probably runs on a mine in the Sicilian Channel and is lost. *Taku* attacks convoys off Tobruk on 18 Sept and 20 Sept, but the torpedoes are out-manoeuvred as is an attack by *Thrasher* on 22 Sept in the same area. *P46/Unruffled* (Lt Stevens) sinks from 20 Sept to 22 Sept three ships of 5305 tons off the Tunisian coast. Near Rhodes the Greek *Nereus* sinks one small ship of 622 tons on 24 Sept. *P35/Umbra* (Lt-Cdr Maydon) attacks a convoy with the destroyers *Da Verazzano* and *Lampo* and the torpedo boats *Partenope*, *Clio*, *Aretusa* and *Lince* near Navarino and sinks one ship of 6343 tons.

10 Sept-5 Nov   Indian Ocean
British operations to occupy Madagascar: operation 'Stream'. A force under Rear-Adm Tennant, comprising the cruisers *Birmingham*, *Gambia* and *Jacob van Heemskerck* (Dutch) and the destroyers (7th DD Flotilla) *Napier*, *Nizam*, *Nestor*, *Norman* (RAN), *Van Galen*, *Tjerk Hiddes* (Dutch) and *Nepal* brings a transport force to Majunga (West Coast) where on 10 Sept the 29th Infantry Brigade is landed. *Napier*

lands commando troops in Morandova. Air escort is provided by the carrier *Illustrious* and aircraft depot ship *Albatross* with the destroyers *Hotspur*, *Express*, *Fortune* and *Inconstant*. While some forces make a sortie over land, to the capital Tananarive, operation 'Jane' is carried out on 18 Sept. The 29th Infantry Brigade is re-embarked and landed near Tamatave. The transports are escorted and supported by a force consisting of the carrier *Illustrious*, the battleship *Warspite*, the *Jacob van Heemskerck*, *Van Galen*, *Tjerk Hiddes*, *Napier*, *Norman* *Nizam*, *Nestor* and *Hotspur*. On 23 Sept Tananarive is occupied and the Vichy French Governor withdraws. After landing a South African regiment in Thelar on 29 Sept the French troops are pursued until they surrender in Ihosy on 5 Nov. *Nizam* captures two French transports S of Madagascar on 24 Sept and 30 Sept which are sunk.

12-17 Sept   South Atlantic
Laconia incident: on 12 Sept *U156* (Cdr Hartenstein) sinks the British transport *Laconia* (19695 tons) with 1800 Italian prisoners of war on board NE of Ascension. *U156* begins at once with the rescue and in W/T plain language appeals to all ships in the area for help. The Commander U-boats orders *U506* (Lt-Cdr Würdemann) and *U507* (Cdr Schacht) and the Italian submarine *Cappellini* (Lt-Cdr Revedin) to the scene and they arrive on 15 Sept and 16 Sept. He also requests, through diplomatic channels, the French Navy in West Africa for support. When the report is picked up in Freetown, the British merchant ship *Empire Haven* and the auxiliary cruiser *Corinthian* from Takoradi are ordered to the spot. The US 1st Composite Air Squadron on Ascension, which has received the *U156's* W/T message in garbled form and is not informed of the rescue action by the U-boats, is asked to provide air escort for the British ships. In the meantime, the U-boats have taken aboard a large number of British, Polish and Italian survivors and taken the rest in tow in lifeboats in order to proceed to the rendezvous with the French ships. A Liberator bomber of the USAAF 343rd Bombardment Sqdn

(Lt Harden), which happens to be in Ascension on the way to Africa, sees the U-boats when escorting the British ships and, after referring to the Commander of the 1st Composite Sqdn, Capt Richardson, receives an order to attack. It attacks *U156* with bombs in spite of the clear Red Cross flags. Thereupon the Commander U-boats gives orders on 17 Sept to all German U-boats that the rescue of survivors from sunken ships is forbidden ('Laconia' order). On 17 Sept the cruiser *Gloire*, the sloop *Dumont D'Urville* and the minesweeper *Annamite* arrive, having been sent to sea on the instructions of the Vichy government by Adm Collinet, the naval commander in French Equatorial Africa. They take on 1041 survivors from the German U-boats and lifeboats and on 18 Sept *Dumont D'Urville* takes on another 42 from *Cappellini*.

12-18 Sept Arctic
Operation against Allied supply convoy PQ.18 in the Arctic.
12 Sept: German reconnaissance aircraft locate the convoy consisting of 39 freighters, one rescue ship, one tanker, three minesweepers and two fleet tankers. Escort is provided by the destroyers *Achates* and *Malcolm*, the AA ships *Alynbank* and *Ulster Queen*, two submarines, four corvettes, three minesweepers and four trawlers and, in addition, the escort carrier *Avenger* with two destroyers. As close support, divided into two groups, there is: the light cruiser *Scylla* (Rear-Adm Burnett) with the destroyers *Onslow*, *Onslaught*, *Opportune*, *Offa*, *Ashanti*, *Eskimo*, *Somali*, *Tartar*, *Milne*, *Marne*, *Martin*, *Meteor*, *Faulknor*, *Intrepid*, *Impulsive* and *Fury*. Covering force: the heavy cruisers *Norfolk* (Vice-Adm Bonham-Carter), *London* and *Suffolk*. Distant cover: the battleships *Anson* (Vice-Adm Fraser) and *Duke of York*, the light cruiser *Jamaica* and five 'Hunt' class destroyers. The rescue ship *Copeland* is part of the convoy.
13 Sept: *U405* (Cdr Hopmann) and *U589* (Lt-Cdr Horrer) sink the US freighter *Oliver Ellsworth* (7191 tons) and the Soviet steamer *Stalingrad* (3559 tons). Bombers of K.G. 30 (Maj Bloedorn) and torpedo aircraft of

I/K.G. 26 (Maj Klümper) and elements of III/K.G. 26 (Capt Nocken) destroy in several attacks the freighters *Wacosta* (5432 tons), *Oregonian* (4826 tons) *Macbeth* (6131 tons), *Africander* (5441 tons), *Empire Stevenson* (6209 tons) *Empire Beaumont* (7044 tons) and the Soviet steamer *Sukhona* (3124 tons). On 13-14 Sept Hurricanes of the *Avenger* shoot down five German aircraft and four Hurricanes are lost. 14 Sept: in the night *U457* (Cdr Brandenburg) torpedoes the British tanker *Atheltemplar* (8992 tons) which later has to be abandoned. In the afternoon, in a renewed attack by K.G. 30 the freighter *Mary Luckenbach* (5049 tons) sinks. In all these attacks, I/K·G 26 loses 12 aircraft and seven crews and III/K.G. 26 eight aircraft and seven crews.
16 Sept: bad weather prevents further air attacks. 17 Sept: the convoy is again located, but an attack by K.G. 26 is broken off.
18 Sept: renewed attack by K.G. 26 and K.G. 30 in poor visibility. K.G. 26 has many torpedo failures. A Hurricane of the catapult ship *Empire Morn* shoots down two He 115s. The convoy, whose escort the Soviet destroyers *Gremyashchi, Kuibyshev, Sokrushitelny* and *Uritski* have now joined, loses the freighter *Kentucky* (5446 tons). The freighter *Troubador* (6458 tons) is damaged by bombs and beached in the Kola Inlet. She is later dismantled. In all, PQ.18 loses three ships of 19742 tons to U-boats and 10 ships of 55915 tons to air attacks. The German U-boats *U88* (Lt-Cdr Bohmann), *U457* and *U589* are sunk in the course of the fighting by the British escort vessels *Onslow, Faulknor* and *Impulsive*.

12-27 Sept Indonesia
After several journeys, since May, by the small vessels *Kuru* and *Vigilant* from Port Darwin to supply the Dutch and Australian troops left on Timor, the Australian corvette *Kalgoorlie* brings reinforcements from 12 Sept to 17 Sept. The transportation of a relief company in the Australian destroyer *Voyager* fails because the ship runs on a reef off Timor on 23 Sept and has to be blown up. The corvettes *Kalgoorlie* and *Warnambool* rescue the survivors.

13-20 Sept North Atlantic

On the way to a patrol line 'Pfeil' planned for 14 Sept *U216* (Lt-Cdr Schultz) sights the convoy SC.99 (61 ships, EG C.1) on 13 Sept but is at once driven off. Of the boats *U615*, *U258*, *U221*, *U617* (Lt-Cdr Brandi), which sinks one trawler on the way out, *U618*, *U356* and *U440*—all of which are ordered to the scene—only *U440* comes up on 14 Sept but is attacked by escort vessels with depth charges and severely damaged. Before a new patrol line can be taken up on 16 Sept *U221* (Lt Trojer) sights on 15 Sept the convoy ON.129 (30 ships, EG C.2) but loses contact in the mist. On 16 Sept the boats which approach are driven off by the escort which makes skilful use of smoke. With the exception of *U440* the boats are ordered to take part in a new patrol line and are directed to SC.100 (EG A.3) on 2 Sept.

13 Sept Western Atlantic

From the convoy TAG.5 *U558* (Lt-Cdr Krech) sinks in two approaches three ships of 21828 tons.

13-14 Sept Mediterranean

Operation 'Agreement': British raid on Tobruk. 13 Sept: the destroyer *Sikh* (Capt Micklewait) and *Zulu* with 350 Marines on board set out from Alexandria and meet at sea the AA cruiser *Coventry* and the 5th DD Flotilla ('Hunt' class). In addition, there arrive 18 MTBs and three launches with 150 landing troops. In the night 13-14 Sept there are heavy attacks by the RAF on Tobruk. 14 Sept: an attempt is made to land. Only a few soldiers are able to get ashore. *Sikh* sinks in the fire of the AA battery I/43 (Maj Wegener) near the coast. Most the crew and the surviving Marines are taken prisoner. Ju 87s (Lt Göbel) of III/St. G. 3 sink the *Coventry*, the Italian 13th Fighter Bomber Group (Maj Viale) the destroyer *Zulu* and the *MTB308*, *MTB310* and *MTB312*. In addition, *ML352* and *ML353* sink in the fire of the AA battery. *MTB314* is brought in by boats of the 6th MMS Flotilla (Lt-Cdr Reischauer) with 117 men on board. A simultaneous Commando operation from the land side (Col Haselden†) also fails. In all, the German and Italian defenders of Tobruk take 576 prisoners.

15 Sept Gibraltar

Italian frogmen sink the British freighter *Ravens Point* (1787 tons) in Gibraltar.

18-30 Sept Baltic

Break-out of the first group of the third wave of Soviet submarines—*S-9*, *Shch-310*, *S-12*, *M-102*, *D-2* and *Shch-307*—through the mine barrages. In spite of some detonations close to several boats, the operations are continued. The returning *Shch-407* runs on a mine near Porkkala on 25 Sept but is brought in heavily damaged. *Shch-308* is probably lost on a mine on the return.

19 Sept-14 Oct South West Pacific

In the Indonesian area the US submarines *Sargo* (Lt-Cdr Gregory) and *Seadragon* (Lt-Cdr Ferrall) each sink one ship of 4472 tons and 1579 tons respectively. *Searaven* (Lt-Cdr Cassedy) torpedoes the German blockade-runner *Regensburg* (8068 tons) off Sunda Strait. In the area of the Bismarck Islands and N of the Solomons *Amberjack* (Lt-Cdr Bole) sinks two ships of 5231 tons and torpedoes two ships of 24120 tons including the large whaler *Tonan Maru*. *Sculpin* (Lt-Cdr Chappell) sinks two ships of 6652 tons and *Sturgeon* (Lt-Cdr Piaczentkowski) one ship of 8033 tons.

20-22 Sept Arctic

The German U-boats *U251*, *U255*, *U403*, *U408*, *U435*, *U592* and *U703* operate in the Arctic against the convoy QP.14. The convoy consists of 15 merchant ships, escorted by two AA ships and 11 corvettes, minesweepers and trawlers with the rescue ships *Rathlin* and *Zamalek*. They set out from Archangel on 13 Sept. Close escort is provided by Rear-Adm Burnett's force (see PQ.18). 20 Sept: *U435* (Lt-Cdr Strelow) sinks the minesweeper *Leda*, *U255* (Lt-Cdr Reche) the freighter *Silver Sword* (4937 tons) and *U703* (Lt-Cdr Bielfeld) and destroyer *Somali*. 22 Sept: Although the convoy is still escorted by 11 destroyers and nine smaller units after the withdrawal of a part of Adm Burnett's force, *U435* is able to come up to attack again and to sink the freighters *Bellingham* (5345 tons), *Ocean Voice* (7174 tons) and the tanker *Grey Ranger* (3313 tons).

s

20-26 Sept   North Atlantic

Of the 10 boats of the "Vorwärts' group refuelled from *U461* (Lt-Cdr Stiegler) from 16 Sept to 18 Sept, *U380, U404, U584, U211, U407, U91* and *U96* form a new patrol line E of the Newfoundland Bank on 20 Sept and they are joined by *U260, U582* and *U619* in the next few days. From 18 Sept to 24 Sept the following each sink one independent or straggler: *U380* (Lt-Cdr Röther) (2994 tons); *U211* (Lt-Cdr Hauser) (11237 tons); *U582* (Lt-Cdr Schulte) (2993 tons); and *U619* (Lt Makowski) (7176 tons). On 23 Sept *U404* (Lt-Cdr von Bülow) sights the convoy RB.1 (eight passenger steamers from the Great Lakes; escort: British destroyers *Vanoc* and *Veteran*) whose steamers are mistakenly taken for large troop transports. Apart from the 'Vorwärts' group, the 'Pfeil' group comprising *U618, U216, U356, U595, U607, U410* and *U617*, is accordingly ordered to the scene from the E on the completion of the operation against SC.100. But because of the high speed of the convoy, the boats have difficulty in getting to it. In the night 24-25 Sept *U211* and *U260* attack unsuccessfully. In the afternoon of 25 Sept *U216* (Lt-Cdr Karl-Otto Schultz) sinks one ship of 4989 tons and in the evening *U96* (Lt Hellriegel) sinks one ship also of 4989 tons. Attacks by *U410* (Cdr Sturm, twice), *U91* and *U356* fail. On the morning of 26 Sept *U404* sinks the destroyer *Veteran* and in the evening *U619* one straggler of 1547 tons.

20 Sept-6 Oct   Mediterranean

In the Eastern Mediterranean *U431* (Lt-Cdr Dommes) and *U561* (Lt Schomburg) sink four sailing ships. The Italian submarines *Ametista* and *Nereide* operate SE of Crete, *Argo, Alabastro, Argente* and *Nichelio* off Algeria.

24 Sept   Gibraltar

P 108s of the Italian 274th Long-Range Bomber Sqdn attack Gibraltar. The attack is repeated in the nights 19-20 Oct and 20-21 Oct.

24-28 Sept   Arctic

Offensive mining operation 'Zarin' by the heavy cruiser *Admiral Hipper* (Rear-Adm Meisel) and the destroyers *Z28, Z29, Z30* and *Richard Beitzen*, off the NW coast of Novaya Zemlya.

24 Sept-9 Oct   South Pacific

Both sides continue to try to supply Guadalcanal. From 24 Sept to 27 Sept US Marine Corps Companies brought by sea in assault boats try to prevent a Japanese concentration on the Matanikau River but have to retire again under cover from the APD *Ballard*. The Japanese 3rd and 4th DD Flotillas (see 1-9 Sept) continue their night missions to Guadalcanal. On 24 Sept the destroyers *Kawakaze* and *Umikaze* whilst thus engaged, are slightly damaged by dive bombers from Henderson Airfield and on 25 Sept the cruiser *Yura* suffers the same fate from B17 bombers from Espiritu Santo. In a raid on Rabaul on 2 Oct the cruiser *Tenryu* is damaged.

To prevent Allied supplies, the Japanese submarine group A, comprising *I-4, I-5, I-7, I-8, I-22* and *I-176*, is deployed in the area of Guadalcanal. *I-5* is damaged on 25 Sept when she tries to attack. *I-4* (Cdr Kawasaki) torpedoes the US transport *Alhena* (7440 tons) off Lunga Point on 29 Sept. *I-22* misses a convoy on 29 Sept and is lost on 1 Oct after reporting a further convoy.

To cover and support the US operations TF 17 (Rear-Adm Murray) sets out on 2 Oct from Nouméa with the carrier *Hornet*, the cruisers *Northampton, Pensacola, San Diego* and *Juneau* and the destroyers *Morris, Anderson, Hughes, Mustin, Russell* and *Barton* and carries out two raids on Japanese shipping in the roads of Shortland on 5 Oct But because of the weather they are not pressed home. US Marine Corps bombers from Henderson Field, however, damage the destroyers *Minegumo* and *Murasame* in the area.

On 9 Sept a Japanese force, comprising the cruiser *Tatsuta* and five destroyers, brings the C-in-C of the 17th Army (Lt-Gen Hyakutake) to Tassaforonga on Guadalcanal. In addition, elements of the Japanese 2nd Inf Div (Lt-Gen Matsuyama) are landed.

24 Sept-15 Oct   Indian Ocean

Off the coasts of India and Ceylon the Japanese submarine *I-162* (Cdr Shimose) sinks two ships of 7929 tons and damages one more of 4161 tons; *I-165* (Cdr Torisu) sinks one ship of 5549 tons and one unidentified ship; *I-166*

(Cdr Tanaka) sinks one ship of 1201 tons and damages one unidentified ship. In addition, she lands agents on the coast of Calicut.

26-30 Sept North Atlantic
On 26 Sept *U617* (Lt-Cdr Brandi), which has been directed to SC.100, sights the convoy ON.131 (EG C.3, leading destroyer *Skeena*) but her immediate attack fails because of torpedo defects. From the boats which were widely scattered after the operations against RB.1 and SC.100, *U615*, *U258*, *U221*, *U617*, *U618*, *U216*, *U356*, *U595*, *U607*, *U410*, *U599*, *U755*, *U373*, *U569* and *U176* are ordered to the scene as the 'Tiger' group. After losing contact, a systematic search is impossible because of the uncertain position of the boats and an incipient storm. The operation has to be broken off. Eight boats go S to refuel —four with *U118* and four with *U116*.

26 Sept-24 Oct Pacific
On the Japanese East Coast the US submarine *Nautilus* (Lt-Cdr Brockman) sinks two ships of 7426 tons; *Kingfish* (Lt-Cdr Lowrance) sinks two ships of 5540 tons; *Greenling* (Lt-Cdr Bruton) sinks four ships of 19871 tons; *Trigger* (Lt-Cdr Lewis) sinks one ship of 5870 tons and damages two ships of 14517 tons; *Drum* (Lt-Cdr Rice) sinks three ships of 13208 tons. In addition, *Greenling* lightly hits the Japanese carrier *Hiyo* on 20 Oct. Off Formosa *Guardfish* (Lt-Cdr Klakring) sinks one ship of 6362 tons and *Finback* (Lt-Cdr Hull) sinks one ship of 7007 tons and torpedoes one more ship of 5359 tons. Near Truk *Trout* (Lt-Cdr Ramage) torpedoes the Japanese escort carrier *Taiyo* on 28 Sept. Off the Kuriles *Nautilus* (Lt-Cdr Brockman) and *S31* (Lt Sellars) each sink one ship of 4643 tons and 2864 tons respectively.

26 Sept-20 May Pacific/Arctic
Soviet submarines of the Pacific Fleet are transferred to the Northern Fleet via the Panama Canal. On 26 Sept *L-15* and *L-16* and on 15 Oct and 18 Oct *S-51*, *S-54*, *S-55* and *S-56* set out from Petropavlovsk and proceed under Capt 1st Class Tripolski via Dutch Harbour, San Francisco and the Panama Canal to Halifax (*L-16* is sunk on 11 Oct). *S-51* goes from there

via Iceland direct to Polyarnoe, where she arrives on 24 Jan 1943. *S-55*, *S-56* and *S-54*, after stops in Rosyth, proceed to the Kola Inlet, where they arrive in March 1943. *L-15* follows in May after being repaired in Greenock.

27 Sept South Atlantic
In the South Atlantic the German auxiliary cruiser *Schiff 23 Stier* (Capt Gerlach) comes unexpectedly in poor visibility across the US freighter *Stephen Hopkins* (Capt Paul Buck, 7181 tons), sinks her but receives such heavy damage in the engagement that she has to be abandoned. The crew reach the Gironde Estuary in the blockade-runner *Tannenfels* on 2 Nov. Sinkings by *Schiff 23*: four ships of 29409 tons.

27 Sept-5 Nov Baltic
Of the Soviet submarines of the third wave which have broken through the mine barrages *S-9* operates in the Gulf of Bothnia; *D-2*, *Shch-310* and *Shch-406* between Rixhöft and Bornholm; *S-12* on the Baltic Coast; *Shch-307*, *S-7*, *Shch-305* and *Shch-306* in the Aaland Sea; *Schh-303* in Swedish waters and *M-102* in the western part of the Gulf of Finland. *L-3* (Capt 2nd Class Grishchenko) lays mine barrages off Utö, Libau and the Irben Strait on which three ships of 11789 tons are probably lost. Of the other boats, *S-9* (Lt-Cdr Mylnikov with the Divisional Commander, Capt 2nd Class Yunakov on board) sinks one ship of 290 tons, torpedoes one of 6370 tons and misses one; *Shch-310* (Capt 3rd Class Yarosevich) sinks one ship of 1419 tons and misses one; *S-12* (Capt 3rd Class Turaev) damages two ships of 12326 tons; *M-102* (Lt-Cdr Gladilin) misses one; *D-2* (Capt 2nd Class Lindenberg) sinks one ship of 4090 tons and damages one of 2972 tons; *Shch-307* (Capt 3rd Class Momot) sinks one ship of 2478 tons and misses three; *Shch-406* (Capt 3rd Class Osipov) sinks two ships of 3855 tons and misses one; and *Shch-303* (Capt 3rd Class Travkin) misses four. *Inter-alia*, *Shch-406* sinks the Swedish steamer *Bengt Sture* in the night 28-29 Oct and takes six prisoners.

28 Sept-28 Nov Western Atlantic
SE of Trinidad *U202* (Lt Poser) sinks one ship of 1815 tons; *U201* (Lt

Rosenberg) sinks two ships of 8505 tons and *U201* and *U202* jointly sink one ship of 7191 tons; *U332* (Lt-Cdr Liebe) sinks two ships of 11004 tons; and *U67* (Lt-Cdr Müller-Stöckheim) sinks four ships of 20467 tons and damages two ships of 11781 tons.

28-30 Sept   Black Sea
The Soviet destroyer *Nezamozhnik* and the patrol ship *Shtorm* transport 8000 men of the 408th Rifle Div to Tuapse.

29 Sept-6 Oct   North Atlantic
It is proposed to form a new large patrol line 'Luchs' for 1 Oct on the E side of the Atlantic from outward-bound boats. The first outward-bound boats *U620*, *U610* and *U253* are temporarily stationed in the Denmark Strait from 20 Sept and here *U253* (Lt-Cdr A. Friedrichs†) is lost on 23 Sept thanks to a Catalina flying-boat of No 210 Sqdn RAF. *U610* (Lt-Cdr Frhr von Freyburg) sinks one straggler of 1774 tons from the convoy SC.101 (EG C.4). On the way *U442* (Cdr Hesse) sinks one ship of 1774 tons from a small convoy and *U382* (Lt-Cdr Juli) one independent of 1324 tons. On 29 Sept the outward-bound U-tanker, *U118* (Cdr Czygan), sights an ON convoy with the result that the line of the 'Luchs' group is moved to the N on 1 Oct. It consists of *U437*, *U597*, *U442*, *U254*, *U382*, *U620*, *U610*, *U706*, *U260*, *U582*, *U619*, *U753*, *U755*, *U257*, *U602*, *U183* and *U757*. Whilst the U-boats proceed slowly to the SW, the most northerly boat, *U260* (Lt-Cdr Purkhold), sights the convoy HX.209 (31 ships, E G B.4). Storms, rain and hail squalls delay the approach of the other boats from an unfavourable stern position. Only *U254* (Lt-Cdr Loewe) finds an abandoned drifting tanker of 11651 tons and sinks her. Atmospheric interference prevents the reception of a contact signal on 4 Oct from *U437* (Lt-Cdr Lamby) with the substantially better-situated ON convoy. Most of the boats continue the pursuit of HX.209 despite the air escort that it gets on 4 Oct. But on 5-6 Oct *U582* (Lt-Cdr Schulte) and *U619* (Lt Makowski) are lost through air attacks and *U257* (Lt-Cdr Rahe) is damaged. On 6 Oct the operation has to be broken off.

1-3 Oct   Black Sea
The Soviet patrol ship *Shtorm* shells Anapa on 1 Oct. The destroyer *Boiki* (with the Commander of the Squadron, Vice-Adm L. A. Vladimirski, on board) and *Soobrazitelny* shell Yalta in the night 2-3 Oct (406 rounds).

1-20 Oct   Central Atlantic
In operations by Italian submarines in the area SW of Freetown and in the Gulf of Guinea *Barbarigo* (Cdr Grossi) attacks the British corvette *Petunia* on 6 Oct which she mistakes for a US battleship and thinks depth detonations are hits. On 9 Oct *Archimede* (Lt-Cdr Saccardo) sinks the British troop transport *Oronsay* (20043 tons) and attacks the transport *Nea Hellas* (16991 tons) on 10 Oct which, however, is hardly damaged. *Bagnolini* has no success.

1-26 Oct   Black Sea
In Soviet submarine operations *M-118* (Lt-Cdr Savin) sinks on 1 Oct the German transport *Salzburg* (1742 tons) but is herself sunk by the gunboat *Ghigulescu* in an attack on a Rumanian convoy. *M.111* (?) sinks the Rumanian tug *Oituz*; *Shch-216* (Capt 3rd Class Karbovski) the Rumanian steamer *Carpati* (4336 tons); *M-35* (Capt 3rd Class Greshilov) the tanker *Le Progrès* (511 tons). Among others *M-32* and *Shch-207* make unsuccessful attacks.

1-30 Oct   Central Atlantic
Of the U-boats *U87*, *U107*, *U590* and *U333* which have just been refuelled and deployed off Freetown, only *U107* (Lt-Cdr Gelhaus) and *U87* (Lt-Cdr Berger) each sink one ship of 14943 tons and 7392 tons respectively. *U333* (Lt-Cdr Cremer) has a gun duel at short range with the British corvette *Crocus* on 6 Oct in which both ships suffer damage and loss of personnel.
The *U156*, stationed W of Freetown since the *Laconia* affair, has no success at first in this phase, like the newcomers *U552*, *U128* and *UD5*. Only on 29 Oct does *UD5* (Cdr* Mahn) sink one ship of 7628 tons.

2 Oct   English Channel
In an attack by the 5th MTB Flotilla, consisting of *S65*, *S77*, *S82* and *S112*, on a British convoy off Eddystone, *S112* (Lt Karl Müller) sinks the British trawler *Lord Stonehaven*.

2 Oct North Atlantic
Off the British South-West Coast the AA cruiser *Curacao* sinks with 338 members of the crew after a collision with the troop transport *Queen Mary* (81236 tons).

2-3 Oct Mediterranean
The Italian tankers *Scrivia*, *Sesia* and *Tirso* which are equipped as auxiliary minelayers, lay with the destroyers *Ascari* and *Mitragliere* the mine barrage S.61 (400 mines) S of Marettimo (Western Sicily). Simultaneously, the destroyer *Da Verazzano* lays hear Cape Bon 194 protection and explosive floats in two sections.

2-10 Oct Mediterranean
In the Adriatic the British submarine *P.211/Safari* (Cdr Bryant) attacks four ships and torpedoes two of 1052 tons. On 8 Oct and 9 Oct on the Cyrenaican coast *Turbulent* (Cdr Linton) sinks one ship of 853 tons and *P.37/Unbending* (Lt Stanley) sinks two ships of 2230 tons and a small sailing ship. *P.43/Unison* (Lt Halliday) sinks on 10 Oct W of the Peloponnese a ship of 4652 tons escorted by the torpedo boat *Bassini*. *Porpoise* (Cdr Bennington) lays a mine barrage on 3 Oct near Tobruk.

5-27 Oct Baltic
Break-out of the last group of the third wave of Soviet submarines through the mine barrages: *Shch-320*, *Shch-303*, *Shch-302*, *Shch-311*, *S-7*, *Shch-306*, *Shch-406*, *Shch-304* and *L-3*. On the way out *Shch-320*, *Shch-302*, *Shch-311* and *Shch-304* are lost on the barrages. Of the submarines which, at the same time, return, *Shch-310* is badly damaged near Suursaari by a mine on 9 Oct; and *S-13* escapes attacks by the Finnish submarine-chasers *VMV-13* and *VMV-15* near Vaindlo on 15 Oct. In operations to guard the mine barrages, the German submarine-chaser *UJ1204* runs on a Soviet mine near Pien-Tytärsaari and sinks. Of the Finnish submarines deployed in submarine-hunting in the area of the Aaland Sea *Vesihiisi* (Lt-Cdr Aittola) sinks *S-7* near Söderarm on 21 Oct and takes four prisoners including the Commander, Capt 3rd Class Lisin. On 26 Oct *Iku-Turso* (Lt-Cdr Pakkala) sinks *Shch-305* and on 5 Nov *Vetehinen* (Lt-Cdr Leino) probably *Shch-306*.

6 Oct-3 Dec Western Atlantic
In October *U43* operates in the Gulf of St Lawrence, *U183* and *U518* off the Belle Isle Strait and *U106* (Lt-Cdr Rasch) off Cabot Strait where she sinks one ship of 2140 tons. On 2 Nov *U518* (Lt Wissmann) enters Conception Bay and sinks two ore ships of 13336 tons. An attack by *U183* (Cdr Schäfer) remains unclarified. On 18 Nov *U43* (Lt Schwantke) torpedoes NE of the Newfoundland Bank from the convoy SC.109 (EG C.3, with the rescue ship *Bury* equipped with effective HF/DF) a tanker of 9132 tons which is at first taken in tow but then sinks on 25 Jan 1943 on the way to the repair yard. From the convoy ON.145 (EG A.3) *U518* sinks off Newfoundland on 21 Nov a ship of 6140 tons and torpedoes two of 15440 tons. On 3 Dec *U183* sinks one ship of 6089 tons from the convoy ONS.146 off Nova Scotia.

7 Oct English Channel/North Sea
Sortie by the 2nd MTB Flotilla, comprising *S101*, *S46*, *S62*, *S80*, *S105* and *S108*, as well as *S63*, *S79* and *S117* of the 4th MTB Flotilla against a British convoy off Cromer: three British freighters of 7576 tons, one RN tug (444 tons) and the launch *ML339* are sunk. The German auxiliary cruiser *Schiff 45 Komet*, escorted by the 2nd MMS Flotilla, runs on a newly-laid minefield off Dunkirk and loses *R77*, *R78*, *R82* and *R86*.

7 Oct-13 Nov South Africa
The 'Eisbär' group operates off South Africa. After *U68* has sunk two ships of 12157 tons on 12 Sept to 15 Sept in the Central Atlantic on the outward journey and all boats have refuelled from *U459* (Cdr von Wilamowitz-Moellendorf) on 24-25 Sept S of Ascension, the four boats simultaneously attack the traffic off South Africa on 7-8 Oct. Up to 3 Nov *U172* (Lt-Cdr Emmermann) sinks six ships of 48054 tons; *U159* (Lt-Cdr Witte) eight ships of 47233 tons; *U68* (Cdr Merten) seven ships of 44173 tons; and *U504* (Cdr Poske) sinks six ships of 36156 tons.

In addition, *U179* (Cdr* Sobe) of the second wave of IX-D2 boats, which arrives on 8 Oct sinks one ship of 6558 tons but is then sunk by depth charges and ramming from the British destroyer *Active*.

8-16 Oct   North Atlantic

On the E side of the Atlantic the 'Panther' group is formed from 8 Oct from the boats coming from the HX.209 convoy and from new arrivals. It consists of *U84*, *U454*, *U353*, *U437*, *U597*, *U442*, *U254*, *U706*, *U260*, *U753*, *U575*, *U602* and *U757*, to which in the following days are added *U662*, *U382*, *U620*, *U610*, *U301*, *U443*, *U563*, *U621* and *U441*. *U254* (Lt-Cdr Loewe) sinks an independent of 6098 tons. On the evening of 11 Oct *U620* (Lt-Cdr Stein) sights the convoy ONS. 136 (36 ships, EG B.3). *U353*, *U662*, *U437*, *U597*, *U442*, *U254*, *U382* and *U620* are directed to it as the 'Leopard' group. With winds of Force 8-10 only *U597* (Lt-Cdr Bopst) is able to fire— twice unsuccessfully but she is sunk on 12 Oct by a Liberator bomber of No 120 Sqdn RAF. After that only independents and stragglers are sighted. *U382* (Lt-Cdr Juli) misses a destroyer and *U706* (Lt-Cdr von Zitzewitz) sinks one ship of 4265 tons. On 14 Oct the operation is broken off and the 'Leopard' group is directed to the oncoming SC.104.

With the boats *U615*, *U258*, *U221*, *U618*, *U356*, *U607*, *U410* and *U599*, which have been refuelled from *U116* and *U118*, the 'Wotan' group is formed E of Newfoundland on 8 Oct and to this are added by 12 Oct *U216* and *U661*, replenished by the newly-arrived *U463*. On 11 Oct *U615* (Lt-Cdr Kapitzky) sinks one independent of 4219 tons. On the same day *U258* (Lt-Cdr von Mässenhausen) sights a corvette of the convoy SC.104. This consists of 48 ships and the EG B.6 (Cdr Heathcote) with the British destroyers *Fame* and *Viscount* and the Norwegian corvettes *Potentilla*, *Eglantine*, *Montbretia* and *Acanthus* with the rescue ship *Goathland* with HF/DF. Radio atmospherics prevent the contact report from coming through before 12 Oct and the deployment of the 'Wotan' group is delayed by the sighting of the convoy ON.135 (EG A.3) by *U356*. Only in the night 12-13 Oct, therefore, does *U221* (Lt-Trojer) approach SC.104 and in three skilfully executed approaches sinks three ships of 11354 tons. By day on 13 Oct *U221* keeps contact and brings up *U599*, *U216*, *U607* and *U258*, but they are driven off by *Viscount*, *Potentilla* and *Eglantine*, the last of which shells *U258* with gunfire. In the night 13-14 Oct *U221* attacks again whilst three escorts remain astern and sinks one ship of 5929 tons and torpedoes the whale factory ship *Southern Empress* (12398 tons) which is later finished off. A little later *U607* (Lt-Cdr Mengersen) and *U661* (Lt von Lilienfeld) attack almost simultaneously and each sinks one ship of 4826 tons and 3672 tons respectively. *U607* is attacked by *Viscount* and damaged with depth charges. Towards morning *U618* (Lt Baberg) sinks one ship of 5791 tons. *Montbretia* drives off *U615* which is located with radar. At mid-day on 14 October contact is re-established by *U216* but before dark the escorts drive off *U661*, *U258* and *U599* which are found by HF/DF near the convoy. The 'Leopard' group is directed from ONS.136 to SC.104. In the night first *Montbretia* (Lt-Cdr Söiland) drives off *U661*; *U607* is forced to submerge by *Acanthus* (Lt-Cdr Bruun). *Viscount* (Lt-Cdr Waterhouse) locates *U661* by radar and rams the boat at 26 knots. *Potentilla* (Lt-Cdr Monssen) forces *U254* to submerge and *Eglantine* (Lt-Cdr Voltersvik) damages the boat with depth charges). By day on 15 Oct *U410* (Cdr Sturm) sinks an unknown disabled ship; *Fame* and *Acanthus* drive off *U258* and *U599* and in the afternoon, *Acanthus* attacks *U442* with depth charges. The first Liberator 'H' of No 120 Sqdn RAF bombs *U615* and forces *U437* underwater. Contact is only re-established by *U258* in the morning of 16 Oct but Liberators and Catalinas of No 120 Sqdn RAF and of USN-VP 84 drive off all boats. At mid-day *U353* is located by ASDIC by *Fame* when she attempts an underwater attack: she is compelled by depth charges to surface and is sunk by ramming. In the evening *U571*, which has just arrived in the operational area, approaches the convoy now only escorted by the four Norwegian corvettes, but she is slightly damaged by gunfire and depth charges from *Potentilla*. Before *U258* once again sights the convoy on the morning of 16 Oct the 'Wotan' group is directed to the nearby convoy ON.137 (EG C.4) reported by *U704*.

9-13 Oct   South Pacific
Naval battle off Cape Esperance. On 9 Oct a US convoy (Rear Adm Turner), comprising the transports *McCawley* and *Zeilin* and eight fast transports (APDs) with the 164th Inf Regt, sets out from Nouméa for Guadalcanal. It is escorted by destroyers. To cover the operation there cruise TF 17 (Rear-Adm Murray) with the carrier *Hornet*, four cruisers and six destroyers (see below) 180 nautical miles S of Guadalcanal, a force (Rear-Adm Lee) comprising the battleship *Washington*, two cruisers and five destroyers 50 nautical miles E of Malaita and TF 64 (Rear-Adm Scott) with the cruisers *San Francisco*, *Salt Lake City*, *Boise* and *Helena* and the destroyers *Farenholt*, *Duncan*, *Laffey*, *Buchanan* and *McCalla* near Rennell Island.
On 11 Oct a Japanese transport force (Rear-Adm Joshima) approaches Tassafaronga from Rabaul with the seaplane carriers *Chitose* and *Nisshin* and the destroyers *Akizuki* (Rear-Adm Takama, 4th DD Flotilla), *Asagumo*, *Natsugumo*, *Yamagumo*, *Murakumo* and *Shirayuki* with 728 men of the 2nd Inf Div and heavy artillery and tanks on board. The uneventful disembarkation is to be covered by the 6th Cruiser Sqdn (Rear-Adm Goto†) with the cruisers *Aoba*, *Furutaka*, *Kinugasa* and the destroyers *Fubuki* and *Hatsuyuki* with orders to shell Henderson Airfield. But this force is located on 11 Oct by US air reconnaissance and Rear-Adm Scott is able to bar its way. Shortly before midnight he attacks the Japanese force with the help of radar from a 'crossing the T' position, *Fubuki* and *Furataka* sink; *Aoba* and *Hatsuyuki* are hit and Adm Goto is killed. The US force loses *Duncan*: *Boise* is severely, and *Salt Lake City* and *Farenholt*, lightly, damaged. An attack by the Japanese submarine *I-2* on the destroyer *McCalla* fails in the morning. On the morning of 12 Oct the Japanese destroyers *Murakumo* and *Shirayuki* rescue 400 survivors

but the returning destroyers *Murakumo* and *Natsugumo* are sunk by dive bombers from Henderson Field. In the course of 12 Oct the APDs, *Hovey* and *Southard*, tow four motor torpedo boats to Tulagi and on 13 Oct some 3,000 troops of the convoy are landed near Lunga Point. The destroyers *Gwin*, *Nicholas* and *Sterett* of the escort shell Japanese artillery positions in the NW of the island where on the day before disembarked guns were brought into position. A Japanese attack with 24 and 15 bombers on the ships has no success. On the evening of 13 Oct Turner sets out again.

10 Oct-31 Dec   Black Sea
Soviet ships transport 14527 troops and 3000 to 4000 tons of supplies and ammunition off the Caucasian coast.

11-20 Oct   Mediterranean
The British submarine *P.46/Unruffled* (Lt Stevens) sinks two ships of 2452 tons off Capri and *Utmost* (Lt Coombe) one ship of 2070 tons off Sardinia. In the Aegean *Thrasher* (Lt-Cdr Mackenzie) sinks two ships of 2110 tons and two sailing ships. The Italian submarines *Dandolo* and *Mocenigo* operate S of the Balearics.

11-22 Nov   South Pacific
Naval operations off Guadalcanal (compare 9-13 Oct). On 11 Oct the Japanese Combined Fleet leaves Truk to cover and support the major attack on Guadalcanal planned for 21 Oct. 2nd Fleet (Vice-Adm Kondo) comprises the heavy cruisers *Atago* and *Takao* (4th Cruiser Sqdn), *Maya* and *Myoko* (5th Cruiser Sqdn, Rear-Adm Omori), the battleships *Haruna* and *Kongo* (3rd BB Sqdn, Rear-Adm Kurita) the carriers *Hiyo* and *Junyo* (2nd Carrier Sqdn, Rear-Adm Kakuta) and the 2nd DD Flotilla (Rear-Adm Tanaka) with the cruiser *Isuzu* and the destroyers *Naganami*, *Makinami*, *Takanami*, *Isonami* (31st DD Div), *Umikaze*, *Kawakaze*, *Suzukaze* (24th DD Div), *Kagero*, *Oyashio*, *Hayashio*, *Kuroshio* (15th DD Div) and *Inazuma*. 3rd Fleet (Vice-Adm Nagumo) comprises the carriers *Shokaku*, *Zuiho* and *Zuikaku* (1st Carrier Sqdn), the battleships *Hiyei* and *Kirishima* (11th BB Sqdn, Rear-Adm Abe), the cruisers *Kumano* and *Suzuya* (7th Cruiser Sqdn, Rear-Adm

Nishimura), *Chikuma* and *Tone* (8th Cruiser Sqdn (Rear-Adm Hara) and the 10th DD Flotilla (Rear-Adm Kimura) with the cruiser *Nagara* and the destroyers *Kazegumo, Makigumo, Yugumo, Akigumo* (10th DD Div), *Amatsukaze, Tokitsukaze, Yukikaze, Hatsukaze* (16th DD Div), *Isokaze. Tanikaze, Urakaze,* (17th DD Div), and the attached *Arashi, Maikaze, Nowake* (4th DD Div), *Hamakaze* and *Terutsuki* and a supply force of four tankers and three freighters. A submarine line B with the 1st SM Flotilla, comprising *I-9, I-15, I-21, I-24, I-174* and *I-175*, operates as a vanguard whilst the submarine group A (see 24 Sept- 9 Oct) remains in the Guadalcanal area. *I-7* has reconnoitered Espiritu Santo on 7 Oct with her aircraft and carries out shellings of the island on 14 Oct and 23 Oct.

After the battle of Cape Esperance (see 9-13 Oct) the forces of the Japanese fleet reach the area E of the Solomons on 13 Oct. On 13 Oct Japanese air reconnaissance reports US forces S of Guadalcanal.

In the night 13-14 Oct Rear-Adm Kurita makes a sortie towards Guadalcanal with the battleships *Haruna* and *Kongo* and the cruiser *Isuzu* (Rear-Adm Tanaka) and the destroyers *Takanami, Makinami, Naganami, Hayashio, Oyashio, Kuroshio* and *Kagero* and bombards Henderson Airfield with 918 rounds of 35·6cm shells including about 300 with HE fuses. Of 90 aircraft 48 are destroyed; the remainder are damaged except for one. The attempt by the four US motor torpedo boats *PT46, PT48, PT60* and *PT38*, to attack the force from Tulagi is frustrated by *Naganami.* The Japanese 2nd and 3rd Fleets reach the area of Ndeni on 14 Oct. Japanese air reconnaissance reports US convoys S of Guadalcanal and US air reconnaissance sights Japanese naval forces NE of the Solomons.

In the night 14-15 Oct Vice-Adm Mikawa again bombards Henderson Airfield with 752 rounds of 20·3cm shells from the cruisers *Chokai* and *Kinugasa.* But they have much less effect. At the same time Rear-Adm Takama (4th DD Flotilla) brings six transports with 11 destroyers to Tassafaronga. They

land some 4500 men of the 2nd and 38th Inf Divs there. On the morning of 15 Oct. the *Azumasan Maru, Kyushu Maru* and *Sasago Maru* from among the transports have to be beached after US air attacks and are lost. The destroyer *Samidare* is slightly damaged. In order to bring petrol to Guadalcanal for the aircraft of Henderson Airfield the US transports *Alchiba, Bellatrix* and *Jamestown* and the tug *Vireo* each set out with a lighter in tow, escorted by the destroyers *Meredith* and *Nicholas.* They are recalled when reports are received of Japanese forces in the NE. Only *Meredith* and *Vireo* proceed: they fall victims to an attack force from the Japanese carrier *Zuikaku* on 15 Oct.

In the night 15-16 Oct Rear-Adm Omori makes a sortie towards Guadalcanal with the cruisers *Maya* and *Myoko.* Rear-Adm Tanaka does likewise with the *Isuzu* and the above-mentioned destroyers. They bombard Henderson Field with nearly 1500 rounds of 20·3cm shells.

Whilst the Japanese 2nd and 3rd Fleets replenish from the tanker force N of the Equator on 17-18 Oct, the 3rd and 4th DD Flotillas continue their night supply missions to Guadalcanal. In the process the cruiser *Yura* is slightly damaged on 18 Oct in an attack by the US submarine *Grampus.* On 19 Oct the destroyer *Ayanami* suffers the same fate in an air attack. In US supply operations the destroyers *Aaron Ward* and *Lardner* shell Japanese concentrations on 21 Oct. The Japanese submarine *I-176* (Lt-Cdr Tanabe) torpedoes on 20 Oct the heavy cruiser *Chester* from US TF 64 (Rear-Adm Lee) operating in the area S of Rennell Island. On 23 Oct *I-7* again shells Espiritu Santo.

On the Allied side Vice-Adm Halsey relieves Vice-Adm Ghormley as C-in-C South Pacific on 18 Oct.

11 Oct-10 Dec Western Atlantic
U-boats operate against convoys and independents both sides of Trinidad. *U516* (Cdr Wiebe) and *U160* (Lt-Cdr Lassen) shadow an east-bound convoy on 16 Oct and also *U67* (Lt-Cdr Müller-Stöckheim) and *U332* (Lt-Cdr Liebe (J)) on 17 Oct and 18 Oct but

only *U160* sinks one ship of 730 tons and torpedoes one of 6197 tons. From 1 Nov to 4 Nov *U160* shadows the convoy TAG.18 and in three approaches sinks four ships of 25855 tons. On 5 Nov *U129* (Lt-Cdr Witt) establishes contact with TAG.18 near Aruba and sinks two ships of 14622 tons. At the same time *U160* sinks one ship of 5431 tons from an approaching GAT convoy. Further E *U508* (Lt-Cdr Staats) locates the convoy TAG.19 (?) in the night 5-6 Nov and sinks in two approaches two ships of 12424 tons on 7 Nov. On 12 Nov *U219* misses near Aruba a feeder convoy for TAG.20 which *U163* (Cdr Engelmann) attacks a little later. The first approach is beaten off but in the second the US gunboat *Erie* is hit. She has to be beached and is burnt out. In attacks on independents *U160* also sinks two ships of 12849 tons; *U129* three ships of 17991 tons; *U154* (Cdr Schuch) three ships of 17936 tons; *U505* (Lt-Cdr Zschech) one ship of 7173 tons; *U508* seven ships of 37841 tons; *U163* three ships of 15011 tons and damages one ship of 7127 tons. *U505* is unexpectedly attacked on 10 Nov by an aircraft from Trinidad: the bomb explodes on the barrel of the 3·7cm AA gun and causes heavy damage and losses on the boat. The aircraft crashes in the explosion.

12-31 Oct   Indian Ocean
In the Gulf of Oman the Japanese submarine *I-27* (Cdr Kitamura) sinks one ship of 7174 tons.

13-14 Oct   English Channel
Unsuccessful attempt to bring the auxiliary cruiser *Schiff 45 Komet* (Capt Brocksien†) through the Channel from Le Havre. In spite of a strong escort of minesweepers and the 3rd TB Flotilla (Cdr Wilcke), comprising *T4*, *T10*, *T14* and *T19*, a British force of eight MTBs *MTB49*, *MTB55*, *MTB56*, *MTB84*, *MTB95*, *MTB203*, *MTB229* and *MTB236* and the escort destroyers *Cottesmore*, *Quorn*, *Glaisdale*, *Eskdale* and *Albrighton* are able to intercept the German force near Cape de la Hague when *Schiff 45* is sunk in the morning hours of 14 Oct by two torpedoes from *MTB236* (Sub-Lt Drayson). None of the crew can be rescued. The German torpedo boats and coastal

batteries later damage the destroyer *Brocklesby* from a second group which also includes the destroyers *Fernie*, *Tynedale* and *Krakowiak* (Polish).

13-14 Oct   Mediterranean
The Italian 15th DD Flotilla (Capt Mirti della Valle), comprising *Pigafetta*, *Zeno*, *Da Noli* and *Da Verazzano*, lays N of Cape Bon the mine barrage S.71 with 258 mines and 286 explosive floats.

13-15 Oct   Arctic
Offensive mining operation by the destroyers *Richard Beitzen*, *Friedrich Eckoldt*, *Z27* and *Z30* off Kanin Nos. The Soviet ice-breaker *Mikoyan* runs on this barrage. On 13 Oct *U592* (Lt-Cdr Borm) lays the barrage 'Paul' off the Yugor Strait; the Soviet steamer *Shchors* (3770 tons) is hit on it and damaged.
Whilst *U212* and *U586* reconnoitre near Jan Mayen *U377* (Lt-Cdr Köhler) disembarks the weather detachment 'Nussbaum' on Spitzbergen.

13-14 Oct   Black Sea
The Soviet destroyer *Nezamozhnik* and the patrol ship *Shkval* shell land targets near Sarygol and Kiik-Atlama (121 rounds) in the night 13-14 Oct.

13-28 Oct   Arctic
The British cruiser *Argonaut* and the destroyers *Intrepid* and *Obdurate* proceed from Scapa Flow to Murmansk and back to take hospital equipment and medical personnel and to bring back survivors from PQ.18.

14 Oct   North Sea
The German 6th MTB Flotilla, comprising *S69*, *S71*, *S74* and *S75*, attacks a British convoy off Cromer and torpedoes two freighters of 2905 tons.

15-19 Oct   Norway
In operations by Allied submarines off Norway the Norwegian *Uredd* (Lt Rören) sinks the transport *Libau* (3663 tons). The French *Junon* (Lt Querville) attacks two convoys without success. A Norwegian steamer (726 tons) sinks on a mine barrage laid on 19 Sept by the French *Rubis* (Lt-Cdr Rousselot).

16-29 Oct   North Atlantic
On 16 Oct *U704* (Lt-Cdr Kessler) sights in the southern half of the 'Panther' patrol line the convoy ON.137 (40 ships, EG C.4 with the Canadian destroyers *Restigouche* and *St Croix*

and the corvettes *Amherst, Arvida, Orillia* [Canadian] and *Celandine* [British] with the rescue ship *Bury* equipped with HF/DF). From the 'Panther' group *U609, U658, U132, U71, U571, U438, U402, U89, U381, U84, U454* and from the 'Wotan' group from convoy SC.104 *U615, U258, U618, U216, U356, U410, U599, U662, U437* and *U442* are ordered to the convoy. *U704* sinks one straggler of 4212 tons. *U609* (Lt Rudloff) in bad visibility comes up against the *Celandine* in trying to attack, submerges and is heavily attacked by shallow depth charges, but is able to escape. In a heavy westerly wind the boats do not get up to the convoy on 17-18 Oct. The 'Wotan' group has to start the journey home on 18 Oct and on 19 Oct the operation is broken off. The 'Panther' group goes either to refuel from *U463* or to the new 'Veilchen' patrol line. On the way the boats encounter independents: *U610* (Lt-Cdr Frhr von Freyberg-Eisenberg-Allmendigen) sinks one ship of 5718 tons; *U615* (Lt-Cdr Kapitzky) the large motor ship *Empire Star* (12656 tons); and *U618* (Lt Baberg) one ship of 4772 tons.

From the boats *U441, U621, U602, U563, U757, U753, U301* and *U443* which were not directed to ON.137, the 'Puma' group is formed on 16 Oct. It is sent S to the convoy ONS.138 (EG B.2) reported by the 'B' service. On 22 Oct *U443* (Lt von Puttkamer), the most southerly boat, sights the ON.139 (EG C.2) and, since an operation by the other boats from the stern is hopeless, receives permission to attack. She sinks two ships of 17843 tons. Together with *U301*, she tries to keep contact in order to bring up *U260, U706, U620* and *U662* which are advancing after refuelling from *U463*. But on 25 Oct contact is lost after the boats have shadowed an OS convoy instead of the ON.139 from 23 Oct. After *U441* and *U621* (Lt-Cdr Schünemann) have sighted independents on 22 Oct, of which *U621* sinks one ship of 6113 tons, the 'Puma' group, reinforced up to 26 Oct by *U436, U624, U606, U383* and *U224*, proceeds westwards. On 26 Oct the convoy HX.212 (45 ships, EG A.3 [Cdr Lewis], leader US

coastguard cutter *Campbell*) runs into the patrol line and is reported by *U436* (Lt-Cdr Seibicke) which keeps contact until the next day, while several other boats of the group are driven off. In the night 26-27 Oct first *U436* attacks and with five hits sinks one ship of 10107 tons and damages two others of 7350 tons and 8225 tons respectively. The latter is finished off later by *U606* (Lt Döhler). This boat torpedoes beforehand the whale factory ship *Kosmos II* (16966 tons), which is later finished off by *U606* and *U624*. Attacks by *U621* and *U563* fail. In the course of 28 Oct *U443, U606, U624, U441* and *U436* come up but are repeatedly forced to submerge by the air escort of No 120 Sqdn RAF sent out from Iceland. In the night 28-29 Oct *U224* (Lt Kosbadt) sinks one straggler of 4000 tons and *U624* (Lt Count Soden-Fraunhofen) sinks one ship of 7700 tons from the convoy. On 29 Oct the boats are again driven off by the air escort. On the way to a new station *U436* sinks one ship of 4998 tons and *U575* (Lt-Cdr Heydemann) the transport *Abosso* of 11330 tons.

16-30 Oct   Central Atlantic
A sortie by *U161* and *U126* to the Congo Estuary is unsuccessful apart from the torpedoing of the British cruiser *Phoebe* on 23 Oct by *U161* (Lt-Cdr Achilles).

18 Oct-8 Nov   South West Pacific
In the Malacca Straits the Dutch submarine *O23* (Lt-Cdr Valkenburg) torpedoes one ship of 4621 tons. On the coast of Indo-China and in the Gulf of Siam the US submarines *Thresher* (Lt-Cdr Millican), *Gar* (Lt-Cdr McGregor), *Grenadier* (Lt-Cdr Charr), *Tambor* (Lt-Cdr Ambruster) and *Tautog* (Lt-Cdr Willingham) lay mine barrages. *Tautog* sinks one guard boat of 33 tons by gunfire and *Tambor* one ship of 2461 tons by torpedo. In the area of Davao *Seawolf* (Lt-Cdr Warder) sinks three ships of 13501 tons. Off the Bismarck Archipelago *Gudgeon* (Lt-Cdr Stovall) torpedoes one ship and *Grayback* (Lt-Cdr Stephan) two ships of 6783 tons and 13858 tons respectively. *Grampus* (Lt-Cdr Craig) torpedoes on 18 Oct the Japanese cruiser *Yura* which is slightly damaged.

19-26 Oct Mediterranean

An Italian convoy of four steamers from Naples to Tripoli, which is escorted by the destroyers *Pigafetta, Da Verazzano, Oriani, Gioberti, Da Noli, Ascari* and the torpedo boats *Centauro* and *Sagittario,* is located by a British submarine formation. On 19 Oct *P.37/Unbending* (Lt Stanley) sinks one ship of 4459 tons and the *Da Verazzano.* On 20 Oct *P.42/Unbroken* (Lt Mars) torpedoes one ship of 5397 tons, which is sunk by *P.211/Safari* (Cdr Bryant) when being towed by *Ascari. P.35/ Umbra* (Lt-Cdr Maydon) destroys on 23 Oct one ship of 8670 tons beached after an air torpedo hit and sinks one small vessel of 182 tons. In the Aegean *Taku* sinks one ship of 2238 tons.

19-28 Oct Black Sea

The Soviet cruisers *Krasny Krym* and *Krasny Kavkaz,* the flotilla leader *Kharkov* and the destroyers *Besposhchadny* and *Soobrazitelny* transport the 8th, 9th and 10th Guards Rifle Brigades (12600 troops, 50 guns, 65 mortars and 100 tons of ammunition) from Poti to Tuapse from 20 Oct to 23 Oct. In the night 22-23 Oct four motor torpedo boats of the 1st MTB Flotilla (Lt-Cdr Christiansen) attack the incoming force: two torpedoes explode on the mole, the others go ashore. From 24 Oct to 28 Oct the destroyers *Nezamozhnik, Boiki* and *Besposhchadny* and the patrol ships *Shkval* and *Shtorm* and transports bring more troops and supplies from Sochi to Tuapse.

19 Oct-6 Nov North Atlantic

After the conclusion of the ON.137 operation the boats *U71, U438, U84, U89, U704, U381, U658, U402, U571, U454* and *U132* receive orders to form the 'Veilchen' group E of Newfoundland from 24 Oct. From 27 Oct it is reinforced in the S by *U437* and *U442. U522, U520* and *U521* are stationed S of Newfoundland and *U183* and *U518* on the North-East Coast. On 30 Oct *U658* is sunk in the patrol line by a Hudson of No 145 Sqdn RCAF. A little later *U522* (Lt-Cdr Schneider) sights the convoy SC.107 SW of Cape Race which has just joined up with the feeder convoys from Halifax and Sydney and is met by EG C.4 (Lt-Cdr Piers). The convoy (Commodore Vice-Adm

Watson) consists of 42 ships with an escort of the Canadian destroyer *Restigouche,* the Canadian corvettes *Algoma, Amherst* and *Arvida* and the British *Celandine* and, initially, the destroyers of the Western Local Escort Group *Walker* (British) and *Columbia* (Canadian). There is also the rescue ship *Stockport* with HF/DF. An attack by *U522* on *Columbia* fails. *U520* is sunk in the area of the convoy by a Digby bomber of No 10 Sqdn RCAF. On 31 Oct *U522* is driven off by a destroyer and *U521* by a Hudson of No 145 Sqdn RCAF. As a result of a 'B' service report, the Commander U-boats has moved the 'Veilchen' patrol line to the S with the result that SC.107 is sighted on 1 Nov by *U381* (Lt-Cdr Count von Pückler und Linpurg). Located by HF/DF, the first boats to approach *U381, U704, U402,* are driven off by *Celandine* and *Restigouche.* Shortly after sunset, *U71* is located by radar and forced to submerge. *U89* passes by. After midnight *U402* (Lt-Cdr Frhr von Forstner) attacks for the first time and torpedoes one ship of 7459 tons which is later finished off by *U84* (Lt-Cdr Uphoff). An attack by *U381* on *Restigouche* is out-manoeuvred. In the night *U402* and *U522* with a three-hour interval each attack the convoy twice—almost simultaneously. *U402* sinks three ships of 15270 tons and torpedoes one ship of 4558 tons which is later sunk by *U438* (Lt-Cdr Franzius). *U522* sinks two ships of 11466 tons and torpedoes one ship of 5496 tons which *U521* (Lt-Cdr Bargsten) later sinks. An attack by *U442* (Cdr Hesse) misses the convoy. By day on 2 Nov *U132, U402* and *U522* keep contact with SC.107, whose escort is reinforced by the Canadian corvette *Moosejaw.* In an underwater attack by day *U522* sinks one ship of 3189 tons. In the evening mist sets in, contact is lost and the convoy falls into disorder. The destroyer *Vanessa* is detached from convoy HX.213 and joins SC.107. When visibility improves, *U438, U402, U84, U381, U571, U71, U704, U521* and *U522* in turn establish contact by day on 3 Nov, because the convoy, after several zigzag moves, again proceeds on its general course. An attempt to attack by the boat in contact, *U438*, fails and *Celandine* and *Vanessa* drive off other U-boats detected by HF/DF. Only at mid-day does *U521* attack when she sinks one tanker of 6855 tons. *U522* misses the *Restigouche*. Until evening the escorts drive off all U-boats: only *U438* attacks the detached rescue ship *Stockport*—unsuccessfully. After dark on 4 Nov *U89* (Lt-Cdr Lohmann) comes up and sinks the ship of the convoy commodore, *Jeypore* (5318 tons). Later in the night *U132* (Lt-Cdr Vogelsang) sinks two ships of 11886 tons and torpedoes one ship of 6690 tons which is later sunk by *U442*. *U132* is probably lost in this attack as a result of an explosion in an ammunition steamer. Further attacks by *U71*, *U438* and *U442* have no success. By day on 4 Nov the tugs *Uncas* and *Pessacus*, overcrowded with 240 survivors, and the rescue ship *Stockport*, which is likewise overcrowded, one tanker and the corvettes *Arvida* and *Celandine* are detached to Iceland. The US destroyers *Schenck* and *Leary* and the US coastguard cutter *Ingham* arrive in the late evening from Iceland shortly after *U89* has sunk one more ship of 4640 tons. On the morning of 5 Nov *U84*, *U381*, *U571*, *U454*, *U442*, *U522* and *U521*, which are still operating against the convoy, are driven off by Liberators of No 120 Sqdn RAF which are directed by the HF/DF beams of the command boat *Restigouche*. The operation is broken off on 6 Nov.

21-23 Oct Lake Ladoga
A German attempt to land on the island of Suho in the southern part of Lake Ladoga fails.

22-23 Oct South Pacific
The Australian destroyers *Arunta* and *Stuart* land an assault team of one battalion numbering 640 men on Goodenough Island which has been evacuated by the Japanese.

22-27 Oct South Pacific
Carrier air battle near the Santa Cruz Islands/battle for Guadalcanal. Because of the difficulties in concentrating the Japanese troops of the 17th Army (Lt-Gen Hyakutake) brought to Guadalcanal, the original aim to take Henderson Airfield by 21 Oct is postponed

more than once until 24 Oct. On 22 Oct the Japanese Army units attack but this repeatedly comes to a halt thanks to the resistance of the US marines. When the airfield is prematurely reported to be taken in the night 24-25 Oct, the Combined Fleet which has been at sea since 11 Oct and which has been partly able to replenish its destroyers again on 24 Oct, makes a sortie E of the Solomons to the S in several groups.

NE of Malaita there is the Advance Force (Vice-Adm Kondo) with the heavy cruisers *Atago*, *Takao*, *Myoko* and *Maya*, the battleships *Haruna* and *Kongo* and the 2nd DD Flotilla with the cruiser *Isuzu* and the destroyers *Takanami*, *Makinami*, *Naganami*, *Umikaze*, *Kawakaze*, *Suzukaze*, *Oyashio* and *Kagero* and the 2nd Carrier Sdqn (Rear-Adm Kakuta) with the carrier *Junyo* and the destroyers *Hayashio* and *Kuroshio* stationed further to the W. The second carrier, *Hiyo*, has had to return to Truk with engine trouble on 22 Oct, escorted by the destroyers *Inazuma* and *Isonami*.

SE of the Kondo Force is the Striking Force (Vice-Adm Nagumo) with the carriers *Shokaku*, *Zuikaku* and *Zuiho*, the heavy cruiser *Kumano* and the destroyers *Amatsukaze*, *Tokitsukaze*, *Hatsukaze*, *Yukikaze*, *Arashi*, *Maikaze*, *Hamakaze* and *Teruzuki*. And stationed to the S is the Vanguard Group (Rear-Adm Abe) with the battleships *Hiyei* and *Kirishima,* the heavy cruisers *Tone*, *Chikuma* and *Suzuya* and the 10th DD Flotilla with the cruiser *Nagara* and the destroyers *Akigumo*, *Yugumo*, *Makigumo*, *Kazegumo*, *Tanikaze*, *Urakaze* and *Isokaze*. In addition, the 4th DD Flotilla (Rear-Adm Takama) sets out from Shortland with the transport force with the cruiser *Yura*, the new destroyer leader *Akizuki* and the destroyers *Harusame*, *Yudachi*, *Murasame* and *Samidare* (2nd DD Div) and a bombardment force with the destroyers *Akatsuki*, *Ikazuchi* and *Shiratsuyu*. The latter, as they advance to a first daylight bombardment of Lunga Point, encounter the US APDS *Trever* and *Zane* coming from Tulagi. The APDs escape through the Sealark Channel after a short engagement but the Japanese destroyers then sink the tug *Seminole* and the harbour craft *YP-284* off Lunga. In the process *Akatsuki* is hit by a coastal battery. Dive-bombers flown off from Henderson Field obtain hits on the cruiser *Yura* which is coming up to shell and on the *Akatsuki*. The former has to be abandoned in the afternoon after further attacks by B-17 bombers and dive bombers. The four Japanese carriers have 87 fighters, 68 dive bombers and 57 torpedo aircraft. The 11th Air Fleet (Vice-Adm Kusaka), stationed on land on the Solomons and in the area of Rabaul, has about 220 aircraft at the beginning of the operations, but in the period 16-25 Oct these sustain considerable losses at the hands of the new fighters flown into Henderson Field. The Japanese shore-based reconnaissance repeatedly locates on 21 Oct, 23 Oct and 24 Oct US TF 64 (Rear-Adm Lee), comprising the battleship *Washington*, the cruisers *San Francisco* (Rear-Adm Scott), *Atlanta* and *Helena* and the destroyers *Aaron Ward, Lansdowne, Lardner, McCalla, Benham* and *Fletcher*. But it is not able to find the US carriers.

TF 61 (Rear-Adm Kinkaid) which sets out from Pearl Harbour on 16 Oct with the carrier *Enterprise*, the battleship *South Dakota*, the cruisers *Portland* (Rear-Adm Tisdale) and *San Juan* and Desron 5 with the destroyers *Porter, Mahan, Cushing, Preston, Smith, Maury* and *Conyngham* joins up on 24 Oct 273 nautical miles NE of Espiritu Santo with TF 17 (Rear-Adm Murray), comprising the carrier *Hornet*, the cruisers *Northampton* (Rear-Adm Good), *Pensacola, San Diego* and *Juneau* and the destroyers *Morris, Anderson, Hughes, Mustin, Russell* and *Barton*. Both groups go to meet the Japanese Vanguard Group reported on 23 Oct by a Catalina flying boat of TF 63 (Rear-Adm Fitch—shore based air units). On 25 Oct Catalina flying boats report, in addition to the Vanguard Group, the Japanese carrier force behind it. Rear-Adm Fitch deploys against them B-17 bombers and Catalinas temporarily equipped as torpedo carriers. They secure near-misses by the *Kirishima, Zuikaku* and *Isokaze*.

But reconnaissance aircraft from the *Enterprise* and the Japanese carriers do not find their targets. Aircraft of the *Junyo* carry out a raid on US positions near Lunga Point. Early on 26 Oct a reconnaissance aircraft from the Japanese cruiser *Tone* sights the US carrier forces. The three carriers *Shokaku, Zuiho* and *Zuikaku* fly off 65 and 44 aircraft in two waves, followed by 29 planes from the *Junyo*, which tries to close up to the Nagumo force. About the same time several of the 16 dive bombers from the *Enterprise*. flown off for armed reconnaissance, sight the Abe and Nagumo forces and obtain two hits on the *Zuiho* which can no longer operate aircraft but which remains manoeuvrable. When this is reported, the *Enterprise* and *Hornet* fly off three attack groups totalling 73 aircraft. Although the 38 aircraft of the US carriers' fighter cover shoot down almost half the Japanese attackers, the latter, operating in several waves, obtain four bomb and two torpedo hits on the *Hornet* (Capt Moran). Two other aircraft crash onto the ship which is halted. The second wave concentrates on the *Enterprise* group, as does the *Junyo* force. They obtain two hits and one near-miss on the *Enterprise*, but the ship avoids all the torpedoes and, despite damage, remains substantially operational. The *South Dakota, San Juan* and *Smith* are damaged by bomb hits and their own AA fire. *Portland* remains operational in spite of three torpedoes which fail to detonate. The *Hornet* is damaged by another torpedo from the last Japanese aircraft and the *Hughes* is lightly damaged.

Of the two attack groups from the *Hornet* the first meanwhile attacks the Japanese carrier force and obtains three bomb hits on the *Shokaku* (Adm Nagumo has later to transfer to the destroyer *Arashi*). The *Suzuya* out-manoeuvres torpedoes. The second group, with the *Enterprise* group, attacks the Abe force and obtains five heavy hits on the *Chikuma*. The *Tone* and *Kirishima* just avoid torpedo and bomb hits respectively.

In the evening the Abe force (without

Chikuma) and Kondo force make a sortie to the SE in the direction of the stricken US ships, while the carriers retire to the N. The US forces have to retire to the SE in face of the advancing Japanese heavy ships. The destroyers *Mustin* and *Anderson*, each using eight torpedoes with three and six hits respectively and 430 rounds of 5in shells, are unable to sink the wreck of the abandoned *Hornet*. Because it is impossible to tow her away, the Japanese destroyers *Akigumo* and *Makigumo* finish the ship off with torpedoes. A night Catalina torpedo flying boat damages the destroyer *Teruzuki*.

Of the Japanese submarine groups A and B (see 24 Sept-9 Oct) deployed in support of the operations, *I-21* (Cdr* Matsumura) attacks the *Hornet* group during the carrier air battle and sinks the destroyer *Porter*. On 27 Oct *I-15* (Cdr* Ishikawa) just misses Adm Lee's flagship, the battleship *Washington*. On the same day the battleship *South Dakota* and the destroyer *Mahan* suffer damage in a collision in trying to avoid an attack by another Japanese submarine.

The battle of Santa Cruz ends with a tactical victory for the Japanese, but they are unable to exploit it because the Army's offensive by land on Guadalcanal has failed. The remaining carrier aircraft are no longer sufficient to eliminate Henderson Field; in addition, the Fleet has to return to Truk because of fuel shortages. It is therefore not possible to free the route for the transports from Rabaul to Guadalcanal.

23 Oct   Mediterranean
Beginning of a British offensive on the Alamein front.

23-31 Oct   North Atlantic
From 23 Oct *U510*, *U509*, *U572*, *U134*, *U409*, *U203*, *U604* and *U659* proceed, as the 'Streitaxt' group, in line abreast to the S, west of Africa. On 25 Oct *U510* sights one steamer, *U659* two escorts and *U203* one escorted tanker (7705 tons) which is shadowed by *U134* on 27 Oct and sunk by *U604* (Lt-Cdr Höltring). On the morning of 27 Oct *U409* (Lt Massmann) reports the convoy SL.125 (37 ships and four corvettes including the British *Petunia* [Lt-Cdr Rayner]]. In the eve-

ning *U203*, *U509* and *U659* are brought up. They attack but only *U509* (Lt Witte) sinks two ships of 14099 tons. On 28 Oct *U203* (Lt Kottmann) keeps contact and brings up *U409*, *U659*, *U509*, *U510* and *U604*. *U103* and *U440*, coming from the N, are also directed to the scene. After a miss in the morning *U509* torpedoes in the evening one ship of 5283 tons which is later sunk by *U203*. On 29 Oct *U134* (Lt-Cdr Schendel) keeps contact from mid-day and brings up *U103*, *U510*, *U509* and *U604*. In the night *U509* attacks twice and each time torpedoes one ship of 4772 tons and 7131 tons respectively. Both receive finishing-off hits from *U659* (Lt-Cdr Stock); the second ship is sunk by torpedo and gunfire from *U203*. *U409* sinks one ship of 7519 tons and in the morning *U509* misses one of the corvettes. On 30 Oct *U509* and *U604* continually keep contact and bring all except three boats up. In the night *U604* in two attacks sinks the transport *President Doumer* (11898 tons) and one ship of 3642 tons; *U659* one ship of 6373 tons; *U409* one ship of 6405 tons; and *U510* (Cdr Neitzel) torpedoes one ship of 5681 tons. *U103* (Lt Janssen) misses one corvette and two ships of the scattered convoy. *U659* is damaged by depth charges. On 31 Oct *U509* and *U604* keep contact with the remainder but towards evening all boats are driven off when air escort is provided and there is reinforced sea escort. As this operation involves the U-boats in the area W of Morocco and Gibraltar, the simultaneous 'Torch' convoys reach their destinations unmolested by U-boats.

25 Oct-14 Nov   South Atlantic
The Italian submarines *Da Vinci* (Lt-Cdr Gazzana-Priaroggia) operates until 30 Oct W of the Cape Verde Islands and then off the NE coast of Brazil. She sinks four ships of 26042 tons from 2 Nov to 11 Nov. On 3 Nov the Dutch steamer *Frans Hals* escapes when she forces the submarine to submerge with gunfire after a torpedo miss.

28-30 Oct   Mediterranean
British Force H with the carrier *Furious*, the cruisers *Aurora* and *Charybdis* and eight destroyers proceeds from

Gibraltar into the area S of the Balearics and flies off 29 Spitfire fighters to Malta. The Italian submarines *Emo*, *Brin*, *Corallo*, *Turchese*, *Topazio* and *Axum* S of the Balearics and *Porfido*, *Nichelio*, *Asteria* and *Argo* off Cape Bon sight nothing. At the end of October and the beginning of November the fast minelayer *Welshman* and the submarines *Parthian*, *Clyde*, *Traveller* and *Thrasher* have again to be employed to bring aviation petrol, food and ammunition to Malta. The Italian submarines *Micca*, *Sciesa*, *Bragadino*, *Narvalo*, *Atropo* and *Zoea* transport fuel and ammunition to North Africa.

28 Oct-8 Nov   South Pacific
Continuation of the supply operations for Guadalcanal.
The Japanese 8th Fleet (Vice-Adm Mikawa) continues the transport of supplies at first with the 3rd DD Flotilla (Rear-Adm Hashimoto), comprising the cruiser *Sendai* and destroyers *Shirayuki*, *Hatsuyuki*, *Uranami*, *Shikinami* and *Ayanami*, and the 4th DD Flotilla (Rear-Adm Takama) comprising the destroyers *Murasame*, *Yudachi*, *Harusame*, *Samidare*, *Asagumo*, *Yugure*, *Shiratsuyu* and *Shigure*. From 5 Nov they are relieved by the 2nd DD Flotilla (Rear-Adm Tanaka), comprising the cruiser *Isuzu* and the destroyers *Hayashio*, *Oyashio*, *Kagero*, *Umikaze*, *Kawakaze*, *Suzukaze*, *Naganami*, *Makinami* and *Takanami*. These ships, together with the cruiser *Tenryu* and the destroyers *Arashio*, *Asashio*, *Michishio*, *Amagiri* and *Mochizuki*, which are with the 8th Fleet, undertake, in all, two cruiser and 65 destroyer missions in the course of which there are repeated air attacks and engagements with US PT boats from Tulagi. US TG 62.4 (Rear-Adm Scott) with the cruiser *Atlanta* and the destroyers *Aaron Ward*, *Benham*, *Fletcher* and *Lardner* brings the transports *Alchiba* and *Fuller* with two 155mm batteries to Guadalcanal and from 30-31 Oct supports the attack of the 1st Marine Div over the Matanikau River to the W. On 2-3 Nov the attack is supported by the destroyers *Conyngham* and *Shaw* with 803 rounds of 5in shells and reaches Point Cruz on 3 Nov. But

in the same night a Japanese force of one cruiser, three destroyers and one transport lands 1500 men of the 230th Inf Regt near Koli Point E of the US bridgehead, while other units of the 'Tokyo Express' land elements of the 228th Inf Regt in the W near Kokumbona. The 1st Marine Div temporarily halts its attack towards the W and regroups forces for a counter-attack in the E. Simultaneously, TG 67.4 (Rear-Adm Callaghan) arrives off Lunga Point on 4 Nov and disembarks the 8th Marine Inf Regt (2nd Div) as reinforcement. The cruisers *Helena* and *San Francisco* with the destroyer *Sterett* from the covering forces shell the Japanese troops which have landed near Koli Point. The latter are wiped out by 9 Nov in the counter-attack.
A second US group, consisting of the transports *Neville*, *Heywood* and *Fomalhaut* and the destroyer transports *McKean* and *Manley*, lands on 4 Nov near Aola Bay on the E coast of Guadalcanal 1700 men of the 147th Inf Regt and a Marine Raider Battalion, as well as 500 Seabees to construct an airfield. But this proves impossible because of the difficulties of the terrain.
On 7 Nov the Japanese 2nd DD Flotilla under Capt Sato with the destroyers *Oyashio*, *Kagero*, *Umikaze*, *Kawakaze*, *Suzukaze*, *Naganami*, *Makinami*, *Takanami* and *Yugumo*, *Makigumo* and *Kazegumo* from the 10th DD Div sets out from Shortland for Guadalcanal with an advance party of 1300 men from the 38th Inf Div. On the way they are attacked by dive bombers from Henderson Field which damage *Naganami* and *Takanami*. A successful disembarkation is made in the night 7-8 Nov. In the following night (8-9 Nov) the destroyers *Asashio*, *Arashio*, *Michishio*, *Amagiri* and *Mochizuki* also arrive with reinforcements and supplies. The US motor torpedo boats *PT61*, *PT39* and *PT37* attack from Tulagi and obtain a light torpedo hit on *Mochizuki*.
The Japanese deploy the SM Group A (*I-16*, *I-20* and *I-24*) against the US supply transports. *I-20* (Cdr* Yoshimura) torpedoes the transport *Majaba* (2227 tons) on 7 Nov and evades pursuit by the destroyers *Lansdowne*

and *Lardner*, the first of which has landed 90 tons of ammunition.

29 Oct-4 Nov Mediterranean
In the nights 29-30 Oct and 3-4 Nov the Italian destroyers *Pigafetta* (Captain Del Minio), *Da Noli*, *Zeno* and the torpedo boat *Castelfidardo* lay the mine barrages S.72 and S.73 with 388 and 338 mines respectively N of Cape Bon.

29 Oct-9 Nov Arctic
At the wish of the Russians 13 single freighters sail on 29 Oct from Reykjavik to Murmansk and Archangel with 200 nautical miles between them and five independents return from Soviet harbours to Iceland. Of the eastward-bound ships six are lost. On 2 Nov *U586* (Lt-Cdr v. d. Esch) sinks the *Empire Gilbert* (6640 tons). On 4 Nov the first ships are located by K.Fl.Gr. 406. The Soviet *Dekabrist* (7363 tons) is sunk by Ju 88s of I/K.G.30 sent to the scene, while II/K.G.30 damages two ships. Of them the *William Clark* (7176 tons) is finished off by *U354* (Lt-Cdr Herbschleb) and the *Chulmleigh* (5445 tons) by one torpedo from *U625* (Lt Benker) on 16 Nov—having been beached by another bomb hit on 5 Nov on the S Cape of Spitzbergen. *U625* also sinks the *Empire Sky* (7455 tons). The heavy cruiser *Admiral Hipper* (Capt Hartmann with the Commander Cruisers, Vice-Adm Kummetz, on board) and the 5th DD Flotilla (Capt Schemmel), comprising *Z27*, *Z30*, *Friedrich Eckoldt* and *Richard Beitzen*, are also used against the traffic on 5 Nov. K.G.30 flies reconnaissance flights. On 7 Nov the westward-bound Soviet tanker *Donbass* (7925 tons) is located and sunk by *Z27*. Likewise the Soviet submarine-chaser *BO-78*.

30 Oct-15 Dec South Atlantic
Between St Paul and the Brazilian coast *U174* (Cdr Thilo) sinks five ships of 30813 tons; *U128* (Lt-Cdr Heyse) three ships of 15571 tons; and *U172* (Lt-Cdr Emmermann) and *U159* (Lt-Cdr Witte), which are returning from South Africa, two ships of 11994 tons and three ships of 16497 tons respectively.

1-8 Nov North Atlantic
The 'Natter' group is formed W of Ireland from the U-boats *U224*, *U383*, *U436*, *U606*, *U624* coming from HX.212 and from the newly-arrived *U98*. By 4 Nov *U566*, *U613*, *U92*, *U564*, *U563* and the newly-replenished *U753* are added to it. On 4 Nov *U92* (Lt Oelrich) sights the convoy ON.143 (EG C.1) but contact is soon lost and is not re-established until 6 Nov because most of the boats have not yet reached their position. On 7 Nov *U566* (Lt Remus) and *U613* (Lt-Cdr Köppe) each sink a straggler of 4252 tons. On 8 Nov the boats with adequate fuel supplies are sent to the area W of Gibraltar, those short of fuel to the 'Kreuzotter' group.

1 Nov-16 Dec South Africa
After *U178* has sunk the transport *Duchess of Atholl* (20119 tons) on the way on 10 Oct, three type IX-D2 boats operate as a second wave off South Africa. *U178* (Capt Ibbeken) sinks five ships of 26978 tons and damages one ship of 6348 tons; *U177* (Lt-Cdr Gysae) sinks eight ships of 49371 tons, and *U181* (Lt-Cdr Lüth) sinks twelve ships of 58431 tons. In addition, the Italian submarine *Cagni* (Cdr* Liannazza), coming from the Mediterranean, sinks one ship on the way out and another off South Africa, totalling 5840 tons.

3-7 Nov Mediterranean
The German 3rd MTB Flotilla (Lt-Cdr Kemnade) lays off Malta the barrages MT 25-27 with 108 UMB mines, 18 protection and 29 explosive floats.

4-8 Nov Atlantic
In preparation for operation 'Torch' the US submarines *Shad*, *Gunnel*, *Herring*, *Barb* and *Blackfish* reconnoitre off the Moroccan harbours of Rabat, Fedala, Casablanca, Safi and off Dakar. *Herring* (Lt-Cdr Johnson) sinks the French steamer *Ville du Havre* (5083 tons) on 8 Nov. The submarines are then deployed in the Bay of Biscay from British bases. First operation with *Gurnard* takes place in early December.

4-19 Nov Western Atlantic
U608 (Lt Struckmeier), operating off New York, sinks one ship of 5621 tons and lays an unsuccessful mine barrage on 10 Nov.

5-15 Nov Mediterranean
All available German U-boats are stationed in the area W of the line

Balearics/Algiers in the western Mediterranean as a precaution against the heavy concentrations of ships observed in Gibraltar. They include *U73*, *U77*, *U81*, *U205*, *U331*, *U431*, *U458*, *U561*, *U565*, *U593*, *U605* and *U660* from the Mediterranean boats as well as *U595*, *U407*, *U617*, *U596*, *U755*, *U259* and *U380* which have just come from the Atlantic. In the area of Algiers and to the E the Italian boats *Axum*, *Topazio*, *Argo*, *Platino*, *Mocenigo*, *Emo*, *Nichelio*, *Asteria*, *Porfido*, *Velella*, *Brin*, *Dandolo*, *Argento*, *Acciaio*, *Bronzo*, *Turchese*, *Corallo*, *Aradam*, *Diaspro*, *Alagi* and *Avorio* are deployed. They achieve the following successes: on 7 Nov *U205* (Lt-Cdr Reschke) probably torpedoes the US transport *Thomas Stone* (9255 tons) which is later beached off Algiers; on 10 Nov *U431* (Lt-Cdr Dommes) sinks the British destroyer *Martin* and *U81* (Lt-Cdr Guggenberger) the transport *Garlinge* (2012 tons); on 11 Nov *U380* (Lt-Cdr Röther) the transport *Nieuw Zeeland* (11069 tons); *U407* (Lt-Cdr Brüller) the transport *Viceroy of India* (19627 tons) and *U595* (Lt-Cdr J. Quaet-Faslem) the transport *Browning* (5332 tons). On 12 Nov *U77* (Lt-Cdr Otto Hartmann) torpedoes the British sloop *Stork* and the Italian submarine *Argo* (Lt-Cdr Gigli) attacks in the roads of Bougie the transports *Awatea* and *Cathay*, respectively damaged by mines and air attacks, and damages them again. On 13 Nov *U431* sinks the Dutch destroyer *Isaac Sweers* and *U73* (Lt-Deckert) the transport *Lalande* (7453 tons). The Italian submarine *Platino* (Lt-Cdr Rigoli) torpedoes the British transport *Narkunda* (16632 tons), already damaged in an air attack. On 14 Nov *U81* sinks the transport *Maron* (6487 tons) and on 15 Nov the Italian submarine *Ascianghi* (Lt-Cdr Erler) sinks the minesweeper *Algerine* off Bougie. Lost in these operations as a result of enemy action; *Emo*, *U660*, *U605*. *U595*, *U259* and *U331*.

5-17 Nov   Pacific
The US submarine *Haddock* (Lt-Cdr Taylor) sinks three ships of 10413 tons off Japan and torpedoes two more of 8560 tons.

5-20 Nov   Baltic
Because it begins to ice up the Soviet submarines have to return from the Baltic to Lavansaari through the mine barrages of the Gulf of Finland. *D-2*, *Shch-406*, *Shch-307*, *Shch-303*, *S-12* and *L-3* are in turn met by minesweeper forces, patrol cutters and torpedo cutters with air support. *M-96* operates in November in the Gulf of Finland as the last boat to set out. In the escort operations and submarine escorts the following Soviet vessels are lost between May and November 1942: the minesweepers *T-204/Fugas*, *Udarnik*, *T-48*, the patrol cutters *MO-211*, *MO-212*, *MO-308* and *MO-225*.

7-9 Nov   Mediterranean
In the night 7-8 Nov the new Italian cruiser *Attilio Regolo* with the destroyers *Pigafetta* (Rear-Adm Gasparri), *Ascari*, *Da Noli*, *Mitragliere* and *Zeno* lay the barrage S.8 with 241 mines E of Cape Bon, whilst, at the same time, the destroyer *Corazziere* lays the explosive float barrage St. 2. On the return the cruiser *Regolo* is torpedoed by the British submarine *Unruffled* (Lt Stevens) W of Sicily, but is taken in tow by the tug *Polifemo*, escorted by the torpedo boats *Cigno*, *Lince* and *Abba*. An attack by the British submarine *United* misses the towing convoy.

8 Nov   North Africa
Operation 'Torch': Allied landing in French North Africa.
Western Task Force (landing on the West Coast of Morocco between Safi and Mehedia with the main target Casablanca): Rear Adm-Hewitt (USN) —Maj-Gen Patton (USA). Naval forces: the battleships *Massachusetts* and *Texas*, the aircraft carrier *Ranger*, the escort carriers *Sangamon*, *Chenango*, *Suwanee* and *Santee*, the heavy cruisers *Wichita*, *Tuscaloosa* and *Augusta*, the light cruisers *Savannah*, *Brooklyn*, *Cleveland* and *Philadelphia*, 38 destroyers, three minelayers, eight minesweepers, one flying boat tender, four submarines, 23 troop transports, eight supply transports and five tankers.
Land forces: the 2nd US Armoured Div, the 3rd US Inf Div, two-thirds of the US 9th Inf Div, comprising 34305 troops, 54 medium and 198 light tanks.
Centre Task Force (landing in the area of Oran): Commodore Troubridge (RN) —Maj-Gen Fredendall (USA).
Naval forces: the headquarters ship

T

Largs, the escort carriers *Biter* and *Dasher,* the light cruisers *Aurora* and *Jamaica,* the AA cruiser *Delhi,* one AA ship, 13 destroyers, four sloops, six corvettes, eight minesweepers, eight trawlers, ten launches, two submarines, 19 landing ships and 28 supply transports.

Land forces: the 1st US Inf Div, half of the US Armoured Div, comprising 39000 troops.

Eastern Task Force (landings in the area of Algiers): Rear-Adm Burrough (RN)—Maj-Gen Ryder (USA).

Naval forces: the headquarters ship *Bulolo,* the monitor *Roberts,* three AA ships, eight destroyers, three sloops, six corvettes, seven minesweepers, eight trawlers, eight launches, three submarines, 17 landing ships, 16 supply transports and Force O (Rear-Adm Harcourt) with the carrier *Argus,* the escort carrier *Avenger,* the light cruisers *Sheffield, Scylla* and *Charybdis* and five destroyers.

Land forces: the 34th US Inf Div, one-third of the 9th US Inf Div, one-half of the 1st US Armoured Div, 78th British Inf Div, comprising 33000 troops.

The operations in the Mediterranean are covered by Force H (Vice-Adm Syfret): the battleships *Duke of York, Nelson* and *Rodney,* the battlecruiser *Renown,* the carriers *Victorious* (Rear-Adm Lyster), *Formidable* and *Furious,* the light cruisers *Argonaut, Bermuda* and *Sirius* and 17 destroyers.

The French forces put up considerable resistance in places to the Allied landing fleets. Attempts by the sloops *Walney* and *Hartland* to enter the harbour of Oran (Naval Commander: Vice-Adm Rioult) to prevent the French ships scuttling themselves fail, as does a similar operation in Algiers (HQ: Adm Darlan, Naval Commander: Vice-Adm Leclerc) with the destroyers *Broke* and *Malcolm.* Apart from *Malcolm* the participating ships are sunk by French coastal artillery and warships. The submarines *Caiman* and *Marsouin* break out of Algiers for Toulon. In the fighting for Oran the French Navy loses the flotilla leader *Epervier* (Cdr* Laurin), the destroyers *Tornade, Tramontane* and *Typhon,* the mine-

sweeper *La Surprise* and, in addition to smaller vessels, the submarines *Actéon, Ariane, Argonaute, Cérès, Diane* and *Pallas.* The submarine *Fresnel* attacks the cruiser *Southampton* without success and is able to escape to Toulon. In Casablanca (Naval Commander: Vice-Adm Michelier) too, the French Navy resists strongly. The unfinished battleship *Jean Bart* is severely damaged by shelling and air attacks. Attempts by Rear-Adm de Lafond to attack the Western Task Force with the cruiser *Primauguet* (Capt Mercier†), the flotilla leaders *Albatros* and *Milan* and the destroyers *Boulonnais, Brestois, Fougueux* and *Frondeur* fail. All ships are lost or have to be beached. *Albatros* is severely damaged. Of the 11 submarines present in Casablanca, *Amazone* attacks the *Brooklyn* on 8 Nov, *Le Tonnant* the *Ranger, Meduse* and *Antiope* the *Massachusetts* and *Tuscaloosa* on 10 Nov, but all torpedoes are narrowly evaded. *Amphitrite, La Sibylle, Méduse, Oréade, La Psyché, Sidi Ferruch* and *Le Conquérant* are lost. *Le Tonnant* scuttles herself off Cadiz, *Amazone* and *Antiope* go to Dakar and the eleventh boat, *Orphée,* returns to Casablanca after the fighting.

The French Navy loses, in all, 462 dead, the Army 326 and the Air Force 15. In addition there are over 1000 wounded.

For successes by German and Italian submarines against the landing forces see 5-15 Nov (Mediterranean) and 8-26 Nov (Central Atlantic).

German bombers and torpedo aircraft damage and sink from 8 Nov to 14 Nov off the North African coast the troop transports *Awatea* (13482 tons) and *Cathay* (15225 tons), the landing ship *Karanja* (9891 tons), the transports *Glenfinlas* (7572 tons) and *Leedstown* (9135 tons) and the gunboat *Ibis.* The carrier *Argus* is hit by bombs and the monitor *Roberts* severely damaged.

8-15 Nov   South Pacific
Japanese and US forces seek a decision in the battle for Guadalcanal. On 8 Nov US TG 67.1 (Rear-Adm Turner) sets out from Nouméa with the transports *McCawley, President Jackson, President Adams* and *Crescent City,* on which

6000 troops of the reinforced 182nd Inf Regt are embarked. Escort is provided by the cruisers *Pensacola* and *Portland* and the destroyers *Barton, Monssen,* and *O'Bannon* (from TG 67.4). It is followed on 9 Nov from Espiritu Santo by TG 62.4 (Rear-Adm Scott) with the cruiser *Atlanta* and the destroyers *Aaron Ward, Fletcher, Lardner* and *McCalla* and the transports *Zeilin, Libra* and *Betelgeuse* with some 1000 troops and a construction battalion. TG 67.4 (Rear-Adm Callaghan) puts out to sea from Espiritu Santo as a covering force with the cruisers *San Francisco, Helena* and *Juneau* and the destroyers *Cushing, Laffey, Sterett, Buchanan, Shaw, Gwin* and *Preston.* It joins the Turner Group on 11 Nov. In the night 11-12 Nov TF 16 (Rear-Adm Kinkaid) also puts to sea from Nouméa as a covering group, consisting of the carrier *Enterprise,* the cruisers *Northampton* and *San Diego* and the destroyers *Clark, Anderson, Hughes, Morris, Austin* and *Russell,* together with TF 64 (Rear-Adm Lee), comprising the battleships *South Dakota* and *Washington* and the destroyers *Benham* and *Walke.*

On the Japanese side the destroyers *Makinami, Suzukaze, Yugumo, Makigumo* and *Kazegumo* bring another 600 men and the Commander of the Japanese 38th Inf Div, Lt-Gen Sano, to Guadalcanal in the night 10-11 Nov. Air and PT boats attacks are repelled.

To protect the Japanese operation the submarines of Group D (*I-122, I-175, I-172* and *Ro34,* are concentrated in the approaches to the N coast of Guadalcanal. *I-172* is sunk on 10 Nov by the US minesweeper *Southard.* On 11 Nov the submarines *I-7, I-9, I-21* and *I-31* fly off their aircraft to reconnoitre over Vanikoro/Santa Cruz, Espiritu Santo, Nouméa and Suva/Fiji. In the process *I-21* (Cdr* Matsumura) sinks one transport of 7176 tons. On the US side 24 submarines are distributed in the area of the Solomons. On the Japanese side the 2nd Fleet (Vice-Adm Kondo) sets out from Truk on 9 Nov in order to carry out the following plan in co-operation with the 8th Fleet (Vice-Adm Mikawa) operating

from Rabaul and Shortland: in the night 12-13 Nov Vice-Adm Abe is to shell Henderson Airfield with the battleships *Hiyei* and *Kirishima* (11th BB Sqdn), screened by the 10th DD Flotilla (Rear-Adm Kimura), comprising the cruiser *Nagara* and the destroyers *Yukikaze* and *Amatsukaze,* (16th DD Div), *Akatsuki, Ikazuchi* and *Inazuma* (6th DD Div) and *Teruzuki* and the 4th DD Flotilla (Rear-Adm Takama) with the destroyers *Asagumo, Murasame, Samidare, Yudachi* and *Harusame* (2nd DD Div), *Shigure, Shiratsuyu* and *Yugure* (27th DD Div). In the following night (13 -14 Nov) the shelling is to be repeated by a force (Rear-Adm Nishimura) consisting of the cruisers *Maya* and *Suzuya,* screened by the light cruiser *Tenryu* with the destroyers *Kazegumo, Makigumo, Yugumo* (10th DD Div) and *Michishio.* Vice-Adm Mikawa is to cover this operation with the cruisers *Chokai, Isuzu* and *Kinugasa* and the destroyers *Arashio* and *Asashio* (8th DD Div). At the same time Rear-Adm Tanaka with the 2nd DD Flotilla, comprising the destroyers *Hayashio, Kagero, Oyashio* (15th DD Div), *Kawakaze, Suzukaze, Umikaze* (24th DD Div), *Makinami, Naganami, Takanami* (31st DD Div) and *Amagiri* and *Mochizuki* is to land 11 large transports with the bulk of the 38th Inf Div and its heavy equipment near Cape Esperance and Kokumbona. The main body of the 2nd Fleet (Vice-Adm Kondo) comprising the cruisers *Atago* (F) and *Takao,* the battleships *Kongo* (Vice-Adm Kurita, 3rd BB Sqdn) and *Haruna,* the carriers *Junyo* (Rear-Adm Kakuta, 2nd Carrier Sqdn) and *Hiyo,* the cruisers *Tone* and *Sendai* (Rear-Adm Hashimoto, 3rd DD Flotilla) and the destroyers *Hatsuyuki, Shirayuki* (11th DD Div), *Uranami, Shikinami* and *Ayanami* (19th DD Div) take up a covering position NE of the Solomons.

On 11 Nov Rear-Adm Scott arrives with his TG 62.4 off Lunga Point and begins at once the disembarkation from the three transports. In an attack by 12 Japanese aircraft from the *Hiyo,* the transport *Zeilin* is damaged and detached with the destroyer *Lardner.* A Japanese bomber force from the 11th

Air Fleet (Vice-Adm Kusaka) from Rabaul attacks Henderson Field. On the morning of 12 Nov the transports of Rear-Adm Turner and the covering force of Rear-Adm Callaghan arrive off Guadalcanal and begin to disembark. The cruiser *Portland* is detached to TF 16 and the destroyers *Gwin* and *Preston* to TF 64. In an air attack by bombers from Rabaul the destroyer *Buchanan* is damaged by her own AA and the cruiser *San Francisco* by a crashing Japanese aircraft. When air reconnaissance reports come in about the approaching Japanese naval forces, Adm Turner breaks off the disembarkation and withdraws with the transports escorted by the destroyers *Buchanan, McCalla* and *Shaw* and the minesweepers *Hovey* and *Southard*. US TG 67.4 in the order the destroyers *Cushing, Laffey, Sterett, O'Bannon* and the cruisers *San Francisco* (Rear-Adm Callaghan), *Portland, Helena,* and *Atlanta* (Rear-Adm Scott) and the destroyers *Aaron Ward, Barton, Monssen* and *Fletcher* tries to intercept the approaching Japanese bombardment force of Vice-Adm Abe (see above) between Savo Island and Lunga Point. Abe, who has left the three destroyers of the 27th DD Div behind, as defence to the westwards, comes up against Callaghan's force in the dark on 13 Nov. In fierce engagements, at very short range, the US force is broken up. Both US admirals perish in the first minutes. *Atlanta* (Capt S. P. Jenkins), *Laffey, Barton, Monssen* and *Cushing* sink after gun and torpedo hits; *San Francisco* (Capt Cassin Young†), *Juno, Portland, Aaron Ward* and *Sterett* are badly damaged. On the Japanese side the *Akatsuki* sinks and the disabled *Yudachi* is sunk in the morning by the *Portland*. The *Hiyei* receives more than 50 shell hits and sinks in the morning after receiving two air torpedo hits from aircraft of the *Enterprise* operating S of Guadalcanal and a bomb hit from a B 17/Fortress, the crew having been saved. Of the Japanese submarines, *I-17* and *I-26* (Cdr* Yokota), the latter attacks the returning US force, misses the flagship *San Francisco* but sinks the *Juneau* (Capt Swenson†).

In order to knock out Henderson Field on 14 Nov the Japanese cruisers *Suzuya* (Rear-Adm Hashimoto) and *Maya* shell the airfield, as planned, in the night 13-14 Nov, but with little success. The remaining ships of this force and of the Support Group (Vice-Adm Mikawa) guard the N and the W. The landing of the troops from the 11 transports, which have set out from Shortland on 12 Nov with the 2nd DD Flotilla, is postponed for 24 hours to give another bombardment group under Vice-Adm Kondo an opportunity to shell Henderson Field again in the night 14-15 Nov and to provide cover for the landing. It comprises *Atago, Takao, Sendai, Uranami, Shikinami, Ayanami,* and *Kirishima, Nagara, Teruzuki, Inazuma, Asagumo* and *Samidare* which join from the 1st Bombardment Group, and *Hatsuyuki* and *Shirayuki* from the carrier force. After further reconnaissance reports, the US C-in-C South Pacific, Adm Halsey, detaches Rear-Adm Lee to Guadalcanal on the afternoon of 13 Nov with the battleships *South Dakota* and *Washington* and the destroyers *Walke, Benham, Preston* and *Gwin*. Rear-Adm Kinkaid receives orders to remain S of Guadalcanal with the carrier *Enterprise* and the remaining ships. Early on 14 Nov US reconnaissance aircraft sight Mikawa's and Nishimura's forces withdrawing from Guadalcanal. In several waves aircraft of the Marine Corps from the carrier *Enterprise* and from Henderson Field attack. They sink the *Kinugasa* and damage the cruisers *Chokai, Isuzu* and *Maya* and the destroyer *Michishio* with hits and near-misses with the result that these ships take no further part in the operation. After sighting by reconnaissance aircraft of the *Enterprise,* aircraft from the carrier and from Henderson Field and B-17/Fortress bombers from Espiritu Santo attack the Japanese landing force in several waves as it proceeds down the 'Slot'. In the first attack the transports *Canberra Maru* and *Nagara Maru* are sunk; the *Sado Maru* is damaged and detached with the destroyers *Amagiri* and *Mochizuki*. Fighter protection from the

carriers *Hiyo* and *Junyo* is able to shoot down some aircraft but cannot prevent the attacks. In the second attack the *Brisbane Maru*, in the third the *Arizona Maru* and *Shinanogawa Maru* and in the last the *Nako Maru* are sunk: the destroyers *Kawakaze*, *Makinami*, *Naganami* and *Suzukaze* rescue some 5000 men, 400 are lost with the ships. Rear-Adm Tanaka continues the advance with the remaining four transports, the *Kinugawa Maru*, *Yamatsuki Maru*, *Hirokawa Maru* and *Yamaura Maru* in order to beach these ships in the night 14-15 Nov on the NW corner of Guadalcanal. This, together with the landing of the rescued survivors from the destroyers, succeeds. The transports are destroyed by air attacks on 15 Nov.
In the night 14-15 Nov the main body of the Japanese 2nd Fleet (Vice-Adm Kondo), comprising the heavy cruisers *Atago* and *Takao*, the battleship *Kirishima* and two escort groups with the cruiser *Nagara* and the destroyers *Teruzuki*, *Hatsuyuki*, *Shirayuki*, *Asagumo* and *Samidare* and the cruiser *Sendai* with the destroyers *Uranami*, *Shikinami* and *Ayanami*, tries to shell Henderson Field. In the process the *Sendai* group and then the other ships encounter the US force under Rear-Adm Lee (see above), as it enters 'Iron Bottom Sound'. The latter's van destroyers *Walke*, *Benham* and *Preston* at first fall victim to the Japanese torpedoes and gunfire and the *Gwin* is damaged. In manoeuvring, the *South Dakota* (Capt T. L. Gatch) with her radar out of action comes up against the *Kirishima*, *Atago* and *Takao* and is badly damaged by 42 hits in her superstructure. A torpedo attack by Rear-Adm Kimura's destroyers fails and the *Ayanami* is lost. Then the *Washington* (Capt G. B. Davis), which has remained unnoticed, approaches within 8000 metres with the help of radar and in 7 minutes destroys the *Kirishima* by shellfire. As she retires, she avoids the torpedo attacks of the destroyers *Kagero* and *Oyashio* detached by Rear-Adm Tanaka from the landing force.
In the next 14 days both sides carry out individual supply operations. On the Japanese side the submarines *I-16* and

I-20 with midget submarines are deployed against the supply operations on 15 Nov and 29 Nov. *Ha-10* torpedoes the transport *Alchiba* (6198 tons) on 29 Nov and she has to be beached. The Japanese destroyer *Hayashio* is sunk by US dive bombers on 24 Nov when engaged in a supply mission.
8-26 Nov   Central Atlantic
On the report of the Allied landing in North Africa all U-boats with sufficient fuel are brought at top speed from the North Atlantic to the area off Morocco. 'Schlagetot' group, comprising *U572*, *U173*, *U130*, *U108*, *U103*, *U510*, *U509*, *U752* and *U511*) and off Gibraltar 'Westwall' group, comprising *U515*, *U155*, *U411*, *U564*, *U86*, *U91*, *U98*, *U218*, *U566*, *U613*, *U92*, *U413*, *U653*, *U519*, *U185* and *U263*.
In the roads of Fedala *U173* (Lt Schweichel) attacks the convoy UGF.1 at anchor on 11-12 Nov and sinks the troop transport *Joseph Hewes* (9359 tons) and torpedoes the tanker *Winooski* (10600 tons) and the destroyer *Hambleton*. In the following night *U130* (Cdr Kals) sinks the troop transports *Edward Rutledge*, *Hugh L. Scott* and *Tasker H. Bliss* totalling 34507 tons. On 15 Nov *U173* torpedoes the transport *Electra* (6200 tons) which has to be beached. *U173* is sunk on the following day by the US destroyers *Woolsey*, *Swanson* and *Quick*. Attempted attacks by *U572*, *U108*, *U510*, *U511* and *U752* from 11 Nov to 18 Nov fail. *U108* is damaged by bombs on 18 Nov. Of the 'Westwall' group *U515* (Lt-Cdr Henke) attacks the submarine depot ship *Hecla* (10850 tons) on 12 Nov and sinks her in many approaches: the escorting destroyer *Marne* is torpedoed. The returning transport convoy MKF.1, which is escorted, *inter alia*, by the escort carriers *Argus* and *Avenger*, the destroyers *Wrestler*, *Amazon* and *Glaisdale* (Norwegian) and the close escort group with the new frigate *Exe* as leader, loses on 14 Nov the troop transport *Warwick Castle* (20107 tons) to *U413* (Lt Poel). On 15 Nov *U155* (Lt. Cdr. Piening) sinks the carrier *Avenger* (Cdr Colthurst) and the troop transport *Ettrick* (11279 tons) and torpedoes the transport *Almaak* (6737 tons). On 16 Nov

U92 (Lt Oelrich) sinks one ship of 7662 tons. *U515* misses a carrier and *U218* is damaged when trying to attack a carrier force.
On 17 Nov *U566* suffers depth charge damage. On 18 Nov *U155* misses a convoy and *U613* and *U91* are damaged by aircraft bombs and depth charges respectively. On 20 Nov *U413* misses the convoy KRS.2 and is damaged by the defence. *U263* (Lt-Cdr Nölke) sinks two ships of 12376 tons from the convoy.
On 24 Nov *U263* and *U510* are damaged and from 26 Nov the boats have to leave for the W or proceed to *U118* to refuel.

9 Nov   North Sea
The German 2nd MTB Flotilla (Lt-Cdr Feldt), comprising *S46*, *S48*, *S66*, *S70*, *S73*, *S80*, *S83*, *S101*, *S104* and *S113*, attacks a British convoy off Lowestoft and sinks a freighter (1843 tons) and torpedoes a second (1482 tons).

9-18 Nov   Mediterranean
Deployment of the British submarines of the 8th, 10th and 1st Flotillas to cover the operation 'Torch': *Ursula* and *P.54/Unshaken* off Oran; *P.45/Un-rivalled*, *P.48* and *P.221/Shakespeare* off Algiers; *P.211/Safari*, *P.212/Sahib* and *P.213/Saracen* between Sardinia and Sicily; *P.44/United*, *P.46/Unruffled*, *P.37/Unbending*, *P.35/Umbra* and *P.43/Unison* N of Sicily and Messina; *Una* and *Utmost* S of Messina; and S of the French south coast *P.51/Unseen* and *P.222* and, with special missions (the landing of Gen Clay and the collecting of the French Gen Giraud), *P.219/Seraph* and *P.217/Sibyl*. *Traveller*, *Parthian*, *Clyde*, *Thrasher*, *Proteus* and *Porpoise* are engaged in transport journeys to Malta and then partly deployed on the Tunisian and Libyan coasts.
In these operations many attacks are made. *Turbulent* (Cdr Linton) sinks one ship of 1554 tons; *P.211/Safari* (Cdr Bryant) two ships of 2914 tons and three small craft; *P.212/Sahib* (Lt Bromage) finishes off one ship of 1579 tons; *P.213/Saracen* (Lt Lumby) sinks one ship of 209 tons; *Porpoise* (Cdr Bennington) two ships of 11273 tons; and *Proteus* torpedoes one ship of 1579 tons.

9-21 Nov   North Atlantic
The 'Kreuzotter' group is formed from the U-boats *U84*, *U522*, *U521*, *U753*, *U224* and *U383* which are left behind in the Atlantic because of their limited fuel supplies. To it are added by 17 Nov *U454*, *U606* and *U624* which have been refuelled and *U184*, *U262*, *U264* and *U611* fresh from home. On 12 Nov *U224* (Lt Kosbadt) sinks an independent of 5614 tons. On 15 Nov *U521* (Lt-Cdr Bargsten) reports the convoy ONS.144 (33 ships, EG B.6 Norwegian Lt-Cdr Monssen) with the Norwegian corvettes *Potentilla*, *Eglantine*, *Montbretia*, *Rose* and the British *Vervain* and the rescue ship *Perth* fitted with HF/DF. *U521* unsuccessfully attacks and is driven off by depth charges from *Rose*. In the mist *U611* (Lt-Cdr von Jakobs) also loses the briefly-established contact. Only on the afternoon of 17 Nov does *U521* and, shortly after, *U184* (Lt-Cdr Dangschat) come up. The latter leads the other boats to the scene with D/F bearings. In the night 17-18 Nov *U262*, *U264*, *U184*, *U521*, *U224*, *U383*, *U454* and *U624* attack successively. *U264* (Lt Looks) and *U184* each sink one ship of 6696 tons and 3192 tons respectively. *U624* (Lt Count Soden-Frauenhofen) sinks two ships of 10076 tons and torpedoes one more of 5432 tons which is later sunk by *U522* (Lt-Cdr Schneider). She just misses the *Eglantine*. The other boats miss their targets and are attacked with depth charges from *Rose*, *Montbretia* and *Potentilla*. Towards morning *U262* (Lt Franke) sinks the *Montbretia*. *U753* (Cdr von Mannstein) misses the rescue ship *Perth* with the *Rose*. Because of the expenditure of torpedoes and lack of fuel most of the boats have to break off on 18 Nov. Only *U184*, *U262*, *U264* and *U611* continue the operation. On the afternoon of 18 Nov and on the morning of 19 Nov salvoes from *U264* and *U184* miss their targets.
The escort, reinforced in the evening by the destroyers HMS *Firedrake* and USS *Badger*, drives the boats off. Towards morning on 20 Nov *Potentilla* sinks *U184*, which is keeping contact, and shortly afterwards *U264* misses the *Rose*. In the morning the Western

Local Escort Group meets the convoy and the U-boats break off the operation.

11 Nov Indian ocean
The Japanese auxiliary cruisers *Aikoku Maru* (10500 tons) and *Hokoku Maru* (10438 tons) attack about 500 nautical miles SW of the Cocos Islands the Dutch tanker *Ondina* (6341 tons) travelling from Fremantle to Diego Garcia, escorted by the Indian minesweeper *Bengal* (Lt-Cdr W. J. Wilson). In the engagement the *Bengal* succeeds in hitting the vastly superior-armed *Hokoku Maru* so often that the ship explodes, whereupon the second auxiliary cruiser, which has in the meantime set the tanker on fire, breaks off the engagement. *Ondina* can be brought to Fremantle severely damaged.

12 Nov-17 Dec Arctic
Soviet mining operations on the Norwegian Polar Coast. On 12 Nov nine Soviet MO-IV patrol cutters lay mines off the harbours of Varangerfjord. By the end of the year 14 are laid by them off Vardö, 20 off Kirkenes and 34 off Petsamofjord. There sink on these barrages *Schiff 18* (419 tons) on 19 Nov off Kirkenes, the freighter *Akka* (2646 tons) on 29 Nov off Vardö and the freighters *Hans Rickmers* (5226 tons) and *Westsee* (5911 tons) on 30 Nov off Petsamo. The latter two are partly beached. On 7 Dec the 56th MS Flotilla partly clears the barrages off Petsamo.
The newly-operational minelaying submarines *L-20* and *L-22* lay, *inter alia*, mine barrages in Porsangerfjord in several operations. On these the patrol boats *V6116/Ubier* and *V6117/Cherusker* sink on 6 Dec.

14 Nov Black Sea
The Soviet submarine *L-23* (Capt 3rd Class Fartushny) torpedoes the German tanker *Ossag* (2793 tons) which has been met off the Bosphorus by the Rumanian destroyers *Regele Ferdinand* and *Regina Maria*. The tanker is towed into the Bosphorus by a Turkish tug.

15 Nov-19 Dec Central Atlantic
Of the U-boats again deployed off Freetown and in the area of the Cape Verde Islands, following refuelling from *U462* (Lt Vowe), *U134* (Lt-Cdr Schendel) sinks one ship of 4827 tons; *U552* (Lt-Cdr Popp) one ship of 3157 tons; *UD3* (Cdr* Rigele) one ship of 5041 tons; and *U176* (Lt-Cdr Dierksen) three ships of 13432 tons. Between the Gulf of Guinea and the Cape Verde Islands *U161* (Lt-Cdr Achilles) sinks three ships of 16284 tons and damages one ship of 5161 tons and *U126* (Lt-Cdr Bauer) four ships of 19672 tons.

16 Nov Mediterranean
In escorting a German convoy from Piraeus to the Dardanelles *UJ2102* (Lt Kleiner) sinks the Greek submarine *Triton* located by the destroyer *Hermes* (Capt Johannesson) and takes the crew prisoner.

17-18 Nov Baltic
The Finnish motor torpedo boats *Syöksy*, *Vihuri* (Lt Kajatsalo) and *Vinha* (Lt Vuorensaari) attack the Soviet gunboat *Krasnoe Znamya* lying in the harbour of Lavansaari and sink her with torpedo hits. She is later raised and repaired.

17-20 Nov Mediterranean
Operation 'Stone Age'. British convoy of four merchant ships, escorted by the 15th Cruiser Sqdn (Rear-Adm Power), comprising *Arethusa*, *Dido* and *Euryalus* and 10 destroyers, proceeds from Alexandria to Malta. Despite German air attacks in which the *Arethusa* is so badly hit N of Derna on 18 Nov that she has to return, all four transports reach Malta. With this the island can be regarded as relieved.

17-21 Nov South-West Pacific
In the Malacca Straits the British submarine *Trusty* (Lt-Cdr King) torpedoes one ship of 5617 tons and the US submarine *Searaven* (Lt-Cdr Cassedy) sinks one ship of 333 tons near Christmas Island. In the area of the Philippines *Seal* (Lt-Cdr Hurd) and *Salmon* (Lt-Cdr McKinney) each sink one ship of 5487 tons and 5873 tons respectively. *Stingray* (Lt-Cdr Earle) torpedoes one ship of 8360 tons.

17-23 Nov Arctic
On 17 Nov the convoy QP.15 sets out from the Kola Inlet with 28 ships escorted by one AA ship, five minesweepers, four corvettes and one trawler and the Soviet destroyers *Baku* and *Sokrushitelny*. It is met in the Barents Sea by five British destroyers and, further W, by the British cruisers *London* and *Suffolk* and another five

destroyers. Three British and one Soviet submarine take up positions off the North Norwegian fjords against German surface ships. On 20 Nov the convoy is much dispersed in a heavy storm and parts of the *Baku's* superstructure are blown away in the sea. With a big leak in her bows and boiler rooms, the ship only reaches harbour with difficulty. The *Sokrushitelny* breaks in two. The destroyers *Razumny*, *Kuibyshev* and *Uritski*, which are sent to help, are able to rescue 187 men in very heavy seas and the destroyer sinks on 22 Nov. German air reconnaissance does not locate the convoy in the bad weather. *U625* (Lt Benker) and *U601* (Lt-Cdr Grau) each sink one ship of 5851 tons and 3974 tons respectively from convoy groups.

19 Nov English Channel
The German 5th MTB Flotilla (Lt-Cdr Klug), comprising *S68*, *S77*, *S82*, *S112*, *S115* and *S116*, attacks a British convoy S of Plymouth and sinks the trawler *Ullswater* and three freighters of 3528 tons.

20 Nov-10 Dec Indian Ocean
The Japanese submarine *I-166* (Cdr Tanaka), operating SW of the Malabar Coast, sinks one ship of 5332 tons and *I-29* (Cdr* Izu) two ships of 16329 tons in the Gulf of Aden. *I-27* has no success in the Gulf of Oman.

21 Nov-6 Dec Mediterranean
In the Bay of Naples the British submarine *P.228/Splendid* (Lt-Cdr McGeogh) attacks several convoys from 16 Nov to 22 Nov, including on 21 Nov one of two ships and the destroyers *Bombardiere*, *Legionario* and *Velite*, the last of which is torpedoed. Off the Tunisian Coast and S of Marettimo *P.44/United*, *Utmost*, *Una* and *P.219/Seraph* attack convoys without success. *Utmost* is damaged by depth charges from the torpedo boat *Ardente*. At the beginning of December *Ursula* (Lt Lakin) sinks two ships of 1962 tons off Corsica; *P.35/Umbra* (Lt-Cdr Maydon) one ship of 1097 tons off Sousse; and *P.45/Unrivalled* (Lt Sprice) the hospital ship *Città di Trapani* (1467 tons) and one sailing ship off Tunis. In the Aegean the Greek submarine *Papanicolis* reports successful attacks.

Off Sicily *P.217/Sibyl* misses the German transport *Ankara* escorted by the Italian destroyers *Granatiere* and *Saetta* and the torpedo boats *Partenope* and *Perseo*. Off Sardinia *Tigris* sinks the Italian submarine *Porfido* on 6 Dec.

24 Nov-3 Dec North Atlantic
From the U-boats coming from ONS.144 the 'Drachen' group is formed NE of Newfoundland, consisting of *U454*, *U522*, *U262*, *U611*, *U623*, *U663* and *U445*. On 26 Nov *U262* (Lt Franke) and *U663* (Lt-Cdr Schmid) each sink one ship of 7178 tons and 5170 tons respectively. Convoys are not sighted.

26 Nov Indian Ocean
In escorting the convoy OW.1 from Fremantle to Diego Garcia with the corvettes *Cessnock* and *Toowoomba*, the cruisers *Adelaide* (RAN) and *Jacob van Heemskerck* (Dutch) encounter the German blockade-runner *Ramses* (7983 tons) proceeding from Djakarta to France. The German ship scuttles herself.

27 Nov Mediterranean
Operation 'Lila': occupation of Toulon by the II S.S. Armoured Corps. By order of the C-in-C of the Fleet, Adm de Laborde, the French Navy is scuttled in Toulon: the battleships *Strasbourg*, *Dunkerque* and *Provence;* the heavy cruisers *Algérie*, *Foch*, *Colbert* and *Dupleix;* the light cruisers *La Galissonnière*, *Marseillaise* and *Jean-de-Vienne*, the aircraft depot ship *Commandant Teste*, the destroyers *Lion*, *Gerfaut*, *Lynx*, *Panthère*, *Tigre*, *Vauban*, *Aigle*, *Cassard*, *Guépard*, *Kersaint*, *L'Indomptable*, *Mogador*, *Tartu*, *Valmy*, *Vauquelin*, *Vautour*, *Verdun*, *Volta*, *Bison*, *Casque*, *La Foudroyant*, *L'Adroit*, *Lansquennet*, *Le Hardi*, *Mameluk*, *Le Siroco*, *Bordelais*, *La Palme*, *Le Mars* and *Trombe*, the torpedo boats *Baliste*, *La Bayonnaise* and *La Poursuivante*, the submarines *Achéron*, *Aurore*, *Caiman*, *Diamant*, *Eurydice*, *Fresnel*, *Galatée*, *Henri Poincaré*, *L'Espoir*, *Naiade*, *Pascal*, *Redoutable*, *Sirène*, *Thétis*, *Vengeur* and *Vénus*, 11 gunboats and smaller craft.

28 Nov-19 Dec Indonesia
On 28-29 Nov the auxiliary vessel *Kuru* and the corvettes *Armidale* and *Castlemaine* set out for Timor from

Port Darwin to bring 63 relief personnel and to evacuate 77 Portuguese refugees. On a second journey *Armidale* is sunk on 1 Dec by Japanese torpedo aircraft. The Dutch destroyer *Tjerk Hiddes* evacuates 950 persons from Timor to Port Darwin in three journeys in the period 10-19 Dec.

29 Nov Mediterranean
The British fast minelayer *Manxman* lays a barrage of 156 mines near Cani in the neighbourhood of Tunis. On 8 Dec it is extended by another 36 mines.

29 Nov-1 Dec Bay of Biscay
The Italian blockade-runner *Cortellazzo* (Capt Paladini, A.) sets out from Bordeaux on the way to Japan, escorted by the German torpedo boats *T23*, *Kondor*, *Falke* and *T22*. After the torpedo boats have left, the ship is found on 30 Nov by a Sunderland flying-boat of No 10 Sqdn RAAF and is located on 1 Dec by the destroyers *Quickmatch* (RAN) and *Redoubt*, detached from convoy KMF.4 (SOE on the sloop *Egret*). After the crew has left the ship, she is sunk by a torpedo from the *Redoubt*.

29 Nov-2 Dec Black Sea
First sortie by the Soviet Squadron (Vice-Adm Vladimirski) against shipping on the Rumanian-Bulgarian coast. The first group, consisting of the cruiser *Voroshilov*, the flotilla leader *Kharkov* and the destroyer *Soobrazitelny*, is to shell the harbours of Sulina and Burgas and the radio station at Fidonisi; the second group, comprising the destroyers *Besposhchadny* and *Boiki*, is to attack shipping targets near Cape Kaliakra and Cape Shabla and to shell Mangalia. On 1 Dec the destroyers of the second group fire torpedoes at ships in the roads of Kalytch-Kiap, but they go ashore. *Voroshilov* and *Soobrazitelny* shell Fidonisi, but the cruiser is damaged by a mine detonation in the bow paravane of the destroyer and the force returns. *Kharkov* does not find targets near Gibrieni.

29 Nov-11 Dec North Atlantic
On 30 Nov the 'Draufgänger' group is formed W of Ireland from the newly-arrived U-boats *U455*, *U221*, *U553*, *U610*, *U600*, *U604*, *U569*, *U615* and *U609* to operate against

an OS convoy suspected as a result of listening observations on 29 Nov. No convoy is found. On 2 Dec *U604* (Lt-Cdr Höltring) sinks one ship of 7057 tons. Two attacks by *U435* and *U615* fail. The group is moved to the N for 6 Dec to operate against the convoys ONS.150 (EG B.4) expected according to convoy schedule, and on 7 Dec boats are directed against HX.217 from her unsuccessful patrol line (see below). On 29 Nov the 'Panther' group is formed in the Central North Atlantic from the newly-arrived U-boats *U439*, *U254*, *U758*, *U465*, *U135*, *U211* and *U524* to operate against the convoy ONS.148 (EG B.2). The group proceeds westwards to the NE of Newfoundland until 4 Dec in accordance with the day's run of an ONS convoy without finding targets. *U524* (Lt-Cdr Frhr von Steinaecker), which carries a 'B' service team to listen to UK telephone talk, listens on 4 Dec to the convoy's talk and the group is directed to the NE. At mid-day on 6 Dec *U524* sights the convoy HX.217 (33 ships, EG B.6-[Cdr Heathcote] with the destroyers *Burza*, *Fame* (Polish) and the corvettes *Vervain* (British) and *Potentilla*, *Rose* and *Eglantine* (Norwegian) and the rescue ship *Perth* fitted with HF/DF). The four U-boats which approach on the afternoon of 6 Dec lose contact in deteriorating visibility and are diverted by the destroyer *Montgomery* of the Western Local Escort Group which is firing flares on the flank. On morning of 7 Dec *U524* again establishes contact and brings up *U254*, *U465*, *U439* and *U135* but they are driven off by the Liberator H/120. In the night 7-8 Dec *U524* sinks a ship of 8194 tons and just misses the *Fame*. *U254*, *U465*, *U623* (coming with *U611* from refuelling) and *U758* are located by *Eglantine*, *Rose*, *Burza* and *Potentilla* before being able to fire and are driven off. On 8 Dec the boats of the 'Draufgänger' group —*U455*, *U221*, *U553*, *U610*, *U600*, *U604*, *U569*, *U615* and *U609*— approach. *U600* (Lt-Cdr Zurmühlen) has already sunk one independent of 6762 tons on 7 Dec. On the afternoon of 8 Dec *U610* and *U553* establish contact but after a miss on a destroyer, they, with three other boats, are forced to submerge by the Liberator bombers B/120 and M/120. In the evening of 8 Dec *U221* (Lt Trojer) in an attack rams *U254* (Lt-Cdr Gilardone), which sinks. Two boats are driven off by *Potentilla* and *Rose*. On the morning of 9 Dec *U455* misses one escort vessel and *U553* (Cdr Thurmann) sinks one scattered ship of 5273 tons. Two further attacks are frustrated by *Eglantine* and *Potentilla*. During 9 Dec *U553* keeps contact; in the night 9-10 Dec only *U758* (Lt-Cdr Manseck) fires—a miss on the *Burza*. Six other attacks are frustrated by *Potentilla*, *Rose*, *Potentilla* again, *Vervain*, *Burza* and *Rose*. Despite strong air escort from six Hudsons of No. 269 Sqdn RAF, Fortresses of No 220 Sqdn RAF and Catalinas of USN Sqdn VP-84, *U628* (Lt Hasenschar) is able to keep contact until the night of 11 Dec. But all boats i.e. *U610*, *U615* and *U623*, are driven off and *U611* is sunk by the Catalina H/84. A further operation against the strong air escort on 11 Dec has no prospect of success.

29 Nov-12 Dec   Mediterranean
Flanking mine barrages are laid out from Bizerta in a north-easterly direction as far as the area W of Sicily to protect Axis supply traffic to Tunis. On 29-30 Nov the destroyer *Da Noli* (Cdr* Valdambrini) and the auxiliary ship *Barletta* in two missions lay the barrages S.91 and S.92 with 172 mines and 154 mines respectively. On 30 Nov-1 Dec the destroyers *Maestrale* (Capt Bedeschi), *Grecale*, *Mitragliere* and *Ascari* lay the barrage S.96 (224 mines). On 4-5 Dec the destroyers *Pigafetta* (Capt del Minio), *Da Noli* and the minelayer *Barletta* lay the barrage S.93 (172 mines) and the destroyers *Maestrale*, *Graecale*, *Ascari* and *Corazziere* the barrage S.97 (224 mines). On 11-12 Dec the destroyers *Pigafetta*, *Da Noli*, *Zeno*, *Mitragliere*, *Ascari*, *Corazziere* and *Graecale* lay the barrage S.94 (224 mines.)

30 Nov   Pacific
Destruction of the German auxiliary cruiser *Schiff 10/Thor* (Capt Gumprich) in the harbour of Yokohama as a result of an explosion in the supply ship *Uckermark* (Cdr von Zatorski) lying alongside her. In addition to Japanese harbour craft and a freighter the prize ship *Leuthen* is also destroyed. *Schiff 10* captured, or sank, on her last voyage, 10 merchant ships totalling 56037 tons.

30 Nov-1 Dec   South Pacific
Night battle of Tassafaronga. A Japanese destroyer force (Rear-Adm Tanaka), comprising *Naganami*, *Makinami*, *Oyashio*, *Kuroshio*, *Kagero*, *Kawakaze*, *Suzukaze* and *Takanami*, tries to get through to Guadalcanal with supplies. The Americans learn of the operation through their W/T interception service, whereupon Adm Halsey sends out TF 67 (Rear-Adm Wright) from Espiritu Santo to oppose the force; the heavy cruisers *Minneapolis*, *New Orleans*, *Northampton* and *Pensacola*, the light cruiser *Honolulu* and the destroyers *Drayton*, *Fletcher*, *Maury*, *Perkins*, *Lamson* and *Lardner*.
With the help of radar, Rear-Adm Wright is able to surprise the Japanese force and in the engagement to damage the destroyer *Takanami* so badly that she has later to be abandoned. Rear-Adm Tanaka then orders half of his ships to keep on for Guadalcanal in order to throw the supply containers they have brought overboard (they are later recovered from the water) and attacks with the remaining force the superior US group with torpedoes. All four heavy cruisers are hit: *Northampton* (Capt W. A. Kitts) sinks, *New Orleans* loses her bow and *Minneapolis* and *Pensacola* are badly damaged.

1 Dec   English Channel
S81 (Lt Wendler) sinks the British trawler *Jasper*.

1-2 Dec   Mediterranean
Attack by British Force Q (Rear-Adm Harcourt), comprising the cruisers *Aurora*, *Sirius* and *Argonaut* and the destroyers *Quiberon* and *Quentin* on the Italian convoy traffic on the route Trapani-Tunis. Of four convoys at sea totalling 13 transports, escorted by seven destroyers and 12 torpedo boats, three can be recalled after being located by British air reconnaissance. The convoy H with four ships and the destroyers *Da Recco* (Capt Cocchia), *Camicia Nera* and *Folgore* and the torpedo boats *Clio* and *Procione* is encountered near the Skerki Bank. The four ships and the destroyer *Folgore* are

sunk and *Da Recco* and *Procione* damaged. On the return the British force is attacked by bombers and torpedo aircraft and loses the *Quentin* by torpedo hit. The Italian submarines *Nichelio*, *Asteria*, *Dandolo* and *Giada* make no contact.

1-10 Dec Black Sea
The Soviet cruiser *Krasny Krym*, the destroyers *Besposhchadny* and *Nezamozhnik* and minesweepers bring the 9th Mountain Rifle Div from Batumi to Tuapse.

1-28 Dec Mediterranean
In the Western Mediterranean *U375* (Lt-Cdr Könenkamp) torpedoes the British fast minelayer *Manxman* on 1 Dec and *U602* (Lt-Cdr Schüler) the destroyer *Porcupine* on 9 Dec. On 11 Dec *U443* (Lt von Puttkamer) sinks the British destroyer *Blean* and on 14 Dec one ship of 1592 tons. *U565* (Lt-Cdr Franken) sinks the British destroyer *Partridge* on 18 Dec and torpedoes the troop transport *Cameronia* (16297 tons) on 22 Dec. On 21 Dec the troop transport *Strathallan* (23722 tons) is sunk by *U562* (Lt Hamm). In the eastern Mediterranean *U617* (Lt-Cdr Brandi) attacks various convoys off the Cyrenaican coast and sinks one fleet tug (810 tons). Of the Italian submarines *Alagi*, *Bronzo*, *Galatea*, *Porfido*, *Volframio*, *Argento*, *Corallo*, *Mocenigo*, *Diaspro* and *Malachite* in the Western Mediterranean only *Mocenigo* (Lt-Cdr Longhi) torpedoes the British cruiser *Argonaut* and *Bronzo* misses one destroyer. *Porfido* and *Corallo* are sunk by the British submarine *Tigris* and the sloop *Enchantress*.

3 Dec English Channel
The 5th MTB Flotilla (Lt-Cdr Klug), comprising *S81*, *S82*, *S115* and *S116*, attacks British convoys in the Channel and sinks one freighter (383 tons). *S115* (Lt Klocke) sinks the British escort destroyer *Penylan*.

3-11 Dec South Pacific
The Japanese 2nd DD Flotilla under Rear-Adm Tanaka carries out supply operations from Shortland to Guadalcanal.
On 3-4 Dec the destroyers *Oyashio*, *Kuroshio*, *Kagero*, *Kawakaze*, *Suzukaze*, *Nowake* and *Arashi*, covered by the destroyers *Naganami* (Rear-Adm Tana-

ka), *Makinami* and *Yugure*, transport 1500 canisters with supplies to Cape Esperance and throw them overboard. But only 310 are brought ashore by the troops. In the night 7-8 Dec another attempt is made under Capt Sano with the destroyers *Oyashio*, *Kuroshio*, *Kagero*, *Kawakaze*, *Suzukaze*, *Nowake* and *Ariake* and the same covering force. On the way *Nowake* is put out of action by bomb hits and the operation has to be abandoned because of attacks by the US motor torpedo boats, *PT109*, *PT43*, *PT48*, *PT40*, *PT59*, *PT44*, *PT36* and *PT37*.
A new attempt is made on 11-12 Dec with the destroyers *Teruzuki* (Rear-Adm Tanaka), *Oyashio*, *Kuroshio*, *Kagero*, *Tanikaze*, *Urakaze*, *Kawakaze*, *Suzukaze*, *Yugure*, *Ariake* and *Arashi* when the seven transport destroyers throw 1200 canisters overboard. The leading destroyer *Terezuki* falls a victim to torpedoes from the US *PT37* and *PT40* off Guadalcanal; *PT44* sinks.

3-22 Dec North Atlantic
Continuation of the operations against the Allied supplies for 'Torch' in the area W of Gibraltar and Morocco by the 'Westwall' group: it consists of *U185*, *U515*, *U155*, *U130*, *U103* and the replenished *U106*, *U92*, *U564*, *U653*, *U519* and *U86*. *U618* and *U432* are deployed off the Moroccan harbours. On 6 Dec *U106* misses one auxiliary ship; *U155* (Lt-Cdr Piening) and *U103* (Lt Janssen) each sink one ship of 8456 tons and 5026 tons respectively. On 7 Dec *U515* (Lt-Cdr Henke) sinks the troop transport *Ceramic* (18713 tons) and *U185* (Lt-Cdr Maus) one ship of 4576 tons. On 13 Dec *U103* torpedoes the transport *Hororata* (13945 tons). Attacks by *U519* and *U185* on 9 Dec and 20 Dec are not successful. Off Fedala *U432* (Lt-Cdr H. O. Schultze) sinks one guard boat of 310 tons and misses two transports.

4 Dec Mediterranean
First attack on Italy by the US 9th Air Fleet: target the Fleet in Naples. The cruiser *Attendolo* is hit and destroyed. *Montecuccolo* is badly, and *Eugenio di Savoia* and four destroyers less seriously, damaged. Then the 9th Div, comprising the battleships *Littorio*, *Roma*, and *Vittorio Veneto* is moved

to La Spezia and the 3rd Div, consisting of the heavy cruisers *Gorizia* and *Trieste*, is moved from Messina to Maddalena (Sardinia). The 8th Div, comprising the cruisers *Garibaldi*, *Duca degli Abruzzi* and *Duca d'Aosta*, remains in Messina.

5-25 Dec   South Pacific

Of the Japanese submarines *I-2*, *I-3*, *I-4*, *I-5* and *I-6* employed in transport duties in the area of the Solomons, *I-3* is lost on 10 Dec through a torpedo attack by the US motor torpedo boat *PT59* and *I-4* on 20 Dec through one torpedo from the US submarine *Seadragon*. The 7th SM Flotilla, reinforced by new construction, operates from Rabaul with *Ro-101* off Milne Bay, *Ro-102* off the Jomard Channel and *Ro-103* in a transport mission.

7-28 Dec   Pacific

Off Japan the US submarine *Kingfish* (Lt-Cdr Lowrance) sinks two ships of 9779 tons; *Halibut* (Lt-Cdr Gross) four ships of 12651 tons and torpedoes one more ship of 6376 tons. *Drum* (Lt-Cdr McMahon) torpedoes the Japanese carrier *Ryuho* and lays a mine barrage off Bungo Suido on 17 Dec. *Trigger* (Lt-Cdr Benson) lays a barrage off Inubozaki on 20 Dec. In the area of Ponape *Triton* (Lt-Cdr Kirkpatrick) sinks two ships of 5306 tons.

8 Dec   Mediterranean

A small German battle group (Maj-Gen Gause) occupies the coastal batteries of Bizerta and captures in the harbour the destroyer *L'Audacieux*, the torpedo boats *La Pomone*, *L'Iphigénie* and *Bombarde*, the submarines *Circé*, *Calypso*, *Dauphin*, *Requin*, *Phoque*, *Espadon*, *Saphir*, *Turquoise* and *Nautilus*, the sloops *Commandant Rivière* and *La Batailleuse* and the minelayer *Castor*.

8 Dec   Black Sea

In operations off the Bosphorus the Soviet submarine *D-5* (Lt-Cdr Trofimov) sinks the small Turkish sailing ship *Koçiboglu*.

8-29 Dec   South West Pacific

In the South Asian area the US submarine *Gar* (Lt-Cdr McGregor, D.) sinks one ship of 661 tons; *Tambor* (Lt-Cdr Ambruster) one ship of 2558 tons; and *Thresher* (Lt-Cdr Millican) one ship of 2733 tons. *Tautog* (Lt-Cdr Willingham) torpedoes one ship of 1000 tons. In the area of the Bismarck

Archipelago *Wahoo* (Lt-Cdr Kennedy) sinks one ship of 5355 tons; *Grouper* (Lt-Cdr McGregor R. R.) one ship of 4003 tons and torpedoes one more ship of 4861 tons; *Albacore* (Lt-Cdr Lake) sinks on 18 Dec the cruiser *Tenryu* and torpedoes one ship of 10438 tons; *Greenling* (Lt-Cdr Bruton) sinks one unknown warship; and *Seadragon* (Lt-Cdr Ashley) torpedoes one ship of 6187 tons. Off Wake *Triton* (Lt-Cdr Kirkpatrick) sinks one ship of 3393 tons.

9-18 Dec   Mediterranean

Off the Tunisian coast the British submarine *P.35/Umbra* (Lt-Cdr Maydon) sinks two ships of 3572 tons. On 12 Dec *P.222* is sunk by the torpedo boat *Fortunale* when she attacks an Italian convoy off Naples. In the area of Bizerta *P.212/Sahib* (Lt Bromage) and *P.46/Unruffled* (Lt Stevens) attack on 14 Dec an Italian convoy of four steamers and the torpedo boats *Ardito*, *Fortunale*, *Groppo* and *Orione*: each sinks one ship of 4959 tons and 6666 tons respectively. Off Sardinia *P.228/Splendid* (Lt-Cdr McGeogh) sinks on 15 Dec one ship of 5048 tons and on 17 Dec the destroyer *Aviere* which is escorting the German transport *Ankara* with the *Camicia Nera*. *Rorqual* (Lt-Cdr Napier) lays a mine barrage off Ischia and attacks one ship on 18 Dec. In the Aegean *Taku* sinks one ship of 5322 tons and one sailing ship.

9-26 Dec   North Atlantic

From 9 Dec the 'Büffel' group is deployed S of Greenland on the course of convoy HX.218 (EG B.3), as deciphered by the 'B' Service. It consists of *U663*, *U445* and *U373*. On 13 Dec *U373* (Lt-Cdr Loeser) sights HX.218 with 54 ships, but is driven off four hours later by two destroyers. *U663* (Lt-Cdr Schmid) is attacked by depth charges from one destroyer in the night 13-14 Dec and, because she is damaged, has to start the homeward journey. In the hope that the convoy will keep to the familiar course, the 'Ungestüm' group, stationed S of Iceland from 13 Dec and comprising *U435*, *U628*, *U336*, *U591*, *U604*, *U569*, *U615*, *U455* and *U524*, is sent to meet the convoy. On 14 Dec *U373* and *U445* are forced to submerge because of the strong air escort and on 15 Dec the

HX.218 goes round S of the 'Ungestüm' patrol line. In the course of the search on 16 Dec *U373* sights the approaching ONS.152 (EG C.3) with 22 ships. *U524*, *U615* and *U445* come up but the boats lose contact in the deteriorating visibility and with the approach of a severe storm which reaches Force 12 on 18 Dec. The search is continued until 22 Dec but only independents and scattered ships are sighted. Of these *U591* (Lt-Cdr Zetzsche) sinks one ship of 3077 tons. The ten 'Ungestüm' boats and *U373* form a new patrol line on 25-26 Dec.

10-17 Dec Norway
The heavy cruiser *Lützow* (Capt Stange) moves from Gotenhafen to Northern Norway (Altafjord) without incident.

10-25 Dec Indian Ocean
After an unsuccessful operation in the Arafura Sea the Japanese submarines *I-165* and *I-166* shell Port Gregory and the Cocos Islands respectively.

10-25 Dec South Atlantic
The Italian submarine *Tazzoli* (Cdr* Fecia di Cossato) sinks four ships of 20480 tons off the North-East Coast of Brazil. *Finzi* has to break off the operation because of a mechanical fault.

11-14 Dec Black Sea
Sortie against the Rumanian coast by two Soviet minesweeper groups (Rear-Adm V. G. Fadeev). The first group includes the minesweeper *T-407-Mina* and *T-412-Arseni Rasskin;* and the second group *T-406-Iskatel* and *T-408-Yakor*. Cover is provided by the destroyer *Soobrazitelny*. The first group attacks a German convoy between Gibrieni and Burgas comprising the steamers *Oituz* and *Zar Ferdinand*, the Rumanian torpedo boat *Smeul* and four motor minesweepers of the 3rd MMS Flotilla (Lt-Cdr Klassmann), but is driven off by the motor minesweepers feigning a motor torpedo boat attack, whilst *Smeul* covers the steamers in smoke.

11-29 Dec South Pacific
Australian landings near Buna (Papua). To support the Australian and American troops advancing on land, the Dutch steamer *Karsik*, escorted by the corvette *Lithgow*, brings eight armoured vehicles into Oro Bay S of Buna on 10-12 Dec

and 14-16 Dec. On 14 Dec the corvettes *Ballarat*, *Broome* and *Kolac* land one battalion of 762 men and on 19 Dec another battalion of 699 men in Oro Bay. On 29 Dec the corvettes *Broome*, *Kolac* and *Whyalla* transport 615 men from Goodenough Island into Oro Bay.
Five Japanese destroyers bring 800 men from Rabaul to Cape Ward Hunt N of Buna from 12 Dec to 14 Dec.

12 Dec Mediterranean
Italian guided torpedoes (SLCs) and frogmen, disembarked from the submarine *Ambra* (Cdr Arillo), penetrate the harbour of Algiers and badly damage the freighters *Ocean Vanquisher* (7174 tons), *Berto* (1493 tons), *Empire Centaur* (7041 tons) and *Harmattan* (4558 tons).

12 Dec North Sea
The 4th MTB Flotilla (Lt-Cdr Bätge), comprising *S48*, *S63*, *S80*, *S110* and *S117*, attacks the British convoy FN.889 off Lowestoft and sinks five freighters of 7113 tons.

12 Dec-3 Feb Western Atlantic
E of the Caribbean *U217* (Lt Reichenbach-Klinke) sinks two ships of 10576 tons. One other sinking and two torpedoings remain unclarified. *U124* and *U214* shadow a convoy on 15-16 Dec and *U124* (Lt-Cdr J. Mohr) reports two tankers from it sunk (so far unidentified). On 28 Dec the boat sinks one ship from a convoy and on 9 Jan 1943 four steamers totalling 28259 tons from the convoy TB.1 (12 ships). From 3 Jan to 23 Jan *U214* (Lt-Cdr G. Reeder) and *U105* (Lt Nissen) enter the Caribbean. In all, they sink one ship of 4426 tons and three ships and one sailing ship of 20444 tons respectively. *U109* (Lt-Cdr Bleichrodt) has to return prematurely.

15-21 Dec North Atlantic
The 'Raufbold' group is formed W of Ireland on 15 Dec from the U-boats coming from HX.217 and new arrivals. It consists of *U623*, *U609*, *U610*, *U600*, *U211*, *U135*, *U439*, *U410*, *U203*, *U664*, *U356*, *U409* and *U621)* On 15 Dec *U609* (Lt-Cdr Rudloff. sights the convoy ON.153 (EG B.7) with 43 ships. *U609* maintains contact until the evening of 16 Dec and bring-up *U610* (Lt-Cdr von Freyberg-Eisens

berg-Allmendigen), *U356* (Lt Ruppelt) and *U621* (Lt Kruschka) which each sink a ship of 9551 tons, 6125 tons and 5936 tons respectively, and also *U664* (Lt Graef). In the night *U211* (Lt-Cdr Hause) sinks the leading destroyer *Firedrake*. On 17 Dec *U609* keeps contact for some time in spite of heavy seas, but an attack fails in the swell. On 18-19 Dec *U621* and *U609* keep contact in turns but none of the six boats still operating comes up. *U621* sinks on 18 Dec and 20 Dec another two scattered ships totalling 10691 tons. On 18 Dec the outward-bound *U563* (Lt-Cdr von Hartmann) also sinks one ship of 4906 tons W of the Bay of Biscay. On 15 Dec *U626*, which is on the way out, happens to be overtaken by the Escort Group of the Iceland section on ONS.152 (EG C.3) and is sunk by the US coastguard cutter *Ingham*.

15-25 Dec   Arctic
The British convoy JW.51A sets out for Murmansk from Loch Ewe with 16 freighters (over 100000 tons of cargo). Escort Group: the destroyers *Beagle* and *Boadicea*, the corvettes *Honeysuckle* and *Oxlip*, the minesweeper *Seagull* and the trawlers *Lady Madelaine* and *Northern Whale*. In addition, there is a destroyer force from Seidisfjord comprising *Faulknor*, *Fury*, *Echo*, *Eclipse* and *Inglefield*. A distant cover is provided by the Home Fleet. The convoy reaches Murmansk on 25 Dec without having been located by German reconnaissance. Five ships are lost in the Kola Inlet as a result of German air attacks and mines.

15-25 Dec   South Pacific
The Japanese 2nd DD Flotilla (Rear-Adm Tanaka) with the destroyers *Naganami*, *Makinami*, *Oyashio*, *Kuroshio*, *Kagero*, *Kawakaze*, *Suzukaze*, *Tanikaze*, *Urakaze*, *Yugure* and *Ariake* and units of the 8th Fleet, including the minelayer *Tsugaru*, carry out transport missions in six operations from Rabaul and Shortland to Munda in the New Georgia Archipelago in order to construct an airfield there to support Guadalcanal.

18-21 Dec   Mediterranean
In the Gulf of Hammamet the British submarine *P.211/Safari* (Cdr Bryant) sinks five vessels of 1757 tons. *P.45/Unrivalled* (Lt Sprice) sinks two ships of 414 tons. Off Naples *P.42/Unbroken* (Lt Mars) torpedoes one ship of 2835 tons and *Turbulent* (Cdr Linton) sinks one ship of 5290 tons. Near Cape Bon *P.48* misses the destroyer *Lampo* in an attack on a convoy and is damaged by the torpedo boat *Perseo*. In another attempted attack on 25 Dec the submarine is sunk by the torpedo boats *Ardente* and *Ardito*. *Ursula* (Lt Lakin) sinks on 28 Dec one ship of 4140 tons near Marettimo and is rammed and damaged two days later by a merchant ship.

20 Dec   Black Sea
The Soviet flotilla leader *Kharkov* and destroyer *Boiki* shell Yalta in the night 19-20 Dec and the destroyer *Nezamozhnik* and the patrol ship *Shkval* Feodosia. On the way back they encounter the returning German 1st MTB Flotilla. Both sides fail to secure hits.

21 Dec-31 Jan   South Atlantic
In Brazilian waters *U507* (Cdr Schacht) and *U164* (Cdr Fechner) sink three ships of 14230 tons and one ship of 2608 tons respectively. On 13 Jan and 6 Jan respectively they are sunk by Catalina flying boats of USN VP-83 operating as escorts.

21 Dec-25 Jan   Central Atlantic
In operations in the area of Dakar and Freetown *U175* (Lt-Cdr Bruns) sinks one ship of 7177 tons.

24 Dec   General Situation
The High Commissioner for French North and West Africa, Admiral Darlan, is murdered in Algiers by a fanatical supporter of Gen de Gaulle.

24-31 Dec   North Atlantic
From the newly arrived U-boats the 'Spitz' group is formed on 24 Dec on the E side of the North Atlantic. It consists of *U260*, *U662*, *U123*, *U659*, *U225*, *U406*, *U440*, *U203*, *U664* and *U356*. S of the patrol line the advancing *U664* (Lt Graef) sights on 26 Dec the convoy ONS.154 with 45 ships (Commodore Vice-Adm Egerton†), escorted by the EG C.1 (Cdr Windeyer) with the Canadian destroyer *St Laurent* and the corvettes *Battleford*, *Chilliwack*, *Kenogami*, *Napanee* and *Shediac* with the rescue ship *Toward* equipped with

HF/DF. Apart from the 'Spitz' group the 'Ungestüm' group, stationed a little further to the W, and consisting of *U373*, *U435*, *U628*, *U336*, *U591*, *U615*, *U455*, *U409* and *U441*, is deployed against the convoy. On the afternoon of 26 Dec *U662* (Cdr Hermann) establishes contact and in the night 26-27 Dec *U356* (Lt Ruppelt) in two approaches sinks three ships of 13649 tons and torpedoes one ship of 7051 tons which *U441* (Lt-Cdr Hartmann) sinks. The latter also misses the *St Laurent* and one ship. *U356*, after her second attack, is herself sunk by *St Laurent*, *Chilliwack*, *Battleford* and *Napanee*. The lost contact is re-established in the afternoon of 27 Dec by *U225* (Lt Leimkühler), which torpedoes in the night one tanker of 7087 tons then taken in tow by the *Chilliwack*. In the morning, after an interruption of nine hours, contact is re-established by *U260* (Lt-Cdr Purkhold) which, after reconnaissance on 28 Dec, brings up by day *U336*, *U203*, *U615*, *U123*, *U406*, *U591*, *U664*, *U225*, *U440* and, after dark, *U435*, *U628* and *U662*. In the night 28-29 Dec the boats attack, sometimes repeatedly, in quick succession. After misses by *U203* and *U435*, *U591* (Lt-Cdr Zetzsche) torpedoes one ship of 5701 tons, which is later sunk by *U435* (Lt-Cdr Strelow). *U225* sinks one ship of 5273 tons and torpedoes one ship of 5598 tons, which is sunk by *U662*. *U260* sinks one ship of 4893 tons; after a miss by *U203*, *U406* (Lt-Cdr Dieterichs) torpedoes three ships of which one ship of 3385 tons is sunk by *U123* (Lt v. Schroeter), one ship of 5029 tons by *U628* (Lt Hasenschar) and one ship of 4871 tons by *U591*. At midnight *U225* torpedoes one ship of 4919 tons, which is sunk by *U225* and *U336* (Lt-Cdr Hunger), as well as the Commodore's ship of 7068 tons, which is sunk by *U123* and *U435*. Further attacks by *U203*, *U435*, *U628*, *U664* and (again) *U628* on escorts and merchant ships fail. When day breaks on 29 Dec the British Destroyers *Milne* and *Meteor* arrive as additional escort and drive off *U260*, *U591* and *U455*. Only *U435* sinks one ship of 5701 tons in a daylight underwater attack. On the

evening of 29 Dec *U225* and *U615* repeatedly attack the auxiliary warship *Fidelity* (2456 tons), which sails with a French crew, but she is able to avoid the attacks. Only on the afternoon of 30 Dec is she sunk by *U435*. *U455*, which keeps contact with the convoy until the night 30-31 Dec, is unable to bring up any other boat. The boats proceed to *U117* for replenishment.

26-27 Dec   North Atlantic
The outward-bound *U357* (Lt-Cdr Kellner) sights on 26 Dec NW of Ireland the convoy HX.219 with the EG B.2 (Cdr Macintyre) consisting of the destroyers *Hesperus* and *Vanessa* and the corvettes *Gentian*, *Clematis*, *Heather*, *Campanula*, *Mignonette* and *Sweetbriar*. Her contact signal is located by HF/DF and *Hesperus* and *Vanessa* sink *U357* before she can send further signals and bring up the outward-bound *U384* and *U525* which have been directed to the convoy.

26-29 Dec   Black Sea
Second sortie by a Soviet minesweeping division (Rear-Adm V. G. Fadeev) against shipping on the Rumanian coast. With the minesweepers *T-406-Iskatel*, *T-407-Mina*, *T-408-Yakor* and *T-412-Arseni Rasskin* it proceeds to the area between Gibrieni and Burgas. The destroyers *Besposhchadny* and *Soobrazitelny* cover the operation and make a sortie, without success, on 28 Dec into the area S of Fidonisi. Two minesweepers shell Burgas.

31 Dec   Arctic
Operation 'Regenbogen': attack by a German naval force on the British convoy JW.51B in the Arctic.
22 Dec: the convoy JW.51B leaves Loch Ewe: 14 freighters, escorted by the destroyers *Onslow* (Capt Sherbrooke) *Oribi*, *Obedient*, *Obdurate*, *Orwell*, *Achates* and *Bulldog*, the minesweeper *Bramble*, the corvettes *Hyderabad* and *Rhododendron* and two trawlers, *Ocean Gem* and *Vizalma*. Close escort: the light cruisers *Sheffield* (Rear-Adm Burnett) and *Jamaica*, the destroyer *Opportune* and from 29 Dec *Matchless*. Distant cover: the battleship *Anson* (Vice-Adm Fraser), the heavy cruiser *Cumberland*, the destroyers *Forester*, *Icarus* and *Impulsive*. Flanking cover:

the submarines *Trespasser*, *Seadog*, *Unruly* and *Graph* (ex-*U570*).

24 Dec: the convoy is located for the first time by a German reconnaissance aircraft. It is also sighted by *U354* (Lt-Cdr Herbschleb).

30 Dec (afternoon): the German force puts to sea from Altafjord, consisting of the heavy cruiser *Admiral Hipper* (Capt Hartmann with the Commander Cruisers Vice-Adm Kummetz, on board) and *Lützow* (Capt Stange), the 5th DD Flotilla (Capt Schemmel) comprising the destroyers *Friedrich Eckoldt* (Cdr Bachmann), *Z29* (Cdr* Rechel), *Richard Beitzen* (Cdr von Davidson), *Theodor Riedel* (Cdr Riede), *Z30* (Cdr* Kaiser) and *Z31* (Cdr Alberts).

31 Dec: the German force is directed to the area of *U354*'s contact signals. At first *Admiral Hipper* advances on the convoy in bad weather. But the convoy is skilfully defended by the destroyer group of Capt Sherbrooke and is covered by a smoke screen.

Obedient and *Onslow* are damaged and *Achates* is sunk. *Eckoldt*, *Beitzen* and *Z29* sink the minesweeper *Bramble*. Shortly before mid-day the British close escort intervenes in the fighting. *Admiral Hipper* receives three hits in the engagement, one of which reduces the speed of the cruiser. *Eckoldt* is sunk by the *Sheffield* (Capt A. W. Clarke) and *Obdurate* is badly damaged by the *Lützow*. Because of the confused situation, the poor visibility and the Navy Staff's W/T message ('In spite of operational orders, exercise restraint if you contact enemy of comparable strength, since it is undesirable to run excessive risks to the cruisers') Vice-Adm Kummetz breaks off the engagement.

The convoy RA.51 proceeds to the W with the escort of JW.51 without making contact with the enemy and arrives in Loch Ewe on 9 Jan 1943.

31 Dec   South Pacific
Imperial Headquarters in Tokyo decides to abandon the island of Guadalcanal.